# Working with Ideas

As part of Houghton Mifflin's ongoing commitment to the environment,
this text has been printed on recycled paper.

# Working with Ideas

## Reading, Writing, and Researching Experience

**Donna Dunbar-Odom**
*Texas A&M, Commerce*

**Houghton Mifflin Company**     Boston   New York

*Senior Sponsoring Editor:*   Suzanne Phelps Weir
*Associate Editor:*   Janet Young
*Project Editor:*   Gabrielle Stone
*Production/Design Coordinator:*   Jodi O'Rourke
*Cover Coordinator:*   Deborah Azerrad Savona
*Senior Manufacturing Coordinator:*   Sally Culler
*Senior Marketing Manager:*   Nancy Lyman

*Cover design:*   Len Massiglia/LMA Communications
*Cover image:*   Sin Takahashi/Photonica

*(Acknowledgments continued on page 645, which constitutes an extension of the copyright page.)*

Printed in the U.S.A.

Library of Congress Catalog Card Number: 99-71998

ISBN: 0-395-88154-4

ABCDEFGHIJ-VB-04 03 02 01 00

# Contents

# Preface

*Working with Ideas* is for first-year English composition courses that emphasize academic writing, critical thinking, and research. What makes this text unique is that its sequenced reading and writing assignments build on students' personal experiences *as students* to help them focus their reading and writing and enable them to develop an understanding of argument and research as a dialectical process rather than a series of formulaic steps. Toward this end, *Working with Ideas* emphasizes the role that active, critical reading plays in academic reading and writing. It is also unique in that it stresses field research, to enrich student researchers' sense of expertise and to help them see themselves as participants in an ongoing academic conversation rather than mere eavesdroppers.

## *How* Working with Ideas *is organized*

The book is divided into two sections. Part One introduces students to academic reading and writing, rhetorical strategies, and library and field research. Part Two consists of eight "themed" reading and writing assignment sequences that help students develop the intellectual skills stressed in Part One.

## *What* Working with Ideas *does* not *do*

This book is an outgrowth of my frustration with the usual research and argument books in the field, which continue to encourage students to think about arguments in terms of polarized positions and debate. Few of these texts find ways to show students how sophisticated research requires the researcher to synthesize a variety of positions and points of view. Toulminian and Aristotelian approaches to argument are valuable, but I have found time and again that they break down when students are faced with assignments that ask them to work through complex issues and make use of library research. The worst scenario is the "research paper" in which a student takes a side—say, for gun control or against animal testing—comes up with several reasons for her position, locates three articles agreeing with her position and one opposed, and then builds a predictable paper that rarely if ever reflects the richness of the ongoing discussion and—consequently—never speaks with anything resembling real authority.

## *What* Working with Ideas *does*

Deborah Tannen's most recent book *The Argument Culture: Moving from Debate to Dialogue* (1998) clearly demonstrates, via numerous examples, that our culture has come to equate argument with debate, to the detriment of civil discourse in general. I see this book as an effort to move students beyond what Tannen describes as an "ethic of aggression" to an ethic that instead stresses reflection.

*Working with Ideas* uses eight themed, sequenced assignments, all related to the central theme of student life, to develop students' abilities to do academic reading, writing, and research. In a certain sense, I see argument and research as integrally related, in that research is largely the extended development of an argument that considers critically the positions and perspectives of others. To that end, students and teachers will probably move back and forth between Part One and Part Two. This book, therefore, combines argumentation, research, and critical thinking.

## *Unique features and strengths*

The unique features of this book include an emphasis on active reading strategies (largely ignored in traditional composition textbooks and classrooms) and assignment sequences that attempt to reproduce as much as possible the experience of doing ongoing research. Each sequence begins with a writing assignment that asks students to make an argument based on their own experience and preliminary thinking in relation to the sequence topic—for example, their idea of what a college or university should be and should include. Next they are asked (1) to read essays that will add to and, it is likely, complicate their initial approach to the topic, and (2) to write new essays of their own that reflect their increasingly complex understanding of the issue. In other words, the sequenced assignments require students to synthesize progressively more and more new information in a series of reading and writing assignments, each building on the one before, and to consider their position from a number of perspectives. The sequences cover such themes as intellectual life, religion on campus, diversity, women's and men's experiences as students, and environmentalism.

In addition, *Working with Ideas* positions students to speak with some measure of authority from the first assignment. Every student has expertise on which to draw; every student is the "star" of his or her own experience of college, whether he or she is a traditional student, a nontraditional student, an athlete, a commuter, a part-time student, and so on. The assignment sequences enable students to build on that expertise so that they can enter into a larger conversation—the one that educators and administrators carry on every day in every college in every part of the country.

I invite my students to compare what I'm asking them to do with juggling. It takes them a short while to learn to juggle two balls, and once they've acquired some competence, I toss in a third ball. Of course, it's a struggle at first, but eventually they are able to manage three balls. Then here comes the fourth ball, and so on. This approach is valuable not only because it forces students to move beyond binary, reductive forms of thinking but also because it challenges all students, from the brightest to the weakest, requiring all to test their limits.

A further strength of *Working with Ideas* is its voice and style, which make it accessible without being patronizing or simplistic. My goal is to introduce students to the real intellectual pleasure of ongoing research and to position them to teach others about what they know and what they learn in doing their college work. Thus I've tried to make this text as accessible as possible, to encourage students to participate enthusiastically in their own intellectual growth and development.

## *Acknowledgments*

*Working with Ideas* has a long history. It began years ago, when, as a teacher of basic writing, I knew there had to be something more to teach my students than five-paragraph formula essays. It grew when that desire for something more led me to study with David Bartholomae, Jean Ferguson Carr, Mariolina Salvatori, and others who helped me begin to see what I teach and how I teach as intellectually rigorous and exciting. I then had the good fortune to become a part of a department where I was given the intellectual freedom to experiment, fail, and experiment again as a new writing program administrator, and I am grateful to and continue to learn from Liz Buckley, Gerald Duchovnay, and Dick Fulkerson, extraordinary colleagues. Colin and Jonikka Charlton "road-tested" assignment sequences in their classes and offered valuable suggestions and feedback. In addition, I am in the debt of the many students in my classes who worked with me in the early stages of this project—especially Daniel Clayton, Bunnie Cummings, Charolette Gardner, Nickole Hatchett, Vince Leibowitz, Liz Mahaffey, Allison Mellen, Shelle Smith, Monica Tabor.

I am also extremely grateful to the many folks at Houghton Mifflin who have helped me shape and form the idea into a real book. My sincere thanks to Suzanne Phelps Weir, who oversaw the whole process; to Jayne Fargnoli, who got me started; to Janet Edmonds, who got me through the middle process; and to Jennifer Roderick, who got me to the finish line. Because I am a writer who requires lots of revision, it was my profound good luck to work with editors who had the patience to push and guide me through every stage. I greatly appreciate the able assistance of Bruce Crabtree and Janice Okoomian, who did so much of the polishing and who both deserve a lot of the credit for the completion of this project. My thanks also go to the many reviewers who offered such thoughtful and useful feedback:

Nancy Blattner, Southeast Missouri State University
Lori Catallozzi, Massachusetts Bay Community College
John Champagne, Penn State Erie, The Behrend College
Charles Clifton, University of Southern Colorado
Allysen Todd Croyle, Community College of Allegheny County
Pamelyn Dane, Lane Community College (OR)
Stephen John Dilks, University of Missouri-Kansas City
Kathryn T. Flannery, Indiana University
Charles Lewis, Westminster College (MO)
Rebecca Board Liljenstolpe, DeAnza College (CA)
Robert Lyman, California State University, Sacramento
Barbara W. McCarthy, Massachusetts Bay Community College
Mark Reynolds, Jefferson Davis Community College (AL)

Throughout the entire process, I have drawn on the intellectual and emotional support from my dear friends Barbara W. McCarthy and Richard E. Miller. Via email, long distance conversations, and CCCC, these two have sustained me. Most significantly, however, Michael Odom has been my companion and ally and is the one who, more than anyone else, has helped me see myself as someone ready for the "big leagues."

*Donna Dunbar-Odom*

# Learning Habits of Reflection

How do you approach your college writing assignments? Like many students, you might think of them primarily in terms of the finished products you must eventually present to your instructors—for example, a 15-page, double-spaced paper that cites at least 8 secondary sources and is due in 8 weeks—instead of as opportunities to learn new material or to persuade an audience to support a particular point of view. If you do, then your projects can become like empty containers or molds into which you haphazardly toss material to fill up a certain required volume. This approach might satisfy the minimum requirements of your college courses, but it won't help you genuinely understand your subject matter or produce compelling pieces of writing. Any writing project (whether it's a simple essay, a research paper, or an entire book) on any topic (whether it's one you've already made up your mind about or one you're not that familiar with) will benefit from a systematic approach that gets you to reflect on what you're writing about and what you want to say. That kind of approach—one centered on certain habits of reflection—is what this book is all about.

What process do you follow to complete a writing assignment? Do you test the waters before you begin writing, or do you plunge right in? Do you carefully consider the assignment and brainstorm different points of view before you commit yourself to a thesis? Or do you go with the first position that occurs to you and then construct your researching process and your paper around it? Do you cull some material from the library and then piece together a thesis based on what you happened to find on your topic? Or do you start with a carefully considered thesis and then perform library and field research to test it and back it up? Do you assess your audience beforehand and pursue a rhetorical strategy appropriate to it and to your thesis? Or do you assume that just because you're convinced of the rightness of your position, your readers will naturally agree with you? In the chapters that follow, we'll discuss researching and writing processes, rhetorical strategies, and formatting conventions that will help you produce persuasive papers that conform to academic and professional standards. We'll discuss these writing processes, strategies, and formatting norms in practical, step-by-step terms to help you complete your college writing assignments efficiently and effectively.

Although this book is designed for use in college composition courses, at its heart it is more about thinking than about writing. It's about breaking free of formulaic or just-get-it-done approaches to research and writing and instead actively engaging with ideas. It's about the intellectual growth that should accompany every writing assignment you complete in college—and that characterizes the thinking and writing people do in their professional lives. To be successful after college, you'll need to develop strategies for working with ideas that spark this kind of growth. Therefore, in addition to discussing writing processes and norms, this book discusses strategies for active, critical reading and research that will make your academic experience richer and, in turn, your writing more successful and convincing.

## Breaking out of Formulas

Many years ago, I used to teach my students a formulaic method for writing a persuasive five-paragraph essay. You may be familiar with the formula:

- The introduction begins with a couple of general statements about the topic that then lead to a thesis statement (usually the last sentence of the first paragraph).

- The thesis also follows a formula: a point of view or stance on an issue is presented and then either defended or attacked, depending on the writer's position on the subject, because of Reason 1, Reason 2, and Reason 3.

- Each body paragraph that follows includes a topic sentence—that is, a full-sentence version of one of the three reasons stated in the thesis sentence—and offers an example. The third paragraph is likely to begin with "In addition" and the fourth with "Finally."

- The concluding (fifth) paragraph begins, predictably, with "In conclusion" and restates the thesis.

This formula is extremely useful in certain limited circumstances—essay exams or brief writing assignments—but as I quickly found out from my students, it will not serve a writer well in many academic or professional writing situations.

By the end of each term, my students would have little problem producing five-paragraph essays. But when they went on to more advanced courses, courses that required them to grapple with demanding reading and longer writing assignments, many had serious difficulty. The formula I had taught them simply wasn't adequate to the more complex tasks they were being given to perform. One student came back to see me after getting a D on a paper in a more advanced class. Danny had written lively, humorous five-paragraph essays in my class and had developed a facility in writing that he had never experienced before, so he had begun the next class with high expectations of success. But the advanced class required that he synthesize substantive reading and library research on complex subjects into essays that communicated not only his own understanding of and judgments about the material but also the points of view of other authors—and to conform to the norms of academic discourse. In other words, he was expected to read and produce complex academic writing.

Danny reported that he originally felt like he had something to say about the topics assigned but that once he had read what published experts had to say in the sources he found in the library, he began to forget what he had thought he wanted to say in the first place. He had felt secure with the formula that required only that he decide what his position was and then come up with three reasons why he thought that way. But what was he supposed to do with all these other positions and reasons? How was he supposed to bring them all together into some form that made sense? He confessed that he felt overwhelmed by these demands, and he worried that a D was the best he could hope for.

I won't claim that "the truth" about how writing should be taught was suddenly revealed to me at that moment. I also won't say that everything I had taught Danny was wrong. He *had* written funny, smart five-paragraph essays, and these had taught him something of value about organization and logic. However, I will say that Danny's visit and his distress made me begin a long process of re-examining what a first-year college writing course should include and accomplish.

## *Reading and writing to stimulate thinking*

The conclusion I arrived at is that first-year college students need to learn how to bring their reading and writing together in increasingly meaningful and complex ways. For students to accomplish this, the reading and writing they do should be relevant to their own lives and should exercise their critical-thinking abilities. Such assignments should give students a sense of the pleasure that active engagement with ideas can produce. I came to realize that the researching and writing processes students follow should do more than just culminate in a finished research paper; they should encourage robust reflection and provide students with true "ownership" of the end result. I found that a course organized around a series of multistage assignments, each consisting of a reading–writing–research sequence and with students' own experience at the core, offered the most intellectually satisfying results. These "sequenced" assignments help students grapple with intellectual complexity and move beyond writing "canned" research papers.

Part One introduces the kinds of reading and writing required in college settings. Chapter 1 discusses strategies for reading actively and critically, and Chapter 2 offers an overview of writing processes. Chapter 3 addresses the elements of argument and persuasion, whereas the last two chapters focus on research—in the library and in "the field."

Part Two includes eight "sequenced" reading, writing, and research assignments, all revolving in one way or another around college life and your own experience, both as a college student and in the greater world beyond campus. (For example, the first assignment focuses on the idea of a university or college; the second one focuses on campus politics and its effect on the world outside of school; the third concerns race, class, and ethnicity on campus and in society.) Each assignment sequence begins with a thinking and writing exercise that asks you to reflect on the issue and respond to it on the basis of your own experience. Next you are asked to read an essay by another writer on the same issue and complete a second writing exercise in which you compare his or her position with yours. At this point, you're juggling two viewpoints: your original outlook and the point of view you've just read. Once you're comfortable with these first two frames of reference, I'll toss in a third, and so on.

### Conducting meaningful research

At the same time you're completing these thinking and writing exercises, you will also begin to do your own library and field research on the issue, in order to gain additional expertise from which to speak in a final research paper on the topic. Library research allows you to engage with and draw on the work of others who have expertise on your topic. Field research enables you to incorporate the power of a personal narrative into your paper, by describing your role as a participant or an observer in your research process, while sidestepping the pitfalls of more traditional personal-narrative forms. For example, Sequence 5, "Striking Balances," focuses on the complexity of most students' lives. In this sequence, you read about others' experiences in balancing student life with home, family, and work life, but as you read, you consider how your own experience in college compares with these accounts and then offer your own perspective on the problems that students, teachers, administrators, and others on every campus address every day. Your perception can then serve as a place to begin further research among your fellow students and in library and Internet resources. Supplementing your personal story with such research lends authority to what might otherwise be a hackneyed treatment of a limited topic.

The problem with taking a "fill the container" approach to research writing assignments is that it tends to produce a "just enough" attitude toward secondary sources. Many students try to find "just enough" outside sources to meet the minimum requirements of the assignment. The question "How many pages do we have to have?" naturally leads to "How many sources do we need?" and "How many quotations do we have to include?" With a "just enough" attitude toward secondary sources, "researching" often comes down to scavenging sundry information from magazines or other periodicals and assembling it piecemeal, and the student's own words are relegated to gluing together the required number of quotations.

You'll produce stronger and more interesting papers if you adopt a "more than enough" attitude, amassing ample material with which to work and from which to choose and draw conclusions. Sorting through "too much" information means, for one thing, that you can make choices as a writer, rather than having to find ways to include every bit of information you've gathered. For another thing, it hones your critical-thinking skills as you sort through your secondary sources and make connections between them and your own observations. When you make ethnographic methods the foundation of your research—that is, when you begin by considering your own experiences and by conducting surveys and interviews—supporting materials become just that, *support* for the position *you* develop yourself.

### Becoming an expert

At its core, research is motivated by the desire or need to become an expert, and effective writing generally presents the writer as an expert on the subject matter it covers. Including field research as a key element of your research projects positions you as an expert on your topic. No one can argue powerfully from a position of ignorance; we all argue more effectively about what we know. Therefore, this book asks that you carve out an area of interest from your own experience and then conduct surveys and interviews with others to gauge their attitudes toward the issues you are investigating. Those who complete this stage in their research naturally speak with greater confidence and authority than those who do not. Their contributions to class discussion and their writing assignments reflect that confidence: "*My* research shows . . ." they say, or "According to the people *I* interviewed. . . ." No one else will have conducted the particular surveys or interviews that *you* conduct, so no one else will be able to speak with quite the same expertise on your topic.

Because I ask you to begin with your own experience, I have chosen, as a unifying theme for the assignment sequences, a subject that all students are at least somewhat familiar with—the culture of higher education. Although this topic is of universal concern to students, it is not monolithic; there is enough conflict and variety associated with this topic to allow for a multiplicity of viewpoints and strong positions. The very definition of a college student, for example, has shifted in recent years. More and more people now enter or return to college later in life, balancing school with work and family, or otherwise don't fit the stereotype of a middle-class recent high school graduate. Even the definition of college itself has shifted. Some colleges and universities now make it possible for students to obtain a degree via the Internet, without ever setting foot on a traditional college campus. With all of this in mind, then, the assignments give you an opportunity to consider several issues related to college life today. They challenge you to begin with your personal experience with an issue related to student life, to absorb different viewpoints on that issue and respond in increasingly complex ways, to perform library and field research on one aspect of the issue that strikes you as particularly significant, and then finally to produce a paper in which you make an argument that will engage and perhaps persuade intelligent readers.

## How this book is organized

*Working with Ideas* offers you a series of reading and writing assignments that introduce you to the complexities and pleasures of speaking with authority about research to which you are connected and committed. Toward that end, the book is divided into two parts.

Part One contains five introductory chapters. Chapter 1 discusses strategies for active and critical reading, to help you build strengths in this area. Chapter 2 describes the writing process, paying special attention to prewriting and revision strategies. Chapter 3 examines the elements of argument and persuasion, particularly the norms involved in writing and academic argument, with special attention to audience, proof, and organization. Chapter 4 introduces library research and briefly explains the proper way to format and document academic writing. Chapter 5 discusses field research.

Part Two contains eight assignment sequences, each centered on a broad issue confronting college students. Each sequence contains readings in meaningful groupings that lead you toward developing an extended research project. The reading and writing assignments are sequenced in this way to encourage you to see your work as an ongoing process—an intellectual enterprise—rather than as a series of discrete, unconnected tasks or hoops that the teacher (or text-book writer) wants you to jump through. For example, one sequence focuses on student attitudes toward faith and religion. The first writing assignment asks you to consider and describe your own attitudes about the role that religion plays in your life and the lives of other students you know. The first reading, Robert Johnson's "Teaching the Forbidden: Literature and the Religious Student," argues that conservative religious views hamper students' ability to engage in the kind of critical thinking demanded in literature classes. The next writing assignment asks you to respond to Johnson's essay, drawing on your own experience and the observations you recorded in the first writing assignment. Each subsequent reading and writing assignment then adds to and complicates the debate. At the same time, you are asked to conduct field research on the topic to gain a sense of how other students' attitudes compare with your own. The final stage is to conduct library research; you are now ready to approach the work of published experts as an expert in your own right. The final project, then, reflects weeks of work and integrates an increasingly complex understanding of a complex issue. It will be a project in which you will have a real stake.

Take some time to browse through this book and to reflect on the questions you have about college life and on the many things you already know about the place of higher education in contemporary society. Whatever your situation, you're in a position to consider, respond to, test, and refine the ideas in this book. My goal for *Working with Ideas* is to make it a useful and engaging tool for your continued growth as a critical, thoughtful person—and to help you write better, now and for the rest of your life.

# Working
# with Ideas

# PART I

# Reading, Writing, and Researching

# CHAPTER 1

# Active Reading

THE MAJORITY OF the writing you produce in college will be done to demonstrate how well you have read and understood something. For exams and short papers, you'll have to show how well you've understood your textbooks and other class readings. For long papers or projects, you'll have to demonstrate how well you have comprehended and synthesized some of the written work of several experts or other authors in the field you're studying. Indeed, virtually all of the academic writing you will do will be in response to close, active reading of the work of others. To produce effective academic discourse, then, you must be able to understand fully what you read, and to do this, you must learn to read actively and critically.

*Active* may seem an odd adjective to associate with reading; after all, we usually think of reading as a passive pursuit done lying on a couch or with our feet up on a hassock. Reading is not like watching television, however. A book does not spoon-feed meaning to its readers; rather, each reader must actively construct meaning from the words on every page. The more engaged and active a reader is in this task of constructing meaning from the text, the richer his or her construction of meaning will be. This chapter is included here to give you some guidelines for active reading and to get you into the habit of reading actively and critically.

## Getting Ready for Active Reading

Many students enter or return to college without having read extensively. Those who have read a lot have generally read for pleasure (science fiction novels, mysteries, thrillers) or for information (textbooks) or for a combination of the two (magazines, newspapers, web sites). Novels carry readers along via a plot and characters, making us want to find out what happens next. Textbooks help readers along with the use of bold type, subheadings, chapter summaries, and review questions. You may not find the readings in this book quite so "user-friendly." Therefore, some suggestions and guidelines may help you prepare yourself to approach more demanding reading assignments.

To begin with, follow these practical steps to prepare for serious, active reading:

1. *Make sure your work environment is comfortable and helps you concentrate.* You need a quiet place free of television or stereo noise. If you're using music to drown out dorm or family noise, choose music that can become part of the background, and turn it up just enough to camouflage other people's noise but not so much that it detracts from your attention to your studies. Good lighting is important, so invest in a reading lamp if you don't already have one. Sit upright so as to stay alert and focused.
2. *Read with the dictionary within easy reach, and use it.* Avoid the temptation to skip words you don't know—doing so will cut down on your comprehension. When you look up a word, write its definition in your book so that you can refresh your memory easily.

## Strategies for Active Reading

Reading, whether for pleasure, for information, or for a college course, requires varying amounts of concentration, depending on the particular piece of writing you're engaged with. You'll find, for instance, that some of the readings in this text are harder to comprehend than others, perhaps because of arcane vocabulary, complex organization, or challenging ideas and concepts. Some difficulties can get worked out in class discussions or journals; others may be resolved when you read additional assignments. None of these difficulties can be overcome, however, without paying close attention to each reading the first time you encounter it. The following strategies will help you improve your comprehension each time you delve into a written work.

### Contemplate the title

The title is your first point of entry into the text. Short though it may be, it contains key information. Take a minute, for example, to consider the title of Alexander W. Astin's essay "The Cause of Citizenship." It's not as simple as it first appears in that *cause* can be read two ways: both in terms of the process that produces citizens (as in "cause and effect") and in terms of the goal of promoting citizenship (as in "a worthy cause"). The reader who pays close attention to this title may get the sense that Astin will be discussing both definitions of *cause*—and may thus have a head start in constructing meaning from the essay.

It can help you to stop and contemplate even a very simple title, such as "The Idea of a University," before you begin reading the actual work. An excerpt from Cardinal John Henry Newman's piece by that name is included in Part Three. Newman describes what he believes a university should be, and keeping his title in mind can help you navigate his nineteenth-century prose style.

Some titles may seem at first to make no sense at all. The title of Sven Birkerts's piece "Mahvahhuhpuh," for example, looks like nonsense. But once you've read the essay (actually an excerpt from his book *The Gutenberg Elegies*—another title worth deciphering), you'll see what the title refers to, and keeping the title in mind as you read will help you gain additional insight into his argument. In other words, titles aren't just filler; they're important to the meaning of the texts you'll be working with.

## *Read the introduction*

If any kind of introductory text precedes the main part of the reading, pay close attention to the information it contains. It's there to provide context for the reading and help you better understand it. "Head notes" and other introductory comments are included to acquaint you with the writer and perhaps to explain his or her purpose in writing that particular piece. Sometimes specific information in the head note gives you a good indication of what the writer wants you to take from your reading. In this book, for example, each reading begins with a brief head note to provide you with general background information on the writer or the specific piece and a sense of what the writer's focus or argument will be. The head note to Lynne Cheney's "Students of Success" briefly explains Cheney's purpose for writing the piece and invites you to compare your experience of choosing a major with what she argues a "good student should consider when doing so.

## *Respond to focus and journal questions*

In Part Two, prereading focus or journal questions accompany each assigned reading. These are included to help you define a personally meaningful approach to each reading and use your own experience to make sense of the readings and get more out of them. As you answer these questions, make predictions about the reading on the basis of what each question asks.

Before Robert Johnson's essay "Teaching the Forbidden: Literature and the Religious Student," for example, I ask you to consider whether you've ever been in a classroom where one or more persons' religious beliefs affected anyone else in any way. If not, was that because everyone there thought in pretty much the same ways about religion's place in the classroom, or was something else involved? Considering these questions will put you in a position to approach Johnson's argument as someone who also has personal experience with the issue. In other words, the questions are there to help you find a way into the "conversation" each reading represents and to help you begin to think about where you stand in relation to the issue being addressed.

The assignment sequences include many more focus questions than you can or should try to answer. And they are not roadmaps to organizing your essay. Simply compiling a sequence of discrete paragraphs responding to the focus questions would not result in an effective essay. Use the questions to help you think critically and generate ideas about different ways to get into and respond to the readings. Then, for your essay, pursue those focus questions that strike you as most promising or about which you have the most to say.

### Skim the reading

Before you begin to read in earnest, skim through the essay once. Try to get a sense of where the writer is coming from and what point he or she is arguing (although this won't always be clear from a quick pass-through). Pay close attention to subheadings, terms printed in boldface type or italics, photos and other illustrations, and captions, and use them to help you make predictions about the argument. What do the closing paragraphs indicate about the writer's argument? Knowing something about where the writer is going can help you read the beginning and the body of the essay more closely and with greater comprehension. You can practice that strategy on this book. Before you read the following chapters, take a few minutes to skim each one. Jot down what you think the key terms and arguments are. What is the most important information in each chapter? Spending just a short time skimming the material you are about to read can make a real difference in your comprehension and retention of it.

### Annotate the reading

Sit down to read with a pen or pencil and two highlighters of different colors. Designate one color to highlight sections of the reading that you find important or significant, for whatever reason, and use the other color to mark passages you find confusing, obscure, or completely impenetrable. Then use the pen or pencil to write brief comments to yourself about what you've highlighted—why you connected with a certain passage or why you found others completely off base. These steps may seem time-consuming at this point, but they'll save you considerable time when you move on to writing about the essay. You'll also be more likely to remember material that you've paid such close attention to.

In Figure 1.1, you'll see the first paragraph of Cardinal John Newman's "The Idea of a University" with my annotations in the margins to give you an example of what I'm talking about.

## *Take part in the argument*

As you read, highlighters and pencil in hand, think of yourself as entering into a dialogue with the writer about what he or she has written. To provide intelligent responses to the writer's work, you'll need to read it with two purposes in mind. First, you'll want to gain a strong sense of what the writer is trying to communicate and what she or he wants to accomplish by doing so. Thus your first goal should be to identify the writer's central argument and the reasons for advancing it. Second, you'll want to pinpoint where and why you do or don't agree with the writer, where and how

**FIGURE 1.1**
**Discourse V    Knowledge Its Own End**

1

I have said that all branches of knowledge are connected together, because the subject-matter of knowledge is intimately united in itself, as being the acts and the work of the Creator. Hence it is that the Sciences, into which our knowledge may be said to be cast, have multiplied bearings one on another, and an internal sympathy, and admit, or rather demand, comparison and adjustment. They complete, correct, balance each other. This consideration, if well-founded, must be taken into account, not only as regards the attainment of truth, which is their common end, but as regards the influence which they exercise upon those whose education consists in the study of them. I have said already, that to give undue prominence to one is to be unjust to another; to neglect or supersede these is to divert those from their proper object. It is to unsettle the boundary lines between science and science, to <u>disturb</u> their action, to <u>destroy</u> the harmony which binds them together. Such a proceeding will have a corresponding effect when introduced into a place of education. There is no science but tells a different tale, when viewed as a portion of a whole, from what it is likely to suggest when taken by itself, without the safeguard, as I may call it, of others.

*Margin annotations:*

Is he saying everything is connected because God made it?

What kind of Sciences is he talking about?

Sciences have to be brought together to provide the "big picture." Is this one of the purposes for colleges, then?

But isn't destruction a bad thing?

you think he or she made a particularly strong point or perhaps missed something. Once you understand the writer's argument, you can begin to compare it with your personal experience, or with other reading you've done, and to make judgments about its validity and persuasiveness.

Consider Robert Johnson's "Teaching the Forbidden." In this essay, Johnson describes the culture shock he experienced after coming to teach at a university in north central Texas. He argues that the religious, political, and intellectual conservatism in his "Bible belt" classroom interferes with his students' ability to think critically and that this is a sign of things to come in other classrooms around the country. As a teacher at a university in the same part of the country, I identify with much of what he has to say. I tread carefully and work to respect my students' religious and political positions, but even so I have shocked a few students on more than one occasion.

Yet even though I understand Johnson's concerns and agree with parts of his argument, I also strongly disagree with him in places. For one thing, the majority of the students I have taught who come from the same part of the country Johnson describes have proved to be as willing to question authority as students from any other part of the country where I've taught. For another thing, I myself was born and raised in the Bible belt. The fact that I have always questioned authority and thought critically leads me to think that Johnson has made too broad a generalization. In addition, other reading I've done helps me see gaps in Johnson's essay. For example, one book I was reading at the time that I wrote this chapter argues that people in positions of power (professors, in this case) may not be aware of what the people over whom they hold power (students, in this case) are really thinking, because their communication rarely goes beyond polite exchanges.

## *Reread*

At some point in the process of working with the ideas of a text or texts, it's important to reread. Especially with a more challenging reading assignment, we usually find we haven't remembered or understood as much about it as we wish. We tend to think that others only have to read once and are able to retain every word, but no one achieves any kind of real acquaintance with a text after only one reading. In fact, one of the pleasures of teaching for me is returning to texts time and again and finding something more each time I read and reread. Note also that if you've annotated your text, you'll find rereading much more productive.

### Assume authority and take responsibility

Notice two things about my reaction to Johnson's essay. First, I both agree and disagree with Johnson's position. Readers often approach a difficult reading assignment thinking that they must either agree with it totally or disagree totally, but the more complex a reading the more likely it is that both the writer's argument and your response to it will be much less clear-cut. Second, my personal experience makes it possible for me to begin to read "against the grain" of Johnson's essay, maintaining a healthy skepticism about his argument. Likewise, you will draw on *your* own experience as you read for this and other college courses. I've chosen the culture of higher education as a unifying theme for the readings specifically to draw out this aspect of close reading—to get you into the habit of reflecting on how your reading resonates with your personal experience. This habit will help you approach your academic reading as an authority in your own right. You can be an authority and at the same time remain open to the ideas you encounter in your reading, some of which may even persuade you to modify your own position on an issue.

The fact that you have this book in front of you indicates that you've considered the importance of higher education in your life. The fact that you've survived orientation, registered, acquired an e-mail account, bought books, and attended this class long enough to reach this point indicates that you've already invested considerable energy in your pursuit of higher education. All of this places you in the perfect position to enter into a dialogue with every writer in this book. And as you read more and more essays in each assignment sequence, you'll be able to marshal the authority of multiple writers to help you continue to develop and complicate your position.

### Make connections with the ideas of others

To see yourself in conversation with the writers you read, you must first find ways to make connections with their ideas. Where do you agree with them (and where do they agree with you)? Where and what are the disagreements? When you begin to "speak back" to the essays in this book, you're making connections. These connections can help you see yourself in a kind of conversational chain.

Why, you might ask, should you engage in conversation with the writers you read for this and other courses? First, you should do it because it is a way of working with ideas that characterizes educated persons—work that will serve you well in your professional life beyond your college years. Engaging in conversation with other writers enables you to present yourself as an authority and to take a position of responsibility on issues that concern you personally. The issues addressed by the readings in this book provide a good example. In my state, educators, legislators, and citizens are arguing over legislation that will affect general education requirements. Debates in other parts of the country concern affirmative action and its alternatives, whether or not to get rid of remedial courses in four-year colleges and universities, and many, many other issues. As both a student and a citizen, you have a vested interest in these discussions, which may affect where you can take classes, how many classes you can take, and how much you'll pay for them. If you don't enter the conversation, your voice won't be heard, and these decisions will be left entirely to others.

Second, engaging in conversation with the many materials you read will give you the ability to bring together, comprehend, and synthesize a variety of sources of information and ultimately to make critical judgments about their validity and relevance. As we enter the twenty-first century, we need to keep up with lightning-fast changes in technology, deal with threats to the global environment, and make wise decisions that will position us well in the global economy. As the world continues to shrink, it becomes more and more vital that we be able to hear, evaluate, and respond to others' concerns and desires. It has never been more crucial for our society to be able to draw on a diverse pool of educated, thoughtful citizens who are critically aware and capable of producing reasonable, clear discourse. A major goal of this book is to help you become a contributing member of such a pool.

## Closing Thoughts on Active Reading

Finally, I challenge you to take responsibility for your own confusion. Some of these readings are difficult, it's true, but the ones that are hard challenge all readers, not just you alone. I tell my students each term, "It's hard because it's hard." In other words, it isn't difficult to read scholarly or demanding texts because you're not smart enough or tall enough or experienced enough; they're hard because they're hard. Serious scholars don't read quickly; they read slowly, pen or pencil in hand, over and over again. What I've tried to do in this chapter is to help you learn to work with "difficult" texts and challenging ideas so that you no longer have to feel that any reading is "over your head" and so that you can approach any reading you have to do with the confidence that comes from knowing you can find your way into it and take something valuable away from it. With this chapter, you now have strategies at hand to help you approach any reading you need to do, for any class, as an active, critical participant.

# CHAPTER 2

# Writing as a Process

I'VE BEEN TEACHING writing in one form or another and at one school or another for a long time now, and I can safely say that there is no one tried-and-true writing process, system, or method that will work for everyone. I've come to this realization by observing my own writing efforts as well as those of my colleagues and students. I've learned that my writing process differs markedly from the way some other people get words down on paper. For example, I'm a slow writer, for whom producing every page is a struggle, but I'm usually able to keep what I write very focused. By contrast, a friend of mine can rapidly produce page after page, but what she writes is usually "all over the place." We were in a study group together some time ago, and although we created a first draft by entirely different methods, we were a good team when it came time to revise, because she could help me expand and develop, and I could help her cut. We learned from observing each other's methods.

Exposure to other people's writing processes has made me a better, less constricted writer. I'm still slow, but I don't approach my writing projects with quite the same level of anxiety as before, because I have more strategies to rely on now. This chapter offers you some strategies that you may not have tried for writing an essay or research paper. Sample some of the methods that are less familiar to you to see whether you can improve your own writing process.

## Enhancing Your Repertoire of Writing Strategies

The writing assignments in this book may be unlike any you've tackled before, and you may need to refine your repertoire of writing strategies to respond to them. You may need to try different ways of planning and drafting—that is, to experiment with your writing process.

On the following pages you'll find an overview of a writing process you can use to complete the assignment sequences in this book. But remember, it's up to you to customize your own strategies for writing successfully. I'll offer suggestions, but you need to keep in mind the kind of learner, thinker, and writer you are so that you can come up with creative strategies specifically geared to your inclinations and needs. Talking about how to write is like trying to explain how to dance or how to serve a volleyball; there are certain moves everyone must make, but not everyone executes those moves in the same way. Most people who become truly proficient at an activity develop their own unique style.

## Developing a Writing Process That Works for You

What follows is a step-by-step description of a thinking and writing process that you can use or adapt to suit your own requirements and preferences. Although the process is specifically geared to completing the assignment sequences in this book, it is applicable to other writing projects as well. It is provided here as a model, a starting point that you can use to develop your own unique and proficient learning and writing style.

### Before you write anything

Maybe you keep a personal journal or diary. Perhaps you're a fine, productive poet. You might even be a songwriter. Personal or creative writing usually does not require you to respond to specific assignments or readings. Academic writing, on the other hand, nearly always does, so you will benefit from some prior consideration of the assignment, the readings, your goals, and your potential audience. The following paragraphs describe some preliminary steps to take, in any academic writing project, before you ever put pen to paper.

#### Assess the assignment

The first step in the academic writing process is to assess the assignment, or "prompt." Always read your assignment through at least twice before you begin to write anything. Underline or highlight words that indicate how you're expected to approach the assignment, such as *argue, compare, contrast, summarize, persuade,* and *analyze.*

For example, if an assignment asks for an analysis of another writer's arguments, then an essay that merely restates those arguments won't fill the bill. An analysis requires that you not only make observations but also draw conclusions from them. For instance, if your instructor were to ask you to analyze a television talk show, you would, of course, describe the set, the format, and who appeared and what happened in the episodes you watched. You would then have a report. To move beyond a report to an analysis, you would have to draw conclusions from your observations, explaining the significance of certain details and identifying the show's strengths and weaknesses. You might, for example, note that although the advertisements for the show seem to be aimed at attracting a young audience, its guests seem geared to much older viewers. Then you would go on to discuss your conclusions concerning why this is so and offer evidence to support those conclusions.

### Ask for help if you need it

If at any time it is not clear what the assignment requires, don't hesitate to ask your instructor to go over it with you. Even if you feel you have a pretty solid understanding of the assignment, ask yourself, "If I *had* to come up with a question about this assignment for my instructor, what would it be?" This step may seem like a waste of time, but I've often found that what I think I've asked students to do and what my students think I've asked them to do aren't necessarily the same thing. When I have my students write questions about an assignment, even if they think they understand it completely, it helps us get a better sense of each other's goals and expectations. Finally, make notes on the assignment as you hear other people's questions and your teacher's responses. You never know what might help you later when it's just you and the blank page or computer screen.

### Read the reading

With your answers to key focus or prereading journal questions in mind, highlight and annotate sections of the text that you think might be useful as supporting evidence or that you might want to argue against. (For a detailed discussion of active-reading strategies, see Chapter 1. Also, as noted in Chapter 1, don't try to answer all of the prereading questions for the assignment sequences in this book. Instead, pursue those questions that, for whatever reason, attract your attention most forcefully.)

### Define your purpose

Defining your reasons for writing and for whom you are writing is related to the step of assessing your assignment, insofar as it will cause you to focus your assessment further. For example, suppose you are asked to analyze Robert Johnson's argument in his essay "Teaching the Forbidden: Literature and the Religious Student." Right off the bat, you know that your overall purpose is to perform that analysis. But let's say you are put off by the way Johnson represents his students in his essay. You would want to communicate that concern as part of your analysis, and this would become part of your purpose in writing your essay. At this point you probably wouldn't know exactly how you would accomplish this, but it would be part of your purpose, nonetheless. Defining your purpose in writing is an important habit that will help you go beyond simply reacting to your assignments and craft unique, carefully considered responses to them.

### *Identify your audience*

You also need to begin thinking about your audience at this stage. Certainly, you know that writing for your best friend is radically different from writing for a college course. Not only does your purpose for writing differ, but the expectations of your readers differ as well. Your friend will be a generous, interested, and sympathetic reader, disposed to be persuaded by whatever you have to say. Academic readers, who do not know you, are much more demanding. In general, academic audiences have a standard set of expectations: that you use solid logical argumentation and backing, that your prose be precise and well structured, and that you rely as little as possible on emotional appeals. The assignment sequences in this book ask you to produce papers that conform to these conventions. However, expectations may vary even among academic readers. Your biology or history or business professors will have different expectations than your English professors concerning what a successful writing project should include and how it should look. Even two English professors at the same college can differ in what they find valuable or what they want you to emphasize in your writing. Thus each writing situation requires that you shift "rhetorical gears" and that you consider for whom you are writing. Don't let this keep you from getting started, however. If you're not sure how to write for a particular audience, you can always revise your paper later to suit that audience once you've figured out what its expectations are likely to be.

The next time you read the newspaper, take a longer-than-usual look at the letters to the editor and consider how well each writer has imagined and addressed his or her audience. What kind of person do you assume each letter writer to be, and what kind of people do you think each was writing for? In other words, what is each writer's rhetorical stance? Did these writers imagine a particular audience and try to communicate their concerns to that audience, specifically? How persuasive were they?

Each time you write, you want to accomplish something—to get a good grade, secure a job interview, or obtain more votes for the candidate you favor. If you want to be as successful as possible, then you should take the time to define exactly whom you are trying to convince and what you are trying to convince them of—this will help you adopt an effective rhetorical stance. Once you've done this, then you can consider how best to approach your project for the specific audience and purpose you've defined:

- What will your audience know about your topic? What background information will you need to provide?
- Will your audience understand your approach to your topic, or do you need to explain it?
- Where is your audience likely to stand on the issue you're addressing? Will they agree with you or disagree?
- Will you have to convince them that your approach or position is worth caring about?

All of the assignments in this book ask you to keep your experience as a student (in whatever setting and at whatever point in your life) at the center of your responses. If you're a student who has been out of school for several years, you'll have to decide how likely it is that your audience will know how your experience of student life differs from that of someone right out of high school. If you're a first-generation college student at a school where most of the students have college-educated parents, you'll need to decide whether your background enables you to see some things your classmates can't. If it does, you'll need to explain something of that background to your audience so you can teach them what you've observed. Your answers to the questions in the preceding list will affect what you include in your draft and how you shape it. They'll also help you decide how to help your audience to appreciate and understand where your responses come from.

## The invention and planning stage

Now that you've analyzed your assignment, done some reading on your topic, defined your purpose for writing, and identified your audience, you're ready to start planning the content of your essay. You are still very much in the thinking stages of your writing process, and you should strive to remain as unfettered as possible. At this stage you need to discover new possibilities and explore various avenues. Later you'll pick and choose among the options you develop now, so don't limit your choices at this point; let your mind roam free.

### Revisit the readings and the prereading questions

You will often find that at this stage of your writing process, it is useful to reflect on any reading you've done on your topic. Because this book specifically asks you to read and respond to a number of essays for each assignment sequence, you'll definitely have done some reading on your topic by this point. In fact, you'll probably have done some reading of outside sources by this stage no matter what your assignment is, and whether or not you've yet done any formal library research.

At this point you might want to revisit your answers to the pre-reading focus questions in the assignment sequences (or, for other assignments, any prereading questions you compiled yourself). If you took the trouble to highlight and annotate your reading the first time through, then you'll have a head start. If there were sections that struck you as especially true or compelling or that angered you, copy them down (if they're not too long) and take notes about what made them work, or not work, for you.

If you found nothing worth pursuing in the readings, then you'll have your work cut out for you in terms of completing the assignment sequences. When students find a reading "boring," it's usually because there are obstacles to their understanding it. The writing may be above their reading level. Or perhaps they couldn't find a way into the text and were unsure how to proceed. It can also mean that they tried to read the material too quickly. You may encounter difficulties with some of the readings in this book, for a variety of reasons. If you do, stick with the readings. Believe that you'll find a way to make yourself interested in them. In this class, you're learning intellectual strategies and skills, not just information to be repeated for a test, and engaging with the readings in the assignment sequences is an important part of learning those skills.

### Answer the prewriting questions

If you're unsure how or where to begin, try working with the prewriting questions that appear after each essay in the assignment sequences (for other assignments, try compiling prewriting questions yourself). The prewriting questions should serve as prompts to help you move from the readings into the writing assignments that follow them. After you've answered some of the prewriting questions, choose two or three of the questions within the writing assignment itself that you feel are the most promising. Next revisit the readings briefly, with those particular questions in mind. Mark the places that seem to connect, and make quick notes that convey some sense of what those connections are.

### Brainstorm to get ideas

What you do next will largely depend on how you work as a writer. I generally brainstorm on the topic at this point, trying to write down as many ideas and observations as I can. I used to try to formulate a thesis sentence and outline at this point, but I (slowly) learned that doing this too soon kept me from developing ideas and associating those ideas with other ideas that would make my writing more interesting and complex. Also, on a number of occasions, I'd think of something I'd left out after I had completed the outline.

When you brainstorm, try to associate your topic with as many other ideas as you can. Leave nothing out. Some writers prefer to do this with nothing more than a pen and a pad of unlined paper. Others do it at the computer keyboard. Some people use huge numbers of sticky notes of different sizes and colors. Still others use lots of different-colored pens. Whatever method you use, cover the page or screen with as many directions as you can think of that your writing can take.

### *Branch-map or cluster-map your ideas*

This variation on brainstorming offers the added advantage of helping you organize your ideas sooner. At the center of a sheet of paper, write down a possible idea or argument that you think you might want to work with (perhaps a key term from the assignment). Then, as related ideas occur to you, draw lines branching out from that central point. (See Figure 2.1 for an example.) If you were working with the first assignment in the "Idea of a University" sequence, you might write that phrase at the center of your page. Your branching lines might go to topics like "career preparation," "leave

**FIGURE 2.1**
**A Sample Branch Map or Cluster Map**

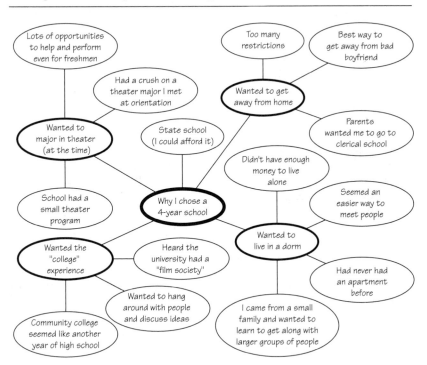

home," and "meet diverse people." From each of these you would then draw more lines, branching out to still more specific kinds of information. For instance, branching out from "leave home" might be "time management," "handle own problems," or "budget money." From there you could keep going, jotting down examples and specifics that support or clarify each idea or point. Just keep going until you run out of "twigs" for your branches.

### Make a chart or table

If your writing assignment seems too complicated for a cluster map, try making a chart or table of the different issues involved. For example, if the assignment asks you to compare your idea of a university to John Henry Newman's or Caroline Bird's ideas, draw three lines down your paper and list what you can about each viewpoint in the appropriate column. Include a fourth column for ideas that don't seem to fit in any of the other three columns but may be helpful as you begin drafting your essay.

### Freewrite

You can also try freewriting to get your ideas flowing. To do this, write for several minutes without stopping, and see what ideas emerge. Even if you get stuck, don't stop writing. If you have to, write "stuck, stuck, stuck" over and over again until the flow of ideas resumes; the point is to break through writer's block to find possibilities to develop in your draft. If you find this strategy useful, you can do a series of freewritings, taking the best parts of each as the jumping-off place for the next.

### Think out loud

If you're more comfortable talking through ideas than writing them down, experiment with a tape recorder or a very good friend who is willing to listen and take notes on what you say. Many of my students have found this an effective strategy. When you "replay" your comments, jot down or otherwise indicate which parts seem worth exploring further or about which you had the most to say or became the most animated and engaged.

### Collaborate with others

A variation on thinking out loud is to work with a study group composed of other people in your class. When you work with a group of peers committed to helping one another, this technique can be fun as well as effective. The purpose is to bounce ideas off one another and help one another develop ideas by asking questions and making suggestions. Of course, each member of the group does his or her own work and writes his or her own essay. I only ask that my students who work together like this include in their essays a note acknowledging the collaboration.

### Stay flexible

Remember that nothing is cast in stone in the early stages. These are just a few strategies for getting your ideas out where you can see and work with them. Your job is to find some way to begin writing—one of the ways just discussed, or one you invent for yourself, or one you see a classmate using—so that when you begin to draft your essay, you have more than enough material to work with and you are in a position to make choices about what to include and what to leave out as you write.

Planning what you're going to write in your first rough draft should always be seen as provisional—that is, it can be changed and reworked and redirected. When I used to require outlines, I found that most of my students did them after they had written their essays. Most strong writers, however, have some sort of plan from which to begin. Experiment with loose, quick outlines (you don't have to use Roman numerals) or notes to help you find and follow a direction for your draft. It may seem like extra work, but it will pay off in the long run.

### Organizing and drafting your essay

It is always tempting to write an exploratory draft before you decide how to organize your final paper. But thinking about possibilities for organization before you begin to write can give you a sense of direction that will help you as you face that first blank page.

The writing assignments in this book ask you to try out a variety of organizational methods. One assignment in the "Higher Learning/Cyber-Learning" sequence asks that you work through some of the ideas and terms in Paul Saffo's essay "Quality in an Age of Electronic Incunabula" and see how those ideas and terms fit or do not fit your experience of computers and learning. Whether or not you're a computer programmer or "hacker," as a college student you are in a position to speculate about the future of technology in both your college career and your economic career. As you tell how computers have "transformed [your] intellectual life," you will probably be able to incorporate stories and examples drawn from your own experience to either reinforce or contrast with Saffo's own. You'll need to narrate those events in detail, providing a chronological description of who said and did what. You'll also have to show clearly how your position compares with Saffo's. And, of course, you'll need to present your point of view—your argument—in the most effective, persuasive way possible. This is a lot to juggle, and it will help to at least sketch out where in your essay you want to perform each of these tasks: narrating events, making comparisons, and presenting your arguments.

As I sat writing the first exploratory draft of this part of this book, I was surrounded by many pieces of paper—notes, brainstorming cluster maps, a very rough outline, suggestions from others, old handouts I'd given classes. I shifted these around as I worked, staring at them, making more notes on them, and pawing through them each of the many times that I got stuck. It was a messy sight. I suggest that as you begin to write your first draft of an essay, you spread your notes, your plans, your prewriting questions, and your readings around you. For one thing, having all this *writing* around makes your blank page or computer screen less intimidating! For another, you'll be less likely to leave things out. And finally, ideas can generate other ideas.

### Observe your writing rituals

Do you have writing rituals? What can you do to make your writing time as productive as possible? I try to compose at the computer, but when my brain won't work fast enough, I find I'm more comfortable writing longhand. (Of course, I then have to find exactly the right pen.) Do you find that music helps you think, or do you need silence? Do you need a clear desk, or do you prefer to sprawl out on the floor? Is the library a place where you find it easier to get writing done, or is your kitchen table a better workplace? Are you an early-morning writer or a late-night writer? Spend some time thinking about what you might do to get yourself in the frame of mind for some serious writing. You might also ask other students what works for them. Experiment, and perhaps you'll find new rituals that can help you get down to work more quickly and efficiently.

### Find a good starting point

Where to begin is another consideration. Do you feel you absolutely *must* have a solid introduction before you can move on, or does the introduction seem to be something you should come back to once you've worked on the body of your essay? Beginning is difficult, so experiment with different ways to get yourself going. Do you find it hard to make that first mark? Try freewriting again. Sometimes when you're stuck on a particular paragraph, try brainstorming material for just that one paragraph to see what the possibilities are and where you can go with it. Keep in mind that you can always change it. (In fact, I require that my students revise their essays extensively to help them get over the idea that the first draft they turn in has to be perfect.)

If you can, formulate at least a rough thesis or central claim to start out with. It can be a single sentence or several sentences. Doing this will help you focus your essay and pin down what point of view you are going to express. A thesis statement is like a memorable, effective photograph: It gives the reader a sense of what's happening and what the story is behind it. A good photograph not only shows the subject but also gives the viewer a sense of what the photographer wants him or her to think about that subject. Similarly, your thesis can convey what you personally find significant about your topic.

### *Maintain your momentum*

Don't let yourself get blocked if a perfectly formulated thesis doesn't flow effortlessly from your brain to the page. Instead, try to come up with a "working" thesis. You can always narrow and sharpen it as your ideas evolve. Let it be as broad as you need it to be at this point, as long as it gives you some sense of direction to follow in the rest of your draft.

As you write the body of your essay, keep your plan and notes at hand, and find ways to get as much done as possible. Ask yourself questions and make notes with different colored pens or sticky notes on your paper or in brackets and capital letters on your screen. If you get stuck, make a note and work on another section; then come back later, when you're fresh or when an idea shakes loose as you work on that other section.

Here's a key tip: When you take a break, don't stop at a place where you're stuck; stop at a place where you have a good idea what's coming next. If you stop because you're blocked, you'll probably dread picking up where you left off, and once you make yourself begin again, it will be even harder to gather writing steam. Again, if you've begun with a rough outline, you'll have other sections you can work on when you run dry. Remember that it doesn't have to be perfect at this stage—it just has to get written!

### *Revision doesn't mean just fixing the commas*

The revision stage of the writing process is where the real craft of writing comes in. Some students think revising is the same thing as editing or proofreading (that is, checking spelling, punctuation, and grammar), but these are two radically different stages in the writing process. Think of revising as re-envisioning your project and where you can take it. If you can do this, many more writing opportunities will open up for you.

It is especially helpful at this stage to be writing on a computer. After making a copy of your draft, try experimenting with major changes to your copy—and I really do mean *major*. What happens if you move your conclusion to the beginning? What other stories could you offer in your introduction to lead up to and clarify your thesis? Or, now that you've done all this thinking and writing to produce this draft, is there a more interesting or compelling argument you could make in your thesis? Are there big block quotes in the middle that need to be broken down and explained? What anecdotes, examples, or personal observations could you add to make your essay more engaging?

Even though it may not seem like it, your writing is the result of a series of choices: Will I argue from this point of view or that one? Will I include this example or that one? Does this phrase say exactly what I want it to, or can I say it differently? As I tell my students, no draft is ever "final"; there's always something else that could be developed or reimagined. Writing is an intellectual process, and as you write, new ideas take shape. The revision stage is the perfect time for you to reflect—and even shuffle—on the ideas you've developed so far. The more time you can devote to playing with your writing at this stage, the better your paper is likely to be.

When you have your paper or essay pretty much in the shape you want to stick with, try to let it get "cold." If you've been writing for four hours straight, you're not going to have much perspective if you try to evaluate its quality immediately. A day or two can help you "hear" it much more clearly. I realize that one practically never completes an academic paper in time to let it sit for two days, but if you do, the payoff can be amazing. When you read your revised draft, make notes in the margins or on another sheet of paper so you'll know where to focus your attention after you finish reading the whole thing. Also ask someone else to read the paper and note what sections he or she thinks are particularly strong and what sections need more work—and why. The following is a kind of checklist you can use to help "road test" your essay.

1. Analyze the argument and organization.
   - What's the focus or thesis of your paper, and where can you find it?
   - Does the way you have arranged or organized your essay—that is, what comes first, second, third, and so on—make sense?
   - How much support have you provided for your thesis? Have you broken your main argument down for your reader and provided examples and supporting information to back up your arguments?
   - Could your introduction be more effective or compelling?
   - Does your conclusion bring your essay to a satisfying close without relying on stock closing phrases?
   - Where could you add more, or what could you leave out?
   - Is everything in your essay relevant to your thesis?

2. Analyze the rhetorical stance.
   - For whom is your essay written?
   - Will that audience need more background information about your topic before you introduce your thesis?
   - How would you describe your essay's tone? Have you addressed your audience as you would want to be addressed? (People don't like being talked down to or being told things they already know.)
   - How do you come across to your audience? Are you someone others will want to listen to?
   - Where and how have you attempted to engage your audience's interest?
   - Does your essay get bogged down anywhere? Does it move too quickly through any difficult issues or ideas?
3. Analyze the style.
   - What are your key terms? Are they clearly and adequately defined?
   - What section of your essay is the strongest? What makes it strong? Can you exploit that source of strength in other sections of your essay to strengthen them as well?
   - How many of your sentences begin with *there* or *this* or *it*? If you find more than a couple, rewrite those sentences.

### Editing and proofreading your essay

Editing and proofreading, or reading your essay for correct grammar, punctuation, and spelling, is the very last thing you should do before sharing it with a serious reader. Read your essay aloud, as though you had an audience right there to keep interested. Don't mumble through it in a monotone. If any sentences or sections make you stumble, make a mark in the margin as a signal to go over them again. Anything that confuses you is likely to do the same to your reader.

Run a spell-checking program if you've used a word processing program on a computer. If you haven't written with a computer, read your essay backward with a dictionary at hand. Look up the words you're not sure about. If you're still not sure after checking your dictionary, ask your teacher before you turn your essay in. Also be aware that spell checkers are not foolproof. A spell-checking program won't catch incorrect homonyms (words that sound alike but have different spellings and meanings), for instance. The most common homonym errors involve *they're, their,* and *there; to, too,* and *two; you're* and *your,* and *accept* and *except.* Just remember that the ultimate responsibility for making sure your essay is error-free is yours, not your computer's.

Over the course of this term, keep a list in your notebook of problems that occur in your writing. For example, if you've had trouble remembering the difference between *there, they're,* and *their,* include these in a chart in your notebook, and consult that chart as part of your final editing process. Finally, ask someone you trust to read your essay to catch anything you might have missed.

### *Responding to the comments of others*

Your job as a writer doesn't end when you turn your essay in. You will doubtless receive feedback about what you've written, from either your peers or your teachers—or from both. These comments can reveal how others have received and perceived your writing and may suggest ways to extend the intellectual project you've begun. They also help you see whether you've succeeded in reaching your audience.

Because these people have gone to the trouble to read and respond to your work, you owe it to them to pay close attention to that response. Did they understand your purpose and your argument? What did they see as the strengths in your work? Where did they have questions? Only you can decide which comments will help you extend and strengthen your writing project and which won't. But it's your job to respond meaningfully and fully to the comments you find most relevant.

In my own classes, I ask my students to highlight the revisions they do in response to my comments and those of their peers. This way, they and I can immediately see how "deeply" they've revised. For example, if I see single sentences highlighted in a few paragraphs, I can pretty quickly tell that rather than reevaluating their project in light of the questions raised, they've tried to "silence" those questions. What I look for are whole sections highlighted, showing that significant portions of the student's writing has been reworked. Real revision offers a considered response to the questions and comments of the reader—whether that reader is the teacher or a classmate.

## Closing Thoughts on Writing as a Process

The idea behind this chapter was not to overwhelm you with rules to follow and hoops to jump through but to let you know that people aren't born writers; they learn to be writers. Think about yourself as a writer—your pleasures, your anxieties, your strengths, your weaknesses. How can you use what you know about yourself and what you've read here to expand and refine those pleasures and strengths? There is no one "right" step-by-step formula, but there are strategies available to you if you're willing to experiment and invest the necessary time.

# CHAPTER 3

# Argument and Persuasion

Have you ever been in an argument with someone who refused to listen to your point of view or even let you try to explain it? Such arguments are not fun. They are not even interesting. The only possible outcome is a standoff, unless the person who isn't allowed to get his or her point of view across simply gives in out of frustration. Rarely does any learning take place in such an argument, on either side— and an opportunity for learning is just what an argument should be. Instead of something to be "won" by one side or the other, an argument can be a way for two or more people to discuss difficult issues and fully appreciate their complexity. In this type of argument, it is possible for people to change their minds without feeling they have "lost." That's because the goal of such arguments is not to win but to engage in reasonable civil discourse, which is exactly the kind of communication that is appropriate for an academic setting. It is this kind of argumentation that this chapter describes.

The term *discourse* refers to the means we all use to communicate with one another, whether orally, in writing, or even through gestures (such as nodding our heads to mean "yes"). The meaning of the term *civil discourse* is a bit more restrictive. After all, when one driver yells and gestures at another driver in traffic, it's a form of discourse—the second driver undoubtedly understands what the first one is communicating—but it can hardly be called civil. In the context of social and academic communication, then, *civil* means "respectful." Participants in civil discourse listen closely to one another's positions and present their own views in ways that rely more on reason than on emotion and that seek to convince those with a different outlook rather than to brainwash or bully them.

The issues you'll encounter in the assignment sequences are meant to stimulate civil discourse. I tried to avoid topics that lead to polarization. For example, it's almost impossible to have a civil, critical discussion about abortion, because many people are so passionately attached to their positions that they cease to hear alternative points of view. The topics in the assignment sequences, by contrast, steer you away from simplistic, "pro" versus "con" positions and encourage you to consider multiple arguments and points of view.

The academic world has its own set of expectations regarding discourse. For example, academic writing frequently refers to previous scholarship; therefore, the rules for quoting and crediting other sources are important. Academic discourse is also characterized by careful, dispassionate explorations of ideas for a specialized, patient audience. (This makes it in many ways the opposite of newspaper writing, which is aimed at a general audience, usually strives to be brief, and sometimes plays to readers' emotions.) Thus, although you can't help but be influenced by your personal background and experiences—including your heritage, the culture of the region where you grew up, your previous education, and so on—you must try to remain somewhat intellectually aloof when participating in academic discussions, whether written or spoken.

For example, my personal background and history position me well to discuss growing up in a small family, growing up in the South, being a nontraditional student, being a parent and a student, being a part-time student, as well as many other roles, circumstances, and issues. When I communicate within the academic arena, I draw on this experience and on what I've learned from people with different personal backgrounds, but I don't put that personal experience in the foreground. I use it to enhance my arguments, not as their sole basis. And I add another dimension to my arguments: scholarship. Academic discourse draws on the research and writings of others, which are made available to the academic community in a variety of ways (journal articles, books, lectures, Internet mailing lists, and so on) and add to the stock of knowledge on innumerable subjects. Academic discourse makes it possible for us to come together and learn from one another's efforts—to participate in the continuing creation of knowledge in our fields of study. Arguments (of the civil sort) are an indispensable part of academic discourse.

## Crafting an Argument

An argument makes a claim about an issue and attempts to convince others of the correctness of that claim. In an essay or research paper, your argument is the position you take—your thesis—which you will try to support with reasons and evidence throughout your work. For your essay to be compelling, you need to adopt a stance that others can reasonably disagree with. For example, suppose your thesis is "People should not abuse children." Because no reasonable person can argue the opposite position, that people *should* abuse children, this thesis does not really make an argument; it just states a truism. But if you define your thesis more clearly and focus your argument more precisely—stating, for example, that child abuse includes all forms of corporal punishment, even spanking—then you are on your way to writing a compelling essay, built around a genuine argument that can engender dialogue about your topic.

### Offer reasons, not opinions

Just as a thesis must be more than a self-evident truth, it must also be more than an opinion. It must rest on valid underlying claims or evidence rather than on your personal beliefs or preferences. For example, you probably like some forms of music better than others. In college dorms, battles rage over whether rap or country music is the superior art form. This is a question of personal preference, however, which ultimately doesn't provide a basis for an arguable position. I can state my opinion, based on my personal musical taste, that polkas should not be taken seriously as an art form. But this is not a thesis; it is merely a statement of my opinion about polkas. If, by contrast, someone presents me with quantities of evidence showing that the polka is indeed a valuable art form—for instance, because it reflects the heritage of a particular ethnic group or because it has evolved through the efforts and artistry of polka musicians—I will have to concede the validity of their argument, even if I don't necessarily agree with their conclusion.

Valid underlying claims provide the reasons why your thesis makes sense to you and can make sense to others. You can think of these underlying claims as "because" statements. For example, you might state that colleges have a responsibility to monitor students' on-campus behavior because they can be held legally liable in case of accidents or serious problems. Another person could respond that colleges do not have a responsibility to monitor students' on-campus behavior because students are adults and, as such, are responsible for themselves.

### Define key terms

In almost any serious argument, whether written or spoken, the participants need to define the key terms of their position. When you consider that we come from so many different backgrounds, age groups, and experiences, the need to clarify what we're saying becomes obvious. Our way of seeing things will seem natural to us, but it probably won't be so natural to others. If you and I are arguing about *conservative* politics, for example, we must make sure we share the same understanding of this key term, which helps us set some ground rules.

Deciding which terms need defining takes some practice and a lot of thought about who your audience is. An important step when you define a term is to consult a dictionary, but don't assume that a dictionary definition will do the job by itself. For instance, some students find the label *feminist* objectionable, even though the dictionary definition of feminism seems to match their own views about women's roles in society. For example, most agree that women should earn equal pay for equal work, that parents should share child care responsibilities, and that women should be free to pursue any career they desire. But some see the word *feminist* as meaning something more than or different from the dictionary definition. Therefore, writers need to sort out and make clear what definitions they wish to use for terms such as this.

Note that *feminism* is what is called an abstract term. Abstract terms don't have precise or specific or obvious meanings. In this they are unlike concrete terms whose meanings, which are called denotative definitions, are immediately clear. If you tell a friend you ate tuna salad for lunch, she may not know precisely how it was prepared, but she will have a pretty clear idea what you consumed, and unless she has a particular passion for collecting tuna salad recipes, she probably won't ask for further details. Other terms, however, aren't so easy to pin down to a singular definition. We refer to their meanings as *connotative* because their definitions depend on experiences and feelings. For instance, because of the variety of understandings that different people bring to the word *morality,* you're going to have to provide abundant information about how *you* are using this word.

Another step—arguably more important than looking in a dictionary—is to draw distinctions between your use of the term and another use. Drawing such distinctions enables you to make clear what you mean by ruling out what you don't mean. Here is an example. Read the following clear and thorough definition of a slippery term, *criticism,* from Terry Barrett's *Criticizing Photographs: An Introduction to Understanding Image.*

> Throughout this book the term *criticism* will not refer to the act of negative judgment; it will refer to a much wider range of activities and will adhere to this broad definition: Criticism is informed discourse about art to increase understanding and appreciation of art. This definition includes criticism of all art forms including dance, music, poetry, painting, and photography. "Discourse" includes talking and writing. "Informed" is an important qualifier that distinguishes criticism from mere talk and uninformed opinion about art. Not all writing about art is criticism. Some art writing, for example, is journalism rather than criticism: It is news reporting on artists and art world events rather than critical analysis.

Notice Barrett's use of italics and quotation marks. Using punctuation in these ways in your own writing will alert your readers that you're offering your own special definitions of terms. Barrett works through his definition of *criticism* with great patience. This patience indicates his awareness of his audience: beginning college students who may see "criticism" as an unpleasant, mean-spirited, activity. Barrett begins with a distinction (*"criticism* will not refer to the act of negative judgment") and then proceeds to what he *will* use the term to mean ("informed discourse about art to increase understanding and appreciation of art"). Note also that he defines terms used within his definition ("'Discourse' includes talking and writing.") Each sentence works with the one before it to make the ground rules clear to his audience.

In general, when you use a term that's important to your argument, consider how likely a wide audience is to share your understanding of that term. Be ready to question what seems to you to be obvious and to question the assumptions that underlie your understanding and use of the term. The meaning of the word *privacy,* for example, seems pretty straightforward, but if you're an only child and your dormitory roommate or spouse is the youngest of seven children, you may find your definitions to be surprisingly different. Try to view your term from different perspectives.

### Provide supporting evidence

How, after you have taken a position and defined your terms, will you start to persuade people to agree with your argument? You will need to produce evidence to back up your claims—in other words, the reasons for your reasons. These reasons are your supporting details. Imagine your readers asking you, in response to your claims, "Why do you say that?" How would you answer? The most effective response is to provide proof in the form of examples drawn from others' research or your own (research is discussed in greater detail in Chapters 4 and 5).

Providing supporting evidence accomplishes several goals. First of all, it shows you know what you're talking about and that you speak either from experience or on the basis of research. Second, supporting evidence is what your reader may find to be the most interesting part of your essay. Finally, supporting evidence is what persuades your reader to agree or disagree with you if he or she is unsure about what position to hold or holds another position. Bear in mind that an essay without adequate supporting detail is very likely to be boring and not very persuasive. Details can make an enormous difference in the effectiveness of your writing.

### Present opposing points of view

Another major consideration when formulating your overall argument is what claims or reasons would probably be offered to refute your position by those who disagree with your argument. Your position and the reasoning behind it should be strong enough to withstand such a challenge. To demonstrate this strength, your essay should include, at various points, discussions of opposing views and explanations of why they don't convince you. For instance, if you are going to argue in an essay that colleges should be responsible for monitoring students' behavior, then you have to be able to address counterarguments to this position as well. You might mention the counterargument that some students are financially independent at the age of eighteen or nineteen and that some are even married and have children. You might mention that many students live in fraternity or sorority houses or in other off-campus housing, and you might present the arguments offered by students who have protested (or "rioted," as some news reports have called it) over the complicated set of issues characterized by the media as "the right to party." As you work on preparing to write your essay, you have to consider and respond to all these points—and even try to come up with more. This doesn't mean that in the final product you have to include a lengthy list of all your opposition's arguments. Rather, your essay should ultimately include only your strongest claims and the strongest claims from alternative points of view.

You should also be aware that for many subjects, particularly in academic writing, there are more than two sides. Most serious issues can be viewed from multiple perspectives. As Deborah Tannen explains in *The Argument Culture* (26),

> I do not believe we should put aside the argument model of public discourse entirely, but we need to rethink whether this is the *only* way, or *always* the best way, to carry out our affairs. A step toward broadening our repertoires would be to pioneer reform by experimenting with metaphors other than sports and war, and with formats other than debate for framing the exchange of ideas. The change might be as simple as introducing a plural form. Instead of asking "What's the other side?" we might ask . . . "What are the other sides?" Instead of insisting on hearing "both sides," we might insist in hearing "all sides."

In other words, many people tend to see all issues as having only two sides, but as Tannen points out, there are often many positions worth exploring. This observation doesn't mean that there should be no disagreement but that there are a variety of ways to approach an issue, ways that can include both agreement and disagreement.

## Using the Three Appeals

As you develop your argument, you must consider not only what your position is but also how best to present that position to your audience. To make your argument as persuasive as possible, consider how to employ the "three appeals," or the three ways in which writers attempt to appeal to their readers. The first way is to present yourself as an authority on your topic—as someone worth listening to. This is known as making an ethical appeal, or using the rhetorical strategy of *ethos*. The second way is to offer examples that will invoke an emotional response in your readers. This is known as making an emotional appeal, or using the strategy of *pathos*. The third way is to appeal to your readers' reason. This is known as making a logical appeal, or using the strategy of *logos*. All three appeals are necessary components of all persuasive, argumentative writing.

## Ethos

When you write, you have to take pains to demonstrate to your audience that you are believable and that you speak with authority on your topic. The term *ethos* is related to the word *ethics* in that both refer to legitimacy. To make a successful ethical appeal, an author must make the reader believe that this writer is telling the truth as he or she sees it and has struggled to make sure that it is indeed the truth. Your goal as a writer, then, is to establish a credible *persona*. Your persona is the person your readers imagine you to be as they read. Obviously, you want to come across as trustworthy, reasonable, and thorough.

In some respects, establishing your *ethos* is closely related to the responsibility to provide your reader with opposing viewpoints on your topic. Doing so demonstrates that you are presenting your side of the issue fairly. You also enhance your credibility by using examples to show that you know what you're talking about. If you were to write a paper about the difficulty of balancing college and family or work, you would strengthen your credibility by drawing from your specific experience, detailing a particular time when you felt pulled in too many directions.

## Pathos

During the recent impeachment trial of President Bill Clinton, Representative Henry Hyde, the chief House "manager" in charge of prosecuting the president, invoked the memory of those Americans who had fought and died for their country in World War II. Likewise, President Clinton's attorneys invoked the civil rights movement in their arguments in defense of the President. Although most commentators agreed that war deaths and civil rights had little to do with the charges against the President, these appeals received more attention than most of the rest of the arguments presented to the Senate. If they had nothing to do with the issue at hand, why were they mentioned? They were included in the debate because of the emotional pull they brought to each side's argument.

*Pathos* is the attempt to persuade people through their emotions, and it can be very effective for drawing people in and getting them to consider your broader argument. Thus both the House managers and the President's lawyers were able to use this strategy to capture the attention of the press and of a scandal-weary public. The problem with appealing to people strictly through their emotions, however, is that it generally works for only a short time. An emotional appeal will get your readers' attention, but it is unlikely to convince them of the rightness of your position. Once the immediate effect wears off, your audience will no longer be persuaded unless your appeal is made—and holds up—on other levels as well.

### Logos

Recently I attended a forum to discuss drug testing for high school students involved in extracurricular activities. As you know, the issue of drug abuse scares most parents deeply, and the parents at this gathering were no exception. Hence pathos was much in evidence: The discussion was charged and emotional, and many people stood up and talked about their fears. People also were careful to establish their ethos—as a paramedic, a parent, a social worker, a teacher, and so on. What was largely lacking was any appeal to logic. No facts or figures were presented to show what people's fears were based on. There was no account of how many drug-related problems had occurred at the school, no estimate of the cost of testing, no details on how and where testing would be carried out, no evidence from the local police indicating that the school had a serious drug problem, little discussion of how drug testing would avoid violating students' constitutional rights, and so on. This kind of information and support—the kind that was missing from this discussion—is what is meant by the term *logos*. Without a firm foundation in logical reasoning, an appeal based on ethos and pathos won't support a strong, effective argument.

## Writing for a Specific Audience

To integrate the three appeals successfully in your essays, you must take some time to think about whom you're writing for. This is one of the hardest things writers must do. Although it may be easy to figure out how to address one particular audience that you're familiar with (for example, you undoubtedly speak differently to your grandmother than to your friends, and you know automatically how to address each), in academic writing it's often hard to get a sense of whom you're writing for and what their needs are. One rule should always prevail: Make sure you treat your audience with respect. After the drug testing discussion, an editorial in our local newspaper stated that anyone who opposed drug testing "was not living in the real world." The writer of that editorial was not respectful of his audience and their legitimate concerns about the constitutionality and cost of drug testing, and as a result he may have alienated more people than he convinced. Always assume that your audience is your equal. Also note that it's best to avoid irony or sarcasm when making an argument. For one thing irony and sarcasm easily backfire, irritating an audience into taking the opposition's side. For another, a shift in tone from ironic or sarcastic to sincere is jarring and hard to carry off.

Part of treating your audiences as your equal is conforming to standard English usage. The essays you will be writing for the assignment sequences in this book are largely formal, and therefore they call for formal language and usage. Adhering to standard usage means, among other things, avoiding colloquial language, such as slang. If your topic specifically calls for slang or would be best treated by including slang terms (say, for example, you're reporting on binge drinking on campus), then it's fine to use nonstandard terms. Just be sure to define them for your audience, which might not be familiar with them or might use other expressions to describe the same things.

### Adopt an appropriate rhetorical stance

Look back at Chapter 2, "Writing as a Process," and think again about the questions you are advised to use to analyze your rhetorical stance and style (pages 22–23). As discussed in that chapter, *rhetorical stance* refers to the way in which you attempt to engage with and persuade your audience. Thus, to adopt an effective rhetorical stance, you need to think about who your audience is, what kind of background information they'll need, how likely they are to agree or disagree with you, and whether or not you'll need to persuade them to care about the issue you are discussing. The answers to these questions will help you decide how to shape your paper. For example, if your audience will need considerable background information to understand your argument, then you'll want to provide the necessary information near the beginning of your essay.

Let's say that you spent one Christmas vacation working at a homeless shelter and that the experience had a profound impact on you. As part of your response to an assignment in a research writing class, you want to argue that community service should be a graduation requirement for all students at your college. You can first assume that your audience will need to know what *community service* means. Therefore, you'll need to include a definition in your introduction or very near the beginning of your essay. You can also assume that a number of your fellow students will respond that they don't have time for such a requirement, so you'll need to offer several reasons to persuade them that such an activity would be worth their time. You might also find faculty members and administrators reluctant to organize such a requirement. Therefore, you'll need to use the three appeals appropriately for an academic audience, by showing them that you are, like them, busy yet concerned about the problem of homelessness (ethos); by describing what you saw and learned from your experience (pathos); and by explaining how service learning can be implemented, how other colleges have established this requirement, and how it is ultimately of real benefit on a practical as well as a moral level (logos).

### Clarify your underlying assumptions and anticipate those of your audience

When we analyze arguments, whether our own or those we encounter in class or in readings, we need to have a sense of what foundation they rest on. In other words, we need to discover the beliefs from which they have emerged. Often these underlying beliefs or assumptions go unexamined. If they're never challenged, we may not even become aware of them. Nonetheless, they are there in the background, invisible yet omnipresent, like the air we breathe. I learned about the hazards of leaving such assumptions unanalyzed from an ongoing argument with a former colleague who had been educated in France. Our disagreement concerned the nature and quality of the students in our classes. Our arguments were passionate but unproductive, and neither of us able to understand why the other "couldn't see reason."

Finally we realized that our dissimilar backgrounds and our different experiences with institutions of higher education had shaped what we regarded as reasonable. That is, we weren't arguing from *shared* assumptions. She was the product of an educational system that begins testing students at an early age and in which access to higher education is largely state-controlled. I came through a state university system that gave me access to higher education even though I hadn't yet figured out what I wanted to do with my life. Her assumption was "of course college attendance should be based on intellectual merit." My assumption was "of course higher education should be open to all people, at any time in their lives." Once these unspoken assumptions became clear, each of us was able to understand why the other clung so tenaciously to her position, even though we were still unable to agree. Our "of courses"—our underlying assumptions—were intensely important to both of us. In a certain sense, they were part of how we saw ourselves.

It's important both to pinpoint your own underlying assumptions, because they will inevitably crop up in your writing, and to anticipate those of your audience, because their reactions to your argument will depend in part on their preconceptions, previous knowledge, and biases. You need to make sure your assumptions are accurate and that they in fact support your thesis; otherwise, you'll end up arguing against yourself. Likewise, you need to consider your audience's assumptions as you decide which rhetorical strategy to emphasize. Remember that you want to convince your audience, not win a debate with them. When our assumptions are challenged or threatened, we generally respond passionately, sometimes defensively. Therefore, it's important to at least consider whether your thesis will be challenging readers' closely held assumptions. If so, your argument will have to be especially sensitive and persuasive and your rhetorical stance particularly effective.

Consider the opening sentence from "Radical English," a column by George F. Will: "At the University of Texas at Austin, as on campuses across the country, freshmen are hooking up their stereos and buckling down to the business of learning what they should have learned in high school—particularly English composition." Reread this sentence a couple of times carefully. Now take some time to answer the following questions:

- What is Will assuming about you as a student and about all beginning college students? How does this make you feel? Does this sentence describe you? Your friends?

- Why does he connect "hooking up their stereos" to "buckling down to the business of learning what they should have learned in high school"?

- What do you think Will's argument is going to be in this essay? Do you agree with it? What examples can you offer to support or counter it?

Note the range of responses that this one sentence can potentially evoke, depending on the reader's assumptions and on what the reader takes to be the author's assumptions.

The fact that you and someone else hold different underlying assumptions does not mean that you will necessarily disagree with each other on a particular issue. Several years ago, feminists on the political left and Christians on the political right formed an alliance in an effort to eliminate "adult" businesses in Indiana. The general public was surprised by this unlikely coalition, because the two groups' positions on so many issues seemed utterly opposed. Yet, even though these groups had different underlying assumptions about pornography sellers—the feminists saw these businesses as engendering violence against women, whereas the Christian groups saw them as contributing to the community's overall moral decline—their goal was the same, and therefore they were able to pool their resources and have a real impact on their community.

## Closing Thoughts on Argument and Persuasion

"Moving from Debate to Dialogue," the title of the final section in Deborah Tannen's book *The Argument Culture,* sums up my goals for this chapter. We all live in communities—families, academic institutions, professions, workplaces, neighborhoods, and so on. As part of a community, we daily communicate to those around us our hopes, fears, plans, needs, discoveries, and opinions. Expressing ourselves through debate, although it is sometimes our tendency, limits us to win–lose scenarios that often cause more problems than they solve. When we nurture a dialogue, however, we create a greater possibility for understanding and compromise and acquire a greater sense of the complexity of the issues that move us. When you write an essay or a paper, you are likewise communicating your hopes, fears, plans, needs, discoveries, and opinions to a community—your readers—and the same distinction between a debate and a dialogue holds true. Crafting an effective argument isn't about winning; it's about teaching and communicating. And that's what academic writing is really all about.

# CHAPTER 4

# Conducting Library Research

MANY STUDENTS HAVE little sense of the purpose or value of doing library research; it just seems like a hoop they must jump through at several points in their academic lives. At the same time, many such students think of researching as a relatively easy, mindless task. The problem, they believe, lies not so much in how to do research as in what to do with their research once they've conducted it. This attitude reveals a basic lack of understanding about the role research plays in learning and intellectual growth. Yes, there's a lot of information available on almost any topic you can think of, but conducting meaningful research is not the same as just casting a wide net and then scrambling to use whatever you happen to catch in it.

Imagine a student who decides to write a paper about the war on drugs. She looks up *drugs* in the most recent *Reader's Guide to Periodical Literature* and is briefly horrified by the large number of entries, but then she skims the list and jots down (or prints out) items in periodicals that she's sure will be readily available in the library: *Time, Newsweek, U.S. News and World Report.* Once she has located her articles, she carefully copies down a line or two from each, making sure that at least one quote includes statistics. More or less by chance, the quotation she selects emphasizes the social costs of Drug addiction and educational efforts to reduce drug use among teens. A night or two before her paper is due, she sits down with these quotes and a blank page or computer screen. The statistics go into the introduction as a "hook," which becomes her thesis; the rest get arranged in some sort of order, and she writes around them.

Such use of "research" resembles the tail wagging the dog. Unfortunately, though, students often let this type of haphazard research determine what they're going to say in their papers. That view of research is not part of this book's approach or goals. Instead, I hope you'll begin to think of library research as another way of working with ideas—an intellectual exercise in which you can enter into a special kind of dialogue or correspondence with others interested in the same topics you are investigating. One person offers an analysis of a particular topic (the meaning of a work of fiction, for example) or makes observations about a collection of data (such as the results of a scientific experiment or fluctuations in the stock market) in a published book, in an article in a professional journal, or on a web site. Countless others can then access that analysis or those observations and offer feedback in their own writings. As you perform library research, think of yourself as a participant in the academic and professional conversations going on about your topic, and think of the paper you are preparing to write as a potential contribution to that dialogue.

To enter the conversation, you need to learn a few rules that will help you do so on an equal footing. If you want to be taken seriously, you have to display an awareness of what others in your field have done and are doing. Therefore, you must read accounts of prior and current research done by professionals working in that area and mention their research in your own project. You need to build on what's been done before and use it as a foundation for your own arguments. You also need to style and format your writings in accordance with the appropriate academic and professional conventions.

The key point to remember is that the purpose of consulting others' research is *to support your own research,* not to tell you what to write. You can use general-interest publications (such as newsmagazines) and general reference books (such as encyclopedias) to help you initially investigate and narrow your topic, but once you've developed your thesis, you'll need to consult specialized academic sources (such as monographs and professional journals) for meatier information to bolster your arguments. This chapter provides some guidelines to help you conduct meaningful research and participate successfully in the world of academic and professional discourse.

## Narrowing Your Topic

Now imagine that our student interested in writing about the war on drugs starts out by reading several general-interest publications actively and critically, using the techniques described in Chapter 1. She photocopies a number of newspaper and newsmagazine articles so that she can annotate them. She poses and answers several pre-reading focus questions for each article, and she does some post-reading journal writing as well. Before she began these investigations, she had a vague sense that the war on drugs is worthwhile and should be rigorously supported. On the basis of her commonsense understanding that drug abuse destroys people's lives and often begins before adulthood, she had planned to argue in her paper for tougher drug laws and earmarking more money for antidrug education efforts aimed at teenagers. Her active investigations into the topic suggested to her, however, that existing U.S. drug policy has been extremely expensive, has not demonstrably reduced drug use among U.S. teens, has resulted in many long jail terms for casual users, and may have violated the civil rights of a large number of Americans. Since she is a pre-law student, the last point makes an especially strong impression on her. Therefore, as a result of her active reflection on the topic, she decides to argue that the war on drugs has had a disturbing, negative impact on civil rights in the United States—a position that not only is much more specific but also differs substantially from her initial notion about how she would approach the topic. Now she's ready to do some more de-tailed research to determine whether she can adequately back up this claim or needs to modify it further.

As this example suggests, there's a big difference between ana-lyzing information and merely collecting it and spitting it back out. Analyzing information deepens our understanding of the topics we research. Just as our analytical ability is a large part of what makes us human, an analytical approach to library research is a large part of what makes it worthwhile. This is the approach this book stresses, in which library research becomes another habit of reflection, not a rote process.

The example also illustrates the relationships among research-ing, reflecting, and narrowing your topic. It's OK to start with general-interest sources like newsmagazines and encyclopedias, as long as you reflect on what you learn from those sources, use them to narrow your thesis (not define it), and then move on to more detailed and specific investigations. You should continue to analyze the informa-tion you collect at each stage of your researching process, working from the most general to the most specific. Keep in mind as you con-duct your investigations that broadening a too-narrow topic is easier than narrowing a too-broad one.

You can consult general-interest publications in just about any library. To locate more specialized sources of information, however, it helps to know how to use a large research library. The next sec-tion provides a general overview of research libraries to help you get the most out of your library time.

## Getting to Know Your Library

A trip to the library evokes different feelings in different people. Although I don't always love doing research, I do love being in li-braries. I have positive memories of sitting in comfy kid-sized chairs in a cool room on hot Texas summer days. Also, I love to read and just like being around books. But I realize that for many students, a library—especially a large university research library—can be in-timidating. If you've never spent much time in a library or if your college library is much bigger than any other library you've seen, set aside some time just to go in and figure out where things are. When you first walk into your library, you'll probably see the main desk, where you can ask general questions and check out books. You may also see the reserve desk, where you can pick up books and other materials that teachers have asked the library to keep available for students to consult in the library for brief periods of time. You're likely to see computer terminals for the library's online catalogue. You may or may not also find its old card catalogue, a bank of drawers filled with paper cards; in most libraries this time-honored but cumbersome fixture has been permanently retired. The computer will provide you with general instructions on how to search for materials by subject, author, or title—just as you would search using an old-fashioned card catalogue—and by "keyword" as well. (Performing computerized searches using keywords is discussed later in the chapter.) These instructions might resemble those on the screen in Figure 4.1.

Somewhere in the library, you will find the reference desk. Here you can ask specially trained reference librarians for help in locating information on your topic. The reference desk is often a good place to begin. Reference librarians are a gold mine of information about reference resources and often about the library's general holdings as well, including old-fashioned books and journals as well as cutting-edge computerized and online databases. No one will expect you to be familiar with the mind-boggling number of reference

**FIGURE 4.1**
**Instructions for an Online Library Catalogue**

```
        You may search the catalog by one of the following:

AUTHOR    To find authors, composers, performers, illustrators,
          editors, conferences, corporate authors.

          EXAMPLES: >>A=shakespeare william (enter last name first)
                    >>A=American Bar Assoc

TITLE     To find a work by title.
          EXAMPLE: >>T=HAMLET

SUBJECT   To find material on a subject.
          EXAMPLES: >>S=CHILD PSYCHOLOGY
                    >>S=Twain Mark

KEYWORD   To search the catalog by keyword,
          type the command KEYWORD at the >> prompt.

          PRESS <CTRL>Z TO RETURN TO MAIN MENU

Enter your search below, or press the (NextScreen) key for more
information.
>>
```

resources available in a large research library, so don't feel reluctant to ask for help. You'll find that most reference librarians genuinely like what they do and enjoy helping people learn their way around the library. And most important, they don't mind when students ask them really basic questions.

## The Library of Congress Classification System

In most university libraries, students can go into the rows of shelved books ("the stacks") and look for books and bound journals themselves. Rare books and other special collections are often stored in closed stacks; library patrons must request these materials, and library employees then fetch them. But most library holdings are stored in open stacks, which students can access freely. Books are shelved in library stacks according to their call numbers. A call number is a unique identifier that tells library patrons where a particular book is shelved and also provides some general information about the book's content. In U.S. libraries, call numbers are based on one of two major classification systems: the Dewey decimal system or the system developed by the Library of Congress. Most academic libraries use the Library of Congress system, so to find what you're looking for in a university library, you'll need to understand and know how to use this system. Because public and high school libraries are more likely to use the Dewey decimal system instead, you may not be familiar with the Library of Congress system. Therefore, I've included a brief overview of it here.

In the Library of Congress system, materials are classified according to their subject matter. Subject areas, or classes, are identified by letters. The main classes are as follows:

A - General works
B - Philosophy, psychology, religion
C - Auxiliary sciences of history
D - General and Old World history
E-F - American history
G - Geography, maps, recreation, anthropology
H - Social sciences (such as sociology and economics)
J - Political science
K - Law
L - Education (all levels)
M - Music
N - Fine arts
P - Literature, linguistics, languages
Q - Science and mathematics

R -        Medicine
S -        Agriculture
T -        Technology
U -       Military science
V -       Naval Science
Z -       Library science

These letters correspond to the first letter in the call numbers assigned to specific books. Each main class is broken down further, using additional letters and then numbers. For example, the call numbers of materials on U.S. federal law begin with KF. Materials on the laws of the individual states are classed as follows:

KFA
1–599          Alabama
1201–1799    Alaska
2401–2999    Arizona
3601–4199    Arkansas

KFC
1–1199        California
1801–2399    Colorado
3601–4199    Connecticut

KFD
1–599          Delaware
1201–1799    District of Columbia

and so on. The Library of Congress web site describes the classification system in complete detail. You can access the top level of the classification system at

http://www.lcweb.loc.gov/catdir/cpso/lcco/lcco.html

Links from that page provide a detailed breakdown of each main class.

Your library probably has handouts or displays telling you on what floor or in what section you'll be able to find various letter and number combinations. The Library of Congress system classifies materials by subject, so you'll find that books on similar topics are shelved near one another in the stacks. For example, all books on U.S. federal law will have call numbers beginning with KF. Because books are shelved by call number, first alphabetically and then numerically, all of the library's books on this topic will be shelved together in the stacks. Thus if you know the two- or three-letter combination that indicates the particular subtopic you're interested in, you can simply go to that section in the stacks and browse through the books shelved there. (It is still helpful to check your library's online catalogue, however. Some books are likely to have been checked out or to be in use somewhere else in the library, so they will be missing from the stacks.)

Figure 4.2 shows a sample computer screen from my university library's computer cataloguing system. The catalogue displays the book's author, title, publisher, year of publication and call number. The first part of the call number—"PZ4"—tells you that this book can be found in the contemporary fiction section. The second part, following the period—"M8489"—tells you precisely where this book is shelved in that section. (For a detailed explanation of Library of Congress call numbers and how books are shelved first alphabetically and then numerically, see http://www.jsu.edu/depart/library/graphic/callno.htm. Or ask at your library's front desk; there may be a handout available that explains the system in detail.)

## Finding Materials

Your college library contains a wide variety of sources. Besides books, a typical library's holdings include newspapers and magazines, professional and academic journals, government documents, maps, documents on microfilm (including back issues of many periodicals), printed catalogues and indexes, electronic catalogues and indexes (online and on CD-ROM), special collections, bound dissertations and dissertation abstracts, and more. And what your library doesn't possess in its holdings, it can often borrow through interlibrary loan programs. The interlibrary loan office will order

**Figure 4.2**
**Sample Screen from an Online Library**

```
       AUTHOR: Morgan, Marlo.
       TITLE: Mutant message down under

   PUBLISHER: HarperCollins Publishers, c1994.
    SUBJECTS: Australian aborigines--Fiction.
             Americans--Travel--Australia--Fiction.
             Adventure stories.

LIBRARY HOLDINGS:
    Gee Library Main Stacks
    1.     CALL NUMBER: PZ4.M8489 Mu -- Book -- Available



No more holdings. Enter 'H' to redisplay all Holdings
information.
Select a line number for detailed information about that line.
Enter:  B          to backup.
        F          to see the Full title record.
        R          to Request the material.


   >>                              Enter ? for HELP.
```

whatever you need; all you have to do is fill out a form telling them what you need and who you are. Many libraries have these forms online. In addition, either your library or a special computer lab at your school will offer access to the vast amount of information available on the Internet.

How do you begin sifting through this mountain of information? To do a complete job of researching your topic, you'll need to consult both print and electronic indexes. The most basic of these is your library's online card catalogue. You'll also want to find out what information is available on your topic in various periodicals. To do this, you'll first look up your topic in a scholarly index, either print or electronic, to get a list of articles you can possibly use, and then you'll consult another list to see which of the periodicals you need are available in your campus libraries. You should also consult on-line database indexes, such as First Search and EBSCOhost, some of which let you get the entire text of many articles without ever leaving your computer.

### Define your search terms

Whether you search in an electronic catalogue, an online index or database, or a print index, your success in finding useful information on your topic will depend in part on what terms you use to search by. Sit down with a piece of paper and, thinking in terms of your needs at the moment, list words that will either focus your search or yield as many sources as possible. For example, a search using the term *civil rights movement* will probably yield many more sources than a search for *freedom riders.*

If your first terms don't yield many results, play with them. One helpful strategy is to consult the *Library of Congress Subject Headings Index,* a two-volume print index that is usually placed conveniently near the online catalogue terminals. This index lists all of the subject headings developed for the Library of Congress classification system. The Library of Congress subject heading for the book in Figure 4.2, for example, is "Australian Aborigines—Fiction." These subject headings can help you put together a list of search terms. Start with the term you think is most obvious for your topic, and see whether the Library of Congress uses that term in its classification system. If there's nothing there, try another term. Many times, this index will point you to alternative terms you might not have thought of yourself. For example, you might be surprised to find that "Native American" is not a Library of Congress subject heading; instead, the heading "Indians of North America" is used.

Note that there is a difference between searching by subject and searching by "keyword" in your library's computerized catalogue.

Whereas subject searches identify sources that match the specific subject heading you indicate, keyword searches enable you to search for particular words that appear in the title, the subject heading, or anywhere else in the bibliographic information stored for each catalogued item. As you can imagine, however, you need to control such searches via the strategic use of keywords. If you use too general a search term, the system will return many more sources than you have time to examine. Strategies for keyword searching are discussed in detail later in this chapter, in the section on the Internet.

### Explore indexes and abstracts

In addition to your library's online catalog, there are a number of print indexes and online databases that you can use to find countless journal and periodical articles. (Note that *journal* usually refers to scholarly publications, whereas *periodical* generally refers to any publication that is published periodically, such as newspapers and magazines.) The most commonly and most easily used index is the *Reader's Guide to Periodical Literature,* which lists general, non-scholarly articles in a wide variety of periodicals. The *Reader's Guide* is published in both a print and an electronic version. If you're using the print version, make sure you have the most recent edition. The print version lists articles in alphabetical order by author as well as by subject, although you'll probably do a subject search. Look for subject headings related to your topic, using your search term as keywords. Once you find the right subject heading, you'll then find a list of articles on the topic. Write down all the information given for the article titles that sound most useful or promising. You might even want to photocopy the page if there are a substantial number of articles listed and if your assignment is an extensive writing project. At the front of the *Reader's Guide,* you'll find a key explaining what all the abbreviations mean.

You might also want to try the online version of the *Reader's Guide.* If you've never used a computer database before, you might be a little nervous about this approach, but once you try it, you may never want to go back to using print indexes again. In fact, the only real challenge when using the computer is making sure you have the correct spelling for the words you type in, because computers don't forgive typographical or spelling errors. The online edition of the *Reader's Guide* differs from the bound edition mainly in that instead of searching through an alphabetical list of terms, you'll type terms in and see whether they produce a match. The computer tells you what to do, and the directions are very clear. Another advantage of using the computerized *Reader's Guide* is that you can print out the citations you think might be useful, which not only saves time but also helps you make sure you have all the bibliographic information you'll need to find sources and document them.

Other, more scholarly indexes are also available. Many of these are in electronic form, available either online or on CD-ROM. Generally, they are arranged according to subject area. The following are some of the subject area indexes available in many college libraries:

Art: *Art Index*
Athletics: *SportDiscus*
Biology: *Biological Abstracts*
Business: *Business Periodicals Index*
Chemistry: *Chemical Abstracts*
Computer science: *Applied Science and Technology Index*
Current news and events: *New York Times Index*
Education and physical education: *Education Index*
English and literature: *MLA International Bibliography*
Environmental science: *Environmental Bibliography*
Humanities: *Humanities Index*
Medicine: *Medline*
Psychology: *Psychological Abstracts*
Religion: *Religion and Theological Abstracts*
Sciences: *General Science Index*
Social sciences: *Social Science Index*
Women's studies: *Women's Studies Index*

An index is a list of articles and resources; an abstract is a very brief summary of an article. *Psychological Abstracts,* therefore, includes brief summaries of each of the articles it lists—a service very useful to researchers. Each of these resources is accessed in a slightly different way, but once you have a good idea of the general principles, you should find them easy to use. If you run into trouble, your reference librarian can help you get back on track.

### *E-mail and Mailing Lists*

E-mail was the first widely used Internet technology, and it remains the most heavily used Internet technology to this day. E-mail enables individuals all over the globe to send and receive messages almost instantly, at whatever time is most convenient for them. Most e-mail programs now allow users to send large data files, too. (The chapters of this book, for example, were all sent to the publisher as e-mail attachments.) It has become nearly as common for people to have an e-mail address as a phone number, and you'll notice when you begin researching that many authors now include an e-mail address as part of their contact information.

In terms of performing research, e-mail can make it possible to ask the author of a book or article you've read for clarification or additional information on the subject he or she has written about. An author who has supplied an e-mail address with his or her research won't mind if you do this, so long as you observe the conventions of "netiquette" and don't ask obvious questions. (If no e-mail address is supplied, you might be able to find it on the Web, as discussed later.) "Netiquette" refers to the proper way to communicate over the Internet, whether by e-mail or in newsgroups, in "chat rooms," or in posts to electronic mailing lists. Although e-mail is generally less formal than conventional mail, it is nevertheless important to be polite and respectful, especially if the person you're writing to doesn't know you. Introduce yourself and quickly ask your question. Although e-mail is not so intrusive as a dinnertime call from a telemarketer, it still represents a use of someone's valuable time; if you want to get a response, it's important to show the proper respect for that time. Most researchers will gladly respond to a politely worded request for information from someone interested in what they've written about. Be sure to include your return e-mail address in your message, in case the recipient's e-mail program does not include a "reply" button.

If you have an e-mail account, then you can subscribe to electronic mailing lists. An electronic mailing list (or "e-conference" or "e-mail discussion group") is another very helpful tool for conducting research. It is like a club where people interested in a particular topic gather and post notes for each other to read, including notes responding to previous notes. To join such a club, you must "subscribe" to a mailing list by submitting your e-mail address to the server (a computer that "serves" files to other computers) that "hosts" the list. Each day or week (or according to some other schedule), all messages sent to the list server are compiled and mailed out to all of the list subscribers.

The research applications of this tool are obvious. With an electronic mailing list, you can pose a specific question to a group of individuals who are specialists in an area you are researching and whom you would otherwise have no way of contacting or even finding. Again, remember the importance of "netiquette" when you participate in electronic mailing lists. Many of these lists have been around for years, and you may be joining a very exclusive club. Before you post a message to a list, read what other members have to say for a few days or weeks (depending on how much time you have). Try to get a feel for their level of expertise on the list topic and for how long they've been members. You'll notice that list members respond to one another's posts. A message that generates a response from another list member may grow into a "thread" (a subject that is discussed over a period of time), the first response generating another response, and so on. Your question might have been a thread on the list some time ago, and long-standing members might have already discussed it, perhaps repeatedly. If you feel this might be the case, identify yourself as a newcomer to the list, and rather than abruptly asking your questions, politely inquire whether they've already discussed it. Most important, don't ask an obvious question that you could find the answer to yourself in your college library. If you do this, you're likely to be ignored or, even worse, "flamed." A "flame" is a rude or confrontational response to a message that some list member (the one doing the "flaming") took to be uninformed or otherwise inappropriate.

Here are a few web sites that list different electronic mailing lists and provide information on how to join and participate in them:

- *The Directory of Scholarly E-Conferences* is a guide to academic and professional mailing lists that you can browse by subject or search using keywords. You can access this site at http://www. n2h2.com/KOVACS.

- *E-Mail Discussion Groups* is a site that describes how to find a mailing list and explains common list commands. You can access it at http://alabanza.com/kabacoff/InterLinks/listserv.html.

- The *Liszt* site lets you browse for lists by topic or search for keywords. It also includes helpful summaries of the mailing lists it catalogues. Access it at http://www.liszt.com.

- *Publicly Accessible Mailing Lists* is a web version of the "list of lists" in the news.list newsgroup. Access it at http://www.neosoft. com/internet/paml.

- *TileNet* is a directory of mailing lists, organized by subject. To find it, point your browser to http://tile.net/lists.

### Newsgroups

Newsgroups are electronic "discussion groups" on the Usenet network. (Technically, Usenet is not part of the Internet; it is another network, *like* the Internet, that uses its own protocol to send and receive messages. About half of all Usenet newsgroups are accessible via the Internet, however.) Newsgroups are similar to mailing lists, but they are more like public forums than exclusive clubs. Messages posted to a newsgroup are stored on a Usenet server for a set period of time; they are not e-mailed to a group of subscribers or members. Anyone with a newsreader program can post to a newsgroup and read what others have posted. Like mailing lists, newsgroups deal with specific topics. Nobody knows for sure how many Usenet newsgroups there are, but estimates range as high as 50,000. New groups are formed every day, and old groups die off each day as well. Usenet newsgroups are divided into eight broad categories, identified by the following abbreviations:

- *.alt* newsgroups (such as alt.adoption and alt.music.alternative) are groups formed by "alternative" methods, bypassing the standard Usenet requirement of discussion and voting on new group formation. The *.alt* category is a catch-all, and there are many, many *.alt* newsgroups to choose from.
- *.comp* newsgroups cover computer-related topics.
- *.misc* newsgroups cover miscellaneous topics (a catch-all, like *.alt*).
- *.news* newsgroups discuss issues specifically related to newsgroups.
- *.rec* newsgroups discuss recreation and hobbies.
- *.sci* newsgroups discuss scientific topics.
- *.soc* newsgroups discuss social issues.
- *.talk* newsgroups are devoted to debating controversial issues.

In general, newsgroups are a somewhat less reliable source of information than mailing lists. Many mailing lists are moderated, which means that someone somewhere reviews posts to the list and weeds out inaccurate or inappropriate messages. And even those lists that are unmoderated reflect a somewhat more restrained culture than do newsgroups. (Mailing list messages resemble interoffice memos, whereas newsgroup posts can be like the graffiti scrawled on the wall outside the office.) But this doesn't mean newsgroups aren't worth investigating. At the very least, they can give you new ideas and help you find new sources of information on the Internet. Sometimes the graffiti scrawled outside corporate headquarters is more revealing than the memos circulated inside!

The best place to start investigating newsgroups is a newsgroup—news.announce.newusers, which describe how to post to newsgroups and discusses the particular conventions and etiquette of Usenet. Your e-mail program may include a newsreader. If not, ask in your school's computer lab how to access newsgroups. You can also access some newsgroups via the World Wide Web, using a web browser such as Netscape or Microsoft Internet Explorer. Two web sites that allow you to read and post to newsgroups from your web browser are DejaNews, at http://www.dejanews.com, and the Liszt site's newsgroup page, at http://www.liszt.com/news. (Although this may appear easier at first, and although it is a good way to introduce yourself to newsgroups if you're familiar with the Web but not with Usenet, you'll probably find that it is faster to use a newsreader than the Web to access Usenet.)

### FTP and Telnet

FTP, for File Transfer Protocol, is an Internet protocol that enables you to transfer files from one computer on the Internet to another. If your e-mail program doesn't allow you to attach large files or to receive file attachments from others, then you might have to learn to use FTP to transfer files. Although FTP programs and commands are somewhat outdated tools, because so many files can now be transferred using e-mail programs and web browsers (often using the FTP protocol transparently—more on this later), it's still useful to know how to use them. Many free computer programs are still available only via regular FTP, for example. There are many FTP programs; your school's computer system will have at least one and possibly more, and a computer lab technician or reference librarian can show you how to use it. If you'd like to get an FTP program for your own computer, many are available free or for little money; ask in your school's computer lab.

Telnet goes one step beyond FTP, enabling you to log on to a remote computer as though you were a local user. This allows you to search large remote databases, including databases at many academic libraries around the world. Like FTP, Telnet is somewhat outdated today: The World Wide Web allows much the same functionality as Telnet, and nearly every database on the Internet has a web version available for you to search. However, if you're using a computer terminal that is connected to the Internet but doesn't have a web browser, Telnet can still be a valuable tool. Again, ask your school's computer lab personnel or a reference librarian how to access and use Telnet.

### Gopher

Gopher, a program developed at the University of Minnesota and named for that institution's mascot as well as for its ability to "go for" information, represents the next step up from Telnet in terms of user-friendly Internet access. With Telnet, the user has to know where he or she wants to go, must have the Internet addresses of the sites he or she wants to access at hand, and must remember a number of commands to be entered at a "prompt" on a blank screen (such as in old MS-DOS and UNIX systems). Gopher, by contrast, lets users connect to different Internet sites by choosing from menus; they need not remember a lot of complicated commands or know the addresses of the sites they want to visit. Gopher was the first tool that made it possible to browse, or "surf," the Internet, allowing users to move from site to site, accessing different menus with links to more and different external sites. Some Gopher connections are actually Telnet connections, but the

Gopher software takes care of the details for you, so you don't have to know any Telnet commands.

A program called Veronica (For Very Easy Rodent-Oriented Netwide Index to Computerized Archives) enables users to search "gopherspace"—the more than 5,500 known gopher servers on the Internet, which together offer more than 10 million menu or directory choices. A Veronica search covers only those menu or directory items, not the actual documents stored in the gopher databases. Like FTP and Telnet, Gopher has been partially subsumed by the World Wide Web but can still be a valuable research tool in its own right, particularly if you're limited to a terminal without Web access. Ask in your computer lab how to use Gopher and Veronica.

### *The World Wide Web*

With the development of the World Wide Web, the Internet made the shift from command- and menu-driven access to a graphical user interface, or GUI. Instead of entering commands at a prompt or choosing items from a menu, a web user clicks on underlined or highlighted text or graphics ("hyperlinks") on web "pages" to move from server to server on the Internet. The rise of the hypertext markup language (HTML), the computer code that is the basis for the Web, is analogous to the rise of the Macintosh and Windows operating systems in the late 1980s, which quickly left the arcane UNIX and MS-DOS operating systems behind for the majority of users. If you have access to the Web on your student account, it will probably be the first way you access the Internet, because it is by far the easiest and most entertaining way to "surf the Net." (If the computer terminal you're using includes a web "browser," a software program used to display Web pages, then you can access the Web. The most popular browsers, as you probably know, are Netscape's Communicator and Microsoft's Internet Explorer.) Once you become familiar with the Web, however, you might want to go back and learn to use FTP, Telnet, and Gopher as well, because these older tools can be faster than the Web for some purposes.

The World Wide Web is the largest information haystack in the world. There are millions of web pages in cyberspace. New ones appear every day, and old, inactive ones linger and clutter things up, sometimes for months or years. This mass of information presents two problems for the researcher: finding the particular needle you seek within that haystack, and ensuring that what you find is reliable (given that anyone can post information to the Web, and no one controls what gets posted).

**Search Engines and Directories.** Recognizing the Web's explosive potential, several visionary individuals invented web search engines and directories in the early 1990s to help people find what they were looking for on the Web. The best known of these tools is probably the Yahoo! web site, which was invented by a couple of college students who are now multimillionaires. Yahoo! is both a search engine and a directory. A search engine, or web "spider," is a computer program that accesses registered web sites, searching the text of their pages and indexing them. A visitor to the search engine's web site enters one or more keywords to search by, and the program then presents the user with a list of web addresses for pages that contain those keywords, ranked in some way (usually according to how many times those keywords appear in the text of the page and in the embedded code behind the scenes). The user next enters the web address (or URL, for Uniform Resource Locator) into his or her browser's locator or navigation field, and the browser will then access that particular web site and download the page to the user's own computer. A directory is like a Yellow Pages for the Web, with sites listed under various categories. Sites like Yahoo! include categories and also "spider," or search, the sites within each category to come up with rankings. The following are some of the major web search engines, with the URL for each.

- Yahoo! (http://www.yahoo.com)
- Lycos (http://www.lycos.com)
- AOL NetFind (http://www.netfind.com)
- AltaVista (http://www.altavista.com)
- HotBot (http://www.hotbot.com)
- Infoseek (http://www.infoseek.com)
- Northern Lights (http://www.northernlights.com)
- Excite! (http://www.excite.com)
- WebCrawler (http://www.webcrawler.com)

There are many more new ones appearing all the time, and there are thousands of directories, including many very specialized ones. Ask your reference librarian which directories to try to research the topic you are investigating.

**Performing Boolean Searches.** Most web search engines use Boolean logic for keyword searches. Veronica also uses Boolean logic to search gopherspace, and it is used by most computerized databases, including most online library catalogues. Performing a Boolean search sounds more intimidating than it is. It just requires that you understand how to use a few simple Boolean terms, or "operators," to combine keywords. Sometimes you need to capitalize operators; each web search engine and online database will include instructions to acquaint you with its own particular conventions. Here are the most common Boolean operators:

- ADJ: Place this between search terms that must be adjacent to each other in the documents you want to locate.
- AND: Place this between search terms if both must be present somewhere in the documents you want to locate, but not necessarily next to each other.
- OR: Place this between search terms if either one, but not necessarily both, must be present somewhere in the documents you want to locate.
- NOT or AND NOT: Place this between search terms if one of the terms must not be present. Use this to eliminate irrelevant items.

In most web search engines, you can place quotation marks around phrases that you want to find (instead of using ADJ), to let the engine know you want to find documents that contain all of the keywords you've entered, in the same order and all together. Finally, you can often use parentheses to group keywords together for more complicated searches. The following examples were taken from the Excite! web site's help page.

- wizard AND oz AND movie: This will find documents that contain all three of these words (but not documents that contain only one or two of them) anywhere in the documents.
- cat OR kitten: This will find documents that contain either *cat* or *kitten,* but not both.
- pets AND NOT dogs: This will find documents that contain *pets* but not *dogs.*
- fruit AND (banana OR apple): This will find documents that contain *fruit* and either *banana* or *apple.*
- "better business bureau": This will find documents that contain this complete phrase, but not documents that contain only one or two of these words.

You might find that your searches turn up lots of irrelevant material. If this happens, try to refine them using Boolean operators and more exact keywords. As you do more and more research on the Internet, it will become easier to find what you need. You'll learn about valuable web directories that are "gateways" to other resources. You'll learn which search engines return the most relevant results and which are overly cluttered with commercial sites. Like any tool, the Internet takes time to become familiar with. But the time you invest in learning how to use it to your best advantage will pay off handsomely later.

**Verifying the Accuracy of Web Sources.**  Anyone with the right software and a $5-per-month FTP web hosting account can publish a web site. As you probably already know, there are scores of commercial sites, personal sites, political sites, news sites—sites about pretty much anything you can think of—on the web, and the quality of these sites varies widely. Don't assume that something is valid just because it's posted on a web site. It is your responsibility to ensure that you can reasonably rely on the information you uncover on the web. There's a lot of garbage on the web, but there's also a lot of valuable and valid information. In particular, there's a lot of very recent information that is not available anywhere else. If you find a site that you'd like to quote or that has statistics you'd like to use to bolster your arguments, find out who published it.

This is really just a question of common sense. You wouldn't quote the *National Enquirer* in a research paper, so don't quote the web equivalents of it (and there are many of them). You'd have no problem quoting the *Journal of the American Medical Association,* however, so you shouldn't hesitate to quote *its* web equivalents (and there are many of these, too). Think twice about relying on any site that you believe has a commercial interest. If it exists to sell you something, quoting from it would be like quoting from a television commercial. Judge where the site owner's prejudices or biases might lie. This information should be available to you in documentation contained on the web site. In addition, make sure that the page offers contact information for the person or organization maintaining it. If none of this information is there, don't use it. Also note how long the site has been on the web and how recently it's been updated. If it is not being frequently updated, don't trust the information. Finally, make sure you get the *exact* URL for the site to include in your Works Cited list. For clear guidelines for evaluating web sites, a very useful place to check is

>  http://www.library.ucla.edu/libraries/college/instruct/web/critical.htm

This web site takes you through a series of questions to help you systematically judge the value of the site that interests you.

### *"I can't find anything on my topic!"*

If you just can't find any information on your topic, follow these steps:

1. Check your list of search terms. Brainstorm to come up with other terms. Use the Library of Congress subject headings to find still more terms.
2. Make sure you've checked all available databases, not just the *Reader's Guide to Periodical Literature.*

3. Go through the bibliographies of the articles you've already found to find other useful sources.
4. Ask your reference librarian for help.

If you still can't find much, you should rethink your topic. Can it be broadened? Is there another way to approach it? Can you add to it? For example, if you want to research steroid use among non-athletes but can't find much on this topic, you may need to expand your focus to include athletes as well.

## Choosing and Documenting Secondary Sources

The reason to conduct library research is to support your own ideas and arguments. That is why this book asks you to delay doing detailed library research until after you've done quite a lot of thinking, reading of general sources, and focus writing. Sometimes when students consult specialized academic or professional sources too soon, they find themselves overwhelmed by the research of others. You need to have an idea of your position and what you want to say about it before you consult others in the field.

Once you've begun consulting specialized secondary sources, you have to decide when it's necessary, or even appropriate, to cite them in your own work. First-year college students frequently have trouble figuring out whether support for a generalization is needed. For example, do you need to cite a source to back up the statement that U.S. voters are increasingly apathetic, or is it common knowledge? You may have read statements to this effect in many secondary sources, but does that mean you have to cite those sources in your paper if you repeat this assertion? To determine whether you need to document a particular assertion you make in your paper, apply the "Who says?" test to it. You need to anticipate the places where readers who disagree with your position or who haven't yet made up their minds are likely to say, "Who says?" Another trick is to try to read your piece as though you were representing "the other side." Where would you object? Where would you be skeptical? Where would you ask for more evidence?

As you can see, deciding when (and when not) to refer to others' research is something of a balancing act. Try to establish some distance from your topic. Stand back if you feel too strongly about a topic, because otherwise it will be difficult to see where others could reasonably disagree with you. A former student of mine wanted to argue that fraternities and sororities should be abolished on all college campuses. Unfortunately, she had just been rejected by the sorority she had wanted to join and was still hurt, angry, and unable to take a balanced view of this topic.

Finally, any time you use other people's ideas, whether you quote them directly or paraphrase them, you must give credit. For one thing, the person you're quoting or paraphrasing did work that you are building on and so deserves recognition. For another, you're providing a trail that subsequent researchers can follow and use. Think of crediting others as a form of courtesy as well as an honest practice.

## Choose credible sources to cite

Deciding what and whom to consult and possibly quote or paraphrase in your paper can be a difficult task, particularly when you're not very familiar with the topic or field you're investigating. Try to draw on credible sources to back up the work you do. If you quote Dennis Rodman in a paper on adoption law, your audience won't take you seriously, even though what he has to say might be very entertaining. To enhance your own credibility, you need to cite credible outside authorities.

As we have noted, the need to evaluate web sites is obvious. What may seem less obvious is the need to evaluate print sources in the same way. The fact that something has been printed, bound, and marketed doesn't make it valid or correct. And even if a source can be considered perfectly valid, it may not be appropriate for a Works Cited page. Remember that the more general your source, the less appropriate it is as a secondary source for a research project. Therefore, an encyclopedia is not a good resource to cite or quote in a research paper, and neither are general magazines such as *Time* and *Newsweek*. Scholarly publications are the most authoritative sources. Scholarly articles and books are published only after a painstaking peer-review process that solicits the opinions of other experts in the same field as the writer. Trade books (general-interest books published by major publishing houses) and government documents fall between scholarly publications and newsmagazines in terms of their authoritativeness.

## Incorporate secondary sources into your work

There are three ways to incorporate others' research, ideas, and words into your research project: summarizing, paraphrasing, and quoting.

### Summarizing

Summarizing is useful when you need to restate as briefly as possible ideas or arguments that are too lengthy to quote or paraphrase. Although it seems that it should be simple enough, summarizing actually requires careful analysis and consideration. You have to read closely and thoroughly. You have to identify the key points and have a good sense of the writer's purpose and the main thrust of the argument. A summary should reveal the essence of the text.

### Paraphrasing

To paraphrase is to translate another's words into your own. Paraphrasing is most useful for brief passages. It restates the original more precisely than does a summary, and it may be nearly the same length. Generally, you should use quotation marks if you repeat more than two words of the original text or if you use a word the author employed in a special way.

In "The Study of Popular Culture Has Acquired Legitimacy, But Still Lacks Cohesion," Michael Kammen draws from a number of current books on the significance of American popular culture. In the following excerpt from his article, he summarizes one book's main argument and then ends the paragraph with what he found to be an effective phrase from the book.

> From Steven Ross, a professor of history at the University of Southern California, for example, we learn that the growth of Hollywood limited the influence of cinema as an agent of democratization. His *Working-Class Hollywood: Silent Film and the Shaping of Class in America* shows that, early in this century, unionists and political radicals produced silent films that presented with great empathy class conflict and the movement for workers' rights. Then, following World War I, these polemical films, which appealed to a working-class audience, gave way to more sentimental and consensus-oriented movies that, Ross says, "emphasized fantasies of love and harmony among the classes."

Here is one way to paraphrase the second sentence from this excerpt: "In *Working-Class Hollywood: Silent Film and the Shaping of Class in America,* Steven Ross demonstrates that overtly political forces made silent movies that clearly addressed and sympathetically portrayed working-class interests."

### Quoting

How do you decide when it's more appropriate to quote than to summarize or paraphrase? Here are several useful rules of thumb:

- Quote when you really like both *what* the writer said and *how* he or she said it.

- Quote when the passage in question contains numbers, statistics, or details that are difficult to paraphrase or summarize.

- Quote when your purpose is to critique what the writer says point by point.

When you quote another's words, you must copy them *exactly,* including any punctuation. Each time you quote, you should also introduce the quotation ("Robert Johnson writes, . . .") and follow it up by giving your readers a sense of what you took the writer to mean or why you found this particular passage important ("As you can see, Johnson is arguing here that . . ."). Before you plunge readers into someone else's words, offer a sense of who the writer is, where the quotation comes from, and why it's relevant. In this way you create a meaningful context for the material. At the end of the quotation—and especially after extracts (long, indented quotations)—let your readers know what you want them to notice about or learn from it. In a sense, you're telling them how the other writer's work amplifies or enhances (or contradicts) your own. You're making it clear to your readers exactly why the quotation was included, either as support for your argument or as something it critiques.

When you quote more than four lines of text, type it as an extract. That is, indent the entire quotation ten spaces from the left-hand margin. Note that an extract does not have quotation marks around it. Consider, though, whether a long quotation is necessary or appropriate. Some students confess that they skip long extracts when they come across them in their reading, and I have to admit that I'm daunted by page-long (or longer) ones myself. If you can do so without damaging the sense or flow of the writer's words, try to keep the quotation as brief as possible or break it up into more manageable chunks, interspersed with your explanation, interpretations, and arguments.

In a long research paper, try to maintain a balance in the ways you incorporate others' research in your work. That is, maintain a balance among direct quotations, summaries, and paraphrases, and between long extracts and shorter quotations. Also maintain a balance between your own words and ideas and those of others (that is, not too much you and not too many outside sources). Your instructor may give you a sense of the minimum and maximum number of sources he or she requires.

### Document your sources

As we have noted, one reason to cite secondary sources in your work is to leave a bibliographic trail for other scholars with similar interests to follow. The "trail markers" you provide should be clear and consistent so that your readers can readily access the knowledge you have incorporated into your work. To make it as easy as possible for those who read your work to find the outside sources you have used, you must adhere to a standard citation system that includes parenthetical citations in the body of your paper and, at the end, a list of works cited. Following is an explanation of the two citation and documentation styles most commonly used by college students and professional researchers: the MLA (Modern Language Association) documentation style and the APA (American Psychological Association) documentation style.

## MLA Documentation Style

In the humanities, you will use the MLA (Modern Language Association) documentation style to document your sources. The following sections offer examples of citations and references lists in MLA style. If you come up with a source that doesn't seem to fall into any of these categories, consult a handbook that explains documentation methods and forms in greater detail.

### *Parenthetical Citations*

To show your readers that you are quoting or referring to an outside source, and to indicate which source that is, you need to include a parenthetical citation within the body of your paper at the appropriate place. Parenthetical citations in MLA style follow this format:

> Pattison argues that rather than serving to "transcribe the vitality of our culture," writing "reflects our ennui" (60).

or

> One literacy theorist argues that rather than serving to "transcribe the vitality of our culture," writing "reflects our ennui" (Pattison 60).

Include the author's name in the parentheses following the quotation only when you haven't used it as part of your introduction to the quotation, as in the second example above. In the first example, mentioning the name afterward isn't necessary, because it's clear from the introductory phrase that Pattison wrote the words that follow. From this combination of information, the reader can go to the Works Cited page, find the Pattison reference, and know that the quoted material can be found on page 60 of that book.

In MLA format, if there are more than three authors, the abbreviation *et al.* (a Latin abbreviation for "and others") is used after the first name, as in "(Applebee et al. 123)." APA style requires the use of *et al.* for six or more authors.

When referring to a text by an unknown, or anonymous, author, begin with the first major word of the title. When you quote a quotation (that is, if you read in your source something that writer quoted and you want to quote it too), indicate this in an MLA parenthetical citation as follows: "(qtd. in Pattison 60)."

Again, for more complicated citations, check a handbook or ask your instructor.

### *The Works Cited Page*

The examples that follow show how to format the references you list on your Works Cited page, or References page, in MLA style.

*Citing Books.* Following are examples of how to cite complete books using MLA documentation style.

**ONE AUTHOR**

Pattison, Robert. <u>On Literacy</u>. New York: Oxford UP, 1982. [UP stands for University Press.]

**TWO AUTHORS**

Conklin, Nancy Faires, and Margaret A Lourie. <u>A Host of Tongues: Language Communities in the United States</u>. New York: The Free Press, 1983.

**THREE AUTHORS**

Applebee, Arthur, Judith A. Langer, and Ina V.S. Mullins. <u>The Writing Report Card: Writing Achievement in American Schools</u>. Princeton: ETS, 1986.

**FOUR OR MORE AUTHORS**

Belenky, Mary F., et al. <u>Women's Ways of Knowing: The Development of Self, Voice, and Mind</u>. New York: Basic Books, 1986.

**ANONYMOUS AUTHOR**

<u>Film Actors Guide</u>. Los Angeles: Lone Eagle, 1995.

**EDITOR**

Johnson, Clifton, ed. <u>God Struck Me Dead: Religious Conversion Experiences and Autobiographies of Ex-Slaves</u>. Philadelphia: Pilgrim P, 1969. [P stands for Press.]

**TWO OR THREE EDITORS**

McMahan, Elizabeth, Susan X. Day, and Robert Funk, eds. <u>Literature and the Writing Process</u>. 4th ed. Upper Saddle River, NJ: Prentice-Hall, 1996.

**MORE THAN THREE EDITORS**

Delahoussaye, Harry, et al., eds. <u>Black Orpheus: Rhetoric and Readings</u>. Needham Heights, MA: Simon and Schuster Custom Publishing, 1996.

**MULTIPLE EDITIONS**

Bernstein, Basil. <u>Class, Codes, and Control: Toward a Theory of Educational Transmissions</u>. 3 vols. 2nd ed. Boston: Routledge & Kegan Paul, 1977.

*Citing Parts of Books.* Following are examples of how to cite parts of books, such as book chapters or articles from edited collections.

**ESSAY OR SECTION FROM A BOOK**

Doane, Mary Ann. "The Voice in Cinema: The Articulation of Body and Space," in <u>Narrative, Apparatus, Ideology: A Film Theory Reader</u>. Ed. Philip Rosen. New York: Columbia UP, 1986: 335-48.

**ESSAY, POEM, OR SHORT STORY IN AN EDITED ANTHOLOGY**

Walker, Alice. "Everyday Use." <u>Responding to Literature</u>. 2nd ed. Ed. Judith A. Stanford. Mountain View, CA: Mayfield, 1996: 371-78.

**ARTICLE FROM A REFERENCE WORK**

"Arthritis." <u>The Columbia Encyclopedia</u>. 1993.

*Citing Other Book Forms.* Following are some other conventions for citing books.

**BOOK WITHOUT COMPLETE PUBLICATION INFORMATION**

Generally, you should start where you can and include everything you can. If you can find no author named, begin with the title. Other abbreviations to show you couldn't find the information are as follows:

**NO DATE**

Seattle: Smith Publishing, n.d.

**NO PUBLISHER**

Seattle: n.p., 1998.

**NO PLACE OF PUBLICATION**

N.p.: Smith Publishing, 1998.

*Citing Periodicals.* Following are examples of how to list journals and other periodicals.

**ARTICLE IN JOURNAL PAGINATED BY VOLUME**

Emig, Janet. "Writing as a Mode of Learning." <u>College Composition and Communication</u> 28 (1977):122-128.

**ARTICLE IN JOURNAL PAGINATED BY ISSUE**

Young, Elizabeth. "The Silence of the Lambs and the Flaying of Feminist Theory." <u>Camera Obscura</u> 27 (Sept. 1991):5-35.

**ARTICLE IN WEEKLY OR MONTHLY MAGAZINE**

Kauffmann, Stanley. "Odd Couples." <u>New Republic</u> 26 Feb. 1990:26-7.

**ARTICLE IN A NEWSPAPER**

Chira, Susan. "Tiny Black Colleges Take High Road in Science." New York Times 28 Mar. 1990:B8.

**EDITORIAL**

"Comments Interpreted as Sexual Harassment." Editorial. The East Texan. 18 Feb. 1998:4.

**REVIEW**

Bolotin, Susan. "The Man Who Raised America." Rev. of Dr. Spock: An American Life, by Thomas Maier. New York Times Book Review 17 May 1998:7.

*Citing Other Sources.* Following are examples of how to cite other types of sources.

**PERSONAL LETTER**

Butterfield, Bev. Letter to the author. 8 Mar. 1998.

**PUBLISHED LETTER**

Larsen, Patricia. Letter. Chronicle of Higher Education. 3 July 1998:B9.

**PERSONAL INTERVIEW**

Ramone, Joey. Personal interview. 1 Jan. 1998.

**TELEPHONE INTERVIEW**

Lydon, Johnny. Telephone interview. 13 May 1998.

**FILM**

Psycho. Dir. Alfred Hitchcock. Perf. Anthony Perkins, Janet Leigh. MCA, 1960.

**TELEVISION OR RADIO PROGRAM**

The Simpsons. Dir. Matt Groening. Fox Network. WPGH Pittsburgh. 1998-99 season.

**RECORDING (CD OR LP)**

Doe, John. Meet John Doe. David Geffen Company, 9 24291-D2, 1990.

**SONG**

Brown, Junior. "Parole Board." Semi Crazy. MCG/Curb, D2-77843, 1996.

**COMPUTER PROGRAM**

Corel WordPerfect. Vers. 7.0 Computer software, 1996.

**CARTOONS**

Shanahan, Danny. Cartoon. New Yorker 22 Sept. 1997:98.

**GOVERNMENT DOCUMENTS**

English language amendment, 1984: Hearings on
    S.J. Res. 167 before the subcommittee on the
    constitution of the Senate Judiciary Committee,
    98th Cong., 2nd Sess. 1284 (1984). Washington,
    D.C.: Government Printing Office.

*Citing Internet Sources.* Following are examples of how to list sources you find on the Internet.

In general, MLA format follows this basic pattern:

1. Author's name
2. Publication information (in MLA format if possible)
3. Title
4. Date
5. Specific publishing information—for example, volume numbers, page numbers, or paragraph numbers
6. An indication of where the document came from (such as "On-line, Internet")
7. Date you accessed the site
8. Site address

# APA Documentation Style

In the social sciences, you will use the APA (American Psychological Association) documentation style. In the following sections are examples of citations and references lists in APA style. If you come up with a source that doesn't seem to fall into any of these categories, consult a handbook that explains documentation methods and forms in greater detail.

## Parenthetical citations

To show your readers that you are quoting or referring to an outside source, and to indicate which source that is, you need to include a parenthetical citation within the body of your paper at the appropriate place. In APA style, include the year of publication and the abbreviation "p." or "pp." (for page or pages) before the page number, with a comma separating the date from the page number. For example:

> Pattison (1982, p. 60) argues that rather than serving to "transcribe the vitality of our culture," writing "reflects our ennui."

APA style requires the use of *et al.* for six or more authors. When referring to a text by an unknown, or anonymous, author, begin with the first major word of the title. When you quote a quotation (that is, if you read in your source something that writer quoted and you want to quote it too), indicate this in an APA parenthetical citation as follows: (cited in Pattison, 1982).

Again, for more complicated citations, check a handbook or ask your instructor.

### *The Works Cited Page*

The following examples show how to format the references you list on your Works Cited page, or References page, in APA style.

*Citing Books.* Following are examples of how to cite complete books using APA documentation style.

**ONE AUTHOR**

Pattison, Robert. (1982). <u>On literacy</u>. New York: Oxford.

**TWO AUTHORS**

Conklin, N.F., & Lourie, M.A. (1983). <u>A host of tongues: Language communities in the United States</u>. New York: Free Press.

**THREE AUTHORS**

Applebee, A., Langer, J. A., and Mullins, I.V.S. (1986). <u>The writing report card: Writing achievement in American Schools</u>. Princeton: ETS.

**SIX OR MORE AUTHORS**

Whack, D., et al. (1996). <u>Developing the mind through exercise</u>. New York. Fitness Books.

**ANONYMOUS AUTHOR**

<u>Film actors guide</u>. (1995). Los Angeles: Lone Eagle.

**EDITOR**

Johnson, C. (Ed.). (1969). <u>God struck me dead: Religious conversion experiences and auto-biographies of ex-slaves</u>. Philadelphia: Pilgrim.

**TWO OR THREE EDITORS**

McMahan, E., Day, S. X., and Funk, R. (Eds.). (1996). <u>Literature and the writing process</u> (4th ed.). Upper Saddle River, NJ: Prentice-Hall.

**MORE THAN THREE EDITORS**

Delahoussaye, H., et al. (Eds.). (1996). <u>Black Orpheus: Rhetoric and readings</u>. Needham Heights, MA: Simon and Schuster Custom Publishing.

**MULTIPLE EDITIONS**

Bernstein, B. (1977). <u>Class, codes, and control:
Toward a theory of educational transmissions</u> (2nd
ed.). (Vols. 1-3). Boston: Routledge & Kegan Paul.

*Citing Parts of Books.* Following are examples of how to cite parts of books, such as book chapters or articles from edited collections.

**ESSAY OR SECTION FROM A BOOK**

Doane, M. A. The voice in cinema: The articulation of
body and space," in P. Rosen (Ed.), <u>Narrative,
apparatus, ideology: A film theory</u> (pp. 335-348).
New York: Columbia.

**ESSAY, POEM, OR SHORT STORY IN AN EDITED ANTHOLOGY**

Walker, A. Everyday use. In J. A. Stanford (Ed.),
<u>Responding to literature</u>. (2nd ed.) (pp.
371-378). Mountain View, CA: Mayfield.

**ARTICLE FROM A REFERENCE WORK**

"Arthritis." <u>The Columbia encyclopedia</u>.

*Citing Other Book Forms.* Following are some other conventions for citing books.

**BOOK WITHOUT COMPLETE PUBLICATION INFORMATION**

Generally, you should start where you can and include everything you can. If you can find no author named, begin with the title. Other abbreviations to show you couldn't find the information are as follows:

**NO DATE**

Seattle: Smith Publishing, n.d.

**NO PUBLISHER**

Seattle: n.p., 1998.

**NO PLACE OF PUBLICATION**

N.p.: Smith Publishing, 1998.

*Citing Periodicals.* Following are examples of how to list journals and other periodicals.

**ARTICLES IN JOURNAL PAGINATED BY VOLUME**

Emig, J. (1977). Writing as a mode of learning. <u>College
composition and communication</u>, 28, 122-128.

**ARTICLE IN JOURNAL PAGINATED BY ISSUE**

Young, E. (1991, Sept.). The silence of the lambs
    and the flaying of feminist theory. Camera
    Obscura 27, 5-35.

**ARTICLE IN WEEKLY OR MONTHLY MAGAZINE**

Kauffmann, S. (1990, Feb. 26). Odd couples. New
    republic, 26-27.

**ARTICLE IN A NEWSPAPER**

Chira, S. (1990, Mar. 28). Tiny black colleges take
    high road in science." The New York Times, p. B8.

**EDITORIAL**

Comments interpreted as sexual harassment
    [Editorial]. (1998, Feb. 18). East Texan, p. 4.

**REVIEW**

Bolotin, S. (1998, May 17). The man who raised
    America. [Review of the book Dr. Spock: An
    American Life]. The New York Times Book
    Review, 7.

*Citing Other Sources.* Following are examples of how to cite
other types of sources.

**PERSONAL LETTER**

Do not list personal letters in your references because they are
not usually recoverable for your readers. However, do document
the source and date of the letter parenthetically in your text.

**PUBLISHED LETTER**

Larsen, P. [Letter to the editor]. (1998, July 3).
    Chronicle of higher education, p. B9.

**PERSONAL INTERVIEW**

Do not list personal interviews in your references because there
is no way for your reader to gain access to this resource. However,
do document the source and date of the interview parenthetically
in your text.

**TELEPHONE INTERVIEW**

Do not list telephone interviews in your references because
there is no way for your reader to gain access to this resource. However, do document the source and date of the interview parenthetically in your text.

**FILM**

Hitchcock A. (Director). (1960). Psycho [Film]. Los
    Angeles: MCA.

**TELEVISION OR RADIO PROGRAM**

Groening M. (Writer, director, and producer). 1993,
    Mar. 15). The Simpsons [Television program].
    Pittsburgh: WPGH, Fox Network.

**RECORDING (CD OR LP)**

Doe, J. (1990). Meet John Doe. [CD]. New York: David
    Geffen.

**SONG**

Brown, J. (Performer). (1996). Parole board. On
    Semi Crazy [CD]. Nashville: MCB/Curb.

**COMPUTER PROGRAM**

Corel WordPerfect Vers. 7.0 [Computer software].
    (1996).

**CARTOONS**

Shanahan, D. (1997, Sept. 22). [Cartoon]. New Yorker, 98.

**GOVERNMENT DOCUMENTS**

United States Congressional Senate Committee on the
    Judiciary. (1984). English language amendment,
    1984: Hearings on S.J. Res. 167. Washington,
    D.C.: Government Printing Office.

*Citing Internet Sources.* Following are examples of how to list
sources you find on the Internet.

In general, APA format follows this basic pattern:

1. Author's name
2. Date (in parentheses)
3. Title
4. Title of electronic text the article or site appears in
5. Specific publishing information—for example, volume numbers,
   page numbers, or paragraph numbers
6. An indication of where the document came from (such as "Online, Internet") in brackets
7. Site address

# Student Essay with MLA Documentation

Following is an example of a complete student essay with citations
and references in MLA format.

Charlotte R. Gardner

Professor Dunbar-Odom

English 102

20 February 1996

Rural North Texas or Hicks in the Sticks?

Imagine, if you will, the following scenario: An instructor walks into a classroom and announces to the class, "Okay, Class, today we are going to do something a little different. It is something that you have obviously never had to do before, but we are going to give it a shot. It is called critical thinking. . . ."

There is no need for the professor to go any further because he has already lost the attention of most of the class. In fact, he could have gone about sending the students into this passive phase in a more timely manner by just saying the words "critical thinking." This scenario is exactly the image that Robert Johnson portrays in his article "Teaching the Forbidden: Literature and the Religious Student": Hicks in the Sticks that do not know better. Now granted there are some students whom this would fit to a "T," but for the most part, rural North Texas students are not afraid of having to give a subject some thought. On the contrary, I thought we were known for our "I'll sleep on it and get back to you," or "Let me go over it and I'll holler at you when I make a decision," or just the plain old, "I'll think about it." Maybe my perception of it is a bit off, but I feel that

---

**Margin notes:**

1" margin ↑

Double space throughout.

1" margin ←→

Gardner uses her title and first paragraph to hook her readers' attention.

Gardner introduces the reading assignment with which she takes issue.

The title of the essay is placed within quotation marks.

many young rural North Texans use that mass
between their ears, and more than just once in
a "blue moon."

When I think of the instances in my personal experience with people who shy away from
critical thought, I think of my high school
days. Laziness, immaturity, and boredom were
the three main factors that kept students from
using their brain cells (for thought, not killing them with alcohol) in my high school days.
Three factors, in my opinion, that help college
students attain brain cell usage (once again, I
must point out that I am referring to thought)
are maturity, knowing that in most cases it is
their money that is being wasted if they goof
off, and knowing that they are working toward a
goal of their professional choice so the information they learn will one day be pertinent.

What gave Johnson the idea that students
do not think critically? I can see where he may
have gotten his idea from, but I am firmly
against him in his thought. There have been
instances in class that the instructor will ask
a question, a very simple question, even, and
not one person in the whole room will call out
the answer. Are they not thinking? Are they not
listening? Or perhaps they are just fearful of
speaking up in front of the group. For the most
part, I can honestly say that I am in the latter
group. I know the answer, but a little voice
inside my head keeps saying, "What if I'm

*In these paragraphs, Gardner is setting up her argument in response to Johnson's.*

wrong? What if I call out the answer and it's wrong? Will everyone laugh at me? Will the instructor ridicule me in front of everyone? Will I be embarrassed?" So, instead of blurting out the answer that is being sought, I sit back in my chair and say nothing. I play it safe. I do not walk on the wild side. Putting myself in my instructor's shoes, I could see Johnson's point of view when he stated, ". . . I have discovered that what I call 'critical writing' and perhaps even 'deep reading' they . . . think to be plain old sin" (37). To me, this point helps to prove, as Clifford Geertz points out in his article "The Interpretation of Cultures," that not every twitch of the eye is intended to be a wink. In describing culture, Geertz says, "Culture . . . is public. . . . [Both] rocks . . . and dreams . . . are things of this world" (10). This seems very applicable to me. It is both the speechless student that the teachers sees and the thinking students that make up culture. Johnson is only looking at this from one perspective.

   To give Johnson some credit, I have encoun-tered some very unintelligent people in my life. Some of these are people you can get to believe anything because they never question a word you say. They are gullible, and the rear end of many jokes. However, they do exist. There are students, as portrayed in a Doonesbury cartoon passed out in class, who go to class and reverently take

Ellipses indicate that material has been omitted from the material she's quoting. Note that the page number is in parentheses, outside the quotation marks, and before the final period.

Note that Gardner follows up the quotation from Geertz with further discussion that supports her point.

down everything the professor says. They never ask questions or make comments on any of the subjects covered in class, and they just assume that any material covered in class is fair game for a test. To show both sides, I must also point out that the shoe could be put on the other foot. Sometimes a teacher will make an extremely out-of-line comment just to shoot the breeze.

As the Doonesbury cartoon depicted, I actually have a history class in which the teacher is constantly throwing out lewd comments on one or more presidential candidates, or former Republican officials, just to spark audience participation in the discussion. On the other hand, I am also in a class where the professor went off on a tangent, just to speak his mind. This was my biology class, in which Dr. [X] was explaining to us the Cell theory. One of the men who came up with the theory had a first name of Theodore. Dr. [X] stopped lecturing for a moment, stared at the dry erase board, then turned to the class and said, "People don't name their kids Theodore anymore, do they? I certainly would not name my kid Theodore." After his little outburst, he went back to the lecture notes. Another angle on this was shown to me by a classmate. Her experience was that if the teacher mentioned something silly (i.e., "Would Dr. [X] use the name Theodore for a child?"), you could rest assured that it would be on there in the form of a bonus questions. These three examples show that, as Geertz points out,

*Gardner omits the name of the professor because this is not a positive example.*

Note how Gardner uses each author's name to introduce the quoted material.

"[One cannot . . . bleach human behavior . . . to] only those properties that interest us" (17). I feel that this is largely what Johnson has done with his analysis of rural North Texans. He wrote this article without fully understanding the goings on of his students' minds.

Johnson surrounded his article around religion. I feel that there are several places in the article where Johnson misuses "religious" examples. He talked about kids being unable to think critically because they see it as "insulting authority" (38). Now if one would really think about it, this may sound prepos- terous to anyone. If teenagers thought that critical thinking would insult anyone, let alone authority, don't you think that this would make them even more anxious to try it out? Teenagers are a rowdy, unpredictable group. This seems to

Square brackets within the quotation show that Gardner has changed the original text to make the sen- tence clearer or to make it grammatical.

be a place where Johnson first shoot[s] the holes in the fence and then paint[s] the bull's-eye around them" (Geertz 26). There is no possible way that so many teenagers could stay away from something if it offended anyone in charge, namely their parents. When Johnson pointed out that ". . . the university is envisioned not necessarily as a place to grow and change your thinking but as an arena in which to garner tech- nical skills that . . . should never alter your beliefs or sense of identity" (38), he left out a couple of big issues, for me anyway. Is he saying then that parents and churches should forget about teaching their children? Is a person only to learn from a university? This gap is too large. Johnson is once again being very one-sided. When he referred to critical writing and deep reading as being "plain old sin" (37), I once again felt that religious terms were being misused. I consider myself to be a religious person. I have read through the entire Bible and continue to do so, among other things. I am from the rural North Texas area that Johnson writes about, yet I have never felt that any kind of "deep thought" would be sinful. In fact, in my readings, of the Bible, I have found that deep thought is the only way I can truly concentrate and get the full meaning of what is before me. Even then, I always come across something new to think about. These are just three examples of how Johnson misuses the religious analogy.

*Gardner uses her personal experience here to develop her argument and to refute Jonhson's.*

In conclusion, Johnson seems not to have a good grasp of his subject. Maybe he could benefit from reading Geertz's process of doing ethnographical research. Because some people might confuse a wink with a twitch, or vice versa, it becomes necessary that we try to fully understand each other in order to get along; I know there are some people that I would definitely not want to mistake my twitching eye for a wink. As a rural North Texan, I do not feel that Johnson has an accurate picture of all, or even the majority of us. It seems he has gotten so close to the mural on the wall that one color is

*Gardner's conclusion restates her position, drawing from her earlier use of Geertz and her personal experience.*

all he sees. I feel that he would greatly benefit
from taking a step back and getting a whole new
perspective on the situation. I can and do think
critically. His misrepresentation of me and my
culture shows me how closed-minded he can be.
Talk about the pot calling the kettle black.

- - - - - - - - - - - - - - - - - - - - - - - -

The Works Cited list starts on a new page. Continue numbering the pages.

Double space throughout.

Indent 5 spaces after the first line of each item on your list.

Works Cited

Geertz, Clifford. The Interpretation of          Book
     Culture. New York: Basic Books, 1973.
Johnson, Robert. "Teaching the Forbidden:        Article
     Literature and the Religious Student."
     ADE Bulletin, 112 (Winter 1995): 37-39.
Trudeau, G. B. Cartoon. Writing Logically,       Cartoon
     Thinking Critically. 2nd ed. Eds. Sheila
     Cooper and Rosemary Patton. New York:
     Longman, 1997. 5.

## Closing Thoughts on Conducting Library Research

Conducting library research should become more than a mechanical process. View it as a skill and as a habit of reflection that enables you to argue more clearly and persuasively. Researching does not have to be the mind-numbing drudgery we often think of when we hear the word. However, to transcend that drudgery, your research must have a worthwhile goal driving it. It must be a tool that helps you better understand a subject you care about. I won't try to convince you that writing out Works Cited pages is ever going to be entertaining, but finding that you have something to say to a larger audience and taking part in conversations about major issues can offer you genuine satisfaction and intellectual stimulation.

# CHAPTER 5

# Conducting Field Research

AFTER YOU'VE DONE some active reading on your topic, have come up with a testable thesis, and have performed library research to find scholarly support for that thesis, what's next? Is it time to sit down and draft your final paper? You could, and that's just what many students do at this point. But ask yourself this question: "What would really make this project *mine*?" Imagine that a classmate has selected the same topic as you, has done much of the same active reading, and has consulted many of the same secondary sources. How might you make your paper stand apart from his?

Throughout this book I've been encouraging you to develop habits of reflection that will help you grow intellectually and provide you with true "ownership" of your writing projects. I've encouraged you to think carefully about your writing assignments, to consider what others have said about the topic you are writing about, and to develop and advance your own ideas rather than simply reporting what others have written or said about your topic. That kind of intellectual growth is what this book is really all about. In many ways, then, this chapter is particularly important. Doing field research gives you an opportunity to explore your topic in a hands-on, personal way and enables you to write about it from personal experience. With the firsthand knowledge that field research provides, you can confidently challenge the claims and assumptions made by others. Thus conducting field research is a particularly effective way to achieve the kind of intellectual growth and ownership that this book stresses.

This chapter first explains the need to focus your inquiry so that you can come up with an effective research plan. It then discusses using the field researcher's tools—observation, questioning, and interviewing—to collect data to support your thesis. Finally, the chapter considers the need to analyze the data you collect. My hope is that after you've read this chapter, you'll find ways to use field research to support or challenge some of the arguments made in the readings in Part Two. (Some suggestions are included in the assignment sequences; you can use these or come up with your own field research ideas.) Perhaps you'll wonder how students at your college would respond to the visitation restrictions described in Christopher Shea's "Sexual Tension," or perhaps you'll be sure that students on your campus are more politically active than those described in Paul Rogat Loeb's "I Feel a Little Fearful." You can use field research to test whether the way college students are perceived in our society accurately reflects students at your campus. Are there as many binge drinkers on your campus as media reports suggest? Are students as ignorant of current events as people say? Do college athletes fit the "dumb jock" stereotype? Is hazing still common in fraternities? Are more students living at home to save money? Are older, returning students always serious achievers? All of these questions could serve as a jumping-off point for field research.

When, in a paper, you can describe the outcome of your own field research, you can do much more than just react to what others have written, thought, or done. You can offer a fresh contribution to the academic discourse on your topic. Of course, much of value can be offered by reacting to the investigations and interpretations of others, but when you inject new and unique information into the conversation, you are more likely to gain the attention of the other participants in the discourse on your topic. Which story is likely to be more interesting—a friend's account of his roommate's spring break trip to Florida or his account of his own trip? Those in the crowd who can offer personal experiences to discuss are the ones who will keep the conversation going. The difference between discussing other researchers' findings and presenting your own, then, is the difference between just going along with the conversation and actively leading it. The goal of this chapter is to help you lead the conversation.

## Planning Field Research

*Field research* is a general term that encompasses a wide range of activities. For a marine biologist, field research might consist of observing the migratory patterns of whales off the coast of Hawaii. For a psychologist, field research might involve interviewing prison inmates about the psychological effects of incarceration. For a sociologist, field research might mean collecting survey data on the relative level of education and the wages of men and women in a particular profession. There are a number of ways to collect field data; the one you choose will depend on the essential focus of your inquiry. Once you've established what form your research will take, you can decide whether you should use observation, surveys, or interviews (or a combination of these methods) to get the data you need and how you should structure your research process.

## *Focus your inquiry*

By "the essential focus of your inquiry," I mean this: exactly what you need to find out in order to support your thesis and specifically who or what you need to examine to get that information. The focus of your field research is likely to be more specific than your overall topic or even your thesis. That is, the data you collect from your field research are more likely to be details that support your thesis (such as the secondary sources you cite in your paper) than comprehensive examples or illustrations of what your thesis states. Indeed, your inquiry might have multiple small foci, requiring several distinct research plans. How, then, do you go about boiling down your topic to determine where to focus your field research?

As an example, consider how you might focus field research for the assignment sequences in this book. The sequences ask you to investigate and write about the culture of higher education in relation to a number of different issues that affect college students. Therefore, you might decide, they are essentially asking you to produce ethnographic analyses.[1] But what does this mean? How do you investigate and analyze a culture? It seems a very broad task. Can you narrow it? Exactly whom or what will you examine, and how? To make your task manageable and in order to approach it systematically, you need to focus your inquiry.

You'll be doing ethnographic research, so you might begin by distilling the concept of "culture." What is a culture? Cultural differences are evident when we visit many foreign countries (for example, the Japanese tea ceremony is a deeply meaningful custom that is almost incomprehensible to many Americans). You don't have to travel abroad to find distinct cultures, however. Ethnographers have studied the "drug culture," "criminal culture," "football culture," and "bar culture," among many others. You might decide, then, that a culture is simply any group with distinct behaviors, beliefs, or activities. Thus fraternity members, dorm residents, student activists, commuter students, and college athletes can all be considered members of distinct cultures or subcultures within the overall culture of higher education. You might determine that you will have to investigate one or several such subcultures for each of the assignment sequences in this book, depending on what you need to find out to support your thesis.

---

[1]Ethnography is the branch of anthropology that describes specific societies or cultures. The roots of the word are *ethno-*, meaning "peoples," and-*graphy*, meaning "writing." Or, as Linda Brodkey states in "Writing Ethnographic Narratives" (*Written Communication*, Vol. 4 No. 1, January 1987, 25–50), "ethnography is the study of lived experience."

You might go even deeper than this and dissect each culture or subculture you've chosen to study, to identify its elements. For example, James Spradley, who has written ethnographies of the experience of cocktail waitresses and alcoholics, breaks culture down into nine components:

1. Space—the location of the group or subgroup
2. Actors—the members of the group or subgroup
3. Activities—what the members do within the context of the group or subgroup
4. Acts—single actions within a group activity
5. Objects—objects used by the group as part of their activities
6. Events—related activities carried out by the group
7. Times—times when events or activities take place and how long they take
8. Goals—what members of the group or the group as a whole want to achieve or accomplish
9. Feelings—how members of the group feel about the events or activities

You could use components such as these to sharpen the focus of your research efforts. If you were conducting field research on dating behavior among college students, for example, you might attend a party (event) at a fraternity house (space). You would probably focus on a few people (actors) and observe how they approach one another (activity). As part of this activity, you might also watch how males hold and handle beer bottles or how females handle their hair (acts and objects). You would take note of how long their interactions take (time). To determine the goals and feelings of the actors, you would need to talk to the individuals involved.

### Choose the populations you want to sample

As the preceding example illustrates, distilling your topic in this way will help you clarify which population you are studying, how you will sample that population for your research, and what details about the sample's behavior, characteristics, and opinions you wish to investigate. In other words, focusing your inquiry will help you decide whom to interview, what groups to survey, what or whom to observe, and when to make your observations. Some projects will require that you limit your research to particular groups (for example, members of the women's soccer team), whereas others will allow a wider focus (say, commuters), and still others can be done with a random sample of the student population (such as students who happen to be in the student center at a particular time on a particular day); it all depends on what data you need to collect to support your thesis.

You will need to explain in your paper why you chose the particular populations you selected and how you sampled them. For example, suppose that for Sequence 3, "Negotiating Differences: Race, Class, and Ethnicity," you decide to write a paper challenging Barbara Ehrenreich's argument in "The Professions as Class Fortress" (from *Fear of Falling*) that the educational requirements for entry into various occupations (law, medicine, social work, academic research, and so on), such as obtaining an advanced degree or taking specific courses as an undergraduate, "serve as much to exclude as to educate." (Ehrenreich argues, for example, that the requirement that pre-med students take organic chemistry serves no real purpose other than to "screen out students who have not had the benefit of a high-quality, middle-class, secondary education" from gaining admittance to medical school.) After actively reading the selections in Sequence 3, you decide to argue in your paper that by and large, the educational requirements of the professions serve to protect the public by ensuring the competence of practitioners and that the exclusionary effect Ehrenreich suggests is at most a secondary by-product of such requirements, not an intentional goal.

Now suppose that you go to the library and find lots of scholarly responses to Ehrenreich's argument, many of them supporting her position. You remain unconvinced by her argument, however, and are eager to conduct some field research to help you refute her claims. What populations might you study to achieve this goal? Because Ehrenreich stresses the medical profession in her essay, you decide to start there. This leaves you with a new choice: Should you study pre-med students? students who are enrolled in medical school? practicing physicians? all three of these populations? some other population? Complicating matters further, you also want to test Ehrenreich's assertions in a second profession, one that she did not use as an example to bolster her claim. In keeping with the theme of this book, you decide to test whether her assertions hold up for the teaching profession. Thus, to keep your field research manageable, you decide to survey a group of practicing medical interns, who have recently completed medical school and have begun practicing medicine, and a group of public school teachers.

Your next decision is how big a sample to survey from each of these populations. At this point in your college career, this will probably depend more on practical factors, such as the time and resources you have available, than on such formal research considerations as the statistical significance of your sample sizes. Later you may learn how to determine when a sample is statistically significant. If you decide to major in psychology, for example, you will have to learn how to conduct statistically significant field research. This concern is beyond the scope of this book, however. (If you're interested in learning about statistical sampling methods now, ask your instructor or a reference librarian for help.) But for our purposes, just try to get as wide a sample from the population you're studying as you can reasonably handle. Use common sense: A survey of your suitemates or the members of your carpool won't be likely to convince your reader of much of anything. I suggest that you keep the number a round one to make figuring percentages easier. The size of your sample will also depend on what method you use to collect your data. You can probably survey many more individuals than you can interview, for example, and you might be able to observe many more individuals than you can survey.

### Understand your relationship to your subject populations

When you begin designing your research process and tools, remember that it makes a difference whether you are an outsider or an insider to the group you are studying. An outsider can see things insiders can't. For example, when I observe another teacher's class, I can see how the students seat themselves around the room, see who dominates the conversations, see patterns in the way the teacher asks questions and the way students answer, and see who's engaged with the class discussion and who isn't. The teacher, immersed in trying to keep the class on schedule and following a coherent chain of activities, may or may not be able to see all of these things, because he or she is juggling so many tasks. But I, as an outsider, don't have to do anything but watch.

Outsiders can lack important information about the groups they study, however. For example, I once observed a class and saw a student reading a newspaper. I immediately assumed that he was not paying attention. It turned out that each day, one student was responsible for reporting on a current event related to the day's assignment; the student I had thought was inattentive was actually making sure he was ready to make his brief presentation to the class. If I hadn't talked to the teacher after class, I wouldn't have had an accurate picture of the class. The moral of this story is that to make sense of the populations and cultures you will be studying, you need to be aware of your relationship with them and to use more than one method—observing, talking, reading, and so on—to learn as much as possible about them and their activities.

As a current student, you are an insider to the culture of higher education, compared with someone who has never gone to college or someone who went to college thirty years ago. You know something about what college is because of your position on the inside. Yet there are different ways of being inside. For example, you may be a student at a community college or at a four-year private college. You may be fresh out of high school or returning after raising a family. You may live on campus or you may commute. Even different majors affect the different ways students experience college. In fact, then, you are an outsider in relation to certain groups on your campus. If you've never commuted, for instance, you can only guess what it would be like to drive back and forth to and from campus each day. If you've never lived in a dormitory, you can only guess what it would be like to live on a floor with a great many other people near your age. Therefore, you have to consider your relationship to the specific group or subgroup you've decided to study.

## Gather background information

To find out what another group's experiences are like, you can interview or survey group members, read about the group, observe where group members congregate, and watch members of the group when they are together and apart. Your job is to interpret for your audience a particular group's experience. To do a good job analyzing your focus group's behavior, you will probably need some background information about it. For example, what are the rules of membership of this group (informal or formal)? What are the codes of acceptable behavior? Do group members ever break the rules? What happens if they do? What determines whether someone will "fit in" with this group? The type of background information you need will affect how you plan your researching process, and your research tools and methods will themselves become background information in your paper. For example, you'll need to report any problems you encountered in the course of your research. Did you have to change any of your questions after you got some sample responses? If so, why? And how did you change them? How many people, overall, did you observe or attempt to contact? What did your respondents have in common? Were there any variables that ultimately had a significant effect on your results? When did you conduct your research and over how long a time?

Field research gives you a variety of options for what may be counted as a resource. For example, you may want to collect and analyze artifacts as part of your field research. Artifacts are objects that are commonly used by a culture or subculture. Artifacts on a college campus might include the campus newspaper, items displaying school or school organization emblems or logos, announcements and flyers posted to attract student attention, materials given to students in their classes, and so on. Many times we can tell something about a group by what the members of that group wear and by the objects they commonly use. Although the focus of your research in the assignment sequences will be human populations, don't forget, as you plan your research, that artifacts attached to those populations may provide you with valuable background information about them.

# Designing and Executing Your Field Research

Once you've focused your inquiry, identified your subject populations, and gathered any background information you can, it's time to think about which method or methods to use to get the specific data you need to support your thesis. You have many options for how to design your research, but your three basic tools as a field researcher are observing, surveying, and interviewing.

To ensure the validity of their results, professional researchers in the sciences and the social sciences create detailed research designs based on accepted scientific methods and complex statistical principles. Again, such considerations are beyond the scope of this book. What I want you to do in this course is to begin thinking about field research goals and methods in broader strokes—to begin making a habit of taking a hands-on approach to your intellectual investigations. Informal research designs are fine for this purpose and for the assignment sequences in this book.

Obviously, you must design your research before you can execute it. But if you've never done field research before, you might not yet have a clear idea about how to design it. It's like trying to break into a new profession—how do you get the required experience if you can't get a job without experience? That's why this book aims to get you out into the field now, early in your college career, before field research is usually stressed or required. You may have to try out a research plan, go back and refine it, and then try it again until you get usable results. Sometimes the best way to gain needed experience is simple to "learn by doing."

## Observing your subjects

You might begin by just observing. You can learn much this way. For instance, if I were to walk on a sunny afternoon through the campus where I presently teach, I could tell that this is a college with a significant number of commuters. How could I tell? After 3:00 P.M., the sidewalks are almost deserted. Parking lots are plentiful and are located near almost every building on campus, but at this hour, many empty spaces are available in prime spots, so I can see that a lot of students have left for the day. I can tell all of this just from observing my surroundings and "reading" the evidence—I haven't asked one person a single question.

Try it yourself. Look around you and try to "read" what you see as you walk across your own campus. Think of yourself as an anthropologist. What can you tell about your college from the number of people and the ages, ethnicities, and genders represented? Is it still a busy place at 3 P.M., or does it seem deserted? What kinds of activities are advertised around campus? What can you learn from observing the grounds? Are there lots of places to sit and talk? Where are the parking lots? Are many bike racks available? Are they used? Are there businesses located near the campus that cater to students, or is your school a "suitcase" college that makes little economic impact on the community around it? Simple observation can tell you a lot about your topic if you take the time to read the evidence before you.

Of course, you won't just rely on chance and serendipity to produce relevant data; you'll plan your observations—what or whom you observe and when and how you observe them—on the basis of the nature of the data you need to collect to support your thesis. For example, suppose you want to test Paul Rogat Loeb's claim in "I Feel a Little Fearful" (in Sequence 2, "Campus Politics, Global Politics") that American college students are apolitical and reluctant to voice what political opinions they do have. How might you determine the extent to which the students at your campus have political opinions and are willing to voice them? You could ask them in a survey or in interviews, but you decide that observation is likely to give you a more accurate, objective picture of this behavior. But whom should you observe, and where and when should you observe them? How you focus your efforts will affect your results. Maybe you're a women's studies major or part of another group that frequently discusses political issues in class, and so you think Loeb has overstated his claim. In that case, you might compare observations of one of your own classes with observations of a class in which political issues could be relevant but students might be less inclined to speak up or to challenge the opinions of others (a history class, for example). This would probably produce different results than would parking yourself on the quad or in a cafeteria and eavesdropping on any conversation that just happened to fall within earshot. Planning plays an important role in research, whether it's library research, observation, surveying, interviewing, or some other means of uncovering information. What you choose to scrutinize and how you go about doing it will affect your findings, so think carefully about these choices, and explain them and their possible effects on your conclusions in your paper.

The type of observation you can do will also be determined by the time and resources you have available. If you were writing a paper about "ecoterrorism," for example, you might want to go and observe a protest by a fringe environmental group at a logging site in Oregon. But this might not be feasible if you don't live in Oregon, so you might decide that you could gain some valuable information by observing a nearby protest sponsored by a mainstream environmental group such as the Sierra Club.

When you observe people, remember to take their body language into account. If one person in a conversation is leaning in and the other is edging away, then you can infer that the first is interested in extending the interaction between them but the second is interested in ending it. As a teacher, I read body language every day in the classroom. I can tell who is engaged in the discussion and who is thinking more about the upcoming weekend. I can tell who didn't get enough sleep. I can tell who is angry and who is frustrated. Many times, body language tells me who is prepared to participate in a discussion and who isn't.

Also pay attention to the dynamics within a group. For example, in my classes I soon learn who the leaders are and who the followers are. Others act as "facilitators," helping the discussion along with supportive comments. I learn who the shy people are and who the extroverts are. In many classes, there will be one person whom the rest of the class finds to be extremely irritating, and I can see how the class responds to that individual when he or she attempts to participate in the discussion (discreet eye rolling, whispering, significant eye contact with others, and so on). The next time you're in a group, look around you and try to "read" how people are feeling and who plays what roles. Who are the leaders? Who is the person people listen to and respect the most? Who is the least respected member of the group? What effects do these roles have on the group's activities or discussions?

### Surveying your subjects

Compiling an effective survey takes a great deal of thought and patience. Questions must be clear, unambiguous, and neutral, and they should have an air of professional detachment. They should not lead respondents to answer in a certain way, and they shouldn't be too nosy. For instance, a student of mine a couple of years ago wanted to include a question asking single students to reveal whether they were virgins, in order to determine whether they were—according to her definition—"truly religious." Her fellow classmates helped her see the problems in asking a question like that, a question that revealed far more about *her* assumptions than it would have about her respondents' religious practices on campus. Analyze your questions to make sure they are not leading and are not influenced by your own assumptions, and test them out on a willing roommate, friend, or spouse *before* you administer your survey.

Figure 5.1 shows a sample survey asking students questions about religion on campus. Notice some of the assumptions and biases this survey reveals. Questions 2, 3, and 5, in particular, seem to assume that respondents will be the stereotypical eighteen- or nineteen-year-old college students living away from home for the first time. If this accurately represents the population of your campus, then such questions are not necessarily a problem (you would

**FIGURE 5.1**
**A Sample Survey**

---

I am currently enrolled in a research writing class at this college. We are attempting to learn more about student attitudes toward faith and religion at this school. Please take a few minutes to answer the following questions.

1. Are you a member of a church, synagogue, mosque, or other religious organization?

_____ Yes          _____ No

If yes, which type of organization do you belong to?

_____ Roman Catholic church          _____ Synagogue

_____ Protestant church          _____ Mosque

(denomination:          _____ Other (please indicate:

_____)          _____)

2. What sort of role, if any, do religious practices play in your daily life as a student?

_____ Very important role          _____ Somewhat important role

_____ Little or no role

3. Would you say, in general, that students today are more or less religious than they were when your parents were your age?

_____ More          _____ Less

Why do you think this is the case?

_____

4. Do many of the students you know well actively practice a religion?

_____ Yes          _____ No

5. Did you attend religious services regularly when you lived at home?

_____ Yes          _____ No

6. If yes, do you find it more difficult to do so now that you're in college?

_____ Yes          _____ No          _____ I haven't tried

7. If yes, what factors contribute to this?

_____

_____

Personal information:

1. Sex:    _____ Male          _____ Female

2. Age:  _____

3. Marital status:  _____ Married          _____ Single

4. Children: how many and what age?

want to point this out in your paper, however). These questions would not be likely to yield useful data if distributed to older students or commuter students, however.

Depending on your research design and goals, your survey might include closed questions, open-ended questions, or both. With closed questions, you control the range of responses. See, for example, Question 1 in Figure 5.1. The question asks simply whether the respondent belongs to a religious organization, and if so which one; it doesn't allow for any responses beyond the options provided. An open-ended question, by contrast, leaves the door open for a wide range of responses. Open-ended questions give the researcher an opportunity to learn more about respondents' characteristics, opinions, beliefs, and so on. For example, the second part of Question 3 asks respondents to speculate about why students today are more or less religious than their parents were at the same age. By comparing different respondents' answers to open-ended "Why?" questions such as this, researchers can find out and track factors that might produce a particular opinion. If you're not sure what type of questions to ask, try a mix of closed- and open-ended questions.

### Interviewing your subjects

In general, my students have found interviewing to be the most interesting and engaging type of field research. Interviewing gives you a chance to obtain more detailed information than you can get from a survey, but from a smaller sample. Interviewing is the obvious choice if the subject of your inquiry is one or two individuals or a very small group. You're not likely to have time to interview more than a handful of people for any one writing project, so if you're studying a large population, you'll probably need to include a survey as part of your research plan to get an accurate idea of that population's characteristics. Interviewing a representative few may add valuable additional insight to your study, however. For example, an interview can reveal and debunk erroneous theories or assumptions you may hold. One student I know interviewed a couple of members of a fraternity and a couple of members of his college's gay and lesbian student organization concerning their religious beliefs and practices. He had assumed that the responses from these two groups would be radically different and that the gay and lesbian students would be far less likely than the fraternity members to consider themselves religious. He was surprised to find that their responses were not much different from each other and that both gay students were deeply religious. Because interviews provide greater detail, they can help us recognize the complexity of a group or an issue and confute false generalizations.

Figure 5.2 contains a list of some sample interview questions, focusing again on religion on campus and designed for a student interviewee. In an interview, pretty much all of the questions are open-ended, except for those that ask for specific information about your interviewee (age, employment history, marital status, and the like). As an interviewer, your job is to get answers that are as detailed as possible, to probe beyond generalities to concrete examples and experiences. For example, consider Question 6. The point of asking such a question is not just to get a "yes or no" response but to elicit details that reveal something about the interviewee—his or her background, standards, beliefs, and so on.

Here are some broad guidelines to help you with interviewing:

- Think of yourself in professional terms and conduct your interviews as professionally as you can, even if you're interviewing a buddy.

- Make an appointment and, of course, make sure that you keep it. Give yourself plenty of time before your assignment's due date so that your interviewee won't feel under pressure to pitch in at the last minute to help you out.

**FIGURE 5.2**
**Sample Interview Questions**

---

### Sample Interview Questions

1. Does your religious faith play an important role in your life as a student? In what ways?

2. Do you attend organized religious services? How often?

3. Have you ever seen someone's religious beliefs get in the way of their ability to participate or to think critically in one of your classes? What happened?

4. William Bennett, author of *The Book of Virtues*, has argued that "we desperately need to recover a sense of the fundamental purpose of education, which is to provide for the intellectual *and* moral education of the young." Do you agree? Why or why not? What might a school like this one do to further this aim?

5. Do you ever discuss your religion with others at school? Under what circumstances?

6. Have you ever felt that someone on campus has "pushed" his or her religious beliefs on you? What happened, and how did it make you feel?

7. Is organized religion important to a "successful" life? How do you define success?

- Come prepared with written questions, paper, and a couple of pens.

- If you want to tape the session, make sure it's all right with your interviewee; tape recorders make some people nervous. Remember to bring extra batteries and a spare tape, just in case.

- Ask some easy questions at the beginning of the interview to help both of you relax. Most people love to talk about themselves and will usually warm up once the interview is under way.

- Use your prepared questions, but also remember to ask follow-up questions based on the interviewee's responses, and feel free to ask any other questions that occur to you during the conversation.

- Remember that your interviewee is doing you a big favor, so be sure to follow up with a written thank you note. Later, if you find that you left something important out of the interview, or if you think of a great question you didn't ask, you can call back. If you've sent a proper thank you, the person will probably be happy to answer another question or two.

- Get permission to use the information from your interviewee in your written work. This is called getting an "informed consent." Type up a form that says something like "I, [name of interviewee] give [your name] my consent to use what I say during this interview in his written research. I understand that I will have a chance to read and comment on a draft before it is turned in or published in any form." Then include blanks for a signature and the date.

- When your draft is done, the ethical thing to do is to give each of your interviewees a chance to read it and respond to how you used their responses. This way they can be assured that they won't be made to look foolish, and you can be assured that you've "gotten it right" and that you haven't written anything that would cause them distress.

It's important to provide your reader with background information about any interviews you refer to in your paper. For example, where did you conduct your interviews? What were the circumstances? Were you sitting across a table from your interviewee? Did you tape the interview or take notes? Did you do any of the interview over the telephone? Was anyone else present? Did you ask everyone the same questions in the same order, or did you vary the order depending on the circumstances? Were some interviews longer than others? Why? Was anyone reluctant to speak? How did your interviewees seem to respond? How did they seem at the end of their interviews?

You should also mention any observations of your own that serve either to confirm or to raise doubts about individual responses. In other words, if your interviewee says one thing but observation tells you something else, speculate about the possible reasons for the discrepancy. For example, if you ask two people who are flirting with each other what they hope will be the result of their behavior, it's possible that they might not be willing to share certain goals with you. Both might say they are just enjoying themselves and have no goals beyond that, for instance, when in fact one might be hoping to meet someone to begin a lasting relationship and the other might be trying to make someone else jealous. Motives are complicated and are worth considering at length. Many of us do things with very little sense of why we're doing them.

Finally, when you transcribe your interviewee's words, it is standard practice to do a certain amount of editing. Where I live, many people have a thick Texas accent. Some people say "git" rather than "get," for example. I would never use "git" in a written transcript of an interview, however. Emphasize *what* your interviewees say, not *how* they say it. Emphasizing quirks in how an interviewee speaks only serves to demean the person who was kind enough to give you an interview.

## Analyzing Your Data

The final step in field research is to analyze your data. It's not enough to gather and compile information about your target population; you also need to draw conclusions from that information. By the time you get to the end of any of the assignment sequences in this book, you will have read several essays, consulted scholarly research on your subject, and conducted your own field research. You might be tempted to write up a list of observations—yours and others'—along the lines of "I read this and then I saw that and then I heard this. . . ." But remember that your job is not only to collect information but also to *shape* it. Suppose you observed dating behavior on your campus. Don't just describe that behavior in your paper—speculate about what purposes it serves. Or suppose you observed that students at your campus are more likely to discuss politics with members of their own gender than with members of the opposite sex. Can you infer something from this about the students on your campus? about American society in general? Why or why not?

In other words, use the data you collect from your field research to test your thesis and to back it up, if possible. Throughout this book I've urged you to come up with a carefully considered thesis and then to make it your goal to find evidence, from library research and from field research, to support it. This doesn't mean, however, that your thesis must be immutable. You might find ample information from library research to support your thesis but then gather field research data that leads you to modify or even completely reverse it. Or you might find that your field research gives you the confidence to strengthen your thesis and take issue with the prevailing scholarly view on your topic. Such changes can become part of your dialogue on your topic. The basic point is this: Plan your research carefully, and then put the same amount of care into analyzing whatever information you collect, and your argument will be as persuasive as it can be.

## Sample Student Paper

Following is a research project by Shelle Smith. Shelle is a nontraditional, returning student who felt a little out of place and a little put out by traditional students, whom she believed took going to college for granted and didn't know how easy they had it. Her original idea was to prove how much more complicated the lives of nontraditional students are than those of students just out of high school. But then, in the course of her field research, she found that on her campus, at least, *everybody's* lives are complicated. Her final paper describes her research findings and her conclusions.

---

Shelle Smith

Professor Dunbar-Odom

English 102

27 Apr 1997

Going to College: A Balancing Act

There was once a time when going to college was an all-expense-paid opportunity reserved for recent high school graduates. Times have changed. Because of increasing tuition costs and decreasing grant money, many students must rely on income from jobs, student loans, or both. The College Board reports that three-quarters of full-time students held down jobs in 1989-90 (Kramer 6). According to my own student survey, that still holds true almost a decade later.

There has also been a change in the type of student attending college. According to the College Board and the U.S. Census Bureau, in 1996 forty percent of undergraduates were 25 or older (Hube 137). Since older students usually have responsibilities such as family and full-time jobs, the additional task of attending college can be very stressful. I must admit that when I started this research project, I assumed that the dilemma of balancing school, work, and family was mostly a problem for nontraditional students (described as part-time, independent, or over 24). Since I am a nontraditional student, my perception may be biased, but it seems that older students are better able to handle large amounts of stress than are younger traditional students (described as full-time, dependent, and under 24). However, I realize that the task as well as the stress of balancing responsibilities is not limited to nontraditional students; many students must make personal and financial sacrifices to attend college.

I conducted a random survey of fifty college students attending Texas A&M University—Commerce. Most surveys were completed by students in freshman-level classes; therefore, there was not a large variation in age. Of the students surveyed, the average age was 21, and 70 percent commute to school. Seventy percent of students also said that their main motivation for going to college was to get a good job while only 20 percent said they wanted to better themselves. Forty-five percent of students said that the most difficult thing about going to college was doing homework and going to class, while 25 percent said managing time was the hardest. I asked students what their biggest stress while attending school was, and most of the answers related to studying, homework, and tests. Some of the most surprising results to me were that 75 percent of the students surveyed worked and that 60 percent of those held down full-time jobs. Unfortunately, only 10 percent of the students said that they studied ten hours or more per week, and 40 percent said they studied 0 to 5 hours per week.

Apparently, they are too busy to study, but I don't understand how any student could pass a college course without studying. In an article in *Change*, Theodore Marchese said, "Gone everywhere, it seems, is the old understanding that college takes three hours outside class for every one in" (4) He also claims that it is not entirely the fault of the student. He states:

> When federal and state policymakers decided to shift college costs from the public and parents to the student, and to move from low tuition and grants to student work and loans, they all but ordained that a culture of "work now, study in-between" would take hold (Marchese 4).

For research purposes, I interviewed a non-traditional student and a traditional student to

get two different views on balancing responsibilities. Robin Smith is a 27-year-old female Animal
Science major at TAMU—Commerce. She attended
college immediately after high school but quit to
get married and have a family. Seven years later,
she decided to go back to school to pursue her
dream of being a veterinarian. She is currently a
sophomore taking fifteen college hours and commutes 120 miles round trip every day. She is
married with two children and works about twenty-
five hours per week. Robin says she studies about
eight hours a week and has a GPA of 3.35 but
claims her grades are much better now than they
were when she was younger. She said, "At 19, I was
happy if I passed a class; now I'm upset if I
don't get an A." Robin admits that as a 27-year-
old, she gets aggravated at incoming freshmen who
want to be "spoon fed." She says, "They aren't
mentally mature. . . . They don't have critical
thinking or understand what they are learning and
how to apply it to life."

Robin said that her biggest stress was trying
to manage her time between work, family, and school
so that nothing gets left out. She also said that
sometimes the pressure makes her snap and she has
to have a tantrum. When I asked Robin if she was
an organized person, she replied, "I don't have
time to get organized; I go on adrenaline." She
admits that a person has to be slightly insane to
do what she is doing and that not everyone can
handle the stress. It takes a certain kind of

person to go in all directions at the same time and still be able to accomplish goals. Robin gave up a job paying $45,000 a year to go back to school. She is willing to sacrifice almost any-thing to accomplish her goal.

Billy Fowler is a traditional male student. He is a 20-year-old Agricultural Economics major at TAMU—C with a GPA of 3.0, and he lives at home with his parents. He is currently taking fifteen college hours and says that he studies about seven hours a week while working two part-time jobs. He believes that his biggest stress is trying to balance his time among school, work, being an FFA (Future Farmers of America) officer, and his duties as a Scoutmaster. Billy said that it is difficult trying to fit in study time with all his other responsibilities. He said, "By the time I figure out a system, the semester is half over." Billy realizes that he should probably cut out some of his activities but feels that he needs the diversion. He also said that most of the students that he knows work, and some students even skip class to study for a test if they had to work the night before. Billy said that school comes first, and he believes that better planning and better time management could be the key ingredient for being better prepared for classes.

In an article in *Change* magazine, Martin Kramer stated, "The present generation of students can surely be labeled the over-scheduled genera-tion, and not only those who are nontraditional.

They have appointment books that must be checked whenever there is a matter of 'fitting in' an activity" (6). I believe that there are a large number of today's students, myself included, who stretch themselves pretty thin. Unless students are lucky enough to receive a full scholarship, to be awarded grants, or to have parents who pay their expenses, their only options are working and student loans. Because of the rising cost of college, most of us have to work to be able to afford going to school. However, many of us not only work full-time while attending college but also have families, mortgages, and various other responsibilities.

Both of my interviewees, Billy and Robin, said that balancing responsibilities was their biggest stress factor while attending college. It is difficult enough to go to school and work, but add family responsibilities to that, and things really get complicated. There was a recent study published in the *Journal of Psychology* about the conflicting demands of work, family, and school. In it the authors stated:

> Research has shown that when people experience a great amount of stress in coping with the demands of work and family, there are negative consequences both on and off the job. Logically, those negative consequences may also exist when people attempt to balance work, family, and student roles simultaneously (Hammer, Grigsby, Woods 221).

As Robin said earlier, a person has to be slightly
insane to attempt to go to school and work while
trying to maintain some sort of family life. The
stress involved could affect grades, relationships, or mental and physical health.

So how does a student balance the stress of
all these responsibilities? Billy mentioned
better planning and time management. Good organizational skills would definitely be a plus, but I
think it takes more than that. I think it takes a
fierce determination, an inner drive that not
everyone has. A person must be willing to make
great sacrifices to achieve a balance for this
juggling act.

The face of the college campus is changing.
It appears that college is no longer just a party
time for 19-year-olds. According to the Office of
Admissions, the average age of undergraduates
here at TAMU—Commerce is 23.4 (*Lion Facts*). That
obviously means that there are a large number of
older students on this campus, and older students
usually tend to have more responsibilities and
more stress. However, as I stated earlier, my survey results showed that 75 percent of the students
that I survey on this campus work, and their
biggest stressor is studying and getting homework
done. Since my survey included many 19-year-olds,
I can conclude that young students are also under
stress. Of my two interviewees, Robin appears to
have more demands put on her than Billy; however,
both students may feel equally stressed. There are

varying degrees of stress, and everyone copes differently. Usually, a person who feels stressed is
stressed. I think that age and maturity may play a
part in being able to handle larger amounts of
stress. However, my research has proven that
students of all ages are trying to deal with the
stress of balancing responsibilities. Regardless
of a student's age, trying to balance work, studying, going to class, family, and various other
responsibilities is very difficult. Therefore,
the present generation of students all must make
sacrifices to attend college.

## Works Cited

Fowler, Billy. Telephone interview. 26 Apr. 1998.

Hammer, Leslie B., Tenora D. Grigsby, and Steven
    Woods. "The Conflicting Demands of Work,
    Family, and School Among Students at an
    Urban University." The Journal of
    Psychology Mar. 1998: 220-6.

Hube, Karen. "How Older Students Can Cut the
    Cost of a College Degree in Half." Money
    Sept. 1996: 137.

Kramer, Martin. "Forum: Earning and Learning."
    Change Jan.-Feb. 1994: 6-7.

Lion Facts. Commerce, TX: Texas A&M University—
    Commerce Office of Admissions, 1997.

Marchese, Theodore J. "Resetting Expectations."
    Change Nov.-Dec. 1996: 4.

Smith, Robin. Personal interview. 28 Apr. 1998.

What I value about this paper is that Shelle's own interests fueled its development. And I respect Shelle's ability to change her mind as a result of her research. I also admire the way she brings others' ideas and words into her paper; she integrates quotations, for instance, into her own arguments and doesn't let them control how she structures her arguments or her paragraphs. In other words, she learned from the work she did and was able, as a result, to see beyond the limits of her own experience. That seems to me to be a crucial hallmark of real research.

## Closing Thoughts on Field Research

Field research gives you an opportunity to teach yourself and others something real, immediate, and unique about your subject— something you probably wouldn't find in a book or journal. It gets you involved in your project in a way that library research just can't match. As a teacher, I find the prospect of my students' experiencing that kind of involvement extremely exciting. Each term, my students learn things about their lives and experiences as members of a college community and teach those things to me, and the prospect of learning from them has transformed my own experience as a teacher.

Performing field research helps you grow intellectually and helps you claim true ownership of your writing. As I said in the Introduction, at its heart this book is more about thinking than it is about writing. It's about breaking free of formulaic approaches and actively engaging with ideas. It's about growing intellectually and cultivating a richer academic experience. Because of the personal involvement it entails, field research is a vital contributor to these processes.

As you move on to the sequenced assignments in Part Two, remember to practice the habits of reflection that will help you write convincing and illuminating papers: Read and think critically, carefully consider your theses, plan your research, thoughtfully analyze your results, and carefully consider how best to frame your arguments. Then you'll be ready to write excellent papers. I hope you find the work you do with this book worthwhile, and I hope you choose to share some of that work with me and others. I welcome your e-mail at Donna_Dunbar-Odom@tamu-commerce.edu.

# PART II

# Readings and Assignment Sequences

# What Is an Assignment Sequence?

BROADLY STATED, AN assignment sequence is a series of reading, writing, and research assignments that build on one another to provide you with a progressively deeper understanding of a complex issue. Each sequence centers on a general theme related to higher education. Each asks you to move gradually from your diffuse personal perceptions on that topic to a series of increasingly complex responses based on the reading and writing you do throughout that sequence of assignments. The sequence culminates in a research paper that draws from that reading and writing and from library and field research, still on the topic with which you began. Thus each sequence asks you to progress in two directions—from the personal to the global, in terms of your audience, and from the general to the specific, in terms of your subject matter. The ultimate goal of the sequences is to encourage you to approach your college reading and writing projects as opportunities for intellectual growth, by helping you acquire the habits of reflection described in this book.

## How the Sequences Are Structured

Each assignment sequence is structured to help you make connections between what you experience, what you read, and what you write. You'll start each sequence by writing down some of your own ideas about the sequence's theme—ideas based on your personal experience as a college student. Next you'll read an essay that deals with the same general theme and then reconsider your original ideas in light of what that reading says about the topic. After that you'll consider yet another essay and again measure your current perspective on the issue against what that reading has to say. You'll repeat this process for each reading in the sequence. The goal is for you to bring together ideas from a number of writers, combine them with your own thoughts and experiences, and ultimately develop a carefully considered thesis for a final research project that focuses in depth on some aspect of the sequence's theme.

Each sequence begins with a Getting Started assignment, for which you will answer some general questions, to get you thinking, and then write a preliminary brief essay on the overall theme of the sequence. You'll then move on to the readings. Every sequence includes from five to six readings, each focusing on one specific issue related to the sequence's theme. Before-reading and after-reading questions are included for each reading selection, to get you thinking about the specific issue the readings cover and to prompt you to enter into a "conversation" with the authors of the readings. After each reading, you'll write a brief essay that integrates the thoughts you expressed in your previous essay with the content of the current reading. After you've completed all of the readings, you'll develop a thesis for a formal research project, conduct library and field research to test and support that thesis, and then write a traditional research paper.

### The Getting Started exercises

Each assignment sequence begins with a brief overview of the sequence's theme and then asks a few questions designed to elicit your thoughts and opinions on the issues addressed in the sequence. You can base your responses to these questions on your own experiences and observations or even on things you've heard others say or do. For example, the Getting Started assignment for Sequence 2, "Campus Politics, Global Politics," asks you to characterize the political atmosphere on your campus, to describe your own level of political involvement, and then to consider what factors enter into students' decisions about whether to participate in campus political activities. The purpose of the assignment is to get you started thinking about political activism on your campus (and thus noticing it more) and about why some students are politically active and others aren't. Finally, the Getting Started segment of each sequence asks you to write a brief preliminary essay based on your responses to one or more of these beginning questions.

### The readings

The next step is for you to read and respond to the first reading of the sequence. The first reading in Sequence 2, for example, is an article from the *Washington Post* about a survey indicating that conservatism is on the rise on college campuses. Using the active reading skills and strategies described in Chapter 1, you'll answer the pre-reading questions and then read the article critically, considering where and how you agree or disagree with its claims and how well it seems to represent your own experience on campus. You will probably also discuss some of the readings in class, which will enable you to get other students' perspectives as well.

Following each reading are several after-reading, before-writing questions designed to help you enter into a "conversation" with the author of the reading. These questions are meant to give you a running start on the essay you'll write about the reading and to provide you with examples and ideas you can draw on when you begin writing. Each of the reading assignments in the rest of the sequence is designed to build on the preceding readings, enriching your understanding of the issues at the center of the sequence.

## *The final project*

Each sequence culminates in a final research project on an issue related to the general theme of the sequence. One reason I've structured the sequences in a layered fashion, with each reading and the written response to it building on prior readings and responses, is to help you craft a carefully considered thesis for the final research project. The reading and writing you will have done by the time you get to this stage in a sequence will provide you with a strong foundation for contributing to the academic discourse on the issue you choose to explore in your final paper.

At the end of each sequence you will find suggestions for library and field research activities and a list of questions you might address in your final paper. You may use these to guide your research, or you might find that they help you think of other, related issues to explore.

You should begin the final assignment by reviewing the materials from the course: the information in Part One of the text, the readings, your essays, other students' papers, your teacher's comments, notes you have from class discussions, and the library and field research you've done on your topic. Pay special attention to your own writing, both your early responses to the readings and your subsequent revisions. Your job in this essay is to explain, describe, and argue *your* position on the issue you write about, not the views of other writers.

As you gather your materials and begin to shape your paper, consider one last time just what you want to convince your readers of. What experiences, examples, and viewpoints can you share that will do the most to bolster your argument? Also, as you write your final paper, remember that you are now an expert on this topic. No one else will have done exactly the same research that you have done on it, so no one else can match your unique viewpoint. Now it's up to you to share your findings with the world.

## How to Approach the Assignment Sequences

The number of questions in the assignment sequences may perplex you. Each of the assignments asks more questions than you can or should answer. Approach the questions as jumping-off places. They are meant to stimulate your creativity and to help you begin to formulate a position. Please do *not* attempt to answer each question in a separate paragraph. Take two or three and run with them. Try to make connections between them.

When you write, draw on your own experience and expertise as well as that of the other writers you've read. I encourage you to make use of personal examples, speaking in the first person and using personal pronouns (*I, me, my,* and so on). Personal examples are nearly always the most interesting parts of academic writing, and they are the most powerful way to establish your authority to speak on the issues you're writing about. Think of yourself as having a conversation with the authors of the readings and the authors of materials you find in the library. They are not present to speak for themselves, so you'll have to bring them into the conversation yourself. Quote these authors to demonstrate your understanding of their views, but leave ample room to state and develop your own. Remember that you're in a conversation with these authors, and neither of you should dominate that conversation.

# Ideas of Higher Education

## Getting Started

As you know, this term you will be reading and writing essays that center on issues of education—particularly college education and the ways in which you do and do not participate in the education process as a student—and on the stories we tell ourselves about education and learning. You have probably invested a great deal of time, energy, and money in getting to occupy the seat you're in right now. Therefore, it should be worth more time and energy to think further about the decisions you've made, the decisions that have been made for you, and the spectrum in between.

The theme addressed in this sequence of readings can be loosely described as *what a college education should make available to individuals and to society*. Should it be preparation of "the best and the brightest"? John Henry Newman holds that a university education prepares students to be future leaders. Should it be strictly preparation for a job? Caroline Bird argues that for many students, money spent on college tuition is wasted money, and Lynne V. Cheney claims that in picking their majors, students should "follow their hearts" and not worry about how much money they can make in that field. Should a college education "liberate" people from their prejudices? Olivia Castellano argues passionately that higher education should make people aware of the ways they have been oppressed and should help them begin to overcome that oppression. Should a university education be available for everyone? Mike Rose says yes and then discusses how complicated that process can be for less-prepared students. Working through these readings and through your answers to the questions in the reading and writing assignments that follow will lead you to a much fuller understanding of what your own "idea of a university" is.

Before you do any of the reading, please reflect on your "ideas of higher education"; then respond to several of the following questions. I use the Getting Started questions as the first writing assignment on the very first day of the course. Your teacher may also do this, or he or she may ask that you write out your responses either in a journal or in your notebook. Your teacher may use these questions as a jumping-off place for class discussion as well. No matter how you use these questions in your class, you'll be able to draw on what you write here both in your contributions to discussion and in your responses to the assignments that follow.

1. Why did you come to college in general? Why this college in particular? What factors did you consider in deciding to attend college? Was it entirely your decision?
2. What do you think a college education should make possible for you? What do you think it will make possible for you?
3. What is the university's responsibility to you? What is your responsibility to the university?
4. Have you heard stories about college life or about earning a college education that you found appealing or intimidating? Why did they affect you this way?
5. How is being a college student different from being in high school?
6. Beyond serving your individual needs, what should the college's educational mission be for the community or for the world at large?

## READING 1

*John Henry Newman*

# The Idea of a University

Cardinal John Henry Newman (1801–1890) wrote *The Idea of a University* in 1852 to bring about the establishment of a Catholic university in the face of the fierce anti-Catholic sentiment of the period. *The Idea of a University* also serves as a description of what a liberal arts education should be and what it should make possible. The first time I taught this piece, I was concerned that my students would find it inaccessible, but in class after class, the majority have voted it their favorite essay of the sequence.

### Before you read

1. Contemplate the term *liberal arts*. What do you think a "liberal arts" education is?
2. In what ways do you expect to be changed by your education?
3. Is the pursuit of knowledge for its own sake a worthwhile goal for college students? Why or why not?
4. What were some of the factors that made you decide to come to college?

### Discourse V
### Knowledge Its Own End

*1*

I have said that all branches of knowledge are connected together, because the subject-matter of knowledge is intimately united in itself, as being the acts and the work of the Creator. Hence it is that the Sciences, into which our knowledge may be said to be cast, have multiplied bearings one on another, and an internal sympathy, and admit, or rather demand, comparison and adjustment. They complete, correct, balance each other. This consideration, if well-founded, must be taken into account, not only as regards the attainment of truth, which is their common end, but as regards the influence which they exercise upon those whose education consists in the study of them. I have said already, that to give undue prominence to one is to be unjust to another; to neglect or supersede these is to divert those from their proper object. It is to unsettle the boundary lines between science and science, to disturb their action, to destroy the harmony which binds them together. Such a proceeding will have a corresponding effect when introduced into a place of education. There is no science but tells a different tale, when viewed as a portion of a whole, from what it is likely to suggest when taken by itself, without the safeguard, as I may call it, of others.

Let me make use of an illustration. In the combination of colours, very different effects are produced by a difference in their selection and juxta-position; red, green, and white, change their shades, according to the contrast to which they are submitted. And, in like manner, the drift and meaning of a branch of knowledge varies with the company in which it is introduced to the student. If his reading is confined simply to one subject, however such division of labour may favour the advancement of a particular pursuit, a point into which I do not here enter, certainly it has a tendency to contract his mind. If it is incorporated with others, it depends on those others as to the kind of influence which it exerts upon him. Thus the Classics, which in England are the means of refining the taste, have in France subserved the spread of revolutionary and deistical doctrines. In Metaphysics, again, Butler's Analogy of Religion, which has had so much to do with the conversion to the Catholic faith of members of the University of Oxford, appeared to Pitt and others, who had received a different training, to operate only in the direction of infidelity. And so again, Watson, Bishop of Llandaff, as I think he tells us in the narrative of his life, felt the science of Mathematics to indispose the mind to religious belief, while others see in its investigations the best parallel, and thereby defence, of the Christian Mysteries. In like manner, I suppose, Arcesilas would not have handled logic as Aristotle, nor Aristotle have criticized poets as Plato; yet reasoning and poetry are subject to scientific rules.

It is a great point then to enlarge the range of studies which a University professes, even for the sake of the students; and, though they cannot pursue every subject which is open to them, they will be the gainers by living among those and under those who represent the whole circle. This I conceive to be the advantage of a seat of universal learning, considered as a place of education. An assemblage of learned men, zealous for their own sciences, and rivals of each other, are brought, by familiar intercourse and for the sake of intellectual peace, to adjust together the claims and relations of their respective subjects of investigation. They learn to respect, to consult, to aid each other. Thus is created a pure and clear atmosphere of thought, which the student also breathes, though in his own case he only pursues a few sciences out of the multitude. He profits by an intellectual tradition, which is independent of particular teachers, which guides him in his choice of subjects, and duly interprets for him those which he chooses. He apprehends the great outlines of knowledge, the principles on which it rests, the scale of its parts, its lights and its shades, its great points and its little, as he otherwise cannot apprehend them. Hence it is that his education is called "Liberal." A habit of mind is formed which lasts through life, of which the attributes are, freedom, equitableness, calmness, moderation, and wisdom; or what in a former Discourse I have ventured to call a philosophical habit. This then I would assign as the special fruit of the education furnished at a University, as contrasted with other places of teaching or modes of teaching. This is the main purpose of a University in its treatment of its students.

And now the question is asked me, What is the *use* of it? and my answer will constitute the main subject of the Discourses which are to follow.

### Discourse VI
### Knowledge Viewed in Relation to Learning

*5*

Now from these instances, to which many more might be added, it is plain, first, that the communication of knowledge certainly is either a condition or the means of that sense of enlargement or enlightenment, of which at this day we hear so much in certain quarters: this cannot be denied; but next, it is equally plain, that such communication is not the whole of the process. The enlargement consists, not merely in the passive reception into the mind of a number of ideas hitherto unknown to it, but in the mind's energetic and simultaneous action upon and towards and among those new ideas, which are rushing in upon it. It is the action of a formative power, reducing to order and meaning the matter of our acquirements; it is a making the objects of our knowledge subjectively our own, or, to use a familiar word, it is a digestion of what we receive, into the substance of our previous state of thought; and without this no enlargement is said to follow. There is no enlargement, unless there be a comparison of ideas one with another, as they come before the mind, and a systematizing of them. We feel our minds to be growing and expanding *then,* when we not only learn, but refer what we learn to what we know already. It is not the mere addition to our knowledge that is the illumination; but the locomotion, the movement onwards, of that mental centre, to which both what we know, and what we are learning, the accumulating mass of our acquirements, gravitates. And therefore a truly great intellect, and recognized to be such by the common opinion of mankind, such as the intellect of Aristotle, or of St. Thomas, or of Newton, or of Goethe, (I purposely take instances within and without the Catholic pale, when I would speak of the intellect as such,) is one which takes a connected view of old and new, past and present, far and near, and which has an insight into the influence of all these one on another; without which there is no whole, and no centre. It possesses the knowledge, not only of things, but also of their mutual and true relations; knowledge, not merely considered as acquirement, but as philosophy.

Accordingly, when this analytical, distributive, harmonizing process is away, the mind experiences no enlargement, and is not reckoned as enlightened or comprehensive, whatever it may add to its knowledge. For instance, a great memory, as I have already said, does not make a philosopher, any more than a dictionary can be called a grammar. There are men who embrace in their minds a vast multitude of ideas, but with little sensibility about their real relations towards each other. These may be antiquarians, annalists, naturalists; they may be learned in the law; they may be versed in statistics; they are most useful in their own place; I should shrink from speaking disrespectfully of them; still there is nothing in such attainments to guarantee the absence of narrowness of mind. If they are nothing more than well-read men, or men of information, they have not what specially deserves the name of culture of mind, or fulfils the type of Liberal Education.

In like manner, we sometimes fall in with persons who have seen much of the world, and of the men who, in their day, have played a conspicuous part in it, but who generalize nothing, and have no observation, in the true sense of the word. They abound in information in detail, curious and entertaining, about men and things; and having lived under the influence of no very clear or settled principles, religious or political, they speak of every one and every thing, only as so many phenomena, which are complete in themselves, and lead to nothing, not discussing them, or teaching any truth, or instructing the hearer, but simply talking. No one would say that these persons, well informed as they are, had attained to any great culture of intellect or to philosophy.

The case is the same still more strikingly where the persons in question are beyond dispute men of inferior powers and deficient education. Perhaps they have been much in foreign countries, and they receive, in a passive, otiose, unfruitful way, the various facts which are forced upon them there. Seafaring men, for example, range from one end of the earth to the other; but the multiplicity of external objects, which they have encountered, forms no symmetrical and consistent picture upon their imagination; they see the tapestry of human life, as it were on the wrong side, and it tells no story. They sleep, and they rise up, and they find themselves, now in Europe, now in Asia; they see visions of great cities, and wild regions; they are in the marts of commerce, or amid the islands of the South; they gaze on Pompey's Pillar, or on the Andes; and nothing which meets them carries them forward or backward, to any idea beyond itself. Nothing has a drift or relation; nothing has a history or a promise. Every thing stands by itself, and comes and goes in its turn, like the shifting scenes of a show, which leave the spectator where he was. Perhaps you are near such a man on a particular occasion, and expect him to be shocked or perplexed at something which occurs; but one thing is much the same to him as another, or, if he is perplexed, it is as not knowing what to say, whether it is right to admire, or to ridicule, or to disapprove, while conscious that some expression of opinion is expected from him; for in fact he has no standard of judgment at all, and no landmarks to guide him to a conclusion. Such is mere acquisition, and, I repeat, no one would dream of calling it philosophy.

## 6

Instances, such as these, confirm, by the contrast, the conclusion I have already drawn from those which preceded them. That only is true enlargement of mind which is the power of viewing many things at once as one whole, of referring them severally to their true place in the universal system, of understanding their respective values, and determining their mutual dependence. Thus is that form of Universal Knowledge, of which I have on a former occasion spoken, set up in the individual intellect, and constitutes its perfection. Possessed of this real illumination, the mind never views any part of the extended subject-matter of Knowledge without recollecting that it is but a part, or without the associations which spring from this recollection. It makes every thing in some sort lead to every thing else; it would communicate the image of the whole to every separate portion, till that whole becomes in imagination like a spirit, every where pervading and penetrating its component parts, and giving them one definite meaning. Just as our bodily organs, when mentioned, recall their function in the body, as the word "creation" suggests the Creator, and "subjects" a sovereign, so, in the mind of the Philosopher, as we are abstractedly conceiving of him, the elements of the physical and moral world, sciences, arts, pursuits, ranks, offices, events, opinions, individualities, are all viewed as one, with correlative functions, and as gradually by successive combinations converging, one and all, to the true centre.

   To have even a portion of this illuminative reason and true philosophy is the highest state to which nature can aspire, in the way of intellect; it puts the mind above the influences of chance and necessity, above anxiety, suspense, unsettlement, and superstition, which is the lot of the many. Men, whose minds are possessed with some one object, take exaggerated views of its importance, are feverish in the pursuit of it, make it the measure of things which are utterly foreign to it, and are startled and despond if it happens to fail them. They are ever in alarm or in transport. Those on the other hand who have no object or principle whatever to hold by, lose their way, every step they take. They are thrown out, and do not know what to think or say, at every fresh juncture; they have no view of persons, or occurrences, or facts, which come suddenly upon them, and they hang upon the opinion of others, for want of internal resources. But the intellect, which has been disciplined to the perfection of its powers, which knows, and thinks while it knows, which has learned to leaven the dense mass of facts and events with the elastic force of reason, such an intellect cannot be partial, cannot be exclusive, cannot be impetuous, cannot be at a loss, cannot but be patient, collected, and majestically calm, because it discerns the end in every beginning, the origin in every end, the law in every interruption, the limit in each delay; because it ever knows where it stands, and how its path lies from one point to another. It is the τετράγωνος of the Peripatetic, and has the "nil admirari" of the Stoic,—

> Felix qui potuit rerum cognoscere causas,
> Atque metus omnes, et inexorabile fatum
> Subjecit pedibus, streptiumque Acherontis avari.

There are men who, when in difficulties, originate at the moment vast ideas or dazzling projects; who, under the influence of excitement, are able to cast a light, almost as if from inspiration, on a subject or course of action which comes before them; who have a sudden presence of mind equal to any emergency, rising with the occasion, and an undaunted magnanimous bearing, and an energy and keenness which is but made intense by opposition. This is genius, this is heroism; it is the exhibition of a natural gift, which no culture can teach, at which no Institution can aim; here, on the contrary, we are concerned, not with mere nature, but with training and teaching. That perfection of the Intellect, which is the result of Education, and its *beau ideal,* to be imparted to individuals in their respective measures, is the clear, calm, accurate vision and comprehension of all things, as far as the finite mind can embrace them, each in its place, and with its own characteristics upon it. It is almost prophetic from its knowledge of history; it is almost heart-searching from its knowledge of human nature; it has almost supernatural charity from its freedom from littleness and prejudice; it has almost the repose of faith, because nothing can startle it; it has almost the beauty and harmony of heavenly contemplation, so intimate is it with the eternal order of things and the music of the spheres.

### Discourse VII
### Knowledge Viewed in Relation to Professional Skill

*10*

But I must bring these extracts to an end. To-day I have confined myself to saying that that training of the intellect, which is best for the individual himself, best enables him to discharge his duties to society. The Philosopher, indeed, and the man of the world differ in their very notion, but the methods, by which they are respectively formed, are pretty much the same. The Philosopher has the same command of matters of thought, which the true citizen and gentleman has of matters of business and conduct. If then a practical end must be assigned to a University course, I say it is that of training good members of society. Its art is the art of social life, and its end is fitness for the world. It neither confines its views to particular professions on the one hand, nor creates heroes or inspires genius on the other. Works indeed of genius fall under no art; heroic minds come under no rule; a University is not a birthplace of poets or of immortal authors, of founders of schools, leaders of colonies, or conquerors of nations. It does not promise a generation of Aristotles or Newtons, of Napoleons or Washingtons, of Raphaels or Shakespeares, though such miracles of nature it has before now contained within its precincts. Nor is it content on the other hand with forming the critic or the experimentalist, the economist or the engineer, though such too it includes within its scope. But a University training is the great ordinary means to a great but ordinary end; it aims at raising the intellectual tone of society, at cultivating the public mind, at purifying the national taste, at supplying true principles to popular enthusiasm and fixed aims to popular aspiration, at giving enlargement and sobriety to the ideas of the age, at facilitating the exercise of political power, and refining the intercourse of private life. It is the education which gives a man a clear conscious view of his own opinions and judgments, a truth in developing them, an eloquence in expressing them, and a force in urging them. It teaches him to see things as they are, to go right to the point, to disentangle a skein of thought, to detect what is sophistical, and to discard what is irrelevant. It prepares him to fill any post with credit, and to master any subject with facility. It shows him how to accommodate himself to others, how to throw himself into their state of mind, how to bring before them his own, how to influence them, how to come to an understanding with them, how to bear with them. He is at home in any society, he has common ground with every class; he knows when to speak and when to be silent; he is able to converse, he is able to listen; he can ask a question pertinently, and gain a lesson seasonably, when he has nothing to impart himself; he is ever ready, yet never in the way; he is a pleasant companion, and a comrade you can depend upon; he knows when to be serious and when to trifle, and he has a sure tact which enables him to trifle with gracefulness and to be serious with effect. He has the repose of a mind which lives in itself, while it lives in the world, and which has resources for its happiness at home when it cannot go abroad. He has a gift which serves him in public, and supports him in retirement, without which good fortune is but vulgar, and with which failure and disappointment have a charm. The art which tends to make a man all this, is in the object which it pursues as useful as the art of wealth or the art of health, though it is less susceptible of method, and less tangible, less certain, less complete in its result.

---

## Now that you've read

1. How does Cardinal John Henry Newman think that intellectual enlargement takes place, and what does the learner do to make this happen?
2. What is Newman's claim about the different branches of knowledge?
3. What do you think makes the most sense in what Newman has to say? Why? Do you find any of his ideas dated? Which ones?
4. Newman writes, "But a University training is the great ordinary means to a great but ordinary end. . . ." What does he mean here? How is he using the words *ordinary* and *great*?

# READING 2

*Caroline Bird*

# The College Mystique

In *The Case Against College,* written in 1975, Caroline Bird has some pretty harsh things to say to people who think that college is the automatic next step after high school. Bird interviewed college students across the country and came to the conclusion that most have no clear idea what they want from their education and see their time in college more in terms of drudgery than in terms of intellectual stimulation and growth. She goes on to argue that college is a waste of money for a great many students. See if you think what she has to say still has merit today, over twenty years later.

### Before you read

1. If you could get a well-paying job without coming to college, would you quit school? Why or why not?
2. Do you have friends who decided not to go to college? How do they seem to be doing? Do they miss not coming to college?
3. Is everyone ready for college right out of high school? Why or why not?

---

This is a book about what happens to young people when they get out of high school.

It is about college only because college is where we put as many of them as possible to get them out of the way. It isn't about education, really, or the virtues of an educated citizenry. It is not about the value of college for those young people who love learning for its own sake, for those who would rather read a good book than eat. They are a minority, even at the big-name prestige colleges which recruit and attract the intellectually oriented. For them college is intellectual discovery and adventure.

But a great majority of our nine million postsecondary students who are "in college" are there because it has become the thing to do or because college is a pleasant place to be (pleasanter at least than the "outside," sometimes called "the real," world); because it's the only way they can get parents or taxpayers to support them without working at a job they don't like; because they can't get any job at all;

because Mother wanted them to go; or for some other reason utterly irrelevant to the courses of studies for which the college is supposedly organized.

It is dismaying to find, as I did, that college professors and administrators, when pressed for a candid opinion, estimate that no more than 25 percent of the students they serve are really turned on by classwork. For the other 75 percent, college is at best a social center, a youth ghetto, an aging vat, and at worst a young folks (rhymes with old folks) home, a youth house (rhymes with poorhouse) or even a prison. However good or bad it might be for the individual students, college is a place where young adults are set apart because they are superfluous people who are of no immediate use to the economy and are a potential embarrassment to the middle-aged white males who operate the outside, or "real," world for their own convenience.

### Educational Huckstering

This segregation of the young began, as many evil institutions do, with the noblest of motives. We believed at the end of World War II that a grateful nation owed every veteran a chance at a college education. Older and eager to make up for lost career time, the veterans who used their G.I. Bill of Rights proved what educators had long contended: that millions of potential lawyers and doctors were working out their lives as factory hands and taxi drivers simply because they didn't have the money to go to college. During the affluent and expanding 1950s, we became convinced that a college education should be available to *every* qualified high-school graduate regardless of ability to pay. After the Russians beat us to space in 1957, it became patriotic as well as noble to promote advanced education, particularly in the sciences.

Educators tapped the bottomless reservoir of national defense appropriations to fund lavish research and educational development programs aimed at "catching up." We overlooked the fact that all other nations, including Russia, educate at public expense only as many of the most talented young people as the economy actually needs. Just as we were the first nation to aspire to teach every small child to read and write, so we were the first and remain the only great nation that aspires to *higher* education for all.

It was a generous ideal in the best American tradition: a door open to talent wherever it occurred. And in grandeur the concept paralleled the nineteenth-century vision of a nation united by railroad tracks from coast to coast. The ideal was especially popular, of course, with the politically articulate middle class in the 1950s and

'60s when their families were having trouble finding places in existing colleges.

Americans pride themselves on implementing impossible dreams. In the 1960s we damned the expense and built the great state university systems as fast as we could, blinking at waste and graft as we went. And like the building of railroads, the building of a state-supported college system offered riches for contractors, power for a new class of administrators, employment for many workers languishing in dead-end jobs, rising land prices for property owners—something, in short, for everyone. The effort transformed the landscape. Small farming and shopping centers that used to be dots on the map, like Mount Pleasant, Michigan, home of Central Michigan University, blossomed into glittering new cities—great plush youth ghettoes of high-rise dormitories sitting in the middle of cornfields. In 1974 Dr. Ernest Boyer, chancellor of the State University of New York, estimated that students could take over the communities of New Paltz, Fredonia, Oneonta, Geneseo, Old Westbury, Plattsburgh, and Potsdam if residency rules permitted those who were eighteen and over to vote in local elections.

Education became a mammoth industry. In the 1970s institutions of higher education were spending more than $30 billion annually. And though tuition rises priced thousands of students out of the colleges their parents had attended, the taxpayers were still providing more than half of all the money spent on higher education.

But in spite of these huge sums, less than half the high-school graduates were going on to higher education, raising a new question of equity. Is it fair to make all the taxpayers pay for the minority who actually go to college? We decided, long ago, that it is fair for childless adults to pay school taxes because everyone parents and nonparents alike, profits by a literate population. But does the same reasoning apply to *higher* education? Would college for everyone benefit society enough to be worth it? We will not try to answer that question in this book; we are concerned here only with what college can and cannot do for individual students. It is interesting to notice in passing, however, that those who argue the public value of a college education are very apt to be the affluent, college-educated parents who have always sent their children to college—even when they had to foot the whole bill themselves. Social critics who are concerned with social equality have begun to point out that state-supported higher education is regressive taxation of the majority of noncollege users—who are more likely to be poor—for the benefit of the children of the middle-class.

The response from educators has been to ask for more. They have argued that simple justice requires tax-supported higher education for *every* high-school graduate, and damn the expense. But the expense would be formidable. Fritz Machlup, an economist who specializes in putting dollar values on knowledge and human capital, has estimated that universal schooling to age twenty-two would have cost $47.5 billion in 1970–71, a year in which corporate profits aggregated $35 billion and the total proceeds of agriculture, fisheries, and forests came to $25 billion. And as costs, both total and per capita, have continued to mount faster than per capita personal income, even the establishment-oriented Carnegie Commission on Higher Education, organized in 1967 to study higher education and its future in the United States, has conceded that there is a limit to what the taxpayers are willing to spend for higher education—and the limit is in sight. Programs for getting *everybody* into college turn out to cost more for each full-time student than programs for educating the traditionally collegebound. By dint of remedial instruction, counseling, tutoring, and extra financial assistance, SEEK (Search for Education, Elevation, and Knowledge) has been helping educationally and economically disadvantaged New Yorkers through the free-tuition City University of New York. But the program costs an average of $2,500 per student in books, stipends, services, overhead, and financial aid, in addition, of course, to the $800 CUNY spends per student on instructional costs in general.

Equality has begun to look like a prohibitive luxury, particularly now that colleges have all they can do to keep their regular programs afloat. Predictable demography has caught up with the empire builders. The power-hungry academics built plants on the assumption that enrollments would continue rising indefinitely. Only a few demographers in the Census Bureau had pointed out, and then mostly in footnotes, that the "market" could not continue to grow at the boom rates of the 1960s, but that the rate of growth would have to decline as the war-boom babies moved out of college and into the job market. That's exactly what happened. While few colleges would confess to actual vacancies, observers estimated that another half million students could have been accommodated each year in the early '70s at a time when inflation was pushing costs up at unprecedented rates. College administrators began to panic.

Most have turned to the hard sell. Admissions officers have put down rugs, put on help, and retained Madison Avenue public relations and advertising firms to woo applicants. Catalogues have grown fatter, glossier, and more pictorial. Kent State University in Ohio bought time for radio commercials. In 1973 Northern Kentucky State College borrowed the giveaway technique used to promote toothpastes. During Christmas vacation, when students were free to move around outdoors, they launched 200 helium balloons, 103 of which carried scholarship offers on the basis of finders keepers.

Some colleges offered tuition rebates to students who recruited other students. High scorers on the Scholastic Aptitude Tests administered by the supposedly noncommercial College Entrance Examination Board found themselves the target of high pressure direct mail and telephone solicitations from respectable colleges, and the very highest scorers of all were offered scholarships even when they did not need the money. And as the economy cooled down, big corporations were slower to recruit executives, and the headhunters turned to the college field. One entrepreneurial operator in Boston was said to have charged colleges $100 for each freshman procured and enrolled.

The Madison Avenue campaigns sell colleges like soap, promoting those features that market analysts think the customers really want: innovative programs, an environment conducive to meaningful personal relationships, and a curriculum so free that it doesn't sound like college at all—"We shape our curriculum to your individual needs." But pleasing the customers is something new for college administrators, and many alumni and parents blame the financial crunch for what they feel to be an undignified, if not immoral capitulation to student whim.

Colleges have always known that most students don't like to study and are, at least part of the time, ambivalent about the college experience as a whole, but they have never thought it either right or necessary to pay any attention to these student feelings. Then, in the 1960s, students rebelling against the Vietnam War and the draft discovered that they could disrupt a campus completely, and even force cancellation of the hated final examinations. News of riots discouraged donors and applicants, and so, when it didn't cost too much in money or power, administrators acted on some student complaints.

But what nobody really understood was that the protests had tapped the basic discontent with the idea of college itself—a discontent that did not go away when the riots subsided. Students now protest individually rather than in concert. They turn inward and withdraw from active participation. They drop out to travel to India or to feed themselves on subsistence farms. Some refuse to go to college at all.

Most, of course, have neither the funds nor the self-confidence for a constructive articulation of their discontent. They simply hang around college because they can't think of anything better to do. As the costs of college to parents, taxpayers, and students themselves have escalated, as jobs for college graduates have begun to dry up, many people—on campus and off—have become disturbed by the mood of college students and have begun to pay more attention to what students themselves are saying about the college experience.

## The Mood on Campus

The unhappiness of young people is nothing new. Like everyone else, I have always assumed that many young people have personal problems. And, like everyone else, I expected them to cope with these problems on an individual basis. But as I traveled around the country speaking at colleges, I was overwhelmed by the prevailing sadness. It was as visible on campuses in California as in Nebraska and Massachusetts. I encountered just too many young people who spoke little—and then only in drowned voices.

Sometimes the mood surfaced as diffidence, wariness, or "coolness," but whatever its form, it began to look like a defense mechanism, and that rang a bell. This is the way it used to be with women! Like everyone else in the 1950s and 1960s, I used to think that the troubles of women were personal, to be dealt with by psychoanalysis if necessary. Now we all recognize that the malaise of women and blacks are normal responses to the limited role society has assigned to them. I began to suspect that the same thing was happening to young adults: just as society has systematically damaged women by insisting that their proper place was in the home, so we may now be systematically damaging eighteen-year-olds by insisting that their proper place is in college.

Campus watchers everywhere know what I mean when I ask why students are so sad, but they don't agree on the answer. My first thought was that it might be an expression of the drug culture. But the mood survived the decline of drugs. Students were as withdrawn in 1974, when a national magazine announced the end of the drug culture, as they were several years earlier when drug usage made daily headlines.

During the Vietnam War, sadness could be ascribed to the draft. But peace did not revive enthusiasm for the future. Students, as well as their mentors, frequently blame "the mess the world is in." This isn't convincing. The world has always been in a mess and never more so than when everyone was optimistic in the so-called Gay Nineties of the last century and the misnamed Roaring Twenties of this one.

"Affluence," say parents and older folks. Young people are jaded and sated because they have received too much too soon, and there's nothing left to look forward to. They are used to instant gratification, and since unlimited wishes cannot be instantaneously gratified, they are doomed to chronic disappointment. But there is more envy than logic to this diagnosis. Whatever affluence does to people, it ought not to make them as cast down as Watteau's clown. On the contrary, in a recent psychological study "having money" is identified as the only factor that reliably correlates with happiness.

A more rational theory, advanced by a forty-year-old college professor, is that his students are sad because of their permissive upbringing. He says that parents have been too lazy or timid to teach children how to get along with people, so they have grown up to be monsters their own parents can't bear to have around the house. And if your own mother is against you, who can be for you?

I don't buy the moralistic undertone of the hard-hat, law-and-order attack on permissiveness, but that bit about parents fearing, hating, and rejecting their grown children sounds plausible to me. The mood that worries me, come to think of it, is exactly the mood of a person jilted in love.

Are young people being rejected on a mass basis in supposedly youth-oriented America? Do we really hate our young? Are we covering up this hate and fear when we talk about how much we love them, how much we are sacrificing for them? Are the kids really living off the fat of the land, suffering from "too much, too soon"? Or do we glorify, envy, and pet them—and send them to college—in order to put them down and leave them out of the so-called real world, the same as we do to women? Is there anything else or anything better we can do for them except send them to college?

This book is the record of what I found out when I tried to answer these questions with the journalistic tools of my trade—scholarly studies, economic analyses, and historical record, the opinions of the specially knowledgeable, conversations with parents, professors, college administrators, and employers, all of whom spoke as alumni, too. Mainly, it reports what hundreds of college students on campuses all over the country, and young people not in college, told us in 1973 and 1974.

My unnerving conclusion is that students are sad because they are not needed—not by their own parents, not by employers, not by the society as a whole. They were not, for the most part, unwanted babies. Their fate is more awkward. Somewhere between the nursery and the employment office they became *unwanted adults.* No one has anything in particular against them. But no one has anything in particular for them either, and they don't see any role for themselves in the future. There are too many people in the world of the 1970s already, and we do not know where to put newcomers. The neatest way to get rid of a superfluous eighteen-year-old is to amuse him all day long at a community college while his family feeds and houses him. This is not only cheaper than a residential college, but cheaper than supporting him on welfare, a make-work job, in prison, or in the armed forces.

### Reluctant Students

The enormity of our hypocrisy about the young is not readily apparent. We assume that we are sending them to college for their own best interests and sell them college the way we sell them spinach—

because it's good for them. Some, of course, learn to like it, but most wind up still preferring green peas. College students are forced to eat spinach—to go to college—even when they don't like it.

Educators admit as much. Nevitt Sanford, a distinguished student of higher education, says students feel they are "capitulating to a kind of voluntary servitude."

Some of them talk about their time in college as if it were a sentence to be served. A Mount Holyoke graduate of 1970 told us that she would have to write a long essay to explain exactly what Mount Holyoke had done to her and her friends. "For two years I was really interested in science," she said. "But in my junior and senior years, I just kept saying, 'I've done two years, I'm going to finish.' When I got out I made up my mind that I wasn't going to school anymore, because so many of my courses had been bullshit. I was just really miserable."

If students feel they are being coerced, it's hard to tell exactly who is coercing them. Parents, of course, are the nearest culprits. Shirley Ann Lee is a black student who feels it's up to her to "put her best foot forward" at Wright State University in Dayton, Ohio, because her mother gave her the opportunity to learn.

"My mother had the chance to go to college, but she gave it up so that her sister and brother could go instead," Shirley Ann told us. "Since I've gotten here, it's not that I thoroughly want to quit, but sometimes you feel down and say like 'I want to take a week away from school.' But I didn't want to quit or anything like that. I think that would hurt my parents."

How parents feel about college is sometimes the key to whether a student applies, goes, and stays. Educators are very much interested in the reasons why students go to college. Because their bread and butter depends on it, they have done extensive market research on their potential customers. They have weighed the impact of place of residence, the income and occupations of parents, the type of secondary school, and even the influence of a young person's peer group. But to some questions there are no answers. Very few people know exactly why they go. However, the studies do suggest some interesting patterns. A big survey of more than 10,000 Wisconsin high-school seniors showed that for all I.Q. levels and both sexes, youngsters from families of limited income whose parents talked up college to them were more apt to plan on going than classmates from affluent families whose parents didn't seem to care whether they went or not.

If parents don't push, high-school counselors may conceive it to be their duty to do the pushing for them. They talk about their responsibility to "detect" and "motivate" scholastically able "college material." And when confronted with youngsters who don't know what they want to do with themselves, counselors who don't know what to do with them either can export the sticky problem to college on the ground that while college may not help the undecided student find his path, it probably won't do him any harm.

During the 1950s and 1960s, high-school counselors pushed and shoved the reluctant into college with a clear conscience. Society needed to "save talent." Parents called up counselors to beg them to help persuade children who were balking at the idea of more school. School authorities eager to increase the ratio of their graduates going "on" to college approved this pressure. Ben Cohn, who supervises guidance counselors for the Board of Cooperative Educational Services in the Northern Westchester-Putnam area of New York State, says that counselors who felt that a youngster was being railroaded into college tried to give him adult support for his intuition against it by urging him to go along with what his parents so badly wanted "just for one year."

When railroaded freshmen get into trouble at college, the college psychiatrist frequently blames the high-school counselor. An occasional problem at selective women's colleges is the bright girl who did very well in high school but never really wanted to go to college. The guidance counselor who "saved" her from the domesticity for which her parents reared her isn't around when she goes to pieces in the competitive environment of the preprofessional campus he chose for her.

Debbie Lewis entered Kirkland, an experimental women's college in upstate New York, because "my mom thinks of college as a step between high school and marriage." That's all right with Debbie, but she didn't bargain for a campus where every other woman is headed for graduate school. Debbie is quite frank to say that she "isn't the kind of person who can benefit from a liberal arts education," and she has the spunk to rebel. "This is too unreal," she told us. "It isn't what I want to do." Debbie thinks she might like to be a cabinetmaker, but she quickly adds she might not be dedicated enough to undergo a seven-year apprenticeship. "Actually, there isn't anything I'm dedicated to. For me it's more important to develop personal things than to have a career."

For every woman pushed into unwonted ambition, there are, of course, a dozen men, and in the unisex world of the young, more of them have now become liberated to join Debbie in asserting that "it's more important to develop personal things than to have a career." Debbie's male analogue has long been the staple client of the psychiatrists of good men's colleges. Classically he is a sensitive, intellectually gifted, and socially isolated young man who feels he cannot bear to carry on the family business or carve out the distinguished career his parents hope for him. The pressure on young males to succeed may be more important than any hormonal fragility in explaining the high suicide rate of male college students. Now that women are expected to succeed, more of them break under the pressure too, and the suicide rate of young women, particularly young black women, is rising.

Luckily, the picture is changing somewhat. Parents who have read up on the latest theories are ashamed to pull and haul on their young the way they used to do. Ben Cohn says that sophisticated Westchester County, New York, parents now tell the high school counselor, "I want my kid to do what he really wants to do." But what they really do, he adds, is to apply the pressure in a more subtle way.

An important and not-so-subtle pressure is, of course, financial. Many families are happy to support their children only as long as they are in college. "College is like welfare," one Bennington dropout explained. "It's what you do when you run out of money and have to go back to your parents for help."

The more thoughtful college psychiatrists don't like to blame parents. "It's the whole society—the whole system that pushes them into college," says Dr. Jane Ranzoni, a psychologist at Vassar. Students say as much themselves. While a substantial proportion told us, in response to the direct question, that they were in college because their parents wanted them to go, many others couldn't identify any particular person or force that impelled them. "I really don't know why I came," one student told us. "It's just something everybody does. My family went and all my friends, so I came, too." "The name locks you in," said a Wellesley student.

The pressure of what "everybody" does is both visible and measurable. According to the same study of high-school graduates that established the importance of parental encouragement, those who live in a poverty neighborhood are less likely to go to college than those who have no more money but who live in a more affluent neighborhood where it looks as if everyone really did go.

Reluctant students who come to college primarily because they can't get up the courage to do anything else may stick it out for the same reason, beefing no more than drafted soldiers. A Russell Sage junior who told us she stayed on because of "the tears of my mother" added that she would have disregarded those tears if she could have found a friend to go jobhunting with. "I just couldn't see myself getting off a bus all alone in a strange city with $50 in my pocket and looking for a policeman to ask where the Y was," she said, obviously disgusted by her own timidity.

Students often say college is an alternative to a far worse fate. They are sticking it out because it is "better" than the army, better than a job—and it has to be pretty bad before it is worse than staying at home.

Student after student told us what college counselors told us, too: The main thing college does for students is to get them away from home without having to break with their parents or earn their own living. In his book *No Time for Youth,* Joseph Katz reported the results of a massive psychological study that followed students through four years of Berkeley and Stanford. A high proportion felt that physical separation from their families was what really changed them. This was true even for the great majority who wanted the same sort of life as their parents were leading.

Students aren't belligerent about this. Some seem surprised at their own answer. "What did I learn in college, really? Well, I learned to do things on my own. At college there are no parents to get you up in the morning and tell you when to study."

Occasionally, of course, college is an alternative to an intolerable home situation. We talked to several students who were glad to be in college because their parents were separating. Steve is the youngest of his family, and both of his parents were married very young. By the time he was in high school, he was the only one left at home. "When they weren't taking out their frustrations on each other, they were inflicting them on me. Sure, I'm glad to get away from home. I don't exactly like college, but it's better than the hassles I'd get at home."

One student we talked to was breaking away from the religious faith of his family and welcomed a chance to "get off by myself and think things out." Many like the feeling of freedom. "At college you don't have to tell anyone where you are going and when you are coming back," one woman exulted. More women than men mentioned personal freedom to come and go—testimony to the perpetuation of a double standard of parental supervision. The prospect of freedom to experiment sexually looms large, but no larger, perhaps, than freedom to choose friends, clothing, manners, and language without explaining them.

Most students want autonomy, not a quarrel with their parents. Shirley Ann Lee, the student whose mother wants her to learn, thinks she got more out of going to a residential college far from home. "Here your attitudes and all your views change because you have the last word on what you're going to do," she told us. "A lot of my friends are still home. They're independent, but they're not really independent. Like right now, I say, I'm going to do this. And I make the last decision. I still have my parents' views—they will always be with me—but right now I have my own views and my own attitudes. So when I get my degree, I'm going to be happy, but I'm going to say, 'Hey, Mom. *I* did it.'"

College is a graceful way to get away from home. It is also a graceful way for a parent to push an overly dependent young one out of the nest. Richard Baloga, the son of a policeman, describes himself as shy. Going away from home to Wright State University in Dayton, Ohio, "forced me out of my freshman shell. I wanted to drop out because I was homesick. I was down here at college and my girl was back home."

Richard's freshman homesickness is classic, and his policeman father handled it in a straight-armed way that seems to have worked for a son brought up to it. "My father straightened me out," Richard related. "He said, 'Don't think about now, think about the future.' I hate school. I don't like it now any more than I ever did. But at the same time the underlying feeling to do it for my father made it worthwhile. It gave me a reason to go." This is, of course, growing up by the book, and it does happen. College sometimes turns the neat trick of getting a young person away from home while doing exactly what the home folks wanted him to do all along.

Many students frankly told us that they were in college because they couldn't find a job. "I'd go again for really poor reasons," Candy Chayer, an eighteen-year-old freshman at Augsburg, said. "I have no options. Some kids have gone through high school taking courses that prepared them for jobs right after high school, but I never did that. College was the only 'job' I could get when I was through with high school."

The economy of the 1970s is biased against beginners in two ways. First, they are hurt by the changing economic structure— there are fewer "entry" jobs which lead to promotion. Young people used to start working as office boys, assistants, apprentices, go-fors, and learners in whom employers invested training. Now machinery does much of the routine work which made it possible for beginners to earn as they learned. Most of the new jobs for beginners that were created during the 1960s and '70s are service jobs—waiting on people who have money to spend in hotels, restaurants, gas stations, retail stores, banks, hospitals, resorts, and the schools that service young people themselves. With few exceptions, these jobs are unskilled, low-paid, routine, and, above all, dead-end.

Second, young people are hurt by cyclical unemployment. When the economy is expanding and employers are hiring, beginners get a chance. When the economy falters, or even if expansion slows, employers don't hire new people. That's why teen-age unemployment is more volatile than the unemployment rate of family heads, the rate most frequently quoted. During the slower growth of 1974 the unemployment rate of teenagers fluctuated around 20 percent.

In Pittsburgh, a West Virginia Wesleyan junior who couldn't find a job during the summer of 1973 after applying to "all the department stores, a health spa, drugstores, and supermarkets" reported that "a lot of kids I know are going to summer school because they can't find a job." College has become a glamorous and expensive way for the affluent society to keep its unemployed young people off the streets. In 1974, William James McGill, the president of Columbia, warned against the danger of using universities "as storage houses for bored young people."

College is, at the least, a voluntary, rather than an involuntary, servitude. A senior at Augsburg College told us what went through his mind when he thought about quitting college. "God, studying is really a drag, and, gee, it would be neat to earn money and always have enough money to spend, to be on your own, but you know it's really kind of a dream. Besides, who wants to work when you've got four years to get your head together?"

A substantial number of students on every campus feel a little like Daniel Sanderson did when he told us that "college is a wonderful life compared with prison." Danny was busted for selling a half-pound of marijuana to an undercover policeman. Instead of the parole his family expected for a first offender, he wound up behind bars. After two and a half years, he was chosen for an experimental program under which selected prisoners are given an educational furlough, and went to Wright State University. Like many other college students, he would like to quit college and travel, but his case is rather special. If he quits before his term is up, he'll be sent back to jail.

The remarkable thing about Danny is not that he is a furloughed prisoner. It is that he should and feels so much like the other students who are glad to be in college primarily because of the fate from which college is saving them.

How many are reluctant? Estimates depend on how reluctant you have to be to be counted. The conservative Carnegie Commission estimates 5 to 30 percent. Sol Linowitz, former chairman of the board of Xerox, who was at one time chairman of a special committee on campus tensions of the American Council on Education, found that "a significant number were not happy with their college experience because they felt they were there only in order to get the 'ticket to the big show' rather than to spend the years as productively as they otherwise could."

There may, of course, be nothing very new about this reluctance except the seriousness with which educators now take it. Students have always wished themselves away, especially when examinations loom and the work piles up. As one student told us, "Clerking in the drugstore, I'd at least have my evenings." "Academics" are generally held a "drag," or as another student put it, "College wouldn't be so bad if it weren't for all the studying you have to do."

Older alumni will identify with Richard Baloga, the policeman's son who stayed in school even though he "hated it" because he thought it would do him some good, but fewer feel this way every year. Daniel Yankelovich has surveyed undergraduate attitudes for a number of years, and reported that in 1971, 74 percent thought education was "very important," but just two years earlier, in 1969, 80 percent had thought so.

The doubters don't mind speaking up. Leon Lefkowitz, chairman of the department of social studies at Central High School in Valley Stream, New York, interviewed 300 college students at random and reports that 200 of them didn't think that the education they were getting was worth the effort. "In two years I'll pick up a diploma and I can honestly say it was a waste of my father's bread," one of them said.

"I don't think I was cut out for college," another young man told us. "I thought of dropping out, but what would I have done? I just don't know. I'd probably have just bummed around for a while until I got myself straightened out." It would be cruel to tell this over-earnest young man that his predicament is not unique. A majority of the population "bums around" this way from birth to death—and without noticeably straightening themselves out.

As a sociologist explained to me, you don't have to have a reason for going to college—it's an institution. If I understand him correctly, an institution, sociologically speaking, is something everyone accepts without question. The burden of proof is not on why you go, but why anyone thinks there might be a reason for *not* going. The implication—and some educators express it quite frankly—is that an eighteen-year-old is too young and confused to know what he wants to do, let alone what is good for him. Later on, you'll be glad you went. Most successful and happy people seem to have gone to college, so why take a chance with *your* life?

Mother knows best. The reasoning recalls the dubious comfort administered by nineteenth-century mothers of reluctant brides: "You're too young to realize that every woman has to be married to be happy, but you'll see. In time you'll learn to love him."

It has always been comfortable for people to believe that authorities like Mother or outside specialists like educators could determine what was best for them. I don't agree. I believe that what is good for me is what feels good for me. I believe that college has to be judged not on what other people think is good for students, but on how good it feels to students themselves. Specialists and authorities no longer enjoy the credibility former generations accorded them. Patients talk back to doctors and are not struck suddenly dead. Clients question the lawyer's bills and sometimes get them reduced. It is no longer so obvious that adolescents are better off studying a core curriculum that was constructed when all educated men could agree on what made them educated, or that professors, advisors, or parents can be of any particular help to young people in choosing a major or a career.

It is now safer to assume that people have an inside view of what's good for them. If a child doesn't want to go to school some morning, better let him stay at home, at least until you find out why. Maybe he knows something that you don't know.

So with college. If high-school graduates don't want to go—or if they don't want to go right away—they may perceive more clearly than their elders that college is not for them. High-school graduates see college graduates driving cabs and decide it's not worth going. College students find no intellectual stimulation in their studies and drop out or stop out with the encouragement of college authorities.

And if students believe that college isn't necessarily good for them, you can't expect them to stay on for the general good of mankind. Young people may be more altruistic than their elders, but no great number are going to spend four years at hard intellectual labor, let alone tens of thousands of family dollars, for "the advancement of human capability in society at large," one of the many purposes of higher education invoked by a Carnegie Commission report. Nor do any considerable number of them go to college to beat the Russians to Jupiter, improve the national defense, increase the Gross National Product, lower the crime rate, improve automobile safety, or create a market for the arts—to mention some of the benefits taxpayers are supposed to get for supporting higher education.

Nor should we expect young people to go to college to bring about social equality—even if it could be attained by putting everyone through four years of academic rigor. On the contrary, this seems to be a very roundabout and expensive way to narrow the gap between the highest and the lowest in our society. And it is worse than roundabout. Equalizing opportunity through universal higher education subjects the whole population to the intellectual mode natural only to a few. It violates the fundamental egalitarian principle of respect for the differences between people.

The simple thesis of this book is that college is good for some people, but it is not good for everybody. The great majority of high-school graduates aren't sure what they want to do. They, and their parents, need some realistic help in deciding whether the promotional claims for the product college are what they want to buy.

---

## Now that you've read

1. Now that you've read Caroline Bird's "case against college," what is the main thing you'd like to say to her if she were to walk into the room this second?

2. What do you find convincing in her arguments? In what respect
   might she be out of touch with today's college student and today's
   economy?
3. What does she mean by "educational huckstering"?
4. Why does she say the students she met were sad?
5. Bird writes, "Equalizing opportunity through universal higher
   education subjects the whole population to the intellectual
   mode natural only to a few." What do you take her to mean here?
   Do you agree? Why or why not?

# READING 3

*Mike Rose*

# Entering the Conversation

Mike Rose teaches at UCLA and still lives in the city he grew up in. This reading from his book *Lives on the Boundary* argues in favor of continuing academic support for students who don't come from "traditional" family backgrounds. Rose shares his own experience as a "nontraditional" college student to illustrate how foreign a university can seem to many of its students and to show us how giving someone a chance can make a dramatic difference in that person's life. With the help of his teachers, Rose came to see education as an exciting process, a process far more valuable than mere memorization and endurance.

## *Before you read*

1. Have you ever felt left out in some way in a class or in school? What were the circumstances?
2. Have you ever been actively encouraged by a teacher? Have you ever been actively discouraged by a teacher? Describe the situation.
3. What can schools do to encourage students to take a more active role in their learning? What can teachers do?

---

If you walked out the back door of 9116 South Vermont and across our narrow yard, you would run smack into those four single-room rentals and, alongside them, an old wooden house-trailer. The trailer had belonged to Mrs. Jolly, the woman who sold us the property. It was locked and empty, and its tires were flat and fused into the asphalt driveway. Rusted dairy cases had been wedged in along its side and four corners to keep it balanced. Two of its eight windows were broken, the frames were warped, and the door stuck. I was getting way too old to continue sharing a room with my mother, so I began to eye that trailer. I decided to refurbish it. It was time to have a room of my own.

Lou Minton had, by now, moved in with us, and he and I fixed the windows and realigned the door. I painted the inside by combining what I could find in our shed with what I could afford to buy: The ceiling became orange, the walls yellow, the rim along the windows flat black. Lou redid the wiring and put in three new sockets. I got an old record player from the second-hand store for five dollars. I had Roy Herweck, the illustrator of our high school annual, draw women in mesh stockings and other objets d'redneck art on the yellow walls, and I put empty Smirnoff and Canadian Club bottles on the ledges above the windows. I turned the old trailer into the kind of bachelor digs a seventeen-year-old in South L.A. would fancy. My friends from high school began congregating there. When she could, my mother would make us a pot of spaghetti or pasta fasul'. And there was a clerk across the street at Marty's Liquor who would sell to us: We would run back across Vermont Avenue laughing and clutching our bags and seal ourselves up in the trailer. We spun fantasies about the waitress at the Mexican restaurant and mimicked our teachers and caught touchdown passes and, in general, dreamed our way through adolescence. It was a terrible time for rock 'n' roll—Connie Francis and Bobby Rydell were headliners in 1961—so we found rhythm and blues on L.A.'s one black station, played the backroom ballads of troubadour Oscar Brand, and discovered Delta and Chicago blues on Pacifica's KPFK:

I'm a man
I'm a full-grown man

As I fell increasingly under Mr. MacFarland's spell, books began replacing the liquor bottles above the windows: *The Trial* and *Waiting for Godot* and *No Exit* and *The Stranger*. Roy sketched a copy of the back cover of *Exile and the Kingdom,* and so the pensive face of Albert Camus now looked down from that patch of wall on which a cartoon had once pressed her crossed legs. My mother found a quilt that my grandmother had sewn from my father's fabric samples. It was dark and heavy, and I would lie under it and read Rimbaud and not understand him and feel very connected to the life I imagined Jack MacFarland's life to be: a subterranean ramble through Bebop and breathless poetry and back-alley revelations.

In 1962, John Connor moved into dank, old Apartment 1. John had also grown up in South L.A., and he and I had become best friends. His parents moved to Oregon, and John—who was a good black-top basketball player and an excellent student—wanted to stay in Los Angeles and go to college. So he rented an apartment for forty dollars a month, and we established a community of two. Some nights, John and I and Roy the artist and a wild kid named Gaspo would drive into downtown L.A.—down to where my mother had waited fearfully for a bus years before—and roam the streets and feel the excitement of the tenderloin: the flashing arrows, the blue-and-orange beer neon, the burlesque houses, the faded stairwell of

Roseland—which we would inch up and then run down—brushing past the photos of taxi dancers, glossy and smiling in a glass display. Cops would tell us to go home, and that intensified this bohemian romance all the more.

About four months after John moved in, we both entered Loyola University. Loyola is now coeducational; its student center houses an Asian Pacific Students Association, Black Student Alliance, and Chicano Resource Center; and its radio station, KXLU, plays the most untamed rock 'n' roll in Los Angeles. But in the early sixties, Loyola was pretty much a school for white males from the middle and upper middle class. It was a sleepy little campus—its under-graduate enrollment was under two thousand—and it prided itself on providing spiritual as well as intellectual guidance for its students: Religion and Christian philosophy courses were a required part of the curriculum. It defined itself as a Catholic intellectual com-munity—promotional brochures relied on phrases like "the social, intellectual, and spiritual aspects of our students"—and made avail-able to its charges small classes, a campus ministry, and thirty-six clubs (the Chess Club, Economics Society, Fine Arts Circle, Debate Squad, and more). There were also six fraternities and a sports pro-gram that included basketball, baseball, volleyball, rugby, soccer, and crew. Loyola men, it was assumed, shared a fairly common set of social and religious values, and the university provided multiple op-portunities for them to develop their minds, their spirits, and their social networks. I imagine that parents sent their boys to Loyola with a sigh of relief: God and man strolled together out of St. Robert Bellarmine Hall and veered left to Sacred Heart Chapel. There was an occasional wild party at one of the off-campus fraternity houses, but, well, a pair of panties in the koi pond was not on a par with crises of faith and violence against the state.

John and I rattled to college in his '53 Plymouth. Loyola Boule-vard was lined with elms and maples, and as we entered the campus we could see the chapel tower rising in the distance. The chapel and all the early buildings had been constructed in the 1920s and were white and separated by broad sweeps of very green grass. Palm trees and stone pines grew in rows and clumps close to the build-ings, and long concrete walkways curved and angled and crossed to connect everything, proving that God, as Plato suspected, is always doing geometry.

Most freshman courses were required, and I took most of mine in St. Robert Bellarmine Hall. Saint Robert was a father of the church who wrote on papal power and censored Galileo: The ceiling in his hallway was high, and dim lights hung down from it. The walls were beige up to about waist level, then turned off-white. The wood trim was dark and worn. The floor combined brown linoleum with brown and black tile. Even with a rush of students, the building maintained its dignity. We moved through it, and its old, clanking radiators warmed us as we did, but it was not a warmth that got to the bone. I remember a dream in which I climbed up beyond the third floor— up thin, narrow stairs to bell tower that held a small, dusky room in which a priest was playing church music to a class of shadows.

My first semester classes included the obligatory theology and ROTC and a series of requirements: biology, psychology, speech, logic, and a language. I went to class and usually met John for lunch: We'd bring sandwiches to his car and play the radio while we ate. Then it was back to class, or the library, or the student union for a Coke. This was the next step in Jack MacFarland's plan for me— and I did okay for a while. I had learned enough routines in high school to act like a fairly typical student, but—except for the historical sketch I received in Senior English—there wasn't a solid center of knowledge and assurance to all this. When I look back through notes and papers and various photographs and memorabilia, I begin to remember what a disengaged, half-awake time it really was. I'll describe two of the notebooks I found. The one from English is a small book, eight by seven, and only eleven pages of it are filled. The notes I did write consist of book titles, dates of publication, names of characters, pointless summaries of books that were not on our syllabus and that I had never read (*The Alexandria Quartet:* 5 or 6 characters seen by different people in different stages of life"), and quotations from the teacher ("Perception can bring sorrow."). The notes are a series of separate entries. I can't see any coherence. My biology lab notes are written on green-tint quadrille. They, too, are sparse. There is an occasional poorly executed sketch of a tiny organism or of a bone and muscle structure. Some of the formulas and molecular models sit isolated on the page, bare of any explanatory discussion. The lecture notes are fragmented; a fair number of sentences remain incomplete.

By the end of the second semester my grades were close to dipping below a C average, and since I had been admitted provisionally, that would have been that. Jack MacFarland had oriented me to Western intellectual history and had helped me develop my writing, but he had worked with me for only a year, and I needed more than twelve months of his kind of instruction. Speech and Introductory Psychology presented no big problems. General Biology had midterm and final examinations that required a good deal of memorizing, and I could do that, but the textbook—particularly the chapters covered in the second semester—was much, much harder than what I read in high school, and I was so ill-adept in the laboratory that I failed that portion of the class. We had to set up and pursue biological problems, not just memorize—and at the first sign of doing rather than memorizing, I would automatically assume the problem was beyond me and distance myself from it. Logic, another requirement, spooked me with its syllogisms and Venn diagrams—they were just a step away from more formal mathematics—so I memorized what I could and squirmed around the rest. Theology was god-awful; ROTC was worse. And Latin, the language I elected on the strength of Jack MacFarland's one piece of bad advice, had me suffocating under the dust of a dead civilization. Freshman English was taught by a frustrated novelist with glittering eyes who had us, among other things, describing the consumption of our last evening's meal using the images of the battlefield.

I was out of my league.

Faculty would announce office hours. If I had had the sense, I would have gone, but they struck me as aloof and somber men, and I felt stupid telling them I was . . . well—stupid. I drifted through the required courses, thinking that as soon as these requirements were over, I'd never have to face anything even vaguely quantitative again. Or anything to do with foreign languages. Or ROTC. I fortified myself with defiance: I worked up an imitation of the old priest who was my Latin teacher, and I kept my ROTC uniform crumpled in the greasy trunk of John's Plymouth.

Many of my classmates came from and lived in a world very different from my own. The campus literary magazine would publish excerpts from the journals of upperclassmen traveling across Europe, standing before the Berlin Wall or hiking through olive groves toward Delphi. With the exception of one train trip back to Altoona, I had never been out of Southern California, and this translated, for me, into some personal inadequacy. Fraternities seemed exclusive and a little strange. I'm not sure why I didn't join any of Loyola's three dozen societies and clubs, though I do know that things like the Debate Squad were way too competitive. Posters and flyers and squibs in the campus newspaper gave testament to a lot of connecting activity, but John and I pretty much kept to ourselves, ragging on the "Loyola man," reading the literary magazine aloud with a French accent, simultaneously feeling contempt for and exclusion from a social life that seemed to work with the mystery and enclosure of the clockwork in a music box.

It is an unfortunate fact of our psychic lives that the images that surround us as we grow up—no matter how much we may scorn them later—give shape to our deepest needs and longings. Every year Loyola men elected a homecoming queen. The queen and her princesses were students at the Catholic sister schools: Marymount,

Mount St. Mary's, St. Vincent's. They had names like Corinne and Cathy, and they came from the Sullivan family or the Mitchells or the Ryans. They were taught to stand with toe to heel, their smiles were inviting, and the photographer's flash illuminated their eyes. Loyola men met them at fraternity parties and mixers and "CoEd Day," met them according to rules of manner and affiliation and parental connection as elaborate as a Balinese dance. John and I drew mustaches on their photographs, but something about them reached far back into my life.

Growing up in South L.A. was certainly not a conscious misery. My neighborhood had its diversions and its mysteries, and I felt loved and needed at home. But all in all there was a dreary impotence to the years, and isolation, and a deep sadness about my father. I protected myself from the harsher side of it all through a life of the mind. And while that interior life included spaceships and pink chemicals and music and the planetary moons, it also held the myriad television images of the good life that were piped into my home: Robert Young sitting down to dinner, Ozzie Nelson tossing the football with his sons, the blond in a Prell commercial turning toward the camera. The images couldn't have been more trivial— all sentimental phosphorescence—but as a child tucked away on South Vermont, they were just about the only images I had of what life would be without illness and dead ends. I didn't realize how completely their message had seeped into my being, what loneliness and sorrow was being held at bay—didn't realize it until I found myself in the middle of Loyola's social life without a guidebook, feeling just beyond the superficial touch of the queen and her princesses, those smiling incarnations of a television promise. I scorned the whole silly show and ached to be embraced by one of these mythic females under the muted light of a paper moon.

So I went to school and sat in class and memorized more than understood and whistled past the academic graveyard. I vacillated between the false potency of scorn and feelings of ineptitude. John and I would get in his car and enjoy the warmth of each other and laugh and head down the long strip of Manchester Boulevard, away from Loyola, away from the palms and green, green lawns, back to South L.A. We'd throw the ball in the alley or lag pennies on Vermont or hit Marty's Liquor. We'd leave much later for a movie or a football game at Mercy High or the terrible safety of downtown Los Angeles. Walking, then, past the *discotecas* and pawnshops, past the windows full of fried chicken and yellow lamps, past the New Follies, walking through hustlers and lost drunks and prostitutes and transvestites with rouge the color of bacon—stopping, finally before the musty opening of a bar where two silhouettes moved around a pool table as though they were underwater.

I don't know what I would have found if the flow of events hadn't changed dramatically. Two things happened. Jack MacFarland privately influenced my course of study at Loyola, and death once again ripped through our small family.

The coterie of MacFarland's students—Art Mitz, Mark Dever, and me—were still visiting our rumpled mentor. We would stop by his office or his apartment to mock our classes and the teachers and all that "'Loyola man' bullshit." Nobody had more appreciation for burlesque than Jack MacFarland, but I suppose he saw beneath our caustic performances and knew we were headed for trouble. Without telling us, he started making phone calls to some of his old teachers at Loyola—primarily to Dr. Frank Carothers, the chairman of the English Department—and, I guess, explained that these kids needed to be slapped alongside the head with a good novel. Dr. Carothers volunteered to look out for us and agreed to some special studies courses that we could substitute for a few of the more traditional requirements, courses that would enable us to read and write a lot under the close supervision of a faculty member. In fact, what he promised were tutorials—and that was exceptional, even for a small college. All this would start up when we returned from summer vacation. Our sophomore year, Jack MacFarland finally revealed, would be different.

When Lou Minton rewired the trailer, he rigged a phone line from the front house: A few digits and we could call each other. One night during the summer after my freshman year, the phone rang while I was reading. It was my mother and she was screaming. I ran into the house to find her standing in the kitchen hysterical—both hands pressed to her face—and all I could make out was Lou's name. I didn't see him in the front of the house, so I ran back through the kitchen to the bedroom. He had fallen back across the bed, a hole right at his sideburn, his jaw still quivering. They had a fight, and some ugly depth of pain convulsed within him. He left the table and walked to the bedroom. My mother heard the light slam of a .22. Nothing more.

That summer seems vague and distant. I can't remember any specifics, though I had to take care of my mother and handle the affairs of the house. I probably made do by blunting a good deal of what I saw and navigating with intuitive quadrants. But though I cannot remember details, I do recall feelings and recognitions: Lou's suicide came to represent the sadness and dead time I had protected myself against, the personal as well as public oppressiveness of life in South Los Angeles. I began to see that my escape to the trailer and my isolationist fantasies of the demimonde would yield another kind of death, a surrender to the culture's lost core. An alternative was somehow starting to take shape around school and knowledge. Knowledge seemed . . . was it empowering? No, that's a word I would use now. Then I felt freed, as if I were untying fetters. There simply were times when the pain and confusion of that summer would give way to something I felt more than I knew: a lightness to my body, an ease in breathing. Three or four months later I took an art history course, and one day during a slide show on Gothic architecture I felt myself rising up within the interior light of Mont-Saint-Michel. I wanted to be released from the despair that surrounded me on South Vermont and from my own troubled sense of exclusion.

Jack MacFarland had saved me at one juncture—caught my fancy and revitalized my mind—what I felt now was something further, some tentative recognition that an engagement with ideas could foster competence and lead me out into the world. But all this was very new and fragile, and given what I know now, I realize how easily it could have been crushed. My mother, for as long as I can remember, always added onto any statement of intention—hers or others'—the phrase *se vuol Dio,* if God wants it. The fulfillment of desire, no matter how trivial, required the blessing of the gods, for the world was filled with threat. "I'll plant the seeds this weekend," I might say. "Se vuol Dio," she would add. *Se vuol Dio.* The phrase expressed several lifetimes of ravaged hope: my grandfather's lost leg, the failure of the Rose Spaghetti House, my father laid low, Lou Minton, the landscapes of South L.A. *Se vuol Dio.* For those who live their lives on South Vermont, tomorrow doesn't beckon to be defined from a benign future. It's up to the gods, not you, if any old thing turns out right. I carried within me no history of assurances that what I was feeling would lead to anything.

Because of its size and because of the kind of teacher who is drawn to small liberal arts colleges, Loyola would turn out to be a very good place for me. For even with MacFarland's yearlong tour through ideas and language, I was unprepared. English prose written before the twentieth century was difficult, sometimes impossible, for me to comprehend. The kind of reasoning I found in logic was very foreign. My writing was okay, but I couldn't hold a candle to Art Mitz or Mark Dever or to those boys who came from good schools. And my fears about science and mathematics prevailed: Pereira Hall, the Math and Engineering Building, was only forty to fifty yards from the rear entrance to the English Department but seemed an unfriendly mirage, a malevolent castle floating in the haze of a mescaline dream.

We live, in America, with so many platitudes about motivation and self-reliance and individualism—and myths spun from them, like those of Horatio Alger—that we find it hard to accept the fact that they are serious nonsense. To live your early life on the streets of South L.A.—or Homewood or Spanish Harlem or Chicago's South Side or any one of hundreds of other depressed communities—and to journey up through the top levels of the American educational system will call for support and guidance at many, many points along the way. You'll need people to guide you into conversations that seem foreign and threatening. You'll need models, lots of them, to show you how to get at what you don't know. You'll need people to help you center yourself in your own developing ideas. You'll need people to watch out for you. There is much talk these days about the value of a classical humanistic education, a call for an immersion in the humanities, a return to the great books. These appeals raise lots of suspicions, for such curricula have traditionally served to exclude working-class people from the classroom. It doesn't, of necessity, have to be that way. The teachers that fate and Jack MacFarland's crisis intervention sent my way worked at making the humanities truly human. What transpired between us was the essence of humane liberal education, and it enabled me to move far beyond the cognitive charade of my freshman year.

From the midpoint of their freshman year, Loyola students had to take one philosophy course per semester: Logic, Philosophy of Nature, Philosophy of Man, General Ethics, Natural Theology, and so on. Logic was the first in the series, and I had barely gotten a C. The rest of the courses looked like a book fair of medieval scholasticism with the mold scraped off the bindings, and I dreaded their advent. But I was beginning my sophomore year at a time when the best and brightest of the Jesuit community were calling for an intellectually panoramic, socially progressive Catholicism, and while this lasted, I reaped the benefits. Sections of the next three courses I had to take would be taught by a young man who was studying for the priesthood and who was, himself, attempting to develop a personal philosophy that incorporated the mind and the body as well as the spirit.

Mr. Johnson could have strolled off a Wheaties box. Still in his twenties and a casting director's vision of those good looks thought to be all-American, Don Johnson had committed his very considerable intelligence to the study and teaching of philosophy. Jack MacFarland had introduced me to the Greeks, to Christian scholasticism, eighteenth-century deism, and French existentialism, but it was truly an introduction, a curtsy to that realm of the heavens where the philosophers dwell. Mr. Johnson provided a fuller course. He was methodical and spoke with vibrance and made connections between ancients and moderns with care. He did for philosophy what Mr. MacFarland had done for literary history: He gave me a directory of key names and notions.

We started in a traditional way with the Greek philosophers who preceded Socrates—Thales, Heraclitus, Empedocles—and worked our way down to Kant and Hegel. We read a little Aquinas, but we also read E. A. Burtt's *The Metaphysical Foundations of Modern Science,* and that gave me entry to Kepler, Copernicus, Galileo (which I was then spelling *Galelao*), and Newton. As he laid out his history of ideas, Mr. Johnson would consider aloud the particular philosophical issue involved, so we didn't, for example, simply get an outline of what Hegel believed, but we watched and listened as Don Johnson reasoned like Hegel and then raised his own questions about the Hegelian scheme. He was a working philosopher, and he was thinking out loud in front of us.

*The Metaphysical Foundations of Modern Science* was very tough going. It assumed not only a familiarity with Western thought but, as well, a sophistication in reading a theoretically rich argument. It was, in other words, the kind of book you encounter with increased frequency as you move through college. It combined the history of mathematics and science with philosophical investigation, and when I tried to read it, I'd end up rescanning the same sentences over and over, not understanding them, and, finally, slamming the book down on the desk—swearing at this golden boy Johnson and angry with myself. Here's a typical passage, one of the many I marked as being hopeless:

> We begin now to glimpse the tremendous significance of what these fathers of modern science were doing, but let us continue with our questions. What further specific metaphysical doctrines was Kepler led to adopt as a consequence of this notion of what constitutes the real world? For one thing, it led him to appropriate in his own way the distinction between primary and secondary qualities, which had been noted in the ancient world by the atomist and skeptical schools, and which was being revived in the sixteenth century in varied form by such miscellaneous thinkers as Vives, Sanchez, Montaigne, and Campanella. Knowledge as it is immediately offered the mind through the senses is obscure, confused, contradictory, and hence untrustworthy; only those features of the world in terms of which we get certain and consistent knowledge open before us what is indubitably and permanently real. Other qualities are not real qualities of things, but only signs of them. For Kepler, of course, the real qualities are those caught up in this mathematical harmony underlying the world of the senses, and which, therefore, have a causal relation to the latter. *The real world is a world of quantitative characteristics only; its differences are differences of number alone.*

I couldn't get the distinction that was being made between primary and secondary qualities, and I certainly didn't have the background that would enable me to make sense of Burtt's brief historical survey: from "atomist and skeptical schools [to] . . . Campanella." It is clear from the author's italics that the last sentence of the passage is important, so I underlined it, but because Burtt's discussion is built on a rich intellectual history that I didn't know, I was reading words but not understanding text. I was the human incarnation of language-recognition computer programs: able to record the dictionary meanings of individual words but unable to generate any meaning out of them.

"What," I asked in class, "are primary and secondary qualities? I don't get it." And here Don Johnson was very good. "The answer," he said, "can be found in the passage itself. I'll go back through it with you. Let's start with primary and secondary qualities. If some qualities are primary and others secondary, which do you think would be most important?"

"Primary?"

"Right. Primary qualities. Whatever they are. Now let's turn to Kepler, since Kepler's the subject of this passage. What is it that's more important to Kepler?"

I pause and say tentatively, "Math." Another student speaks up, reading from the book: "Quantitative characteristics."

"All right. So primary qualities, for Kepler, are mathematical, quantitative. But we still don't know what this primary and secondary opposition really refers to, do we? Look right in the middle of the paragraph. Burtt is comparing mathematical knowledge to the immediate knowledge provided by—what?"

My light bulb goes on: "The senses."

"There it is. The primary-secondary opposition is the opposition between knowledge gained by pure mathematical reasoning versus knowledge gained through our five senses."

We worked with *The Metaphysical Foundations of Modern Science* for some time, and I made my way slowly through it. Mr. Johnson was helping me develop an ability to read difficult texts—I was learning how to reread critically, how to tease out definitions and basic arguments. And I was also gaining confidence that if I stayed with material long enough and kept asking questions, I would get it. That assurance proved to be more valuable than any particular body of knowledge I learned that year.

For my second semester, I had to take Philosophy of Man, and it was during that course that Mr. Johnson delivered his second gift. We read Gabriel Marcel and Erich Fromm, learning about phenomenology and social criticism. We considered the human animal from an anthropological as well as philosophical perspective. And we read humanistic psychologist Abraham Maslow's *Toward a Psychology of Being*. Maslow wrote about "the 'will to health,' the urge to grow, the pressure of self-actualization, the quest for one's identity." The book had a profound effect on me. Six months before, Lou Minton's jaw quivered as if to speak the race's deepest sorrow, and through the rest of that summer I could only feel in my legs and chest some fleeting assurance that the world wasn't a thin mask stretched over nothingness. Now I was reading an articulation of that vague, hopeful feeling. Maslow was giving voice to some delicate possibility within me, and I was powerfully drawn to it. Every person is, in part, "'his own project' and makes himself." I had to know more, so I called Mr. Johnson up and asked if I could visit with him. "Sure," he said, and invited me to campus. So one Saturday morning I took a series of early buses and headed west.

Mr. Johnson and the other initiates to the priesthood lived in an old white residence hall on the grassy east edge of campus, and the long walk up Loyola Boulevard was quiet and meditative: Birds were flying tree to tree and a light breeze was coming in off Playa del Rey. I walked up around the gym, back behind Math-Engineering to his quarters, a simple one-story building with those Spanish curves that seem simultaneously thick and weightless. The sun had warmed the stucco. A window by the door was open, and a curtain had fluttered out. I rang the bell and heard steps on a hardwood floor. Mr. Johnson opened the door and stepped out. He was smiling and his eyes were attentive in the light . . . present . . . there. They said, "Come, let's talk."

Dr. Frank Carothers taught what is generally called the sophomore survey, a yearlong sequence of courses that introduces the neophyte English major to the key works in English literary history. Dr. Carothers was tall and robust. He wore thick glasses and a checkered bow tie and his hairline was male Botticelli, picking up somewhere back beyond his brow. As the year progressed, he spread English literary history out in slow time across the board, and I was introduced to people I'd never heard of: William Langland, a medieval acolyte who wrote the dream-vision *Piers Plowman*; the sixteenth-century poet Sir Thomas Wyatt; Elizabethan lyricists with peculiar names like Orlando Gibbons and Tobias Hume (the author of the wondrous suggestion that tobacco "maketh lean the fat men's tumour"); the physician Sir Thomas Browne; the essayist Joseph Addison; the biographer James Boswell; the political philosopher Edmund Burke, whose prose I could not decipher; and poets Romantic and Victorian (Shelley and Rossetti and Algernon Charles Swinburne). Some of the stuff was invitingly strange ("Pallid and pink as the palm of the flagflower . . ."), some was awfully hard to read, and some was just awful. But Dr. Carothers laid it all out with his reserved passion, drew for us a giant conceptual blueprint onto which we could place other courses, other books. He was precise, thorough, and rigorous. And he started his best work once class was over.

Being a professor was, for Frank Carothers, a profoundly social calling: He enjoyed the classroom, and he seemed to love the more informal contacts with those he taught, those he once taught, and those who stopped by just to get a look at this guy. He stayed in his office until about four each afternoon, leaning back in his old swivel chair, hands clasped behind his head, his bow tie tight against his collar. He had strong opinions, and he'd get irritated if you missed class, and he sometimes gave quirky advice—but there he'd be shaking his head sympathetically as students poured out their troubles. It was pure and primary for Frank Carothers: Teaching allowed him daily to fuse the joy he got from reading literature—poetry especially—with his deep pleasure in human community. What I saw when I was around him—and I hung out in his office from my sophomore year on—was very different from the world I had been creating for myself, a far cry from my withdrawal into an old house trailer with a silent book.

One of Dr. Carothers's achievements was the English Society. The English Society had seventy-eight members, and that made it just about the biggest organization on campus: jocks, literati, C-plus students, frat boys, engineers, mystics, scholars, profligates, bullies, geeks, Republicans—all stood side by side for group pictures. The English Society sponsored poetry readings, lectures, and card games, and best of all, barbecues in the Carotherses' backyard. We would caravan out to Manhattan Beach to be greeted by Betsy, the youngest of the seven Carothers children, and she'd walk us back to her father who, wrapped now in an apron, was poking coals or unscrewing the tops from jugs of red wine.

Vivian Carothers, a delicate, soft-spoken woman, would look after us and serve up trays of cheese and chips and little baked things. Students would knock on the redwood gate all through the late afternoon, more and more finding places for themselves among flowers and elephant ears, patio furniture, and a wizened pine. We would go on way past sunset, talking to Dr. Carothers and to each other about books and sports and currently despised professors, sometimes letting off steam and sometimes learning something new. And Frank Carothers would keep us fed, returning to the big domed barbecue through the evening to lift the lid and add hamburgers, the smoke rising off the grill and up through the telephone lines stretching like the strings of Shelley's harp over the suburbs of the South Bay.

When I was learning my craft at Jack MacFarland's knee, I continually misused words and wrote fragments and run-on sentences and had trouble making my pronouns agree with whatever it was that preceded them. I also produced sentences like these:

> Some of these modern-day Ramses are inherent of their wealth, others are self-made.

> An exhibition of will on the part of the protagonist enables him to accomplish a subjective good (which is an element of tragedy, namely: the protagonist does not fully realize the objective wrong that he is doing. He feels objectively justified if not completely right.)

I was struggling to express increasingly complex ideas, and I couldn't get the language straight: Words, as in my second sentence on tragedy, piled up like cars in a serial wreck. I was encountering a new language—the language of the academy—and was trying to find my way around in it. I have some more examples, written during my first year and a half at Loyola. There was inflated vocabulary:

> I conjectured that he was the same individual who had arrested my attention earlier.

> In his famed speech, "The American Scholar," Ralph Waldo Emerson posed several problems that are particularly germane to the position of the young author.

There were cliches and mixed and awkward metaphors:

> In 1517, when Luther nailed his 95 theses to the door of Wittenburg Cathedral, he unknowingly started a snowball rolling that was to grow to tremendous reprocussions [sic].

And there was academic melodrama:

> The vast realm of the cosmos or the depths of a man's soul hold questions that reason flounders upon, but which can be probed by the peculiar private insight of the seer.

Pop grammarians and unhappy English teachers get a little strange around sentences like these. But such sentences can be seen as marking a stage in linguistic growth. Appropriating a style and making it your own is difficult, and you'll miss the mark a thousand times along the way. The botched performances, though, are part of it all, and developing writers will grow through them if they are able to write for people who care about language, people who are willing to sit with them and help them as they struggle to write about difficult things. That is what Ted Erlandson did for me.

Dr. Erlandson was one of the people who agreed to teach me and my Mercy High companions a seminar—a close, intensive course that would substitute for a larger, standard offering like Introduction to Prose Literature. He was tall and lanky and had a long reddish brown beard and lectured in a voice that was basso and happy. He was a strong lecturer and possessed the best memory for fictional detail I'd ever witnessed. And he cared about prose. The teachers I had during my last three years at Loyola assigned a tremendous amount of writing. But it was Ted Erlandson who got in there with his pencil and worked on my style. He would sit me down next to him at his big desk, sweep books and pencils across the scratched veneer, and go back over the sentences he wanted me to revise.

He always began by reading the sentence out loud: "Camus ascented to a richer vision of life that was to characterize the entirety of his work." Then he would fiddle with the sentence, talking and looking up at me intermittently to comment or ask questions: "'Ascent'. That sounds like 'assent', I know, but look it up, Mike." He'd wait while I fluttered the dictionary. "Now, 'the entirety of his work' . . . try this instead: 'his entire work.' Let's read it. 'Camus assented to a richer vision of life that would characterize his entire work.' Sounds better, doesn't it?"

And another sentence. "'Irregardless of the disastrous ending of *Bread and Wine,* it must be seen as an affirmative work.' 'Irregardless' . . . people use it all the time, but 'regardless' will do just fine. Now, I think this next part sounds a little awkward; listen: 'Regardless of the disastrous ending of *Bread and Wine,* it . . . 'Hear that? Let's try removing the 'of' and the 'it': 'Regardless of the disastrous ending, *Bread and Wine* must be seen as an affirmative work.' Hmmm. Better, I think."

And so it would go. He rarely used grammatical terms, and he never got technical. He dealt with specific bits of language: "Try this here" or "Here's another way to say it." He worked as a craftsman works, with particulars, and he shuttled back and forth continually between print and voice, making me breathe my prose, making me hear the language I'd generated in silence. Perhaps he was more directive than some would like, but, to be truthful, direction was what I needed. I was easily frustrated, and it didn't take a lot to make me doubt myself. When teachers would write "no" or "awkward" or "rewrite" alongside the sentences I had worked so hard to produce, I would be peeved and disappointed. "Well, what the hell *do* they want?" I'd grumble to no one in particular. So Ted Erlandson's linguistic parenting felt just right: a modeling of grace until it all slowly, slowly began to work itself into the way I shaped language.

When Father Albertson lectured, he would stand pretty much in one spot slightly to the left or right of center in front of us. He tended to hold his notes or a play or a critical study in both hands, releasing one to emphasize a point with a simple gesture. He was tall and thin, and his voice was soft and tended toward monotone. When he spoke, he looked very serious, but when one of us responded with any kind of intelligence, a little smile would come over his face. Jack MacFarland had told me that it was Clint Albertson's Shakespeare course that would knock my socks off.

For each play we covered, Father Albertson distributed a five- to ten-page list of questions to ask ourselves as we read. These study questions were of three general types.

The first type was broad and speculative and was meant to spark reflection on major characters and key events. Here's a teaser on *Hamlet:*

> Would you look among the portrait-paintings by Raphael, or Rembrandt, or Van Gogh, or El Greco, or Rouault for an ideal representation of Hamlet? Which painting by which of these men do you think most closely resembles your idea of what Hamlet should look like?

The second type focused on the details of the play itself and were very specific. Here are two of the thirty-eight he wrote for *As You Like It:*

ACT I, SCENE 2

> How is Rosalind distinguished from Celia in this scene? How do you explain the discrepancy between the Folio version of lines 284–287 and Act I, scene 3, line 117?

ACT II, SCENES 4–6

> It has been said these scenes take us definitely out of the world of reality into a world of dream. What would you say are the steps of the process by which Shakespeare brings about this illusion?

The third kind of question required us to work with some historical or critical study. This is an example from the worksheet on *Romeo and Juliet:*

> Read the first chapter of C. S. Lewis's *Allegory of Love,* "Courtly Love." What would you say about Shakespeare's concept of love in relation to what Lewis presents as the traditional contradictory concepts in medieval literature of "romantic love" vs. "marriage."

Father Albertson had placed over 150 books on the reserve shelf in the library, and they ranged from intellectual history to literary criticism to handbooks on theater production. I had used a few such "secondary sources" to quote in my own writing since my days with Jack MacFarland, but this was the first time a teacher had so thoroughly woven them into a course. Father Albertson would cite them during lectures as naturally as though he were recalling a discussion he had overheard. He would add his own opinions and, since he expected us to form opinions, would ask us for ours.

I realize that this kind of thing—the close, line-by-line examination, the citing of critical opinion—has given rise to endless parodies of the academy: repressed schoolmen clucking along in the land of lost language. It certainly can be that way. But with Clint Albertson, all the learning furthered my comprehension of the play. His questions forced me to think carefully about Shakespeare's choice of words, about the crafting of a scene, about the connections between language and performance. I had to read very, very closely, leaning over the thin Formica desk in the trailer, my head cupped in my hands with my two index fingers in my ears to blot out the noise from the alley behind me. There were times when no matter how hard I tried, I wouldn't get it. I'd close the book, feeling stupid to my bones, and go find John. Over then to the liquor store, out into the night. The next day I would visit Father Albertson and tell him I was lost, ask him why this stuff was so damned hard. He'd listen and ask me to tell him why it made me so angry. I'd sputter some more, and then he'd draw me to the difficult passage, slowly opening the language up, helping me comprehend a distant, stylized literature, taking it apart, touching it.

I would then return to a classroom where a historically rich conversation was in progress. Other readers of Shakespeare—from Samuel Johnson to the contemporary literary critic Wylie Sypher— were given voice by Father Albertson, and we were encouraged to enter the dialogue, to consider, to take issue, to be seated amid all that potentially intimidating shoptalk. We were shown how to summarize an opinion, argue with it, weave it into our own interpretations. Nothing is more exclusive than the academic club: its language is highbrow, it has fancy badges, and it worships tradition. It limits itself to a few participants who prefer to talk to each other. What Father Albertson did was bring us inside the circle, nudging us out into the chatter, always just behind us, whispering to try this step, then this one, encouraging us to feel the moves for ourselves.

---

## Now that you've read

1. What is Mike Rose's argument? What does he want to persuade you to think or see about education?
2. What do you make of his use of stories from his own life to make his argument?
3. Which of his stories did you find most effective? Why?
4. Which of his stories apply most specifically to your experience or to the experiences of your friends?
5. What role does Jack MacFarland play in Rose's education? Has anyone ever played a similar role in your own education?

## READING 4

---

*Lynne V. Cheney*

# Students of Success

Lynne V. Cheney has made a career in education, beginning with an undergraduate degree in education and continuing with a term as chair of the National Endowment for the Humanities under President Ronald Reagan. In "Students of Success," she argues that students should be passionately interested in and committed to the majors they choose in order to be "successful." She also argues that liberal arts degrees can be both financially and intellectually rewarding.

### *Before you read*

1. What major have you chosen (or are you thinking of choosing)? Why did you (or might you) choose it?
2. If you didn't have to be concerned about making a living, would you choose the same major? Why or why not?
3. What is your definition of "success"? What kind of career do you hope to have?

---

### Politics in the Schoolroom

Not long ago, my college-age daughter read about a software genius who became a multimillionaire before he was 30. "That does it," she said, "I'm going into computers."

This daughter, who has never met a political-science course she didn't like, was only joking. But a study conducted by the Carnegie Foundation shows that many young people do think seriously along these lines. Instead of choosing college majors—and careers— according to their interests, they are channeling themselves into fields that promise to be profitable: business, engineering, computer science, allied health programs.

Given the high cost of a college education, this trend is not surprising. A bachelor's degree now costs $40,000 at an average independent college. Can we expect students to major in the liberal arts when their starting salaries will be significantly lower than they are for business and professional majors? Shouldn't they get the best possible return on their investment?

They should, but I would suggest that there are better ways to calculate profit and loss than by looking at starting salaries. Consider, first of all, that very few people stay in the same line of work over a lifetime. They switch jobs, even change professions, and what is crucial for advancement is not specialized training but the ability to think critically and judge wisely. Given the difficulty of predicting which skills will be in demand even five years from now, let alone over a lifetime, a student's best career preparation is one that emphasizes general understanding and intellectual curiosity: a knowledge of how to learn and the desire to do it. Literature, history, philosophy and the social sciences—majors that students avoid today—are the ones traditionally believed to develop such habits of mind.

I recently conducted an informal survey of successful Americans, and while several dozen phone calls aren't proof of the value of a liberal-arts major, the results are suggestive. The communications world, for example, is dominated by liberal-arts majors. Thomas H. Wyman, chairman of CBS, majored in English, as did Cathleen Black, publisher of USA Today. Washington Post columnist William Raspberry studied history; NBC News anchorman Tom Brokaw, political science.

In public life, too, leaders more often than not were students of the liberal arts. They form a majority in the president's cabinet. Secretary of State George Shultz and Secretary of Energy John Herrington majored in economics. Interior Secretary Donald Hodel majored in government, and Transportation Secretary Elizabeth Dole, political science. Secretary of the Treasury James Baker read history with a minor in classics; Secretary of Education William Bennett studied philosophy.

The president himself majored in economics and sociology. His communications director, Pat Buchanan, majored in English and philosophy. White House chief of staff (and former treasury secretary) Donald Regan was an English major and before he came to government had a remarkably successful business career as the head of Merrill Lynch. Secretary of Commerce Malcolm Baldrige headed Scovill Manufacturing, and now the former English major is leading a campaign for clear writing in government.

Executives like Regan and Baldrige are not unusual. According to a recent report in Fortune magazine, 38 percent of today's CEO's majored in the liberal arts, and a close reading of The New York Times shows that 9 of the top 13 executives at IBM are liberal-arts majors. At AT&T, a study showed social-science and humanities graduates moving into middle management faster than engineers and doing at least as well as their business and engineering counterparts in reaching top management levels.

For several years now, corporate executives have extolled the wide range of knowledge and interests that a study of the liberal arts encourages. And now under Tom Wyman's direction, CBS has funded an organization that investigates exactly why it is that liberal-arts training is valuable to the American corporation. "In an increasingly competitive, internationally oriented and technologically innovative society," Wyman recently wrote, "successful executives will be those who can understand—and interpret—complex relationships and who are capable of continually reconsidering assumptions underlying old operating practices."

In the past, such top-level views did not always filter down to where entry-level hiring is done. But reports from that front are encouraging. A study by Northwestern University shows that many major companies plan to increase their hiring of liberal-arts graduates by some 20 percent in 1986. Or as one employer recently told "Today" show viewers, "Those that are involved in recruiting people to the company are looking for . . . broader skills. . . . Then we will worry about teaching them terminology, specifics of the jobs."

I don't mean to argue that liberal arts is the only road to success. The average starting salary for engineers remains impressively high, almost $30,000 compared to $21,000 for a liberal-arts graduate. In fact, my informal survey also shows that engineers are doing well in a variety of fields. Chrysler chairman Lee Iacocca was an engineering major, as was former Delaware Governor Pete du Pont. My point is that there are many paths to success and students shouldn't force themselves down any single one if their true interests lie elsewhere. College should be a time for intellectual enthusiasm, for trying to read one's way through the library, for heated debate with those who see the world differently. College should be a time for learning to enjoy the life of the mind rather than for learning to tolerate what one doesn't find interesting.

Students who follow their hearts in choosing majors will most likely end up laboring at what they love. They're the ones who will put in the long hours and intense effort that achievement requires. And they're the ones who will find the sense of purpose that underlies most human happiness.

---

## Now that you've read

1. What is Cheney's main argument? What evidence does she offer to support that argument?
2. Are you convinced? Why or why not?
3. What does Cheney mean by "intellectual curiosity"? How many of the courses you're taking now encourage you to exercise your intellectual curiosity? In what ways?
4. Do you love your major field of study? Why or why not?

# READING 5

*Olivia Castellano*

# Canto, Locura, y Poesia

Olivia Castellano is a poet and college professor in California. Her essay brings together her personal history, her sense of responsibility to others who struggle as she did, her love of language, and her views on what it takes to become the kind of teacher who can make a difference in students' lives. For Castellano, a teacher's first job is to deal with students' anger.

### Before you read

1. At what point in your life did you decide to go to college?
2. Did you ever have to worry about whether or not you would be able to go to college?
3. What are your goals for your life after you complete your undergraduate degree?
4. Who has helped you the most in college so far? How have they helped?
5. Have you ever had a teacher take a special interest in you? Was that important to your decision to be in or stay in college? How?

I am a walking contradiction. I have no Ph.D. yet I'm a full professor of English at a state university. By all definitions and designs I should not even have made it to college. I am the second of five children of a Southern Pacific Railroad worker with a fifth-grade education and a woman who dropped out of the second grade to help raise ten siblings—while her mother worked ten hours a day cleaning houses and doing laundry for rich Texan ranchers.

In Comstock, the Tex-Mex border town about fifteen miles from the Rio Grande where I spent the first twelve years of my life, I saw the despair that poverty and hopelessness had etched in the faces of young Chicano men who, like my father, walked back and forth on the dusty path between Comstock and the Southern Pacific Railroad station. They would set out every day on rail carts to repair the railroad. The women of Comstock fared no better. Most married early. I had seen them in their kitchens toiling at a stove, with one baby propped on one hip and two toddlers tugging at their skirts. Or they followed their working mothers' route, cleaning houses and doing laundry for rich Texan ranchers who paid them a pittance. I decided very early that this was not the future I wanted.

In 1958 my father, tired of seeing his days fade into each other without promise, moved us to California where we became farmworkers in the San Jose area (then a major agricultural center). I saw the same futile look in the faces of young Chicanos and Chicanas working beside my family. Those faces already lined so young with sadness made me deadly serious about my books and my education.

At a young age—between eleven and fourteen—I began my intellectual and spiritual rebellion against my parents and society. I fell in love with books and created space of my own where I could dare to dream. Yet in school I remained shy and introverted, terrified of my white, male professors. In my adolescence I rebelled against my mother's insistence that Mexican girls should marry young, as she did at eighteen. I told her that I didn't care if my cousins Alicia and Anita were getting married and having babies early. "I was put on this earth to make books, not babies!" I announced and ran into my room.

Books were my obsession. I wanted to read everything that I was not supposed to. By fourteen I was already getting to know the Marquis de Sade, Rimbaud, Lautr amont, Whitman, Dostoyevsky, Marx. I came by these writers serendipitously. To get from home to Sacramento High School I had to walk through one of the toughest neighborhoods in the city, Oak Park. There were men hanging out with liquor in brown paper bags, playing dice, shooting craps and calling from cars: "Hey, baby, get in here with me!" I'd run into a little library called Oak Park Library, which turned out to have a little bit of everything. I would walk around and stare at the shelves, killing time till the shifty-eyed men would go away.

The librarians knew and tolerated me with skepticism: "Are you sure you're going to read the Marquis de Sade? Do your parents know you're checking out this material? What are you doing with the *Communist Manifesto?*" One librarian even forbade me to check the books out, so I'd sit reading in the library for hours on end. Later, at sixteen or seventeen, I was allowed to check anything and everything out.

So it was that I came to grapple with tough language and ideas. These books were hot! Yet I also was obsessed with wanting to be pretty, mysterious, silent and sexy. I wanted to have long curly hair, red lips and long red nails; to wear black tight dresses and high heels. I wanted desperately to look like the sensuous femmes fatales of the Mexican cinema—María F liz, one of the most beautiful and famous of Mexico's screen goddesses, and Libertad Lamarque, the smoky-voiced, green-eyed Argentinian singer. These were the women I admired when my mother and I went to the movies together. So these were my "outward" models. My "inward" models, the voices of the intellect that spoke to me when I shut the door to my room, were, as you have gathered, a writer of erotica, two mad surrealists, a crazy Romantic, an epileptic literary genius and a radical socialist.

I needed to sabotage society in a major, intellectually radical way. I needed to be a warrior who would catch everyone off guard. But to be a warrior, you must never let your opponent figure you out. When the bullets of racism and sexism are flying at you, you must be very clever in deciding how you want to live. I knew that everything around me—school, teachers, television, friends, men, even my own parents, who in their internalized racism and self-hatred didn't really believe I'd amount to much though they hoped like hell that life would prove them wrong—everything was against me, and I understood this fully.

To protect myself I fell in love with language—all of it, poems, stories, novels, plays, songs, biographies, "cuentos" or little vignettes, movies—all manifestations of spoken and written language. I fell in love with ideas, with essays by writers like Bacon or Montaigne. I began my serious reading crusade around age eleven, when I was already convinced that books were central to my life. Only through them and through songs, I felt, would I be free to structure some kind of future for myself.

I wanted to prove to anyone who cared to ask (though by now I was convinced no one gave a damn) that I, the daughter of a laborer-farmworker, could dare to be somebody. Try to imagine what it is like to be always full of rage—rage at everything: at white teachers who could never even pronounce my name (I was often called anything from "Odilia" to "Otilia" to "Estela"); rage at those teachers who asked me point-blank, "But how did you get to be so smart? You are Mexican, aren't you?"; rage at my eleventh-grade English teacher who said to me in front of the class, "You stick to essay writing; never try to write a poem again because a poet you are not!" (This, after I had worked for two diligent weeks on an imitation of "La Belle Dame Sans Merci"! Now I can laugh. Then it was pitiful.)

From age thirteen I was also angry at boys who hounded me for dates. When I'd reject them they'd yell, "So what do you plan to do for the rest of your life, fuck a book?" I was angry at my Chicana classmates in high school who, perhaps jealous of my high grades, would say, "What are you trying to do, be like the whites?" I regret to say that I was also angry at my parents, exasperated by their docility, their limited expectations of me. Oh, I knew they were proud; but sometimes, in their own misdirected rage (maybe afraid of my little successes), they would make painful comments. "Te vas a volver loca con esos jodidos libros" (You'll go nuts with those fucking books") was my mother's frequent statement. Or the even more sickening, "Esta nunca se va a casar." ("Give up on this one;

she'll never get married.)" This was the tenor of my adolescent years. When nothing on either side of the two cultures, Mexican or Anglo-American, affirms your existence, that is how rage is shaped.

While I managed to escape at least from the obvious entrapments—a teen pregnancy, a destructive early marriage—I did not escape years of being told I wasn't quite right, that because of my ethnicity and gender I was somehow defective, incomplete. Those years left wounds on my self-esteem, wounds so deep that even armed with my books and stolen knowledge I could not entirely escape deep feelings of unworthiness.

By the time I graduated from high school and managed to get a little scholarship to California State University in Sacramento, where I now teach (in 1962 it was called Sacramento State College), I had become very unassertive, immensely shy. I was afraid to look unfeminine if I raised my hand in class, afraid to seem ridiculous if I asked a "bad" question and all eyes turned on me. A deeper part of me was afraid that my rage might rear its ugly head and I would be considered "an angry Mexican accusing everybody of racism." I was painfully concerned with my physical appearance: wasn't I supposed to look beautiful like F liz and Lamarque? Yet while I wanted to look pretty for the boys, the thought of having sex terrified me. What if I got pregnant, had to quit college and couldn't read my books anymore? The more I feared boys, the more I made myself attractive for them and the more they would make advances, the more I rejected them.

The constant tension sapped my energy and distracted me from my creative journeys into language. Oh, I would write little things (poems, sketches for stories, journal entries), but I was afraid to show them to anyone. Besides, no one knew I was writing them. I was so frightened by my white, male professors, especially in the English department—they looked so arrogant and were so ungiving of their knowledge—that I didn't have the nerve to major in English, though it was the major I really wanted.

Instead, I chose to major in French. The "Parisiens" and "Qu - becois" in the French department faculty admired my French accent: "Mademoiselle,  tes-vous certaine que vous n' tes pas parisienne? they would ask. In short, they cared. They engaged me in dialogue, asked why I preferred to study French instead of Spanish. ("I already know Spanish," I'd say.) French became my adopted language. I could play with it, sing songs in it and sound exotic. It complemented my Spanish; besides, I didn't have to worry about speaking English with my heavy Spanish accent and risk being ridiculed. At one point, my spoken French was better than my oral Spanish; my written French has remained better than my written Spanish.

At 23, armed with a secondary school teaching credential and B.A. in French with an English minor, I became a high school teacher of French and English. Soon after that I began to work for a school district where the majority of the students were Chicanos and Blacks from families on welfare and/or from households run by women.

After two years of high school teaching, I returned to Cal State at Sacramento for the Master's degree. Professionally and artistically, it was the best decision I have ever made. The Master's program to which I applied was a pilot program in its second year at CSUS. Called the Mexican American Experienced Teachers' Fellowship, it was run by a team of anthropology professors, central among whom was Professor Steven Arvizu. The program was designed to turn us into *"agents of cultural change."* It was 1969 and the program was one of the first federally funded (Title V) ones to address Mexican American students' needs by re-educating their teachers.

My interests were literary, but all twenty of us "fellows" had to get an M.A. in social anthropology, since this experiment took the "anthropologizing education" approach. We studied social dynamics, psycholinguistics, history of Mexico, history of the American Southwest, community activism and confrontational strategies and the nature of the Chicano movement. The courses were eye-openers. I had never heard the terms Chicano, biculturalism, marginality, assimilation, Chicanismo, protest art. I had never heard of Cesar Chavez and the farmworkers nor of Luis Valdez and the Teatro Campesino. I had never studied the nature of racism and identity. The theme of the program was that culture is a powerful tool for learning, self-expression, solidarity and positive change. Exploring it can help Chicano students understand their bicultural circumstances.

The program brought me face to face with nineteen other Chicano men and women, all experienced public school teachers like myself, with backgrounds like mine. The program challenged every aspect of my life. Through group counseling, group encounter, classroom interaction, course content and community involvement I was allowed to express my rage and to examine it in the company of peers who had a similar anger. Most of our instructors, moreover, were Chicano or white professors sensitive to Chicanos. For the first time, at 25, I had found my role models. I vowed to do for other students what these people had done for me.

Eighteen years of teaching primarily white women students, Chicanos and Blacks at California State University, Sacramento, have led me to see myself less as a teacher and more as a cultural worker, struggling against society to undo the damage of years of abuse. I continue to see myself as a warrior empowered by my rage. Racism and sexism leave two clear-cut scars on my students; internalized self-hatred and fear of their own creative passion, in my view the two most serious obstacles in the classroom. Confronting this two-headed monster has made me razor-sharp. Given their tragic personal stories, the hope in my students' eyes reconfirms daily the incredible beauty, the tenacity of the human spirit.

Teaching white women students (ages 30–45) is no different from working with Chicano and Black students (both men and women): you have to bring about changes in the way they view themselves, their abilities, their right to get educated and their relation to a world that has systematically oppressed them simply for being who they are. You have to help them channel and understand the seething rage they carry deep inside, a rage which, left unexpressed, can make them turn against each other and, more sadly, against themselves.

I teach four courses per semester: English 109G, Writing for Proficiency for Bilingual/Bidialectal Students (a course taken mainly by Chicano and Black students, ages 19–24); English 115A, Pedagogy/Language Arts for Prospective Elementary School Teachers (a course taken mainly by women aged 25–45, 50 percent white, 50 percent Chicano); English 180G, Chicano Literature, an advanced studies General Education course for non-English majors (taken by excellent students, aged 24–45, about 40 percent white, 40 percent Chicano, 20 percent Black/Vietnamese/Filipino/South American). The fourth course is English 1, Basic Language Skills, a pre-freshman composition course taken primarily by Black and Chicano freshmen, male and female, aged 18–22, who score too low on the English Placement Test to be placed in "regular" Freshman Composition.

Mine is a teaching load that, in my younger days at CSUS, used to drive me close to insanity from physical, mental and spiritual exhaustion—spiritual from having internalized my students' pain. Perhaps not fully empowered myself, not fully emplumed in the feathers of my own creativity (to borrow the wonderful "emplumada" metaphor coined by Lorna Dee Cervantes, the brilliant Chicana poet), I allowed their rage to become part of mine. This kind of rage can kill you. And so through years of working with these kinds of students I have learned to make my spirit strong with "canto, locura y poesia" (song, madness, and poetry). Judging from my students' progress, the songs have worked.

Truly, it takes a conjurer, a magus with all her teaching cards up her sleeve, to deal with the fragmented souls that show up in my classes. Among the Chicanos and Blacks I get ex-offenders (mostly men but occasionally a woman who has done time), orphans, single women heads of household, high school dropouts who took years to complete their Graduation Equivalency Diploma.

I get women who have been raped and/or who have been sexually abused either by a father figure or by male relatives—Sylvia Tracey, for example, a 30-year-old Chicana feminist, mother of two, whose parents pressured her to marry her (white) rapist and who is going through divorce after ten years of marriage. I get women who have been battered. And, of course, I get the young Chicano and Black little yuppies who don't believe the world existed before 1970, who know nothing about the sixties' history of struggle and student protest, who—in the case of the Chicanos—feel ashamed that their parents speak English with an accent or were once farmworkers. I get Chicanos, Blacks and white women, especially, who are ashamed of their writing skills, who have never once been told that they could succeed in school.

Annetta Jones is typical. A 45-year-old Black woman, who single-handedly raised three children, all college-educated and successful, she is still married to a man who served ten years in prison for being a "hit man." She visited him faithfully in prison and underwent all kinds of humiliation at the hands of correctional officers—even granting them sexual favors just to be allowed to have conjugal visits. When her husband completed his time he fell in love with a young woman from Chicago, where he now lives.

Among my white women students (ranging in age from 25 to 40, though occasionally I get a 45-year-old woman who wants to be an elementary or high school teacher and "help out young kids so they won't have to go through what I went through"—their exact words) I get women who are either divorced or divorcing; rarely do I get a "happily" married woman. This is especially true of the white women who take my Chicano literature and my credential-pedagogy classes. Take Lynne Trebeck, for instance, a white woman about 40 years old who runs a farm. When she entered the university her husband objected, so she divorced him! They continue to live in the same house (he refused to leave), "but now he has no control over me," she told me triumphantly midway through the semester. She has two sons, fifteen and eighteen years old; as a young woman she did jail time as the accomplice of a convicted drug dealer.

Every semester I get two or three white lesbian feminists. This semester there was Vivianne Rose, about 40, in my Chicano literature class. Apparently sensing too much conservatism in the students, and knowing that she wanted to be an elementary school teacher, she chose to conceal her sexual orientation. On the first day of class she wore Levi pants, a baggy sweatshirt, white tennis shoes and a beige baseball cap. By the end of the first week she had switched to ultrafeminine dresses and skirts, brightly colored blouses, nylons and medium-heeled black shoes, not to mention lipstick and eye makeup. When she spoke in class she occasionally made references to "my husband who is Native American." She and Sylvia Tracey became very close friends. Halfway through the course they informed me that "Shit, it's about time we tell her." (This, from Sylvia.) "Oh hell, why not," Vivianne said; "my 'husband' is a woman." The woman *is* Native American; Vivianne Rose lived on a reservation for years and taught young Native American children to read and write. She speaks "Res" talk (reservation speech) and has adopted her "husband's" last name.

Among my white women students there are also divorced women who are raising two to four children, usually between the ages of eight and seventeen. Sometimes I get older widowed white women who are taking classes for their own enjoyment, not for a degree. These women also tell stories of torment: rapes, beatings, verbal and emotional harassment from their men. On occasion I get women who have done jail time, usually for taking the rap for drug-connected boyfriends. I rarely get a married woman, but when I do there is pain: "My husband doesn't really want me in school." "My husband doesn't really care what I do in college as long as I take care of his needs and the kids' needs." "My husband doesn't really know what I'm studying—he has never asked and I've never told him."

Most of the white women as well as the minority students come to the university under special programs. There is the "Educational Opportunity Program" for students who do not meet all university entrance requirements or whose grade point average is simply too low for regular admission. There is the "Student Affirmative Action Program" for students who need special counseling and tutoring to bring their academic skills up to par or deal with emotional trauma. There is the "College Assistance Migrant Program" for students whose parents are migrant farmworkers in the agricultural areas surrounding Sacramento. There is a wonderful program called PASAR for older women students entering the university for the first time or returning after a multiple-year absence. The Women's Resource Center also provides small grants and scholarships for re-entry women. A large number of my students (both white and minority women) come severely handicapped in their basic language, math and science skills; many have never used a computer. It is not uncommon (especially among Chicanos and Blacks) to get an incoming student who scores at the fifth- and sixth-grade reading levels.

The task is herculean, the rewards spiritually fulfilling. I would not have it any other way. Every day is a lesson in humility and audacity. That my students have endured nothing but obstacles and putdowns, yet still have the courage and strength to seek a college education, humbles me. They are, like me, walking paradoxes.

They have won against all the odds (their very presence on campus attests to that). Yet really they haven't won: they carry a deeply ingrained sense of inferiority, a firm conviction that they are not worthy of success.

This is my challenge: I embrace it wholeheartedly. There is no place I'd rather be, no profession more noble. Sure, I sometimes have doubts: every day something new, sad, even tragic comes up. Just as I was typing this article, for instance, Vicky, one of the white students in my Chicano literature class, called in tears, barely able to talk. "Professor, I can't possibly turn in my paper to your mailbox by four o'clock," she cried. "Everything in my house is falling apart! My husband just fought with my oldest daughter [from a previous marriage], has thrown her out of the house. He's running up and down the street, yelling and threatening to leave us. And I'm sitting here trying to write your paper! I'm going crazy. I feel like walking away from it all!" I took an hour from writing this article to help her contain herself. By the end of our conversation, I had her laughing. I also put her in touch with a counselor friend of mine and gave her a two-day extension for her final paper. And naturally I was one more hour late with my own writing!

I teach in a totally non-traditional way. I use every trick in the book: lots of positive reinforcement, both oral and written; lots of one-on-one conferences. I network women with each other, refer them to professor friends who can help them; connect them to graduate students and/or former students who are already pursuing careers. In the classroom I force my students to come up in front of their classmates, explain concepts or read their essays aloud. I create panels representing opposing viewpoints and hold debates—lots of oral participation, role-playing, reading their own texts. Their own writing and opinions become part of the course. On exams I ask them questions about their classmates' presentations. I meet with individual students in local coffeehouses or taverns: it's much easier to talk about personal pain over coffee or a beer or a glass of wine than in my office. My students, for the most part, do not have a network of support away from the university. There are no supportive husbands, lovers (except on rare occasions, as with my lesbian students), no relatives saying, "Yes, you can do it."

Is it any wonder that when these students come to me they have a deep sense of personal shame about everything—poor skills, being older students? They are also very angry, not only at themselves but at the schools for having victimized them; at poor, uninspired teaching, at their parents for not having had high enough expectations of them or (in the case of the women) for having allowed them to marry so young. Sylvia, my Chicana feminist student, put it best when I was pointing out incomplete sentences in her essay: "Where the hell was I when all this was being taught in high school? And why didn't anybody give a damn that I wasn't learning it?"

I never teach content for the first two weeks of any of my courses. I talk about anger, sexism, racism and the sixties—a time when people believed in something larger than themselves. We dialogue—about prisons and why so many Chicano and Black young men are behind bars in California; why people fear differences; why they are so homophobic. I give my students a chance to talk about their anger ("coraje" in Spanish). I often read them the poem by my friend and colleague Jose Montoya, called "Eslipping and Esliding," where he talks about "locura" (craziness) and says that with a little locura, a little eslipping and esliding, we can survive the madness that surrounds us. We laugh at ourselves, sharing our tragic, tattered pasts; we undo everything and let the anger out. "I know why so many of you are afraid of doing well," I say. "You've been told you can't do it, and you're so pissed off about it, you can't concentrate." Courage takes pure concentration. By the end of these initial two or three weeks we have become friends and defined our mutual respect. Only then do we enter the course content.

I am not good at endings; I prefer to celebrate beginnings. The struggle continues and the success stories abound. Students come back, year after year, to say "Thank you." Usually I pull these visitors into the classroom: "Tell my class that they can do it. Tell them how you did it!" They start talking and can't stop. "Look, Olivia, when I first came into your class," said Sylvia, "I couldn't even put a fucking sentence together. And now look at me, three years later I'm even writing poetry!"

---

## Now that you've read

1. What were some of the turning points in Castellano's life?
2. In what ways was language a form of "protection" for her?
3. What roles did anger play in Castellano's own education?
4. What is Castellano trying to accomplish as a teacher? How is she trying to accomplish it?

# SEQUENCE 1 ASSIGNMENTS

## Reading 1: John Henry Newman, "The Idea of a University"

A habit of mind is formed which lasts through life, of which the attributes are, freedom, equitableness, calmness, moderation, and wisdom; or what in a former Discourse I have ventured to call a philosophical habit. This then I would assign as the special fruit of the education furnished at a University, as contrasted with other places of teaching or modes of teaching. This is the main purpose of a University in its treatment of its students.

### *Prewriting*

In your notebook or on a separate sheet of paper, respond to the following questions:

1. Summarize the quotation that begins this assignment in two or three sentences.
2. Give a real example of intellectual enlargement from your personal experience. What did you do to bring it about?
3. In the last section, what does Newman say are the practical characteristics (three or four) of a University-educated person in society? How valuable do you think these characteristics are?
4. Reread your responses to the Getting Started questions. What connections can you make between them and Newman's essay?

### *Writing assignment*

Write a brief essay in which you compare Newman's idea of higher education with your own. Cite significant differences and similarities between your respective visions of, and goals for, higher education. Are you the same kind of student that Newman was writing about or for? Feel free to draw on your personal experience and background. Quote from Newman's essay, too, being careful to present his words and punctuation exactly and to include the page number. After you quote, make sure that your understanding of what Newman is saying is clear for your readers.

## Reading 2: Caroline Bird, "The Case Against College"

We assume that we are sending them [students] to college for their own best interests and sell them college the way we sell them spinach—because it's good for them. Some, of course, learn to like it, but most wind up still preferring green peas. College students are forced to eat spinach—to go to college—even when they don't like it.

## Prewriting

1. Summarize the quotation above in two or three sentences.
2. List as many reasons as you can imagine for a student to go to college and to choose a particular course of study or major. When you've finished your list, make a mark by those that apply to you.
3. List as many reasons as you can imagine why students should avoid going to college or, once they're in college, should avoid declaring a major for a couple of semesters or so.
4. For what reasons do you choose your classes? How do you justify your decisions?
5. Bird writes that students feel coerced into going to college. Is coercion necessary for educational achievement?

## Writing assignment

Newman's and Bird's essays have asked you to consider the importance of higher education to life in general and to your life in particular. Reread your previous essay, reviewing your position in relation to Newman. Reconsider what you want a college education to make possible for you. What is the "something more" that this school can give you that a technical school cannot? Now write an essay in which you clarify, refine, or expand on your original position regarding your "idea of a university." You will need to make clear your understanding of Bird's and Newman's arguments as you present your own point of view.

## Reading 3: Mike Rose, "Entering the Conversation"

The teachers that fate and Jack MacFarland's crisis intervention sent my way worked at making the humanities truly human. What transpired between us was the essence of humane liberal education, and it enabled me to move far beyond the cognitive charade of my freshman year.

## Prewriting

1. What do you take the quotation above to mean?
2. Would Mike Rose or the friends he describes fit into the university Newman describes? Why or why not? (Be prepared to support your answer with quotations from each text.)

3. List three specific passages from Newman and three from Rose that apply specifically to you and your educational experience and expectations.
4. What does Rose mean by "the cognitive charade of my freshman year"? What is "the essence of humane liberal education"?

## Writing assignment

Reflecting on your reading of Newman, Bird, and Rose, where do you position yourself in this conversation? How are the kind of reading that Rose is asking students to do (and teachers to teach) and the kind of university he is calling for radically different from the kind of reading and the kind of university Newman is calling for and Bird is describing? What role do teachers play in Rose's discussion? Where do you as a student and reader fit in?

Note that Rose quite literally tells stories about his own experiences. What larger story do these smaller stories enable him to tell? What does your experience teach you about learning? Rose says that he learns to enter a "conversation." Compare the conversations you enter with the one Rose learns to enter. This difficult assignment asks you to weigh different writers' arguments, as well as your own.

## Reading 4: Lynne V. Cheney, "Students of Success"

Students who follow their hearts in choosing majors will most likely end up laboring at what they love. They're the ones who will put in the long hours and intense effort that achievement requires. And they're the ones who will find the sense of purpose that underlies most human happiness.

## Prewriting

1. In two or three sentences, explain what Cheney means in the quotation above.
2. What were the most important things you took into consideration when you decided what your major would be? If you are still undecided about your major, what factors have prevented you from making a final decision?
3. How realistic is it to expect today's college students to "follow their hearts"?

## Writing assignment

Cheney encourages students to rethink their definitions of "success" when they select their majors. If students were to do so, how might they change their educational or life goals? In what ways does your own definition of "success" resemble or differ from Cheney's?

Does Cheney describe an ideal that cannot exist for students concerned about finishing school, making a living, and paying back thousands of dollars in student loans? What might Cheney say to Bird or Rose? Using your reading of Cheney and the previous essays, discuss how the "idea of a university" has changed from Newman's time to the present and what accounts for the change. Include specific examples, drawing on your own concerns in choosing a major and a career path.

## Reading 5: Olivia Castellano, "Canto, Locura y Poesia"

> You have to help them channel and understand the seething rage they carry deep inside, a rage which, left unexpressed, can make them turn against each other and, more sadly, against themselves.

### Prewriting

1. In two or three sentences, draw from the context of the essay to explain what Castellano means in the quotation above.
2. Can anger play a productive role in a person's education? Why or why not?
3. How likely is it that your race, class, or sex will affect your experience of college? Offer an example.

### Writing assignment

Castellano argues that anger can be a positive force, a force that can be channeled to produce knowledge and make connections. Take time to work through her argument, and then respond to it. Do you see any of your teachers as "agents of cultural change"? What do you take this to mean? Is this a teacher's job?

Finally, what might Rose or Cheney say in response to Castellano's essay? How does Castellano's definition of "success" differ from Cheney's? Rose works with some of the same students. How does his argument differ from Castellano's? Where do you stand among these positions?

### Final Project

Review what you've written in the writing assignments for this sequence. What is your "idea of a university" now that you've done a lot of thinking and writing about the subject? Does the reality measure up to your ideal? Mine your essays for a specific issue you'd like to investigate in further detail, and formulate a concise thesis you can develop into a research paper. If you can't decide on a topic to investigate further, consider these questions:

Why did students at your school choose to attend?
How would students at your school describe the "ideal" university?
Is college worth the time and money?

## Library Research Ideas

Try one of the following library research activities, or come up with your own ideas for library research to support your thesis.

1. Find your school's mission statement. (Try looking on the World Wide Web.) Does your school live up to its stated mission? Is the mission statement appropriate? Compare the mission statements of several other different types of schools (for example, community colleges, vocational schools, four-year universities, elite graduate schools). For whom do you think the mission statements were written? Current students? Potential students? Administrators? Teachers? Alumni? Potential donors? Is this appropriate?
2. Investigate trends, for as far back as you can find relevant information, in the following areas:
   a. The differences in income earned by people with a high school diploma, by people with a bachelor's degree, and by people with a Ph.D.
   b. The professions people train for in college
   c. Rates of increases in tuition
3. Now compare these trends, draw conclusions, and use the information you find to support your thesis.

## Field Research Ideas

Try one or more of the following field research ideas, or use your own field research ideas to get data to support your thesis.

1. Choose two majors, one that some might consider impractical and one that many consider very practical (in terms of employment prospects after graduation). Compile a survey to get information from students in these two majors about why they chose their major. Ask what their career plans are, how important a consideration those plans were in their choice of major, and whether they enjoy their classes. Then survey a group of alumni from each major (people who graduated, say, ten years ago) and inquire about their job satisfaction and whether they would

choose a different major if they had to do it over again. Ask your respondents anything else you feel will provide relevant information for your paper.

2. Interview three or four seniors who do not plan to go on to graduate school. Ask about their immediate plans for the future. Do they feel prepared? Do they feel they've gotten what they needed and wanted from their college education? Now interview several graduate students or seniors who want to attend graduate school. Ask about their career plans and their feelings about their college education.

# Campus Politics, Global Politics

### READINGS

## Getting Started

Around the world, college students have frequently felt called to take action in the political arena. Often college students have greater freedom to protest political and social conditions than the rest of society—or at least they're more willing than others to risk staging such protests. Students have sometimes assumed the role of political and social conscience, and sometimes they have acted as political thugs. Think of the Chinese students who stood up to their government in Tiananmen Square in 1989, and compare them to those who terrorized their countrymen during the Cultural Revolution. Or think of the French students who led the Paris general strike in 1968, the American students killed at Kent State in 1970, or the Iranian students who took over the American embassy in Tehran in 1979. Clearly, college campuses serve as magnets for political activists of all stripes.

Not too long ago, this country's college campuses were perceived as hotbeds of political radicalism. Today, however, U.S. college students are often regarded as completely apathetic and concerned only with making money. This sequence asks you to *look at your own political awareness and involvement and that of your fellow students.* Where do you stand in relation to how college students have been and are currently portrayed in terms of political activism? Are students on your campus aware of political issues? Are some more likely to be politically aware than others?

The first reading in this sequence is a *Washington Post* article that reports on a survey that found college students more conservative than ever. Paul Rogat Loeb, author of the second reading ("I Feel a Little Fearful"), went to college campuses and asked students to talk about why they hesitate to speak out about political issues. Alexander W. Astin argues in "The Cause of Citizenship" that all of us need to exercise our rights as citizens with much greater passion and frequency. Paul Berman, in an excerpt from the first chapter of his book *A Tale of Two Utopias,* provides us with a "global" history of events leading to political activism on college campuses all over the world in 1968. Patricia Williams's essay "Crimes Without Passion" brings the personal and the political together as she shows how seemingly neutral language is in fact politically charged. And finally, historian Barbara Tuchman argues in "History as Mirror" that we have a great deal to learn from the distant past about ourselves and our political health. Work through the readings, and as you answer the questions in the related reading and writing assignments, consider how local or global your own politics are.

Before you do any of the reading, however, please reflect on your own political consciousness and on the level of political activism on your campus; then respond to several of the questions that follow. I use the Getting Started questions as a preliminary exercise on the first day my class works on a particular sequence. Your teacher may also do this, or he or she may ask that you write out your responses either in a journal or in your notebook. Your teacher may use these questions as a jumping-off place for class discussion as well. No matter how you use these questions in your class, you'll be able to draw on what you write here both in your contributions to class discussion and in your responses to the assignments that follow.

1. How would you describe the political atmosphere on your campus? Apathetic? Activist? In between? What, if anything, prevents students from being more politically involved on your campus? On college campuses in general?

2. How would you describe your own level of political awareness and activism? What kinds of problems or situations motivate you (or might motivate you) to speak out?

3. What happens to students' political activism and involvement after they leave college and enter the "real world"? Do people tend to become more or less active politically after they leave college? Why do you think this is so?
4. Where are the most intense sites of activism on your campus right now? What sorts of activism take place there?
5. Can the politics of the past teach us anything today? What?

READING 1

---

# College Freshmen More Conservative in Survey

"College Freshmen More Conservative in Survey" reports that today's first-year college students take, on the whole, more conservative political positions and more civic responsibility than their counterparts have since the 1960s when the survey was first administered. The article includes a number of details from the survey and suggests a few factors that may contribute to these changes in attitude.

### Before you read

1. Would you describe your fellow students as conservative? If so, why? If not, how would you describe them?
2. How would you describe your own political views in relation to those of other students you know?
3. If the article's title is correct, why might college freshmen be more conservative? What factors contribute to this trend?

---

The nation's largest annual survey of college freshmen portrays a class that is more civic-minded, more self-confident and more supportive of a range of conservative social values than students have been in decades.

The survey, an important gauge of attitudes and aspirations among college freshmen since it began in the 1960s, reveals many striking trends this year: Record numbers of them are doing volunteer work, interest in careers in law or business have hit new lows, and students seem to think more highly of themselves than ever.

On social issues, the survey shows that student support for keeping abortion legal has declined for the fourth consecutive year. And the percentage of students endorsing casual sexual relationships has dwindled to a new low.

More than 250,000 freshmen at nearly 500 universities nationwide took part in the survey, which is being released Monday by UCLA's Higher Education Research Institute. The results are based on responses that freshmen gave to hundreds of questions on their interests, issues in American society and their plans for the future.

In recent years, college analysts have expressed dismay with the growing apathy that students have shown in the survey about government and politics. That remained low again this year; only about 30 percent said they considered keeping up with current events "very important." But it did not decline, as it has for most of this decade.

In this year's survey, researchers said they were heartened most by the rise of community service. About 72 percent of freshmen said they had performed volunteer work in the past year, which is 10 points higher than it was in 1989. About 38 percent said they volunteer once a week. Both figures are the highest the survey has ever recorded.

College officials said they believed the trend is the result of growing campaigns in the nation's high schools to encourage, even require, students to do community work.

"There is clearly more genuine interest in that among students," said Robert Canevari, the dean of students at the University of Virginia. "We're seeing much more of it on campus, and I don't think it's just for most students to pad their resumes."

More freshmen than ever rated themselves "above average" or in the "highest 10 percent" of their class in academics, public speaking and leadership, and artistic skill.

In 1971, for example, only about 35 percent of freshmen in the survey said they had strong leadership ability. Now, 54 percent say they do. Overall, 58 percent of freshmen said they were "above average" compared with their peers.

One reason for that, researchers said, could be grade inflation. The survey reports that the nation's high schools appear to be awarding students higher marks than at any other time in the survey's history.

For example: In 1969, only 12 percent of freshmen said they had "A" averages. Now, 32 percent say they do. In 1969, about 33 percent of freshmen said they had "C" averages. Now, only 15 percent do.

Researchers expressed caution about the trends in student confidence.

"This improved self-concept may be more the result of current self-esteem-raising programs in kindergarten through 12th grade rather than actual gains in ability," said Linda Sax, an education professor at UCLA who helped direct the survey.

On social issues, survey results were mixed. Strong majorities of freshmen want more gun control, favor tougher environmental laws and support gay rights. But on other prominent subjects, many more students are embracing staunchly conservative views.

Support for abortion rights, for example, continues to decline after peaking at 65 percent in 1990. This year, 56 percent of students favor it, one of its lowest levels since the survey began. Support for abortion was similar among male and female freshmen. Seventy-two percent of freshmen also said society shows "too much concern for criminals." About 80 percent of them want to keep the death penalty.

---

### Now that you've read

1. Are you convinced by the survey's results? Why or why not?
2. The survey states that more students are doing volunteer work than did so in the past. It goes on to suggest that this may be the result of high schools encouraging, and sometimes requiring, their students to volunteer in their communities. Why might high schools be doing this? What effect could this have on those students, especially on their political outlooks? If you yourself have done any volunteer work, what effect, if any, has the experience had on your politics?
3. The article states that "Overall, 58 percent of freshmen said they were 'above average' compared with their peers." Can 58 percent be "above average"? If this is the case, what does "average" mean? Why might students rate themselves so highly?
4. How well do you think these results reflect general thinking on your campus?

## READING 2

*Paul Rogat Loeb*

# I Feel a Little Fearful:
# The Reluctance to Speak

For his book *Generation at the Crossroads: Apathy and Action on the American Campus* (1994), Paul Rogat Loeb interviewed college students all over the United States to learn the truths behind the myths of student apathy and student activism. In this chapter from the book, he looks particularly at why some students are hesitant to express their political views publicly. Consider to what extent he describes people you know.

### Before you read

1. Do you ever feel "fearful" about speaking out? Why or why not?
2. Why do you think some students are more willing than others to speak out about political issues?
3. What kind of reception do the most politically active students receive on your campus?

---

In April 1988, I was in Chicago, the second largest Polish city in the world, at the urban commuter campus officially named University of Illinois at Chicago, but which students continue to call Chicago Circle. I spent much of my time there with the Polish American Student Association (PASA), which included students who had grown up in the city's longstanding ethnic neighborhoods as well as others who had come after December 1981, when the Polish imposition of martial law crushed Solidarity's initial hope.

In Poland, meanwhile, citizens were striking. Fifteen thousand workers walked out at the massive Polish steel complex at Nowa Huta. Strikers occupied the Lenin shipyard in Gdansk, the birthplace of Solidarity, while supporters fought with police. In Warsaw, thousands of people marched in the streets, then were beaten and dispersed. Poland had strikes and demonstrations in Krakow and Lublin, Poznan and Lodz. The strikes lasted two weeks, until State security forces stormed the Nowa Huta steelworks and the Gdansk shipyard workers gave in. The challenges seemed to have failed.

Marching in Chicago's annual Polish Day parade with the Chicago Circle group, I met a student named Andrzej. Just two years out of Warsaw, he still burned with memories of marches and strikes. Because America proclaimed democracy as its promise, he assumed that, in contrast with Jaruzelski's Poland, ordinary citizens would routinely participate in shaping their nation's destiny. He found ample career opportunity: part-time jobs with United Parcel Service and with a design firm, training for his intended vocation in economics. But though he saw no one punished for their opinions, political concerns seemed almost wholly absent from his workplace and school.

Responses seemed muted even toward the latest events in Poland. True, Chicago's Polish community sent money and supplies. Parade marshals handed out red and white *Solidarnosc* signs for people to carry alongside floats from restaurants, churches, butcher and sausage shops. But when Andrzej handed out copies of *New York Times* articles on the Lenin shipyard strikes, none but the most recently arrived students were interested.

The parade ended, and we adjourned to a nearby Greek restaurant. "Viva Solidarity. Viva Lech Walesa," the owner said again and again, slapping down free bottles of dark red wine on our table. We talked about Poland and about America. PASA's new members had entered the United States as political refugees, but once here, they pursued just the hope of decent private lives. "People in Poland know what rights they don't have and fight for them," observed a woman studying to be an engineer. "Here, you know your rights. You're satisfied. That keeps people from participating."

At the restaurant, Andrzej talked on as the wine took hold. He spun faster and faster, handsome, charismatic, and drunk. He flirted with the group's president and the other women at the table. "I don't want to be just a mainstream white American," he said. "I want to become a Polish hero." But that meant he had to strike it rich in this land of opportunity, "because ordinary workers don't have power." When he'd earned enough, he'd start a new career, running weapons to Poland, "like another IRA." Or maybe return to be "the next Lech Walesa, the next Martin Luther King." "I'm glad you're not totally selfish," teased his PASA friends, indulging his grand dreams.

Later the group moved to Andrzej's small apartment and put on the music that had gotten them through the darkest times back home. "This brings me back to Warsaw," Andrzej stated sadly as he inserted a Dire Straits cassette into a tape deck. "More than Chopin?" I asked, a bit surprised. Far more, the others agreed. Far more than any music except Leonard Cohen's, whom another student called "the guru of Polish society," relating how his generation was raised on Cohen's mournful dirges.

The night ended with Andrzej crying for everything he'd left behind, repeating again and again, "No one here acts. No one here cares." He was drunk, to be sure, and missed home and family. Yet I believe he missed as well the sense of working to shape a better society. American freedom offered a chance for private gain, and the right to be left alone in personal affairs. But people didn't talk, Andrzej said, about the kind of country they'd like to build. "They just don't talk about it at all."

### Isolation set the tone

It's hard to act when dissenting movements are remote or invisible. In times of great upheaval, as at the height of the Vietnam era, students often have to consciously choose whether or not to get involved. In recent years, political withdrawal has been the automatic track at most schools. Students have to consciously work to depart from it.

A student named John from [the] University of Southern Mississippi at Hattiesburg was chosen in his high school senior year as a 1983 Presidential Scholar. Joining 140 other seniors from around the country, he traveled to Washington to meet President Reagan. Although the meeting was purely ceremonial, a New Jersey woman, Ariella Gross, took the audacious step of circulating a letter among the scholars to ask Reagan to support a nuclear freeze.

Gross's actions caused a major controversy, although only a dozen others in the largely conservative student group ended up signing the letter. Like most of the rest, John held back. He felt he didn't know enough to judge, and considered it impolite for Gross to bring her personal concerns into a situation in which she should have just felt honored and grateful. But he left D.C. wanting to learn more about the arms race.

Returning home with his newfound concern, John hit a political void. When he went off to the University of Southern Mississippi the next fall, few students seemed interested in such issues. John knew of no local groups addressing them, and no individuals. He ended up keeping his questions to himself, then barely noticed as they faded away.

In fact, several faculty at the Southern Mississippi campus were interested in issues of global war and peace. And some time later, a group of socially concerned students coalesced around a campus AIDS benefit. But to John, the school seemed wholly isolated and apathetic. He hadn't known where to look.

Some colleges are more politically quiescent than others. Yet until the nascent turn toward concern of the early 1990s, I heard similar explanations of retreat throughout the country. "If I were only at Michigan or Berkeley," students would say, "I'd join in for sure." "I wish I were at Yale or Wesleyan, where people care." "If I was just near Washington, D.C., or had a car . . ." These explanations came from small-town colleges where "problems seem far away and you really can't do anything," from schools in entrenched conservative communities where "if you speak out here, they call you un-American," and from urban commuter campuses where "everyone works and drives straight off to their jobs." They even came from elite residential colleges, including campuses romanticized at other schools as radical meccas. These students, too, talked of "a sort of bubble of insulation," beyond which the outside world receded in the distance.

It's frustrating to want to act but to find no context. It's frustrating to try to speak out against the current, only to be stereotyped and dismissed. I respect greatly students who worked to forge the first necessary steps toward concern, who persisted even when others of like mind seemed few. Yet most students use talk of isolation not to describe the frustrations of trying to act for change but to justify retreat—to shore up their more general belief that if peers were involved, they were elsewhere, far away.

From the mid-1970s to the late 1980s, isolation set the dominant campus tone. Colleges, by and large, were politically quiet. Surveys found dramatic downturns in the numbers of incoming students who wanted to participate in environmental or community action programs, or who valued goals beyond material success. Most instead focused overwhelmingly on their careers. Even where campus or community activism occurred, the major media rarely covered it, so only those involved enough to tap into alternative information sources got much of a sense that anyone else in their generation cared.

### I don't think it's worth it

Politically involved students place large public issues at the center of their lives. Their apolitical counterparts view these same issues as abstract and remote. During a visit to Dartmouth, I crossed paths with visiting speaker Elizabeth Linder, the activist mother of a twenty-seven-year-old University of Washington engineering graduate who was murdered by Nicaraguan contras while working on a dam. I asked two students I was interviewing whether they'd considered going to hear her. They said they probably wouldn't. "It's just something that doesn't directly affect me," explained a junior named Bryan. "Maybe we're drawn into ourselves a little more than people were twenty years ago. But if you take her son's life, he died in El Salvador, no, Nicaragua. As I see my life right now, it just has no bearing."

Bryan lived less for material dreams than many. He made it a point to regularly take classes "just because they look interesting," regardless of how they might contribute to his career. Yet the very autonomy he prized set him in opposition to political involvement. "If you think you can't control things," he said, "you probably won't worry about them. The more interesting question, though, is whether I should radically change the way I live my life to do something about any of these issues. And pragmatically, I don't think it's worth it."

We talked of recent campus demonstrations around South African divestment, and about antiapartheid shanties that right-wing students from the *Dartmouth Review* had burned down. "It's all just a tennis match," Bryan commented. "Watching these people yell at these people, yell at those people. I think the general consensus is not to get involved. Students see it all as more closed-mindedness."

"The apartheid issue was particularly strange," added Bryan's friend Peter, who joined us in an elegantly paneled lounge near a main student eating area. "They wanted to get the college to divest because that would help end apartheid in South Africa, which is questionable. What bothered me, though, was that because I wasn't marching for companies to take their holdings out, everybody who did assumed I was against divestment, for apartheid, and a racist, right here on this campus. I had a little trouble with that. I became almost rebelliously apathetic."

Bryan talked further about the "marchers with their marcher face on," then paused for a moment and reflected. "I don't know why I put in three or four hours a day on the crew team," he continued, "but won't write my congressman or a government that's torturing someone to ask, 'Why the hell are you doing this?' Maybe I just don't want to get involved."

"I know for me," said Peter, "I might still be reacting to high school. I spent it racing from activity to activity, whether with the yearbook, my athletic teams, an Amnesty chapter, or the chorus, I got here . . ." He stopped to take a breath, ". . . and just wanted to sit in the woods, look at the trees, and wander around with no particular destination."

"Is there anything that would involve you?" I asked.

"I don't know," Peter responded. "I joined a pro-fraternity march, because I'm in one, we were under attack, and it felt like the right thing to do at the time. I don't know if it had any impact. But on causes like the South Africa shanties, I've gotten wary. I don't know what people could do to get me involved. Maybe it would have to be personal. I'm getting awfully tired of fliers in my mail box."

Politically engaged students succeed best when they enlist broad support beyond their core numbers. They have to constantly reach out. Yet when they do, skeptical peers accuse them of trying to mandate particular passions as universal concerns. "I've always wanted just to get on with my life," said a student at Western Michigan University. "And I feel you guys get mad at us for not being active. I don't get mad at you if you want to change your carpet from red to blue and I don't approve. That's your choice. I don't tell you what to do or how to act. But when you want me to pay attention to your cause and I don't, you look at me like 'He's a jerk.'"

Educator and theologian Paulo Freire describes a "culture of silence" that emerges when individuals are denied the opportunity to reflect on their situation and to participate in shaping their destinies. Instead, Freire writes, their voice becomes merely an echo of the powerful, of the dominant voices of their time.

Equivalent silences on American campuses leave students who try to act on what they believe in a bind. Nothing has threatened their peers so dramatically as the draft and the Vietnam War threatened a previous generation. More recent shifts to greater concern are related to a growing sense of crisis around issues like environmental degradation, threats to abortion choice, the crumbling of America's cities, and the skyrocketing costs of education. Yet most students still feel uneasy challenging social wrongs. And the less these issues are discussed, the more they recede from view.

Those who try to break this prevailing silence risk being tarred as evangelists. Should they succeed, and mobilize hundreds, hostile students call it "just a fad" or "part of a group mentality." If they draw out only the loyal few, these same critics dismiss them as marginal. "When I see a march on the Dartmouth green," said Peter, "I pretty much know who's going to be there, whether for divestment, or against CIA recruiting, or whatever. There's a certain group who've been involved in every protest since freshman fall. It's OK to feel strongly on many issues, but it undermines them when they constantly go from one to another." Most marched, he believed, "just for the sake of marching."

The adapters call politically engaged students self-serving. They say they plead the causes of peace, the environment, or the poor—yet really want just power or attention. Of course, any group will include individuals who are ego-bound, intolerant, and who seek largely to prove their moral righteousness. But the adapters damn those who make claims on the common conscience, regardless of their actual strengths or weaknesses of character. They do so not because they've known scores of activists who've proven themselves craven and hypocritical, but because they've bought into prevailing myths that levy these judgments against all who question America's dominant political and economic arrangements.

They end up blaming the ills of their schools and of America not on institutional choices that promote short-sightedness, callousness, or greed, but on the citizen efforts that challenge them.

## The good that they do

Apolitical students, far more than those politically involved, tend to trust America's leaders. Atomic weapons workers I studied for my book *Nuclear Culture* used the phrase "the men who know best" to describe those to whom they delegated the choice of whether or not the bombs they built were necessary. Students of the eighties and nineties grew up in a time that encouraged similar unquestioning faith. They witnessed presidents deriding even token congressional participation in shaping national policy, as when Reagan exclaimed after losing a vote on contra aid, "We have got to get to where we can run a foreign policy without a committee of 535 telling us what we can do." National media constantly celebrated the wealthy and powerful, rarely asking how ordinary citizens might have a say in shaping the common future. If even senators were granted little right to challenge the president, and history was to be made exclusively by those at the top, it's understandable why nineteen-year-old sophomores might feel intimidated.

Some students approved of this antidemocratic current, or accepted its premises as necessary. Fairfield University's George Lipson praised Reagan "because he uplifted our national morale and was a strong figure who made our opinion of ourselves a whole lot better." "We have to leave policy to the specialists," said a University of Minnesota student, "They're the ones who've studied it and made it their careers." "The world would be lots better off," suggested a University of Michigan engineering major, "if people attended to their own work."

In an upper division government class at Saint Joseph's College, I mentioned the 1973 CIA-assisted overthrow of Salvador Allende's democratically elected government in Chile. Only one of the forty students knew the coup had occurred—consistent with responses I'd been getting at other schools—but several nonetheless defended it. It did sound appalling, they agreed. "But there must have been something going on that we don't know. Maybe Chile was shipping drugs or supplying terrorists with arms. I can't see us overthrowing a government or assassinating a leader without a reason." A Dartmouth student defended the Reagan-era CIA in similar terms: "Maybe we just don't know the good that they do."

Surveys throughout the 1980s suggested a substantial number of America's young felt an obligation to believe that those in charge were doing their best. A 1987 Times Mirror study found young adults eighteen to thirty years old the least likely of any generation to criticize business or government for lack of responsibility. In a poll two years later, this group more than any other believed Ronald Reagan would go down in history as "an outstanding or above average president." "We've been taught," explained an Indiana woman, "that God is in control, our leaders are in control, and there's nothing we can do."

### Marshmallows and wieners

Stereotypes suggest that student separation from politics stems from active conservatism. If most don't identify with liberal-left causes, why should they get involved? Yet, even in the depoliticized heart of the 1980s, surveys showed students consistently disagreeing with the Republican thrust of expanding the military, attacking sexuality, and allowing an increasingly corporatized global economy to hold sway. The students disagreed on virtually every major policy, even as many embraced Reagan's image of "morning in America."

As a result, conservative student activists found little campus support for their efforts. They hit both specific disagreements around issues and the general antipathy to politics. At the University of Texas, San Antonio, a self-described "staunch young Reaganite" complained that his peers seemed to care about no ideas at all "except how to grub best for the almighty dollar." At a Williams environmental studies seminar, the head of the Young Republicans told a leading campus radical, "No one takes our leaflets either." Williams students, he said, wanted "moderation, the mainstream," were wary of political causes, and mistrusted all sources less respectable than the *Washington Post* and *New York Times*.

National surveys confirmed this mistrust. From the early seventies to the early eighties, the number of students calling themselves "liberal" or "far left" dropped nearly in half before rebounding at the decade's end. Yet the numbers of self-defined conservatives increased only slightly, even at their peak in the early eighties. The real gain was in students who called themselves "middle of the road."

The media has made much of a new crop of campus conservatives, such as *Dartmouth Review* editors who made national headlines by burning an antiapartheid shanty, harassing a black music professor until he quit, and attacking women's studies, affirmative action, minority scholarships, and all other manifestations of what they called a decline in their school's traditional values. Yet the prominence of the *Review* and similar campus publications did not come from widespread student embrace of their viewpoints or journalistic integrity. It came, rather, from massive outside support spearheaded by the money and contacts of a consortium of right-wing foundations that included Scaife, Bradley, John M. Olin, Smith-Richardson, Coors, Earhart, and the corporate foundation of Mobil Oil, as well as conservative alumni.

I'll discuss later the role of these foundations in whipping up media hysteria around "political correctness." For now, it's worth noting that, working through the Institute for Educational Affairs (which later became the Madison Center for Educational Affairs), they helped fund over seventy conservative campus papers, with the John M. Olin Foundation alone giving the *Dartmouth Review* over $300,000 during the 1980s. Their networks supported and nurtured young conservatives, linking them up with legal and journalistic advice, financial support in the form of donations and joint ads, and jobs and internships at conservative publications and think tanks and in government offices. These same foundations also poured millions of dollars into endowed chairs for conservative professors. They joined with the Reagan-Bush administrations and allied networks of right-wing intellectuals and activists to give college conservatives a clout and status vastly disproportionate to either their minimal intellectual contributions or the degree of their campus support.

When I visited Dartmouth in 1987, staffers were regularly leaving copies of the *Review* in the halls of the dorms. One day, while students in the dorm where I was staying were partying and listening to Jimi Hendrix, a man lit a match to one of the stacks. The papers caught fire, triggering the alarms, and the student and his friends threw the burning copies out the window onto the concrete plaza below. As fire marshals cleared the halls, a crowd gathered by the stacks of flaming papers, talking and laughing as if at any fine October bonfire.

Just that afternoon, dorm residents had voiced their mistrust of peers involved in a planned march to challenge U.S. intervention in El Salvador. They were equally skeptical of others who'd built anti-apartheid shanties on the quad. But they seemed perfectly delighted about the burning of the *Review,* joking how someone should get marshmallows and wieners, and more copies of the newspaper to feed the fire. Whether politics was left or right, rhetorical or reasoned, they kept their distance.

Even students who admired Reagan and Bush rarely seemed stirred by their specific prescriptions. Particularly as supply-side dreams began to crumble, students less and less praised the vision, wisdom, or courage of America's leaders. Instead they insisted we had no choice but to trust those in charge. "Bush tries," they said, repeatedly. "He's doing the best he can." "If you could meet Ronald Reagan, he'd give you the shirt off his back." "I know Barbara Bush really cares." Until the U.S. economy blatantly collapsed in the early

1990s, and student activism rose, they continued to excuse all manner of dubious actions by America's leaders, insisting that what really mattered was whether they were personally kind.

## The perfect standard

Apolitical students alternate between feeling they have no right to challenge "the men who know best," and a forgiveness so all encompassing they find it impossible to hold institutions accountable. They respond to their activist peers, in contrast, with unforgiving judgments, holding up a Perfect Standard that the activists must meet before they will tender their support. They require politically involved peers to know every fact, reference every figure, be eloquent enough to debate Henry Kissinger on *Nightline,* yet remain constantly humble and self-effacing. Maybe then, they suggest, they'll take their arguments seriously.

Mistrust of activism often accompanies faith in those who wield power. "Say you're walking down the street," explained an education major from Minnesota's Mankato State University, "and someone asks you to sign a petition. You'd be reluctant because you don't know enough. Activists at the rallies take a look at what's going on in the country, and immediately find fault with it. But they aren't well informed. The people who are running things, the heads of the corporations, they understand the whole picture. They know what they're doing and are doing it for a reason."

Other students mistrust both groups. It angered a Dartmouth student in an arms control class when, at a campus forum, neither a Defense Department representative nor local peace activists could tell him the accurate range of Soviet SS 20 missiles. "Why is it that a twenty-one-year-old Dartmouth student has been able to discover this, but not the policy makers? The government doesn't know what it's talking about. The peace groups don't either. Nobody knows the facts." This student knew his weapons technologies better than many who acted to challenge them. Yet to insist that citizens understand every policy detail before taking a stand allows them no ethical basis for judgment except technical knowledge.

Some of this is information overload. Too many cable channels. Too many crises. Too many authorities with competing, clashing claims. But to hold to a perfect standard is ultimately a way of reserving judgment not only on any given issue or controversy, but on the entire prospect of taking responsibility for the future.

This standard demands not only perfect intellectual consistency, but flawless moral piousness. At Saint Benedict College in northern Minnesota, a half dozen students slept out in makeshift cardboard shelters to dramatize the plight of America's homeless.

"Lots who passed by treated us like a slumber party," one participant recalled. "They acted like we were so cute, then when we kept on for a couple days they began to get annoyed. One girl yelled, 'Homeless people don't have blankets.' I was half asleep and told her, 'Yes they do. They have blankets and friends. They just don't have homes.' She looked like she'd only be satisfied if we stood outside and got soaked in the freezing rain."

If the radicals are truly sincere, this sensibility insists, they'll sleep in their shacks without blankets. They'll "sell their cars and give the money to Africa," as suggested by the University of Washington woman who called them "the granolas." They'll prove their commitment with vows of poverty, and never get foolish or frivolous. But the watchers also accuse them of being too "ultraserious" and holy. Maybe they'd get involved, they explain, if activists had a better sense of humor.

The Perfect Standard creates an abstract hierarchy of issues, in which the causes at hand never quite muster up. "I think South Africa is a reprehensible situation," a Columbia student said, "and maybe I should have made my actions correspond more to my beliefs when they were trying to get the school to divest. But when I watched people protesting, I thought, 'How paradoxical. They're so fervent about how awful it is over there, yet they aren't doing much for immediate situations, like racial issues here at home.'"

Why then, I asked, didn't he get involved when students took on precisely that set of questions two years later? "It all seemed diluted," he responded. "It wasn't so much standing up for fair housing or racial justice. It was almost like standing up for being a liberal or radical. Like the chance to be a protestor supersedes the issue itself."

Students used such arguments not only to challenge peers who acted, but to beat down their own impulses toward concern. "I get a little fearful," said a woman in the Mankato State education class, "when someone approaches me and I don't have enough knowledge about the subject. Instead of diving in and trying to learn about it afterward, I tend to ignore it. We feel we need to know so much just to understand what people are talking about."

A Clarkson student feared political involvement would make him "part of a mob. You'd have no say and lose your individualism." He'd just finished describing his hopes to work for IBM. I asked how much individuality he'd retain as part of that global multinational. "I don't worry about that," he said. "They break things down into different divisions."

Apolitical students also believed they had to agree with each and every aspect of any issue they took on—or else be exposed themselves as inconsistent. At Minnesota's Saint Olaf college, some activists held a "gay jeans day"—one of many nationwide—where students asked peers to support gay and lesbian rights by wearing the clothes they'd most often put on in any case. Some did, either because they were gay or acted in solidarity. Others wore the same clothes as always, then explained sheepishly that they hadn't intended this as a statement. Distressingly large numbers turned preppie.

I was struck by one woman who strongly believed in gay rights, but balked at gays adopting children. Because of that exception, she felt she couldn't wear jeans in support. She saw no way to endorse what she generally believed in, even though she could have readily enough have explained her own particular take on the gay adoption issue if it came up in conversation.

A political science major at Columbia described how she considered getting involved in a series of campus issues, but each time held back. She sat out the school's highly successful antiapartheid campaign, although many of her friends took part. She almost joined a fight over the eviction of a Latina tenant from a Columbia-owned apartment, "but I wasn't sure of my information." She was interested in homelessness, "but you can always doubt conflicting sources." She rejected cause after cause, down to her final conclusion, "I guess I'm just not a political person."

In contrast to more hostile others, she admired political commitment. But she exempted herself from responsibility. She described herself accurately, as did others who explain, "I'm not that kind of person" or "I'm just not the kind who speaks out." These students do hold back from marches, rallies, electoral campaigns, issue-oriented courses, controversial speakers, or any other form of social involvement. They do shy away from trying to change the world. Yet their phrases also reflect deeper assumptions. They draw an absolute line separating the rare few who emerge from the womb with protest signs in their hands and the reasonable majority who leave, and always will leave, these troublesome common issues to others. They judge activists and adapters as fundamentally different human breeds, with the dividing lines never to be crossed.

Character differences and differences in upbringing do play a role in political involvement. Some students, especially men from comfortable professional backgrounds, have been groomed for center stage, and eagerly speak their piece. Others, shy by nature or nurture—including family, class, or gender socialization—may require initial forms of engagement more gentle to their souls. As a Columbia woman said, "I guess I just don't like hearing my voice too loud. I don't speak out in my courses either." But if an entire generation consider themselves so fragile they dare not act as citizens, we cannot write this off to individual upbringings or circumstances.

Fear of speaking unwisely mixes with fear of consequences. "It's almost like, if I make an action," said a man in the Mankato State education class, "then I'm responsible for it. I have to justify it. If I go in and take a side, I'm risking my comfort zone. If I'm wrong, I might be scapegoated."

The students in this class were future teachers, preparing to train a new generation. A woman began to raise her hand, then said she hadn't intended to speak. When I asked if she had any reactions, she mentioned how much she feared creating conflict. "If you have a job in a school and you conform to what the administration wants, they like you. People want to be liked. You might lose job security by doing something different."

"Teachers already struggle for respect," the first speaker continued. He suggested that controversial stands would erode his credibility, and concluded "It's so much easier and safer to keep quiet."

---

## Now that you've read

1. What did Loeb learn as he talked to students around the country about their levels of political involvement?
2. According to Loeb, what prevents some students from speaking out?
3. What do you make of the young woman's statement that "We've been taught . . . that God is in control, our leaders are in control, and there's nothing we can do"?
4. Where do you place yourself among the different positions represented? Why?

## READING 3

### *Alexander W. Astin*

# The Cause of Citizenship

In this article, which originally appeared in *The Chronicle of Higher Education,* Alexander W. Astin is concerned over what he sees as a decline in Americans' understanding and appreciation of democratic values. In particular, he is worried that most of us no longer understand what it means to be a good citizen. See whether you agree with his analysis of the problem and his suggestions for what it will take to "turn things around."

### *Before you read*

1. What do you think are the key elements of citizenship?
2. What makes a person a "good" citizen?
3. Do you think of yourself as a good citizen? Why or why not?
4. How would you feel if your college were to implement a program to educate its students about the responsibilities of citizenship? How do you think your classmates would respond?

---

Something is terribly wrong with the state of American democracy. Most citizens don't vote, negative campaigning reigns, and public distrust, contempt, and hostility toward "government" have reached unprecedented heights. Student interest and engagement in politics are at all-time lows, according to the most recent surveys that we have done at the Higher Education Research Institute at the University of California at Los Angeles. While academics occasionally comment on this sorry state of affairs, they seldom suggest that higher education may have played a part in creating these problems, or that it can or should do anything about them.

Most of us probably think of democracy primarily as an *external* process, in which people do such things as discussing public-policy issues, campaigning for candidates, and voting. While these activities are indeed important elements of a healthy democracy, none is likely to occur in the absence of appropriate *internal* conditions: an understanding of how democratic government is supposed to function, an appreciation of the individual's responsibilities under this form of government, and a willingness, if not a determination, to be an active participant. In other words, a person is more likely to become an active citizen if he or she has acquired certain knowledge, beliefs, and values. Such intellectual qualities are precisely the ones that educational institutions are in an ideal position to foster.

The problem for us in higher education is that we have not done a very good job of developing a solid understanding and appreciation of democracy in our students. Many of my faculty colleagues might argue that the failure or success of our representative democracy is not higher education's responsibility or concern, but they forget that promoting "good citizenship" is one of the most commonly stated values in the mission statements of our colleges and universities. We are on record as committing ourselves and our institutions to the value of promoting good citizenship.

But comprehending our democracy involves a lot more than knowing what's in the Constitution and being able to describe the three branches of government. The poor condition of our democracy today is a product of complex forces that have little to do with what we learn in high-school civics courses. Those forces include broad economic and corporate trends, the influence of lobbyists, financing of political campaigns, and the role of the mass media.

We need to help all students—not just political-science majors—understand how our system actually works today. Take the most basic of all ingredients in any functioning democratic system: *information.* Even the most elementary understanding of how a democratic political system is supposed to operate recognizes its central role: A democracy works only to the extent that the voter is well informed. And if citizens really understood and appreciated the importance of information to our system, I believe that they would take a much greater interest in learning about the mass media.

The majority of Americans, for example, get their political news from primetime TV newscasts. That this particular medium is *not* doing an acceptable job is revealed in a disturbing finding from a survey conducted during the last Presidential campaign: It showed that the more people relied on TV for their news, the less they knew about the three major Presidential candidates.

Our educational system should help students to become better critics and analysts of contemporary mass media and of the political information they produce. Most faculty members put a high premium on the development of students' "critical thinking" skills, but we still have a long way to go before we can say that we are producing graduates who have sufficient critical understanding of the media *and* the motivation to demand better information. I'm reminded here of a wonderful little book by Neil Postman and Charles Weingartner called *Teaching as a Subversive Activity* (Dell, 1987), in which they argue that in an information society heavily dependent on commercial mass media, an important function of education should be to help young people become expert "crap detectors." Given what we see happening in contemporary politics, the need to develop those capabilities in our students has never been greater.

What kind of new "citizenship curriculum" would help students become better-informed and more-involved participants in the democratic process? First, students need to understand that the media that produce most of their political "news" are large businesses run for profit. In this very basic sense, then, the news media do not really play the role of critical mavericks traditionally assigned to them. Rather, they are an integral part of the business community and therefore subject to the same pressures, values, and motivations that govern the operation of any other large business: marketing, competition, profit.

News media become profitable by selling advertising and by getting as many people as possible to read, listen to, or watch what they produce; the more people they attract, the more they can charge their advertisers. As a result, we shouldn't be surprised if they try to avoid offending the thousands of corporate advertisers on whom they are so dependent for revenue.

Institutions will have their own appropriate ways to educate students about these facts, but several alternatives come to mind. What about an interdisciplinary freshman seminar that contrasts the theory of representative democracy with the role actually played by the various media today in informing or misinforming citizens? What about a required seminar for all students that focuses directly on the news media (especially television) and their impact on our thinking about and engagement in, or disengagement from, politics?

In designing our citizenship curricula, we also need to consider the possibility that our students' alienation from government may be symptomatic of larger societal forces that tend to promote the values of individualism, materialism, and competitiveness over the values of community, service, and cooperation. These latter values, of course, are central to any democracy: We pool our wisdom when we vote, and we pool our resources through taxes so that we can receive services and benefits that we cannot obtain on our own. Uninformed citizens are bamboozled by rhetoric denigrating "bureaucracy" and "tax and spend" government, as if there were some other more responsible way for government to function. Informed citizens, by contrast, understand that the real issues are how tax money actually is spent and who pays how much in taxes. Informed citizens will demand that their politicians design tax and budget policies that will address the nation's real problems.

Our students, then, need to be taught how to inform themselves so that they can formulate the right questions. How about taking a hard look at our journalism-and-communications programs with this idea in mind? All told, these programs graduate thousands of students each year, many of whom will help determine what their fellow citizens learn from the media. How much emphasis does each of these programs put on training its students to understand the most important questions citizens should ask concerning public issues—as opposed to training them to pursue the most obvious or sensational facets of a story?

Why has higher education failed for so long to make good on its professed commitment to promote citizenship? Many institutions are caught up in the "pursuit of excellence," which usually means competing to acquire as many resources as possible and jockeying to build up their reputations so that they move up the pecking order among similar institutions. Those traditional approaches to excellence can lead us to ignore academe's own "citizenship" responsibilities, embodied in our basic purposes of teaching and public service. It is not that we don't *need* reputations or resources, but rather that the efforts to achieve them can become ends in themselves, leading us to forget that they ultimately should contribute to improving the education and service we provide.

Just as excessive materialism and narcissism can interfere with the individual's ability to be a good citizen, so can an academic institution's preoccupation with acquisitiveness and self-aggrandizement interfere with its ability to be a good citizen in the community of institutions and in the larger society.

If we want our students to acquire the democratic virtues of honesty, tolerance, empathy, generosity, teamwork, and social responsibility, we have to demonstrate those qualities not only in our individual professional conduct, but also in our institutional policies and practices. To emphasize the importance of these democratic virtues, why not begin a campus-wide effort to determine how citizenship and democracy can be given a more central place in the general-education curriculum? And why not explore how we might integrate "service learning" into the general educational program—beyond the scattered courses or internships in which it may be emphasized now?

Some of my academic colleagues might argue that "a traditional liberal education" is the best way to prepare young people for the responsibilities of citizenship. While there may be some truth in that argument, the uncomfortable reality is that whatever we are currently providing—call it liberal learning if you like—simply isn't getting the job done. Most of our citizenry—and that includes most of our college-educated citizenry—seems neither to understand what democracy is all about nor to accept responsibility for making it work.

And for people who might think that we in higher education have no real power to strengthen American democracy, consider the following: We educate a large proportion of the citizens who bother to vote, not to mention most of the politicians, journalists, and news commentators. We also educate all of the school administrators and teachers, who in turn educate everyone at the pre-college level. And we do much to shape the pre-college curriculum through what we require of our college applicants. In short, not only have we helped to create the problems that plague American democracy, but we are also in a position to begin doing something about them.

If higher education doesn't start giving citizenship and democracy much greater priority, who will? Corporate business? The news media? Politicians? How can we ever expect the democratic dream to become a reality unless education changes its priorities? The future of American democracy is, to a certain extent, in our hands, and if we want to improve it, we have to change some of our ways of doing business.

In light of the reduced budgets and other external pressures that many of us face today, it is fair to ask whether we have the wherewithal to undertake any such initiatives as citizenship development. I would argue that most of the educational resources and personnel needed to develop a greater emphasis on educating citizens for democracy already exist on campus; educators just need to recognize that they have the capacity to draw those resources and personnel together in new and creative ways. Citizenship development should not be considered an "add on," to be pursued only if new money ever becomes available. Rather, it needs to be viewed as an integral part of the educational program.

The academic autonomy that we constantly seek to protect may be the most powerful tool that we have for refocusing our programs to better promote democracy and citizenship. The fact remains that, despite increased public attacks on colleges in recent years, we still retain control over practically all of the decisions that really matter: whom to admit and how to admit them; what to teach and how to teach it; how to assess and evaluate our students; how to structure extracurricular programs; what subject matter we choose for our research; and how we hire, reward, and tenure our colleagues.

If we genuinely believe that it is in our own best interests—not to mention those of our students and of the society that supports us—to introduce a focus on democracy and citizenship into our curriculum and other campus activities, we have both the autonomy and the intellectual skill to do it.

---

## Now that you've read

1. What do you think Alexander W. Astin's strongest arguments are? Why? Which do you think are his weakest? Why?
2. Astin asks, "Why has higher education failed for so long to make good on its professed commitment to promote citizenship?" How do you respond to this question from your perspective as a student in a particular college?
3. He suggests that colleges find ways to "explore how we might integrate 'service learning' into the general educational program." What do you think he means by service learning?
4. Do you consider yourself to be an expert "crap detector"? Why is that, or why is it not, a worthwhile goal?

## READING 4

*Paul Berman*

# The Moral History of the Baby Boom Generation

Paul Berman's book *A Tale of Two Utopias,* from which this reading is an excerpt, focuses on the political events and circumstances around the world that led so many young people to question the status quo and take action against it in 1968. In this reading, Berman helps us understand the politics of the 1960s in richer, more complicated ways.

### Before you read

1. What do you see as the main problems or important issues on your campus? Is there an issue that might move students to sit in or demonstrate publicly in some form or another?
2. Has your campus ever been the site of demonstrations? When? Over what?

I

Every few decades, a pure flame of political rebellion shoots up somewhere and with amazing speed spreads in all directions, until half the countries on earth have been scorched.

The first time such a thing happened was in the American Revolution of 1776, though in that instance the flame, spreading with less than amazing speed, took thirteen years before reaching as far away as France. But then, yes, the main ideas of the American and French revolutions went leaping fairly quickly across whole regions of Europe and even into the distant exotic zones of colonial Latin America, until a good many countries on three continents were undergoing republican agitations and experiments with constitutional government, which was a wildly revolutionary thing to have happen. A clearer example of the same phenomenon took place in 1848. An insurrection broke out in Paris. That time the uprising invoked the ideals of liberal nationalism and hinted at socialism, too—and within a few months, powerful movements affirming those same ideas swept across Germany, the Austrian Empire, Italy, Spain, and several other countries, not always with the same heat or intensity.

A few radical sparks spread all the way to the United States. A republican uprising shook the Seneca nation of America in 1848, which is odd to consider. The first convention for women's rights assembled in upstate New York.

The uprisings that broke out in 1917 showed the same pattern. There was an idea of constructing a new socialist society on the basis of locally organized workers' councils. The workers' councils arose in St. Petersburg under the name of "soviets." Then, when the First World War came to an end, the councils spread to Germany, Hungary, Italy, Spain, and several other countries. The faraway city of Seattle, Washington, underwent a general strike in 1919, and even there, in Wild West America, the strikers took over the management of the town, as if in distant lunar reflection of St. Petersburg's insurrectionary events. Still another example took place in 1936–38, that time in the form of trade union movements and factory takeovers. The union takeovers spread across France (the Popular Front agitations), Spain (the anarchosyndicalist revolution), the American Midwest (the rise of the CIO), and a few other places, too. And if you keep in mind the historical pattern of those several revolutionary upheavals, it's obvious that student rebellions in the years around 1968 should count as one more instance of the same mysterious phenomenon, except on a bigger geographical scale than ever before.

The student movements rose up all over Western Europe and in parts of Central and Eastern Europe, parts of North and West Africa, all over the United States, Mexico, Central and South America, the Caribbean, Japan, and the Philippines. You could point to China, where student insurrections played a big role in the Great Proletarian Cultural Revolution during the entire period from 1966 to 1976. Yet in the case of 1968, as in every instance back to 1848 and even back to 1776, it's hard to understand how so many rebellions could have taken place at the same time. There were some obvious causes of tension around the world: the Vietnam War and the anti-colonial revolutions, the theological reforms within the Catholic Church, the rise of the hippies, new styles in pop music, the civil rights movements and the race riots in the United States, a few eye-opening indications of discontent in the Soviet empire.

Each of those events created a pressure, which made for excitement, which sometimes was exhilarating. But it's hard to see what turned the excitement into rebellion, or what could have caused the rebellion to spread around the world. In 1968 no single, great trauma was devastating the world economy or putting an unbearable strain on the young. Social conditions were entirely different from one country to the next. It's hard even to identify a common ideology or doctrine in the '68 rebellions. We had our own beliefs in the student movement in the United States, but in the Eastern

Bloc the students clung to beliefs that were quite different. In some places the student movement leaned toward Communism, and in other places, leaned away. In France the students managed to lean in both directions at once.

How to explain those many simultaneous uprisings, then? You could argue (A) that student rebellions broke out around the world circa 1968 for reasons of pure coincidence, and in each country the causes were local, and no larger phenomenon needs to be explained. But that was not how it felt in 1968. The student rebels in different parts of the world definitely recognized one another, felt themselves to be part of a worldwide movement, adopted one another's slogans. Alternatively, you could argue (B) that a desire for freedom is deeply rooted, and when desire turns to rebellion in any part of the world, people in other places will look at the rebels and recognize their own feelings and will feel prompted to stage uprisings of their own—even if freedom in one country is pictured as Communism and in another country as anti-Communism. Hannah Arendt devoted several moving passages of her book *On Revolution* to expounding a version of that idea. You could argue (C) that a desire to wreak havoc is just as deeply rooted, and may spread in exactly the same way. Unfortunately, both (B) and (C), the desire for freedom and the desire for havoc, are exceedingly vague as explanations of human behavior. And so the best way to understand what occurred would seem to be (D) to look for common features among the separate movements, in the hope that common features will point to a common motive.

What were the common features in the rebellions of circa 1968? Everyone will agree that in each country the students followed their own national traditions, and one country's uprising was never exactly like another's. And yet, in quite a few places there was, as everyone recognized at the time, a common theme. It was the split between the young and the old. In the Great Proletarian Cultural Revolution of China, the generational split was not quite genuine, and behind the rampaging young Red Guards stood some very old Reds from the Communist leadership. But in other places the split between the young and the old was exactly what it seemed to be—a sharp split in the United States and Western Europe, less sharp in other regions, yet clear enough for the young people to identify with one another across the borders. And if you look a little closer, still another common trait looms into focus.

It is the story of how the split between the generations, taken as a political disagreement, got its earliest start. In one country after another, the split made its first appearance in the early and mid-1960s, as a fairly obscure argument deep within the ranks of the old working-class parties of the left. No more than a handful of people were ever involved. The brightest young people in the old left-wing parties or in their youth affiliates somehow got into a dispute with the adult leaders of their own organization. The arguments grew testy. Finally the irritated adults grabbed a few of the uncooperative young people by the hair and grandly expelled them from the organized ranks of the international left—only to gaze out the window a few years later, circa 1968, to see those same uncooperative young troublemakers marching through the street with fists in the air and several hundred thousand followers marching behind.

In West Germany in 1961, the student wing of the Social Democratic Party, the Sozialistische Deutsche Studentenbund (whose abbreviation happened to be SDS, just like the American student movement of the 1960s), fell out with the adult Social Democrats and was expelled. And by 1967 and '68, that same German SDS ended up leading the mass radical youth movement in West Germany. The split in France took place mostly within the French Communist Party. The party's student wing, the Communist Student Union, was led in Paris by young people from the Sorbonne. The young activists met with the Communist adults, and the meetings went so badly that by 1965 the adults felt they had no choice but to drive the uncooperative students out of the Communist movement together. A similar argument took place in the French Socialist Party. Then came 1968 and popular uprisings broke out in Paris and all over France, and the leaders were young people who had learned their politics in the little Parisian student world of the expelled Communists and the ex-Socialists.

Social and political conditions in Latin America—to leap across the hemispheres for a moment—were nothing like those in Western Europe. Yet in Mexico, where the most important of Latin America's 1968 movements took place, the split between young and old came about in exactly the same way. The semi-clandestine Mexican Communist Party stood at the center of the Mexican left, and at the center of the party's student organization, the Communist Youth, stood some very talented young people, including Gilberto Guevara Niebla and Ra l Alvarez Garín. The young people quarreled with their elders over the importance of student issues, which the adults were reluctant to acknowledge, and beginning in 1964 the young leaders either were expelled from the party or drifted away. Then came the uprisings of 1968, and three hundred thousand people were parading along the boulevards of Mexico City under the leadership of a National Strike Council based in the universities. And the two people who had founded that council and who figured throughout the uprising among its most prominent and revered leaders happened to be the ex-Communists Gilberto Guevara and Ra l Alvarez.

In other Latin American countries the split within the Communist movement took place earlier in the sixties and pitted pro-Cuban or pro-Chinese supermilitants against the traditional pro-Moscow leadership, who were more conservative. Generational issues were not so prominent; yet neither were they missing. There was the example of Nicaragua. The old-fashioned working-class party of the left was the Nicaraguan Socialist Party, which despite its name was Marxist-Leninist and pro-Moscow. In the 1950s a handful of middle-class students joined the party but couldn't get along with the traditional leaders, and in the early sixties the students—Carlos Fonseca, Tom s Borge, and a couple of others—put together their own organization. The year 1968 came and went in Nicaragua without a major rebellion by the student population. Yet the news from Mexico, France, and the United States had its effect on the Nicaraguan universities, and the tiny group that had broken away from the Nicaraguan Socialist Party began to flourish, and in 1970 the breakaway group—by then it was called the Sandinista National Liberation Front—succeeded, through its campus wing, in taking over the national student organization, and the 1968 phenomenon (a couple of years later) had taken place in Nicaragua, too.

The specific controversies or debates that led to the divisions between young and old in the traditional left-wing parties were different in each of these countries, as you would expect. And yet, if you peer still closer into the story of those splits, a single point of contention pops up over and over. The young people were eager for risk; the elders, not. Ultra-radicalism versus left-wing caution was the crucial division. Why were the young people so enamored of risky radicalism? Now, on this point it would make no sense to look for a single explanation, applicable to all countries. In a place like Nicaragua, risky radicalism was a logical political gamble, and people who took that gamble and threw themselves into guerrilla war had reason to think that, with perseverance and luck, they might win, and a revolution might break out, and they might end up as the new government—which in Nicaragua is exactly what happened, by 1979. But what could radical action expect to achieve in the stable, democratic, industrial countries? Neither patience nor impatience was going to make a revolution there. Whatever pushed the students into radical action could not have been political calculation in any ordinary sense.

Were the students pressured into radicalism by the special anxieties of university life in those days? All over the world during the sixties, the universities swelled in population but not necessarily in resources, which led to unhappy feelings and a lot of talk of "alienation." To cite the three countries where the '68 student movements were largest: In France, the student population increased by nearly 50 percent between 1960 and 1963. In Mexico, the student population tripled between 1964 and 1970. In the United States, the student population of the universities tripled between 1955 and 1970.

But then, it's not immediately obvious why crowded lecture halls and feelings of impersonality on campus (those were the fashionable complaints) would necessarily lead the students into left-wing adventures. Conceivably, the ever-increasing gap between the students and the faraway world of their professors and deans made it easier for the students to picture themselves as a distinct generation, and in that respect the growth of the student population may very well have contributed to the new political attitude. Yet the growth of the student population had little or nothing to do with the squabbles that broke out within the organizations of the traditional left. *Those* squabbles, the tiny left-wing disputes between young and old that anticipated the big student uprisings by a few years, can only be understood with a sympathetic glance at what it was like to be a student leftist in the early or middle 1960s and to find yourself sitting across the room from the adult leaders of the left-wing parties.

Exactly who were those student leftists, the ones who got the student movement underway? In Paris, for instance? The pioneers of the student movement there were not necessarily typical of the French university population. France is a Catholic country with a small Protestant minority and a Jewish population that has never risen above 1 percent of the total. Yet of the students who quarreled with their left-wing elders and who would later turn up as leaders of their own generation, a very high number came from Jewish backgrounds. These were people with not very pleasant family histories. The parents of those students, some of them, had spent the Nazi era living like hunted animals, fleeing from place to place, taking part in guerrilla actions when they could. Some of them had ended up in the Nazi camps; others, fleeing eastward from Poland, had ended up in the Soviet camps. The oldest among the children were born under extremely grim circumstances. Andr  Glucksmann, who as a young philosopher played a notable role in the uprisings of 1968 and after, was born in 1937 to immigrant parents who spent the war years as part of the Comintern's nucleus within the Resistance.

Jeanette Pienkny, the Trotskyist leader, born the year after Glucksmann, was seven years old by the time her father came home from a German prison. Another important Trotskyist student leader, Henri Weber, was born during the war in a Soviet camp. Pierre Goldman—the young man who, among the '68 generation in France, came to symbolize dedication to revolutionary action—was born during the war to immigrant parents who fought in a Jewish shock brigade of the Lyons-region Resistance. And so forth. Children with backgrounds like those were brought up during the postwar years in the kind of atmosphere that used to be called "militant." For most of those children, that meant the youth groups of the French Communist Party; for others, the Zionist-socialist youth movement Hashomer Hatzair (the Young Guard); in a handful of cases, the anarchist groups.

The children sang the songs and attended the festivals. They listened to the stories of what their parents had done during the war. They knew themselves to be the children of heroes and of people who had suffered. Their own childish lives, on the other hand, were singularly free of suffering or heroism, at least after their earliest years. They grew up during the greatest prolonged boom in the history of capitalism. Everything that the parents had lacked, the children came to possess: comfort, peace, security, democracy, education, opportunity. And as the children got older, the contrast between Marxist memories of the war and the comforts of the present was bound to cast a disagreeable light on their own young lives. For who were they, these children, compared to who their parents had been? For that matter, who were these parents by the 1960s? The old guerrilla heroes of the wartime Resistance who kept prattling to their children about Marxism and courage and the coming revolution and the feats of the past—these people had become, thanks to their own successes and the capitalist boom, middle-aged bourgeois who no longer meant a single word about revolutionary Marxism but did think the children ought to be grateful to have things so easy.

Not every young person growing up in circumstances like those would feel especially tortured by moral self-doubt or self-contempt. But there is a certain kind of young person for whom moral tortures are unavoidable, and the natural place for people like that is in a left-wing youth group. So the students who doubted themselves and worried about their own moral worth, once they had left home for school in Paris, drew together. They browsed at the Communist Party's bookstore and hung out at the editorial office of *Clart* , the party's youth magazine. They drank coffee at Le Champo caf , near the Sorbonne. And they said to themselves, as their elders would never have thought to say: I am privileged, therefore I am nothing. The chief chroniclers of the French student movement, Herv Hamon and Patrick Rotman, the authors of *G n ration,* have coined a phrase to describe what afflicted those anguished students. Some people suffer from an inferiority complex; these people suffered, on moral grounds, from an "illegitimacy complex."

The complex made them wonder if their own privileges weren't based on a lie. Their parents and the elders whom they met in the Communist Party (or in some of the other left-wing organizations) kept saying that life had become better and progress was at hand and, in the future, social conditions would continue to improve. The young people knew that, in regard to their own Parisian student lives, those statements were true. On the other hand, France in the 1960s was fighting an ugly colonial war against the Algerian nationalists, was it not? Soon enough the United States was fighting an exceedingly nasty anti-Communist war against the Vietnamese. Was life any better for the Algerians or the Vietnamese under the bombs of the Western Allies? Was the exploitation of Arab and African immigrant workers in France or of the black proletariat in the United States any different from the racist exploitation that had thrived in earlier times? Things *were* better; but only for oneself.

So the young people embarked on a reverse passion for the "other"—not a hatred for people who are different but a love for them, in eager acknowledgment of their very difference. Faraway solidarity became their religion. They said, in effect: I struggle on behalf of others, therefore I am. They conceived an idea of identity through action. It was a grand idea, morally. They imagined that, through radical action, they were going to revive the heroism and moral clarity of the old Resistance struggle against the Nazis. Pierre Goldman, in his memoirs, was explicit about it: "I think I was trying to recapture the time of my father, the time of my mother." But as soon as they tried to recapture the time of their parents in any kind of practical way, they ran into a terrible obstacle. It was the adult left. The grizzled leaders of the French Communist Party turned out to be people who felt not a single moral qualm about their own adult lives. On the topic of desperado actions by young leftists, the adults regarded themselves as supreme experts; and their expertise told them that in Gaullist France during the glory days of the economic boom, risk-taking adventures were a thing of the past. The young people wanted to aid the Algerian revolutionaries in their struggle against French colonialism; to lend military support to the guerrillas of Latin America; to do *something*. The adults flared their Communist nostrils, smelled petty-bourgeois adventurism, and gave the order "No." And so the young people looked at their elders and felt—contempt. They felt for their elders all the contempt that otherwise they might have felt for themselves, as the do-nothing heirs of heroes and martyrs.

The French children of Jewish Resistance heroes from the Second World War may have undergone these moral stresses with a particular intensity, which could explain why so many of them were quick to get into quarrels with the adult left. But nothing about their experience differed fundamentally from a lot of other people in the younger generation. Of the young French leftists who responded to the sixties cult of action by going to Latin America and joining the Marxist guerrillas, a couple of the better known were Jewish: there was Michelle Firk, who served with the Guatemalan guerrillas, and

Goldman, who spent some time with the guerrillas in Venezuela. But the most famous of all, certainly the most talented political writer of the generation, was R gis Debray, who was not Jewish. Debray was a student of the Communist philosopher Louis Althusser at an elite school in Paris, the  cole normale sup rieure. Debray, too, went to Venezuela to support the guerrilla revolution. By 1964 he was sending reports home to France, and his reports made it seem as if the old French Resistance were alive and well, fighting on in leafy Venezuela against U.S. imperialism (and against Venezuela's social democratic government) instead of against the Nazi occupiers from the European past. Debray expressed the worry of an entire generation in a famous remark about what would happen if the younger people did not, in fact, plunge into radical campaigns or join a revolutionary *maquis:* "After the veterans of Verdun, of Mauthausen [the Nazi death camp] and of Indochina, we will be the veterans of the cinemath que." That was not a small fear.

So the tiny handful of left-wing French students argued with the adult leftists about the need for action, and when the adults lost patience and expelled the young truculents from the official organizations (in the case of the Communist Student Union, this took place in 1965–66, in two waves), the young people went ahead and organized their own solidarity groups to aid the Marxist guerrillas of Latin America. They made pilgrimages to the Venezuelan countryside, to Communist Cuba, to insurrectionary Algeria, and to China. They formed underground Trotskyist support channels for the Algerian nationalists. They discovered that adult backing was unnecessary. That was the fateful revelation. Students who were five or ten years younger began to follow their example. The younger students staged a thousand provocations and classroom coups d' tat. Impudence became their signature. In 1967 a squad of young militants attacked the American Express office in Paris on behalf of the Vietnamese Communists. Groups of young people were soon enough engaged in disputes with the university administration at Nanterre, outside of Paris.

A Nanterre sit-in got under way, then another at the Sorbonne. And the handful of young people suddenly discovered that when they issued calls for a political demonstration tens of thousands of their peers showed up to participate. They acted, and the vibrations penetrated into the student population. For to be young and morally troubled in 1968 was to feel, at least in a small way, the same painful doubts and anxieties that the tiny handful of Jewish and non-Jewish left-wing youth activists had begun to express a few years earlier in their battles with the left-wing elders. It was to feel morally worthless in the face of what the parents' generation had gone through—or had gone along with. And it was to feel contempt

for what the parents had become. The young people wanted to re-
deem their souls. They wanted to leave behind the privileges and
comforts of middle-class student life and go fight in the street and
in the universities for a better world, just the way the heroes of the
Resistance had gone into the street to fight against the Nazis.

You hardly needed to be French to feel those impulses. In large
parts of the world, not just in Western Europe, the twentieth century from the 1930s into the early 1950s had been an age of disaster,
and the parents of the students of the sixties, the left-wing parents
especially, were disaster's veterans. Those people had been the
combatants in the Spanish Civil War. (The Communist Youth club
in Mexico that produced Gilberto Guevara and some other future
leaders of the student uprising in 1968 contained the children of
refugees from Spain.) The parents had struggled through the Great
Depression and the Second World War, and they had endured the
repression of the Communist movements in a number of Western
countries when the war was over, and now they were exhausted,
and the children who were born of those parents had something
in common. They were the after-the-deluge children. And in more
than a few countries around the world those children, just enough
of them to get a movement going, felt that the same agony of conscience and idealism, naturally in a different style in every country.
It was the moral crisis of the baby boom generation.

In one country after another, the way out of that crisis was to
shake off the comforts of a stable bourgeois world and to take up
the risks of radical solidarity. So a small vanguard of privileged
students in place after place proposed risky campaigns of radical
solidarity, and because the risky campaigns and the cult of danger
seemed foolish or irresponsible to the adult left, the young and
their elders fell into bitter arguments, and the young were expelled
by the old. Everywhere the young discovered that adult support was
unnecessary. And at once the newly independent radical campaigns
of the young began to express the wider generational anguish with
perfect fidelity. Tiny flames of pure idealism went up. Everywhere
the effect was intoxicating, even among the great mass of students
whose parents had been anything but left wing. And so the handful
of young militants who had been expelled from the traditional left-
wing parties found themselves with a large following of their own
age or a few years younger, and the sparks of radical action flew
from one country to the next so swiftly that no one could remember
how or where or why the whole thing had gotten started, and the
crowds were marching through the streets with red flags and black
flags and it was 1968.

## Now that you've read

1. In what respects does Berman's account still describe college life over 30 years later? Where do you see him as outdated or missing the mark entirely?
2. How does the political activism that took place in other countries differ from the activism in the United States?
3. What does Berman mean when he writes, "Every few decades, a pure flame of political rebellion shoots up somewhere and with amazing speed spreads in all directions, until half the countries on earth have been scorched"? Why is the flame "pure"? In what ways is it both good *and* bad to be "scorched"?

# READING 5

*Patricia Williams*

# Crimes Without Passion

Patricia Williams is an outspoken writer and teacher. In this chapter from her book *The Alchemy of Race and Rights*, she brings the professional together with the personal in order to communicate her understanding of how we are often blind to the prejudices we hold. As you read, note where you get frustrated and consider the source of that frustration. Is it just Williams's style, or is it what she has to say? Could it be something else as well?

### *Before you read*

1. Have you ever taken an exam you felt to be unfair? What made it unfair?
2. Have you ever had a teacher you felt was prejudiced in some way? Describe the situation. What did you do?
3. What stories have you heard about law school? How do these stories of law school differ from your experience as an undergraduate at your college?

---

It is early on a Tuesday morning. I am feeling most like a law professor—prolific, published, powerful. There is a knock on my office door. It is K., a first-year student, in tears.

"What's wrong?" I ask. A school administrator has called her an activist. My first instinct is to ask again, so what's wrong? But we're in the middle of a presidential election in which the word "liberal" has become a synonym for "better dead," so I try to put myself in tune with this upsidedown new world in which "activist" might mean something like "troublemaker." "Why?" I ask instead.

K. had gone to an administrator to complain about an exam she and her classmates were given by their criminal-law professor. The problem was an updated version of Shakespeare's *Othello*, in which Othello is described as a "black militaristic African leader" who marries the "young white Desdemona" whom he then kills in a fit of sexual rage. Othello is put on trial. The students were to identify the elements of murder. The model answer gives points for ability to "individualize the test" of provocation by recognizing that "a rough untutored Moor might understandably be deceived by the wiles of a more sophisticated European." K. had gone first to the professor and told him she thought the exam racist; the professor denied it, saying it was not he who had dreamed up the facts but Shakespeare. Then K. went to the administrator, who called her an activist but not before he said that she should be more concerned about learning the law and less about the package in which it comes.

As I read the exam, I think about this assertion that the exercise is not racist because, after all, it was Shakespeare who made race part of the problem. But the exam used race in a peculiarly gratuitous fashion; it seems to me that its offensiveness does not depend on whether race and cultural "unsophistication" play any part in the play *Othello;* the issue is what role they played in the fact pattern (Othello-as-legal-problem) that students had to resolve. In fact, the play is irrelevant to the resolution of Othello-as-defendant, and the opening paragraph of the exam says as much (that students don't need to have read the play to understand the dynamic contained in the problem). So the complex dramatic motivations, ironies, subtleties, and complications of character development in the original play are, again, rendered unimportant—gratuitous—in this context.

K. is crying softly in the background. I look up and offer her some tissue. As I continue to read, I reflect that one of the things I find most valuable about the insights of literary theory as applied to law is the recognition of some relation between reader and text, of looking at what the reader does to transform meaning: the issue of what you do with what you read is very important in textual interpretation. It challenges the notion that there is an easily identifiable objective meaning to something like *Othello* which can be sliced from the haunch of the play and served up, essentialism retained, on a law exam.

I grow angry as I continue to read. Even though the problem follows the facts of the original play, the analogy stops there. To say that this is "the same as" is to accept blindly the authority of "Shakespeare" as some universalized canon. Moreover, it does not acknowledge the fact that, while Shakespeare may have produced great literature, he was also a historical being, a product of an Elizabethan world that was in some ways quite as racist as our own. This is not to say that we should therefore suppress *Othello,* for it allows us to view ourselves and to evaluate a range of still valid human dilemmas.

Unfortunately, those human dilemmas do not seem to be the subject of this problem; instead there is a flattening of universal emotions and events to mere stereotype because all the artful, evocative context of the original is missing. The problem presents a defendant who is black, militaristic, unsophisticated, insecure, jealous, and sexually enraged. It reduces the facts to the very same racist generalizations and stereotypes this nation has used to subjugate black people since the first slave was brought from Africa. Moreover, it places an enormous burden on black students in particular who must assume, for the sake of answering these questions, these things about themselves—that is the trauma of gratuitous generalization. The frame places blacks in the position of speaking against ourselves. It forces us to accept as "truth" constructions that go to the heart of who we are.

In the Othello problem, the exam is put in a frame where to contest those subtly generalized "truths" (blacks are sexually dangerous, blacks are militaristic—would the Capulets or the Montagues ever be characterized as "militaristic"?) is not only irrelevant but costs the student points: it is, according to the model answer, *necessary* to argue that "a rough untutored Moor might understandably be deceived by the wiles of a more sophisticated European." In other words, a student who refuses to or cannot think like a racist—most people of color, I would guess—will receive a lower grade. My further guess is that everyone, including perhaps the students of color, will rationalize this result away as an inability to "think like a lawyer."

I agree to speak to the professor on behalf of K. "Just make sure he understands I'm not an activist," implores K. "This could ruin my career."

I visit Professor L. the next day and present our concerns. L's explanation is that this was merely his attempt to respect the minority and feminist quest to bring issues of race, class, and gender more directly into the curriculum. I say I'm concerned that he shares a deep misunderstanding of the struggle, a misunderstanding that threatens to turn the quest for empowering experiential narrative into permission for the most blatant expressions of cynical stereotypification. I cite the example of an exam given by another professor at another school, who handed out to his class a detailed and luridly violent wife-battering hypothetical in which a man knocks out his wife's teeth, urinates on the floor and throws their baby down into it, rips her blouse off, calls her a "castrating bitch," and arranges for a friend to come in and rape her. At the top of the question there is a disclaiming explanation that it only reflects "the world" where "there is a lot of violence directed at women" and that "the legal system has (often in response to organized feminist concerns) at least partly shifted its responses to situations involving that violence." I use this example to question the potential, no doubt unintended, voyeuristic repercussions of well-meaning attempts to include race and gender without also attempting to examine the *way* in which such material is included. I don't do a good job of making this point, and L. sees no comparison.

L. asks me: "Are you suggesting that race and gender issues be censored from the law-school classroom?"

I answer: The catch-22 of using terms like "black" and "white" has to do with fathoming when and why race or gender or violence or anything else is important. On the one hand, race isn't important because it isn't important; most of us devoutly wish this to be a color-blind society, in which removing the words "black" and "white" from our vocabulary would render the world, in a miraculous flash, free of all division. On the other hand, real life isn't that simple. Often we have to use the words in order to acknowledge the undeniable psychological and cultural power of racial constructions upon all our lives; we have to be able to call out against the things that trouble us, whether racism or other forms of suffering.

This is not the same, I say, as retreating to a completely race-neutral point of view for any and all circumstances. That would be like saying we should never study Shakespeare, particularly *Othello* and *The Merchant of Venice*—or, to take it to an extreme, that we should never discuss why racism is racist. (And we desperately need to get past the point of angst about whether we're guilty of guilt-tripping each other.) But it is something quite again if I were to use the authority of what this culture considers "classical" to justify every instance of violent gratuity. It simply would not be valid for me to say, "Well, these are Shakespeare's facts, not mine"—as if "Shakespeare" were some fixed object, some physically determinate piece of marble, as if I could discount all my own interpretive power and responsibility over what I render from it.

"What you are proposing," says L., "sounds like the very antithesis of academic freedom."

Over the next few weeks, I think about ways in which to clarify what I am trying to say. Word has gotten out among my students and friends that I am interested in this sort of thing, and they bring me sheaves of exams; in addition I do my own research. I end up with a stack of exams written on a variety of subjects, and given at schools around the country. I find:

- a tax exam that asks students to calculate the tax implications for Kunta Kinte's master when the slavecatchers cut off his foot.

- a securities-regulation exam in which the professor muses about whether white-collar defendants should go to jail, since "unlike ghetto kids" they are not equipped to fare in that environment.

- a constitutional-law exam in which students are given the lengthy text of a hate-filled polemic entitled "How To Be a Jew-Nigger" and then told to use the first amendment to defend it.

- a description of the "typical criminal" as "a young black male with an I.Q. of 87 who is one of eight children and has always lived on welfare and who spends his time hanging out in pool halls with his best friend Slick."

- numerous criminal-law exams whose questions feature exclusively black or Hispanic or Asian criminals and exclusively white victims.

- many questions depicting gay men as the exclusive spreaders of AIDS, asking students to find the elements of murder.

- many, many questions in which women are beaten, raped, and killed in descriptions pornographically detailed (in contrast to streamlined questions, by the same professors, that do not involve female victims).

I review all these exams and ponder what to do with them, how to raise the issues in a way that can best be heard, and heard in a way that will not be taken as "censorship." Finally I decide to write a memorandum to the faculty, worded generally, without names of professors or schools, but using real exams to illustrate real issues of propriety. I write:

> I have been looking at law-school exams and studying them as a genre of legal writing involving complex relations of power and influence. I am interested in opening discussion about the extent to which what we write into exams, as much as what we teach, conveys stereotypes, delimits the acceptable, and formulates ideals. I have been reviewing a collection of exams that exploit race and gender and violence in ways that I think are highly inappropriate. By "inappropriate" I mean that they use race, gender, and violence in ways that have no educational purpose, that are gratuitous and voyeuristic, and that simultaneously perpetuate inaccurate and harmful stereotypes as "truthful." This is accomplished by a variety of devices:
>
> 1. Compartmentalizing the relevant from the irrelevant is one of the primary skills law students are expected to master during their education. Frequently, professors employ red-herring facts from which the legally dispositive kernel facts must be clearly identified. But in the exams about which I am concerned, race, ethnicity, class, and gender are irrelevant even to the process of winnowing the relevant from the irrelevant. They function as sheer gratuity. Their mention has absolutely nothing to do with the manipulation of rules necessary to resolve the fact patterns as constructed.
>
> Furthermore, in the one or two questions in which a specified characteristic (e.g., a "gay male prostitute" being tried for murder in the spread of AIDS) is arguably important to the disposition, or reflective of some current controversy in the law, students are specifically instructed not to consider it, or to consider it only to a limited extent (e.g., that same exam contained the following instruction: "while we're all concerned about homophobia, don't consider it in answering this

problem"). I found exams whose basic message was: M. is black, N. is a white racist, but you, you're colorblind. O. is battered wife, P. is her vicious spouse-battering husband, but you, you must not consider provocation if O. hits P.

It is thus that information that is quite important in real life and real courtrooms becomes unimportant for purposes of answering a law school exam. Students are left to deal with raised issues of race and gender as unframed information, as mere backdrop—in a society where large numbers of people hold powerful, if not always spoken, impressions that "most blacks are criminals" or "women can't be raped by their husbands" or "all Chicanos belong to gangs."

The message that is reinforced by such exams is that while racist, sexist stereotypes may be part of life, it's not important—or important *not*—to deal with them in the law. (And yet of course we know it is.) Or that it's not so important that it can't be severed, caged, and neatly suppressed. Actual importance is thus not legitimated.

Nevertheless, although devalued expressly or implicitly, race, gender, sexual preference are part of these problems. They're written in them by virtue of some inscrutable design. And they do have a power and a function in such questions, if beyond the answer to that question: yet that function is rendered invisible—not less powerful, just not acknowledged. They become powerful as external markers of what must be suppressed or ignored, of what must be rendered unconscious as "unsightly." These interrogatories, in so directly turning students' attention away from precisely what is most provocative and significant in these problems, reiterates exactly what is so difficult about raising these issues in any kind of social setting: the feeling of impropriety, the sheer discourtesy of talking about what has been, by our teachers at every stage of life, explicitly tabooed: it's o.k. to purvey these unchallenged images as gratuity, but not to talk about them in a way that matters, that changes outcomes.

2. These problems draw for their justification upon one of the law's best-loved inculcations: the preference for the impersonal above the personal, the "objective" above the "subjective." Most of these problems require blacks, women who have been raped, gays and lesbians, to not just re-experience their oppression, but to write *against* their personal knowledge. They actually require the assumption of an "impersonal" (but racist/sexist/homophobic) mentality in order to do well in the grading process. Consider, for example, the exam in which a white woman premeditatedly lures a 13-year old black would-be thief to her balcony and then kills him, her actions motivated by racial hatred. In one interrogatory, students are asked to "make the best argument you can that [the white woman] ought to be exculpated entirely, ignoring arguments (say that she might be diplomatically immune or insane) grounded in general incapacity to be convicted." This requires students either to indulge the imaginative flowering of their most insidious rationalizations for racial hatred; or it requires them to suppress any sense of social conscience. It requires them to devalue their own and others' humanity for the sake of a grade. (This is also how,

over time, perfectly rational and humanitarian insights and concerns are devalued, as a matter of habit rather than wisdom, as "merely experiential" and "irrelevant to the law." Law professors can thus set up irresponsibly authoritarian constructs that give permission to, and legitimize, some really warped world views. The result will be students who are cultured to hate; yet who still think of themselves as very very good people; who will be deeply offended, and *personally* hurt, if anyone tries to tell them otherwise. I think this sort of teaching, rampant throughout the educational system, is why racism and sexism remain so routine, so habitually dismissed, as to be largely invisible).

3. While styled as hypotheticals, these collected exams set themselves up as instructional mirrors of real life. In talking to some of the professors whose exams concerned me, I was always given some version of the following explanation: "Well, (people of color) (women) (gays) do commit crimes after all. It's naive to assume this doesn't happen in the real world." The problem with this reasoning however, is that everything under the sun could be rationalized by the open-ended authority of "what happens," no matter how depraved, singular, or despicable.

We, as law teachers, create miniworlds of reality, by the faith that students put in our tutelage of the rules of reality. We define the boundaries of the legitimate and the illegitimate, in a more ultimately powerful way than almost anyone else in the world. It is enormously important therefore to consider the process by which we include, as well as the process by which we exclude. It is thus that an exam, which includes only three problems, two of which feature black criminality and the third of which deals with gay criminality, constructs a miniworld that reinforces the widely held misperceptions that blacks commit most of the crimes, that only gays carry AIDS, or that all gays are promiscuous.

It is not that there aren't racially or sexually motivated crimes of all sorts in the world; what is problematic about casting problems (directed to a hypothetically diverse student body) repeatedly and persistently in racially or sexually stereotypical terms is that it not only perpetuates the idea, for example, that most blacks commit most crimes, but that it makes invisible white criminality. In any event, race has nothing to do with the resolution of these problems, which for the most part are problems going beyond race and class; yet students are set up to believe that this is "what happens."

Furthermore, there is a relativistic, cynical majoritarianism in the idea that "it happens in the real world," akin to the childish excuse that "everybody does it." I am struck, for example, by the general absence of reference to white people in exams written by people who do specify race when they are referring to nonwhites. Yet we all know that there are white gangs (e.g., skinheads, the White Aryan Resistance) as well as black, Asian, and Chicano gangs. None of these exams, or any I could find, present gratuitous "white-people" problems. "White" is used only to distinguish from blacks and other nonwhites. The absence of "white" thus signals that "everyone" is white. "Blacks" therefore become distanced, different, "othered." In order to deal with such a problem on an exam, moreover, students are required to take the perspective of "everybody"; for black students this requires their taking a stance in which they objectify themselves with reference to the interrogatories. (I use the word "objectify" in the literal, grammatical sense of subject-verb-object: the removing of oneself from the subject position of power, control, and direction over the verb-action. "We," blacks, become "them.") The law becomes less than universally accessible or participatory. The point of view assumes a community of "everybody's" that is in fact exclusionary.

When my sister was in the fourth grade, she was the only black child in the class. One Valentine's Day, when the teacher went out of the room, all her white classmates ripped up the valentines she had sent them and dumped them on her desk. It was so traumatic that my sister couldn't speak again in that class, she refused to participate: so completely had they made her feel not part of that group. For a while she stopped performing altogether. Ultimately my mother convinced her that she could "show them" by outperforming them, but I think the joy of education for its own sake was seriously impaired, in both her and me (for I felt it almost as much as she did; we had made the valentines together).

Our roles repeatedly defined as "outsiders" in both cruel and unintentional ways, we were faced with a curious dilemma: we could continually try to be insiders, which would have been quite frustrating, because "insider" is not an act of will but a cooperative relation, defeated as easily as the turn of a head; or we could resign ourselves to being outsiders. A few exceptionally strong people, usually reinforced by an alternative sense of community, can just ignore it and carry on, despite the lack of that part of education which flows from full participation, perhaps thus resulting in a brand of knowledge that is more abstract than relational. But most others become driven to transform the outsider status into its own excuse, either by obsessional and abstracted overachievement, or by underachievement occasioned by the loss of relation and loss of interest. Either way the outsider status is a kind of unresolved wound, driven by pain, for after all that is the seeded prophecy contained in the word and the concept of those who are designated "outsider."

The students who have been coming to my office have been describing occurrences, in class as well as on exams, that if true are just as powerfully and complexly traumatizing. Perhaps if all we value is toughness of spirit in our interactions, then what happened to my sister was a good lesson. It's certainly not just as easy to inflict the same lesson on women and students of color, or white men for that matter, if the project is only to toughen them up. We will, in the forge of exam pressure and general humiliation, be able to produce a tough human being totally split inside. But I trust that is not the exclusive project of institutions engaged in the training of ethical servants of either private or public interest.

This brings me back to my original issue—how to distinguish the appropriate introduction of race, gender, class, social policy, into law-school classrooms. I don't think there's an easy answer or a formula that can be applied. That's why I think such discussion should be ongoing, constant, among faculties willing to hear divers points of view— as difficult as such conversations are, and as long-term and noisy as they may have to be.

Nor do I think that handling these exams should be limited to discussions of wording in specific instances, or to specific professors who may have suffered momentary lapses of consciousness or whose motives may have been misunderstood. I think that the ultimate resolution has to do with understanding relations of power. It is significant that in my sister's class everyone ripped up her valentines; it might not have been more than a few hours of hurt feelings if only one person had done it. Similarly, it is significant when not just one but many law professors feel free to propagate (if unintentionally) racism in fanciful classroom hypotheticals and in publicly disseminated exams, bound for posterity in volumes in the library. It is significant that professors feel that they *can't talk* about exams like these without interfering with the first-amendment rights or the academic freedom of their colleagues. It is significant that we are teachers and have power over our students. It is significant that significant numbers of students are desperately unhappy about what they consider the abusive exercise of that power, and yet are too afraid to speak openly of their unhappiness. It is significant because people are hired and fired and graded and held to accountability under law, based on factors about which we cannot or will not speak.

The response to my memo is not good. I am accused of being didactic, condescending, "too teacherly." I am told that I have humiliated a number of professors because, although no names were used, identities were easily divined. I have, I am told, "reduced the conversation to one of personalities and pot shots."

These accusations frighten me. I share the lawyerly resistance to the windy, risky plain of exposure that the "personal" represents. I am just as fearful of my own personality having been put into public debate as my critics are of theirs. My instinct is to retreat—the responses to my memo render the debate too subjective, complicated, messy, detailed. Somewhere inside, I know that my fear of being called didactic, condescending, and teacherly is related to K.'s fear of being called an activist.

I sit down and write my sister a long letter, including my memo. I tell her how I have fictionalized the identities of people and collapsed several conversations with different colleagues into the mouths of only a few characters. My sister responds with a phone call: she tells me I'm a coward. She thinks I should write up everything Exactly As It Happened and have it published somewhere. Otherwise, she says, I open myself up to being dismissed as merely literary; people will be able to say It Didn't Happen.

But the exams are all real, I insist, and all the events did happen, just not all in the same instant, not all in that order; it happened, just not exactly that way.

Then it's not true, she says, and you will have committed an act of bad scholarship.

But my point is not to hold individual people or institutions up for ridicule, I persist. I generalized because the power of these events is precisely their generality throughout legal education and practice. The lessons lie in the principles, not in the personalities.

The power of these events, says my sister the historian, is that they happened, and there is no one who is in a more ideal position to document them in detail than you. You are just afraid to do that.

I promise to think about what she has said, and our conversation ends. And I do think about what my sister has said, long and hard, for weeks and weeks.

In the meantime, I avoid K. whenever I see her on the other side of the student union.

I am lured, eventually, from my hibernation by two memos I receive from colleagues. The first is from Q., who inquires about the tone assumed in my memo as well as in my other writing. Q. asks whether I am not afraid that my personal style is "too much" for an academic audience; he says that it is inevitable that my words will be read as "all about me" and speculates that my writing necessarily involves the reader's passing judgment on me. Rather than risking another memo written in the first person, I take Q. to lunch and we talk.

I say: Writing for me is an act of sacrifice, not denial. (I think: I'm so glad I didn't try to write this down.) I deliberately sacrifice myself in my writing. I leave no part of myself out, for that is how much I want readers to connect with me. I want them to wonder about the things I wonder about, and to think about some of the things that trouble me.

What is "impersonal" writing but denial of self? If withholding is an ideology worth teaching, we should be clearer about that as the bottom line of the enterprise. We should also acknowledge the extent to which denial of one's authority in authorship is not the same as elimination of oneself; it is ruse, not reality. And the object of such ruse is to empower still further; to empower beyond the self, by appealing to neutral, shared, even universal understandings. In a vacuum, I suppose there's nothing wrong with that attempt to empower: it generates respect and distance and a certain obeisance to the sleekness of a product that has been skinned of its personalized complication. But in a world of real others, the cost of such exclusive forms of discourse is empowerment at the expense of one's relation to those others; empowerment without communion. And as the comfort of such false power becomes habitual, it is easy to forget that the source of one's power is quite limited, not the fiat of a heavenly mandate. It is easy to forget how much that grandiosity of power depends on the courtesy and restraint of a society of others no less equally endowed than you.

The other thing contained in assumption of neutral, impersonal writing styles is the lack of risk. It is not only a ruse, but a warm protective hole to crawl in, as if you were to throw your shoe out the front door while insisting that no one's home. I also believe that the personal is not the same as "private": the personal is often merely the highly particular. I think the personal has fallen into disrepute as sloppy because we have lost the courage and the vocabulary to describe it in the face of the enormous social pressure to "keep it to ourselves"—but this is where our most idealistic and our deadliest politics are lodged, and are revealed.

The second memo is from R. He writes:

> I can't think of anyone who claims to have liked law school. I haven't taken a poll, but I suspect most students feel like they are suffering in law school . . . I didn't go to Harvard for law school, or Yale. I had messed up the beginning of my undergraduate education. In any event I am a certified member of the class of also-rans. It is possible to generalize about us . . . Some of us, of course, are among the strongest critics of affirmative action. I never really felt that way. I guess I always believed the idea that diversity is more than just a campaign slogan, and that an all-vanilla law school is an insipid place.
>
> But there is another kind of *resentment* which, however irrational, I confess I do share. That directs itself not against the affirmative action candidates but rather against the pampered children of privilege who tell me how terrible it all is. It's not that they're "undeserving" per se; some of them are clearly just as brilliant as the development officers say they are. But they sure do seem unappreciative. "My god!" I find myself saying. "You've got a chance I'd clean out privies for, and you're telling me it isn't worth very much? You should be wearing an MIA bracelet in my name; you should fall down on your knees and whisper prayers of thanks, just for the chance to be in that seat!"

Into my computer I write:

> Dear R.: I do agree with you that most law students are indeed miserable. In the context of my concerns about exams, however, I was not concerned with ranking degrees of pain into some kind of hierarchy, although of course degree is vital to the maintenance of perspective. It is not comforting to me that "everyone," not just particular students, suffer in law school. Misery may love company, but I trust none of us particularly loves misery. It helps me not at all to know that others are unhappy; there is nothing possessive about my unhappiness. I know I

am not the only one. The three (white) students who committed suicide when I was in law school may have complained less than I did, but obviously suffered more; their loss intensified my unhappiness. I do not think my life became easier by the comparison.

Rather, my personal concern is with identifying the specifics of my pain. What causes it, what sustains it, what interferes with my ability to be most fully and most productively myself. My unhappiness, whether alone or among many, makes me inefficient. It makes me hide myself.

None of this, however, should be mistaken for doubts about the value of my education. It should not be taken as a denial of the wonderful people and wonderful moments that have also characterized my schooling and my career. My complaining doesn't mean that I devalue who I am; but just because Harvard admitted me or Stanford hired me doesn't mean that they own me to the extent that I can never speak about my feelings. There would be some element of unthinking fervor in that, I think, akin to blind patriotism: love it or leave it. Not to complain about real inequities and real sources of misery in even the most powerful institutions seems only to kowtow to power rather than participate in a meaningful and great-souled manner.

I never give R. a copy of this response; I'm not sure why. Instead I look for my student K. to see if she wants to have lunch.

It is the end of a long academic year. I sit in my office reviewing my student's evaluations of me. They are awful, and I am devastated. The substantive ones say that what I teach is "not law." The nonsubstantive evaluations are about either my personality or my physical features. I am deified, reified, and vilified in all sorts of cross-directions. I am condescending, earthy, approachable, and arrogant. Things are out of control in my classroom, and I am too much the taskmaster. I am a PNCNG (Person of No Color and No Gender) as well as too absorbed with ethnicity and social victimhood. My braids are described as being swept up over my "great bald dome of a skull," and my clothes, I am relieved to hear, are "neat." I am obscure, challenging, lacking in intellectual rigor, and brilliant. I think in a disorganized fashion and insist that everyone think as I do. I appear tired all the time and talk as if I'm on speed, particularly when reading from texts. My writing on the blackboard is too small.

"The failure of this class was a group effort," writes one student. "When Professor Williams got off to a rocky start, rather than cooperating with her, the class would adopt an adversarial posture. For instance, knowing full well that Professor Williams did not look to the sides of the room very often, certain individuals would raise their hands quietly and leave them up without saying a word, thereby sending titters all through the class; this unnecessarily heightened the perception of students that the professor was in over her head."

My head hurts. In nine years of teaching I have never felt less like a law professor. Who wants to be the worst so-called law professor who ever lived anyway? I marvel, in a moment of genuine bitterness, that anonymous student evaluations speculating on dimensions of my anatomy are nevertheless counted into the statistical measurement of my teaching proficiency. I am expected to woo students even as I try to fend them off; I am supposed to control them even as I am supposed to manipulate them into loving me. Still I am aware of the paradox of my power over these students. I am aware of my role, my place in an institution that is larger than myself, whose power I wield even as I am powerless, whose shield of respectability shelters me even as I am disrespected.

I am always aware of my first years in teaching when students would come in upset that I had yelled at them on paper by virtue of red-ink exclamatory comments in their margins. These days I correct my exams in pencil, faintly, softly. Red pen was too much of a shout to students if I had anything other to say than "Great!" I never say "Wrong" in the margins, but always ask questions: "Are you sure that's the section you mean?" "Have you compared this conclusion with that in the preceding paragraph?" Any occasional imperative begins with "Try to distinguish this thought from . . . ." I circle spelling errors rather than correct them.

I am always aware of the ex-pro-football player/student whom I had told in class to read the cases more carefully; he came to my office to tell me that I had humiliated him in front of everyone and he was going to "get you, lady." At that, I ordered him out of my office, whereupon he walked down to the associate dean's office and burst into tears, great heaving, football-player sobs, the tears dripping off the tip of his nose, as it was described to me later. Now I admit that of all the possible ways in which I thought he might try to get me, this was the one for which I was least prepared; but it could not have been more effective in terms of coalescing both the student body and the administration against me. I became the drill sergeant. A militant black woman who took out her rage on her students. Someone who could make a big man like him cry and cry hard.

And it is true that I did make him cry. I thought long about how a situation in which I thought I was being plucky and self-protective had turned into such a nightmare. How did my self-assertion become so powerful as to frighten, frustrate, or humiliate this man? Part of the answer is that he indeed felt humiliated; it is hard to be criticized in a large classroom, although I had perceived mine to be gentle criticism. Part of it lies in the power I wield as teacher over all my students; each of us seeks unconditional approval even from the teachers we may hate. But I'm not sure this explains sufficiently the intensity of my student's reaction or, even if I conclude that he was simply sensitive, the intensity of the sympathy that rushed in this largely male institution away from me and unto him.

Two students come to visit me in the wake of the evaluations, my scores having been published in the student newspaper. They think the response has to do with race and gender, and with the perceived preposterousness of the authority that I, as the first black woman ever to have taught at this particular institution, symbolically and imagistically bring to bear in and out of the classroom. Breaking out of this, they say, is something we all suffer as pawns in a hierarchy, but it is particularly aggravated in the confusing, oxymoronic hierarchic symbology of me as black female law professor.

That, I tell them in a grateful swell of unscholarly emotionalism, feels like truth to me.

---

### Now that you've read

1. What is Williams's argument? What are the arguments of some of her fellow teachers? Where do you stand?
2. Why is K. worried about being labeled an "activist"? What would be wrong with that?
3. Why did K. bring her exam to Williams? What conclusions did Williams draw from K's exams and the exams other students brought her?
4. How is Williams's concern about her teaching evaluations related to the first two-thirds of her essay?

# READING 5

*Barbara Tuchman*

# History as Mirror

Barbara Tuchman is a widely read historian who has written several accessible histories of a number of times, people, and places: the American Revolution, World War I in Europe, failed leaders throughout the ages, and fourteenth-century Europe (which this essay comes from). "History as Mirror" focuses on the fourteenth century, a time of plague and war and economic change in Europe. At first glance, we might ask what the fourteenth century has to do with anything happening now. But in "History as Mirror," Tuchman suggests that there are parallels between past and present events—and that a better understanding of historical parallels can inform our understanding of politics in the present. In other words, looking backward can actually sharpen our view of today.

## *Before you read*

1. What do you take the title to mean?
2. What is valuable about studying history?
3. Did you (or do you) enjoy studying history? If so, why? If not, why not?
4. What might teachers do to make studying history seem more vital?

---

At a time when everyone's mind is on the explosions of the moment, it might seem obtuse of me to discuss the fourteenth century. But I think a backward look at that disordered, violent, bewildered, disintegrating, and calamity-prone age can be consoling and possibly instructive in a time of similar disarray. Reflected in a six-hundred-year-old mirror, a more revealing image of ourselves and our species might be seen than is visible in the clutter of circumstances under our noses. The value of historical comparison was made keenly apparent to the French medievalist, Edouard Perroy, when he was writing his book on the Hundred Years' War while dodging the Gestapo in World War II. "Certain ways of behaving," he wrote, "certain reactions against fate, throw mutual light upon each other."

Besides, if one suspects that the twentieth century's record of inhumanity and folly represents a phase of mankind at its worst, and that our last decade of collapsing assumptions has been one of unprecedented discomfort, it is reassuring to discover that the human race has been in this box before—and emerged. The historian has the comfort of knowing that man (meaning, here and hereafter, the species, not the sex) is always capable of his worst; has indulged in it, painfully struggled up from it, slid back, and gone on again.

In what follows, the parallels are not always in physical events but rather in the effect on society, and sometimes in both.

The afflictions of the fourteenth century were the classic riders of the Apocalypse—famine, plague, war, and death, this time on a black horse. These combined to produce an epidemic of violence, depopulation, bad government, oppressive taxes, an accelerated breakdown of feudal bonds, working class insurrection, monetary crisis, decline of morals and rise in crime, decay of chivalry, the governing idea of the governing class, and above all, corruption of society's central institution, the Church, whose loss of authority and prestige deprived man of his accustomed guide in a darkening world.

Yet amidst the disintegration were sprouting, invisible to contemporaries, the green shoots of the Renaissance to come. In human affairs as in nature, decay is compost for new growth.

Some medievalists reject the title of decline for the fourteenth century, asserting instead that it was the dawn of a new age. Since the processes obviously overlap, I am not sure that the question is worth arguing, but it becomes poignantly interesting when applied to ourselves. Do *we* walk amidst trends of a new world without knowing it? How far ahead is the dividing line? Or are we on it? What designation will our age earn from historians six hundred years hence? One wishes one could make a pact with the devil like Enoch Soames, the neglected poet in Max Beerbohm's story, allowing us to return and look ourselves up in the library catalogue. In that future history book, shall we find the chapter title for the twentieth century reading Decline and Fall, or Eve of Revival?

The fourteenth century opened with a series of famines brought on when population growth outstripped the techniques of food production. The precarious balance was tipped by a series of heavy rains and floods and by a chilling of the climate in what has been called the Little Ice Age. Upon a people thus weakened fell the century's central disaster, the Black Death, an eruption of bubonic plague which swept the known world in the years 1347–1349 and carried off an estimated one-third of the population in two and a half years. This makes it the most lethal episode known to history, which is of some interest to an age equipped with the tools of overkill.

The plague raged at terrifying speed, increasing the impression of horror. In a given locality it accomplished its kill within four to six months, except in larger cities, where it struck again in spring after lying dormant in winter. The death rate in Avignon was said to have claimed half the population, of whom ten thousand were buried in the first six weeks in a single mass grave. The mortality was in fact erratic. Some communities whose last survivors fled in despair were simply wiped out and disappeared from the map forever, leaving only a grassed-over hump as their mortal trace.

Whole families died, leaving empty houses and property as prey to looters. Wolves came down from the mountains to attack plague-stricken villages, crops went unharvested, dikes crumbled, salt water reinvaded and soured the lowlands, the forest crept back, and second growth, with the awful energy of nature unchecked, reconverted cleared land to waste. For lack of hands to cultivate, it was thought impossible that the world could ever regain its former prosperity.

Once the dark bubonic swellings appeared in armpit and groin, death followed rapidly within one to three days, often overnight. For lack of gravediggers, corpses piled up in the streets or were buried so hastily that dogs dug them up and ate them. Doctors were helpless, and priests lacking to administer that final sacrament so that people died believing they must go to hell. No bells tolled, the dead were buried without prayers or funeral rites or tears; families did not weep for the loss of loved ones, for everyone expected death. Matteo Villani, taking up the chronicle of Florence from the hands of his dead brother, believed he was recording the "extermination of mankind."

People reacted variously, as they always do: Some prayed, some robbed, some tried to help, most fled if they could, others abandoned themselves to debauchery on the theory that there would be no tomorrow. On balance, the dominant reaction was fear and a desire to save one's own skin regardless of the closest ties. "A father did not visit his son, nor the son his father; charity was dead," wrote one physician, and that was not an isolated observation. Boccaccio in his famous account reports that "kinsfolk held aloof, brother was forsaken by brother . . . often times husband by wife; nay what is more, and scarcely to be believed, fathers and mothers were found to abandon their own children to their fate, untended, unvisited as if they had been strangers."

"Men grew bold," wrote another chronicler, "in their indulgence in pleasure. . . . No fear of God or law of man deterred a criminal. Seeing that all perished alike, they reflected that offenses against human or Divine law would bring no punishment for no one would live long enough to be held to account." This is an accurate summary, but it was written by Thucydides about the Plague of Athens in the fifth century B.C.—which indicates a certain permanence of human behavior.

The nightmare of the plague was compounded for the fourteenth century by the awful mystery of its cause. The idea of disease carried by insect bite was undreamed of. Fleas and rats, which were in fact the carriers, are not mentioned in the plague writings. Contagion could be observed but not explained and thus seemed doubly sinister. The medical faculty of the University of Paris favored a theory of poisonous air spread by a conjunction of the planets, but the general and fundamental belief, made official by a papal bull, was the pestilence was divine punishment for man's sins. Such horror could only be caused by the wrath of God. "In the year of our Lord, 1348," sadly wrote a professor of law at the University of Pisa, "the hostility of God was greater than the hostility of men."

That belief enhanced the sense of guilt, or rather the consciousness of sin (guilt, I suspect, is modern; sin is medieval), which was always so close to the surface throughout the Middle Ages. Out of the effort to appease divine wrath came the flagellants, a morbid frenzy of self-punishment that almost at once found a better object in the Jews.

A storm of pogroms followed in the track of the Black Death, widely stimulated by the flagellants, who often rushed straight for the Jewish quarter, even in towns which had not yet suffered the plague. As outsiders within the unity of Christendom the Jews were natural persons to suspect of evil design on the Christian world. They were accused of poisoning the wells. Although the Pope condemned the attacks as inspired by "that liar the devil," pointing out that Jews died of plague like everyone else, the populace wanted victims, and fell upon them in three hundred communities throughout Europe. Slaughtered and burned alive, the entire colonies of Frankfurt, Cologne, Mainz, and other towns of Germany and the Lowlands were exterminated, despite the restraining efforts of town authorities. Elsewhere the Jews were expelled by judicial process after confession of well-poisoning was extracted by torture. In every case their goods and property, whether looted or confiscated, ended in the hands of the persecutors. The process was lucrative, as it was to be again in our time under the Nazis, although the fourteenth century had no gold teeth to rob from the corpses. Where survivors slowly returned and the communities revived, it was on worse terms than before and in walled isolation. This was the beginning of the ghetto.

Men of the fourteenth century were particularly vulnerable because of the loss of credibility by the Church, which alone could absolve sin and offer salvation from hell. When the papal schism dating from 1378 divided the Church under two popes, it brought the highest authority in society into disrepute, a situation with which we are familiar. The schism was the second great calamity of the time, displaying before all the world the unedifying spectacle of twin vicars of God, each trying to bump the other off the chair of St. Peter, each appointing his own college of cardinals, each collecting tithes and revenues and excommunicating the partisans of his rival. No conflict of ideology was involved; the split arose from a simple squabble for the office of the papacy and remained no more than that for the fifty years the schism lasted. Plunged in this scandal, the Church lost moral authority, the more so as its two halves scrambled in the political arena for support. Kingdoms, principalities, even towns, took sides, finding new cause for the endless wars that scourged the times.

The Church's corruption by worldliness long antedated the schism. By the fourteenth century the papal court at Avignon was called Babylon and rivaled temporal courts in luxury and magnificence. Its bureaucracy was enormous and its upkeep mired in a commercial traffic in spiritual things. Pardons, indulgences, prayers, every benefice and bishopric, everything the Church had or was, from cardinal's hat to pilgrim's relic, everything that represented man's relation to God, was for sale. Today it is the processes of government that are for sale, especially the electoral process, which is as vital to our political security as salvation was to the emotional security of the fourteenth century.

Men still craved God and spun off from the Church in sects and heresies, seeking to purify the realm of the spirit. They too yearned for a greening of the system. The yearning, and disgust with the Establishment, produced freak orders of mystics who lived in coeducational communes, rejected marriage, and glorified sexual indulgence. Passionate reformers ranged from St. Catherine of Siena, who scolded everyone in the hierarchy from the popes down, to John Wycliffe, who plowed the soil of Protestant revolt. Both strove to renew the Church, which for so long had been the only institution to give order and meaning to the untidy business of living on earth. When in the last quarter of the century the schism brought the Church into scorn and ridicule and fratricidal war, serious men took alarm. The University of Paris made strenuous and ceaseless efforts to find a remedy, finally demanding submission of the conflict to a supreme Council of the Church whose object should be not only reunification but reform.

Without reform, said the University's theologians in their letter to the popes, the damaging effect of the current scandal could be irreversible. In words that could have been addressed to our own secular potentate although he is—happily—not double, they wrote, "The Church will suffer for your overconfidence if you repent too late of having neglected reform. If you postpone it longer the harm will be incurable. Do you think people will suffer forever from your bad government? Who do you think can endure, amid so many abuses . . . your evaluation of men without literacy or virtue to the most eminent positions?" The echo sounds over the gulf of six hundred years with a timeliness almost supernatural.

When the twin popes failed to respond, pressure at last brought about a series of Church councils which endeavored to limit and constitutionalize the powers of the papacy. After a thirty-year struggle, the councils succeeded in ending the schism but the papacy resisted reform. The decades of debate only served to prove that the institution could not be reformed from within. Eighty years of mounting protest were to pass before pressure produced Luther and the great crack.

Despite the parallel with the present struggle between Congress and the presidency, there is no historical law that says the outcome must necessarily be the same. The American presidency at age two hundred is not a massive rock of ages embedded in a thousand years of acceptance as was the medieval Church, and should be easier to reform. One can wish for Congress a better result than the councils had in the effort to curb the executive—or at least one can hope.

The more important parallel lies in the decay of public confidence in our governing institutions, as the fourteenth-century public lost confidence in the Church. Who believes today in the integrity of government?—or of business, or of law or justice or labor unions or the military or the police? Even physicians, the last of the admired, are now in disfavor. I have a theory that the credibility vacuum owes something to our nurture in that conspiracy of fables called advertising, which we daily absorb without believing. Since public affairs and ideas and candidates are now presented to us as a form of advertising, we automatically suspend belief or suspect fraud as soon as we recognize the familiar slickness. I realize, of course, that the roots of disbelief go down to deeper ground. Meanwhile the effect is a loss of trust in all authority which leaves us guideless and dismayed and cynical—even as in the fourteenth century.

Over that whole century hung the smoke of war—dominated by the Anglo-French conflict known to us, though fortunately not to them, as the Hundred Years' War. (With the clock still ticking in Indochina, one wonders how many years there are still to go in that conflict.) Fought on French soil and extending into Flanders and Spain, the Hundred Years' War actually lasted for more than a century, from 1337 to 1453. In addition, the English fought the Scots; the French fought incessant civil wars against Gascons, Bretons, Normans, and Navarrese; the Italian republics fought each other—Florence against Pisa, Venice against Genoa, Milan against everybody; the kingdom of Naples and Sicily was fought over by claimants from Hungary to Aragon; the papacy fought a war that included unbridled massacre to reconquer the Papal States; the Savoyards fought the Lombards; the Swiss fought the Austrians; the tangled wars of Bohemia, Poland, and the German Empire defy listing; crusades were launched against the Saracens, and to fill up any pauses the Teutonic Knights conducted annual campaigns against pagan Lithuania which other knights could join for extra practice. Fighting was the function of the Second Estate, that is, of the landed nobles and knights. A knight without a war or tournament to go to felt as restless as a man who cannot go to the office.

Every one of these conflicts threw off Free Companies of mercenaries, organized for brigandage under a professional captain, which became an evil of the period as malignant as the plague. In the money economy of the fourteenth century, armed forces were no longer feudal levies serving under a vassal's obligation who went home after forty days, but were recruited bodies who served for pay. Since this was at great cost to the sovereign, he cut off the payroll as soon as he safely could during halts of truce or negotiation. Thrown on their own resources and having acquired a taste for plunder, the men-at-arms banded together in the Free Companies, whose savage success swelled their ranks with landless knights and squires and roving adventurers.

The companies contracted their services to whatever ruler was in need of troops, and between contracts held up towns for huge ransom, ravaged the countryside, and burned, pillaged, raped, and slaughtered their way back and forth across Europe. No one was safe, no town or village knew when it might be attacked. The leaders, prototypes of the *condottieri* in Italy, became powers and made fortunes and even became respectable like Sir John Hawkwood, commander of the famous White Company. Smaller bands, called in France the *tards-venus* (latecomers), scavenged like jackals, living off the land, plundering, killing, carrying off women, torturing peasants for their small horde of grain or townsmen for their hidden goods, and burning, always burning. They set fire to whatever they left behind, farmhouses, vineyards, abbeys, in a kind of madness to destroy the very sources off which they lived, or would live tomorrow. Destruction and cruelty became self-engendering, not merely for loot but almost one might say for sport. The phenomenon is not peculiar to any one time or people, as we know from the experience of our own century, but in the fourteenth century it seems to have reached a degree and extent beyond explanation.

It must be added that in practice and often personnel the Free Companies were hardly distinguishable from the troops of organized official wars. About 80 percent of the activity of a declared war consisted of raids of plunder and burning through enemy territory. That paragon of chivalry, the Black Prince, could well have earned his name from the blackened ruins he left across France. His baggage train and men-at-arms were often so heavily laden with loot that they moved as slowly as a woman's litter.

The saddest aspect of the Hundred Years' War was the persistent but vain efforts of the belligerents themselves to stop it. As in our case, it spread political damage at home, and the cost was appalling. Moreover it harmed the relations of all the powers at a time when they were anxious to unite to repel the infidel at the gates. For Christendom was now on the defensive against the encroaching Turks. For that reason the Church, too, tried to end the war that was keeping Europe at odds. On the very morning of the fatal battle of Poitiers, two cardinals hurried with offers and counter-offers between the two armed camps, trying in vain to prevent the clash. During periods of truce the parties held long parleys lasting months and sometimes years in the effort to negotiate a definitive peace. It always eluded them, failing over questions of prestige, or put off by the feeling of whichever side held a slight advantage that one more push would bring the desired gains.

All this took place under a code of chivalry whose creed was honor, loyalty, and courtesy and whose purpose, like that of every social code evolved by man in his long search for order, was to civilize and supply a pattern of rules. A knight's task under the code was to uphold the Church, defend his land and vassals, maintain the peace of his province, protect the weak and guard the poor from injustice, shed his blood for his comrade, and lay down his life if needs must. For the land-owning warrior class, chivalry was their ideology, their politics, their system—what democracy is to us or Marxism to the Communists.

Originating out of feudal needs, it was already slipping into anachronism by the fourteenth century because the development of monarchy and a royal bureaucracy was taking away the knight's functions, economic facts were forcing him to commute labor dues for money, and a rival element was appearing in the urban magnates. Even his military prowess was being nullified by trained bodies of English longbowmen and Swiss pikemen, nonmembers of the warrior class who in feudal theory had no business in battle at all.

Yet in decadence chivalry threw its brightest light; never were its ceremonies more brilliant, its jousts and tournaments so brave, its apparel so splendid, its manners so gay and amorous, its entertainments so festive, its self-glorification more eloquent. The gentry elaborated the forms of chivalry just *because* institutions around them were crumbling. They clung to what gave their status meaning in a desperate embrace of the past. This is the time when the Order of the Garter was founded by the King of England, the Order of the Star

by the King of France, the Golden Fleece by the Duke of Burgundy—
in deliberate imitation of King Arthur's Knights of the Round Table.

The rules still worked well enough among themselves, with occasional notorious exceptions such as Charles of Navarre, a bad
man appropriately known as Charles the Bad. Whenever necessity
required him to swear loyal reconciliation and fealty to the King of
France, his mortal enemy, he promptly engaged in treacherous in-
trigues with the King of England, leaving his knightly oaths to become, in the White House word, inoperative. On the whole, however,
the nobility laid great stress on high standards of honor. It was vis- -
vis the Third Estate that chivalry fell so far short of the theory. Yet it
remained an ideal of human relations, as Christianity remained an
ideal of faith, that kept men reaching for the unattainable. The effort
of society is always toward order, away from anarchy. Sometimes it
moves forward, sometimes it slips back. Which is the direction of
one's own time may be obscure.

The fourteenth century was further afflicted by a series of con-
vulsions and upheavals in the working class, both urban and rural.
Causes were various: the cost of constant war was thrown upon the
people in hearth taxes, sales taxes, and debasement of coinage. In
France the failure of the knights to protect the populace from incessant ravaging was a factor. It exacerbated the peasants' misery,
giving it the energy of anger which erupted in the ferocious mid-
century rising called the *Jacquerie*. Shortage of labor caused by the
plague had temporarily brought higher wages and rising expectations. When these were met, especially in England, by statutes
clamping wages at preplague levels, the result was the historic Peasants' Revolt of 1381. In the towns, capitalism was widening the gap
between masters and artisans, producing the sustained weavers' re-
volts in the cloth towns of Flanders and major outbreaks in Florence
and Paris. In Paris, too, the merchant class rose against the royal
councillors, whom they despised as both corrupt and incompetent.
To frighten the regent into submission, they murdered his two chief
councillors in his presence.

All these struggles had one thing in common: They were doomed.
United against a common threat, the ruling class could summon
greater strength than its antagonists and acted to suppress insurrection with savagery equal to the fury from below. Yet discontent had
found its voice; dissent and rejection of authority for the first time in
the Middle Ages became a social force. Demagogues and determined
leaders, reformers and agitators came to the surface. Though all
were killed, several by mobs of their own followers, the uprisings
they led were the beginning of modern, conscious, class war.

Meanwhile, over the second half-century, the plague returned with lesser virulence at intervals of every twelve to fifteen years. It is hardly to be wondered that people of the time saw man's fate as an endless succession of evils. He must indeed be wicked and his enemy Satan finally triumphant. According to popular belief at the end of the century, no one since the beginning of the schism had entered Paradise.

Pessimism was a mark of the age and the *Danse Macabre* or Dance of Death its most vivid expression. Performed at occasions of popular drama and public sermons, it was an actual dance or pantomime in which a figure from every walk of life—king, clerk, lawyer, friar, goldsmith, bailiff, and so on—confronts the loathsome corpse he must become. In the accompanying verses and illustrations which have survived, the theme repeats itself over and over: the end of all life is putrefaction and the grave; no one escapes; no matter what beauty or kingly power or poor man's misery has been the lot in life, all end alike as food for worms. Death is not treated poetically as the soul's flight to reunion with God; it is a skeleton grinning at the vanity of life.

Life as well as death was viewed with disgust. The vices and corruptions of the age, a low opinion of one's fellowmen, and nostalgia for the well-ordered past were the favorite themes of literary men. Even Boccaccio in his later works became ill-tempered. "All good customs fail," laments Christine de Pisan of France, "and virtues are held at little worth." Eustache Deschamps complains that "the child of today has become a ruffian. . . . People are gluttons and drunkards, haughty of heart, caring for nought, not honor nor goodness nor kindness," and he ends each verse with the refrain, "Time past had virtue and righteousness but today reigns only vice." In England John Gower denounces Rome for simony, Lollards for heresy, clergy and monks for idleness and lust, kings, nobles, and knights for self-indulgence and rapine, the law for bribery, merchants for usury and fraud, the commons for ignorance, and in general the sins of perjury, lechery, avarice, and pride as displayed in extravagant fashions.

These last did indeed, as in all distracted times, reflect a reaching for the absurd, especially in the long pointed shoes which kept getting longer until the points had to be tied up around the knee, and the young men's doublets which kept getting shorter until they revealed the buttocks, to the censure of moralists and snickers of the crowd. Leaving miniskirts to the males, the ladies inexplicably adopted a fashion of gowns and posture designed to make them look pregnant.

Self-disgust, it seems to me, has reappeared in our time, not without cause. The succession of events since 1914 has disqualified belief in moral progress, and pollution of the physical world is our bubonic plague. Like the fourteenth century, we have lost confidence in man's capacity to control his fate and even in his capacity to be good. So we have a literature of the antihero aimlessly wandering among the perverse, absurd, and depraved; we have porn and pop and blank canvases and anti-music designed to deafen. I am not sure whether in all this the artists are expressing contempt for their fellowman or the loud laugh that bespeaks emptiness of feeling, but whatever the message, it has a faint ring of the *Danse Macabre.*

Historians until recently have hurried over the fourteenth century because like most people they prefer not to deal with failure. But it would be a mistake to imply that it was solid gloom. Seen from inside, especially from a position of privilege, it had beauties and wonders, and the ferment itself was exciting. "In these fifty years," said the renowned Comte de Foix to the chronicler Froissart in the year 1389, "there have been more feats of arms and more marvels in the world than in the three hundred years before." The Count himself, a famous huntsman, was known as Phoebus for his personal beauty and splendid court.

The streets of cities were bright with colored clothes: crimson fur-lined gowns of merchants, parti-colored velvets and silks of a nobleman's retinue, in sky blue and fawn or two shades of scarlet or it might be the all-emerald liveries of the Green Count of Savoy. Street sounds were those of human voices: criers of news and official announcements, shopkeepers in their doorways and itinerant vendors crying fresh eggs, charcoal at a penny a sack, candlewicks "brighter than the stars," cakes and waffles, mushrooms, hot baths. Mountebanks entertained the public in the town square or village green with tricks and magic and trained animals. Jongleurs sang ballads of adventure in Saracen lands. After church on Sundays, laborers gathered in cookshops and taverns; burghers promenaded in their gardens or visited their vineyards outside the city walls. Church bells marked the eight times of day from Matins through Vespers, when shops closed, work ceased, silence succeeded bustle, and the darkness of unlit night descended.

The gaudy extravagance of noble life was awesome. Now and then its patronage brought forth works of eternal beauty like the exquisite illuminated Books of Hours commissioned by the Duc de Berry. More often it was pure ostentation and conspicuous consumption. Charles V of France owned forty-seven jeweled and golden crowns and sixty-three complete sets of chapel furnishings, including vestments, gold crucifixes, altarpieces, reliquaries, and prayer books. Jewels and cloth of gold marked every occasion and every occasion was pretext for a spectacle—a grand procession, or ceremonial welcome to a visiting prince, a tournament or entertainment with music, and dancing by the light of great torches. When

Gian Galeazzo Visconti, ruler of Milan, gave a wedding banquet for his daughter, eighteen double courses were served, each of fish and meat, including trout, quail, herons, eels, sturgeon, and suckling pig spouting fire. The gifts presented after *each* course to several hundred guests included greyhounds in gem-studded velvet collars, hawks in tinkling silver bells, suits of armor, rolls of silk and brocade, garments trimmed with pearls and ermine, fully caparisoned warhorses, and twelve fat oxen. For the entry into Paris of the new Queen, Isabel of Bavaria, the entire length of the Rue St. Denis was hung with a canopy representing the firmament twinkling with stars from which sweetly singing angels descended bearing a crown, and fountains ran with wine, distributed to the people in golden cups by lovely maidens wearing caps of solid gold.

One wonders where all the money came from for such luxury and festivity in a time of devastation. What taxes could burned-out and destitute people pay? This is a puzzle until one remembers that the Aga Khan got to be the richest man in the world on the backs of the poorest people, and that disaster is never as pervasive as it seems from recorded accounts. It is one of the pitfalls for historians that the very fact of being on the record makes a happening appear to have been continuous and all-inclusive, whereas in reality it is more likely to have been sporadic both in time and place. Besides, persistence of the normal is usually greater than the effect of disturbance, as we know from our own times. After absorbing the daily paper and weekly magazine, one expects to face a world consisting entirely of strikes, crimes, power shortages, broken water mains, stalled trains, school shutdowns, Black Panthers, addicts, transvestites, rapists, and militant lesbians. The fact is that one can come home in the evening—on a lucky day—without having encountered more than two or three of these phenomena. This has led me to formulate Tuchman's Law, as follows: "The fact of being reported increases the *apparent* extent of a deplorable development by a factor of ten." (I snatch the figure from the air and will leave it to the quantifiers to justify.)

The astonishing fact is that except for Boccaccio, to whom we owe the most vivid account, the Black Death was virtually ignored by the great writers of the time. Petrarch, who was forty-four when it happened, mentions it only as the occasion for the death of Laura; Chaucer, from what I have read, passes it over in silence; Jean Froissart, the Herodotus of his time, gives it no more than one casual paragraph, and even that second Isaiah, the author of *Piers Plowman,* who might have been expected to make it central to his theme of woe, uses it only incidentally. One could argue that in 1348 Chaucer was only eight or nine years old and Froissart ten or eleven and the unknown Langland probably of the same vintage, but that is old enough to absorb and remember a great catastrophe, especially when they lived through several returns of the plague as grown men.

Perhaps this tells us that disaster, once survived, leaves less track than one supposed, or that man's instinct for living pushes it down below the surface, or simply that his recuperative powers are remarkable. Or was it just an accident of personality? Is it significant or just chance that Chaucer, the greatest writer of his age, was so uncharacteristic of it in sanguine temperament and good-humored view of his fellow creatures?

As for Froissart, never was a man more in love with his age. To him it appeared as a marvelous pageant of glittering armor and the beauty of emblazoned banners fluttering in the breeze and the clear shrill call of the trumpet. Still believing, still enraptured by the chivalric ideal, he reports savagery, treachery, limitless greed, and the pitiless slaughter of the poor when driven to revolt as minor stumbles in the grand adventure of valor and honor. Yet near the end, even Froissart could not hide from himself the decay made plain by a dissolute court, venality in high places, and a knighthood that kept losing battles. In 1397, the year he turned sixty, the defeat and massacre of the flower of chivalry at the hands of the Turks in the battle of Nicopolis set the seal on the incompetence of his heroes. Lastly, the murder of a King in England shocked him deeply, not for any love of Richard II but because the act was subversive of the whole order that sustained his world. As in Watergate, the underside had rolled to the surface all too visibly. Froissart had not the heart to continue and brought his chronicle to an end.

The sad century closed with a meeting between King Charles VI of France and the Emperor Wenceslaus, the one intermittently mad and the other regularly drunk. They met at Reims in 1397 to consult on means of ending the papal schism, but whenever Charles had a lucid interval, Wenceslaus was in a stupor and so the conference, proving fruitless, was called off.

It makes an artistic ending. Yet in that same year Johann Gutenberg, who was to change the world, was born. In the next century appeared Joan of Arc, embodying the new spirit of nationalism, still pure like mountain water before it runs downhill; and Columbus, who opened a new hemisphere; and Copernicus, who revolutionized the concept of the earth's relation to the universe; and Michelangelo, whose sculptured visions gave men a new status; in those proud, superb, unconquered figures, the human being, not God, was captain.

As our century enters its final quarter, I am not persuaded, despite the signs, that the end is necessarily doom. The doomsayers work by extrapolation; they take a trend and extend it, forgetting that the doom factor sooner or later generates a coping mechanism.

I have a rule for this situation too, which is absolute: You cannot extrapolate any series in which the human element intrudes; history, that is, the human narrative, never follows, and will always fool, the scientific curve. I cannot tell you what twists it will take, but I expect, that like our ancestors, we, too, will muddle through.

---

## Now that you've read

1. What were some of the significant events and changes that took place in the fourteenth century, according to Tuchman?
2. What are some of the similarities between the fourteenth century and ours?
3. According to Tuchman, what can closer attention to and knowledge of history teach us about ourselves and about our time in history?

## SEQUENCE 2 ASSIGNMENTS

### Reading 1: "College Freshmen More Conservative in Survey"

> Strong majorities of freshmen want more gun control, favor tougher environmental laws and support gay rights. But on other prominent subjects, many more students are embracing staunchly conservative views.

### *Prewriting*

1. How important is it to you to keep up with current events and why? How do you keep up with current events?
2. How important is doing volunteer work to you and why?
3. Do you think that grades have become "inflated" over the years? Explain your answer.
4. Why is "self-esteem" mentioned as a possible contributing factor to the survey results?

### *Writing assignment*

This article, which originally appeared in the *Washington Post* offers a lot of information on a variety of topics. What kinds of conclusions can you draw from the items covered in the survey? How well do you think these results reflect general thinking on your campus? How well do they describe you? Offer examples.

On the basis of the list of issues surveyed for this article, develop your own short set of questions and do an informal survey to determine the attitudes of people from your dorm or classmates in another class. Discuss their answers and draw conclusions about how well your results concur with those of the *Washington Post* writer.

### Reading 2: Paul Rogat Loeb, "I Feel a Little Fearful"

> It's frustrating to want to act but to find no context. It's frustrating to try to speak out against the current, only to be stereotyped and dismissed. I respect greatly students who worked to forge the first necessary steps toward concern, who persisted even when others of like mind seemed few. Yet most students use talk of isolation not to describe the frustrations of trying to act for change but to justify retreat—to shore up their more general belief that if peers were involved, they were elsewhere, far away.

## Prewriting

1. In two or three sentences, discuss what you think Loeb's quotation above means in the context of the whole reading assignment.
2. Reflect on the contrast Loeb draws between Polish activism and the comparative lack of activism in the United States. What might account for this difference?
3. How would you describe the level of political involvement on your campus?

## Writing assignment

In "I Feel a Little Fearful," Paul Rogat Loeb refers to Brazilian educator Paulo Freire's phrase "culture of silence." What does this phrase seem to mean, according to Loeb, and how is it connected, to students' willingness or unwillingness to speak out about issues on American college campuses? Would you say that Freire is correct? Compare the concept of the culture of silence to the information in the *Washington Post* article and to your own experience in college. Does this phrase describe the atmosphere on your campus? Give examples to support your answer. Quote from both Loeb and the *Washington Post* article as needed.

## Reading 3: Alexander W. Astin, "The Cause of Citizenship"

> Most of our citizenry—and that includes most of our college-educated citizenry—seems neither to understand what democracy is all about nor to accept responsibility for making it work.

## Prewriting

1. How well informed about politics would you say you are? How much of your knowledge of political events comes from television news?
2. Is it the university's responsibility to ensure that students are better informed about political events and the democratic process? Why or why not?

## Writing assignment

Astin makes the charge that most citizens—students and nonstudents alike—know little about how democracy works and even less about what roles they might play in its working. What's the basis for his argument? What does he offer as a solution? Does Loeb's piece necessarily support Astin's argument, or can one "feel a little fearful" about speaking out and still be an informed citizen? What might some of the students Loeb interviewed say in response to Astin? Would Astin be right in claiming that such students have been taught to value individualism, materialism, and competitiveness over community, service, and cooperation?

## Reading 4: Paul Berman, "The Moral History of the Baby Boom Generation"

> In one country after another, the way out of [the moral] crisis [of the baby boom generation] was to shake off the comforts of a stable bourgeois world and to take up the risks of radical solidarity. So a small vanguard of privileged students in place after place proposed risky campaigns of radical solidarity, and because the risky campaigns and the cult of danger seemed foolish or irresponsible to the adult left, the young and their elders fell into bitter arguments, and the young were expelled by the old.

### Prewriting

1. What is your mental picture of college life in the 1960s? Would you want to have been a college student then? Why or why not?
2. In what ways other than protest can an individual make her or his voice heard?
3. Reflect on why people are moved to participate in public forms of protest? What issue might move you to such activity?

### Writing assignment

First spend some time working through the history Berman relates and considering his concerns and arguments. What is he concerned about? What does he want us to know about that era? What was the "moral crisis" the baby boom generation faced? In the second part of your essay, respond to Berman's arguments. How do the main problems on your campus today—as well as student, faculty, and administrative responses to those problems—compare with what Berman describes? What happened to that "moral crisis" he describes? How might Astin in "The Cause of Citizenship" respond to Berman's history? How might Berman respond to Loeb?

## Reading 5: Patricia Williams, "Crimes Without Passion"

> I also believe that the personal is not the same as "private": the personal is often merely the highly particular. I think the personal has fallen into disrepute as sloppy because we have lost the courage and the vocabulary to describe it in the face of the enormous social pressure to "keep it

to ourselves"—but this is where our most idealistic and our deadliest politics are lodged, and are revealed.

## Prewriting

1. Use the context described in Williams's essay to explain what you take the quotation to mean.
2. Why does Williams include the story of her sister's Valentine's Day experience? How is it connected to the rest of the essay?
3. Should there be any limits on academic freedom? Does Williams's critique of the *Othello* exam question seek to curtail academic freedom, as Professor L. claims? Why or why not?

## Writing assignment

Now that you've taken some time to consider Williams's arguments, write a brief essay in which you describe where you stand. You don't have to say one person is right and one is wrong; instead, work through the ways in which both sides can be "right" *and* "wrong." How does Williams's definition of *politics* differ from Astin's or Berman's? What are the larger issues at stake, according to Williams? In what ways is the personal "where our most idealistic and our deadliest politics are lodged, and are revealed"? What are the implications of these issues beyond the college campus?

## Reading 6: Barbara Tuchman, "History as Mirror"

> As our century enters its final quarter, I am not persuaded, despite the signs, that the end is necessarily doom. The doomsayers work by extrapolation; they take a trend and extend it, forgetting that the doom factor sooner or later generates a coping mechanism.

## Prewriting

1. Reflect on the quotation from Tuchman's essay above, and discuss what you think it means.
2. Make a list of the parallels Tuchman identifies between past and present. Were you surprised by any of these parallels? Why?
3. What conclusions does Tuchman want you to draw about present-day politics?

## Writing assignment

First, go through Tuchman's essay and choose one section that seems to you to have something to teach us about an issue currently in the news. What happened in the past? What is happening now? What can you predict about the present on the basis of the event in the past? Then consider your responsibility as a citizen in this day and age. What enables you to make informed judgments about current global political problems and events? What do you believe it is necessary for you to do in order to meet that responsibility? Draw from the other readings in this sequence to compose your response.

## Final Project

Review what you've written in the writing assignments for this sequence. What is your level of political awareness? What is the level of student activism on your campus? Are you satisfied with the level of student activism on your campus and throughout the nation, or would you like to see a change in another direction? Mine your essays for a specific issue you'd like to investigate in further detail, and formulate a concise thesis you can use in a research paper. If you can't decide on a topic to investigate further, consider these questions:

How well informed are students on your campus? How politically active are they?
What are contemporary students' attitudes toward the campus politics of the 1960s?
What prevents students from speaking out on your campus or encourages them to speak out?
What do you believe it is necessary for a person to do in order to consider himself or herself an informed citizen and a participant in the democratic process?

## Library Research Ideas

Try one or more of the following library research activities, or come up with your own ideas for library research to support your thesis.

1. Check out the web site **http://www.proactivist.com**. This site, devoted to political activism, has links to many other web sites devoted to political issues and activism. In addition, check out the page of links to student activist groups: **http://proactivist. com/links/Student_Activism**. Are any of these groups represented on your campus?
2. Compare coverage of one or more controversial issues in your city or state's major newspaper to coverage of the same issues in your school's official student newspaper. Be sure to check the editorials in both papers. Are there student-published underground newspapers on your campus, in addition to the official

student paper? If so, how do their views compare to those of the official student paper? Do you think the official student paper reflects the political views of a majority of students on your campus? Do the underground publications?

3. Research the history of student activism in the United States and in other countries. How politically aware and active have students traditionally been? How active were U.S. students before the 1960s? How politically active and aware have U.S. students been compared with students around the world? Are today's U.S. college students more or less politically active and aware than students in other periods and in other countries?

## Field Research Ideas

Try one or more of the following field research ideas, or use your own field research ideas to get data to support your thesis.

1. Develop a survey to measure student political attitudes—a survey similar to the one summarized in the first reading. Administer it in your dorm, among classmates, or among some other student population, and compare your results with those reported in the *Washington Post* article.

2. Observe your campus for a period of time (say, a couple of weeks) for signs of political awareness and activism. Notice flyers posted on campus kiosks and in the library. Do many of them deal with political issues? Do student activists regularly hand out literature on your campus? If so, can you discern any patterns in terms of their political philosophy? Are they more likely to be liberal or conservative in their views? Do you think they represent the most common views among the students at your school? Are their views more extreme, either toward the right or toward the left, than those of most other students on campus?

3. Interview a student activist. Ask why he or she is involved in politics on campus, what he or she is studying in school, and what he or she plans to do after leaving college. Ask for his or her opinion about the level of student activism on campus. You could also interview an individual who was politically active as a student in the past, such as in the 1960s.

# Negotiating Differences: Race, Class, Ethnicity

## Getting Started

*Political correctness* and *multiculturalism* have become hot-button terms in recent years, sparking strong words and intense debates on college campuses and in living rooms, boardrooms, and legislative halls around the country. This sequence explores how racial, ethnic, and socioeconomic differences—and the perception of difference—affect college life and American society in general.

In "The Professions as Class Fortress," Barbara Ehrenreich argues that the educational requirements of the professions—advanced degrees, certain prerequisite courses—serve as much to lock out working-class people, who haven't had the advantage of a middle-class education, as they do to train competent professionals. In "Dirtbags, Burnouts, Metalheads, and Thrashers," Donna Gaines investigates the role that class plays in how students are labeled and in what type of academic and career advice they receive. bell hooks also makes class a focus of investigation in "Confronting Class in the

Classroom." In "From Outside, In," Barbara Mellix discusses the difference between being an "insider" and being an "outsider" in the world of education. As a reporter covering the Balkans, Janine DiGiorgio shows, in "Lost Generation," how the age-old conflicts between Serbs and ethnic Albanians have destroyed the chances of an entire generation of young adults to go to college or find employment in their own hometowns. Finally, Audre Lorde argues in "The Uses of Anger: Women Responding to Racism" that anger over injustice, if properly channeled, can be empowering and liberating. As you work through these readings and answer the questions in the reading and writing assignments that follow, consider your own thoughts and feelings about multiculturalism and diversity.

Before you do any of the reading, however, please reflect on the issue of diversity on campus and in society in general; then respond to several of the following questions. I use the Getting Started questions as a preliminary exercise on the first day my class works on a particular sequence. Your teacher may also do this, or he or she may ask that you write out your responses either in a journal or in your notebook. Your teacher may use these questions as a jumping-off place for class discussion as well. No matter how you use these questions in your class, you'll be able to draw on what you write here both in your contributions to class discussion and in your responses to the assignments that follow.

1. What do you think the term *multiculturalism* and *political correctness* mean? Do you think the word *multicultural* encompasses class as well as racial or ethnic diversity? Why or why not? Is multiculturalism politically correct? Why or why not?
2. What are some of the advantages of attending an ethnically and racially diverse college or university?
3. What does it mean to be middle-class? What does "class" mean? What are some of the advantages of attending a college or university with students from a broad range of socioeconomic classes?

## READING 1

### Barbara Ehrenreich

# The Professions as Class Fortress

Barbara Ehrenreich has written widely about social class in America. In this excerpt from her book *Fear of Falling: The Inner Life of the Middle Class,* she claims that college training for the professions serves to exclude some people from those professions, and consequently from the middle class, even more than it serves to train professionals. See whether you find her evidence convincing.

### *Before you read*

1. To what socioeconomic class (middle, working, upper, etc.) would you say you belong? Why?
2. Ehrenreich states that when asked, "90% of Americans identified themselves as belonging to the middle class—even those with incomes near or below the poverty level and those who make hundreds of thousands of dollars." Why might that be?
3. How would you define the term *middle class*?
4. Are any classes on your campus known as "weed-out" courses— courses designed to get rid of students? Why would a college or a department want such classes?

---

To step back for a moment from the immediate fray: The professions are indeed tne unique occupational "space" possessed by the middle class. The period in which the professions arose, about 1870 to 1920, was also the period in which the middle class itself appeared in its present form on the American scene. In every field, professionalization was presented as a reform, a bold new measure aimed at replacing guesswork and tradition with science and rationality. But it was also an economic strategy, linked, as historian Samuel Haber has written, with "the 'art of rising in life,' with upward mobility." Through professionalization, the middle class sought to carve out an occupational niche that would be closed both to the poor and to those who were merely rich.

Our modern middle class is the descendant of an older gentry composed of independent farmers, small businessmen, self-employed lawyers, doctors, and ministers. In the fifty years surrounding the turn of the twentieth century, that gentry—the "old" middle class—found itself squeezed between an insurgent lower class and a powerful new capitalist class. As the monopolies tightened their grip on the economy, small business became risky business. At the same time, the old, unregulated professions of medicine and law, which almost anyone could enter simply by hanging out a shingle, were becoming "overpopulated" with upstarts from less genteel backgrounds.

Professionalization was, above all, a way to restrict entry to existing occupations. In medicine, for example, alarm over an oversupply of doctors ultimately convinced the American Medical Association of the value of "scientific" reforms limiting the practice of medicine to those who had completed a college education and four additional years of standardized medical training. At a time when less than 5 percent of the college-age population actually attended college, these reforms guaranteed that medicine would henceforth be limited to "gentlemen" and closed, as reformer Abraham Flexner explained, to the "crude boy or jaded clerk." For those already in practice, it was a matter of pulling the ladder up after oneself. As the famed physician and medical professor William Osler quipped to a colleague, "We are lucky to get in [to the medical profession] as professors, for I am sure that neither you nor I could ever get in as students."

Other occupations adopted a similar strategy. Law and social work declared themselves "scientific," instituted steep educational barriers, and succeeded in closing their ranks to any "crude boys" or (in the case of social work) dilettantish volunteers who might seek entry. Academia sorted itself into most of the familiar disciplines (sociology, political science, psychology, and so forth) and established the equally familiar hierarchy of degrees (bachelor's, master's, doctor's). Even management claimed to be "scientific" and sought (unsuccessfully, at the time) to limit entry to the appropriately, and expensively, educated. Each group publicized its professionalization as a major reform in the interests of science, rationality, and public service. And each succeeded, to a greater or lesser degree, in carving out an occupational monopoly restricted to the elite minority who could afford college educations and graduate degrees.

Through professionalization, the middle class gained purchase in an increasingly uncertain world. Henceforth it would be shielded, at least slightly, from the upheavals of the market economy. Its "capital" would be knowledge or, more precisely, expertise. Its security would lie in the monopolization of that expertise through the device of professionalization. Its hallmark would be higher education and, with it, the exclusive license to practice, consult, or teach, in exchange for that more mundane form of capital, money.

To this day, the educational barriers to the professions serve as much to exclude as to educate. Consider the case of medicine, which is usually regarded, at least by sociologists, as the most secure and least assailable of the professions. The critical barrier—the key "weeding out" course for undergraduate premed majors—is organic chemistry. In fact, organic chemistry was the example Brustein seized on, in his defense of professionalism, to refute student demands in the sixties for socially relevant education. "My very simple point was that in order to become a doctor and help the sick of the ghettos," he wrote in response to a critic of his essay, "you must first study 'irrelevant' subjects like comparative anatomy and organic chemistry." But why should organic chemistry be the critical barrier to becoming a doctor? Why not a course in nutrition, or in the social and environmental causes of disease? (Incidentally, these courses are not even part of the premed program and are only recently being added to medical school curricula.)

Of course premed students *should* study organic chemistry—and so, I believe, should drama students if they are so inclined—because it is an intrinsically fascinating subject. But it should be acknowledged that much of the content of a college course in organic chemistry has little or no relevance to the practice of medicine. Despite the scientific aspirations of early twentieth-century medical reformers, medicine has not reached the point where knowledge of the quantum chemistry of covalent bonds is helpful in the treatment of patients. Calculus, another hurdle for the would-be medical student, is even less defensible: A subject of great charm to many, it is of no conceivable value to the practicing physician or, for that matter, the great majority of medical researchers. Most premed students know perfectly well that these requirements are irrelevant to their future careers. They do not enjoy organic chemistry; they get through it, one way or another, and promptly forget it.

But such courses still serve one of their original functions: to screen out students who have not had the benefit of a high-quality, middle-class, secondary education (as well as those who simply cannot afford to go to college). In other areas, such as law and social work, the requirement of a generic college degree serves the same screening function, regardless of whether one earns it in a subject remotely relevant to the practice of these professions. The academic disciplines appear to be on somewhat more solid ground, since they involve no "practice" apart from research—research which can only be judged by those already within the discipline. No one but a sociologist, say, can judge what constitutes sociology and what is relevant for a would-be sociologist to study. But, here too, a screening function is at work, eliminating not only the poor and underprepared but any amateurs—journalists or free-lance intellectuals, for example—who might wish to dignify their efforts as "sociology," "history," or whatever.

So we can begin to understand the fury and spitefulness of the backlash against the student movement. When students challenged the authority of their professors, when they questioned the validity and relevance of the knowledge from which that authority was said to be derived, they struck at the fundamental assumptions of their class. Judged in the context of that class and its interests, they were guilty of nothing less than treason. They had exposed, in however inarticulate a fashion, the conceit on which middle-class privilege rests: We know more, and are therefore entitled to positions of privilege and authority.

In response, the spokespersons for the backlash fell back on every shibboleth of professional ideology: the reality of purely objective knowledge, untainted by self-interest; the sanctity of the university; the unassailable integrity of the "inherited body of knowledge."* What they abandoned, unfortunately, was the middle class's historical claim to be the agent of reform and rationality. The backlash ultimately degenerated into mere conservatism—the defense of hierarchy for its own sake. "There is no blinking the fact that some people are brighter than others," Brustein wrote, ostensible in defense of a kind of status that is normally achieved only through years of disciplined study, "some more beautiful, some more gifted."

--------------------------------

*In detail, their defense of professionalism was lamentably weak. Consider Brustein's defense of medicine, the only profession for which he actually ventured a substantive defense of any kind. "It is unlikely," he wrote, "(though anything is possible these days) that medical students will insist on making a diagnosis through majority vote, or that students entering surgery will refuse anaesthesia because they want to participate in the decisions that affect their lives and, therefore, demand to choose the surgeon's instruments or tell him where to cut."

But these are not unreasonable demands. First, while diagnostic decisions should not be made by "majority vote," they are—or should be—arrived at through open discussion, preferably involving nurses and technicians as well as physicians. Second, most patients do indeed want to "participate in decisions that affect their lives," which is why they seek second opinions and try to find physicians who are willing to answer questions and discuss alternatives. Finally, it should be observed that the example of surgery is often invoked as a last-ditch defense of professional authority. When community groups demanded a voice in the management of Harlem Hospital in the late sixties, lobbying, for example, for more accessible clinic hours, administrators and doctors responded that "next they'll want to tell the surgeon where to cut." This is a standard professional ploy, using expertise in one area ("where to cut") to legitimize authority in other areas (clinic hours). Similarly, Brustein sought to spread the acknowledged authority of the surgeon *at the time of surgery* to all professionals, including, presumably, the professor of drama holding forth in his lecture hall.

## Now that you've read:

1. What is Barbara Ehrenreich's overall argument? Do you agree or disagree with her? Explain your answer.
2. Would you rather see a doctor who had passed a course in organic chemistry or one who had passed a course in nutrition? Explain your answer.
3. Reflect on your own career aspirations. Are you considering a career in one of the professions (law, medicine, etc.)? Why or why not?

## Reading 2

---

### *Donna Gaines*

## Dirtbags, Burnouts, Metalheads, and Thrashers

Donna Gaines has some harsh things to say about America's claim to being a "classless" society. Her views grew out of her research talking to and learning about the lives of high school dropouts in New Jersey and New York, detailed in her book *Teenage Wasteland*. Here Gaines makes some critically pointed arguments about how students are counseled by school advisors and about how placement can reveal prejudices based on social class. As you read, think about the people you knew in high school that other people labeled as "dirtbags, burnouts, metalheads, and thrashers" and consider how Gaines might respond to them.

### *Before you read*

1. What do you make of the title of this essay?
2. Is there a vocational high school where you come from? What is its reputation? What kind of reputations do the students who go there have?
3. At your high school, did the students in college preparatory classes hang out with those in vocational classes? Explain your answer.

---

Dirtbags, burnouts, metalheads, and thrashers alike could find pride and purpose in Bergen County's trade schools. Here, as in other suburban towns, the local vocational and technical school is usually called "heavy metal high school" because of all the metalheads who attend.

Vocational high school may be viewed by academically oriented educators as a convenient dump site for troublemakers with low test scores. But for the kids who end up there, it's often a pretty cool scene. Especially here in Bergen County, where every dirtbag shuttled over to a vocational school has the additional prestige of knowing S.O.D.'s lead singer went to one. Wherever I went in Bergen County, if music was seriously discussed, people made sure to tell me that S.O.D.'s powerful front man, Billy Milano, was from Bergen County. So what if the jocks were winning state competitions—the dirts had Billy and S.O.D. for their regional pride.

Meanwhile, there were guys like Roy. I had met him on the Ave one night, talking to Jeanne and Nicole. Roy rarely hung out anymore, now that he was learning to labor on the cars of America. It was a great career choice, and it seems to have happened quite by chance. It's a familiar story, though.

This is how it goes: The teacher calls you down to talk about your record. Or maybe it's the guidance counselor. "So, Roy, what do you see yourself doing five years from now?" And Roy is thinking what did I do wrong, what does she want me to say, what is going to come down on me now? And then the guidance counselor will say something about Roy's lack of spectacular grades—"not on any teams or in any clubs, are you, Roy?" And Roy starts feeling stupid and maybe he fiddles with himself nervously, and says the first thing that comes to his head, like how much he enjoys working on his car. Like she shouldn't think he's a total loser. And that's that! He's never really given much thought before now, but today, the future is laid out before him and now Roy's going to vocational high school and he's going to learn about cars.

He's so relieved that he's not in trouble, and that this adult hasn't figured out that he really hasn't got a clue about what he's going to do with his life because nobody ever asked him about it. Or impressed upon him that what he wants might be important. Until today, most of what Roy has been concerned with has been keeping out of trouble, keeping out of his teachers' way. So Roy is satisfied because now he has a future, and with it, an identity and plans. Maybe he'll do well at it. His foster mother is proud of him. He's almost grown, and now he's got a direction.

In the suburban high schools of America the greasers have always been found hanging around outside "shop." There are many "hoody"-looking types who have good academic grades, who are book-smart, but that's not the stereotype. Working-class males smoking cigarettes and bonding around labor. Girls gathered around small office machines and hair-setting apparatus. This territory is now the domain of America's metalheads. Dirtbags, metalheads, thrashers, and burnouts. Black and Hispanic kids are part of this too.

Bergen County's Vocational Technical School, where Roy was now enrolled, was in Hackensack. When I mentioned this to some guy I met at Hav-A-Pizza in the Foster Village Shopping Center, he said, "Oh yeah, that's a real burnout school." The school has a great street rep. So I drove out to Roy's school that afternoon, to find out what this school was doing right.

The campus is situated near Roy Rogers, which is right away a good spot for a school. In the parking lot an unidentifiable thrash band's snarecore drumroll propels two long-haired dudes deep into the engine of an old light-green Chevy Nova. Many of the grand bombs of the Ave will have been resurrected here. Engines and bodies and hoods and fenders and hair. Here, the celebration of car culture becomes a legitimate practice, and it's okay to be yourself. You learn what you like to learn. That's why you're here.

There are greenhouses, and clusters of girls in smocks. Before I introduce myself to the authorities I meander through the halls. The school is clean and cheerful, although clearly "not for kids." Serious business is conducted here. On display are the successful liaisons of youth and industry, career ladders in various trades, union wage schedules. I am stopped by a man who is a teacher. We chat comfortably. This is far from Bergenfield and he is delighted that I am interested in the school.

For more information he suggests the guidance counselor's offices, and directs me there. I am told that someone can see me in about twenty minutes, as a door shuts behind a middle-aged woman with dark hair and a young girl. Meantime, would I mind waiting in the library?

I walk by a room filled with computers. A few moments later I am seated near some kids doing library time, working on a report, relaxing and quietly talking. I pick from a table of magazines: *Psychology Today, BYTE, Horticulture, The Conservationist, Parents, New Jersey Outdoors, Family Computing, Gourmet.* Something for everyone.

A glamorous teenage girl shows off an earring someone made for her in shop. It's [a] delicate metal sculpture, something nice enough to wear to a show. A boy in a concert polo shirt teases her, all the while viewing the librarian for sanctions. The librarian glares once or twice, but goes on to other business. The students seem more physically relaxed than their counterparts in regular schools. They're more stylish too, from a street point of view. That makes sense; these are specialized programs for kids interested in food preparation, cosmetology, carpentry, commercial art, and the interest in grooming and styling is strong. Also, they will be working with the public in some of these fields, so personal appearance is important.

The time passes quickly in this sunlit airy room. I am greeted by the dark-haired guidance counselor, Dolores Bentivegna. We sit down in her office and I ask her, simply, why kids seem to like this school so much. By now I understand the basic breakdown: Kids with behavior problems are sent to special services—emotionally disturbed kids, school phobics, and disabled kids. And kids with low grades are often encouraged to come here, dumped into vocational education. That way teachers can spread scarce resources efficiently, focus on the more intellectually responsive kids, the college material. Keep the school looking good, the test scores robust, all so their "brighter" kids have a better chance.

I also understand from the kids that getting farmed out to the vocational high school involves some degree of coercion. But once they get here, they like it, they are happy. So I ask this guidance counselor what is the secret of this school's success.

Mrs. B. explains that this school has the longest school day in the district, no study hall, a short lunch break. Half the day is academic, half is for work in one's chosen field. The program is highly structured. Not all the kids can handle it. That makes sense, I say, since a number of kids who have been encouraged to come here say they have no real interest in vocational training. . . .

Following a good hour of her time, Mrs. B. gives me her card, and I thank her.

That night it occurs to me that most of the guys I knew from Metal 24, guys in my neighborhood, were "B.O.C.E.S." graduates— New York State's version of Bergen Vo-Tech. The Board of Cooperative Educational Services of Nassau County was famous for many things. Some kids were sent there for vocational training or for programs in the arts, and they spoke lovingly of their high school experiences. Some programs were directly related to Long Island's aerospace and technology industries.

Other kids were "special," like Nicky and Joe and Randy, too "emotionally disturbed" for the mainstream classroom. These guys were sent to the school in Baldwin Harbor because they were even too rowdy for the "rubber rooms" in their own districts. They just took it in stride: the label, the Ritalin, the warehousing.

Then there was "B.O.C.E.S. for chicks"—that's what the guys call the traditionally feminine fields of cosmetology, flower arranging, data processing, food preparation, and dental assisting. I live near Nassau Tech, a major B.O.C.E.S. site that is known for its low-cost, high-quality lunch cafeteria. The kids do the cooking and the public gets a great deal on a meal.

My "research consultants" at the convenience store, Eddie and Cliff, also agreed that life in vocational courses had a lot more dignity than life in regular high school. Eddie says he was coming to his school drunk every day, so they steered him over to B.O.C.E.S. When asked what he wanted to study, Eddie figured food preparation, because this was where all the pretty girls hung out and he wanted to meet them. So he embarked upon a career in "food prep." This eventually landed him a job baking donuts, then making sandwiches at a deli.

Of course Eddie couldn't support himself on five dollars an hour, so, like many local entrepreneurs, he began moonlighting in the underground youth economy. This illicit activity got him sent up for two years. In prison, he had the opportunity to take some college courses. Eddie says he would like to complete his B.S. degree some day, but he's got no money for tuition. Besides, he says, he's not in any rush for school right now. So he's just working at the convenience store and playing in a local band.

Cliff studied graphic arts and printing, but had also worked in a deli. He hoped to buy one of his own but needed a chunk of cash to do it. His parents died before he was twenty-one; there really wasn't anyone to help him out. At one point he was going to go in on a limo partnership, hoping to drive and work for himself. But he needed to put up heavy cash for it. So for now he's working at Metal 24. Late at night it's arts-and-crafts time at Metal 24. Eddie will be writing lyrics, Cliff setting up designs for future tattoos. Sid and a few of the other guys will be playing video games and Cliff's girlfriend, Ann, and I are probably discussing horoscopes.

Sid is another B.O.C.E.S. alum who studied auto body. He offers to do a light compounding on my car. He did an impressive piece of work on his Boxcar; he won't take any money from me because we're friends. He works at the parts counter at Auto Barn.

The "disposable" heroes in my neighborhood are all working in fields related to the training they got at B.O.C.E.S. Ann works in hair, and she sweeps the floors of a local beauty parlor. The other girls have babies now, so they don't hang out anymore. A few hold jobs as cashiers or hostesses and you rarely see them. One girl goes to Nassau Community College at night and works in a video store during the day.

Meanwhile Cliff dreams of being a bass player, Eddie is writing lyrics. Sid plays drums, Ann wants to have a family. Friends from the neighborhood who are my age hung out at Metal 24 when it was a drive-in hamburger stand. Many people here live the same lives, ten years after, with some of the same dreams.

In the scheme of things average American kids who don't have rich or well-connected parents have had these choices: Play the game and try to get ahead. Do what your parents did—work yourself to death at a menial job and find solace in beer, God, or family. Or take risks, cut deals, or break the law. The Reagan years made it hard for kids to "put their noses to the grindstone" as their parents had. Like everyone, these people hoped for better lives. But they lived in an age of inflated expectations and diminishing returns. Big and fast money was everywhere, and ever out of reach. America now had an economy that worked sort of like a cocaine high—propped up by hot air and big debt. The substance was absent. People's lives were like that too, and at times they were crashing hard.

In the meantime, wherever you were, you could still dream of becoming spectacular. A special talent could be your ticket out. Long Island kids had role models in bands like the Crumbsuckers, Ludichrist, Twisted Sister, and Pat Benatar. North Jersey was full of sports celebrities and rock millionaires—you grew up hoping you'd end up like Mike Tyson or Jon Bon Jovi. Or like Keith Richards, whose father worked in a factory; or Ozzy, who also came from a grim

English factory town, a hero who escaped the drudge because he was spectacular. This was the hip version of the American dream.

Kids who go for the prize now understand there are only two choices—rise to the top or crash to the bottom. Many openly admit that they would rather end it all now than end up losers. The nine-to-five world, corporate grunt life, working at the same job for thirty years, that's not for them. They'd prefer to hold out until the last possibility and then just piss on it all. The big easy or the bottomless pit, but never the everyday drone. And as long as there are local heroes and stories, you can still believe you have a chance to emerge from the mass as something larger than life. You can still play the great lottery and dream.

Schools urge kids to make these choices as early as possible, in a variety of ways. In the terse words of the San Francisco hardcore band MDC, "There's no such thing as cheating in a loser's game." Many kids who start out as nobody from nowhere with nothing will end up that way. Nevertheless, everyone pretends that everything is possible if give it your best shot. We actually believe it. While educators hope to be as efficient as possible in figuring out where unspectacular students can plug into the work force, kids try to play at being one in a million, some way of shining, even if it's just for a while.

A few years playing ball, or in a band, and then you get a job. My boyfriend K. had a father employed as a mechanic at Grumman Aerospace. His father offered to get him a job in management there, since K. was "quick with the words." But K. had other plans. He got a part-time job in shipping at the age of seventeen. He kept it after high school, and held on to it for ten years while he played in the Grinders and other bands. The music was always his first priority. Over the years, he's picked up some more hours, and he's glad to have good Teamsters benefits.

But during those years he also got to play at CBGB's and Max's Kansas City, and he cut a few albums. Periodically there was champagne and limousines, and so once in a while K. got to be spectacular.

Girls get slightly different choices. They may hope to become spectacular by virtue of their talents and their beauty. Being the girlfriend of a guy in a band means you might get to live in his mansion someday if you stick it out with him during the lean years. You might just end up like Jon Bon Jovi's high school sweetheart, or married to someone like Cinderella's lead singer—he married his hometown girlfriend and helped set her up in her own business. These are suburban fairy tales.

Around here, some girls who are beautiful and talented hope to become stars too, like Long Island's local products Debbie Gibson and Taylor Dayne. Some hope to be like actress Heather Locklear and marry someone really hot like Motley Crue's drummer, Tommy Lee. If you could just get to the right place at the right time.

But most people from New Jersey and Long Island or anywhere else in America don't end up rich and famous. They have some fun trying, though, and for a while life isn't bad at all.

Yet, if you are unspectacular—not too book-smart, of average looks and moderate creative ability—there have always been places for you. Much of your teacher's efforts will be devoted to your more promising peers, and so will your nation's resources. But your parents will explain to you that this is the way it is, and early on, you will know to expect very little from school.

There are still a few enclaves, reservations. The shop and crafting culture of your parents' class of origin is one pocket of refuge. In the vocational high school, your interests are rewarded, once you have allowed yourself to be dumped there. And if the skills you gather there don't really lead to anything much, there's always the military.

Even though half the kids in America today will never go to college, the country still acts as if they will. At least, most schools seem to be set up to prepare you for college. And if it's not what you can or want to do, their attitude is tough shit, it's your problem.

And your most devoted teachers at vocational high school will never tell you that the training you will get from them is barely enough to get your foot in the door. You picture yourself getting into something with a future only to find that your skills are obsolete, superficial, and the boss prefers people with more training, more experience, more promise. So you are stuck in dead-end "youth employment jobs," and now what?

According to the William T. Grant Commission on Work, Family and Citizenship, twenty million people between the ages of sixteen and twenty-four are not likely to go to college. The "forgotten half," as youth advocates call them, will find jobs in service and retail. But the money is bad, only half that of typical manufacturing jobs. The good, stable jobs that don't require advanced training have been disappearing rapidly. From 1979 to 1985 the U.S.A. suffered a net loss of 1.7 million manufacturing jobs. What's left?

In my neighborhood, the shipping and warehousing jobs that guys like the Grinders took, hedging their bets against rock stardom, are now seen as "good jobs" by the younger guys at Metal 24. I am regularly asked to petition K. to "find out if they're hiring" down at his shipping company. Dead-end kids around here who aren't working with family are working "shit jobs."

The skills used in a typical "shit job" like the ones Cliff and Eddie have involve slapping rancid butter on stale hard rolls, mopping the floor, selling Lotto tickets, making sure shelves and refrigerators are clean, sorting and stacking magazines, taking delivery on news-papers, and signing out videos. They are also advised to look out for shoplifters, to protect the register, and to be sure that the sur-veillance camera is running. Like most kids in shit jobs, they are most skilled at getting over on the boss and in developing strategies to ward off boredom. It is not unusual to see kids at the super-market cash register or the mall clothing shop standing around with a glazed look in their eyes. And you will often hear them complain of boredom, tiredness, or whine, "I can't wait to get out of here." Usually, in shit jobs this is where it begins and ends. There aren't many alternatives.

Everywhere, such kids find getting into a union or having access to supervisory or managerial tracks hard to come by. Some forms of disinvestment are more obvious than others. In a company town, you will be somewhat clear about what is going on. At the end of the 1980s, the defense industry of Long Island seemed threatened; people feared that their lives would soon be devastated.

But the effect of a changing economic order on most kids only translates into scrambling for a new safety zone. It is mostly ex-pressed as resentment against entrepreneurial foreigners (non-whites) and as anomie—a vague sense of loss, then confusion about where they might fit in.

Through the 1980s, people articulated their sense of loss in songs. Springsteen's Jersey was a suicide rap, a death trap. The Pretenders' Chrissie Hynde found that her industrial city, her Ohio, was gone, turned into shopping malls. Billy Joel's "Allentown" mourned for the steelworkers of Pennsylvania who had lost their America. To those of us who relate to music nonlyrically, the middle 1980s "industrial noise" bands, the postpunks, and the death-metal merchants were saying the same thing: when old ways die out, be-fore new ones are firmly established, all that remains is a vacuum, a black hole. . . .

So where are we going? Some people fear we are polarizing into a two-class nation, rich and poor. More precisely, a privileged knowledge-producing class and a low-paid, low-status service class. It is in the public high school that this division of labor for an emer-gent postindustrial local economy is first articulated. At the top are the kids who will hold jobs in a highly competitive technological economic order, who will advance and be respected if they cooper-ate and excel.

At the bottom are kids with poor basic skills, short attention spans, limited emotional investment in the future. Also poor hous-ing, poor nutrition, bad schooling, bad lives. And in their bad jobs they will face careers of unsatisfying part-time work, low pay, no benefits, and no opportunity for advancement.

There are the few possibilities offered by a relative—a coveted place in a union, a chance to join a small family business in a service trade, a spot in a small shop. In my neighborhood, kids dream of making a good score on the cop tests, working up from hostess to waitress. Most hang out in limbo hoping to get called for a job in the sheriff's department, or the parks, or sanitation. They're on all the lists, although they know the odds for getting called are slim. The lists are frozen, the screening process is endless.

Meantime they hold jobs for a few months here and there, or they work off the books, or at two bad jobs at once. They live at home, in a finished basement. If they get pregnant, they still remain with their parents. Nobody has health insurance. Unless they are sucked in by car salesmen who urge them to buy on credit and are paying off heavy car loans, they drive old cars.

And they don't marry. Some think it's hopeless because of the inevitability of divorce. But many girls have told me marriage is their dream, since it is their one shot at a home of their own. In 1985, only 43 percent of high school dropouts had incomes high enough to support a three-person family above the poverty level. That's a decline of 60 percent since 1973. In 1985, 3.1 million family households headed by youths under twenty-five had incomes below the poverty level, nearly double the rate of the early 1970s. If we disengage the romanticism normally ascribed to "adolescence," these are simply poor people with few options and no understanding of the social relations that permit adults to keep young Americans poor, disenfranchised, and without skills. Young people are poor people without rights, poor and powerless even without any added burdens of region, class, race, and sex. In the absence of a "youth" movement of magnitude or any memory of intergeneration politics, many kids are simply stuck.

In *Learning to Labor,* a study of British working-class kids, Paul Willis argued that by messing up at school, kids tricked themselves into reproducing their parents' bad lives. Willis was writing in the middle 1970s. By now, his "lads" and my "kids" don't even have those same bad options, since so many working-class jobs are disappearing. Today, dropping out of school in a society that is curtailing production and moving toward technical knowledge is the kiss of death.

Working-class kids have learned patterns of coping with an educational system originally designed by middle-class reformers to elevate the masses. It is generally agreed that the values and "cultural capital" needed to survive and thrive in this environment have given middle-class kids a bigger advantage. Traditionally, working-class kids had a number of strategies mentioned earlier, shop strategies adapted from the parent culture (sabotage, workplace solidarity, after-hours fraternizing). But if the parent culture itself is dying out, the strategies learned from it have no value. They won't lead to reproducing one's parents' lives in industrial labor. They'll lead you nowhere.

Kids who bomb out at school, who express their outrage and defy the regime by ignoring it, will now pay a worse price than ever before. They have higher expectations because of the inflated rhetoric of the Reagan years, and lower life chances because of global transformations in the economy that most people cannot even comprehend. Older guys I know who are struggling to keep their jobs in American companies say we should be more organized, be like the Japanese. Labor blames management and management blames labor. The public buys American out of loyalty and then curses the shitty product. Beyond that, nobody has a clue.

Responsibility for containing young people, for prolonging their entry into the work force, is now shared among families, school, the military, and juvenile jails. Meanwhile, life outside, in the real world, has changed drastically.

So if kids fuck off in school, they have nothing to fall back on. They are tracked, early on, for life. According to the Grant Commission, kids with math and reading scores in the bottom fifth as compared with their peers in the top half were almost nine times more likely to leave without a diploma, have a child out of wedlock, almost five times more likely to have incomes below the poverty line, and twice as likely to have been arrested the previous year.

In 1986, high school dropouts between the ages of twenty and twenty-four earned 42 percent less than similar kids did in 1973. In 1984, 12 percent of them had no earnings at all. So kids who make up the forgotten half and are unspectacular are now learning to labor at the bottom of the economy. These undereducated and underemployed kids will be tracked into low-paid, futureless jobs. The dropout rates, all the invisible kids bombing out to nowhere, foreshadows the career possibilities available to whole classes of Americans.

Unspectacular children of the baby bust—*Los Olvidados.* And these will become America's invisible classes. They will remain as unseen and unheard as the legions of young people who now serve the baby boom and others, in fancy eateries, video stores, and supermarkets. Adult employers regularly complain that such kids have "poor work habits," are unreliable, "tardy," and perform badly at whatever they're told to do. The kids today lack "basic skills." Half the time they don't even show up for work. The impression is that for most kids, work is a low priority. They lack the discipline. They just don't seem to care about anything except having a good time.

Before I knew better, I asked Nicky what he was planning to do after he graduated. Was he going to college? He had decent grades. He could study music. Nicky was annoyed that I would even suggest something so idiotic. He laughed right in my face. "Yeah, right. I'll go to college for four years, be bored to death, and come out owing all this money and then I can get a job that pays less than what some guy pumping gas is making." For him, school is a joke. He wants the diploma but beyond that, education serves no purpose.

For Nicky, there also doesn't seem to be any desire to try to live differently from his parents. Nicky has dreams; he'd like to make it someday as a drummer. This is his shot at becoming spectacular. He was practicing, he said. Maybe he'd get in a band. Meanwhile Nicky was planning to put in some applications. Maybe get a job as a stock boy at Rickel's, a huge home-improvement chain.

After school he'd go right to work. If he didn't leave north Jersey he would probably look for a place around here. Or stay at home and save money. I asked him if he wanted to get out of here, leave the area for good. Maybe; he might like to move to California someday. Maybe he'd move there with his old girlfriend. But Nicky also told me he didn't want to leave his friends or his family. He was always saying, "This place sucks." He was always complaining about how boring it was. But when it came down to making a move, he doubted there was any place else he'd rather live. It would be hard to get started where you didn't have people you knew. His friends agreed.

But even for kids who finish school, have good records, and obey the rules, there is no guarantee they'll make it into productive careers. The American dream won't work for them, and nobody has bothered to explain why. So they find their concentrated effort and motivation only lead to an extra dollar an hour. At best, they'll earn a promotion to another boring job.

Stuck without hope, dreaming of jobs that no longer exist, with the myths of better days further convincing them of their individual fate as "losers," kids today are earning almost one-third less, in constant dollars, than comparable groups in 1973. For white kids, the drop in income is almost 25 percent; for black kids, it's 44 percent. The scars of discrimination run deep, and minority youth feel hopeless because they get the message that this nation does not value its nonwhite citizens.

White kids have scars too, but with no attending socioeconomic explanation, they personalize their plights. They are "losers" because they are shit as people. They are failures because they are worthless. Either way, it hurts.

The understanding of how class works in "classless America" eludes everyone. Parents can teach kids what to expect, help shape attitudes toward their "lot in life." If your parents are losers, it's because their parents were. It's just that way.

In nonaffluent white suburbia, all this is hidden. The big picture isn't there. You're middle class, you think. You believe that this country works for you. You do what you are told. It doesn't work, even though you're sure you made all the right moves. So who's fault is it? Yours. You have shit for brains and you'll never be anybody. This feeling becomes part of you.

---

## *Now that you've read*

1. What is Gaines's argument?
2. What is her strongest evidence for that argument?
3. What do you think happens to most students who give up on school while still in high school? Offer an example from your experience or observation.
4. Can you offer another "category" or "label" to go along with Gaines's list? What are some of the problems than can result from labeling others in negative terms?

# READING 3

## bell hooks

# Confronting Class in the Classroom

This author, bell hooks (yes, the use of lower case is intentional), is a college professor as well as a passionate and prolific writer about race, class, gender, and her own background. She was an astute observer of her own undergraduate experience (she published her first book while still an undergraduate at Stanford University). As a teacher, hooks sees one of her primary responsibilities as moving her students to think critically about their studies and their surroundings. Use her observations to help you become a keener observer of your own college life.

### Before you read

1. Predict, on the basis of the title, how the word *class* will be used in this essay.
2. Why might class be an important factor in U.S. classrooms? Do you think it has a similar impact in classrooms in any other countries? Explain.
3. Have you ever seen or heard of someone disrupting a class? What happened?
4. Describe a time when you felt that you didn't "fit in" with a particular group. How did you feel? Why?

---

Class is rarely talked about in the United States; nowhere is there a more intense silence about the reality of class differences than in educational settings. Significantly, class differences are particularly ignored in classrooms. From grade school on, we are all encouraged to cross the threshold of the classroom believing we are entering a democratic space—a free zone where the desire to study and learn makes us all equal. And even if we enter accepting the reality of class differences, most of us still believe knowledge will be meted out in fair and equal proportions. In those rare cases where it is acknowledged that students and professors do not share the same class backgrounds, the underlying assumption is still that we are all equally committed to getting ahead, to moving up the ladder of success to the top. And even though many of us will not make it to the top, the unspoken understanding is that we will land somewhere in the middle, between top and bottom.

Coming from a nonmaterially privileged background, from the working poor, I entered college acutely aware of class. When I received notice of my acceptance at Stanford University, the first question that was raised in my household was how I would pay for it. My parents understood that I had been awarded scholarships, and allowed to take out loans, but they wanted to know where the money would come from for transportation, clothes, books. Given these concerns, I went to Stanford thinking that class was mainly about materiality. It only took me a short while to understand that class was more than just a question of money, that it shaped values, attitudes, social relations, and the biases that informed the way knowledge would be given and received. These same realizations about class in the academy are expressed again and again by academics from working-class backgrounds in the collection of essays *Strangers in Paradise* edited by Jake Ryan and Charles Sackrey.

During my college years it was tacitly assumed that we all agreed that class should not be talked about, that there would be no critique of the bourgeois class biases shaping and informing pedagogical process (as well as social etiquette) in the classroom. Although no one ever directly stated the rules that would govern our conduct, it was taught by example and reinforced by a system of rewards. As silence and obedience to authority were most rewarded, students learned that this was the appropriate demeanor in the classroom. Loudness, anger, emotional outbursts, and even something as seemingly innocent as unrestrained laughter were deemed unacceptable, vulgar disruptions of classroom social order. These traits were also associated with being a member of the lower classes. If one was not from a privileged class group, adopting a demeanor similar to that of the group could help one to advance. It is still necessary for students to assimilate bourgeois values in order to be deemed acceptable.

Bourgeois values in the classroom create a barrier, blocking the possibility of confrontation and conflict, warding off dissent. Students are often silenced by means of their acceptance of class values that teach them to maintain order at all costs. When the obsession with maintaining order is coupled with the fear of "losing face," of not being thought well of by one's professor and peers, all possibility of constructive dialogue is undermined. Even though students enter the "democratic" classroom believing they have the right to "free speech," most students are not comfortable exercising this right to "free speech." Most students are not comfortable exercising this right—especially if it means they must give voice to thoughts, ideas, feelings that go against the grain, that are unpopular. This censoring

process is only one way bourgeois values overdetermine social behavior in the classroom and undermine the democratic exchange of
ideas. Writing about his experience in the section of *Strangers in Paradise* entitled "Outsiders," Karl Anderson confessed:

> Power and hierarchy, and not teaching and learning, dominated the
> graduate school I found myself in. "Knowledge" was one-upmanship,
> and no one disguised the fact. . . . The one thing I learned absolutely
> was the inseparability of free speech and free thought. I, as well as
> some of my peers, were refused the opportunity to speak and some-
> times to ask questions deemed "irrelevant" when the instructors didn't
> wish to discuss or respond to them.

Students who enter the academy unwilling to accept without question the assumptions and values held by privileged classes tend to
be silenced, deemed troublemakers.

Conservative discussions of censorship in contemporary university settings often suggest that the absence of constructive dialogue, enforced silencing, takes place as a by-product of progressive
efforts to question canonical knowledge, critique relations of domination, or subvert bourgeois class biases. There is little or no discussion of the way in which the attitudes and values of those from
materially privileged classes are imposed upon everyone via biased
pedagogical strategies. Reflected in choice of subject matter and the
manner in which ideas are shared, these biases need never be
overtly stated. In his essay Karl Anderson states that silencing is
"the most oppressive aspect of middle-class life." He maintains:

> It thrives upon people keeping their mouths shut, unless they are ac-
> tually endorsing whatever powers exist. The free marketplace of "ideas"
> that is so beloved of liberals is as much a fantasy as a free marketplace
> in oil or automobiles; a more harmful fantasy, because it breeds even
> more hypocrisy and cynicism. Just as teachers can control what is said
> in their classrooms, most also have ultra-sensitive antennae as to what
> will be rewarded or punished that is said outside them. And these an-
> tennae control them.

Silencing enforced by bourgeois values is sanctioned in the classroom by everyone.

Even those professors who embrace the tenets of critical pedagogy (many of whom are white and male) still conduct their classrooms in a manner that only reinforces bourgeois models of
decorum. At the same time, the subject matter taught in such
classes might reflect professorial awareness of intellectual perspectives that critique domination, that emphasize an understanding of the politics of difference, of race, class, gender, even though
classroom dynamics remain conventional, business as usual. When
contemporary feminist movement made its initial presence felt in

the academy there was both an ongoing critique of conventional classroom dynamics and an attempt to create alternative pedagogical strategies. However, as feminist scholars endeavored to make Women's Studies a discipline administrators and peers would respect, there was a shift in perspective.

Significantly, feminist classrooms were the first spaces in the university where I encountered any attempt to acknowledge class difference. The focus was usually on the way class differences are structured in the larger society, not on our class position. Yet the focus on gender privilege in patriarchal society often meant that there was a recognition of the ways women were economically disenfranchised and therefore more likely to be poor or working class. Often, the feminist classroom was the only place where students (mostly female) from materially disadvantaged circumstances would speak from that class positionality, acknowledging both the impact of class on our social status as well as critiquing the class biases of feminist thought.

When I first entered university settings I felt estranged from this new environment. Like most of my peers and professors, I initially believed those feelings were there because of differences in racial and cultural background. However, as time passed it was more evident that this estrangement was in part a reflection of class difference. At Stanford, I was often asked by peers and professors if I was there on a scholarship. Underlying this question was the implication that receiving financial aid "diminished" one in some way. It was not just this experience that intensified my awareness of class difference, it was the constant evocation of materially privileged class experience (usually that of the middle class) as a universal norm that not only set those of us from working-class backgrounds apart but effectively excluded those who were not privileged from discussions, from social activities. To avoid feelings of estrangement, students from working-class backgrounds could assimilate into the mainstream, change speech patterns, points of reference, drop any habit that might reveal them to be from a nonmaterially privileged background.

Of course I entered college hoping that a university degree would enhance my class mobility. Yet I thought of this solely in economic terms. Early on I did not realize that class was much more than one's economic standing, that it determined values, standpoint, and interests. It was assumed that any student coming from a poor or working-class background would willingly surrender all values and habits of being associated with this background. Those of us from diverse ethnic/racial backgrounds learned that no aspect of our vernacular culture could be voiced in elite settings. This was especially the case with vernacular language or a first language that was not English. To insist on speaking in any manner that did not conform to privileged class ideals and mannerisms placed one always in the position of interloper.

Demands that individuals from class backgrounds deemed undesirable surrender all vestiges of their past create psychic turmoil. We were encouraged, as many students are today, to betray our class origins. Rewarded if we chose to assimilate, estranged if we chose to maintain those aspects of who we were, some were all too often seen as outsiders. Some of us rebelled by clinging to exaggerated manners and behavior clearly marked as outside the accepted bourgeois norm. During my student years, and now as a professor, I see many students from "undesirable" class backgrounds become unable to complete their studies because the contradictions between the behavior necessary to "make it" in the academy and those that allowed them to be comfortable at home, with their families and friends, are just too great.

Often, African Americans are among those students I teach from poor and working-class backgrounds who are most vocal about issues of class. They express frustration, anger, and sadness about the tensions and stress the experience trying to conform to acceptable white, middle-class behaviors in university settings while retaining the ability to "deal" at home. Sharing strategies for coping from my own experience, I encourage students to reject the notion that they must choose between experiences. They must believe they can inhabit comfortably two different worlds, but they must make each space one of comfort. They must creatively invent ways to cross borders. They must believe in their capacity to alter the bourgeois settings they enter. All too often, students from nonmaterially privileged backgrounds assume a position of passivity—they behave as victims, as though they can only be acted upon against their will. Ultimately, they end up feeling they can only reject or accept the norms imposed upon them. This either/or often sets them up for disappointment and failure.

Those of us in the academy from working-class backgrounds are empowered when we recognize our own agency, our capacity to be active participants in the pedagogical process. This process is not simple or easy: it takes courage to embrace a vision of wholeness of being that does not reinforce the capitalist version that suggests that one must always give something up to gain another. In the introduction to the section of their book titled "Class Mobility and Internalized Conflict," Ryan and Sackrey remind readers that "the academic work process is essentially antagonistic to the working class, and academics for the most part live in a different world of culture, different ways that make it, too, antagonistic to working class life." Yet those of us from working-class backgrounds cannot

allow class antagonism to prevent us from gaining knowledge, degrees and enjoying the aspects of higher education that are fulfilling. Class antagonism can be constructively used, not made to
reinforce the notion that students and professors from working-
class backgrounds are "outsiders" and "interlopers," but to subvert
and challenge the existing structure.

When I entered my first Women's Studies classes at Stanford,
white professors talked about "women" when they were making the
experience of materially privileged white women a norm. It was both
a matter of personal and intellectual integrity for me to challenge
this biased assumption. By challenging, I refused to be complicit in
the erasure of black and/or working-class women of all ethnicities.
Personally, that meant I was not able to just sit in class, grooving on
the good feminist vibes—that was a loss. The gain was that I was
honoring the experience of poor and working-class women in my
own family, in that very community that had encouraged and supported me in my efforts to be better educated. Even though my
intervention was not wholeheartedly welcomed, it created a context for critical thinking, for dialectical exchange.

Any attempt on the part of individual students to critique the
bourgeois biases that shape pedagogical process, particularly as
they relate to epistemological perspectives (the points from which
information is shared) will, in most cases, no doubt, be viewed as
negative and disruptive. Given the presumed radical or liberal nature of early feminist classrooms, it was shocking to me to find
those settings were also often closed to different ways of thinking.
While it was acceptable to critique patriarchy in that context, it was
not acceptable to confront issues of class, especially in ways that
were not simply about the evocation of guilt. In general, despite
their participation in different disciplines and the diversity of class
backgrounds, African American scholars and other nonwhite professors have been no more willing to confront issues of class. Even
when it became more acceptable to give at least lip service to the
recognition of race, gender, and class, most professors and students just did not feel they were able to address class in anything
more than a simplistic way. Certainly, the primary area where there
was the possibility of meaningful critique and change was in relation to biased scholarship, work that used the experiences and
thoughts of materially privileged people as normative.

In recent years, growing awareness of class differences in progressive academic circles has meant that students and professors
committed to critical and feminist pedagogy have the opportunity to
make spaces in the academy where class can receive attention. Yet
there can be no intervention that challenges the status quo if we are
not willing to interrogate the way our presentation of self as well as

our pedagogical process is often shaped by middle-class norms. My awareness of class has been continually reinforced by my efforts to remain close to loved ones who remain in materially underprivileged class positions. This has helped me to employ pedagogical strategies that create ruptures in the established order, that promote modes of learning which challenge bourgeois hegemony.

One such strategy has been the emphasis on creating in classrooms learning communities where everyone's voice can be heard, their presence recognized and valued. In the section of *Strangers in Paradise* entitled "Balancing Class Locations," Jane Ellen Wilson shares the way an emphasis on personal voice strengthened her.

> Only by coming to terms with my own past, my own background, and seeing that in the context of the world at large, have I begun to find my true voice and to understand that, since it is my own voice, that no pre-cut niche exists for it; that part of the work to be done is making a place, with others, where my and our voices, can stand clear of the background noise and voice our concerns as part of a larger song.

When those of us in the academy who are working class or from working-class backgrounds share our perspectives, we subvert the tendency to focus only on the thoughts, attitudes, and experiences of those who are materially privileged. Feminist and critical pedagogy are two alternative paradigms for teaching which have really emphasized the issue of coming to voice. That focus emerged as central, precisely because it was so evident that race, sex, and class privilege empower some students more than others, granting "authority" to some voices more than others.

A distinction must be made between a shallow emphasis on coming to voice, which wrongly suggests there can be some democratization of voice wherein everyone's words will be given equal time and be seen as equally valuable (often the model applied in feminist classrooms), and the more complex recognition of the uniqueness of each voice and a willingness to create spaces in the classroom where all voices can be heard because all students are free to speak, knowing their presence will be recognized and valued. This does not mean that anything can be said, no matter how irrelevant to classroom subject matter, and receive attention—or that something meaningful takes place if everyone has equal time to voice an opinion. In the classes I teach, I have students write short paragraphs that they read aloud so that we all have a chance to hear unique perspectives and we are all given an opportunity to pause and listen to one another. Just the physical experience of hearing, of listening intently, to each particular voice strengthens our capacity to learn together. Even though a student may not speak again after this moment, that student's presence has been acknowledged.

Hearing each other's voices, individual thoughts, and sometimes associating these voices with personal experience makes us more acutely aware of each other. That moment of collective participation and dialogue means that students and professor respect—and here I invoke the root meaning of the word, "to look at"—each other, engage in acts of recognition with one another, and do not just talk to the professor. Sharing experiences and confessional narratives in the classroom helps establish communal commitment to learning. These narrative moments usually are the space where the assumption that we share a common class background and perspective is disrupted. While students may be open to the idea that they do not all come from a common class background, they may still expect that the values of materially privileged groups will be the class's norm.

Some students may feel threatened if awareness of class difference leads to changes in the classroom. Today's students all dress alike, wearing clothes from stores such as the Gap and Benetton; this acts to erase the markers of class difference that older generations of students experienced. Young students are more eager to deny the impact of class and class differences in our society. I have found that students from upper- and middle-class backgrounds are disturbed if heated exchange takes place in the classroom. Many of them equate loud talk or interruptions with rude and threatening behavior. Yet those of us from working-class backgrounds may feel that discussion is deeper and richer if it arouses intense responses. In class, students are often disturbed if anyone is interrupted while speaking, even though outside class most of them are not threatened. Few of us are taught to facilitate heated discussions that may include useful interruptions and digressions, but it is often the professor who is most invested in maintaining order in the classroom. Professors cannot empower students to embrace diversities of experience, standpoint, behavior, or style if our training has disempowered us, socialized us to cope effectively only with a single mode of interaction based on middle-class values.

Most progressive professors are more comfortable striving to challenge class biases through the material studied than they are with interrogating how class biases shape conduct in the classroom and transforming their pedagogical process. When I entered my first classroom as a college professor and a feminist, I was deeply afraid of using authority in a way that would perpetuate class elitism and other forms of domination. Fearful that I might abuse power, I falsely pretended that no power difference existed between students and myself. That was a mistake. Yet it was only as I began to interrogate my fear of "power"—the way that fear was related to my own class background where I had so often seen those with class power coerce, abuse, and dominate those without—that I began to understand that power was not itself negative. It depended on what one did with it. It was up to me to create ways within my professional power constructively, precisely because I was teaching in institutional structures that affirm it is fine to use power to reinforce and maintain coercive hierarchies.

Fear of losing control in the classroom often leads individual professors to fall into a conventional teaching pattern wherein power is used destructively. It is this fear that leads to collective professorial investment in bourgeois decorum as a means of maintaining a fixed notion of order, of ensuring that the teacher will have absolute authority. Unfortunately, this fear of losing control shapes and informs the professorial pedagogical process to the extent that it acts a barrier preventing any constructive grappling with issues of class.

Sometimes students who want professors to grapple with class differences often simply desire that individuals from less materially privileged backgrounds be given center stage so that an inversion of hierarchical structures takes place, not a disruption. One semester, a number of black female students from working-class backgrounds attended a course I taught on African American women writers. They arrived hoping I would use my professorial power to decenter the voices of privileged white students in nonconstructive ways so that those students would experience what it is like to be an outsider. Some of these black students rigidly resisted attempts to involve the others in an engaged pedagogy where space is created for everyone. Many of the black students feared that learning new terminology or new perspectives would alienate them from familiar social relations. Since these fears are rarely addressed as part of progressive pedagogical process, students caught in the grip of such anxiety often sit in classes feeling hostile, estranged, refusing to participate. I often face students who think that in my classes they will "naturally" not feel estranged and that part of this feeling of comfort, or being "at home," is that they will not have to work as hard as they do in other classes. These students are expecting to find alternative pedagogy in my classes but merely "rest" from the negative tensions they may feel in the majority of other courses. It is my job to address these tensions.

If we can trust the demographics, we must assume that the academy will be full of students from diverse classes, and that more of our students than ever before will be from poor and working-class backgrounds. This change will not be reflected in the class background of professors. In my own experience, I encounter fewer and fewer academics from working-class backgrounds. Our absence is no doubt related to the way class politics and class struggle shapes who will receive graduate degrees in our society. However, constructively confronting issues of class is not simply a task for those of us who came from working-class and poor backgrounds; it is a challenge for all professors. Critiquing the way academic settings are structured to reproduce class hierarchy, Jake Ryan and Charles Sackrey emphasize "that no matter what the politics or ideological stripe of the individual professor, of what the content of his or her teaching, Marxist, anarchist, or nihilist, he or she nonetheless participates in the reproduction of the cultural and class relations of capitalism." Despite this bleak assertion they are willing to acknowledge that "nonconformist intellectuals can, through research and publication, chip away with some success at the conventional orthodoxies, nurture students with comparable ideas and intentions, or find ways to bring some fraction of the resources of the university to the service of the . . . class interests of the workers and others below." Any professor who commits to engaged pedagogy recognizes the importance of constructively confronting issues of class. That means welcoming the opportunity to alter our classroom practices creatively so that the democratic ideal of education for everyone can be realized.

---

### Now that you've read

1. How similar or dissimilar is your campus to the college campus that bell hooks describes?
2. How does social class affect the classroom, according to hooks?
3. hooks argues that social class differences are more important than racial or ethnic or gender differences. How do you respond?
4. hooks writes, "Students who enter the academy unwilling to accept without question the assumptions and values held by privileged classes tend to be silenced, deemed troublemakers." How do you respond?

## READING 4

*Barbara Mellix*

# From Outside, In

Barbara Mellix began as a "basic writer" and later became a published writer and a lover of language. Her experience affords us yet another view of education and what it can and cannot do for students. Mellix published this essay in 1987 in *The Georgia Review*. Since then, it has been widely anthologized for its powerful discussion of language, race, and class. As you read, think about how she uses her own experiences to ground her arguments.

### Before you read

1. How important to you is the way you talk (your dialect, accent, slang, usage, etc.)?
2. Have you ever been asked or felt pressure to change the way you talk? Describe the situation.
3. Can an "outsider" always become an "insider"? What does it take?
4. What are some of the reasons to learn to use "proper" English? Can you think of any reasons not to?

Two years ago, when I started writing this paper, trying to bring order out of chaos, my ten-year-old daughter was suffering from an acute attack of boredom. She drifted in and out of the room complaining that she had nothing to do, no one to "be with" because none of her friends were at home. Patiently I explained that I was working on something special and needed peace and quiet, and I suggested that she paint, read, or work with her computer. None of these interested her. Finally, she pulled up a chair to my desk and watched me, now and then heaving long, loud sighs. After two or three minutes (nine or ten sighs), I lost my patience. "Looka here, Allie," I said, "you too old for this kinda carryin' on. I done told you this is important. You wronger than dirt to be in here haggin' me like this and you know it. Now git on outta here and leave me off before I put my foot all the way down."

I was at home, alone with my family, and my daughter understood that this way of speaking was appropriate in that context. She knew, as a matter of fact, that it was almost inevitable; when I get angry at home, I speak some of my finest, most cherished black English. Had I been speaking to my daughter in this manner in certain other environments, she would have been shocked and probably worried that I had taken leave of my sense of propriety.

Like my children, I grew up speaking what I considered two distinctly different languages—black English and standard English (or as I thought of them then, the ordinary everyday speech of "country" coloreds and "proper" English)—and in the process of acquiring these languages, I developed an understanding of when, where, and how to use them. But unlike my children, I grew up in a world that was primarily black. My friends, neighbors, minister, teachers—almost everybody I associated with every day—were black. And we spoke to one another in our own special language: *That sho is a pretty dress you got on. If she don' soon leave me off I'm gon tell her head a mess. I was so mad I could'a pissed a blue nail. He all the time trying to low-rate somebody. Ain't that just about the nastiest thing you ever set ears on?*

Then there were the "others," the "proper" blacks, transplanted relatives and one-time friends who came home from the city for weddings, funerals, and vacations. And the whites. To these we spoke standard English. "Ain't?" my mother would yell at me when I used the term in the presence of "others." "You *know* better than that." And I would hang my head in shame and say the "proper" word.

I remember one summer sitting in my grandmother's house in Greeleyville, South Carolina, when it was full of the chatter of city relatives who were home on vacation. My parents sat quietly, only now and then volunteering a comment or answering a question. My mother's face took on a strained expression when she spoke. I could see that she was being careful to say just the right words in just the right way. Her voice sounded thick, muffled. And when she finished speaking, she would lapse into silence, her proper smile on her face. My father was more articulate, more aggressive. He spoke quickly, his words sharp and clear. But he held his proud head higher, a signal that he, too, was uncomfortable. My sisters and brothers and I stared at our aunts, uncles, and cousins, speaking only when prompted. Even then, we hesitated, formed our sentences in our minds, then spoke softly, shyly.

My parents looked small and anxious during those occasions, and I waited impatiently for our leave-taking when we would mock our relatives the moment we were out of their hearing. "Reeely," we would say to one another, flexing our wrists and rolling our eyes, "how dooo you stan' this heat? Chile, it just too hy*ooo*-mid for words." Our relatives had made us feel "country," and this was our way of regaining pride in ourselves while getting a little revenge in the bargain. The words bubbled in our throats and rolled across our tongues, a balming.

As a child I felt this same doubleness in uptown Greeleyville where the whites lived. "Ain't that a pretty dress you're wearing!" Toby, the town policeman, said to me one day when I was fifteen. "Thank you very much," I replied, my voice barely audible in my own ears. The words felt wrong in my mouth, rigid, foreign. It was not that I had never spoken that phrase before—it was common in black English, too—but I was extremely conscious that this was an occasion for proper English. I had taken out my English and put it on as I did my church clothes, and I felt as if I were wearing my Sunday best in the middle of the week. It did not matter that Toby had not spoken grammatically correct English. He was white and could speak as he wished. I had something to prove. Toby did not.

Speaking standard English to whites was our way of demonstrating that we knew their language and could use it. Speaking it to standard-English-speaking blacks was our way of showing them that we, as well as they, could "put on airs." But when we spoke standard English, we acknowledged (to ourselves and to others—but primarily to ourselves) that our customary way of speaking was inferior. We felt foolish, embarrassed, somehow diminished because we were ashamed to be our real selves. We were reserved, shy in the presence of those who owned and/or spoke *the* language.

My parents never set aside time to drill us in standard English. Their forms of instruction were less formal. When my father was feeling particularly expansive, he would regale us with tales of his exploits in the outside world. In almost flawless English, complete with dialogue and flavored with gestures and embellishment, he told us about his attempt to get a haircut at a white barbershop; his refusal to acknowledge one of the town merchants until the man addressed him as "Mister"; the time he refused to step off the sidewalk uptown to let some whites pass; his airplane trip to New York City (to visit a sick relative) during which the stewardesses and porters—recognizing that he was a "gentleman"—addressed him as "Sir." I did not realize then—nor, I think, did my father—that he was teaching us, among other things, standard English and the relationship between language and power.

My mother's approach was different. Often, when one of us said, "I'm gon wash off my feet," she would say, "And what will you walk on if you wash them off?" Everyone would laugh at the victim of my mother's "proper" mood. But it was different when one of us children was in a proper mood. "You think you are so superior," I said to my oldest sister one day when we were arguing and she was winning. "Superior!" my sister mocked. "You mean I am acting 'big-gidy'?" My sisters and brothers sniggered, then joined in teasing me. Finally, my mother said, "Leave your sister alone. There's nothing wrong with using proper English." There was a half-smile on her face. I had gotten "uppity," had "put on airs" for no good reason. I was at home, alone with the family, and I hadn't been prompted by one of my mother's proper moods. But there was also a proud light in my mother's eyes; her children were learning English very well.

Not until years later, as a college student, did I begin to understand our ambivalence toward English, our scorn of it, our need to master it, to own and be owned by it—an ambivalence that extended to the public-school classroom. In our school, where there were no whites, my teachers taught standard English but used black English to do it. When my grammar-school teachers wanted us to write, for example, they usually said something like, "I want y'all to write five sentences that make a statement. Anybody git done before the rest can color." It was probably almost those exact words that led me to write these sentences in 1953 when I was in the second grade:

The white clouds are pretty.
There are only 15 people in our room.
We will go to gym.
We have a new poster.
We may go out doors.

Second grade came after "Little First" and "Big First," so by then I knew the implied rules that accompanied all writing assignments. Writing was an occasion for proper English. I was not to write in the way we spoke to one another: The white clouds pretty; There ain't but 15 people in our room; We going to gym. We got a new poster; We can go out in the yard. Rather I was to use the language of "other": clouds *are, there are,* we *will,* we *have,* we *may.*

My sentences were short, rigid, perfunctory, like the letters my mother wrote to relatives:

> Dear Papa,
> How are you? How is Mattie? Fine I hope. We are fine. We will come to see you Sunday. Cousin Ned will give us a ride.
>
> > Love,
> > Daughter

The language was not ours. It was something from outside us, something we used for special occasions.

But my coloring on the other side of that second-grade paper is different. I drew three hearts and a sun. The sun has a smiling face that radiates and envelops everything it touches. And although the sun and its world are enclosed in a circle, the colors I used—red, blue, green, purple, orange, yellow, black—indicate that I was less restricted with drawing and coloring than I was with writing standard English. My valentines were not just red. My sun was not just a yellow ball in the sky.

By the time I reached the twelfth grade, speaking and writing standard English had taken on new importance. Each year, about half of the newly graduated seniors of our school moved to large cities—particularly in the North—to live with relatives and find work. Our English teacher constantly corrected our grammar: "Not 'ain't,' but "isn't.'" We seldom wrote papers, and even those few were usually plot summaries of short stories. When our teacher returned the papers, she usually lectured on the importance of using standard English: "I *am;* you *are;* he, she, or it *is,*" she would say, writing on the chalkboard as she spoke. "How you gon git a job talking about 'I is,' or 'I isn't' or 'I ain't'?"

In Pittsburgh, where I moved after graduation, I watched my aunt and uncle—who had always spoken standard English when in Greeleyville—switch from black English to standard English to a mixture of the two, according to where they were or who they were with. At home and with certain close relatives, friends, and neighbors, they spoke black English. With those less close, they spoke a mixture. In public and with strangers, they generally spoke standard English.

In time, I learned to speak standard English with ease and to switch smoothly from black to standard or a mixture, and back again. But no matter where I was, no matter what the situation or occasion, I continued to write as I had in school:

> Dear Mommie,
> How are you? How is everybody else? Fine I hope. I am fine. So are Aunt and Uncle. Tell everyone I said hello. I will write again soon.
> 
> > Love,
> > Barbara

At work, at a health insurance company, I learned to write letters to customers. I studied form letters and letters written by co-workers, memorizing the phrases and the ways in which they were used. I dictated:

> Thank you for your letter of January 5. We have made the changes in your coverage you requested. Your new premium will be $150 every three months. We are pleased to have been of service to you.

In a sense, I was proud of the letters I wrote for the company: they were proof of my ability to survive in the city, the outside world—an indication of my growing mastery of English. But they also indicate that writing was still mechanical for me, something that didn't require much thought.

Reading also became a more significant part of my life during those early years in Pittsburgh. I had always liked reading, but now I devoted more and more of my spare time to it. I read romances, mysteries, popular novels. Looking back, I realize that the books I liked best were simple, unambiguous: good versus bad and right versus wrong with right rewarded and wrong punished, mysteries unraveled and all set right in the end. It was how I remembered life in Greeleyville.

Of course I was romanticizing. Life in Greeleyville had not been so very uncomplicated. Back there I had been—first as a child, then as a young woman with limited experience in the outside world—living in a relatively closed-in society. But there were implicit and explicit principles that guided our way of life and shaped our relationships with one another and the people outside—principles that a new-comer would find elusive and baffling. In Pittsburgh, I had matured, become more experienced: I had worked at three different jobs, as-sociated with a wider range of people, married, had children. This new environment with different prescripts for living required that I speak standard English much of the time, and slowly, imperceptibly, I had ceased seeing a sharp distinction between myself and "others." Reading romances and mysteries, characterized by dichotomy, was a way of shying away from change, from the person I was becoming.

But that other part of me—that part which took great pride in my ability to hold a job writing business letters—was increasingly drawn to the new developments in my life and the attending possibilities, opportunities for even greater change. If I could write letters for a na-tionally known business, could I not also do something better, more challenging, more important? Could I not, perhaps, go to college and become a school teacher? For years, afraid and a little embarrassed, I did no more than imagine this different me, this possible me. But six-teen years after coming north, when my younger daughter entered kindergarten, I found myself unable—or unwilling—to resist the lure of possibility. I enrolled in my first college course: Basic Writing, at the University of Pittsburgh.

For the first time in my life, I was required to write extensively about myself. Using the most formal English at my command, I wrote these sentences near the beginning of the term:

> One of my duties as a homemaker is simply picking up after others. A day seldom passes that I don't search for a mislaid toy, book, or gym shoe, etc. I change the Ty-D-Bol, fight "ring around the collar," and keep our laun-dry smelling "April fresh." Occasionally, I settle arguments between my children and suggest things to do when they're bored. Taking telephone messages for my oldest daughter is my newest (and sometimes most ag-gravating) chore. Hanging the toilet paper roll is my most insignificant.

My concern was to use "appropriate" language, to sound as if I be-longed in a college classroom. But I felt separate from the language—as if it did not and could not belong to me. I couldn't think and feel genuinely in that language, couldn't make it express what I thought and felt about being a housewife. A part of me resented, among other things, being judged by such things as the appearance of my family's laundry and toilet bowl, but in that language I could only imagine and write about a conventional housewife.

For the most part, the remainder of the term was a period of adjustment, a time of trying to find my bearings as a student in a college composition class, to learn to shut out my black English whenever I composed, and to prevent it from creeping into my formulations; a time for trying to grasp the language of the classroom and reproduce it in my prose; for trying to talk about myself in that language, reach others through it. Each experience of writing was like standing naked and revealing my imperfection, my "otherness." And each new assignment was another chance to make myself over in language, reshape myself, make myself "better" in my rapidly changing image of a student in a college composition class.

But writing became increasingly unmanageable as the term progressed, and by the end of the semester, my sentences sounded like this:

> My excitement was soon dampened, however, by what seemed like a small voice in the back of my head saying that I should be careful with my long awaited opportunity. I felt frustrated and this seemed to make it difficult to concentrate.

There is a poverty of language in these sentences. By this point, I knew that the clich d language of my Housewife essay was unacceptable, and I generally recognized trite expressions. At the same time, I hadn't yet mastered the language of the classroom, hadn't yet come to see it as belonging to me. Most notable is the lifelessness of the prose, the apparent absence of a person behind the words. I wanted those sentences—and the rest of the essay—to convey the anguish of yearning to, at once, become something more and yet remain the same. I had the sensation of being split in two, part of me going into a future the other part didn't believe possible. As that person, the student writer at that moment, I was essentially mute. I could not—in the process of composing—use the language of the old me, yet I couldn't imagine myself in the language of "others."

I found this particularly discouraging because at midsemester I had been writing in a much different way. Note the language of this introduction to an essay I had written then, near the middle of the term:

> Pain is a constant companion to the people in "Footwork." Their jobs are physically damaging. Employers are insensitive to their feelings and in many cases add to their problems. The general public wounds them further by treating them with disgrace because of what they do for a living. Although the workers are as diverse as they are similar, there is a definite link between them. They suffer a great deal of abuse.

The voice here is stronger, more confident, appropriating terms like "physically damaging," "wounds them further," "insensitive," "diverse"—terms I couldn't have imagined using when writing about my own experience—and shaping them into sentences like, "Although the workers are as diverse as they are similar, there is a definite link between them." And there is the sense of a personality behind the prose, someone who sympathizes with the workers. "The general public wounds them further by treating them with disgrace because of what they do for a living."

What caused these differences? I was, I believed, explaining other people's thoughts and feelings, and I was free to move about in the language of "others" so long as I was speaking *of* others. I was unaware that I was transforming into my best classroom language my own thoughts and feelings about people whose experiences and ways of speaking were in many ways similar to mine.

The following year, unable to turn back or to let go of what had become something of an obsession with language (and hoping to catch and hold the sense of control that had eluded me in Basic Writing), I enrolled in a research writing course. I spent most of the term learning how to prepare for and write a research paper. I chose sex education as my subject and spent hours in libraries, searching for information, reading, taking notes. Then (not without messiness and often-demoralizing frustration) I organized my information into categories, wrote a thesis statement, and composed my paper—a series of paraphrases and quotations spaced between carefully constructed transitions. The process and results felt artificial, but as I would later come to realize I was passing through a necessary stage. My sentences sounded like this:

> This reserve becomes understandable with examination of who the abusers are. In an overwhelming number of cases, they are people the victims know and trust. Family members, relatives, neighbors and close family friends commit seventy-five percent of all reported sex crimes against children, and parents, parent substitutes and relatives are the offenders in thirty to eighty percent of all reported cases. While assault by strangers does occur, it is less common, and is usually a single episode. But abuse by family members, relatives and acquaintances may continue for an extended period of time. In cases of incest, for example, children are abused repeatedly for an average of eight years. In such cases, "the use of physical force is rarely necessary because of the child's trusting, dependent relationship with the offender. The child's cooperation is often facilitated by the adult's position of dominance, an offer of material goods, a threat of physical violence, or a misrepresentation of moral standards."

The completed paper gave me a sense of profound satisfaction, and I read it often after my professor returned it. I know now that what I was pleased with was the language I used and the professional voice it helped me maintain. "Use better words," my teacher had snapped at me one day after reading the notes I'd begun accumulating from my research, and slowly I began taking on the language of my sources. In my next set of notes, I used the word "vacillating"; my professor applauded. And by the time I composed the final draft, I felt at ease with terms like "overwhelming number of cases," "single episode," and "reverse," and I shaped them into sentences similar to those of my "expert" sources.

If I were writing the paper today, I would of course do some things differently. Rather than open with an anecdote—as my teacher suggested—I would begin simply with a quotation that caught my interest as I was researching my paper (and which I scribbled, without its source, in the margin of my notebook): "Truth does not do so much good in the world as the semblance of truth does evil." The quotation felt right because it captured what was for me the central idea of my essay—an idea that emerged gradually during the making of my paper—and expressed it in a way I would like to have said it. The anecdote, a hypothetical situation I invented to conform to the information in the paper, felt forced and insincere because it represented—to a great degree—my teacher's understanding of the essay, *her* idea of what in it was most significant. Improving upon my previous experiences with writing, I was beginning to think and feel in the language I used, to find my own voices in it, to sense that how one speaks influences how one means. But I was not yet secure enough, comfortable enough with the language to trust my intuition.

Now that I know that to seek knowledge, freedom, and autonomy means always to be in the concentrated process of becoming— always to be venturing into new territory, feeling one's way at first, then getting one's balance, negotiating, accommodating, discovering one's self in ways that previously defined "others"—I sometimes get tired. And I ask myself why I keep on participating in this highbrow form of violence, this slamming against perplexity. But there is no real futility in the question, no hint of that part of the old me who stood outside standard English, hugging to herself a disabling mistrust of a language she thought could not represent a person with her history and experience. Rather, the question represents a person who feels the consequence of her education, the weight of her possibilities as a teacher and writer and human being, a voice in society. And I would not change that person, would not give back the good burden that accompanies my growing expertise, my increasing power to shape myself in language and share that self with "others."

"To speak," says Frantz Fanon, "means to be in a position to use a certain syntax, to grasp the morphology of this or that language, but it means above all to assume a culture, to support the weight of a civilization."[1] To write means to do the same, but in a more profound sense. However, Fanon also says that to achieve mastery means to "get" in a position of power, to "grasp," to "assume." This, I have learned both as a student and subsequently as a teacher—can involve tremendous emotional and psychological conflict for those attempting to master academic discourse. Although as a beginning student writer I had a fairly good grasp of ordinary spoken English and was proficient at what Labov calls "code-switching" (and what John Baugh in *Black Street Speech* terms "style shifting"), when I came face to face with the demands of academic writing, I grew increasingly self-conscious, constantly aware of my status as a black and a speaker of one of the many black English vernaculars—a traditional outsider. For the first time, I experienced my sense of doubleness as something menacing, a built-in enemy. Whenever I turned inward for salvation, the balm so available during my childhood, I found instead this new fragmentation which spoke to me in many voices. It was the voice of my desire to prosper, but at the same time it spoke of what I had relinquished and could not regain: a safe way of being, a state of powerlessness which exempted me from responsibility for who I was and might be. And it accused me of betrayal, of turning away from blackness. To recover balance, I had to take on the language of the academy, the language of "others." And to do that, I had to learn to imagine myself a part of the culture of that language, and therefore someone free to manage that language, to take liberties with it. Writing and rewriting, practicing, experimenting, I came to comprehend more fully the generative power of language. I discovered—with the help of some especially sensitive teachers—that through writing one can continually bring new selves into being, each with new responsibilities and difficulties, but also with new possibilities. Remarkable power, indeed. I write and continually give birth to myself.

---

## Now that you've read

1. What do you learn from Barbara Mellix's opening anecdote?
2. What is "code-switching"? Why is it useful—and even necessary?
3. What is Mellix saying when she describes her relatives as making her family "feel country"? Have you ever had a similar experience?
4. Mellix writes, ". . . I ask myself why I keep on participating in this highbrow form of violence, this slamming against perplexity." What does she mean here? How is she using the word *violence?* What does it mean to "slam against perplexity"?

[1]*Black Skin, White Masks* (1952; rpt. New York: Grove Press, 1967), pp. 17–18.

## READING 5

*Janine DiGiovanni*

# Lost Generation

The Balkans of Eastern Europe have been a site of ethnic conflicts for hundreds and hundreds of years. As a reporter covering this region, DiGiovanni focuses on the damage the most recent violence has done to the lives and hopes of young adults on all sides. Her description of the lives of the young people she interviews enables us to see how such widespread and long-lived violence has effects that go far deeper than we generally imagine.

### Before you read

1. What have you heard about the recent conflicts between Serbians and Croats and ethnic Albanians? What is your understanding of the sources of this conflict? What have you heard about "ethnic cleansing"?
2. Reflect a moment on the title of DiGiovanni's article. What might it mean for a generation to be "lost"?

---

It's Thursday, June 24, the day that all but one member of the Yugoslav federal parliament voted to lift the official state of war. In Belgrade, it's a cold, gray, Balkan kind of day, and nobody is celebrating. Not my 22-year-old friend Ivana, whom I met while she was working as an interpreter in Pristina, nor her tall, baby-faced best friend, Ana. Both of them are hung over from drinking too much cheap domestic vodka the night before.

Their friend Ivan is not celebrating either. He is stuck working at a graphic design firm for $100 a month—when he really wants to be back at university. Ivana's brother, 18-year-old Djordje, and his best friend, Nemanja, don't even know the war is over yet; they're too busy plotting their escape from Serbia. Buried in their MTV videos and Michael Jordan posters, they've already left in spirit.

Seeing these young Yugoslavs trapped by the Milosevic regime, which they did not choose, is painful. (I cannot give their last names because, in Belgrade today, most people are paranoid—with good reason. They fear that their phones may be tapped and that they could be threatened by the police.) These are kids who did not actively oppose the current government, either. But they still seem to be a sort of Lost Generation—only without the glamour and the champagne cocktails. In 1990, when the first of Yugoslavia's wars— the one against Slovenian secession—started, the nation was just about to move closer to the West. Yugoslavia's youths got a tantalizing taste of life in modern society; then, suddenly and terribly, it was snatched from them. Since then, they've known nothing but a series of losing wars, dead soldiers, sanctions, economic meltdown, anti-Milosevic demonstrations, and gloom.

Now, they want to leave this place, but they worry about becoming impoverished immigrants in a strange country that will view them as evil. They feel proud of their heritage but ashamed of the destruction Slobodan Milosevic has caused over the past decade. They want to be open-minded about the atrocities committed in the past three months by their army, but, at the same time, their friends were serving in that army, and they can't believe these friends could have been involved in such monstrous crimes. They resent the United States, Great Britain, France, and the rest of the NATO powers for bombing them, yet they desperately want to go live in those very nations. They are, in short, racked with contradictory emotions that spring from a source far deeper than the usual post-teenage angst.

"We can't go anywhere; we're trapped here," moans Ivana, her face pale from her hangover. She's reading an article in the newspaper that says that, in 40 years' time, the Serbian economy will be back to its 1989, prewar state. According to an independent economic society called G-17, she reads aloud, the GDP is 44.4 percent lower than last year because of the war. The damage caused by NATO is estimated at $29.6 billion.

Ana interrupts to point out that Belgrade took 30 years to reconstruct after World War II. "I know because my grandmother told me," she says. "I don't want to wait thirty years to have a normal life." World War II, of course, caused far more damage here than the NATO bombing campaign, but Ana's susceptibility to the false analogy is itself an indication of how out of whack the thinking of Serbian youths has become. "This is what I call 'Futureless in Belgrade,'" Ivana adds. "Something like *Sleepless in Seattle*, but without jokes."

Elegant and haughty even in her black combat jeans and platform sneakers, Ivana comes from a long line of proud Serbs: her paternal great-grandfather was a colonel in the royal army under King Peter and King Alexander; her father's family once owned big houses in downtown Belgrade that were confiscated under Tito's regime. Now, nearly all the members of her father's family have emigrated. One uncle, an opera singer, lives on the Upper East Side. Her grandfather lives in Washington.

Ivana wants to go, too, but she can't. Her Yugoslav passport carries heavy restrictions, so it's hard to get a visa. Even applying for one is difficult: you have to go Budapest first because there are no embassies here. Meanwhile, Ivana and her friends, all students in the faculty of philosophy at Belgrade University, can't finish their studies: the universities closed during the bombings, and they can't get the funding to study abroad.

These youths also have the inherited sense of Serb victimization—the ingrained certainty that the world is against them. They don't seem to realize how much harder this makes it to sympathize with them. "I wrote to Columbia University," Ivana says. "I've got top grades. Good recommendations. They didn't even bother to reply." She thinks it might be because she's a Serb. Columbia's letter might just as easily have been lost in the mail, but she doesn't consider that. In 1997, she lived in France for three months while her mother was dying of cancer and getting medical treatment there. She felt like a pariah: "When one person heard where I came from—Belgrade, Serbia—he didn't want to talk to me."

Ivana, intelligent, beautiful, and cultured, feels suffocated here by the weight of the past and by the nonexistent future. She is convinced the only way she can start a new life is by leaving. "Emigration is always hanging over my head," she says. "The saddest thing is that all my friends are leaving or want to go. I know that, in ten years' time, none of us will be living in the same country." She lists all her friends who have left for England, the United States, Ireland, and France.

"When I graduated from high school in 1990, the future seemed so amazing," says Ivana's close friend Ivan, who is also a student of archaeology. He's sitting in a downtown Belgrade caf  called Ipanema, drinking a cappuccino that he can't really afford and smoking Marlboro Lights made in Romania. Across the road is the grinding sound of a chain saw: people are chopping down trees to heat homes during the upcoming winter, which is predicted to be a harsh one. "Then, I had hope. The wars hadn't started yet. I was proud of my country. Proud to be a Yugoslav. In those days, you thought: 'Yes, I'll get a good job and be able to buy a car and get an apartment with my girlfriend.' Then, it might have been possible. Now, it's not."

Both Ivan and Ivana live with their families. Ivana says she hates her father's small, dark flat in new Belgrade's wasteland of Soviet-style projects. It is a modern place on the seventh floor with a view of the other depressing, block-style buildings. She yearns for some of the airy, romantic properties her family lost under communism. Inside the flat, you see the schizophrenia of modern Serbia. The charmless Communist-era place is cluttered with remnants from before World War II: a heavy, dark mahogany dining room table from the turn of the century; fading pastel-colored icons with mournful Madonnas; oil paintings by Ivana's grandmother; leather-bound books.

In Ivan's small bedroom, the walls are covered with sheets of paper listing the letters of the Greek alphabet. She's studying ancient

Greek, she says, because it makes her think of a more civilized time. She already speaks perfect English, passable French, and some German. She's nagging Djordje to practice his English "so he can get out of this country."

"I'd rather go to Miami than Connecticut," Djordje interjects, staring at "Lenny Kravitz Unplugged" on MTV. It's partly because he loves Will Smith and saw the music video for his song "Welcome to Miami."

"You're going to Connecticut," interrupts his father, Antonio, an architect. Antonio is trying to arrange a student exchange for his son, a basketball star, through a former Yugoslav basketball player who is charging Antonio about three months' salary to place Djordje in an American suburban family's home for a year. "It's healthier. It's old America. Miami isn't America." Later, Antonio explains to me that "for my kids, getting out is a matter of survival. . . . I don't think you realize how empty their future is."

I think I do, because day after day I plod around Belgrade—gray even when the sun is out—with Ivana. I can feel the desperation pouring out of her, and, when I look at her, I can't help thinking that, had she not been born in Tito's Yugoslavia in 1977 and come of age under Milosevic's regime, she would be destined for a great job, a beautiful flat, a happy life. But, sitting in the Russian Tsar Caf on Kneza Mihajlova, swinging her stork-like legs from a bench, she's just a bored kid with no future, no passport, not even Yugoslav citizenship: she forgot to register with the authorities every six months as required. "I don't exist," she says.

In her postwar Belgrade, the days pass uneventfully. The municipality chops down more trees. People are panicking about possible shortages of petrol, heat, and electricity. Drunk reservists, who have not been paid, block the road near Kraljevo. Few people talk about mass graves or Serbian atrocities committed in Kosovo because they genuinely believe these are all lies and propaganda from the West. Or maybe they just can't face what they, as a people, have done, have created. The anomie felt by Ivana and her compatriots is increasingly being translated into mass demonstrations against Milosevic's regime. Just over the past ten days, in cities across Serbia, thousands of marchers have turned out to call for the strongman to step down. Still, given the fractured nature of the opposition movement, no one is sure how that goal might actually be accomplished. "I don't think anything is going to change," Ivana tells me several days before a major demonstration in the nearby town of Cacak.

It is Saturday, June 26. Ivana and I are sitting in a caf on the Danube. And, as usual, we're plotting her escape. "This way the river runs to Romania," she points out, "this way to Germany." From Germany, I tell her, it's easy: you get a train to France; from France go to England; from England go to America.

My mobile phone suddenly rings. It is an unexpected call from a Kosovar Albanian friend of mine who is exactly the same age as Ivana. I met this friend in Albania, where she was working for Human Rights Watch. Together, we spent three weeks trailing the Kosovo Liberation Army in mid-May. We spent three days in trenches together, getting bombed by NATO planes and Serb MiGs; as a result, we bonded for life.

This friend is also a member of the Lost Generation, but she is going through a different kind of hell than Ivana is. On March 22, two days before the NATO bombing began, she was sitting in a caf in Pristina. One minute, she was drinking coffee; the next minute, she was lying in a pool of blood and broken glass and bullets, the victim of a random attack by Serbian gunmen. When she opened her eyes, she was bleeding from fortunately superficial wounds on her neck and arm.

Soon after, she was forced to flee Pristina in such haste that she didn't have time to change out of her hospital pajamas. Serb soldiers confiscated and destroyed her passport. She was separated from her mother and little sister while crossing the Albanian border. And, finally, upon reaching Tirana, she was brutally attacked by local Albanian men. She has yet fully to confront the horrors she's endured. Instead, she responded immediately throwing herself into her work.

When I tell Ivana my friend's story, it both horrifies and fascinates her. She tries to picture her twin, an Albanian of exactly the same age, who is 300 miles away and as deeply unhappy at the prospects of her future as she is, though for different reasons. "I'm fucked up," Ivana says. "And I didn't go through what she did."

She asks if my friend also wants to emigrate, to start a new life. Yes, I reply, as soon as she can get some documents. Ivana is silent for a moment. She stares at the passing boats, which move slowly over the polluted black water. "But everyone is leaving Yugoslavia!" She corrects herself: "What once was Yugoslavia." Her head droops. "Who's going to be left here?"

---

## Now that you've read

1. What are the disappointments that Ivana and her friends are facing?
2. What might you say to Ivana about her concerns over how Americans will treat her?
3. What might happen if Ivana and DiGiovanni's Albanian friend from Kosovo were to meet? How might their meeting be different if it took place in the United States rather than in Belgrade or Kosovo?

# READING 6

*Audre Lorde*

# The Uses of Anger:
# Women Responding to Racism

Poet Audre Lorde forcefully states that anger can be channeled and focused to become a potent means of achieving social and personal change. She is unapologetic about her anger—in fact, she can be said to celebrate it—as she argues that the clear articulation of that anger is necessary for survival and liberation. She writes, ". . . anger expressed and translated into action in the service of our vision is a liberating and strengthening act of clarification." Consider what this might mean as you read Lorde's essay, in which she argues for the importance of using our anger rather than denying or discounting it.

## Before you read

1. In what ways can anger be "useful"?
2. What issues are important enough to you to get angry about?
3. What are some strategies to help us recognize and overcome racism?
4. What does it mean to come to terms with anger, and why might doing so be important?

---

*Racism.* The belief in the inherent superiority of one race over all others and thereby the right to dominance, manifest and implied.

*Women respond to racism.* My response to racism is anger. I have lived with that anger, ignoring it, feeding upon it, learning to use it before it laid my visions to waste, for most of my life. Once I did it in silence, afraid of the weight. My fear of anger taught me nothing. Your fear of that anger will teach you nothing, also.

Women responding to racism means women responding to anger; the anger of exclusion, of unquestioned privilege, of racial distortions, of silence, ill-use, stereotyping, defensiveness, misnaming, betrayal, and co-optation.

My anger is a response to racist attitudes and to the actions and presumptions that arise out of those attitudes. If your dealings with other women reflect those attitudes, then my anger and your attendant fears are spotlights that can be used for growth in the same way I have used learning to express anger for my growth. But for corrective surgery, not guilt. Guilt and defensiveness are bricks in a wall against which we all flounder; they serve none of our futures.

Because I do not want this to become a theoretical discussion, I am going to give a few examples of interchanges between women that illustrate these points. In the interest of time, I am going to cut them short. I want you to know there were many more.

For example:

- I speak out of direct and particular anger at an academic conference, and a white woman says, "Tell me how you feel but don't say it too harshly or I cannot hear you." But is it my manner that keeps her from hearing, or the threat of a message that her life may change?

- The Women's Studies Program of a southern university invites a Black woman to read following a week-long forum on Black and white women. "What has this week given to you?" I ask. The most vocal white woman says, "I think I've gotten a lot. I feel Black women really understand me a lot better now; they have a better idea of where I'm coming from." As if understanding her lay at the core of the racist problem.

- After fifteen years of a women's movement which professes to address the life concerns and possible future of all women, I still hear, on campus after campus, "How can we address the issues of racism? No women of Color attended." Or, the other side of that statement, "We have no one in our department equipped to teach their work." In other words, racism is a Black women's problem, a problem of women of Color, and only we can discuss it.

- After I read from my work entitled "Poems for Women in Rage,"* a white woman asks me: "Are you going to do anything with how we can deal directly with *our* anger? I feel it's so important." I ask, "How do you use *your* rage?" And then I have to turn away from the blank look in her eyes, before she can invite me to participate in her own annihilation. I do not exist to feel her anger for her.

- White women are beginning to examine their relationships to Black women, yet often I hear them wanting only to deal with little colored children across the roads of childhood, the beloved nursemaid, the occasional second-grade classmate—those tender memories of what was once mysterious and intriguing or neutral. You avoid the childhood assumptions formed by the raucous laughter at Rastus and Alfalfa, the acute message of your mommy's hand-

*One poem from this series is included in *Chosen Poems: Old and New* (W. W. Norton and Company, New York, 1978), pp. 105–108.

kerchief spread upon the park bench because I had just been sitting there, the indelible and dehumanizing portraits of Amos 'n' Andy and your daddy's humorous bedtime stories.

• I wheel my two-year-old daughter in a shopping cart through a supermarket in Eastchester in 1967, and a little white girl riding past in her mother's cart calls out excitedly, "Oh look, Mommy, a baby maid!" And your mother shushes you, but she does not correct you. And so fifteen years later, at a conference on racism, you can still find that story humorous. But I hear your laughter is full of terror and dis-ease.

• A white academic welcomes the appearance of a collection by non-Black women of Color.* "It allows me to deal with racism without dealing with the harshness of Black women," she says to me.

• At an international cultural gathering of women, a well-known white american woman poet interrupts the reading of the work of women of Color to read her own poem, and then dashes off to an "important panel."

If women in the academy truly want a dialogue about racism, it will require recognizing the needs and the living context of other women. When an academic woman says, "I can't afford it," she may mean she is making a choice about how to spend her available money. But when a woman on welfare says, "I can't afford it," she means she is surviving on an amount of money that was barely subsistence in 1972, and she often does not have enough to eat. Yet the National Women's Studies Association here in 1981 holds a conference in which it commits itself to responding to racism, yet refuses to waive the registration fee for poor women and women of Color who wished to be present and conduct workshops. This has made it impossible for many women of Color—for instance, Wilmette Brown, of Black Women for Wages for Housework—to participate in this conference. Is this to be merely another case of the academy discussing life within the closed circuits of the academy?

To the white women present who recognize these attitudes as familiar, but most of all, to all my sisters of Color who live and survive thousands of such encounters—to my sisters of Color who like me still tremble their rage under harness, or who sometimes question the expression of our rage as useless and disruptive (the two most popular accusations)—I want to speak about anger, my anger, and what I have learned from my travels through its dominions.

*This Bridge Called My Back: Writings by Radical Women of Color, edited by Cherríe Moraga and Gloria Anzaldúa (Kitchen Table: Women of Color Press, New York, 1984), first published in 1981.

*Everything can be used / except what is wasteful / (you will need /
to remember this when you are accused of destruction.)* *

Every woman has a well-stocked arsenal of anger potentially
useful against those oppressions, personal and institutional, which
brought that anger into being. Focused with precision it can become a powerful source of energy serving progress and change.
And when I speak of change, I do not mean a simple switch of positions or a temporary lessening of tensions, nor the ability to smile
or feel good. I am speaking of a basic and radical alteration in those
assumptions underlining our lives.

I have seen situations where white women hear a racist remark,
resent what has been said, become filled with fury, and remain
silent because they are afraid. That unexpressed anger lies within
them like an undetonated device, usually to be hurled at the first
woman of Color who talks about racism.

But anger expressed and translated into action in the service of
our vision and our future is a liberating and strengthening act of
clarification, for it is in the painful process of this translation that
we identify who are our allies with whom we have grave differences,
and who are our genuine enemies.

Anger is loaded with information and energy. When I speak of
women of Color, I do not only mean Black women. The woman of
Color who is not Black and who charges me with rendering her invisible by assuming that her struggles with racism are identical
with my own has something to tell me that I had better learn from,
lest we both waste ourselves fighting the truths between us. If I participate, knowingly or otherwise, in my sister's oppression and she
calls me on it, to answer her anger with my own only blankets the
substance of our exchange with reaction. It wastes energy. And yes,
it is very difficult to stand still and to listen to another woman's
voice delineate an agony I do not share, or one to which I myself
have contributed.

In this place we speak removed from the more blatant reminders
of our embattlement as women. This need not blind us to the size
and complexities of the forces mounting against us and all that is
most human within our environment. We are not here as women examining racism in a political and social vacuum. We operate in the
teeth of a system for which racism and sexism are primary, established, and necessary props of profit. Women responding to racism
is a topic so dangerous that when the local media attempt to discredit this conference they choose to focus upon the provision of

*From "For Each of You," first published in *From a Land Where Other People Live*
(Broadside Press, Detroit, 1973), and collected in *Chosen Poems: Old and New* (W. W.
Norton and Company, New York, 1982), p. 42.

lesbian housing as a diversionary device—as if the Hartford *Courant* dare not mention the topic chosen for discussion here, racism, lest it become apparent that women are in fact attempting to examine and to alter all the repressive conditions of our lives.

Mainstream communication does not want women, particularly white women, responding to racism. It wants racism to be accepted as an immutable given in the fabric of your existence, like evening-time or the common cold.

So we are working in a context of opposition and threat, the cause of which is certainly not the angers which lie between us, but rather that virulent hatred leveled against all women, people of Color, lesbians and gay men, poor people—against all of us who are seeking to examine the particulars of our lives as we resist our oppressions, moving toward coalition and effective action.

Any discussion among women about racism must include the recognition and the use of anger. This discussion must be direct and creative because it is crucial. We cannot allow our fear of anger to deflect us nor seduce us into settling for anything less than the hard work of excavating honesty; we must be quite serious about the choice of this topic and the angers entwined within it because, rest assured, our opponents are quite serious about their hatred of us and of what we are trying to do here.

And while we scrutinize the often painful face of each other's anger, please remember that it is not our anger which makes me caution you to lock your doors at night and not to wander the streets of Hartford alone. It is the hatred which lurks in those streets, that urge to destroy us all if we truly work for change rather than merely indulge in academic rhetoric.

This hatred and our anger are very different. Hatred is the fury of those who do not share our goals, and its object is death and destruction. Anger is a grief of distortions between peers, and its object is change. But our time is getting shorter. We have been raised to view any difference other than sex as a reason for destruction, and for Black women and white women to face each other's angers without denial or immobility or silence or guilt is in itself a heretical and generative idea. It implies peers meeting upon a common basis to examine difference, and to alter those distortions which history has created around our difference. For it is those distortions which separate us. And we must ask ourselves: Who profits from all this?

Women of Color in america have grown up within a symphony of anger, at being silenced, at being unchosen, at knowing that when we survive, it is in spite of a world that takes for granted our lack of humanness, and which hates our very existence outside of its service. And I say *symphony* rather than *cacophony* because we have had to learn to orchestrate those furies so that they do not tear us apart. We have had to learn to move through them and use them for strength and force and insight within our daily lives. Those of us who did not learn this difficult lesson did not survive. And part of my anger is always libation for my fallen sisters.

Anger is an appropriate reaction to racist attitudes, as is fury when the actions arising from those attitudes do not change. To those women here who fear the anger of women of Color more than their own unscrutinized racist attitudes, I ask: Is the anger of women of Color more threatening than the woman-hatred that tinges all aspects of our lives?

It is not the anger of other women that will destroy us but our refusals to stand still, to listen to its rhythms, to learn within it, to move beyond the manner of presentation to the substance, to tap that anger as an important source of empowerment.

I cannot hide my anger to spare you guilt, nor hurt feelings, nor answering anger; for to do so insults and trivializes all our efforts. Guilt is not a response to anger; it is a response to one's own actions or lack of action. If it leads to change then it can be useful, since it is then no longer guilt but the beginning of knowledge. Yet all too often, guilt is just another name for impotence, for defensiveness destructive of communication; it becomes a device to protect ignorance and the continuation of things the way they are, the ultimate protection for changelessness.

Most women have not developed tools for facing anger constructively. CR groups in the past, largely white, dealt with how to express anger, usually at the world of men. And these groups were made up of white women who shared the terms of their oppressions. There was usually little attempt to articulate the genuine differences between women, such as those of race, color, age, class, and sexual identity. There was no apparent need at that time to examine the contradictions of self, woman as oppressor. There was work on expressing anger, but very little on anger directed against each other. No tools were developed to deal with other women's anger except to avoid it, deflect it, or flee from it under a blanket of guilt.

I have no creative use for guilt, yours or my own. Guilt is only another way of avoiding informed action, of buying time out of the pressing need to make clear choices, out of the approaching storm that can feed the earth as well as bend the trees. If I speak to you in anger, at least I have spoken to you: I have not put a gun to your head and shot you down the street; I have not looked at your bleeding sister's body and asked, "What did she do to deserve it?" This was the reaction of two white women to Mary Church Terrell's telling of the lynching of a pregnant Black woman whose baby was then torn from her body. That was in 1921, and Alice Paul had just refused to publicly endorse the enforcement of the Nineteenth Amendment for all women—by refusing to endorse the inclusion of women of Color, although we had worked to help bring about that amendment.

The angers between women will not kill us if we can articulate them with precision, if we listen to the content of what is said with at least as much intensity as we defend ourselves against the manner of saying. When we turn from anger we turn from insight, saying we will accept only the designs already known, deadly and safely familiar. I have tried to learn my anger's usefulness to me, as well as its limitations.

For women raised to fear, too often anger threatens annihilation. In the male construct of brute force, we were taught that our lives depended upon the good will of patriarchal power. The anger of others was to be avoided at all costs because there was nothing to be learned from it but pain, a judgment that we had been bad girls, come up lacking, not done what we were supposed to do. And if we accept our powerlessness, then of course any anger can destroy us.

But the strength of women lies in recognizing differences between us as creative, and in standing to those distortions which we inherited without blame, but which are now ours to alter. The angers of women can transform difference through insight into power. For anger between peers births change, not destruction, and the discomfort and sense of loss it often causes is not fatal, but a sign of growth.

My response to racism is anger. That anger has eaten clefts into my living only when it remained unspoken, useless to anyone. It has also served me in classrooms without light or learning, where the work and history of Black women was less than a vapor. It has served me as fire in the ice zone of uncomprehending eyes of white women who see in my experience and the experience of my people only new reasons for fear or guilt. And my anger is no excuse for not dealing with your blindness, no reason to withdraw from the results of your own actions.

When women of Color speak out of the anger that laces so many of our contacts with white women, we are often told that we are "creating a mood of hopelessness," "preventing white women from getting past guilt," or "standing in the way of trusting communication and action." All these quotes come directly from letters to me from members of this organization within the last two years. One woman wrote, "Because you are Black and Lesbian, you seem to speak with the moral authority of suffering." Yes, I am Black and Lesbian, and what you hear in my voice is fury, not suffering. Anger, not moral authority. There is a difference.

To turn aside from the anger of Black women with excuses or the pretexts of intimidation is to award no one power—it is merely another way of preserving racial blindness, the power of unaddressed privilege, unbreached, intact. Guilt is only another form of objectification. Oppressed peoples are always being asked to stretch a little more, to bridge the gap between blindness and humanity. Black women are expected to use our anger only in the service of other people's salvation or learning. But that time is over. My anger has meant pain to me but it has also meant survival, and before I give it up I'm going to be sure that there is something at least as powerful to replace it on the road to clarity.

What woman here is so enamoured of her own oppression that she cannot see her heelprint upon another woman's face? What woman's terms of oppression have become precious and necessary to her as a ticket into the fold of the righteous, away from the cold winds of self-scrutiny?

I am a lesbian woman of Color whose children eat regularly because I work in a university. If their full bellies make me fail to recognize my commonality with a woman of Color whose children do not eat because she cannot find work, or who has no children because her insides are rotted from home abortions and sterilization; if I fail to recognize the lesbian who chooses not to have children, the woman who remains closeted because her homophobic community is her only life support, the woman who chooses silence instead of another death, the woman who is terrified lest my anger trigger the explosion of hers; if I fail to recognize them as other faces of myself, then I am contributing not only to each of their oppressions but also to my own, and the anger which stands between us then must be used for clarity and mutual empowerment, not for evasion by guilt or for further separation. I am not free while any woman is unfree, even when her shackles are very different from my own. And I am not free as long as one person of Color remains chained. Nor is any one of you.

I speak here as a woman of Color who is bent not upon destruction but upon survival. No woman is responsible for altering the psyche of her oppressor, even when that psyche is embodied in another woman. I have suckled the wolf's lip of anger and I have used it for illumination, laughter, protection, fire in places where there was no light, no food, no sisters, no quarter. We are not goddesses or matriarchs or edifices of divine forgiveness; we are not fiery fingers of judgment or instruments of flagellation; we are women forced back always upon our woman's power. We have learned to use anger as we have learned to use the dead flesh of animals, and bruised, battered, and changing, we have survived and grown and, in Angela Wilson's words, we *are* moving on. With or without uncolored women. We use whatever strengths we have fought for, including anger, to help define and fashion a world where all our sisters can grow, where our children can love, and where the power of touching and meeting another woman's difference and wonder will eventually transcend the need for destruction.

For it is not the anger of Black women which is dripping down over this globe like a diseased liquid. It is not my anger that launches rockets, spends over sixty thousand dollars a second on missiles and other agents of war and death, slaughters children in cities, stockpiles nerve gas and chemical bombs, sodomizes our daughters and our earth. It is not the anger of Black women which corrodes into blind, dehumanizing power, bent upon the annihilation of us all unless we meet it with what we have, our power to examine and to redefine the terms upon which we will live and work; our power to envision and to reconstruct, anger by painful anger, stone upon heavy stone, a future of pollinating difference and the earth to support our choices.

We welcome all women who can meet us, face to face, beyond objectification and beyond guilt.

---

### Now that you've read

1. In what ways does Lorde bring race and gender together in her argument? Why not focus on just one or the other?
2. Why does Lorde think it is important to recognize the sources of one's anger?
3. Lorde writes, "I have no creative use for guilt, yours or my own." What does she mean here? What are "creative uses"? What is the alternative to guilt, according to Lorde?

# SEQUENCE 3 ASSIGNMENTS

## Reading 1: Barbara Ehrenreich, "The Professions as Class Fortress"

> To this day, the educational barriers to the professions serve as much to exclude as to educate.

### Prewriting

1. In a couple of sentences, work through what Ehrenreich is saying in the epigraph above.
2. Why do people flunk out of college or leave college before getting their degrees? What factors contribute to their leaving?
3. In what ways can college be said to "screen out" students? Is this an appropriate thing for colleges to do? Why or why not?

### Writing assignment

Write a two-part essay responding to Ehrenreich's piece. In the first part of your essay, discuss Ehrenreich's central claim and the evidence she offers to support it. Make sure that you read closely and develop a clear understanding of the piece, particularly the final paragraph. In the second part of this essay, discuss what kind of training/education is required for entry into your ideal profession. Does that training make sense to you? Explain your answer. Do the requirements for entering that field support Ehrenreich's argument?

## Reading 2: Donna Gaines, "Dirtbags, Burnouts, Metalheads, and Thrashers"

> In the scheme of things average American kids who don't have rich or well-connected parents have had these choices: Play the game and try to get ahead. Do what your parents did—work yourself to death at a menial job and find solace in beer, God, or family. Or take risks, cut deals, or break the law.

### Prewriting

1. In two or three sentences, explain what point Gaines is making in the quotation above.
2. Could you make distinctions between students in the college preparatory classes and those in the "regular" classes or the vocational education classes at your high school? Why or why not?

3. At what point in your life did you decide to go to college? What factors in your life contributed to that plan—such as family, friends, career goals, or other influences?

## Writing assignment

Take some time to analyze Gaines's argument. What is she saying about education? What is she saying about the relationship between education and social class? What examples does she offer and how do those examples prove her points? What examples from your own observation or experience could you offer to support or refute her argument? Do Gaines's and Ehrenreich's essays resonate with each other? What might Ehrenreich contribute to what Gaines is saying, and where do you position yourself in this dialogue?

## Reading 3: bell hooks, "Confronting Class in the Classroom"

> It only took me a short while to understand that class was more than just a question of money, that it shaped values, attitudes, social relations, and the biases that informed the way knowledge would be given and received.

## Prewriting

1. Respond to what hooks is saying in the quotation above.
2. hooks writes that "class is rarely talked about in the United States," especially in educational settings. Why does she think this is so? Do you think there should be more discussion of class, either in U.S. society at large or, more particularly, in college classrooms? Why or why not?
3. hooks claims that her own working-class background makes her "acutely aware of class." Why might students from more privileged backgrounds be less aware of class?

## Writing assignment

In this piece, hooks describes some of the difficult lessons she learned as a college student at an elite university. How similar is the atmosphere at your college or university to the one she describes? Write a brief essay in which you respond to her outlook on how class functions on campuses and shapes our behavior. Do you agree with her that class differences are more important than ethnic or racial or gender differences? Draw on Ehrenreich's and Gaines's pieces, as well as on your own experience, in formulating your response to hooks.

## Reading 4: Barbara Mellix, "From Outside, In"

> Writing and rewriting, practicing, experimenting, I came to compre-
> hend more fully the generative power of language. I discovered—with
> the help of some especially sensitive teachers—that through writing
> one can continually bring new selves into being, each with new respon-
> sibilities and difficulties, but also with new possibilities. Remarkable
> power, indeed. I write and continually give birth to myself.

### *Prewriting*

1. Respond to the above quotation from Mellix's essay. Do you
   agree that writing and language have a generative power? Have
   you ever experienced this generative power? If so, what were the
   circumstances?
2. How is Mellix's example of the experiences with her "city" relatives related to her description of her experiences in college?
3. Has your use of language ever marked you as an "insider" or as an
   "outsider"? Think about the use of jargon (the specialized vocabulary of a particular trade or the language used when a knowledgeable person talks about football, say, or sewing). Or think about
   regional or ethnic accents or about slang.

### *Writing assignment*

In "From Outside, In" Barbara Mellix describes her evolution as a
writer and a college student. What difficulties arise when she has to,
in essence, speak (and write) two languages? What were her experiences and how were they significant? If you have similar experiences,
describe a time when you became aware of the differences between
your home or friends' language and your school language. What does
Mellix have to teach us about language acquisition and writing? What
factors made her experience so difficult? Use your reading of hooks
and Gaines to examine Mellix's and your own experiences with language at home and in the classroom.

## Reading 5: Janine DiGiovanni, "Lost Generation"

> Yugoslavia's youths got a tantalizing taste of life in modern society;
> then, suddenly and terribly, it was snatched from them. Since then,
> they've known nothing but a series of losing wars, dead soldiers, sanc-
> tions, economic meltdown, anti-Milosevic demonstrations, and gloom.

### *Prewriting*

1. What do you know about the ethnic conflicts in the Balkan region
   of Eastern Europe?

2. What causes some people to be prejudiced against people whose religion, race, or ethnic background is different from their own?
3. Is knowledge of history important in helping us develop a greater appreciation for and understanding of groups different from the ones we grew up in? Explain. What might Ivana and her friends say in response?

## Writing assignment

Write a brief essay in which you consider how the young people DiGiovanni describes are "lost." To what extent do they have control over their own futures? How are the problems they face different from those described by Ehrenreich? Would Ivana agree with Gaines's contention that language determines one's status as an insider or outsider? Consider what role education may play in teaching tolerance for diverse cultures and backgrounds. Offer examples from your own experience in the classroom.

## Reading 6: Audre Lorde, "The Uses of Anger: Women Responding to Racism"

> Every woman has a well-stocked arsenal of anger potentially useful against those oppressions, personal and institutional, which brought that anger into being. Focused with precision it can become a powerful source of energy serving progress and change.

## Prewriting

1. What do you take the quotation above to mean in the context of Lorde's essay?
2. Reflect on Lorde's use of anecdotes from her own experience. Did you find any of them particularly compelling? Which ones, and why?
3. How does Lorde differentiate between anger and hatred? Does the distinction make sense to you? Why or why not?

## Writing assignment

As you begin your essay, take some time to work through Lorde's argument. Discuss the sources of her anger and how she proposes to make sure her anger is *con*structive rather than *de*structive. Did you become angry as you read her essay? If so, what was it she said that made you angry, and why? If not, consider what in her argument strikes you as particularly true on the basis of your experience and observations. Finally, bring in at least two of the previous readings and consider how they might contribute to the dialogue between you and Lorde.

## Final Project

Review what you have written in the writing assignments for this sequence. What are your feelings about diversity on campus and in society now that you've done a lot of thinking and writing about the subject? Are you satisfied with the level of diversity on your campus? Is multiculturalism important? Does it receive too much attention on today's college campuses, or not enough? Have the readings in this sequence changed your mind about anything? Have they reinforced your views about anything?

Mine your essays for a specific issue you'd like to investigate in further detail, and formulate a concise thesis you can use in a research paper. If you can't decide on a topic to investigate further, consider these questions:

What contributes to interaction among people from diverse backgrounds? What prevents it?

What kinds of supports are available or should be made available for people who want to overcome racial or ethnic prejudice?

Should classes in multicultural awareness be made mandatory in state colleges?

What are the roots of the movement for multicultural education?

## Library Research Ideas

Try one or more of the following library research activities, or come up with your own ideas for library research to support your thesis.

1. Investigate multiculturalism on the World Wide Web. The site **http://multicultural.miningco.com/** is a "gateway site," with links to many sites concerned with multiculturalism. There is a page devoted to multiculturalism and education, with links to other sites and to book reviews and summaries. Also check the Association of American Colleges and Universities' Diversity web site (**http://www.inform.umd.edu/diversityweb/**), including the electronic journal Diversity Digest (.**http://www.inform.umd.edu/diversityweb/Digest/**).
2. Check current sociological research on class divisions in America, and research the history of academic and philosophical thought on class during the twentieth century. Compare how class was conceived of earlier in this century with how it is viewed now in the United States. Start with your library's online catalog and the *Social Science Index,* and ask your reference librarian to direct you to any other online or print indexes that might be helpful.

3. Look for Internet mailing lists and newsgroups devoted to a topic of interest from this sequence (review Chapter 4 for tips on how to find mailing lists and newsgroups).
4. Compare the American model of higher education to that in other countries. Is vocational education treated differently in other cultures? Also compare accounts of vocational education in general-interest publications to discussions in scholarly journals (such as the *Chronicle of Higher Education*). Do professionals in the field of education view vocational education as a good or a bad thing? What about the popular press and politicians?

## Field Research Ideas

Try one or more of the following field research ideas, or use your own field research ideas to get data to support your thesis.

1. Survey your fellow students about their perceptions of class. Ask them to define the American middle class, and ask which class they see themselves as belonging to.
2. Compile a survey asking students whether a course in multiculturalism or some other form of diversity training should be required at your school. Ask what, if any, such courses respondents have taken. Compare results from different racial and ethnic populations and between men and women.
3. Observe the extent to which different racial or ethnic groups interact in common areas on campus (cafeterias, library study areas, and so on). Then make similar observations at different points off campus (in office building cafeterias, for example, or in public parks). Is your campus more or less racially and ethnically diverse than its surrounding community? Is it more or less racially and ethnically segregated?
4. Interview representatives of several different racial, ethnic, or international organizations on campus about their experiences in college. Ask how the presence or lack of diversity on your campus has helped or hindered them. Ask what your college could do to be more inclusive.

# Faith and Religion on Campus

## Getting Started

For many students, the first year in college is also the first time they come into contact with people of different religions. For some, this contact fascinates and educates; for others, it can prove disorienting and disturbing. Still other students choose to attend colleges where the students and faculty will share their religious beliefs. The readings in this sequence evoke a variety of roles that religion plays on the college campus and in people's lives.

Robert Johnson in "Teaching the Forbidden: Literature and the Religious Student" expresses his concern that religion prevents his students from engaging in critical inquiry. Next, William J. Bennett laments the decline of religious values in American culture at large in his essay "Revolt Against God: America's Spiritual Despair." In the third reading, "Chris Chrisman Goes to State," James W. Sire offers the allegorical story of a student's confusion and disappointment over the ways in which religion is and is not a part of campus life. Christopher Shea's "Sexual Tension" reports on one religious university's efforts to make campus life conform to religious beliefs. Finally, Chana Schoenberger's "Getting to Know About You and Me," David Denby's "Passion at Yale," and Karen Armstrong's "Introduction to *Muhammad: A Biography of the Prophet*" all deal with how people from non-Christian religions are viewed and want to be viewed.

Before you do any of the reading, however, please reflect on your ideas about the role religion plays in your life and on your campus; then respond to several of the following questions. I use the Getting Started questions as a preliminary exercise on the first day my class works on a particular sequence. Your teacher may also do this, or he or she may ask that you write out your responses either in a journal or in your notebook. Your teacher may use these questions as a jumping-off place for class discussion as well. No matter how you use these questions in your class, you'll be able to draw on what you write here both in your contributions to class discussion and in your responses to the assignments that follow.

1. Are religious beliefs and practices important to you? Do they play an important part in your day-to-day life as a college student? Many people assume that religion plays little part in the typical college student's day-to-day life. If this is not true for you, how would you respond to someone who makes this assumption?
2. What observations can you make about your fellow students' religious beliefs? Do you feel comfortable discussing religion with other students or asking about their beliefs? Why or why not?
3. Should a college education include a spiritual component? Why or why not?

## READING 1

*Robert Johnson*

# Teaching the Forbidden: Literature and the Religious Student

Robert Johnson, having moved to Texas from another, very different part of the country, found himself experiencing culture shock. In particular, he argues that the conservative nature of his students' religious beliefs interfere with their willingness to question and discuss ideas. Consider his descriptions of his students and his classes and how they do or do not resemble you, your classmates, and your own classes.

### Before you read

1. What do you think the essay will be about, judging on the basis of the title?
2. Have you ever been in a situation where you thought one way, but everyone else in the room seemed to think another way? Describe the situation.
3. How would you describe the level of religious belief on your campus?
4. How important is your religion to you in your life as a student? Have your religious beliefs and/or practices changed since you started college?

---

The academy is *always* a minority culture. That is to say, because we pursue knowledge for its own sake, we will never regularly share the values of the surrounding community—even though, at least at state-supported institutions, that community pays our bills. Real teachers are always social deviants.

Never has the dangerousness of our profession been made so clear to me as it has of late. Rebounding from a spate of unemployment, I was lucky enough to obtain a faculty position at a university designated a teaching-centered campus within Texas's higher education system. After accepting my new position, I traveled from a sprawling cosmopolitan city not particularly known for its spiritual values to an environment that functions as a spare tire slung over the Lone Star Bible Belt. And I am here to admit that teaching in north Texas has taught me valuable lessons about some of the most essential conflicts we face as a profession.

North Texas has sunsets and dawns right out of the Big Bang. It is a world in extremis, where the mind naturally runs toward musings born of philosophy and conscience. I remain totally unnerved by the Philippine-quality spring rains. They tear houses apart and leave clothing sufficiently transparent that I have become expert, I believe, for my gender and age group, at making precise, steady eye contact during any conversation held roughly from March to early June. In spite of this seasonal reticence I have been watching my students carefully.

What I have seen is that just as Texans cannot escape the rain, they cannot leave their culture behind—nor can anyone—when they come to school. Moreover, facing the assumptions that most of my students bring to class, I have discovered that what I call "critical writing" and perhaps even "deep reading" they (in increasing numbers, I worry) probably think to be plain old *sin.* In addition, if predictions that we are destined to become a nation increasingly "traditional" in its religious and philosophical assumptions are correct, I think that my experience may soon be shared by others. So I would like to describe some of what I have learned.

Central to the professional training of those of us who have completed graduate work in the humanities has been submission. After long hours of explicating and providing intellectual frames for texts, of constructing (and re- and deconstructing) systems of meaning, of surviving roundtable seminars the purpose of which seems to be to parody what my Zen-practicing friends call "dharma combat," most of us eventually accept that all ideas are mutable. That any conception is meant to be pushed. That dismantling notions the way biologists tear down formaldehyde-preserved cats is not only fitting but right.

We learn to treat ideas as malleable substance and to accept an active commerce in and competition with ideas as a sign of health. To watch three professors sitting at the head table going purple in the neck fighting over Yeats is, to our eyes, good.

Today's literature and composition textbooks reflect this set of values. Each winter, they crash into our offices by the armload, crammed with chapters about intellectual surgery, about dismantling, probing, and disintegrating ideas. Most contemporary texts are based on the notion that unfastening ideas and rebuilding them, challenging the reasons we believe what we do, is admirable, is the root of becoming educated, of becoming literate—of becoming better people. So lulled are we in academia by our professional culture that we easily assume ideas are always most respected when they are batted about.

I would suggest to you that, off campus, ideas are not always seen in the same light. In north Texas they assuredly aren't.

For example, to break the ice in a composition section, I dragged in copies of a cartoon showing two football players trotting off the field: enormous characters, done up in imposing athletic armor. Below the drawing, in the caption, one of the men flatters the other's blocking skills, using effete, elevated diction.

Mind you, I did not propose to ridicule athletes or football; I meant to encourage a discussion of why readers might laugh at that cartoon. My hope was that we could begin to feel a bit of the danger and tension of humor. At least, I wanted folks to think about how language can have more than one set of meanings—how readers, that is, always bring value systems to the text.

Well, boy howdy—that last part quickly became clear. My class met the example with stony, angry silence. A dog faced with their response probably would have laid its ears down and retreated. Lacking such instinctual good sense, I instead went into my teacher routine. I pumped up the energy level, began pacing around the class, attempted to engage individual students in discussing their feelings, my motives, the meaning of our experience. Teachers' motto number one: If all else fails, dig.

What I found, though, was that the silence and anger only became more resolute. To probe was not to fix. To dig was to make worse. Whatever line had been broken couldn't be healed by talk. At which point I remembered reading that in Texas there were five times as many guns as humans and that, in some recent years, more folks were shot than were hit by automobiles, and I changed subjects. By a strange mercy of Bergsonian psychological compression, the class seemed immediately to end.

Speaking with the department chair—another transplant, but a man who has lived a decade in north Texas—I was debriefed, as the astronauts say, about what happened. Smiling his infectious smile, he assured me that what I had done wrong was obvious. What I didn't understand, as a foreigner, was that in local culture football was *not* ironic but essential to the social system. Young folks and their parents—indeed, whole towns—defined themselves using football. Everyone fit someplace: as a cheerleader, a player, a member of the homecoming court, a devoted fan, or a booster in local support organizations. It was like Homer's world—each person had a niche. People carried their football-born identities for life! To challenge any link was to challenge the chain.

Oddly enough, at that time I was teaching the *Odyssey* in a world literature survey. As a gambit, and to chase after what I had been told, in class I diagrammed on the board a concept that I had heard Homer experts label with the Greek term *oikos*. The tale, I harangued the class, was about home, about family, about finding one's identity through community. Copying a diagram from a book, I demonstrated on the board how a family could become self-sufficient and then related to surrounding families as a means of protection . . . how in such a world ritual is sacred, a process through which stability is attained, and to break the web at almost any place is to destabilize the whole.

When I turned away from my awkward art, I was met by the usual fifty-eight astounded faces, but this time, most of them were nodding in affirmation. For the first time in weeks, everyone seemed to understand. Significantly, when moments later I introduced into my diagram the problem of what happens to such a vision of life in the face of the need to change and adapt to new circumstances—or to divided loyalties, new knowledge, new desires—most of the same five dozen faces dramatically fell. The ugly silence returned. But this time, I think, I had a glimmer, at least, of why.

A confession: None of the above is a slam at Texas. In Texas, I am a foreigner. And, in my own Yankee way, I've grown to love the place. Nor is it a slam at my students. They're great. How can you not appreciate classrooms full of folks taught by their parents and ministers to call you "Sir"? You've not done Flaubert, I will add, until you have listened to ranch wives passionately explicate *Madame Bovary* as a picture of the lives of women on the lonely open range. On days when the students are excited, teaching in Texas is like camping at ground zero. I fear I should be wearing one of those lead aprons dentists use to cover patients' privates when they take pictures of teeth.

What I do mean to suggest is that there are great stretches of our country in which challenging ideas is not a comfortable behavior. Indeed, it makes people angry.

So what does this situation have to do with teaching? Well, I for one grew up as a teacher celebrating open classrooms, collaborative exchanges, and dialectic as the soul of my professional behaviors. I have developed my composition and literature lesson plans around that sense of soul. Yet, what I have discovered teaching in north Texas is that there my beliefs are heretical.

For instance, parents have told me that some of my students arrive fresh from schools in which the discovery that you have word processed and not typed an essay will lead to your being awarded an *F* for "cheating." Embracing the fluidity of word processing means that you have forsaken discipline, that you are therefore in error, which is to say *bad.* Some of my students come from high schools where students are given failing grades on research essays if they express theses or personal ideas, from communities in which the university is envisioned not necessarily as a place to grow and change your thinking but as an arena in which to garner technical skills that, rightly speaking, should never alter your beliefs or sense of identity. God talks to the reverends, reverends talk to the men, men enlighten women and mothers . . . and kids take orders from everybody. To speak up in class or challenge ideas is to insult authority. To come home from university changed in deep ways is to have been tainted. And these students have to go home again—they have to be able to live there.

The social model I have found myself confronting in class troubles me. To doubt a word is to doubt an idea, which is to doubt the chain, which is to doubt everything. For many of my students, if I ask them to probe and challenge, to rethink conceptions they hold about the world, I ask them to engage an absurdity. If truth is truth, what is there to challenge? I realize I am overstating things a bit, but for at least some of my students, I think that prewriting, brainstorming, adapting to audience-analysis protocols, letting ideas "cook," is—at some psychological level—letting go of moorings that run clear to God.

That's why they get angry, that's why they show a sick nervousness, that's why they protest, "Just tell me what you want . . . just tell me where the footnotes go, which sentence has the quotes in it, how many paragraphs for an *A*? Why would I want to revise—I said it, didn't I?"

None of this explanation is meant to attack religion. While I am not today a religious person, I grew up surrounded by evangelical Protestant fervor, and I feel nothing but respect for religiously confident persons. Heavens, as a boy, I hiked to what I was told had once been William Blake's own home. I stood in the sun, pressing my palms to the walls, hoping there'd still be a charge.

So no, I'm not impugning religion. What I am trying to say, though, is that, as teachers in an increasingly conservative American culture, we are going to have to admit and clarify our own values. For instance: Is it moral for me to build into my lessons requirements that confront not just the thinking but the culture of my students? As an ethical teacher, should I keep using classroom tools that lead to "better" (meaning idea-challenging) papers if those tools threaten the values of the paper writers? If I say yes, threat is healthy, how do I structure my classes to build on the consequences of my actions? And if I say yes, am I not assuming that my values outweigh those of my students? How do I know they do? Is it fair to award risk taking with higher grades than those given students who tell me in their portfolios that they simply think it out of place to speak, or express ideas of their own, in class?

A final confession: I don't pretend to have big answers. My own answer has been to keep my hands to the dialectical plow. To be a comforter when the pain comes. To expand my office hours and always be there, using my little room as a safe house for folks who need to visit and unload. I play Swiss and act neutral, though I am of course the most duplicitous of deep-cover agents. And I keep my eyes peeled, *pardner*.

More important, though, what I have learned as a teacher in Red River country is that, as a profession, we must recognize we have a problem. That problem is called "the future." If the alleged values revolution proceeds apace, how will we survive in the resulting culture, in which values and ideas won't run in fluid rivers but will accumulate in tiers, like stone? How do we adapt, as an ever more deviant and dangerous profession, when *oikos* pays the bills?

---

## Now that you've read

1. What is Johnson's main argument? Do you agree or disagree with him?
2. What does Johnson mean when he writes, "Real teachers are always social deviants"?
3. How does Johnson describe his students? What do you make of this description?
4. What do you make of Johnson's claim that a student's religious beliefs can interfere with his or her performance in the classroom?

## READING 2

*William J. Bennett*

# Revolt Against God: America's Spiritual Despair

William J. Bennett, former "drug czar" under President Ronald Reagan, has been an outspoken critic of what he sees as America's lack of moral values. Much of his recent work has been dedicated to finding ways to instill these values in young people, including his book *The Book of Virtues* and a cartoon version of the stories in his book for children. See whether you agree with his prescriptions for a better society.

### *Before you read*

1. What do you think this essay will be about from reading the title?
2. Do you see America as experiencing "spiritual despair?" Explain your answer.
3. If you see America as experiencing "spiritual despair," what do you think we should do about it? If you don't see America as experiencing "spiritual despair," why do you think so many people seem to believe that it is?
4. How would you characterize the spiritual climate on your campus? Offer examples.

---

We gather in a spirit of celebration. But tonight I speak out of a spirit of concern—for this evening my task is to provide an assessment of the social and cultural condition of modern American society. And while many people agree that there is much to be concerned about these days, I don't think that people fully appreciate the depth, or even the nature, of what threatens us—and, therefore, we do not yet have a firm hold on what it will take to better us. We need to have an honest conversation about these issues.

A few months ago I had lunch with a friend of mine, a man who has written for a number of political journals and who now lives in Asia. During our conversation the topic turned to America—specifically, America as seen through the eyes of foreigners.

During our conversation, he told me what he had observed during his travels: that while the world still regards the United States as the leading economic and military power on earth, this same world no longer beholds us with the moral respect it once did. When the rest of the world looks at America, he said, they see no longer a "shining city on a hill." Instead, they see a society in decline, with exploding rates of crime and social pathologies. We all know that foreigners often come here in fear—and once they are here, they travel in fear. It is our shame to realize that they have good reason to fear; a record number of them get killed here.

Today, many who come to America believe they are visiting a degraded society. Yes, America still offers plenty of jobs, enormous opportunity, and unmatched material and physical comforts. But there is a growing sense among many foreigners that when they come here, they are slumming. I have, like many of us, an instinctive aversion to foreigners harshly judging my nation; yet I must concede that much of what they think is true.

## "You're Becoming American"

I recently had a conversation with a D.C. cab driver who is doing graduate work at American University. He told me that once he receives his masters degree he is going back to Africa. His reason? His children. He doesn't think they are safe in Washington. He told me that he didn't want them to grow up in a country where young men will paw his daughter and expect her to be an "easy target," and where his son might be a different kind of target—the target of violence from the hands of other young males. "It is more civilized where I come from," said this man from Africa. I urged him to move outside of Washington; things should improve.

But it is not only violence and urban terror that signal decay. We see it in many forms. *Newsweek* columnist Joe Klein recently wrote about Berenice Belizaire, a young Haitian girl who arrived in New York in 1987. When she arrived in America she spoke no English and her family lived in a cramped Brooklyn apartment. Eventually Berenice enrolled at James Madison High School, where she excelled. According to Judith Khan, a math teacher at James Madison, "[The immigrants are] why I love teaching in Brooklyn. They have a drive in them that we no longer seem to have." And far from New York City, in the beautiful Berkshire mountains where I went to school, Philip Kasinitz, an assistant professor of sociology at Williams College, has observed that Americans have become the object of ridicule among immigrant students on campus. "There's an interesting phenomenon. When immigrant kids criticize each other for getting lazy or loose, they say, 'You're becoming American,'" Kasinitz says. "Those who work hardest to keep American culture at bay have the best chance of becoming American success stories."

Last year an article was published in the *Washington Post* which pointed out how students from other countries adapt to the lifestyle of most American teens. Paulina, a Polish high school student studying in the United States, said that when she first came here she was amazed by the way teens spent their time. According to Paulina:

> In Warsaw, we would talk to friends after school, go home and eat with our parents and then do four or five hours of homework. When I first came here, it was like going into a crazy world, but now I am getting used to it. I'm going to Pizza Hut and watching TV and doing less work in school. I can tell it is not a good thing to get used to.

Think long and hard about these words, spoken by a young Polish girl about America: "When I first came here it was like going into a crazy world, but now I am getting used to it." And, "I can tell it is not a good thing to get used to."

Something has gone wrong with us.

## Social Regression

This is a conclusion which I come to with great reluctance. During the late 1960s and 1970s, I was one of those who reacted strongly to criticisms of America that swept across university campuses. I believe that many of those criticisms—"Amerika" as an inherently repressive, imperialist, and racist society—were wrong then, and they are wrong now. But intellectual honesty demands that we accept facts that we would sometimes like to wish away. Hard truths are truths nonetheless. And the hard truth is that something has gone wrong with us.

America is not in danger of becoming a third world country; we are too rich, too proud and too strong to allow that to happen. It is not that we live in a society completely devoid of virtue. Many people live well, decently, even honorably. There are families, schools, churches and neighborhoods that work. There are places where virtue is taught and learned. But there is a lot less of this than there ought to be. And we know it. John Updike put it this way: "The fact that . . . we still live well cannot ease the pain of feeling that we no longer live nobly."

Let me briefly outline some of the empirical evidence that points to cultural decline, evidence that while we live well materially, we don't live nobly. Earlier this year I released, through the auspices of the Heritage Foundation, *The Index of Leading Cultural Indicators*, the most comprehensive statistical portrait available of behavioral trends over the last thirty years. Among the findings: since 1960, the population has increased 41 percent; the Gross Domestic Product has nearly tripled; and total social spending by all levels of government (measured in constant 1990 dollars) has risen from $142.7 billion to $787 billion—more than a five-fold increase.

But during the same thirty-year period, there has been a 560 percent increase in violent crime; more than a 400 percent increase in illegitimate births; a quadrupling in divorces; a tripling of the percentage of children living in single-parent homes; more than a 200 percent increase in the teenage suicide rate; and a drop of 75 points in the average S.A.T. scores of high-school students.

These are not good things to get used to.

Today 30 percent of all births and 68 percent of black births are illegitimate. By the end of the decade, according to the most reliable projections, 40 percent of all American births and 80 percent of minority births will occur out of wedlock.

These are not good things to get used to.

And then there are the results of an ongoing teacher survey. Over the years teachers have been asked to identify the top problems in America's schools. In 1940 teachers identified them as talking out of turn; chewing gum; making noise; running in the hall; cutting in line; dress code infractions; and littering. When asked the same question in 1990, teachers identified drug use; alcohol abuse; pregnancy; suicide; rape; robbery; and assault. These are not good things to get used to, either.

Consider, too, where the United States ranks in comparison with the rest of the industrialized world. We are at or near the top in rates of abortions, divorces, and unwed births. We lead the industrialized world in murder, rape and violent crime. And in elementary and secondary education, we are at or near the bottom in achievement scores.

These facts alone are evidence of substantial social regression. But there are other signs of decay, ones that do not so easily lend themselves to quantitative analyses (some of which I have already suggested in my opening anecdotes). What I am talking about is the moral, spiritual and aesthetic character and habits of a society— what the ancient Greeks referred to as its *ethos*. And here, too, we are facing serious problems. For there is a coarseness, a callousness, a cynicism, a banality, and vulgarity to our time. There are just too many signs of de-civilization—that is, civilization gone rotten. And the worst of it has to do with our children. Apart from the numbers and the specific facts, there is the ongoing, chronic crime against children: the crime of making them old before their time. We live in a culture which at times seems almost dedicated to the corruption of the young, to assuring the loss of their innocence before their time.

This may sound overly pessimistic or even alarmist, but I think this is the way it is. And my worry is that people are not unsettled enough; I don't think we are angry enough. We have become inured to the cultural rot that is setting in. Like Paulina, we are getting used to it, even though it is not a good thing to get used to. People are experiencing atrocity overload, losing their capacity for shock, disgust, and outrage. A few weeks ago eleven people were murdered in New York City within ten hours—and as far as I can tell, it barely caused a stir.

Two weeks ago a violent criminal, who mugged and almost killed a 72-year-old man and was shot by a police officer while fleeing the scene of the crime, was awarded $4.3 million. Virtual silence.

And during last year's Los Angeles riots, Damian Williams and Henry Watson were filmed pulling an innocent man out of a truck, crushing his skull with a brick, and doing a victory dance over his fallen body. Their lawyers then built a successful legal defense on the proposition that people cannot be held accountable for getting caught up in mob violence. ("They just got caught up in the riot," one juror told the *New York Times*. "I guess maybe they were in the wrong place at the wrong time.") When the trial was over and these men were found not guilty on most counts, the sound you heard throughout the land was relief. We are "defining deviancy down," in Senator Moynihan's memorable phrase. And in the process we are losing a once-reliable sense of civic and moral outrage.

### Urban Surrender

Listen to this story from former New York City Police Commissioner Raymond Kelly:

> A number of years ago there began to appear, in the windows of automobiles parked on the streets of American cities, signs which read: "No radio." Rather than express outrage, or even annoyance at the possibility of a car break-in, people tried to communicate with the potential thief in conciliatory terms. The translation of "no radio" is: "Please break into someone else's car, there's nothing in mine." These "no radio" signs are flags of urban surrender. They are hand-written capitulations. Instead of "no radio," we need new signs that say "no surrender."

And what is so striking today is not simply the increased *number* of violent crimes, but the *nature* of those crimes. It is no longer "just" murder we see, but murders with a prologue, murders accompanied by acts of unspeakable cruelty and inhumanity.

From pop culture, with our own ears, we have heard the terrible debasement of music. Music, harmony and rhythm find their way into the soul and fasten mightily upon it, Plato's *Republic* teaches us. Because music has the capacity to lift us up or to bring us down, we need to pay more careful attention to it. It is a steep moral slide from Bach, and even Buddy Holly, to Guns 'n' Roses and 2 Live Crew. This week an indicted murderer, Snoop Doggy Dogg, saw his rap album, *Doggystyle,* debut at number one. It may be useful for you to read, as I have, some of his lyrics and other lyrics from heavy metal and rap music, and then ask yourself: how much worse could it possibly get? And then ask yourself: what will happen when young boys who grow up on mean streets, without fathers in their lives, are constantly exposed to music when celebrates the torture and abuse of women?

There is a lot of criticism directed at television these days—the casual cruelty, the rampant promiscuity, the mindlessness of sit-coms and soap operas. Most of the criticisms are justified. But this is not the worst of it. The worst of television is the daytime television talk shows, where indecent exposure is celebrated as a virtue. It is hard to remember now, but there was once a time when personal failures, subliminal desires, and perverse taste were accompanied by guilt or embarrassment, at least by silence.

Today these are a ticket to appear as a guest on the *Sally Jessy Raphael Show,* or one of the dozen or so shows like it. I asked my staff to provide me with a list of some of the daytime talk-shows topics from only the last two weeks. They include: cross-dressing couples; a three-way love affair; a man whose chief aim in life is to sleep with women and fool them into thinking that he is using a condom during sex; women who can't say no to cheating; prostitutes who love their jobs; a former drug dealer; and an interview with a young girl caught in the middle of a bitter custody battle. These shows present a two-edged problem to society: the first edge is that some people want to appear on these shows in order to expose themselves. The second edge is that lots of people are tuning in to watch them expose themselves. This is not a good thing to get used to.

Who's to blame? Here I would caution conservatives against the tendency to blame liberals for our social disorders. Contemporary liberalism does have a lot for which to answer; many of its doctrines have wrought a lot of damage. Universities, intellectuals, think tanks, and government departments have put a lot of poison into the reservoirs of national discourse. But to simply point the finger of blame at liberals and elites is wrong. The hard fact of the matter is that this was not something done to us; it is also something we have done to ourselves. Liberals may have been peddling from an empty wagon, but we were buying.

Much of what I have said is familiar to many of you. Why is this happening? What is behind all this? Intelligent arguments have been advanced as to why these things have come to pass. Thoughtful people have pointed to materialism and consumerism; an overly permissive society; the writings of Rousseau, Marx, Freud, Nietzsche; the legacy of the 1960s; and so on. There is truth in almost all of these accounts. Let me give you mine.

## Spiritual Acedia

I submit to you that the real crisis of our time is spiritual. Specifically, our problem is what the ancients called *acedia*. *Acedia* is the sin of sloth. But *acedia*, as understood by the saints of old, is *not* laziness about life's affairs (which is what we normally think sloth to be). *Acedia* is something else; properly understood, *acedia* is an aversion to and a negation of *spiritual* things. *Acedia* reveals itself as an undue concern for external affairs and worldly things. *Acedia* is spiritual torpor; an absence of zeal for divine things. And it brings with it, according to the ancients, "a sadness, a sorrow of the world."

*Acedia* manifests itself in man's "joyless, ill-tempered, and self-seeking rejection of the nobility of the children of God." The slothful man *hates* the spiritual, and he wants to be free of its demands. The old theologians taught that *acedia* arises from a heart steeped in the worldly and carnal, and from a *low esteem* of divine things. It eventually leads to a hatred of the good altogether. With hatred comes more rejection, more ill-tempered, more sadness, and sorrow.

Spiritual *acedia* is not a new condition, of course. It is the seventh capital sin. But today it is in ascendance. In coming to this conclusion, I have relied on two literary giants—men born on vastly different continents, the product of two completely different worlds, and shaped by wholly different experiences—yet writers who possess strikingly similar views, and who have had a profound impact on my own thinking. It was an unusual and surprising moment to find their views coincident.

When the late novelist Walker Percy was asked what concerned him most about the future of America, he answered:

> Probably the fear of seeing America, with all its great strength and beauty and freedom . . . gradually subside into decay through default and be defeated, not by the Communist movement . . . but from within by weariness, boredom, cynicism, greed and in the end helplessness before its great problems.

And here are the words of the prophetic Aleksandr Solzhenitsyn (echoing his 1978 Harvard commencement address in which he warned of the West's "spiritual exhaustion"):

> In the United States the difficulties are not a Minotaur or a dragon—not imprisonment, hard labor, death, government harassment and censorship—but cupidity, boredom, sloppiness, indifference. Not the acts of a mighty all-pervading repressive government but the failure of a listless public to make use of the freedom that is its birthright.

What afflicts us, then, is a corruption of the heart, a turning away in the soul. Our aspirations, our affections and our desires are turned toward the wrong things. And only when we turn them toward the right things—toward enduring, noble, spiritual things—will things get better.

Lest I leave the impression of bad news on all fronts, I do want to be clear about the areas where I think we have made enormous gains: material comforts, economic prosperity and the spread of democracy around the world. The American people have achieved a standard of living unimagined 50 years ago. We have seen extraordinary advances in medicine, science and technology. Life expectancy has increased more than 20 years during the last six decades. Opportunity and equality have been extended to those who were once denied them. And of course America prevailed in our "long, twilight struggle" against communism. Impressive achievements, all.

Yet even with all of this, the conventional analysis is still that this nation's major challenges have to do with getting more of the same: achieving greater economic growth, job creation, increased trade, health care, or more federal programs. Some of these things are desirable, such as greater economic growth and increased trade; some of them are not, such as more federal programs. But to look to any or all of them as the solution to what ails us is akin to assigning names to images and shadows, it so widely misses the mark.

If we have full employment and greater economic growth—if we have cities of gold and alabaster—but our children have not learned how to walk in goodness, justice, and mercy, then the American experiment, no matter how gilded, will have failed.

I realize I have laid down strong charges, a tough indictment. Some may question them. But if I am wrong, if my diagnosis is not right, then someone must explain to me this: why do Americans feel so bad when things are economically, militarily and materially so good? Why amidst this prosperity and security are enormous numbers of people—almost 70 percent of the public—saying that we are off track? This paradox is described in the Scottish author John Buchan's work. Writing a half-century ago, he described the "coming of a too garish age, when life would be lived in the glare of neon lamps and the spirit would have no solitude." Here is what Buchan wrote about his nightmare world:

> In such a [nightmare] world everyone would have leisure. But everyone would be restless, for there would be no spiritual discipline in life. . . . It would be a feverish, bustling world, self-satisfied and yet malcontent, and under the mask of a riotous life there would be death at the heart. In the perpetual hurry of life there would be no chance of quiet for the soul. . . . In such a bagman's paradise, where life would be rationalised and padded with every material comfort, there would be little satisfaction for the immortal part of man.

During the last decade of the twentieth century, many have achieved this bagman's paradise. And this is not a good thing to get used to.

In identifying spiritual exhaustion as the central problem, I part company with many. There *is* a disturbing reluctance in our time to talk seriously about matters spiritual and religious. Why? Perhaps it has to do with the modern sensibility's profound discomfort with the language and the commandments of God. Along with other bad habits, we have gotten used to not talking about the things which matter most—and so, we don't.

One will often hear that religious faith is a private matter that does not belong in the public arena. But this analysis does not hold—at least on some important points. Whatever your faith—or even if you have none at all—it is a fact that when millions of people stop believing in God, or when their belief is so attenuated as to be belief in name only, enormous public consequences follow. And when this is accompanied by an aversion to spiritual language by the political and intellectual class, the public consequences are even greater. How could it be otherwise? In modernity, *nothing* has been more consequential, or more public in its consequences, than large segments of American society privately turning away from God, or considering Him irrelevant, or declaring Him dead. Dostoyevsky reminded us in *Brothers Karamazov* that "if God does not exist, everything is permissible." We are now seeing "everything." And much of it is not good to get used to.

### Social Regeneration

What can be done? First, here are the short answers: do not surrender; get mad; and get in the fight. Now, let me offer a few, somewhat longer, prescriptions.

1. At the risk of committing heresy before a Washington audience, let me suggest that our first task is to recognize that, in general, we place too much hope in politics. I am certainly not denying the impact (for good and for ill) of public policies. I would not have devoted the past decade of my life to public service—and I could not work at the Heritage Foundation—if I believed that the work with which I was engaged amounted to nothing more than striving after wind and ashes. But it is foolish, and futile, to rely primarily on politics to solve moral, cultural, and spiritual afflictions.

The last quarter-century has taught politicians a hard and humbling lesson: there are intrinsic limits to what the state can do, particularly when it comes to imparting virtue, and forming and forging character, and providing peace to souls. Samuel Johnson expressed this (deeply conservative and true) sentiment when he wrote, "How small, of all that human hearts endure, That part which laws or kings can cause or cure!"

King Lear was a great king—sufficient to all his political responsibilities and obligations. He did well as king, but as a father and a man, he messed up terribly. The great king was reduced to the mud and ignominy of the heath, cursing his daughters, his life, his gods. Politics *is* a great adventure; it is greatly important; but its proper place in our lives has been greatly exaggerated. Politics—especially inside the Beltway politics—has too often become the graven image of our time.

2. We must have public policies that once again make the connection between our deepest beliefs and our legislative agenda. Do we Americans, for example, believe that man is a spiritual being with a potential for individual nobility and moral responsibility? Or do we believe that his ultimate fate is to be merely a soulless cog in the machine of state? When we teach sex-education courses to teenagers, do we treat them as if they are young animals in heat? Or, do we treat them as children of God?

In terms of public policy, the failure is not so much intellectual; it is a failure of will and courage. Right now we are playing a rhetorical game: we say one thing and we do another. Consider the following:

- We say that we desire from our children more civility and responsibility, but in many of our schools we steadfastly refuse to teach right and wrong.

- We say that we want law and order in the streets, but we allow criminals, including violent criminals, to return to those same streets.

- We say that we want to stop illegitimacy, but we continue to subsidize the kind of behavior that virtually guarantees high rates of illegitimacy.

- We say that we want to discourage teenage sexual activity, but in classrooms all across America educators are more eager to dispense condoms than moral guidance.

- We say that we want more families to stay together, but we liberalize divorce laws and make divorce easier to attain.

- We say that we want to achieve a color-blind society and judge people by the content of their character, but we continue to count by race, skin and pigment.

- We say that we want to encourage virtue and honor among the young, but it has become a mark of sophistication to shun the language of morality.

3. We desperately need to recover a sense of the fundamental purpose of education, which is to provide for the intellectual *and* moral education of the young. From the ancient Greeks to the founding fathers, moral instruction was *the* central task of education. "If you ask what is the good of education," Plato said, "the answer is easy—that education makes good men, and that good men act nobly."

Jefferson believed that education should aim at improving one's "morals" and "faculties." And of education, John Locke said this: "'Tis virtue that we aim at, hard virtue, and not the subtle arts of shifting." Until a quarter-century or so ago, this consensus was so deep as to go virtually unchallenged. Having departed from this time-honored belief, we are now reaping the whirlwind. And so we talk not about education as the architecture of souls, but about "skills facilitation" and "self-esteem" and about being "comfortable with ourselves."

4. As individuals and as a society, we need to return religion to its proper place. Religion, after all, provides us with moral bearings. And if I am right and the chief problem we face is spiritual impoverishment, then the solution depends, finally, on spiritual renewal. I am not speaking here about coerced spiritual renewal—in fact, there is no such thing—but about renewal freely taken.

The enervation of strong religious beliefs—*in both our private lives as well as our public conversations*—has de-moralized society. We ignore religion and its lessons at our peril. But instead of according religion its proper place, much of society ridicules and disdains it, and mocks those who are serious about their faith. In America today, the only respectable form of bigotry is bigotry directed against religious people. This antipathy toward religion cannot be explained by the well-publicized moral failures and financial excesses of a few leaders or charlatans, or by the censoriousness of some of their followers. No, the reason for hatred of religion is because it forces modern man to confront matters he would prefer to ignore.

Every serious student of American history, familiar with the writings of the founders, know the civic case for religion. It provides society with a moral anchor—and nothing else has yet been found to substitute for it. Religion tames our baser appetites, passions, and impulses. And it helps us to thoughtfully sort through the "ordo amoris," the order of the loves.

But remember, too, that for those who believe, it is a mistake to treat religion merely as a useful means to worldly ends. Religion rightly demands that we take seriously not only the commandments of the faith, but that we also take seriously the object of the faith. Those who believe know that although we are pilgrims and sojourners and wanderers in this earthly kingdom, ultimately we are citizens of the City of God—a City which man did not build and cannot destroy, a City where there is no sadness, where the sorrows of the world find no haven, and where there is peace the world cannot give.

### Pushing Back

Let me conclude. In his 1950 Nobel Prize acceptance speech, William Faulkner declared, "I decline to accept the end of man." Man will not merely endure but prevail because, as Faulkner said, he alone among creatures "has a soul, a spirit capable of compassion and sacrifice and endurance."

Today we must in the same way decline to accept the end of moral man. We must carry on the struggle, for our children. We will push back hard against an age that is pushing hard against us. When we do, we will emerge victorious against the trials of our time. When we do, we will save our children from the decadence of our time.

We have a lot of work to do. Let's get to it.

---

## Now that you've read

1. What evidence does William J. Bennett offer to support his claims? What are the examples he draws from? Do they seem reasonable to you?
2. Bennett writes, "There *is* a disturbing reluctance in our time to talk seriously about matters spiritual and religious." Then he asks, "Why?" How do you respond to Bennett's question?
3. What do you make of Bennett's list of things to do to bring about "social regeneration"? Which, if any, seem sound to you? Which, if any, do not? Why?

# READING 3

## James W. Sire

# Chris Chrisman Goes to State

"Chris Chrisman Goes to State" is a chapter from *Chris Chrisman Goes to College,* James W. Sire's story of a young Christian man's first year of college and how he manages to "keep his faith." Sire's hook is an allegory: The characters in the book are all "types" of people, and their names reflect those types—such as John Imokay, Chris's roommates who doesn't mind that Chris is religious but doesn't want him to talk about it, and Charlie Potter, who identifies himself as a Rastafarian so that he can claim marijuana as a sacrament. Read the selection here and see where and how Sire gets the types right and where he perhaps stereotypes.

### *Before you read*

1. How much religious diversity was there in the community you grew up in?
2. How religiously diverse is your college campus?
3. Were you surprised by the amount of (or lack of) religious diversity on your campus? Explain your answer.
4. What can be gained from meeting people who practice different religions from your own? Can anything be lost? Offer examples.

---

> We believe in Marxfreudandarwin.
> We believe everything is OK
> as long as you don't hurt anyone,
> to the best of your definition of hurt,
> and to the best of your knowledge.
> —STEVE TURNER, "CREED"

Once upon a time there was a student named Chris Chrisman. Chris was raised in a modestly evangelical Christian family in suburban Central City. He and his family attended church regularly, and Chris gave his life to Christ, as he would put it, the summer before he became a freshman at West Bolling High. He attended his church youth group and was the treasurer his final year. His private spiritual life consisted of more or less consistent ten-minute devotions before retiring each evening.

He knew the plan of salvation his church emphasized, he had a passing acquaintance with one Gospel, and he remembered the close reading that one of his church-school teachers had given of the book of Revelation. That fascinated him a lot, but he wasn't sure his teacher was completely right about what it all meant. The charts and graphs made the book much more specific than he thought the text itself seemed. But that was okay; his teacher had really studied it.

Chris got good grades in high school, and so two years ago he entered Hansom State University, pretty much the top university in his area. He wasn't sure what he wanted to major in, so he enrolled in the basic courses—English Comp, Introduction to Sociology, Biology 101 and World Civilization 120—that he knew would stand him well no matter what field he opted for later.

Then, to top it off, he decided to enroll in a fairly specialized course that he'd noticed on the list of electives. It was called the Religious Options Around the World and was described in the catalog as "introducing Western students to the panorama of both Western and Eastern religions." What especially intrigued him was that the professor would invite guest lecturers from several major religions, some of which, like Zen, Chris had never heard of.

Once the semester began, Chris didn't have much difficulty handling the academic coursework. He found that with modest effort to stay alert in class and modest time to read and do his homework he could get more than modest grades. By the time of midterms he was relaxed and well into the swing of studies. Nothing presented in his classes seemed particularly difficult to understand. But he was beginning to sense that something odd was happening to him. And it seemed to be happening not in the classroom but in the dorm.

Chris had come to college with his Bible. He'd expected that he would continue to read it each evening and try to find some time, maybe when his roommate was out, to pray. And he did this. His roommate, Ralph Imokay, didn't mind. In fact, by the third week Chris was openly but quietly having his devotions whether his roommate was in the room or not. His roommate was, in fact, rather accommodating.

"Hey," he told Chris, "it's your life. Whatever you believe is fine with me."

As Chris soon found out, though, "whatever" did not include the idea that Ralph should believe the same thing as Chris. In fact, Ralph was not at all interested in knowing what Chris believed, let alone in believing it. Chris hadn't been pushy with his faith. In fact, before he could be, Ralph had warned him off.

"Listen," he cautioned, "what you're into is fine. But only fine for you. It doesn't have to be my thing. And it isn't. So just keep your Bible on your side of the room."

Ralph was a decent enough guy. Chris found him easy to get along with as long as he let Ralph think and do his own thing. Actually, Ralph turned out to be quite helpful when Chris got hung up on a concept in sociology he didn't understand and had to write a paper on it due the next day. He even loaned Chris a clean shirt when he came up short. In fact, it was difficult to see just how Chris's faith made him any better than this guy who, as far as Chris could tell, believed in nothing special. After all, he and Chris were really after the same things as far as school was concerned—a good job with a good company, or maybe, if things worked out right, a great job with a great company. Both were good students.

Now the others on his floor—they were a motley bunch. Chris was glad he had drawn Ralph in the great roommate lottery.

Cynthia Sharp, a sophomore who lived across the hall, was always down on Chris and every other guy in the dorm for being sexist. Chris found he could say very little without getting some disgusted retort from her. She introduced Chris to the idea of being "politically correct." She had spent a year at Buckherst College before transferring to Hansom State and now wanted to introduce all the subtleties of PC to Backwater U, as she called Hansom State. All in all, she made a peaceful life in the dorm lounge rather chancy.

Cynthia's roommate, Susie Sylvan, was a quiet and pretty freshman. Chris was immediately attracted to her; she had red hair and a few freckles and was, Chris thought, properly demure. But what, he wondered, was she was doing with a Book of Mormon among her textbooks? Chris had noticed this when, early in the semester, he had bumped into her in the hall and all her books had gone sliding down the corridor.

Down the hall was a guy, Charlie Potter, who said he was a Rastafarian, though Chris thought it was just his excuse to smoke marijuana, which he did in a stall in the john to keep the residential adviser off the track. It didn't work well, and after he was caught for the second time Charlie had to cool it. Charlie's roommate, Phil Corper, was a business major, totally oriented to getting out and getting on. Chris never heard Charlie or Phil say a word to each other.

Two of the more colorful characters were Jane and John. They roomed across the hall from each other but were always together. They could be heard in one or other of their rooms chanting "Om mane padme hum" over and over again. The aroma of incense would waft down the hall, sometimes covering the smell of pot from the guys' john. In the lounge John would throw out the strangest questions. Most of them Chris couldn't recall five minutes later, but one did stick in his mind. It had kicked off the weirdest conversation he'd ever had. "What is the sound of one hand clapping?" John mused. Then everything went up for grabs. An hour later John left with Jane to hum a few bars of Om, and Chris returned to his room and went to bed with a splitting headache.

Jane's and John's roommates—fortunately for their own sakes—were seldom around. Both were living with their lovers somewhere off campus and keeping their dorm rooms largely as mailing addresses for their parents' letters.

One thing all of the thirty students on Chris's floor had in common was that—except for the chanters—they had very little in common. There was one politically active student (a Young Republican in a Democrat-dominated university); one Methodist who never went to church; two Reformed Jews; a Catholic who had attended mass at the Newman Center every morning at 6:00 a.m. for the first month and then never attended mass again as long as he was in school; a Catholic who rarely attended mass but was always reading Thomas Merton; a couple of loud basketball players, biding their time till the season came around. Then there was Abe Knox, a Christian who wore a T-shirt emblazoned with "Knights of Jesus" in red and black; his aggressive evangelistic demeanor made Chris cringe.

Ethnic background was mixed too—blacks, Hispanics, American-born Koreans and Chinese—though predominantly white American with European roots all mixed up and long lost anyway.

It was his experience of dormitory life that gave Chris his first hint that something was changing in him. He was growing up, he was learning a lot of new things in his university classes, but after a couple of months he was beginning to feel odd.

In fact, Chris was coming apart.

The narrative that had sustained him throughout his conscious existence as a human being—that is, since he'd left adolescence behind—was coming unraveled. The world was supposed to be a place where you graduated from high school, went to college, learned which ropes to grab and pull and which to leave swinging, got introduced into a profession, found a modestly beautiful "girl" to marry a few months after college or after professional school, and then set forth to make your way as an adult. And if you were a Christian you kept the faith, let people know you believed in Christ, perhaps even led a person or two to the Lord. Life would unfold in a path that, while it might look crooked while you were on it, would look straight-arrow when you looked back. There was a meaning to life. Christ was that meaning, and one either found him or one didn't. The Christian way is the only true way, Chris had assumed. To miss it is simply to be in error. That meant one would miss a meaningful life with God on this earth, and after death, instead of experiencing a fulfilled life with God and his people one would spend eternity in a rather unpleasant place.

This narrative didn't seem so certain now—for several reasons. The first, though, was not really so much a reason as an experience. It was all those people on his floor in his dorm, and all the others. Multiply the thirty on Chris's floor by four floors of fifteen dorms and thirty floors of five dorms. Floor after floor of individuals, each with a separate way of viewing reality. It made his head hurt. Who is right? Is anyone right? What should I believe? Isn't one thing just as good as another? Why shouldn't I live with a lover—same sex, different sex—why not? Why should I believe anything at all?

Chris now began to notice how his academic coursework was not helping to resolve these difficulties in the least. Most of them never raised the questions he was interested in. In English he struggled with a few foibles of his graduate-student English instructor, but soon learned what he wanted and produced it. It wasn't what Chris wanted.

In Biology everything went smoothly until Professor Barbara Silvera insisted that evolution by chance and necessity was a fact; design had nothing to do with it. Professor Silvera had asked on a test, "By what process did the giraffe come to have a long neck?" and Chris had answered, "In order to reach the leaves at the top of the trees." The professor's comment on that idea was devastating. Silvera's grad-student grader later explained to Chris why the professor's comment was so harsh and what it meant for evolution to be nonteleological, without deliberate direction, strictly accidental. At least that's what Chris thought it meant, though he could never quite get the hang of that notion. In didn't seem to explain what it purported to explain. But Chris couldn't quite figure out why.

Chris found out later that Professor Silvera had once chanced to be battered in a public dialogue with a creationist who, the professor said, pretended to be a scientist but was simply a misguided ideologue. Now in her class presentations she gave no consideration to any of the creationist's arguments; she just flatly denied that they were relevant. This gave Chris a funny feeling. Obviously, Professor Silvera knew biology; she talked and thought circles around the best students in the class. What she said about evolution seemed credible. Yet it went against Chris's notion of God's somehow being in charge.

Sociology didn't help either. Everything had a natural explanation, if it had one at all. Religion was the opiate of the people or the vestige of our primitive origins, a piece of the machinery of society or (and Chris could make very little of this) a language game played in a thousand different dialects. It was anything but true. In fact, the question of religious truth seldom came up in the course; when it did—usually from a puzzled student—it was laid to rest by the comment "We do not deal with the truth or falsity of religious ideas, only with their history and function in the fabric of society. Your question is just not one sociology tries to answer."

World Civilization fascinated Chris. It introduced him not just to Western civilization but to prehistory, primal peoples, African and Asian history and a good deal more, but the course moved so fast that Chris felt like he did on his first commercial jet flight. He had looked forward to seeing the entire United States as he flew from New York to San Francisco, but he found that except for the high mountains and dry desert of the West everything was in a soft haze. So too, in World Civ a few things, like ancient Greece and Egypt, stood out, but most of the course was a big blur. Still, he did well on the many multiple-choice quizzes and the occasional short papers he had to write.

But it was the special course that had interested him at the beginning of the semester that really gave him fits. Religious Options Around the World—that was the right title, all right. That was precisely how the course was taught. Here's an option. There's an option. Here's the potted history of this option. There's the potted history of that option. (Each got a chapter in a book called *Major Religions of the World*.) Chris did like the fact that Professor Comprel asked guests from several of the religions to speak to the class. That gave each option personal credibility.

But that was the problem again. Each faith looked right to each of those who spoke, and each one began to look right to Chris as he heard them and noted their sincerity. Still, that couldn't be so if Christianity was the one true way—and that was what Chris believed. Chris tried several times to raise the question of which if any of the various faiths could be thought to be true. But Professor Comprel would not answer, and when one of the guests would make a stab at answering, the professor would soften his or her argument with something like "Remember, we are talking about religious belief here. Truth is not really the issue. It's beyond the scope of this course. And besides, in a state school we can't advocate any particular religion in a classroom." He did suggest, though, that Chris take a course in the philosophy of religion. He thought that they just might deal with the truth question there, though of course not by way of advocating any specific religion.

With all this confusion, Chris decided that discretion was the better part of valor. The advice his roommate had given him at the beginning of the semester became the principle he decided to live by—at least for a while. He would live and let live. His faith was not so much put on the back burner as confined to his private life. Among his fellow students he would take on the color of his surroundings—accede to the notion that everyone is entitled to his or her own views on anything. All notion of sharing his faith with the idea that others should be converted was laid aside. The wind had gone out of his sails, and the ship of Chris's faith lay dead in the water.

---

## Now that you've read

1. How well does Sire describe the confusion some students experience when they move away from home and are confronted by people whose way of life is radically different from their own?
2. What is the hardest thing about meeting people from different backgrounds? What is the most rewarding thing about it?
3. Have you seen any instances of religious intolerance since you came to college?
4. What can colleges and universities do to help students make the transition from home to college?

# READING 4

*Christopher Shea*

# Sexual Tension

Christopher Shea's article "Sexual Tension" details the University of Dallas's efforts to set campus policy on the issue of sex on campus between unmarried students. As a Catholic university, it believes that it is important to make church teachings a part of the written code of behavior. The issue of how to define morality and who gets to define it is one that continues to spark debates across the country. What do you make of this university's attempt to take a stand?

## Before you read

1. Is there a lot of sexual activity on your campus? If so, were you shocked by the amount of sexual activity on your campus when you first came to college? Explain your answer.
2. Do you think any type of sexual behavior should be banned on your campus? If so, what, and why? If not, why not?
3. What do you think students' responses would probably be if your college were to attempt to "ban sex" on your campus?

---

"Sex at College? Don't Dare in Dallas."

The last time a college's policies on sex inspired witty headlines, Antioch College had announced that its students needed permission from their partners for every step from the kiss to the unbuttoning to the act.

This time, the University of Dallas was talking about banning sex in its dormitories. A newspaper in College Station, Tex., which produced the example above, was among the publications that had fun with the idea.

Some Dallas students wondered what the fuss was all about when the policy was proposed by a committee of students and professors last spring. Unlike Antioch, the University of Dallas is not exactly a haven for free spirits and sexual experimentation.

### Climate of "Reverse PC"

At this Roman Catholic institution, there are no free condoms, no AIDS-awareness programs. Dormitory residents have to keep their doors open during visits by members of the opposite sex. A recent lecture on the rhythm method filled a lecture hall. "It's kind of ironic that we've made the big time because an assumed, unwritten policy became written," says Amanda Palmer, a senior.

There is a debate at Dallas—but it's not really between a pro-abstinence contingent and students fighting for their right to have lots of sex. Instead, it has to do with how a Catholic institution should balance its religious identity with intellectual openness and with its diverse group of students, about 30 per cent of whom aren't Catholic.

Some students worry that making more rules contributes to a climate of "reverse P.C.," making the university more dogmatic than it should be and reinforcing the intellectual complacency that they see among some devout Christians on the campus.

"U.D. has a very good mix of people," says Kathryn Sommers, a sophomore who describes herself as a liberal Catholic. "I think if the task force goes through with what they are proposing, we might lose that mix, and the campus will become a little more one-sided."

The scene of the debate is a liberal-arts institution with 1,100 undergraduates, a curriculum centered on Western texts, and an unusual tone. Its pale-yellow-brick buildings are nestled into rolling hills just off a highway leading into Dallas. The words "truth" and "virtue" seem to make their way into every other conversation. One recent editorial in the student newspaper argued that the television show "The Simpsons" pushes students "to tolerate increased perversity of the human good."

"This is not an 'I'm okay, you're okay' university," says Margaret Devlin, a senior. "People across the board are respected, but people are also willing to say, 'You're wrong.'"

The proposal that bans "inappropriate sexual touching" was part of a larger document on improving student life at the university. Janet E. Smith, an associate professor of philosophy and chairwoman of the group that wrote the document, says it is unfortunate that attention focused on this part, rather than on a philosophical statement about the need for students to unite their academic and social lives with a consistent moral vision, or on proposals to spruce up the dormitories.

### "A Traumatic Experience"

Still, she does not back down from the controversy. "The pendulum from a totally restrictive to a totally non-restrictive environment on campuses has probably gone too far," she says. "There are some of us who think that premarital sexual activity is just as disastrous as alcohol or drug abuse." Her committee's report, she notes, only suggests as an option the punishment of such activity.

Scott D. Churchill, an associate professor of psychology, says Ms. Smith, who is well known in Catholic circles as a defender of the church's stance on contraception, takes "a singularly adamant view" on sexual issues. He doesn't want her position attributed to the college, because he thinks this would hurt both its reputation and its recruiting.

"Most faculty members just shake their heads at a moralist, dogmatic, or fundamentalist appropriation of religious doctrine," he says. He is chairman of a faculty committee that is reviewing the student-life proposals.

Some students at Dallas have no idea how there could be any argument about banning sex. "It's a traumatic experience to be in a room when others are engaging in sexual activities, or to walk in, or even to know they are sharing something like that in your room," says one sophomore, who didn't want her name used because she "walked in on the act" last year.

The same thing happened to one of her friends. "She thought her roommate was an angel, and she walked in, and she just cried."

Alfredo Guastella, who was a vice-president in the student government last year, objected last spring that the policy undermined the value of choosing abstinence. "Choosing the good because it's your only choice is not virtue," he says. He was criticized so harshly for that position, he says, that he is taking a year off to think about whether he belongs at the university. He is doing temporary work in the Dallas area.

## "Not the College's Business"

In another incident illustrating what he calls intolerance, Mr. Guastella says, a student called him a "disgrace to the university" because he was wearing a T-shirt that read, "Hate is not a family value." The student interpreted that as condoning homosexuality.

"There should be respect of all viewpoints—not agreement, but respect," Mr. Guastella says. "I don't think that happens."

Like Mr. Guastella, some other students criticize the policy while upholding abstinence as an ideal. But those who say they don't think premarital sex is always wrong won't say so on the record.

"This campus is small, and small-townish," explains one.

Speaking of premarital sex, she says, "I don't really think of it as morally wrong, within the confines of a relationship in which you trust the other person. I personally think it's just not the college's business."

Although Catholic universities often have debated the special nature of their institutions, the debate usually has focused on the academic freedom of faculty members. The question of how students whose views differ from those of the church fit into campus life arises most heatedly in the case of gay-student groups. Boston

College, for example, is the latest Catholic university to decide not to recognize such groups officially. The question hasn't even been raised at the University of Dallas.

Colleges affiliated with other churches, too, face questions of when religious doctrine should be written into student handbooks: Stetson University, a Baptist institution, recently severed a connection with the Florida Baptist Convention so that it could loosen its prohibition on drinking and more openly combat the problem of students' drinking. Dallas forbids drunkenness, but not drinking, among students of legal age.

Anita Koch, a sophomore, seems to take pleasure in not quite fitting in on the conservative campus. She is wearing a T-shirt that reads, "Our mission: tolerance, peace, social responsibility, indigenous people . . ." She has a poster of the band Nine Inch Nails on her wall, and puts beer labels on her door.

## A Sign of Intellectual Life

She says she chose the university because it has a strong pre-med program, and adds that she has had to endure condescending remarks both because of her politics and because she isn't Catholic. She mentions what one student leader has told her: "She'll say it in the nicest way, but she'll say, 'You're not following the true religion, so you're going to hell.'"

Academically, Dallas is a "great" institution, Ms. Koch says, but she adds, "I wish someone had said to me, 'Oh, you're not Catholic? It might not be as easy as you think.'"

Many students say it's a sign of the college's lively intellectual life that they hold strong views, and some of them think their classmates need tougher skins. "What is generally taken to be intolerance is somebody saying, 'Why do you believe this?'" says John Grant, a second-year graduate student in political philosophy.

Ms. Smith, the philosophy professor, says the complaints about intolerance have persuaded her that the college needs to sponsor public discussions on how to make a theological or political argument without being abrasive. She rejects the suggestion that those students who are the most aggressive about their religion are close-minded. "Some faculty members say those students are uneducable," she says. "I have to admire them for their zeal, although we should help them work on gaining finesse."

One question that has been raised is whether tightening up rules only widens the gap between pronouncement and practice. Some students do seem to pay lip service to ideals they don't always uphold. One student, a junior who believes in both the no-sex policy and the ban on drunkenness, thinks neither should stand in the way of a little innocent partying.

Every year, around Groundhog Day, students throw an off-campus bash that he describes as a pick-up scene and "a drunk fest." "Every year you laugh at yourself and what your friends did—and it's good to feel a little embarrassed," he says. "It's not so much the drinking, but also the scamming that goes along with it."

### "Almost Pleasantly Surprised"

The no-sex rule will be debated through the fall, and many students say they are just happy to be studying at a place where such moral questions are considered. Kimberly Arnold, a junior who is a Methodist, says she did not expect theology to be as dominant in campus life as it has turned out to be.

"I was surprised, but almost pleasantly surprised," the pre-med student says. Conversations in and out of class have helped her not only to define her own faith, she says, but also to work out some problems in medical ethics that deeply interest her.

She remembers recently making the case that genetic engineering can sometimes be a good thing. "My friends who are Catholic don't agree with me," she says, "but they respect me for having a strong argument."

## Now that you've read

1. Would you like to see your college take a stand against "immoral" behavior? Would you like to see moral issues discussed publicly on your campus? Explain your answer.
2. The University of Dallas is a private, religious institution. How does that affect what it can and cannot require of its students?
3. A student from the University of Dallas states, "Choosing the good because it's your only choice is not a virtue." What do you take him to mean by this? How do you respond?

## READING 5

*Chana Schoenberger*

# Getting to Know About You and Me

"Getting to Know About You and Me" was published in *Newsweek* in 1993 when Chana Schoenberger was still in high school. Her essay attempts to teach us something important. Is the lesson needed on your campus?

### *Before you read*

1. How diverse is your college in terms of religious representation?
2. Have you ever been in a position to learn about a religion other than your own? If so, describe the situation.
3. In what ways can people's religions affect their professional or academic lives?

As a religious holiday approaches, students at my high school who will be celebrating the holiday prepare a presentation on it for an assembly. The Diversity Committee, which sponsors the assemblies to increase religious awareness, asked me last spring if I would help with the presentation on Passover, the Jewish holiday that commemorates the Exodus from Egypt. I was too busy with other things, and I never got around to helping. I didn't realize then how important those presentations really are, or I definitely would have done something.

This summer I was one of 20 teens who spent five weeks at the University of Wisconsin at Superior studying acid rain with a National Science Foundation Young Scholars program. With such a small group in such a small town, we soon became close friends and had a good deal of fun together. We learned about the science of acid rain, went on field trips, found the best and cheapest restaurants in Superior and ate in them frequently to escape the lousy cafeteria food. We were a happy, bonded group.

Represented among us were eight religions: Jewish, Roman Catholic, Muslim, Hindu, Methodist, Mormon, Jehovah's Witness and Lutheran. It was amazing, given the variety of backgrounds, to see the ignorance of some of the smartest young scholars on the subject of other religions.

On the first day, one girl mentioned that she had nine brothers and sisters. "Oh, are you Mormon?" asked another girl, who I knew was a Mormon herself. The first girl, shocked, replied, "No, I dress normal!" She thought Mormon was the same as Mennonite, and the only thing she knew about either religion was that Mennonites don't, in her opinion, "dress normal."

My friends, ever curious about Judaism, asked me about everything from our basic theology to food preferences. "How come, if Jesus was a Jew, Jews aren't Christian?" my Catholic roommate asked me in all seriousness. Brought up in a small Wisconsin town, she had never met a Jew before, nor had she met people from most of the other "strange" religions (anything but Catholic or mainstream Protestant). Many of the other kids were the same way.

"Do you all still practice animal sacrifices?" a girl from a small town in Minnesota asked me once. I said no, laughed, and pointed out that this was the 20th century, but she had been absolutely serious. The only Jews she knew were the ones from the Bible.

Nobody was deliberately rude or anti-Semitic, but I got the feeling that I was representing the entire Jewish people through my actions. I realized that many of my friends would go back to their small towns thinking that all Jews liked Dairy Queen Blizzards and grilled cheese sandwiches. After all, that was true of all the Jews they knew (in most cases, me and the only other Jewish young scholar, period).

The most awful thing for me, however, was not the benign ignorance of my friends. Our biology professor had taken us on a field trip to the EPA field site where he worked, and he was telling us about the project he was working on. He said that they had to make sure the EPA got its money's worth from the study—he "wouldn't want them to get Jewed."

I was astounded. The professor had a doctorate, various other degrees and seemed to be a very intelligent man. He apparently had no idea that he had just made an anti-Semitic remark. The other Jewish girl in the group and I debated whether or not to say something to him about it, and although we agreed we would, neither of us ever did. Personally, it made me feel uncomfortable. For a high-school student to tell a professor who taught her class that he was a bigot seemed out of place to me, even if he was one.

What scares me about that experience, in fact about my whole visit to Wisconsin, was that I never met a really vicious anti-Semite or a malignantly prejudiced person. Many of the people I met had been brought up to think that Jews (or Mormons or any other religion that's not mainstream Christian) were different and that difference was not good.

Difference, in America, is supposed to be good. We are expected—at least, I always thought we were expected—to respect each other's traditions. Respect requires some knowledge about people's backgrounds. Singing Christmas carols as a kid in school did not make me Christian, but it taught me to appreciate beautiful music and someone else's holiday. It's not necessary or desirable for all ethnic groups in America to assimilate into one traditionless mass. Rather, we all need to learn about other cultures so that we can understand one another and not feel threatened by others.

In the little multicultural universe that I live in, it's safe not to worry about explaining the story of Passover because if people don't hear it from me, they'll hear it some other way. Now I realize that's not true everywhere.

Ignorance was the problem I faced this summer. By itself, ignorance is not always a problem, but it leads to misunderstandings, prejudice and hatred. Many of today's problems involve hatred. If there weren't so much ignorance about other people's backgrounds, would people still hate each other as badly as they do now? Maybe so, but at least that hatred would be based on facts and not flawed beliefs.

I'm now back at school, and I plan to apply for the Diversity Committee. I'm going to get up and tell the whole school about my religion and the tradition I'm proud of. I see now how important it is to celebrate your heritage and to educate others about it. I can no longer take for granted that everyone knows about my religion, or that I know about theirs. People who are suspicious when they find out I'm Jewish usually don't know much about Judaism. I would much prefer them to hate or distrust me because of something I've done, instead of them hating me on the basis of prejudice.

---

### Now that you've read

1. What is Chana Schoenberger's central purpose in writing her essay?
2. What are her main concerns? What is her final plan?
3. What kinds of questions have people asked her about her religion? How does she respond?
4. What kinds of things can colleges do to educate their students about the different religions represented on campus? Should colleges take this responsibility? Why or why not?

# READING 6

*David Denby*

# Passion at Yale

Chana Schoenberger's "Getting to Know About You and Me" and David Denby's "Passion at Yale" make the same argument but from different positions. Schoenberger's article, which originally appeared in *Newsweek,* argues that the only way to overcome prejudice is to focus on getting to know the individual. Denby's article from *The New Yorker* argues that segregation based on any grounds—even when it's self-selected by the group that is the object of prejudice—harms our culture.

## *Before you read*

1. Can you think of any problems that might arise from living in a coed dorm? What are they? Can you think of any advantages? What are they?
2. If your school requires its students to live in dorms at some time or another, when does an individual student have the right to escape the requirement?

As college students gather in the opening weeks of a new semester, there is, we hear, a scandal brewing, a dirty secret spreading its stain through the life of undergraduates, whose life is conducted, at many campuses, in coed dormitories. The secret (which, of course, is not very new and not entirely secret) is that there isn't very much sex going on. There's *some,* of course: some students are very active sexually (and become either famous or notorious for it), and a few may even have the grace or the misfortune to experience what would have been known in another era as passion. But many students "hook up" only now and then, and others may be defiantly chaste, or perhaps lonely or indifferent, and spend the best part of four years in a state of bluesy sexual withdrawal, rarely experiencing so much as the dip of a window shade.

All this serves as the necessary ironic background for the recent announcement by a group of five Yale freshmen and sophomores of the Orthodox Jewish faith that they may begin a lawsuit against the university in order to fight the requirement that they spend their first two years at Yale living in coed dormitories. (At Yale, freshmen generally live on all-male or all-female floors but share some bathrooms; sophomores live in single-sex suites joined by bathrooms. It may, on occasion, be necessary to knock.) Such a residence requirement, the students declare, contradicts religious rules that demand privacy and modesty as well as sexual abstinence prior to marriage. So far, Yale has refused to waive its requirement that the students live in the dormitories, and, in response, the Yale Five (as they style themselves) have asked for the assistance of a prominent lawyer—Nathan Lewin, of Washington—who describes the affair as a constitutional issue in which the students' rights to free religious expression have been infringed. In the past, Mr. Lewin has successfully sued for the rights of Orthodox Jews in public jobs to maintain elements of religious observance—the right of an Air Force psychologist, say, to wear a yarmulke at work. But no one is prohibiting the exercise of religious observance at Yale, and the students can maintain a kosher diet in an off-campus dining hall. What's at stake for the Yale Five is the *atmosphere* of undergraduate life—the threat it poses to their purity of conduct. But temptations must surround the orthodox of any faith when they leave family and community and enter the world. Though the sensibilities of these students may be affronted, have their constitutional rights been abrogated?

One remains puzzled by the students' notion that dormitory life is a parade of licentious goings on—or, at the least, a series of remorseless intrusions. "There is no way to keep female visitors away," one of the Five was quoted as saying. ("I should be so lucky," his dorm-mates may be thinking.) Yes, every dorm resident does have to put up with occasional annoyances—a floormate, say, who won't turn down a CD-player. But no one is forcing the students to do anything in particular. No one is requiring of them—as certain heretical Christian sects were accused of requiring of members—that they lie next to young virgins as a test of their resolve. One of the Five did complain that during freshman orientation he was subjected to a lecture on condoms. It strikes one as exceedingly curious, however, that any university student should be shocked by mere information. Furthermore, students need not avail themselves of the condoms that Yale—continuing to operate in loco parentis—offers to its charges to prevent the spread of sexually transmitted diseases and, of course, unwanted pregnancies. Doors can always be locked. It is hard to believe that if a student wants to live quietly and privately in a Yale dormitory others will not, after a while, respect the signals he is sending out.

In a *Times* Op-Ed piece that appeared last Tuesday, Elisha Dov Hack, one of the Yale Five, complained of a sign he spied during an orientation tour which touted "100 ways to make love without having sex." One of the advertised ways that offended Mr. Hack was "Take a nap together." The sign, of course, was a joking nudge to behave responsibly. Yet even the notion of a mere coed snooze strikes Mr. Hack as heresy. Unmarried intimacy of any kind—or even proximity— seems to be what disturbs the Yale Five. "We cannot, in good conscience," Mr. Hack writes, "live in a place where women are permitted to stay overnight in men's rooms." In that case, Mr. Hack should avoid living in big-city apartment buildings as well.

The students' grievances appears to be produced by a combination of harsh medieval ardor and culture-of-complaint hypersensitivity. If the students care so much for modesty and chastity, they could, of course, attend a seminary. But it's the Yale degree they want, and they can hardly accuse the university of false advertising. Living in a coed dorm for two years is now part of the known Yale experience, just as taking certain required courses, like the Literature Humanities and the Contemporary Civilization courses at Columbia, is part of the life of other schools.

No modern university can be asked to spare its observant students the chagrins of a secular existence, for almost every aspect of the curriculum itself has been formed by secular assumptions. In class, the students may hear religion discussed in historical, political, and military—rather than sacred—terms; they may even hear religion discussed as a system of illusion. In every discipline, the disenchanted modern world awaits them. One of the Yale Five is a biology major. The Hebrew Bible says nothing about evolution. Will the student boycott his courses? One thing that separates a faith community from a learning community is that in the latter one's preconceptions are constantly, and productively, under duress. The experience of confronting both new ideas and people who think differently from oneself has traditionally formed the heart of a liberal education.

It's bad enough that the dormitories at Berkeley are partly balkanized by special-interest groups and that at many universities African-Americans congregate at meals (often to the dismay of white students who would like to mingle with them and make friends). Such self-imposed separations attack the very idea of a university. By not giving in, Yale no doubt wants to avoid a situation in which separatist communities increase their demands on the university. And Yale is right. If universities continue to humor every group's sensitivities, then what is to stop blacks from demanding protection from exposure to white students, gays from exposure to straights, fundamentalist Christians from exposure to Jews and Muslims? In this society, existence is rarely free from jostling: we all, every day, find our deepest convictions offended, even traduced, by *something*. In that respect, the Yale Five, whether they get their way or not, will have to take their chances along with the rest of us.

------------------------------------------------------

## Now that you've read

1. What are the Yale Five's objections to living in a coed dorm? What do you make of those objections?
2. What is David Denby's position in relation to the Yale Five's efforts to get an exception made in their cases?
3. What might the Yale Five argue if someone were to tell them that they should go to a school other than Yale if they object to Yale's requirements?

## READING 7

*Karen Armstrong*

# Introduction to *Muhammad: A Biography of the Prophet*

Many millions of people around the world are Islamic, including many people in the United States. Karen Armstrong is concerned that recent and ongoing political conflicts in Iraq, Iran, and elsewhere have led many Americans to hold stereotyped views of Muslims and potentially dangerous attitudes toward all believers in Islam. What she has to say has implications that move us from the college campus to the world beyond.

### Before you read

1. Are you a Muslim? If so, do you ever feel discriminated against or stereotyped on campus? If not, do you know much about Islam and Muhammad? Where did your information come from?
2. Are there many Muslim students at your college?
3. What is your impression of the way the U.S. media portray Muslims and Islam?

As we approach the end of the twentieth century, religion has once again become a force to be reckoned with. We are witnessing a widespread revival which would have seemed inconceivable to many people during the 1950s and 1960s when secularists tended to assume that religion was a primitive superstition outgrown by civilised, rational man. Some confidently predicted its imminent demise. At best religion was a marginal and private activity, which could no longer influence world events. Now we realise that this was a false prophecy. In the Soviet Union, after decades of official atheism, men and women are demanding the right to practise their faith. In the West, people who have little interest in conventional doctrine and institutional churches have shown a new awareness of spirituality and the inner life. Most dramatically, perhaps, a radical religiosity, which we usually call "fundamentalism," has erupted in most of the major religions. It is an intensely political form of faith and some see it as a grave danger to world and civic peace. Governments ignore it at their peril. Yet again, as so often in the past, an age of scepticism has been followed by a period of intense religious fervour; religion seems to be an important human need which cannot easily be discarded or pushed to the sidelines, no matter how rational or sophisticated our society. Some will welcome this new age of faith, others will deplore it, but none of us can dismiss religion as irrelevant to the chief concerns of our century. The religious instinct is extremely powerful and can be used for good and ill. We must, therefore, understand it and examine its manifestations carefully, not only in our society but also in other cultures.

Our dramatically shrunken world has revealed our inescapable connection with one another. We can no longer think of ourselves as separate from people in distant parts of the globe and leave them to their own fate. We have a responsibility to each other and face common dangers. It is also possible for us to acquire an appreciation of other civilizations that was unimaginable before our own day. For the first time, people all over the world are beginning to find inspiration in more than one religion and many have adopted the faith of another culture. Thus Buddhism is enjoying a great flowering in the West, where Christianity had once reigned supreme. But even when people have remained true to the faith of their fathers, they have sometimes been influenced by other traditions. Sir Sarvepalli Rudhakrishnan (1888–1975), the great Hindu philosopher and statesman, for example, was educated at the Christian College of Madras and strongly affected the religious thought of people of both East and West. The Jewish philosopher Martin Buber (1878–1965), who wrote his doctoral thesis on the two medieval Christian mystics Nicholas of Cusa and Meister Eckhart, has been read enthusiastically by Christians and has had a profound influence on their ideas and spirituality. Jews tend to be less interested in Buber than are Christians, but they do read the Protestant theologian Paul Tillich (1886–1965) and the modernist thinker Harvey Cox. The barriers of geographical distance, hostility and fear, which once kept the religions in separate watertight compartments, are beginning to fall.

Although much of the old prejudice remains, this is a hopeful development. It is particularly heartening, after centuries of virulent Christian anti-Semitism, to see Jewish and Christian scholars attempting to reach a new understanding. There is an incipient perception of the deep unity of mankind's religious experience and a realisation that traditions which "we" once despised can speak to our own condition and revitalise our spirituality. The implication of this could be profound: we will never be able to see either our own or other people's religions and cultures in quite the same way again. The possible result of this has been compared to the revolution that science has effected in the outlook of men and women throughout the world. Many people will find this development extremely threatening and they will erect new barricades against the "Other," but some are already beginning to glimpse broader horizons and find that they are moved by religious ideals that their ancestors would have dismissed with contempt.

But one major religion seems to be outside this circle of goodwill and, in the West at least, to have retained its negative image. People who are beginning to find inspiration in Zen or Taoism are usually not nearly so eager to look kindly upon Islam, even though it is the third religion of Abraham and more in tune with our own Judaeo-Christian tradition. In the West we have a long history of hosility towards Islam that seems as entrenched as our anti-Semitism, which in recent years has seen a disturbing revival in Europe. At least, however, many people have developed a healthy fear of this ancient prejudice since the Nazi Holocaust. But the old hatred of Islam continues to flourish on both sides of the Atlantic and people have few scruples about attacking this religion, even if they know little about it.

The hostility is understandable, because until the rise of the Soviet Union in our own century, no polity or ideology posed such a continuous challenge to the West as Islam. When the Muslim empire was established in the seventh century CE, Europe was a backward region. Islam had quickly overrun much of the Christian world of the Middle East as well as the great Church of North Africa, which had been of crucial importance to the Church of Rome. This brilliant success was threatening: had God deserted the Christians and bestowed his favour on the infidel? Even when Europe recovered from the Dark Ages and established its own great civilisation, the old fear of the ever-expanding Muslim empire remained. Europe could make no impression on this powerful and dynamic culture: the Crusading project of the twelfth and thirteenth centuries eventually failed and, later, the Ottoman Turks brought Islam to the very doorstep of Europe. This fear made it impossible for Western Christians to be rational or objective about the Muslim faith. At the same time as they were weaving fearful fantasies about Jews, they were also evolving a distorted image of Islam, which reflected their own buried anxieties. Western scholars denounced Islam as a blasphemous faith and its Prophet Muhammad as the Great Pretender, who had founded a violent religion of the sword in order to conquer the world. "Mahomet" became a bogy to the people of Europe, used by mothers to frighten disobedient children. In Mummers' plays he was presented as the enemy of Western civilisation, who fought our own brave St George.

This inaccurate image of Islam became one of the received ideas of Europe and it continues to affect our perceptions of the Muslim world. The problem has been compounded by the fact that, for the first time in Islamic history, Muslims have begun to cultivate a passionate hatred of the West. In part this is due to European and American behaviour in the Islamic world. It is a mistake to imagine that Islam is an inherently violent or fanatical faith, as is sometimes suggested. Islam is a universal religion and there is nothing aggressively Oriental or anti-Western about it. Indeed, when Muslims first encountered the colonial West during the eighteenth century many were impressed by its modern civilisation and tried to emulate it. But in recent years this initial enthusiasm has given way to bitter resentment. We should also remember that "fundamentalism" has surfaced in most religions and seems to be a world-wide response to the peculiar strain of late-twentieth-century life. Radical Hindus have taken to the streets to defend the caste system and to oppose the Muslims of India; Jewish fundamentalists have made illegal settlements on the West Bank and the Gaza Strip and have vowed to drive all Arabs from their Holy Land; Jerry Falwell's Moral Majority and the new Christian Right, which saw the Soviet Union as the evil empire, achieved astonishing power in the United States during the 1980s. It is wrong, therefore, to assume that Muslim extremists are typical of their faith. It would be just as mistaken to see the late Ayatollah Khomeini as the incarnation of Islam as to dismiss the rich and complex tradition of Judaism because of the immoral policies of the late Rabbi Meir Kahane. If "fundamentalism" seems particularly rife in the Muslim world, this is because of the population explosion. To give just one telling example: there were only 9 million Iranians before the Second World War; today there are 57 million and their average age is seventeen. Radical Islam, with its extreme and black-and-white solutions, is a young person's faith.

Most Westerners do not know enough about traditional Islam to assess this new strain and put it in a proper perspective. When Shiites in the Lebanon take hostages in the name of "Islam" people in Europe and America naturally feel repelled by the religion itself, without realising that this behaviour contravenes important legislation in the Qu'ran about the taking and treatment of captives. Regrettably, the media and the popular press do not always give us the help we need. Far more coverage, for example, was given to the Muslims who vociferously supported Ayatollah Khomeini's *fatwa* against the British author Salman Rushdie than to the majority who opposed it. The religious authorities of Saudi Arabia and the sheikhs of the prestigious mosque of al-Azhar in Cairo both condemned the *fatwa* as illegal and un-Islamic: Muslim law does not permit a man to be sentenced to death without trial and has no jurisdiction outside the Islamic world. At the Islamic Conference of March 1989, forty-four out of the forty-five member states unanimously rejected the Ayatollah's ruling. But this received only cursory attention in the British press and left many people with the misleading impression that the entire Muslim world was clamouring for Rushdie's blood. Sometimes the media seems to stir up our traditional prejudices, as was particularly apparent during the OPEC oil crisis of 1973. The imagery used in cartoons, advertisements and popular articles was rooted in old Western fears of a Muslim conspiracy to take over the world.

Many people feel that Muslim society justifies our stereotypical view of it: life seems cheap; governments are sometimes corrupt or tyrannical; women are oppressed. It is not uncommon for people to blame this state of affairs on "Islam." But scholars warn us not to over-emphasise the role of any religion on a given society and Marshall G. S. Hodgson, the distinguished historian of Islam, points out that the aspects of the Muslim world condemned in the West are characteristic of most pre-modern societies: life would not have been very different here three hundred years ago. But sometimes there seems to be a definite desire to blame the faith itself for every disorder in the Muslim world. Thus feminists frequently condemn "Islam" for the custom of female circumcision. This despite the fact that it is really an African practice, is never mentioned in the Qu'ran, is *not* prescribed by three of the four main schools of Islamic jurisprudence, and was absorbed into the fourth school in North Africa where it was a fact of life. It is as impossible to generalise about Islam as about Christianity; there is a wide range of ideas and ideals in both.

A clear example of stereotyping is the common assumption that the Islam practised in Saudi Arabia is the most authentic form of the faith. Seemingly more archaic, it is supposed to resemble that practised by the first community of Muslims. Because the West has long considered the regime in Saudi Arabia obnoxious, it tends to write off "Islam" too. But Wahhabism is only an Islamic sect. It developed in the eighteenth century and was similar to the Christian Puritan sect that flourished during the seventeenth century in England, the Netherlands and Massachusetts. The Puritans and the Wahhabis both claimed to be returning to the original faith, but both were really an entirely new development and a response to the unique conditions of the time. Both Wahhabism and Puritanism exerted an important influence in the Muslim and Christian worlds respectively, but it is a mistake to view either sect as normative in their religion. Reform movements in any faith attempt to return to the original spirit of the founder, but it is never possible to reproduce former conditions entirely.

I am not claiming that Islam is entirely faultless. All religions are human institutions and frequently make serious mistakes. All have sometimes expressed their faith in inadequate and even in abhorrent ways. But they have also been creative, enabling millions of men and women to find faith in the ultimate meaning and value of life, despite the suffering that flesh is heir to. To put "Islam" into an unholy category of its own or to assume that its influence has been wholly or even predominantly negative is both inaccurate and unjust. It is a betrayal of the tolerance and compassion that are supposed to characterise Western society. In fact Islam shares many of the ideals and visions that have inspired both Judaism and Christianity. Consequently it has helped people to cultivate values that it shares with our own culture. The Judaeo-Christian tradition does not have the monopoly on either monotheism or concern for justice, decency, compassion and respect for humanity.

Indeed, the Muslim interpretation of the monotheistic faith has its own special genius and has important things to teach us. Ever since Islam came to my attention, I have been increasingly aware of this. Until a few years ago, I was almost entirely ignorant about the religion. The first inkling I had that it was a tradition that could speak to me came during a holiday in Samarkand. There I found the Islamic architecture to express a spirituality that resonated with my own Catholic past. In 1984 I had to make a television programme about Sufism, the mysticism of Islam, and was particularly impressed by the Sufi appreciation of other religions—a quality that I had certainly not encountered in Christianity! This challenged everything that I had taken for granted about "Islam" and I wanted to learn more. Finally, during a study of the Crusades and the current conflict in the Middle East, I was led to the life of Muhammad and to the Qu'ran, the scripture that he brought to the Arabs. I am no longer a believing or practising Christian nor do I belong to any other official religion. But at the same time as I have been revising my ideas about Islam, I have also been reconsidering the religious experience itself. In all the great religions, seers and prophets have conceived strikingly similar visions of a transcendent and ultimate reality. However we choose to interpret it, this human experience has been a fact of life. Indeed, Buddhists deny that there is anything supernatural about it: it is a state of mind that is natural to humanity. The monotheistic faiths, however, call this transcendence "God." I believe that Muhammad had such an experience and made a distinctive and valuable contribution to the spiritual experience of humanity. If we are to do justice to our Muslim neighbours, we must appreciate this essential fact. . . .

The Gulf War of 1991 showed that, whether we like it or not, we are deeply connected with the Muslim world. Despite temporary alliances, it is clear that the West has largely lost the confidence of people in the Islamic world. A breakdown in communications is never the fault of one party and if the West is to regain the sympathy and respect that it once enjoyed in the Muslim world it must examine its own role in the Middle East and consider its own difficulties vis-à-vis Islam.

---

## *Now that you've read*

1. Did you learn anything about Islam from this reading that you didn't know before? If so, what did you learn? Did anything you learned surprise you?
2. What is Armstrong's attitude toward her subject? How can you tell?
3. What factors have contributed to Americans' prejudices against Islam? Why does Armstrong think Islam has been excluded from the current climate of goodwill and religious tolerance?

# Sequence 4 Assignments

## Reading 1: Robert Johnson, "Teaching the Forbidden: Literature and the Religious Student"

> I realize I am overstating things a bit, but for at least some of my students, I think that prewriting, brainstorming, adapting to audience-analysis protocols, letting ideas "cook," is—at some psychological level—letting go of moorings that run clear to God.

### Prewriting

1. Respond to the above quotation from Johnson's piece. Do you agree that critical thinking tends to cut loose religious "moorings"? Is this a necessary or desirable outcome of critical thinking? Why or why not?
2. In what ways do where we live and with whom we live affect what we say and do? How has this been true for you? For Johnson?

### Writing assignment

You've begun to develop your own definition of critical thinking. Keep that in mind as you consider how Johnson is defining this term. What is it in the acts of critical thinking, reading, and writing that he values? Respond to Johnson's representation of students in his classes. What arguments is he making about them, and what is your position in relation to those arguments? Where does what he says ring true? Where do his attempts to understand the "Other" (students from North Texas) break down because of his own assumptions, prejudices, and cultural "of courses"? What stories can you tell to support his case or argue against it? Please be specific.

## Reading 2: William J. Bennett, "Revolt Against God: America's Spiritual Despair"

> Because music has the capacity to lift us up or to bring us down, we need to pay more careful attention to it.

### Prewriting

1. What do you understand the quotation above to mean? What kind of attention might we pay to music?
2. What is the attraction of daytime talk shows?
3. What does "bagman's paradise" mean?

## Writing assignment

In his essay "Teaching the Forbidden," Robert Johnson expresses his concern that religious beliefs and attitudes interfere with students' performance in the classroom. William J. Bennett's concern is the opposite: that the *lack* of religious beliefs interferes with students' classroom performance. First take some time to work through their arguments and bring them together in a conversation. What might Johnson say to Bennett, and Bennett to Johnson? What might each say to the other in support of his own position? Then join the conversation yourself. You've been in classrooms for over twelve years now. What is your position in relation to these two essays. Offer *specific* examples from your experience and observation. If everyone at your college agreed with Bennett, how might your classes change? What kinds of changes might we have to make in the dorms and other places on campus?

## Reading 3: James W. Sire, "Chris Chrisman Goes to State"

> The world was supposed to be a place where you graduated from high school, went to college, learned which ropes to grab and pull and which to leave swinging, got introduced into a profession, found a modestly beautiful "girl" to marry a few months after college or after professional school, and then set forth to make your way as an adult. And if you were a Christian you kept the faith, let people know you believed in Christ, perhaps even led a person or two to the Lord.

## Prewriting

1. Respond to the above quotation from Sire's piece. Do these expectations seem reasonable to you? Do they seem to go together? Why, or why not?
2. What do you remember of the first time you learned there were different religions?
3. Do people speak openly about their religious beliefs on your campus? What are the responses from those around them?
4. What does Sire think of Chris's decision to "live and let live" rather than try to convert others? What do you think of it?

## Writing assignment

Many people assume college will be the time when students will test or maybe even lose their faith. Some students do find it difficult to maintain the same level of attention to their religious beliefs while in college. And some may be shocked to encounter people of other religions or of no religion. Did you experience any "culture shock" when you began college? Did anyone else you know experience "culture shock"? Why or why not? How have students responded to people from religions different from their own? What stories can you tell? What would Chris Chrisman see if he transferred to your school? Is it easier or harder to maintain religious practice in college than before college? Explain your answer.

## Reading 4: Christopher Shea, "Sexual Tension"

> "This is not an 'I'm okay, you're okay' university," says Margaret Devlin, a senior. "People across the board are respected, but people are also willing to say, 'You're wrong.'"

### Prewriting

1. Respond to the above quotation, and comment on whether you think the ongoing debate at the University of Dallas is a healthy one or a repressive one. Explain.
2. What is the university's responsibility toward its students in regard to their private lives?
3. How would you define "immoral" behavior in the context of the university and in terms of students' responsibility toward the university? How would you define "freedom" in this context?

### Writing assignment

Christopher Shea's article from *The Chronicle of Higher Education* reports on the University of Dallas's attempt to, in a sense, respond to William J. Bennett's call for action. In your essay, work through the arguments in both Bennett's essay and Shea's article. What is it that Bennett and the University of Dallas are trying to accomplish? Why are they doing it? Now clarify and develop your own position in relation to theirs. Would you like to see the university take a stand against "immoral" behavior? How should *immoral* be defined? Who should have the authority to determine it? Take particular care to develop your argument using what you've read in Chapter 4.

## Readings 5 and 6: Chana Schoenberger, "Getting to Know About You and Me," and David Denby, "Passion at Yale"

> People who are suspicious when they find out I'm Jewish usually don't know much about Judaism. I would much prefer them to hate or distrust me because of something I've done, instead of them hating me on the basis of prejudice. (Schoenberger)

If universities continue to humor every group's sensitivities, then what is to stop blacks from demanding protection from exposure to white students, gays from exposure to straights, fundamentalist Christians from exposure to Jews and Muslims? (Denby)

## Prewriting

1. Respond to the two quotations from Schoenberger's and Denby's articles. Both writers suggest that exposure to those of other faiths and beliefs promotes tolerance and respect. Do you agree? Why or why not?
2. What kinds of effects do people's religions have on their professional (or academic) lives?
3. Have you ever been in a situation in which your religious beliefs caused you to feel uncomfortable in your surroundings? Describe the situation.

## Writing assignment

Chana Schoenberger wants people to know that she's not so different from the people around her; the Yale Five, as described in David Denby's essay "Passion at Yale," on the other hand, are eager to set themselves apart. What are the different arguments being made in these two essays? How are they similar? Different? How do you respond to Denby's representation of the Yale Five and their demands? Is he being fair?

In some respects, the Yale Five are demanding what Christopher Shea reports that the University of Dallas is providing and what William J. Bennett is calling for. Both the University of Dallas and Yale are private universities. How are the situations different? How might Bennett respond? How do you respond?

## Reading 7: Karen Armstrong, "Introduction to *Muhammad: A Biography of the Prophet*"

Our dramatically shrunken world has revealed our inescapable connection with one another. We can no longer think of ourselves as separate from people in distant parts of the globe and leave them to their own fate. We have a responsibility to each other and face common dangers.

## Prewriting

1. Respond to the above quotation from Armstrong's piece. Do you agree with her that we have a responsibility to people around the globe of faiths other than our own? What exactly is our mutual responsibility, in your view?

2. How does the image of Muslims conveyed by the U.S. media compare with your personal experience with Muslims (if you have any such experience) or with your knowledge of them from other sources?
3. What, if anything, should colleges do to educate students about Islam or any other religion?

## *Writing assignment*

Write a brief essay focusing on one or more of the readings by Johnson, Bennett, Sire, and Schoenberger in relation to Armstrong's piece. How do you think the students whom Johnson describes would react to Armstrong's arguments? Would Bennett be pleased if American schools started to teach about Islamic law and culture? What if the Koran began outselling the Bible in American bookstores? How would Chris Chrisman react to having a Muslim roommate? Would Schoenberger disagree with anything Armstrong says? Be sure to include your own reaction to Armstrong's arguments, too. Has the West been unfair to Muslims? Should the United States be concerned about how to "regain the sympathy and respect that [the West] once enjoyed in the Muslim world?" Why or why not?

## Final Project

Review the essays you've written for this sequence. What are your feelings about faith and religion on campus now that you've done a lot of thinking and writing on the subject? Is it something you think about much? Are you satisfied with the spiritual and moral atmosphere on your campus? If not, how would you change it? Is unbending faith compatible with critical thinking and intellectual development? Why or why not? Have the readings in this sequence changed your mind about anything? Have they reinforced your views about anything? Mine your essays for a specific issue you'd like to investigate in further detail, and formulate a concise thesis that you can use in a research paper. If you can't decide on a topic to investigate further, consider these questions:

How much religious diversity is there on your campus?
Are people tolerant of other people's exhibitions of faith?
How important is religion to students on your campus?
Are on-campus students as likely to practice their religion as students who still live at home and commute?
Are older students more or less religious than younger students?
What is the religious climate at most U.S. colleges? Does anything need to be done to change this?

## Library Research Ideas

Try one or more of the following library research activities, or come up with your own ideas for library research to support your thesis.

1. Investigate what professors at various divinity schools have published in scholarly journals about one or more of the issues raised in this sequence (or about any other issue related to faith and religions that you'd like to pursue). Ask your reference librarian for help in finding appropriate indexes to search. Compare what has been published about your topic in scholarly journals with what has been published in general-interest books and periodicals.

2. Many books and journals have been published in the field of student services (also called student affairs), a profession devoted to helping students adjust to college life and prosper while at school. (For example, Jossey-Bass publishes a quarterly journal, *New Directions for Student Services,* devoted entirely to student services and published just for professionals in that field.) Research what has been written for student services professionals concerning the role of faith and religion on campuses and in students' lives. Has this topic been given adequate attention in the professional student services literature? Ask your reference librarian for advice on finding books and journals related to student services. You could also research how this issue has been addressed in the wider literature on higher education.

3. Compare scholarly and popular press coverage of issues related to ethnic or racial diversity with coverage of issues related to religious diversity. Is religious diversity given adequate attention in the scholarly and general-interest press? You could approach this in two different ways: you could investigate a broad range of publications covering many different topics, or you could select one or two very specialized publications that cover areas in which diversity is a concern (say, human resources or management journals) and compare how they address religious diversity.

## Field Research Ideas

Try one or more of the following field research ideas, or use your own field research ideas to get data to support your thesis.

1. Survey students about their religious practices. Ask how important a role religion plays in their day-to-day lives as college students. Ask whether their experience in college has changed their religious feelings or faith in any way. Ask whether they think the university does enough to ensure that their religious views are respected. Compare the responses of different target populations.

2. Interview student services professionals and administrators at your school about the efforts your school makes to accommodate and respect students' religious views and practices.

3. Survey a large number of professors about the effects, if any, that students' religious beliefs have on their learning. Compare the responses of professors in different disciplines. (Alternatively, if you want to get more detailed responses, you could interview a smaller group of professors about this question.)

4. Over a certain period of time, say a week or two, notice and record how many times you hear fellow students discuss religion. Do students at your school seem reluctant to discuss religion? Are they more open about their faith in some settings on campus than in others?

# Striking Balances: Work, Home, and Student Life

### READINGS

Michael C. Murphy and James Archer, Jr., "Stressors on the College Campus: A Comparison of 1985 and 1993"

Michael Moffatt, "Coming of Age in a College Dorm"

Anne Matthews, "The Night Campus"

Ellen Rosenberg, "Commuting"

Sandy Smith Madsen, "A Welfare Mother in Academe"

"Family Made Graduation More Difficult"

Arlie Russell Hochschild, "The Third Shift"

## Getting Started

The readings in this sequence consider and examine the many forms that "student life" can take. Michael C. Murphy and James Archer, Jr., in their article "Stressors on the College Campus," offer an overview of the many sources of stress in college students' lives. Michael Moffatt's "Coming of Age in a College Dorm" and Anne Matthews's "The Night Campus" focus on the lives of traditional college students. "Commuting," by Ellen Rosenberg, on the other hand, focuses on students who don't live on campus. Sandy Smith Madsen's "A Welfare Mother in Academe" and "Family Made Graduation More Difficult," a letter to the "Dear Abby" column, offer much grimmer pictures of how little support—emotional as well as financial—some students receive as they struggle to stay in and finish school. Finally, in "The Third Shift," Arlie Russell Hochschild reveals that the balancing act continues for many students even after they finish their formal education and become a part of the working world.

Before you do any of the reading, however, please reflect on your ideas about the stressors in your life and on how you and others around you balance the many demands made on you. What is "student life" like for you personally? Do you fit the traditional stereotype of a college student? That is, are you fresh out of high school, living on campus (and away from your parents for perhaps the first time), and enrolled full time in a general bachelor's degree program? Or are you an older or returning student who works full time, lives in your own home, and commutes to specialized, career-oriented classes? Think about the many demands on your time. Are they the same demands that college students have always faced, or are you grappling with new and unique challenges?

Next, respond to several of the following questions. I use the Getting Started questions as a preliminary exercise on the first day my class works on a particular sequence. Your teacher may also do this, or he or she may ask that you write out your responses either in a journal or in your notebook. Your teacher may use these questions as a jumping-off place for class discussion as well. No matter how you use these questions in your class, you'll still be able to draw on what you write here both in your contributions to class discussion and in your response to the assignments that follow.

1. What assumptions about college life did you hold before you started college? Which ones have proved to be accurate? Which have proved inaccurate?
2. Outside of class, what are the most valuable lessons to be learned from going to college?
3. How is college life usually represented in the media (that is, in movies, television, and newspapers)?
4. How often do our assumptions or media representations include returning students, working students, commuting students, or any others who don't seem to fit the usual idea of the "traditional" student? Now that you're in college, what do you think about these assumptions and representations?
5. Is college life different today from the way it was in the past?

## READING 1

*Michael C. Murphy and James Archer, Jr.*

# Stressors on the College Campus: A Comparison of 1985 and 1993

Michael C. Murphy is a psychologist, and James Archer, Jr. is a professor of counseling psychology, both at the University of Florida. Their study of stress in college students' lives appeared in the *Journal of College Student Development.* Although this essay is written in highly academic style, it still offers those of us who are not professional counselors a good sense of what students find most stressful in their lives. Do you see anything of your own experience in Murphy and Archer's study?

### *Before you read*

1. Do you find college life stressful? If so, what makes it stressful for you?
2. Do you think college students in general feel more stress in 1993 than they did in 1985? Explain your answer.
3. What can colleges and teachers do to help students deal with stress more effectively?

---

### Introduction

The serious and debilitating effects of excessive stress, initially identified some 20 years ago (Pelletier, 1977, 1979; Selye, 1974, 1978), are now widely recognized. College counselors, administrators, and student development educators have focused considerable attention on college student stress and on the general increase in severity of all kinds of psychological problems on our campuses (Stone & Archer, 1990).

O'Malley, Wheeler, Murphey, O'Connell, and Waldo (1990) and Robbins, May, and Corazzini (1985) found that university counseling centers were treating students with more severe problems and pathology than in years past. Data from a study by Koplik and DeVito (1986), who compared student pathology and problem severity over a 10 year period, supported the theory that there are increasingly serious problems for college students. Stone and Archer (1990), after conducting a thorough review of the literature, concluded that there is "evidence from many quarters that the level of psychopathology among college students . . . increased during the 1980's, and there is good reason to believe this increase will continue into the 1990's" (p. 544).

Researchers have attempted to identify stressors on college campuses that could potentially cause or exacerbate student problems. An identification of these stressors can provide information that allows campus counselors and administrators to work toward a less stressful campus environment. Archer and Lamnin (1985) studied the academic and personal stressors reported by students on a university campus. From an open-ended questionnaire format, they derived 13 academic and 15 personal stressor categories. They found the major academic stressors to be (in descending rank order) tests, grade competition, time demands, professors and classroom environment, and career and future success. The major personal stressors identified were (in descending rank order): intimate relationships, parental conflicts, finances, and interpersonal conflicts with friends.

Using the same stressors identified by Archer and Lamnin (1985), Roberts and White (1989) studied the academic and personal stressors of a group of "developmental" college students (i.e., students whose skills, knowledge, and academic abilities were lower than those of "typical" students). Using a Q-sort technique, they found the greatest academic stressors to be (in descending rank order) career and future goals, studying, tests and finals, and procrastination. The greatest personal stressors (in descending rank order) were living conditions, appearance, not enough free time, roommate conflicts, meeting others, parents, and intimacy.

Cahir and Morris (1991) developed an instrument to measure stress in graduate psychology students and identified five areas of stress for these students (in descending rank order): time constraints, feedback from faculty, financial constraints, trouble getting help from faculty, and limited emotional support from friends. They found that females reported more stress than males in all areas.

Blankenstein, Flett, and Koledin (1991), in developing the Brief College Hassles Scale identified seven highly rated "hassles." They were (in descending rank order) organization of time, academic deadlines, money for necessary expenses, financial security, family expectations, future job prospects, and college requirements.

Reporting on student and faculty perceptions of student concerns, Carney, Peterson, and Moberg (1990) found the most pressing concerns were in the areas of career planning, personal finances, and academic effectiveness. They noted that these findings were the same as the results of a previous study (Carney & Savitz, 1980) and argued that this duplicate finding lends credence to there being "core concerns" for university students that remain stable over time.

Finally, Gallagher, Golin, and Kelleher (1992) conducted a study of the personal, career, and learning skills needs of college students. They found the most significant needs to be (in descending rank order) overcoming procrastination, overcoming problems with public speaking, increasing self-confidence, increasing motivation, eliminating self-defeating behavior, becoming more assertive, overcoming fear of failure, controlling anxiety and nervousness, controlling weight, developing positive relationships with faculty, and coping with depression.

A number of researchers have identified the stressors faced by students on a university campus. Carney et al. (1990) even looked at the change in concerns over time, an aspect that is particularly important as shifting societal values, problems, and concerns, as well as shifting political/economic climates, influence the stressors college students experience. For example, did the hard economic times of the 1980s, which included decreasing financial aid to students, create more economic/financial stress for college students? Or, did shifting gender roles cause a change in how males and females experience stress? Likewise do the aforementioned reports of increasing psychopathology in college students signal a concomitant increase in stress among college students?

In the 1993 study, the current researchers attempted to address the change in stressors on university campuses over time by replicating the Archer and Lamnin (1985) study. By applying an established methodology at the same university 8 years later, the researchers addressed the issue of how stressors change over time on a university campus. Such information is important from a theoretical perspective (e.g., Do changing societal values influence the stressors on college campuses?) as well as from a programmatic perspective (e.g., How do programs offered by college counseling centers and other student affairs offices need to change over time?).

## Method

### Sample

The sample for the 1993 study consisted of 639 undergraduate students drawn from a undergraduate population of 24,086 at a large Southeastern university. The students in the sample were enrolled in undergraduate classes at the university in a number of different departments. The authors identified classes from freshman through senior levels across a broad spectrum of departments and requested and received permission from instructors to visit those classes and administer a survey. Undergraduate research assistants then went to the classes, introduced the survey using standardized instructions, and collected the questionnaires. The survey took about 10 minutes to complete. The distribution of the sample approximated the undergraduate population in age, residence, ethnic status, fraternity/sorority affiliation, academic classification, and major.

*Survey*

The 2-page survey consisted of seven demographic items and two open-ended questions. In the open-ended questions, students were asked to describe briefly two situations that they found to be the most stressful in two areas of their lives: (a) academic and (b) personal.

Using the categorization system developed by Archer and Lamnin (1985), two psychologists familiar with the 13 academic and 15 personal categories independently rated the stressful situations on the student surveys. They agreed on 90% of the items and, after discussion, they mutually selected a category for each remaining item.

Because the original survey involved open-ended questions that were then categorized by expert raters, the validity of the survey is based on the assumption that student responses were honest and that raters were able to develop accurate categories from the responses and to classify the responses appropriately. The survey was done anonymously; therefore, students had more reason to be honest. The researchers who originally developed the categories reported a 93% agreement on the academic stressor ratings and a 95% agreement on the personal stress ratings (Archer & Lamnin, 1985), data that support the accuracy of the categories and reliability of the categorizations.

*Analysis*

The frequency and percentage of combined stressor responses (first and second choice) were calculated for each academic and personal stressor. The researchers used a chi-square test of proportions to determine differences in stressors reported between various groups; comparisons included analyses of sex, age, race, class, major, Greek affiliation, and residence. They also used a chi-square test to look at the differences between the 1985 and 1993 survey results.

*Results*

"Academic" and "personal" stressors reported by students in the 1985 and 1993 studies are shown in Tables 1 and 2, respectively. The significance level of changes in reported stressors between 1985 and 1993 is also reported in these tables.

The major *academic* stressors for the 1993 sample were tests and finals, grades and competition, professors and class environment, papers and essay exams, too many demands/not enough

TABLE 1
**Academic Stressors Listed as First or Second Response 1985 & 1993**

| Stressor | % Reporting as 1st or 2nd 1985 | % Reporting as 1st or 2nd 1993 | Chi-square Significance[a] |
|---|---|---|---|
| Tests and Finals | 52 | 37 | $p < .001$ |
| Grades and Competition | 28 | 32 | $p < .02$ |
| Too Many Demands | 21 | 16 | N.S. |
| Professors and Class Environment | 18 | 24 | $p < .01$ |
| Career and Future Success | 15 | 14 | N.S. |
| Procrastination | 9 | 6 | N.S. |
| Studying | 8 | 14 | $p < .01$ |
| Finances | 7 | 3 | $p < .01$ |
| Papers/Essay Exams | 6 | 16 | $p < .001$ |
| Registration | 6 | 7 | N.S. |
| Speaking in Class | 3 | 1 | $p < .01$ |
| Size of Class | 2 | 1 | N.S. |
| Other | 13 | 18 | $p < .02$ |

[a] Significance levels reported are from chi-square comparisons. Because of the large number of chi-square comparisons, some of the differences reported may be a result of chance.

time/deadlines, career and future success, and studying. Major *personal* stressors in 1993 included intimate relationships, finances, parental conflicts and expectations, and roommate conflicts.

A number of differences existed between the 1985 and 1993 studies. In 1993, students less frequently reported academic stress related to tests and finals, finances, and speaking in class; however, they more frequently cited stress related to grades and competition, professors and class environment, studying, and papers/essays exams (see Table 1).

Students in the 1993 study reported personal stress in the areas of finances and current jobs more often while reporting stress in relation to parental conflicts and expectations, interpersonal conflicts, judgment and acceptance by peers, personal achievement and goal setting, approaching and meeting other students, general adjustment to unexpected change, and personal appearance less frequently (see Table 2).

Several significant findings emerged regarding differences in how frequently female and male students listed stressors in 1985 and in 1993 (see Table 3). In both studies, female students more frequently listed roommate conflicts and personal appearance as more stressful. However, in 1993, females listed too many demands/not enough time/deadlines as a stressor more frequently than did males, a change from 1985 when females' and males' responses showed no difference. Also, in 1985, males listed approaching and meeting other students and peer judgment and acceptance more often than did females.

TABLE 2
**Personal Stressors Listed as First or Second Response, 1985 & 1993**

| Stressor | % Reporting as 1st or 2nd 1985 | % Reporting as 1st or 2nd 1993 | Chi-square Significance Levels[a] |
|---|---|---|---|
| Intimate Relationships | 37 | 35 | N.S. |
| Parental Conflicts and Expectations | 29 | 14 | $p < .01$ |
| Finances | 27 | 31 | $p < .01$ |
| Interpersonal Conflicts | 13 | 5 | $p < .01$ |
| Judgment and Acceptance by Peers | 11 | 2 | $p < .01$ |
| Personal Achievement/ Goal Setting | 11 | 7 | $p < .05$ |
| Roommate Conflicts | 11 | 10 | N.S. |
| Approaching and Meeting Other Students | 9 | 6 | $p < .02$ |
| Future and Career Plans | 9 | 8 | N.S. |
| Not Enough Free Time | 9 | 6 | N.S. |
| General Adjustments to Change | 5 | 3 | $p < .01$ |
| Personal Appearance | 4 | 2 | $p < .05$ |
| Living Conditions | 3 | 3 | N.S. |
| Current Job | 2 | 5 | $p < .05$ |
| Other | 14 | 33 | $p < .01$ |

[a] Significance levels reported are from chi-square comparisons. Because of the large number of chi-square comparisons, some of the differences reported may be a result of chance.

In relation to age, a comparison of 1985 and 1993 data yielded a number of differences. In 1985 and in 1993, finances were reported more frequently as a concern for older students. However, stress related to concerns about career/future plans was reported more frequently for older students in 1993, a difference that was nonexistent in 1985. In 1993, papers/essay exams were more frequently reported as stressful for 18-year-olds than for other age groups; no significant differences by age group in this category were reported in 1985.

Judgment and acceptance by peers was more frequently reported as stressful for 18-year-olds than for other age groups in both 1985 and 1993; but in 1993, 20-year-olds also reported this category more frequently than did other age groups. Meeting people was listed more often by 17-, 18-, and 20-year-olds in 1993; in 1985, no differences between age groups had existed. Finally, in 1985, 18- and 19-year-olds more frequently than other age groups reported stress in relation to competition, studying, and peer pressure; whereas in 1993, none of these differences were found.

In terms of significant differences by residence, several interesting results emerged. In 1985, students living in fraternities and sororities

TABLE 3
**Summary of Differences Between 1985 and 1993 Stressors**

| | | 1985 | 1993 |
|---|---|---|---|
| Category | Stressor | Differences | |
| Sex | Roommate Conflict | Women > | Women > |
| | Personal Appearance | Women > | Women > |
| | Peer Judgment/Acceptance | Men > | N.D. |
| | Approaching and Meeting Other Students | Men > | N.D. |
| | Too Many Demands on Time | N.D. | Women > |
| Age | Finances | Older > | Older > |
| | Papers/Essay Exams | N.D. | 18 >[a] |
| | Career | N.D. | Older > |
| | Approaching and Meeting Other Students | N.D. | 17, 18, 19 > |
| | Judgment and Acceptance by Peers | 18 > | 18, 20 > |
| | Competition | 18, 19 > | N.D. |
| | Studying | 18, 19 > | N.D. |
| Residence | Living conditions | Greek > | N.D. |
| | Career | N.D. | Dorm < |
| | Finances | N.D. | Dorm < |
| | Papers/Essays Exams | N.D. | Dorm > |
| | Studying | Dorm > | N.D. |
| | Current Job | N.D. | Off Campus |
| Race/Ethnic | Finances | Black > | N.D. |
| | | White < | N.D. |
| | Intimate Relationships | White > | N.D. |

*Note:* Differences reported are from chi-square comparisons with $p < .05$. Because of the large number of chi-square comparisons, some of the differences reported may be a result of chance. Differences between 1985 and 1993 are designated by: > (*more stress*), < (*less stress*), and N.D. (*no difference*).

[a] Specific numbers represent years.

more frequently reported stress from living conditions than did other residence groups; this difference did not appear in 1993. Regarding finances, in 1993, students living off campus and in fraternities and sororities more frequently reported stress than those living in residence halls; whereas this difference did not exist in 1985. Likewise, in 1993, students living in fraternities and sororities and off campus more frequently reported stress than other residence groups in relation to career/future plans, a difference that did not show up in the 1985 study. In relation to papers/essay exams, in 1993, students living in residence halls more frequently reported stress than did students in other residence groups. This difference did not show up in 1985. On the contrary, in 1985, studying was reported as stressful more frequently for students in residence halls than for other groups; but in 1993, this difference disappeared. Stress related to current job was more frequently reported by off-campus students in 1993, whereas in 1985, this difference did not appear.

Finally, although no significant differences by race or ethnicity were reported in the 1993 study, two differences emerged when the 1985 and 1993 studies were compared. In 1985, White students less frequently reported financial stress than did students from other racial and ethnic groups, and Black students more frequently reported financial stress than the other groups. In 1993, neither of these differences appeared. Also, in 1985, Whites more frequently reported stress from intimate relationships than other groups; but in 1993, this difference disappeared.

## Discussion

The stressors that students reported in this study are certainly familiar to college faculty, counselors, or student affairs practitioners. The general pattern of stressors for the 1993 study was quite similar to that in the 1985 study. Students identified tests/finals, grades/competition, professors/class environment, and time demands as the top academic stressors; and they saw intimate relationships, finances, and parental conflicts as the top personal stressors. Because the structure of the higher education enterprise at the institution studied had not changed significantly during this time period, students reasonably would have encountered similar stressors.

The differences between some stressors in the two studies may be related to various changes that have occurred in the college and university environment. For example, a decrease in higher education resources led to larger classes and higher faculty loads. The higher selection of professors/class environment, studying, papers/essay exams, and grades/competition stressors in 1993 could be related to this resource problem.

The career and future success category under academic stressors did not change from 1985 to 1993. With the deterioration of the job market during these years, students might have been expected to worry more about future careers. Possibly these worries were projected onto more immediate concerns such as grades/competition that have a direct bearing for students on their ultimate career options.

The increase in frequency of papers/essay exams as a stressor from 1985 to 1993 raises an interesting question about writing preparation and experience. As class sizes and teaching loads have increased, student writing assignments have probably decreased. Because students do less writing, they may be becoming more afraid and less able to express themselves in writing.

In the personal stressor categories, students selected several categories less frequently in the 1993 study. They reported stress regarding parental conflicts and expectations, interpersonal conflicts, and judgment and acceptance by peers less often in 1993. The lower ratings on parental conflict and judgment and acceptance may be related to major new university programs on diversity and a brochure for parents focusing on how parents can deal with student stress.

The pattern of academic and personal stressors was more varied in the 1993 study. The "other" category was greater in both the academic and personal stressor categories. In the academic stressor category, there were 18% "other" stressors in 1993 and 13% in 1985, which could mean that a number of new stressors had evolved or that students labeled these stressors somewhat differently. An examination of the increased "other" category in the 1993 study revealed that stressors related to living arrangements, course decisions, not finishing/passing classes, lack of focus/motivation, and getting to class on time were selected most frequently. These categories do not appear to be new or unusual and, in fact, are closely related to general academic stressors.

The "other" category in the personal stressor part of the studies was considerably greater in 1993—33% compared to 14% in 1985. The categories in the 1993 "other" category seem to indicate some interesting emerging stressors. The top "other" category stressors and the number of students who endorsed them are listed in Table 4. These responses would not fit easily into any of the categories that were developed in the 1985 study and used in the 1993 study.

The emerging categories related to sleep and health problems could be a manifestation of a general increasing level of stress and psychopathology. Stone and Archer (1990) cited several studies and surveys demonstrating the increasingly complex and difficult problems experienced by college students.

Although this study was conducted on a single campus, the authors believe that it is reasonable to generalize the results to other large public university populations. A number of implications from these studies should be helpful for counselors and student affairs professionals.

TABLE 4
**Responses Included in the 1993 "Other" Personal Stressors Category**

| Subcategory | No. of Students Endorsing | % of Students Endorsing |
| --- | --- | --- |
| Not Getting Enough Sleep | 50 | 8 |
| Finding Time to Get Everything Done | 17 | 3 |
| Family Member Injured/Ill | 16 | 3 |
| Health Problems | 15 | 2 |
| Pledging | 14 | 2 |

First, students clearly continue to be highly stressed by exams, competition for grades, and too many demands on their time—the core academic stressors for students. Counselors and student affairs workers sometimes find other "hotter" or more interesting areas for outreach and preventive programs, but it is important to keep a strong focus on the "basics" of academic stress.

Second, although the current evidence is sketchy, the authors believe that the general decrease in funding for public higher education and the press to do "more with less" may increase student academic stress considerably. As class sizes increase and faculty is reduced more and more students may experience increasing stress from this educational format and all it entails. Students may have to rely more than ever on each other as teachers and learning facilitators, and counselors and student affairs professionals can take a leadership role in helping develop structures for this to occur.

Third, the authors see the increased competition for professional employment that has occurred over the last several years as the source of increasing stress related to career choice and development and to academic pressure. Making career choices and planning for the future have always been part of a complicated process, but in the future, counselors and student affairs professionals will have to provide even more sensitive and comprehensive services in this area.

Just as there are core or basic academic stress areas, there appear to be core personal stress areas as well. The authors see relationships of all kinds, parental conflicts and expectations, and the financing of a college education as these core issues.

Of these personal stress areas, financial concerns are perhaps the least effectively dealt with on campus. Although financial aid offices administer multifaceted and complex financial aid programs, few ways exist to help students deal with the stress of never having enough money. Perhaps counselors and student affairs professionals should more frequently team up with financial aid officers to attend to the psychological aspects of financing college and the related negotiations with parents.

The authors believe that the trend toward more health-related stress problems indicated in the 1993 "other" personal stressor category increase is real. Today's world, the U.S. economy, and the problems and experiences that students bring with them are not getting any less complex. Educators have an opportunity to teach students how to manage the many stressors with which they must deal. Educators also have a mandate to confront and change aspects of the campus environment that create stress.

An interesting theoretical/practical question emerges from these challenges. How much effort should be directed at helping students "manage" their stress and learn to cope with issues like time management, intimacy, and parental conflicts that are in many respects life-long developmental stressors? Should educators concentrate on this preventive and educational approach, as opposed to a more active and perhaps political effort to modify the campus environment to make it less stressful and more user-friendly? For example, should a counseling center or a student affairs multidisciplinary unit put major effort into making a campus more equitable for women and minorities by lobbying for change in campus institutions (e.g., fraternities), or would this time be spent more effectively in teaching women and minorities how to cope with sexism and racism?

Of course, these are not either/or propositions, and both the theoretical and practical approaches can be undertaken to some extent. The question of scarce resources, however, is an important consideration in designing programs to deal with campus stress. The authors believe that this environmental change versus teaching coping skills question deserves further study with regard to college and university stress management programs. Or perhaps some kind of cost-benefit index methodology would be helpful. Perhaps just making these choices more explicit and evaluating costs and benefits would help educators provide the best possible campus stress management programs.

## References

Archer, J., & Lamnin, A. (1985). An investigation of personal and academic stressors on college campuses. *Journal of College Student Personnel, 26,* 210–215.

Blankenstein, K. R., Flett, F. L., & Koledin, S. (1991). The Brief College Hassles Scale: Development, validation and relation with pessimism. *Journal of College Student Development, 32,* 258–264.

Cahir, N., & Morris, R. D. (1991). The Psychology Student Stress Questionnaire. *Journal of Clinical Psychology, 47,* 414–417.

Carney, C., Peterson, K., & Moberg, T. (1990). How stable are student and faculty perceptions of student concerns and of a university counseling center? *Journal of College Student Development, 31,* 423–428.

Carney, C., & Savitz, C. (1980). Student and faculty perceptions of student needs and the services of a university counseling center: Differences that make a difference. *Journal of Counseling Psychology, 27,* 597–604.

Gallagher, R. P., Golin, A., & Kelleher, K. (1992). The personal, career and learning skills needs of college students. *Journal of College Student Development, 33,* 301–309.

Koplik, E. K., & De Vito, A. J. (1986). Problems of freshmen: Comparison of classes of 1976 and 1986. *Journal of College Student Development, 27,* 124–130.

O'Malley, K., Wheeler, I., Murphey, J., O'Connell, J., & Waldo M. (1990). Changes in levels of psychopathology being treated at college and university counseling centers. *Journal of College Student Development, 31,* 464–465.

Pelletier, K. R. (1997) *Mind as healer, mind as slayer.* New York: Dell.

Pelletier, K. R. (Ed.). (1979). *Holistic medicine: From stress to optimum health.* New York: Delacorte.

Robbins, S., May, T., & Corazzini, J. (1985). Perceptions of client needs and counseling center staff roles and functions. *Journal of Counseling Psychology, 32,* 641–644.

Roberts, G. H., & White, W. G., Jr. (1989). Health and stress in developmental college students. *Journal of College Student Development, 30,* 515–521.

Selye, H. (1974). *Stress without distress.* New York: Signet.

Selye, H. (1978). *The stress of life* (2nd ed.). New York: McGraw-Hill.

Stone, G. L., & Archer, J. A., Jr. (1990). College and university counseling centers in the 1990's: Challenges and limits. *Counseling Psychologist, 18,* 539–607.

---

## *Now that you've read*

1. Have you recently seen anyone at school not handle stress well? Describe what happened.
2. What do Murphy and Archer identify as the most common causes of stress?
3. Why might female students feel more stress than male students?

# READING 2

## Michael Moffatt

# Coming of Age in a College Dorm

Michael Moffatt is an cultural anthropology professor at Rutgers University who decided to study the "natives" who lived in some of the dormitories on his campus. He spent two years in the dorms with them, observing, asking questions, and listening to their answers. The result was his book *Coming of Age in New Jersey* (1989) from which this reading is taken. As you read Moffatt's piece, consider what an anthropologist could learn about students on your campus from living among them as Moffatt did.

### *Before you read*

1. Do you live in a dorm? If so, why? If not, why not?
2. What stories had you heard about dorm life before you came to college? Were they accurate?
3. What's the best thing about living in a dorm? What's the worst?
4. What can dorm life offer that commuting or living at home cannot?

---

Most of the freshmen on Hasbrouck Fourth, interviewed privately in the first weeks of the semester, said they were impressed and relieved by the general friendliness of the other students on the floor, especially of the knowledgeable upperclassmen. They were grateful for the chance to establish personal relationships so quickly in college, particularly given the size, impersonality, and confusion of most of Rutgers outside the dorms. A few of them also said, however, that the ambience of the dorms was more juvenile than they had expected in college, and a few others were surprised at how little studying some of their upperclass exemplars appeared to do. Half a dozen freshmen said they were particularly surprised at the amount of drinking that went on.

The sophomores and some of the other upperclassmen also set examples for the sensible use of daily and weekly time for the freshmen. Avoid classes before eleven or so in the morning. Look for floor friends for lunches and dinners; nap in the afternoon if a morning schedule was absolutely necessary; spend some friendly time in the lounge every day, especially before an early dinner (around four in the afternoon) and after an evening of studying. To bed at one or two in the morning after quieter talks with closer friends, or perhaps after a little "David Letterman" or some other late-night TV comic. Avoid Friday classes. Thursday nights were the big party nights; then home or somewhere else for the long weekend, and back to campus Sunday afternoon, perhaps warming up for the next week with the first real studying of the weekend. . . .

You were not a bad person if you did not hang out on the floor; you were just a nonperson. A much worse thing to be was a person who was around a lot but not friend*ly*. Then you were in trouble. Then you were a snob. If you didn't watch it, you might open your door one day to find some local vigilantes "mooning" you in disapproval, or someone might fill a large garbage can with water, balance it against your door, knock, and disappear.

Accordingly, most of the remaining forty-six residents of Hasbrouck Fourth spent varying amounts of time together in the fall of 1984 in the lounges, in private rooms, at Commons, going out visiting or partying with one another at night, going to classes together when they happened to have them in common, and so on. This was friendly time. You necessarily spent some of it with floor acquaintances you were not especially crazy about as individuals, but you tried to spend more of it with your "real" friends on the floor.

In the lounges, the sophomores also soon taught the freshmen to talk the dominant mode of discourse in the undergraduate peer group. It might be labeled "Undergraduate Cynical." In different forms, it is probably a very old speech genre in American college culture. It can be seen as the polar opposite of Deanly Officialese, or of Faculty Lofty. Its attitudinal stance is "wise to the ways of the world." In it, moral, ethical, and intellectual positions are rapidly reduced to the earthiest possible motives of those who articulate them; in it, everyone who participates or is referred to is treated in the same way—leveled—made equal by the joke-and-insult-impregnated discourse of contemporary American friendly busting.

As the students spoke Undergraduate Cynical in the dorms, friends and acquaintances and one's own self were mocked at firsthand, and other people and other kinds of pretension were made fun of at a distance. The students might complain to one another about the rigors of higher education:

> I really hate the teaching in my poly sci classes. They give you a lot of reading and lectures and then tell you to figure things out for yourself. There's a thousand questions the professor can ask. "Relate this to that." . . . I wish they'd have textbooks that just told you everything you need to know. Enough of this enlightened bullshit!—Freshman male, Erewhon Third, 1978.

Or they might discuss among themselves various ways of beating the system, as did two upperclassmen on Hasbrouck Fourth in the spring of 1985.

> *Al:* Hey, John, how was the exam? Was it a cake exam?
> *John:* Yeah. The prof said up to five answers were correct for every question.
> *Al:* Good, good. That means you can definitely argue points with him.

At first I mistook Undergraduate Cynical for a privileged form of truth, for what the undergraduates really thought among themselves when all their defenses were down. Eventually I realized that, as a code of spoken discourse, Undergraduate Cynical could be just as mandatory and just as coercive as other forms of discourse. You could say some very important things in it, things that you really were not allowed to say elsewhere. It was definitely fun to talk it once you learned its rules, and I certainly enjoyed my regular bouts of it throughout my research. But you could not necessarily say everything that you really thought in it, any more than a dean speaking in public could easily stop emphasizing consensus and community among all those who "worked together" at Rutgers and suddenly start ventilating her or his personal animosities toward a particular administrative rival.

Imagine, for instance, that you were an undergraduate who had been reading a sonnet by the poet Shelley for a classroom assignment, and that it had really swept you away. Unless you enjoyed being a figure of fun, you would not have dared to articulate your feelings for the poem with any honesty in the average peer-group talk in the average dorm lounge. You might, on the other hand, have discussed such sentiments more privately with trusted friends. Ordinarily, the dorm lounge and its near-mandatory code did not allow you to say what the "real you" believed, either intellectually or in other ways. The dorm lounge was more often an arena for peer-group posing in which, acting friend*ly,* you presented the "as if" you.

There were many nuances, subtleties, and variations in the modes of lounge talk, however. In unpredictable ways, peer-group talk could shift from purely cynical into more sincere, earnest expressions of meanings and feelings, even when it was not between close friends. In mid-September, while I was still getting to know the residents of Hasbrouck Fourth and while they were still sorting each other out, I touched off one of these talk sessions. In it, the student voices moved back and forth through a number of stances. Sometimes they were bullshitting. Sometimes they were simply being playful. Sometimes they were talking from the heart, evidently trying to present the "real me." Often they were trying to seize conversational control. And almost always, they were performing.

Louie had been hustling as usual, in an ironic mode he often used, simultaneously making fun of himself for hustling as he hustled: "Here I am, Mike, an unknown college sophomore, lost in the dorms at Rutgers. You're my big chance. You can make me famous. When are you gonna interview me? You *gotta* interview me!" So I decided to give him an interview I had been developing privately to elicit some simple cultural meanings. Except, as an experiment, I decided to give it to Louie around his peers rather than in private. We sat down with a tape recorder in a corner of the high-side lounge at about seven o'clock one evening early in the semester. Fifteen feet away, Carrie was quietly reading a book and apparently minding her own business; two freshmen girls sat near her.

I led off with my standard opening question in this interview. I was a man from Mars, I told Louis, I understood about colleges educationally. Earthlings did not have preprogrammed knowledge like we did on Mars. But I did not understand about college "dorms" on Earth. Why did young Earthlings leave big comfortable homes a few miles away, where all their needs were provided for by their parents, and come to live in these crowded, noisy confines, packed together like sardines?

> *Louie:* Well, part of college is to grow, and not only to grow intellectually but to grow independently wise. . . . When you come to college, it's not exactly the real world but it's one step toward it, it's kinda like a plateau. You become more independent. You have to do your own laundry. . . . And you feel a togetherness because there's sixty of you on the floor and all stuck in the same boat. . . .

Louie went on in this vein for five minutes, answering a few of my Martian's follow-up questions. Then, possibly aware that Carrie and the freshmen women were listening in, he paused and soliloquized: "How I bullshit! You want some real answers now? I don't know why anyone's here. They're all just getting ripped off?"

This gave Carrie her opening. "Do you really believe all that stuff you just said, Louie?" she asked. Louie moved over closer to Carrie, and I followed him, carrying my tape recorder in a visible position, Louie said that he really did not know what he believed, so Carrie offered her answer to the Martian's question:

> College is a place where suburban brats come, to hang out for four years. . . . I think it's a step *away* from the real world. . . . I don't think a lot of people here *want* an education, whether from college itself or from interacting with other people. . . . And when they get out of here, they're just going into Mom and Dad's business, or Mom and Dad is going to pay for their apartment for three years until they get a real job. . . . Which is really fucked up.

Louie recognized the critique, but he did not consider himself a spoiled college kid. He answered Carrie by telling her that his father was divorced from his mother and was not putting him through Rutgers; he had to work hard at several jobs to stay in school. He talked about how hard he worked and how much money he made. A lot of other Rutgers undergraduates were serious, hardworking youths like him, he concluded. Carrie agreed that she was, but she was not sure about many others; and whatever the state of Louie's finances, she still thought his opinions were screwy: "I don't know, I see a lot of bullshit and a lot of bullshit people here. . . . And a lot of that stuff you were saying, I thought that was pretty *zorbo*. I said to myself, Louie man, if that's the way you think, I don't know. . . ."

Louie challenged her to tell him what in the world was *not* bullshit? She made a case for the caring self, for "how you feel about yourself and how you feel about those closest to you. That's all that really matters." "*I'm* proud of myself," Louie replied, "so that's not bullshit, right? According to your definition?" Carrie agreed that it was good that Louie was proud of himself, but she thought Louie's pride was misplaced, since it was really just rooted in his ability to make money. And that, she said, still struck her as "zorbo bullshit."

At this point, one of the freshman listeners cut in. "What exactly is 'zorbo'?" she asked deferentially. "I've never heard the phrase." "Bullshit," Louie explained in a dismissive tone. "Nothing," Carrie added. Later I discovered that Louie had never heard the word either and was bluffing. Carrie had coined it the year before in an old clique on a different dorm floor. It was her synonym for "nerd." A real loser, she had decided for some private reason, a hopeless case, should have the name "Zorbo McBladeoff." Anything that such a character did was a "zorbo" thing to do. She was not able to sell the word to Hasbrouck Fourth in 1984, however; despite Louie's implication that it was a perfectly ordinary term in the talk of knowledgeable upperclassmen at Rutgers, I never heard it again.

Carrie and Louie went back to their argument. Carrie thought that the most important things in life had nothing to do with money. Finding something you really wanted to do was more important. So was helping and influencing others. "If you can do that for a friend, and one friend starts to think the way you do, that's two of you now, and if two of you can go out. . . . I want to be able to change the way America is. I'm serious! This place is so fucked up."

Louie replied that helping others did you no good at all: "Like, if you believe in something, and every time you try to do it, nine times out of ten it gets pushed back in your face. . . . Where does that get you? That and fifty cents and you can buy a cup of coffee." Right now, Louie decided, what *he* believed in was "*nothin'*." And he got bored easily, he said, so he liked to try lots of different jobs and he liked to date lots of different girls. In deference to Carrie, Louie did not refer to his erotic prey with his normal label for them, "chicks."

While Carrie and Louie were in the middle of this colloquy, Jay walked in and sat down. He had been working on a paper for an English course; "Does anyone here understand Isaac Babel?" he asked the group at large. "No," Carrie answered abruptly, and went back to her argument. Jay did not like being ignored; he listened for a minute and then tried to change the mood of the session: "Oh, I get it, we're being *cos*mic!" Carrie told him to shut up, so he began busting on her directly. She had been talking about personal satisfaction through an artistic vocation. "Carrie wants to be a really incredible actress," Jay declared to the group, now augmented by three more passing residents, "perhaps on the order of Bo Derek or Ursula Andress." Carrie did not look much like either of these two ridiculous Nordic icons. That ploy did not succeed either, however, and a few minutes later Jay walked away.

Carrie and Louie went on arguing, and after another ten minutes, an upperclassman strode confidently into the lounge from the elevators. He was a skinny, self-assured young man wearing a worn black sports jacket; I had never seem him before on the floor, and I never saw him again. Carrie stopped talking and gave him a big hello, without introducing him to anyone else, and they alluded briefly to unexplained old intimacies:

> *Carrie:* Heeey! It's you! It's the crazy man! What's up?
> *Stranger:* So good to see you alive, kid.
> *Carrie:* I know. I got through it.

Then Carrie went back to the meaning of life with Louie. The stranger listened for a few minutes, apparently felt he had caught the drift, and then stood up and actually danced around the lounge intoning the following paean to the self. He had a certain hypnotic charm, reinforced by the reiterative phrases he used, and a man-of-the-world authority reinforced by the density of his easy vulgarisms:

> If you want to go out and be a success, you're gonna have to go to school and do well, you're gonna go to college, and you're gonna find out you can live on your own [Louie: "You're 150 percent right!"] And you're gonna find out it's you! You know that song [croons]: "It is yoooou, Oh yeah, Oh yeah"? [Back to normal voice] I can tell a person what's gone right for me, how I've gotten where I've gotten, how I've fucked up.
>
> And that's all I can do. It's them, you know, it's got to come from them. . . . If they want to benefit, that's great. If they want to say, "You're an asshole," that's fine too. It hurts me to see them fuck up, but that's the way it's gonna be. And I don't get upset and say [tone of fake emotion], "You're fuckin' up, you're fuckin' up." I walk up calmly and say [calm tone], "You're fuckin' up." You know, "You could do it this way or you could do it that way." And it's gonna come from you. Nobody's gonna hand you anything.

That's the way I feel. You know, it's different for everyone, but that's the way I feel.

I was not sure what this tone poem had to do with the substance of Carrie and Louie's debate. But the stranger had captured everybody's attention, including my own. Everyone sat in rapt silence as he ended his spiel. Then, apparently deliberately, he punctured the mildly reverent mood he himself had created: "Yeah, and there's another thing. I don't like to *dog* anyone. I present myself, not *de*grade somebody else. And you know, it's rush week, everybody. And this is a lot of what my fraternity's all about. . . ." The audience guffawed. The stranger laughed happily and made a quick exit. He had achieved what Jay had failed to do. He had popped the "cosmic" bubble. This little talk session was over, and the participants wandered off to other interests of the evening.

---

## Now that you've read

1. What do you consider the most important observations Michael Moffatt makes about dormitory living?
2. Is there anything Moffatt observes that does not hold true in your experience? If so, what?
3. How would you respond to Moffatt's "Martian on Earth" question?

## READING 3

*Anne Matthews*

# The Night Campus

Anne Matthews, a college teacher herself, writes about the tensions between what we want college to be ("the best years of our lives") and what it can turn out to be. This selection comes from her book *Bright College Years: Inside the American Campus Today.* Her research took her from some of the richest to the poorest, and the largest to the smallest colleges to get a sense of what "college life" was like in the 1990s. In this excerpt from one chapter, Matthews focuses on the safety of college campuses at night. She gives us some scary things to think about. As you read, think about how safe your own campus is at night.

### *Before you read*

1. How safe do you feel on your campus at night?
2. What precautions do you take when you go out at night?
3. Have you ever been in a situation on campus where someone threatened someone else or otherwise acted inappropriately? What happened?
4. How common or uncommon is this kind of activity on your campus?

---

The ripple effects of the night campus are hardest on those who expected college to be challenging and serious. About 70 percent of students do just fine in higher education; the other 30 percent are a major pain. It is hard to tell, on college applications, who will fall in which category. Many students, of course, drink socially, or choose not to drink at all, or have neither the time nor the money to pursue the party scene: instead, they run investment funds, design solar-powered cars, play soccer, start bands, plunge into union organizing. According to the Harvard study, undergraduates involved in community service or the arts or studying are less likely to be bingers.

The culture of academe—self-centered, trusting, impractical—often assumes a finer, safer, freer world. "I get to do whatever I want, but you have to protect me." Most campus crime is impulsive. Assaults, holdups, and stabbings all tend to occur after concerts or dances or big parties. Like undergraduate drinking, undergraduate violence has an extensive pedigree. From Oxbridge hearties pummeling aesthetes to secret-society hazing, the Anglo-American educational strain has long looked the other way after dark. Young subalterns *will* wreck the mess, all very traditional.

Not all campus crime is drunken impulse. White-supremacist incidents, cool and deliberate, are rising, too. Sometimes student-age townies are responsible, sometimes enrolled students, but the aggressors are nearly always white and male. A Siegel colleague cites a recent Berkeley study suggesting that hate crimes shoot up wherever right-wing foundation money subsidizes conservative student groups and publications. Gay or minority students are favorite targets—flyers shoved under a door, yells in the night, spray paint on a car, beatings behind the gym. Weapons offenses on campus are rising, too. A 1995 survey of seventy-three institutions revealed that 7.5 percent of college students had carried guns, knives, or other weapons to school in the last thirty days. Some armed undergraduates are gang members (an increasing worry for campus security staff) and some students who do not wish to become a statistic while walking to the college library parking lot after dark.

College has always been a place of enthusiasm and excess, of identities tried on and discarded: the Pagan Student Union, the Young Republicans, and Alternative Sexualities Task Force, the Ultimate Frisbee team, the drinking crowd. When trouble hits the night campus, the most likely suspect is the white male, freshman or sophomore, who is both athlete and fraternity member. Only 3.3 percent of the college population, athletes commit 19 percent of campus assaults on women. The strongest predictor for binge drinking is membership in a fraternity or sorority: a startling 80 percent of sorority-house dwellers and 86 percent of those who live in frat houses are bingers. Like the tobacco industry, liquor and brewing companies talk responsible use but advertise hard for the student dollar. (Typical ads from ASU campus publications: "Miller Genuine Draft Ski Utah! Round trip video bus . . . of course all the beer you can drink all weekend long!" "Lake Tahoe All-Greek Blowout . . . Booze Cruise!") Greek life is healthier than ever at U.S. colleges and universities. Of the 3 million full-time male undergraduates, 400,000 are frat members. Though their violences often spill onto the larger campus, such societies are private entities. Not all are animal houses; the gay Greeks are often better-behaved. Delta Lambda Phi now has thirty chapters nationwide, and an official toasting song: "There once was a mighty Lambda man/ Who lived by the sword/Crushed the rogue horde/With a whirl of steel he took the fight/And won the prince's heart that night."

At conference after conference, deans and student-life staffers offer theories and anecdotes on the night campus, shards of a social puzzle. For many the problem is not abstract; they badly want to know why sons and daughters, nephews or nieces were beaten or raped during undergraduate years. Some believe America's problems have come to campus because admissions are no longer selective. Others say campus residents should stop treating their schools like small towns, circa 1935, where no one ever locks a door. Security officers see the results of that attitude daily: full professors who leave keys in ignitions; students who keep homeless people in their dorm rooms like pets, feeding them smuggled peanut-butter sandwiches; alumni who steal computers or office equipment because, years later, their building keys still work.

A great many administrators (and faculty) argue that today's college students are damaged goods. They arrive dragging complicated lives. They did kidnap drill in kindergarten, learned to drink in middle school, thwarted their parents' home drug tests by eating poppyseed bagels or drinking goldenroot tea. Some arrive at college with a "been there, done that" view of campus excess, having seen too much in grade school and high school, or else at home; others plunge right in. Many Nineties students have bad academic skills, and worse social ones; even at expensive private schools like Bryn Mawr, professors find themselves explaining how to perform an introduction, or write a check. Many four-year campuses have seen a clear rise in uncontrollable students, afraid of no one, confident that there is no such thing as a permanent record or a last chance.

Other campus adults blame popular culture. This first generation of day-care kids to reach college has watched 100,000 televised murders, they say; what do you expect, if they grow up playing computer games like Night Trap, in which a troupe of ghouls captures a scantily dressed sorority girl and drains her blood with a neck drill? Administrators fear full reporting of campus crimes will make their schools look bad; many security officers and parents push for enforcement; some faculty worry that outsiders who want to oversee campus life beyond the lecture hall will also soon want to dictate class content. We are not high school, professors snap. We are a republic within the Republic, with many freedoms.

Like its European ancestor, the American college experience was designed for young adolescents. In 1600 and 1700, college students were often fifteen to seventeen. Reforming American high schools pushed ahead the college years; enter at seventeen or eighteen, leave at twenty-one or twenty-two. Many undergraduates today are adult in every sense. They have jobs, families, responsibilities; they pay tuitions, do the work, collect diplomas. Everyone wins. But others treat college as an extended vacation or private club. The most violent partiers often prove to be alumni, or students from other schools, or people in their mid-to-late twenties who are still technically under-grads. (Arizona State's *Greek Review*, a tabloid for fraternities and sororities, prints frequent valedictions to aged colleagues: "Hammer down! . . . we must bid farewell to a couple of finally graduating seniors . . . pledged in '86 for Christs sake . . . good luck out there in the real world, I hear it licks balls!")

Academic liability law struggles to decide how much—and how little—faculty, staff, and students must be protected from one an-other. On a college-sponsored field trip, a drunken student falls off a cliff. Is the university liable for his broken neck? No; he is legally adult, and the accident was not foreseeable. A drunken student falls off a campus trampoline. Again, no liability; bouncing under the in-fluence was a personal safety choice, by one who is of age. Students robbed on a public sidewalk? The college has no duty to protect. Students assaulted in a campus parking garage surrounded by un-trimmed foliage where previous attacks occurred? A-*ha:* the school has failed in reasonable care.

Older campus officials observe that a disordered undergraduate life is nothing new. Since the 1960s, the Association of College and University Housing Officers has been known as the Zookeepers. If you want to see student wildness, members observe, try a high-rise dorm in the mid-1970s, when the parents of today's undergraduates were tossing burning couches out the windows and grand pianos from the roof. On campus all trends recycle, its historians say. Con-temporary students drink more like their grandparents than their parents. College life has always been violent; crisis is the univer-sity's natural state. The decades between World War I and Vietnam were really an extended lull. The passionate religious revivals at Jacksonian-era colleges live on at conservative campuses like Tulsa's Oral Roberts University or suburban Chicago's Wheaton, where students by the hundreds line up to make public confession of racism and drug use. Division I Football looks sedate beside the mass mayhem of "rushing" a century ago, when hundreds of students blindly pushed at classmates on stairs or walkways, or pitched one another into rivers and lakes. (Organized sports were promoted as a character-building alternative, but in 1905 alone, eighteen college boys died on football fields. To clean up a brutal game, Theodore Roosevelt finally had to intervene.)

To the sociologist Neil Smelser, formerly of Berkeley, a taxonomy of undergraduate cultures cuts across the decades, even the cen-turies. One clear group is the highly competitive—pre-laws, pre-meds, bright people who are not very interested in ideas. Work and thought, for them, are two distinct activities. Next is a culture of free spirits, who identify with the faculty, value the life of the mind, and come to college hoping for peers who like to read and speculate. Other students join the politically active campus culture, once mostly liberal or radical, now also libertarian or conservative, but in all cases fond of action, and forcing issues. A culture of expressive protest (centered on personal appearance, drug use, sexual liberty, and calculated intellectual outrage) has flourished on campuses for centuries. When Shelley was sent down from Oxford for advocating atheism, he was being correctly countercultural. Niche worlds also bloom and fade, from drama and music to literary groups and ethnic organizations, though yearbooks in time yield to on-line 'zines, and missionary societies to recycling clubs.

The big man on campus is now a ghost. But the party-hearty collegiate subculture that often spawned him remains, still, extroverted, confident, hostile to ideas and causes, anti-intellectualism personified. At its core are fraternities, sororities, athletes, and rich alumni. Many of these people binge. Later, they also give. Antagonize them now, lose a track-and-field complex in 2030.

We are a family, we handle our own, institutions say. Remember goldfish-swallowing, and kids cramming into phone booths? We will survive this, too. But that mind-set—minimize, deny, deny some more—frequently means trouble in an age of live hand grenades in the cafeteria, in a time when dormitory suicides can require an AIDS-alert team in full decontamination gear to sterilize the bookshelves and bedding, and hose away the blood.

In a crowded basement at the edge of Brown University, the school's chief of police steps forward one perfect military pace. "I wish I could say you will all be safe here," says Dennis Boucher, in a strong New England twang. "But even I've been attacked on the street, in full uniform"—he gestures at his crisp khaki shirt, his mirror-bright shoes—"so you must stay alert. Aware." The international students around him, some just hours off a plane from Vienna or Rangoon, murmur in dismay. Seventy-nine nations are represented in the Brown student body, and Boucher knows some come from countries where a reasonable citizen fears uniforms. "America is full of wooden floors," says a woman from India, clutching a camera, "and rats with furry tails!" Everything about a U.S. campus fall is so strange to them, squirrels included, that senior policemen giving special lectures on how to walk in public seems one more inexplicable.

"Head up, confident stride," Boucher continues. "Use the shuttle or escort service rather than walk alone after dark. If you leave a car or a bicycle unguarded here, I guarantee it will go away. Lock your rooms when you go down the hall to shower. If you feel at risk, anywhere, any time, call me." A hand shoots up in the back row. "Do you recommend that we equip ourselves with Mace or stun guns?"

"Arm yourselves with information," Boucher says. "Memorize the university emergency number: 3322." A hundred pens hurry across notepads, double- and triple-underlining.

Half a mile from downtown Providence, Rhode Island, Brown is a hilltop inner-city campus of 235 buildings. The neighborhoods around it range from working-class grit to a gleaming colonial district with streets named Benefit and Jenckes and vast clapboard houses freshly painted mustard, slate, and pumpkin. Like many campuses—USC, the University of Chicago, Yale, Columbia, Clark, Trinity, Marquette, Yeshiva, Fordham, Oakland's Mills College—Brown must live with the consequences of long-ago real-estate decisions; neighborhoods may alter, often for the worse, but campuses are fixed. The Brown campus is unwalled. Campus police, Chief Boucher says, may receive some two thousand suspicious-person calls each year. Police work here is mostly service—lockouts, free whistle distributions, bike registration, a rumor-control hotline, discreet room checks on behalf of parents who haven't heard from a child in weeks. Brown is the easygoing Berkeley of the Ivies, no course requirements, all grades below C purged from student transcripts, lots of choreographed liberty. "Are you feeling okay?" one Frisbee player asks another as they stroll the college green. "You're actually wearing a Brown sweatshirt." "I know, I'm so sorry. Don't disown me." This is *Brown,* students say every year, with great hauteur; do we really need security police at all? On this campus, everyone jaywalks, even the cops.

In the Brown student union a dozen women, most young, one silver-haired, one heavily pregnant, lie on a carpeted floor looking up at a young Asian-American special-services staffer. "Let's review an oral-sex scenario," she says, her voice level and professional. The sole man present, a visiting student from California, nods politely. "It's called Bite and Volley. If you wake up in your apartment or dorm room and find a 240-pound assailant on your chest, or if what began as consensual activity turns to date rape, chomp down on the offending anatomy ["Sure hope it's someone I know," says a nearby woman], brace your feet against the mattress, bring your locked hands up like a volleyball serve, scraping the scrotum as hard as possible, then heave him off with a strong fast hip thrust and come around with your leg cocked, ready to kick. Try it. Make your intentions clear."

Flailing feet fill the air as the women grunt and lunge. They practice instep stomps, screaming *No! No! No!* They master shin kicks and breast-bone jabs and nostril slams and knees to the gonads. The California student is pressed back against the sofa cushions now, eyes averted, face pale. "Rats, I have physics lab," says a petite senior, sending her last invisible rapist reeling. The instructor bounds to her feet, looking proudly at the panting class. Some are somber, some grinning. "Next week," she tells them, "knockout blows." Brown first-years all discuss sexual assault with peer educators; each group must agree on a definition of consent. After class, I ask the self-defense instructor if classes like hers should be required for every student. As a recent graduate, she finds the idea of requirements disconcerting, distasteful. "This is Brown. We don't do mandatory."

Generational amnesia strongly affects the ebb and flow of campus rules. For thirty years, *in loco parentis* seemed a campus artifact, dead as the bonfires that once hailed debate-team victories. But the concept is again alive. The assumption that a college or university represents a student's parents, safeguarding life and morals, flourished between 1914 and 1945, weakened with the arrival of GI Bill students, vanished following Sixties demands to treat students as adults. Like the Berlin Wall, *in loco parentis* fell bloodlessly. Students sought freedoms and colleges retreated, shrugging; most were glad to escape an administrative Vietnam, despite apoplectic letters from alumni. By the mid-1970s, the lowering of voting and drinking ages to eighteen had cemented the shift from student ward to student citizen.

Yet many contemporary undergrads, trained as consumers from the cradle, prefer service to empowerment. Few schools lack a Food Preoccupation Group, an In-the-Closet Support Group, a Bereavement Group, a Self-Hypnosis for Better Grades Group, a Students with Mentally Ill Family Members Group. Twenty-four-hour campus hot lines flower. Brown alone has offered Dean on Call, Women on Call, Chaplains on Call, Psychologist on Call. Sometimes student protection means tighter rules about who may be in campus housing when. Sometimes it means party monitors, once known as chaperones (today, usually moonlighting police officers). Sometimes the demands for perfect protection and perfect freedom leave student employees caught between their peers and their paycheck. "Should I go to the library now?" inquire resident advisors, when the first kegs roll down the hall.

What, if anything, should administrations do about the night campus? Planning response in advance of violent crime is an excellent policy, and so is a clear behavior code. Researchers Andrea Parrot of Cornell University and Carol Bohmer of the University of Pittsburgh have catalogued the classic administrative reactions to sexual assault cases. Some schools favor the much-parodied Antioch model of step-by-step request and consent—May I kiss you now? May I place one hand on your breast? Ethical campuses (Parrot cites New Jersey's Stockton State, or small Catholic colleges like

St. Norbert's in De Pere, Wisconsin) are realistic but firm. They will suspend students for sexual assault. If asked why, ethical campuses reply that they really don't want people like that around.

But most campuses fall into other Parrot-Bohmer categories, just as clear. At There-but-for-the-grace-of-God institutions, the first reaction is selfish gratitude. Spared big-money lawsuits, they count their public-relations blessings. Protecting students—oh, right, them— is a distant second. For barn-door closers, only extreme discomfort (like a big-money lawsuit) produces policy changes. Ostrich schools stonewall. We've never had an assault reported, they will say. All our students are decent and kind. Victim-blamer campuses are as self-protective as barracuda. A female student files a sexual assault charge. Where? school lawyers demand. A fraternity? How many drinks did you have? What were you wearing? Did you lead him on? Be glad that's all that happened. Soon thereafter, the student finds two administrative letters in her mailbox: a complaint against her for filing false complaint, and an alcohol-violation summons.

Tired of stabbings and shootings when outsiders crash large campus parties, MIT now uses metal detectors to deter non-students packing guns and knives. East Texas Baptist University enforces curfew with electronic locks that confirm the time of late arrival, then transmit data via fiber-optic cable to administration computers. The University of Southern California, in southeast Los Angeles, invested in a $2 million access and surveillance network of TV cameras, alarms, and card-key readers used by seven thousand students over twenty-five thousand times a day. Computer-controlled cameras can zoom in on the license numbers of suspicious cars. Two-way speakers warn intruders to leave USC property. In stairwells and parking garages, voices come out of the air. "Hold up your ID to the camera. Thank you. Move along."

Other institutions take refuge in paralysis by analysis. Campus lawyers point out that undergraduate rapists have rights like anyone else; professors warn against paternalism, defending partying as student cultural expression; administrators wince at student arrests for drugs or drinking because all campuses must (in theory) certify that they are drug-free workplaces to receive public funding. Others try prevention. Howard University, in Washington, D.C., is moving all freshmen back on campus. The University of Minnesota holds mandatory briefings for its five thousand first-years on campus safety, sexual assault, and self-defense. The University of South Carolina offers a for-credit course on being a freshman, and claims that students who take it get better grades and are more confident about their undergrad careers. The University of Rhode Island, long a champion party school, banned alcohol on campus in 1995. Cornell has required athletes to attend awareness sessions on sex, crime, and violence. Try the *cum parentibus* model, suggests Connecticut College; ask not only your students but their parents to read three specified books each summer; have faculty run discussion on the reading at parents'-weekend panels; get parents, students, and faculty to help draft campus drinking policies.

Another possible response to night-campus syndrome is assigning more homework. Many American undergraduates have a lot of time on their hands. The average national college workload hovers near a twenty-nine-hour week, an all-time low, as opposed to about sixty hours of schoolwork in the early 1960s—though whether quantity is quality, then or now, sends faculty instantly into bitter defensive debate. So does the question "What should an educated person know?" Competing answers tumble forth: the information explosion has killed survey courses on common knowledge, and high time. Handing students born in 1980 the mental furniture of an eighteenth-century gentleman is no kindness. Ensuring they have something to think about while doing telemarketing or changing diapers, however is. Why require Western Civ courses in a transcultural America? some faculty demand. Students don't know what they don't know, other professors retort: 80 percent of undergraduates now study anything they want; too much of it warmed-over high school. Meanwhile, only 35 percent of first-years do six or more hours of weekly homework, as opposed to 44 percent as recently as 1987.

The night campus has long been a matter for undergraduates and administrators—but to create a more responsible and engaged campus life, involving faculty is essential. What works? Informed academic advising, as hard to find on expensive campuses as at factory schools. Small, targeted common-sense innovations: the New York nonprofit that helps buy PCs for poor first-year black and Hispanic students interested in engineering and science, since low-income undergrads are 50 percent more likely to arrive on campus without their own computers. The Berkeley professor who formed calculus study groups for black students after noticing that while whites and Asians readily worked together on hard problems, black kids tended to suffer proudly in silence, convinced that asking for help would make them look dumb. The studies noting that many undergrads are growing adolescents still; sleeping late, for them, is not always sloth, and many learn most efficiently from early afternoon on—suggesting that scheduling fifty-minute lectures at 8:00, 9:00, 10:00, and 11:00 may be the worst of all campus learning formats. Seminars of ten or twelve students remain a very effective way to learn in college; taking even one small-group class, especially in the first year, does wonders for undergraduate morale and grade point averages both.

Intensive courses wear out professors but stimulate undergrads, from the language schools at Middlebury College that immerse students in Russian or Arabic 24-7 to Yale's legendary Daily Themes course, its requirements simple and brutal: an essay a day. Honors colleges, especially at enormous state universities like Wisconsin, Michigan, and Michigan State, help smart, serious students find one another in the crowds. Faculty everywhere are famously bad at calm negotiation, or bargaining for change (at many schools, some courses have not been seriously updated for forty and fifty years, because all know the fights with colleagues will be so exhausting), but when professors do take charge they tend to get results: after Louisiana State's faculty senate persuaded the public schools to require a year each of chemistry, biology, and physics as a requirement for LSU admissions, enrollments in Louisiana high school physics classes quickly doubled. And when rich campuses help poor ones, both learn: Sinte Gleska did get its $10 million federal grant for computer instruction, and Stanford faculty have promised both syllabi exchanges and access to Silicon Valley's powerful internship and job-placement network. Some of the National Science Foundation money will also wire the tribe, buying a Powerbook with modem for every Sicangu Lakota who wants one, allowing a good portion of the Sioux nation to surf the Net, and dream in C.

The quality of student resident advisors, or RA's, will either ease or hinder first-year adjustments. Some RA's can recommend a good literature professor, explain the fine points of course-change cards, and locate both the math help room and the best local pizza; some are coolly absentee; some deal drugs in the dorms. At Haverford, a small Quaker school in suburban Philadelphia, entering students are assigned to "customs groups" of twelve to fifteen students, a ready-made tribe for study breaks, hikes, concern trips, birthdays, and moans about exam stress; older students serve as advisors. At Haverford an honor system covers exams and private life. Behavior that bothers others gets discussed to death, the prices of collective civility.

Another way to defuse the night campus—to help students belong—is for all undergrads to help tend the campus infrastructure, spending several days each month in painting, cleaning, grounds work, or helping in food service or library, as happens at Blackburn College in southern Illinois. Expenses fall, emotional investment in the campus climbs. And Duke is trying to break up its entrenched undergraduate partying patterns through social engineering—by recruiting students who study for fun, by persuading faculty to live in freshman dorms, by reworking housing assignments to keep younger students away from upperclassmen, many of whom resent the administration's attempt to introduce intellectual activity onto campus. "You can lead me to college," declare their protest T-shirts, "but you can't make me think."

Behind the clash of cultures—an entrenched student tradition of Dionysian excess, a new protective puritanism—two very old models of what a campus should be are also at war: the college way versus the university way, tradition or sentiment against size and money, the finishing school and the trade school. Design students' time, or let them do it. Provide more structure, prune the choices, or keep the system neutral. A hundred years on, campuses are still debating John Dewey's query: are undergraduates wayward, ignorant, and in need of firm guidance, or is experimenting the best way to become self-confident, self-reliant, self-propelled?

Brown University's president, Vartan Gregorian, suggests that campuses have already discovered a third way out: the frankly commercialized operation. "Campuses today are Athenian city-states," he told me, gazing with urbane weariness at the ceiling of his eighteenth-century office. "Laundry, concerts, parking, catering vegetarian, catering kosher, too much government regulation and not enough government funding—some days I feel like Job: 'Hit me again!' But as Neil Rudenstine up at Harvard said to me recently, 'Where else in America can you get hotel, health club, career advice, and eighteen hundred courses for ninety dollars a day?'" As at any exclusive resort, what you do of an evening becomes your own business.

To say "We are responsible" admits liability, and most campuses will do almost anything to avoid a lawsuit. Professors sue their schools far more than workers in any other industry, but students are right behind: a University of Idaho student mooned friends from a third-floor window, fell out, and sued the school for not explicitly warning him of the dangers associated with upper-story windows. Malpractice insurance for colleges and universities is another hidden reason for high campus price tags.

Between rhetoric and action lies a maze of chasms and canyons, underbrush and dead ends, and undergraduates know it. So administrations mostly repeat what is, after all, true. Our students are adults. We must trust them to make responsible choices. Counseling services say, We are winning battles, but losing the war. Beer companies solemnly urge responsible consumption, then sponsor drink'n'raft bashes. Trustees boards say, What do you mean, we can't have drink trays on our carts when we play the university golf course? Student say Get out of my face, or, I have a right to learn in peace. Parents say, How dare you arrest my daughter? or How dare you fail to safeguard my son? Placating is easier than confronting, entertaining easier than correcting bad sophomore essays phrase by phrase. Keep them distracted. Let them party. Bring on the new class. After all, some undergrads drink enormously and still get good grades. And in two or three years, most will have straightened out, gotten bored, turned toward the daylight world once more. But the human wreckage is real, too.

In the end, in the dark, the underpaid security people offer the most consistent witness to the night campus. I talked to one Rutgers guard, a moonlighting sociology graduate student who found his job professionally instructive, like a duck blind set in a flyway. At twenty-six, he knew he was already too old to understand a lot of what he saw. The strange new music, the unchanneled energy, constantly amazed him.

"Frat row can get very scary," he pointed out, "but in fairness, they aren't the only problems. You get these calls from the science dorms: Naked guy running around with rubber doll. Or: Women screaming in dorm room. That one was a ritual initiation of female scientists, where the group brandings got *way* out of hand."

He thought a moment, moving his fork in precise parallel strokes through the remains of Himalayan chicken tikka and bamboo-shoot curry. We were in a campus restaurant at twilight, and groups of students kept coming to the window and squinting at its hand-lettered menu—papri chat, dal bhat, kothay, seven-bean soup. Some made ape faces, then drifted toward a nearby sports bar. Others brightened at the clean hot scent of lentil chips and jasmine tea, and came shyly in.

"For undergrads in general, the worst time is the first week of fall term, when they don't have enough to do, and the week following midterms, same problem," the young guard said. "I learned one thing very quickly on this job. The kids with green hair and nose rings are totally normal. It's the ones who are weird up here"—he tapped his forehead—"that you need to look out for."

---

## Now that you've read

1. What is your responsibility as a student to do to keep yourself safe at night on your campus?
2. What is your college's responsibility to keep you safe?
3. Someone comments to Anne Matthews that "today's college students are damaged goods." What is the context of that comment? How do you respond to it?
4. What could students and colleges do to make campuses safer?

## READING 4

*Ellen Rosenberg*

# Commuting

"Commuting" is a chapter from Ellen Rosenberg's book *College Life,* which offers first-year students advice about what to expect in college and how to cope with it. "Commuting" spells out clearly what is involved in going to school while living elsewhere, for whatever reasons. Rosenberg explains that it's up to the student to make friends and find a niche, whether that student lives on or off campus. As you read, see whether you recognize yourself or someone you know in the stories that students tell of their own experiences as commuters.

### Before you read

1. How many students on your campus commute to school?
2. Do you commute? If so, why? If not, why not?
3. What are some of the advantages of commuting? What are some of the disadvantages?
4. What's the longest commute you've heard of?

There are many commuter students who have talked with me about not feeling a sense of connection on campus. Beyond attending classes, they found it difficult to also have the time to attend meetings, join clubs, become more socially involved, and find a satisfying balance between living at home and enjoying an active life on campus.

Whether your campus is 100 percent commuter or there is a percentage of students who live in residence halls—no matter what your age or where the beginning of your college experience fits into your life—this chapter will give you an opportunity to think more about the feelings, issues, and personal decisions that can affect your campus life.

### Feelings About Commuting

*Positive:*

> *Nick (sophomore at a four-year college where there is a small percentage of students in residence):*
> "I love commuting. I wouldn't live on campus for anything! I like living at home. I like that commuter students get involved with

each other. There is a commuter student organization and we get informed of the different activities that are on campus through a newspaper. I also like the freedom that I have a car and can go where I need to go . . . and don't have to worry about just being stuck on a campus.

"Sometimes you don't feel as much a part of the campus because you don't live there. Until you meet people who live on campus, you don't really have a connection with those who live there. But I feel more a part of the people who commute. It simply works out that way for me. I do have some good friends who live there. It's just a matter of who you meet and you get involved with. It's a personal thing."

*Erin (sophomore at a two-year, 100 percent commuter campus):*

"Going to a commuting school has been a great convenience for me. I am putting myself through school and it is a lot cheaper than a state school. It also allows me to keep my job and close contact with family and friends. Although I hate the morning traffic and the afternoon rush hour, it feels great to be able to pull into my driveway at the end of a long day.

"I love living home and being with my family. I can't imagine being away from home. Meeting people is not difficult if you don't live in a dorm. The only difference is if you don't live at school, you'll see your friends twice a week and if you want to go out in the evening, you have to make a little effort and ask for their phone number."

*Donna (who has already attended two commuting colleges):*

"I enjoy going to the one I'm at now because I run into many friends from high school and I also meet many others. I think the school really does a lot for its students. There is always something going on and something to do. They hold a club hour on Tuesdays and Thursdays from eleven-thirty to twelve-thirty. During this hour, they might have a concert or there may be something going on at the college union. The only thing the college doesn't have is dorms."

*Sebastian (sophomore at a predominantly resident four-year college):*

"I'm a staunch advocate of commuting and living at home. There are a lot of people, commuters especially, who think that just because you live at home . . . you have to just go to classes and then leave. You are a student of the college. You can do what everybody else is doing. You can join the clubs. You can go to the activities that the college offers.

"Look, I'm a commuter. I pledged two fraternities. Yes, it got a little difficult at points, getting back and forth from the college, especially when my car was in a little accident. But it still worked out fine.

"They say you miss a lot of dorm life and such. Yes, you miss a lot of informal get-togethers. But you also miss people throwing up in the halls, no hot water in the showers, and fire alarms at three A.M."

*Allison (sophomore at an all-computer campus):*

"In high school, you felt like you had to go away. It was the 'in' thing to do. And if you weren't out buying new comforters with everyone, life was over.

"I feel more independent because I've stayed home and didn't go away to college—I get to spend more time with the things I like to do, such as staying at school, going to my job, and being with my boyfriend. And I don't have as many friends here that I have to spend time with.

"I feel that staying home was probably one of the best things I've ever done. I made a whole new life for myself. And I did it on my own.

"I think it's different than my friends who went away to school. I had a different perspective. I feel that when you go away to school, you're going with a group of other people and you're all in the same position, forced to group together and make the most of it.

"But when it comes to a community college, you really have to go out and do it on your own. It's all what you make of it.

"If I never took the chance to get involved at school, I would never have known that there really is life on a community college campus. My involvement changed my whole perspective about being home, right away."

*Negative:*

*Chris (first-year student at an all-commuter campus):*

"I hate commuting to school every day, sitting in traffic. And I'm always late for class. I also think that not living on a campus hurts school spirit.

"I feel that by going to a commuter school, I don't spend much nonclassroom time on campus. If I lived on campus, I would probably spend more time at the library and maybe be involved with clubs or extra activities.

"When you commute, you really just want to come, go to your classes, and go home. And by doing so, it limits you to the number of people you'll meet."

*Jason (freshman at a two-year community college):*

"Attending a community college is much like attending high school, yet now you don't know as many people. The people here are not really interested in meeting new friends. They are only interested in getting to class and then getting home or to work. Most people are here so they can transfer to a four-year school and they're concentrating on their schoolwork rather than their social life.

"Of course, there will be people you are friendly with who share the same classes, but other than that, you keep your high-school friends and wait for them to come home to visit."

*Denise (returning student):*
"I feel attending a commuting college prevents the student from getting all the benefits of college. In prior years, I attended a local college where a majority of the students lived on campus. And I feel the attitudes of the students who live on campus are different. They are a lot more friendly because that is their life. If they don't socialize it would be a boring place for four years. The morale in a live-in college is a lot better. It is normal for a large majority of the college students to attend Saturday football games. At a community college, most students don't make it back to support their team."

*Andrew (freshman at an all-commuter campus):*
"I strongly dislike being home and going to school. I find that by being home, I feel like I'm still in high school. My social life has been fair but I know if I had gone away to school, it would have been a lot better. I know this because I have visited many of my friends who are away at school. In high school, I had a ninety average and at college, my grades have gone down."

*Jimmy (freshman at an all-commuter campus):*
"It's not that I don't like school. It's just that I hate commuting back and forth every day. The parking here stinks because there are so many people in this school. I would much rather be away at school in a dorm so when I walk out of my room, I don't have far to go for my classes. Plus a lot of the friends you make here live far away from you, so you don't always see them after school. When you're away, everybody lives together and you make a lot of friends that way and you only have to look out of your room to see them."

This list could go on and on. If you're commuting, whether to a community college or to a four-year institution, the most important factor is your own feelings. Do any of these issues closely relate to your commuting experience? If haven't started life on your campus yet, what do you anticipate to be your situation? What else would you add, either in the positive or negative category?

If your feelings are positive, consider what it is about commuting that means the most to you. What would you change if you could that might make your life as a commuter even better? If your feelings are negative, what do you wish could be different?

As with most things in life, some aspects of this issue are within your control, some are not. No matter what your circumstances are in school, the best you can do is put your energies into what you *can* do something about. And try as hard as you can to accept and make peace with what is not within your power to change.

With that in mind, let's deal with some of the more common issues that commuter students have told me are high on their list of concerns. Hopefully, my ideas will help you better understand your own reactions as well as what steps you can take to add to the quality of your life as a commuter.

### Parking

Just before giving a recent presentation on a campus where a high percentage of the population commuted, a student said to me, "You want to talk about a hot issue? Deal with parking! It's awful here!" Well, that wasn't why I was there. However, I couldn't help but relate to his frustration. I remember only too well how tough it was to find a space on my own commuter campus where I taught.

It's not a great way to start the day if you end up totally nuts from trying to find a space, especially if you just experienced morning rush hour. And on top of this, if you're late for class because you counted on being lucky in the parking lot and weren't, that's not the happiest of situations!

Perhaps this comes under the category of needing to accept what you can't control. While there are students who make formal parking proposals to administrations who may or may not find them feasible, the plain truth is that some campuses are unbelievably crowded. And parking can be a problem.

So rather than allowing your blood to boil daily, build in extra time to get to school. That way you won't be late. And if you accept that you may have to end up parking all the way on the other side of your campus and accept that it may take far too long to park, then you won't get caught up wasting your energies on being miserable about something that just may be that way throughout all your years at that campus.

Put simply, you may not be able to control the parking. But you can control what you do about your parking situation.

### Commuter Student Organizations

Most if not all campuses have a commuter student organization which can help you with any issue that represents a concern, both personal and academic. It also provides a great way to meet other commuter students as well as coordinate carpools with those who live in your general area.

## Attitudes About Living At Home

The ability to start fresh on your local campus needn't be hindered by the fact that you're living at home. Staying home and commuting doesn't have to feel like or be like high school. As always, you've got choices. You can start commuting with an attitude that because you're home nothing too much has changed. Or you can start campus life and *decide* that this can and will be a terrific new experience for you.

Naturally, this is personal. It very much has to do with what you want for yourself. Understand that probably nothing will be handed to you. The opportunity is there, yes. But it's up to you to take advantage of it, actively seek it out, and make it happen. The good news is that you *can.* All you need to do is want to.

If you just wish to attend classes and don't choose to get more involved with campus life, and you're satisfied with that kind of experience, that certainly is your choice. But if you want to get involved, you can and need to make the decision to do so. Then act on that decision and take it as far as you want to go. It's all there for you. You just have to look. And if you don't find it, ask.

So many commuter students talk about how much better college would be—how much more involved they'd be, how much more socially connected—if they were living away at school instead of at home. Yes, it's certainly true that if you were living on campus you'd be right there and have the chance to attend whatever activities were planned without having to make special trips back to campus in order to do so. You'd have the chance to spend time getting to know people differently because you'd all be living there together.

Perhaps the key focus here is on "the chance." Because it's also true that there are many students who go away to college and do not develop any meaningful relationships on campus, never participate in campus activities, and never quite feel connected throughout however many years they attend. Just because they're away doesn't automatically mean their college experience will be incredible. And just because you commute doesn't mean it can't be terrific. Will it be? Home or away, it depends on whether you act on and make the most of each chance.

That's really all it takes—effort. You need to actively push yourself into campus life. You must decide to *make* your college experience all that it can be. Involvement is yours if you want it, no matter how uninvolved you might have been in high school.

The fact that you're the one to shape how you live your college life is dramatically different from high school. You've got a chance to be more independent, a chance to try vastly different activities that you might not have been exposed to in the past, a chance to meet new people from diverse backgrounds. You've got to balance your time, balance your studying, balance your social life, with no one really looking over your shoulders to remind you to go to your locker before class.

Very simply, college is not high school. Because you're home, it will only feel like you felt in high school because you're not living away. But every other aspect of commuter life can and will be worlds apart from what high school was . . . if you explore what's available to you and stay on campus long enough after classes to get involved.

### Balancing Home, Jobs, and School

During the many years I taught at a commuter campus, there were large numbers of students who told me they held a few jobs, came to campus only to attend classes, and left quickly afterward. Many of my conversations with them centered on their frustration in not feeling like they were part of our campus. I can't say that I was surprised. Beyond going to classes, they weren't involved, either by choice or because there just wasn't time to do anything else but work and go to classes.

If you're supporting yourself and are paying your own way through college, it may be too hard to split yourself in many different directions. You can only do so much. If it bothers you that it's not feasible to participate in other campus activities, hopefully those feelings will be offset by the knowledge that your commitment to making this educational experience possible is more important than anything else.

You still can arrange to see people you meet in classes according to your own time schedule. The weekends may be much freer for you. So just because you can't spend more time on campus during the week, that needn't prevent you from pursuing new relationships.

### Involvement on Campus

If you do have the time and wish to get more involved on your campus, the first step is finding out what your campus has to offer. A reminder: Information about clubs, organizations, and other activities is available from the office of student activities, office of student life, dean of students, and the office of residence life.

Clubs are a great way to meet other students who have interests in common with yours. They provide a chance to develop new areas of interest.

*Allison (sophomore):*
"I did find one very special friend. She's a mixture of all my old best friends from high school. The way I found her was through getting involved at school."

Besides involvement in organizations, your sense of connection can be significantly greater if you develop new friendships on campus. Many commuter student concerns relate to "just being friends in the classroom" or finding it difficult to see people after class because many live farther away and don't have the time to stay around. Still others seem to spend all their time with friends from home.

As a commuter, the idea is to be as campus-based as possible, socially as well as academically. If you limit your friendships to those from high school rather than attempting to build new relationships on campus as well, you'll likely not feel as much a part of your campus life.

If someone lives farther away, try to arrange to meet him or her before or after class, if possible, or on weekends. Even grabbing a coffee to go from a food wagon on campus and sitting under a tree—or in the hall—with one of your classmates for ten minutes before class starts will give you a chance to get to know that person better. He or she will also know you're interested in having more than a superficial relationship.

We often make the mistake of thinking we need many hours for socializing. That's great when you have the hours to spare. But if it's ten minutes before or after class, or while having a quick lunch, or taking a break with someone you meet in the library, you'll find that those brief times can mean more than you might think. If you make an effort to more effectively use the time you have, that can make a difference in your relationships.

### Friends From High School
### Who Are Also Home

Starting fresh can also be affected by how your friends from home relate to you—and you to them. You might find that you present yourself one way to your friends from home and quite another way to the new people you meet on campus.

Some students have talked with me at length about their own surprise at finding they established friendships on campus with people who had very little in common with their friends from home. It sometimes becomes a delicate balance between trying to spend time with new friends and leaving enough time for old ones, especially when they don't seem to blend very well with each other.

Another issue students said could be awkward is commuting to the same college with friends from home and finding that the intensity of friendship that you had with them in high school is gradually lessening. Because schedules can be so different, many have said that they used excuses such as "I can't make it . . . I have class" or "I have to do something for school." But making excuses on an ongoing basis is difficult.

More than likely, if you're feeling something has changed, so is your friend. And if this person has been a good friend, you're better off not making excuses in the first place. A better way to handle this is to talk honestly with each other. Then you can feel freer to see each other when you both wish, but at the same time not feel obligated to do so.

*Allison (sophomore):*

"When you go to a community college and your high-school friends are also going there, people often stick to the friends they went to high school with. They kind of stay in their clique from high school. I feel that they lose out, because they're the ones that make it the thirteenth grade.

"Then I think of one friend from high school. We just went our separate ways, even though we went to the same college, because I took the optimistic route and tried to make the most of it, while she went the other way and was very negative. She didn't want to stay home. She thought it was going to be terrible."

The people who go away to school may have somewhat of an easier time filtering out who from high school they still wish to have actively in their life. When they come home for holidays or isolated weekends, there is naturally a limited amount of time. They can choose who they want to see the most and simply say that they have no time to do anything else.

But if you're commuting and have close friends from high school at home with you, it may take a bit of time to filter out who still means the most and gradually ease any expectations of spending the same kind of time together as you did in high school.

There aren't any rules—only the ones you make for yourself—about how much time you should spend with whom. Perhaps a helpful guide would be what you want to do, rather than what you feel you "should" be doing.

So if you're honest with yourself and respect the fact that time will probably be very precious to you, you'll gradually be able to determine who you would wish to spend your free time with and who you might have to tell "Thanks for asking and I'd really love to see you, but I already made some plans and Saturday night isn't good for me. I'll speak with you soon."

Bottom line, it's your call.

## Family Relationships, Expectations At Home,
## If Parents Aren't "Letting Go"

You need to be honest about any pressures you feel at home that are making it difficult to do all you wish to do at your campus. As much as college is an adjustment for students, parents and other family members need their own time to adjust. And if you're living at home, they also may need to learn that this is no longer high school.

Even if you have an excellent relationship with your parents, in order to keep it excellent, be sure to talk about finding a workable balance between your daily commitments and involvements at college and what might be expected of you at home.

Issues you may need to address are your growing sense of independence, privacy, home rules about alcohol, the freedom to invite people to your home, the ease of coming and going and how concerned you need be about letting your parents and family know about your plans, meal schedules, and academic expectations and pressures. Think about what you need to add to this list.

If you haven't gotten along with your parents as well as you would wish, you can try to initiate positive changes. Set aside private time with them in order to talk openly about any strain you feel exists between you and your wish to reach a better understanding.

Patience is essential. Just because you or your parents agree that you want and need to work at improving your relationship doesn't necessarily mean it will dramatically change overnight. The ability to live together with more give and take will take time—and practice.

If you feel either parent is not "letting go," you might say: "Mom [or Dad], I appreciate everything you're doing for me. And I know how much you care. But you're really on top of everything I'm doing and I'm not getting the chance to fully try being on my own. I need to do that for myself. I know I can come to you if I need your help."

Most students tell me they're afraid of hurting their parents' feelings and usually don't say anything, hoping eventually things will change. I can't promise your mother or father will be receptive or even be able to understand. The statement I've just suggested is simply one way to initiate a discussion of a sensitive issue that is important to confront. If you don't talk about this, your parents may have no idea how you're feeling.

You may find it easier to write down your feelings instead of saying them aloud. Discussion can then follow after they've had a chance to digest what you've said.

This may not be a one-time discussion. As I've said many times, any adjustment takes time. If they don't let up and you feel there is no change on their part, you can attempt to talk further. At the very least, your ability to put into perspective their reactions and pronouncements of who they expect you to be will help strengthen your personal sense of freedom to go forward in your life, even if it seems they're still trying to hold you back.

Allison and I talked at length about her commuting experience. With regard to living at home, she said:

> "The fact that I am home means I still have a large connection with the family. Sometimes it's positive, sometimes negative. My parents don't bother me about going in and out, the time I'm coming home . . . those aren't major concerns.
>
> "And although I might only make dinner once every two weeks, it's really nice to have my family there. At the same time, it can be very difficult to deal with family problems when you have everything else in your own personal life to deal with—such as your parents' arguments or family disagreements. That just adds stress to your life that you don't need. That's probably the only negative aspect about being home and not being away at school."

### Interacting With Nontraditional Students

On most commuter campuses, there are traditional as well as nontraditional students. *Traditional* refers to students who are eighteen or nineteen years old, just out of high school. *Nontraditional* identifies students who are older, often returning to college. In day or evening classes, any roster might include people who may be old enough to be your parent or grandparent.

Some traditional students make the unfortunate mistake of thinking that the age difference is too much of a barrier to even consider friendship with other students a possibility. Many think that if they can't get along with their parents, then how could they expect to relate closely to someone who is about their parents' ages? And unfortunately there are nontraditional students who make the same mistake in reverse.

I saw this happen in my own classes. Group work and open class discussions gave my students a better chance to get to know each other, and they found they had more to gain from each other than they had realized, regardless of age or any other difference. By the end of the semester, the reserve that was so apparent in the beginning no longer existed. I wished that their comfort with each other would have taken less time to build; they could have gained even more.

Besides, you can be a great help. There are many older students who have not written a term paper in many years and would be grateful to you if you offered to share some ideas about, for example, organizing notes or research.

But the giving needn't only be one-way. Nontraditional students have many more years of life experience. Their perspectives about the joys and sometimes the disappointments and pain of everyday living can be powerful lessons that can deeply touch your own life.

Some of my students also told me that because they formed such a positive relationship with the older students, that helped them relate better to their own parents. And it's no surprise that many of my older students found that what they gained from a closer relationship with traditional-age students helped them better understand their own children.

As with any other type of difference—be it race or nationality or appearance or weight or gender or religion or whatever—the more you accept and are open to having a relationship with people because of who they are rather than because of age or other differences, the more you'll find that your world at school, and for the rest of your life, will be that much more enriched.

---

## Now that you've read

1. Rosenberg quotes a number of students who express various sentiments about commuting to college. Which did you find most interesting or provocative, and why?
2. Do you think it's easier to get parents to "let go" if you live on campus rather than at home? Why or why not?
3. What advice that Rosenberg offers strikes you as useful? Why? Does anything strike you as wrong or misguided? Why?

# READING 5

---

*Sandy Smith Madsen*

# A Welfare Mother in Academe

As "A Welfare Mother in Academe," Sandy Smith Madsen has struggled to stay in school while supporting herself and her children. After leaving an abusive marriage, she had to go on welfare, but she also found that successive changes in welfare law made it harder and harder for her to stay in school and earn her degree. Currently, she's working on a Ph.D., so she's been successful on many levels. But she still has some harsh criticisms of a system that seems to want to condemn women and children to lives of poverty and minimum-wage jobs.

### Before you read

1. What is the first image that comes to mind when you hear the term *welfare mother*?
2. Do you think welfare recipients should be required to work in return for their benefits? Should there be any exceptions to this work requirement?
3. Do you know anyone who has ever been on welfare? If so, ask that person how he or she feels about recent changes in state and federal welfare laws.

---

I have been, and will always think of myself as, a "welfare mother." Two years after my escape from an abusive marriage, I signed up for yet more abuse. I signed up for welfare. And I enrolled in academe.

Critics have called women like me "pigs at the trough," and many legislators have agreed: The 1996 welfare-reform law signed by President Clinton was based on the premise that the mothers who are the heads of more than 90 per cent of all welfare families are lazy, irresponsible, dishonest, ignorant, and, yes, sexually promiscuous. It also assumed that neither caring for children nor going to college was work.

I began college in the days before the welfare-reform law was passed, and it was very difficult then to juggle education and caring for my family. Today, it is well-nigh impossible. Welfare reform has severely curbed the opportunities for single mothers to go to college, by requiring those who are full-time college students to work

at low-income jobs if they want to retain their benefits. That requirement does not begin to deal with the basic economic reason
that many women are poor and go on welfare in the first place:
When they do work, they earn less than men and cannot support
their families. (While women now earn 76 cents for every dollar that
men earn, women who are mothers earn 59 cents for every dollar
that men who are fathers earn.)

This month, the Senate adopted an amendment to a bill to extend the Higher Education Act that would allow welfare recipients to
spend two years in postsecondary education or vocational training
without having to undertake paid employment at the same time.
While the provision does not go far enough, it is a step in the right
direction. I urge college leaders and advocates for welfare recipients
to work hard to get the House of Representatives, which did not
pass a similar provision, to accept the amendment when conferees
for the two chambers work out a compromise version of the bill. Because, despite the stereotypes, many welfare mothers have not yet
been permanently damaged by the psychologically abusive assaults
on their character inherent in welfare policy. Many still have the
confidence, intelligence, motivation, and perseverance required for
higher education.

While a student at Tennessee State University (I graduated in
1997), I began a study of students who, like me, were struggling to
meet the often-conflicting demands of welfare requirements and education. What happened to the women with whom I spoke in the wake
of welfare reform is especially telling.

With the August 1996 national welfare law as its paradigm, Tennessee reformed its welfare law in September 1996 to mandate that
welfare mothers of children over the age of 16 weeks must engage in
education and/or work "activity" for at least 40 hours a week. When
caseworkers first encountered college students, they subtracted 15
hours of class time from a 40-hour week and sent the mothers out to
work for 25 hours. No allowance was made for the fact that college
students needed to spend time in the library. Today in Tennessee,
welfare recipients are allowed to count one hour of study per class
hour as work. That's still not enough—and that's why we need the
Senate amendment enacted into law.

Take the experience of one student whom I interviewed at Middle
Tennessee State University. In the fall semester of 1996, she attended
class for 15 hours a week, worked for 20 hours a week to earn a non-
living wage, and studied a minimum of two hours per class hour. In
her leisure, she took care of her children. That semester, her cumula-
tive grade-point average fell from 3.5 to 2.5. This 49-year-old mother
of three was forced to take time off from classes—and from the "work
activity" mandated by law—to recover from exhaustion.

Time limitations on receiving welfare are also a problem for mothers. When the bell tolls the end of the 18 consecutive months (since 1996) that women are allowed to receive welfare in Tennessee, recipients must withdraw from welfare for a minimum of three months and try to support their families with full-time work.

Even Superwoman might not be able to work full time (for low wages), maintain a home, care for children, and pursue a college degree. And so the mandated withdrawal from welfare almost inevitably also becomes a withdrawal from higher education.

The lifetime limit of five years on welfare, mandated by federal law, is a little better, because the average traditional college student takes five years to obtain a four-year degree. But for women handicapped by poverty and oppressive welfare regulations (and who must devote time to the responsibilities of being a single parent), five years is not enough.

By the time welfare reform caught up with me, dropping out of college was not an option—I was a senior who was determined both to graduate and to earn a graduate fellowship. The new rules seemed so onerous that, like thousands of other women faced with welfare reform in Tennessee, I opted to drop out of welfare and to increase the amount of time that I worked for wages. That, of course, meant cutting back on the work of caring for my children. Before welfare reform, I had been able to go to college, care for my children, and supplement my welfare benefits with occasional paid work. I scheduled classes around the lives of my children, helped them with homework, and drove them back and forth across Nashville to three different magnet schools.

After I gave up welfare, I strove to do only two things: pay the bills and stay in college. My children often were unsupervised. My teenage daughter almost died in the emergency room from alcohol poisoning—but we were welfare-free. A recent report in *The New York Times* told a similar tale of divided allegiances: A welfare mother incurred the wrath of program officials for her refusal to allow her 3-year-old child to make a 45-minute bus ride—*alone*—to the babysitter. Mother and child were punished with a reduced check. The article also reported on a woman punished for refusing to leave her child with an abusive babysitter—the only day-care alternative she could find.

What I found most objectionable in the 1996 reforms was that they would have required me to report my children's welfare status to their schools at three-month intervals. While I could have gritted my teeth and endured a welfare policy explicitly designed to humiliate me, I could not see myself inflicting this same humiliation and stigma on my children. I traded my family's food stamps and monthly cash grant back to the state for their rights—as citizens—to privacy.

My study of other welfare mothers found similar concerns about stigma. Despite their portrayal in newspapers as vacuous ninnies in pursuit of fame and glory as "Welfare Mother of the Month," many women on welfare with whom I spoke went to great trouble to conceal this one dimension of their identity, lest the disrespect to which they were so accustomed invade the refuge of academe.

One woman I interviewed enrolled in a special program that allowed women with "viable" majors to receive some perks, such as money for child care and transportation. (Viable majors were considered those very likely to lead to employment, often jobs in traditional women's occupations, such as nursing.) In return, she told me, "I had to get professors to sign a time sheet saying that I was really going to class. Then I had to find someone to sign the adviser's spot. I didn't even have an adviser. It felt so bad to have to find someone to sign that. It was hard to know where I fit in. I used to wonder: Am I really the scum of the earth? Or will I be somebody one day?"

Others told me how hard it was to hold on to self-esteem when caseworkers scheduled appointments at times when the women were supposed to be in class or at a job. The women's welfare payments were reduced if they committed the crime of going to class or work instead of the welfare office for such appointments. Welfare rules, and the way they are enforced, vary greatly—even from caseworker to caseworker. But, while most college students typically question everything, most welfare mothers know their precarious places and, wisely, question nothing.

Although social-science research shows that welfare mothers who graduate from college quickly become taxpayers who double or quadruple their former incomes, the transformative powers of higher education are certainly not limited to material gains. One student whom I interviewed told me: "If I hadn't gone to college, I would not have a will to live. I would have no hope, no dreams, nothing to live for. My driving force is the dream of getting a home for my children. I want my children to grow up in one neighborhood. College has taught me the importance of community."

Although it is common for universities to try to meet the needs of specific groups of students, the needs of welfare mothers go largely unmet. Few colleges have support programs for low-income women—for example, to help demystify the morass of welfare rules or to challenge injurious stereotypes. Few have affordable on-campus family housing. Colleges can do more: decent day care on every campus would help; so would career counseling that didn't include gender biases.

There is, indeed, a "culture of dependency" in America. This nation is exceedingly dependent on women to do the *work* of caring for children whom fathers abandon. These women are willing to be mother, father, and able-bodied worker—they are willing to do it all. But they can't do that unless they can get work that provides a living wage, and many such jobs require a college degree. Women like the woman I was, making good progress toward a degree while also caring for children, need to be allowed up to four years of higher education so that they can eventually make a decent income. And they deserve respect while they study and work and juggle their family responsibilities.

---

### Now that you've read

1. What is Madsen arguing for?
2. Where do you find her argument convincing? Where do you find it less so? Explain your answer.
3. What does she say colleges can do to make it easier for people on welfare to better themselves by getting a college education?
4. Why is our culture generally so unsympathetic to requests like Madsen's?

# READING 6

## Family Made Graduation More Difficult

This letter to "Dear Abby" created quite a stir. Abby devoted later columns to the responses, and the vast majority took this letter writer to task for her position. Unfortunately, this letter concisely reveals what some older (and younger) students face when they go to college.

### *Before you read*

1. How supportive has your family been of your education?
2. Are you an older student returning to college? If so, what has been the most difficult thing about coming to college?
3. Do you know anyone who has a parent or other older relative who has come to college to continue his or her education? What has been that individual's reaction to the older person's return to school?

---

**Dear Abby:** A member of our family recently graduated from college—finally! This woman is in her late 40s. For the past four years, she has spent all her free time and money on studies when she should have been spending more time with her husband, children, grandchildren and ailing parents.

She stopped socializing with friends and occasionally missed family parties because she had "work" to do. She often visited with callers at her door or on the porch because she put her studies before housekeeping and, boy, was it ever obvious! Her house was an unholy mess. It's a good thing her husband is a patient man—otherwise, he would have booted her out and found a real wife.

During her last year of school, she lost her 4.0 average when a family member became ill. She actually cried over it, even though her grades are never going to matter to anyone.

Now that she's a college graduate, she seems hurt that no one has made any fuss about it. When she offered tickets to her graduation ceremony, there was a dead silence. Her own kids didn't even want to attend. I can understand making a fuss when young people graduate because they are at the beginning of their careers, but a degree in "the classics" won't help this woman with the job she's held for 25 years. She's now nearing retirement age, so she doesn't need a new career. Abby, do you think we should have made a big deal out of what was no big deal? Sign this — Alice (Not My Real Name)

**Dear Alice:** Yes, you should have, and shame on you for not doing so. My congratulations to your relative, who had the courage and determination to reach an admirable goal to enhance and enrich her life with knowledge. Furthermore, her accomplishment is all the more admirable considering the difficult obstacles she had to overcome, among them a non-supportive family.

---

### *Now that you've read*

1. Where do you stand in relation to Alice's complaint about her relative?
2. What is the value of a degree in "the classics" for a person with a job held for 25 years? How would you respond to Alice?
3. What can families do to help their family members be successful in college?

## READING 7

*Arlie Russell Hochschild*

# The Third Shift

Arlie Russell Hochschild is a sociologist who has done a lot of research in American Fortune 500 companies to understand how corporate culture affects the lives of all levels of workers. "The Third Shift," a chapter from her most recent book *The Time Bind: When Work Becomes Home and Home Becomes Work,* explores how, as demands on our time and energy increase, we turn to work as a less complicated alternative to our chaotic home lives. In addition, Hochschild found that even when companies have established "family-friendly" policies, managers are reluctant to follow through on the policies and employees are reluctant to take advantage of them. As a sociologist, Hochschild thinks it's important to learn what the underlying reasons might be. What she found indicates that many of us are willing to work longer hours because our work lives are more pleasant than our lives at home.

### Before you read

1. What are your career plans for after college?
2. Do you have (or plan to have) a family? Does (or will) your family include children? If so, who cares (or will care) for them?
3. Which is more important to you, career or family?

___

Amerco, a highly profitable, innovative company, had the budget and the will to experiment with new ways to organize its employees' lives. Its Work-Life Balance program could have become a model, demonstrating to other corporations that workforce talents can be used effectively without wearing down workers and their families. But that did not happen. The question I have asked is: Why not? The answer, as we have seen, is complex. Some working parents, especially on the factory floor, were disinclined to work shorter hours because they needed the money or feared losing their jobs. Though not yet an issue at Amerco, in some companies workers may also fear that "good" short-hour jobs could at any moment by converted into "bad" ones, stripped of benefits or job security. Even when such worries were absent, pressure from peers or supervisors to be a "serious player" could cancel out any desire to cut back on work hours. The small number of employees who resolved to actually reduce their hours risked coming up against a company Balashev. But all these sources of inhibition did not fully account for the lack of resistance Amerco's working parents showed to the encroachments of work time on family life.

Much of the solution to the puzzle of work-family balance appeared to be present at Amerco—the pieces were there, but they remained unassembled. Many of those pieces lay in the hands of the powerful men at the top of the company hierarchy, who had the authority and skill to engineer a new family-friendly work culture but lacked any deep interest in doing so. Other pieces were held by the advocates of family-friendly policies lower down the corporate ladder, who had a strong interest in such changes but little authority to implement them. And the departmental supervisors and managers, whose assent was crucial to solving the puzzle, were sometimes overtly hostile to anything that smacked of work-family balance. So even if the workers who could have benefited from such programs had demanded them, resistance from above would still have stymied their efforts.

But why *weren't* Amerco working parents putting up a bigger fight for family time, given the fact that most said they needed more? Many of them may have been responding to a powerful process that is devaluing what was once the essence of family life. The more women and men do what they do in exchange for money and the more their work in the public realm is valued or honored, the more, almost by definition, private life is devalued and its boundaries shrink. For women as well as men, work in the marketplace is less often a simple economic fact than a complex cultural value. If in the early part of the century it was considered unfortunate that a woman had to work, it is now thought surprising when she doesn't.

People generally have the urge to spend more time on what they value most and on what they are most valued for. This tendency may help explain the historic decline in time devoted to private social relations, a decline that has taken on a distinctive cultural form at Amerco. The valued realm of work is registering its gains in part by incorporating the best aspects of home. The devalued realm, the home, is meanwhile taking on what were once considered the most alienating attributes of work. However one explains the failure of Amerco to create a good program of work-family balance, though, the fact is that in a cultural contest between work and home, working parents are voting with their feet, and the workplace is winning.

In this respect, we may ask, are working parents at Amerco an anomaly or are they typical of working parents nationwide? In search of an answer, I contacted a company called Bright Horizons, which runs 125 company-based childcare centers associated with corporations, hospitals, real estate developers, and federal agencies in nineteen states. Bright Horizons allowed me to add a series of new questions to a questionnaire the company was sending out to seven thousand parents whose children were attending Bright Horizons Children's Centers. A third of the parents who received questionnaires filled them out. The resulting 1,446 responses came from mainly middle- or upper-middle-class parents in their early thirties. Since many of them worked for Fortune 500 companies—including IBM, American Express, Sears, Roebuck, Eastman Kodak, Xerox, Bausch and Lomb, and Dunkin' Donuts—this study offers us a highly suggestive picture of what is happening among managers and professional working parents at Amerco's counterparts nationwide.

These parents reported time pressures similar to those Amerco parents complained about. As at Amerco, the longest hours at work were logged by the most highly educated professionals and managers, among whom six out of ten regularly averaged over forty hours a week. A third of the parents in this sample had their children in childcare forty hours a week or more. As at Amerco, the higher the income of their parents, the longer the children's shifts in childcare.

When asked, "Do you ever consider yourself a workaholic?" a third of fathers and a fifth of mothers answered yes. One out of three said their *partner* was workaholic. In response to the question "Do you experience a problem of 'time famine'?" 89 percent responded yes. Half reported that they typically brought work home from the office. Of those who complained of a time famine, half agreed with the statement "I feel guilty that I don't spend enough time with my child." Forty-three percent agreed that they "very often" felt "too much of the time I'm tired when I'm with my child." When asked, "Overall, how well do you feel you can balance the demands of your work and family?" only 9 percent said "very well."

If many of these Bright Horizons working parents were experiencing a time bind of the sort I heard about from Amerco employees, were they living with it because they felt work was more rewarding than family life? To find out, I asked, "Does it sometimes feel to you like home is a 'workplace'?" Eighty-five percent said yes (57 percent "very often"; 28 percent "fairly often"). Women were far more likely to agree than men. I asked this question the other way around as well: "Is it sometimes true that work feels like home should feel?" Twenty-five percent answered "very often" or "quite often," and 33 percent answered "occasionally." Only 37 percent answered "very rarely."

One reason some workers may feel more "at home" at work is that they feel more appreciated and more competent there. Certainly, this was true for many Amerco workers I interviewed, and little wonder, for Amerco put great effort into making its workers feel appreciated. In a large-scale nationwide study, sociologists Diane Burden and Bradley Googins found that 59 percent of employees rated their family performances "good or unusually good," while 86 percent gave that rating to their performances on the job—that is, workers appreciated *themselves* more at work than at home. In the Bright Horizons national survey, only 29 percent felt appreciated "mainly at home," and 52 percent "equally" at home and work. Surprisingly, women were not more likely than men to say they felt more appreciated at home.

Often, working parents feel more at home at work because they come to expect that emotional support will be more readily available there. As at Amerco, work can be where their closest friends are, a pattern the Bright Horizons survey reflected. When asked, "Where do you have the most friends?" 47 percent answered "at work"; 16 percent, "in the neighborhood"; and 6 percent, "at my church or temple." Women were far more likely than men to have the most friends at work.

Some workers at Amerco felt more at home at work because work was where they felt most relaxed. To the question "Where do you feel the most relaxed?" only a slight majority in the Bright Horizons survey, 51 percent, said "home." To the question "Do you feel as if your life circumstances or relationships are more secure at work or at home?" a similarly slim majority answered "home." I also asked, "How many times have you changed jobs since you started working?" The average was between one and two times. Though I didn't ask how many times a person had changed primary loved ones, the national picture suggests that by the early thirties, one or two such changes is not unusual. Work may not "always be there" for the employee, but then home may not either.

I should have asked what arena of life—work or family—was most engrossing. Amerco parents loved their children but nonetheless often found life at work more interesting than life at home. The workplace, after all, offered a natural theater in which one could follow the progress of jealousies, sexual attractions, simmering angers. Home, on the other hand, offered fewer actors on an increasingly cramped stage. Sometimes, the main, stress-free, "exciting" events at home came during the time Americans spend watching television. (According to one study, Americans spend about 30 percent of their free time in front of the television.)

For this sample, then, we find some evidence that a cultural reversal of workplace and home is present at least as a theme. Unsurprisingly, more people in the survey agreed that home felt like work than that work felt like home. Still, only to half of them was home a main source of relaxation or security. For many, work seemed to function as a backup system to a destabilizing family. For women in particular, to take a job is often today to take out an emotional insurance policy on the uncertainties of home life.

The Bright Horizons parents—middle- and upper-middle-class employees of large corporations who had children in childcare— are a good match for many Amerco parents, and the results of the survey confirm that much of what we have seen in Spotted Deer is in fact happening across the nation. Obviously, however, many working parents do not resemble those in the Bright Horizons group. What kinds of families might be omitted from this sample, and what are *their* experiences of work and home and the relation between the two? As a start, we need to recognize at least four other models of family and work life, each based on the relative emotional magnetism of home and work. Most real families, of courses, blend aspects of more than one of them.

There would be a "haven model," for instance, in which work *is* a heartless world and family still a haven. Amerco workers who fit this traditional "haven model" to any extent tended to be factory hands, who did jobs that were relatively unpleasant and lacked on-the-job community. For many blue-collar men and even more women, home is still often—though as Deb and Mario Escalla's story indicates not always—far more of a haven than work. When I asked women whether they would continue to work if they did not need the money, the proportion who answered "no" rose as occupational level fell. This, in part, may reflect the fact that, over the last decade as the rich have become richer and the poor poorer, those with "desirable" jobs have generally found their jobs to be ever more inviting (with more carefully engineered workplace cultures and more impressive corporate perks). Those with "undesirable" jobs, on the other hand, have generally found them ever less welcoming (with little cultural engineering, growing vulnerability to technological displacement, greater insecurity, and declining pay). Many of these "have-nots" may still look to home as a haven, no matter what the realities of their actual home lives.

Billy and Emily Denton fit another "traditional" model, in which home and work each exhibit gender-specific pulls. Bill, and men like him at the top of the corporate ladder, flee neither a dismal workplace nor a stressful home. They make pleasurable "homes" for themselves at an office to which they devote more of their waking hours, while their real homes become like summer cottage retreats. Wives like Emily are then left to manage home and children. For them, home is not a refuge from the workday world, but a potentially fulfilling world in its own right. This old-style model of work-family balance in which each sphere of life is given to one gender is on the decline even among top executives at corporations like Amerco. The magnetic pull of work is drawing some executive wives out of the house; while for those who remain the appeal of housewifely and motherly duties and pleasures has probably diminished.

There is also a "no-job, weak-family" model, in which neither work nor home has any strong attraction for the individual. Poor people who can't find work and to whom a job may be the economic and emotional prerequisite for a reasonable family life would fit this model. In his book *When Work Disappears,* focusing on the plight of African Americans, the sociologist William Julius Wilson has argued that without a New Deal–style national public works program many blacks will find themselves living in a spreading economic desert. Inner city street corner and gang life, buoyed by an underground economy, loom ever larger as substitute sources of appreciation, relaxation, and security, while drugs help provide the temporary illusion that these ideals are really within one's grasp.

Finally, there is the "work-family balance" model in which parents take advantage of family-friendly options at work and do not crave time on the job so much that they are tempted to steal it from time allotted to their children. Such parents might begin to break the time-deficit cycle and so escape the need for a third shift at home. This model was a reality for a small minority at Amerco, and probably a larger minority nationwide.

If families matching the "haven" and "traditional" models are on the decline, and families matching the "no-job, weak-family" model fluctuate with the economic times, families that fall into the reversal model in which home is work and work is home have been on the increase over the last thirty years. But what social conditions have been fostering this change? The takeover of the home by the workplace is certainly an unacknowledged but fundamental part of our changing cultural landscape.

### Behind Reversing Worlds

Although work can complement—and, indeed, improve—family life, in recent decades it has largely competed with the family, and won. While the mass media so often point to global competition as the major business story of the age, it is easy to miss the fact that corporate America's fiercest struggle has been with its local rival—the family. Amerco company officials worry about their battles for market share with companies in Asia and Europe. But they take for granted their company's expanding share of domestic time. For where the workplace invests in its employees, as at Amerco, it often wins the emotional allegiance of its workers—and so ever more of its workers' time.

The ascendancy of the corporation in its battle with the family has been aided in recent years by the rise of company cultural engineering and, in particular, the shift from Frederick Taylor's principles of scientific management to the Total Quality principles originally set out by Charles Deming. Under the influence of a Taylorist worldview, the manager's job was to coerce the worker's mind and body, not to appeal to his heart. The Taylorized worker was deskilled, replaceable, cheap, and as a consequence felt bored, demeaned, and unappreciated.

Using more modern participative management techniques, companies now invest in training workers to "make decisions" and then set before their newly "empowered" workers moral as well as financial incentives. Under Taylor's system, managers assumed that workers lacked the basic impulse to do a good job. Under Total Quality, managers assume workers possess such an impulse. Under Taylorism, the worker was given no autonomy. Under Total Quality, the worker has a certain amount of autonomy and is drawn further into the world of work by the promise of more.

As the Amerco work environment illustrates, the Total Quality worker is invited to feel recognized for job accomplishments. The company publishes a quarterly magazine, *Amerco World,* that features photos of smiling workers credited with solving problems, anticipating bottlenecks, inventing new products, reducing errors, and otherwise "delighting the customer." In describing its application of the Total Quality system before the House Subcommittee on Science, Research, and Technology, an Amerco vice president noted that the company preferred to reward quality work with personal recognition rather than money. Personal recognition, he pointed out, has proved an extremely effective motivational tool, one far less likely to create the jealousies that often result from giving financial rewards to some workers and not others. Company surveys confirm this.

At Amerco, employees are invited to feel relaxed while on the job. Frequent recognition events reward work but also provide the context for a kind of play. Amerco's management has, in fact, put thought and effort into blurring the distinction between work and play (just as that distinction is so often blurred at home). Fridays during the summer, for instance, are "dress down" days on which employees are urged to dress "as though" they are at home; and the regular rounds of company picnics, holiday parties, and ceremonies are clearly meant to invest work with celebratory good feeling. For white-collar workers at Amerco headquarters, there are even free Cokes, just as at home, stashed in refrigerators placed near coffee machines on every floor.

Amerco has also made a calculated attempt to take on the role of helpful relative in relation to employee problems at work and at home. The Education and Training Division offers employees free courses (on company time) in "Dealing with Anger," "How to Give and Accept Criticism," "How to Cope with Difficult People," "Stress Management," "Taking Control of Your Work Day," and "Using the Myers-Briggs Personality Test to Improve Team Effectiveness." There are workshops in "Work-Life Balance for Two-Career Couples" and "Work-Life Balance for Single Adults." At home, people seldom receive anything like this much help on issues so basic to family life. At home, there were no courses on "Coping with Your Child's Anger over the Time Famine" or "Dealing with Your Child's Disappointment in You or Yours in Him."

As a result, many Amerco managers and professionals earnestly confessed to me that the company had helped them grow as human beings in ways that improved their ability to cope with problems at home. Even in the plants, training in team building sometimes instills similar feelings in the workers. One Amerco handout for its managers lists a series of "qualities for excellence at work" that would be useful at home—an employee would be judged on whether he or she "seeks feedback on personal behaviors," "senses changes in attention level and mood," or "adapts personality to the situation and the people involved." Amerco is also one of about a hundred companies that enrolls its top executives in classes at the Corporate Learning Institute. There, managers learn how to motivate and influence others and manage conflict. The Institute offers an open-ended "personal focus program designed for people from all walks of life who have a genuine desire to explore and expand their unique possibilities." One can, at company expense, attend a course on "Self-Awareness and Being: The Importance of Self in the Influence Process."

The Total Quality worker is invited to feel committed to his company. When, in *Modern Times,* a speedup finally drives the Taylorized Charlie Chaplin crazy, he climbs into a giant complex of cogs and belts and is wound around a huge wheel. He has become part of the machine itself. How could he feel committed to a company that had turned him into a machine part?

Under Total Quality at Amerco, the worker is not a machine; he's a believer. This became clear to me when I witnessed a "Large Group Change Event," held in a high school cafeteria one summer morning in 1992. The event, Amerco's response to losing customers to a growing competitor, was staged somewhat like a revival meeting. Its purpose was to convince each worker to renew his commitment not to his spouse or church but to his workplace. It was one of a series of such events held at underproducing plants in the valley. Two banners hanging at the entrance said, "Show Our Commitment." Four hundred workers, most of them white men between the ages of twenty and forty, were assembled eight to a table. They tended to sport tee-shirts, blue jeans, and baseball caps worn back to front. One young man in sunglasses casually lifted his leg over the back of his chair as if mounting a horse and sat down to join his group. "What's frustrating about your job?" the group leader asked.

"A few supervisors don't have anything to do but watch for you to make a mistake," one man responded. "Why don't they just get to work themselves?"

Talk soon turned to the effect the morning's proceedings might have on life at home. George, twenty-two, his hair in a Mohawk, volunteered, "Me and my wife just got back together. We were going down to New Orleans for a trip; but now this event comes along."

"If we keep this plant open," another worker replied wryly, "that will help keep your family together more than going on some trip."

The organizer of the event then introduced three people, a plant manager, an investor, and a union representative, each emphasizing the need to improve production in the next six months. As a revivalist minister might plumb the depths of sin, the plant manager described how "low down" plant production had sunk, how many fewer defects per million parts Amerco's competitors had, and how many more employee-initiated ideas (or, as they were calling them, Corrective Action Requests) their plants were generating each year. He went on to bemoan Amerco's declining share of the market.

The union representative, who had been a mold maker at another company for twenty-six years, told how his plant had merged with another, then closed. "We lost over 400 jobs in a town of 2,000," he said. "This is what American industry and labor face today." To think up good ideas, to concentrate harder, to be more careful, to cooperate with the coworkers on your team—these were, he suggested, patriotic as well as pro-labor acts.

Workers were then handed pads of Post-its and asked to write down good ideas, which would be stuck on a large wall in the cafeteria under the heading, "Action Ideas." Typical Post-its read: "Don't throw safety goggles away." "Recycle the water," "Don't need to wax the floor three times a day—save money." Each eight-person group was then given twenty-one adhesive gold stars and asked to vote for the best suggestions by sticking stars on the wall next to the action ideas of which they most approved. Back at their tables, workers discussed the stars their groups, now renamed "Worker-Manager Improvement Teams," had given out.

Each team was then asked to consider the question "What am I willing to commit to?" Men at one table talked about quitting their horseplay, their back talk, their slowdowns. They vowed to "cast out the devil" of taking petty revenge on the company for the tediousness of their jobs.

The event organizer then asked all the workers to take a Meyers-Briggs Personality Test using pamphlets and pencils set out on the tables. This test focuses on one's capacity for teamwork, one's tendency to lead or follow, to stand up or hide, to work fast or slow. "Who here is an introvert? Who is an extrovert?" People volunteered and were then asked, "Is your personality getting in the way of committing yourself to improvement?" As was the intent of the whole meeting, the test tacitly invited these blue-collar workers to take on a managerial viewpoint in which people skills matter more than brawn, in which you and the company both should care about what type of personality you have and how it best suits the workplace. They were invited to leave their individual fates behind and try, like any executive, to envision, care about, and plan for the fate of the company.

At the end of the event, to signify their new "commitment," workers inscribed their names on one of the immense red banners that hung at the cafeteria entrance. They signed with fancy long *g*'s and tall *t*'s, with lines under their names, and curlicued *s*'s. Under some names they bracketed nicknames, others as in a high school yearbook were cleverly written inside one of the banner's larger letters that corresponded to the beginning letter of a name.

The event had climaxed with a promise of redemption. Workers had offered themselves up, name by name, to be "saved" from unemployment, and to save the company from falling profits. Amerco, too, wanted these workers to be saved, not laid off. It had already spent four million dollars to get the "mission" of Total Quality out to the plants—and now it was spending even more to save plants and jobs. That said something in itself, the workers felt: Amerco cared.

This sense of being cared for encouraged workers to adopt a more personal orientation toward work time. If, in *Modern Times,* Chaplin, like millions of real factory workers of his era, found himself the victim of a company-initiated speedup, Amerco's professionals, managers, and even factory workers were being asked to envision themselves as their own time strategists, their own efficiency experts. They were to improve their own production, to manage their own intensified work pace at their own plants, even in their own lives. Under the moral mantle of Total Quality, however, workers weren't being asked to consider the speed of their work—not directly anyway—only its "quality." Meanwhile at home, the same workers were finding that quality was exactly what they had to let go of in order to do a certain quantity of chores in the few hours left to them.

### The Taylorized Family

If Total Quality called for "reskilling" the worker in an "enriched" job environment, capitalism and technological developments have long been gradually deskilling parents at home. Over time, store-bought goods have replaced homespun cloth, homemade soap and candles, home-cured meats and home-baked foods. Instant mixes, frozen dinners, and take-out meals have replaced Mother's recipes.

Daycare for children, retirement homes for the elderly, wilderness camps for delinquent children, even psychotherapy are, in a way, commercial substitutes for jobs a mother once did at home. If, under Total Quality, "enriched" jobs call for more skill at work, household chores have over the years become fewer and easier to do.

Even family-generated entertainment has its own mechanical replacement—primarily the television, but also the video game, VCR, computer, and CD player. In the Amerco families I observed, TV cartoons often went on early in the morning as a way to ease children into dressing and eating breakfast. For some families in the evening, CNN or network news lent an aura of seriousness to the mundane task of preparing dinner. After dinner, some families would sit together, mute but cozy, watching sitcoms in which *television* mothers, fathers, and children talked energetically to one another. TV characters did the joking and bantering for them while the family itself engaged in "relational loafing." What the family used to produce—entertainment—it now consumes. Ironically, this entertainment may even show viewers a "family life" that, as in the sitcoms *Murphy Brown* and *Ink,* has moved to work.

The main "skill" still required of family members is the hardest one of all—the ability to forge, deepen, and repair family relationships. Under normal circumstances the work of tending to relationships calls for noticing, acknowledging, and empathizing with the feelings of family members, patching up quarrels, and soothing hurt feelings.

In the wake of the "divorce revolution," this sort of emotional work, always delicate, has become even more complicated and difficult. Two-thirds of the marriages that end in divorce involve children. In *Second Chances,* Judith Wallerstein and Sandra Blakeslee report on a fifteen-year study of sixty middle-class parents and children. Within ten years, half of the children whose parents had divorced had gone through a parent's second divorce; typically, one parent happily remarried and the other did not. Only one child in eight saw both parents remarry happily. Half the women and a third of the men were still intensely angry at their ex-spouses a decade later.

The study provided other insights as well. For one thing, parents and children often saw divorce differently. Two-thirds of the women and half of the men claimed they felt more content with the quality of their lives after divorce, but only one in ten children felt the same way. Three out of four children felt rejected by their fathers. Yet Wallerstein and Blakeslee found, poignantly enough, that these "rejecting" fathers often maintained phantom relations with the children they didn't see or support, keeping their photographs near at hand. One national study found that half of children aged eleven to sixteen living with a divorced mother had not seen their fathers during the entire previous year.

Family life can be baffling under the best of circumstances. But in a society based on the nuclear family, divorce creates extra strains. Blending and reblending people into remarriage "chains" can be much harder than the word "blend" implies. Stepsiblings in such families are rarely as close as biological siblings—and that's only one of many problems such new families face. One divorced Amerco employee complained that his stepchildren refused to obey him and instead confronted him with the challenge "You're not my *real* Dad!" On the other hand, many divorced mothers also deeply resented the ways their remarried ex-husbands favored their new families. One divorced wife, for instance, observed bitterly that her ex-husband had managed to buy a new car and boat while remaining in arrears on his child support payments. Faced with such issues and in need of emotional "reskilling" few parents at home have the faintest idea where to look for "retraining."

At Amerco, successful completion of on-the-job training is rewarded with a recognition ceremony, a Total Quality pin, and possibly even a mention in the company magazine. At Amerco, large sums of money are spent to stage "commitment ceremonies" between the company and its workers whenever a "divorce" seems to threaten. But who rewards a difficult new kind of emotional work or watches for declining profit margins at home? Who calls for renewed vows of commitment there?

### The Hydro-Compressed Sterilized Mouth Wiper

Working parents often face difficult problems at home without much outside support or help in resolving them. In itself time is, of course, no cure-all. But having time together is an important precondition for building family relations. What, then, is happening to family time?

Working parents exhibit an understandable desire to build sanctuaries of family time, free from pressure, in which they can devote themselves to only one activity or one relationship. So, for instance, the time between 8 and 8:45 P.M. may be cordoned off as "quality time" for parents and child, and that between 9:15 and 10 P.M. as quality time for a couple (once the children are in bed). Such time boundaries must then be guarded against other time demands—calls from the office, from a neighbor to arrange tomorrow's car pool, from a child's friend about homework. Yet these brief respites of "relaxed time" themselves come to look more and more like little segments of job time, with parents punching in and out as if on a time clock. When Denise Hampton read *The Narnia Chronicles* to her two sons at night, for instance, she made a special effort not to think about the e-mail piling up for her in cyberspace and the memos she might soon have to compose and e-mail back. Thus, for her, "relaxed" quality time actually took special discipline, focus, and energy, just like work. Even when Denise was at home, even when her mind was on domestic matters, she often found herself approaching time in a quasi-industrial way.

Paradoxically, what may seem to harried working parents like a solution to their time bind—efficiency and time segmentation—can later feel like a problem in itself. To be efficient with whatever time they do have at home, many working parents try to go faster if for no other reason than to clear off some space in which to go slowly. They do two or three things at once. They plan ahead. They delegate. They separate home events into categories and try to outsource some of them. In their efficiency, they may inadvertently trample on the emotion-laden symbols associated with particular times of day or particular days of the week. They pack one activity closer to the next and disregard the "framing" around each of them, those moments of looking forward to or looking back on an experience, which heighten its emotional impact. They ignore the contribution that a leisurely pace can make to fulfillment, so that a rapid dinner, followed by a speedy bath and bedtime story for a child—if part of "quality time"—is counted as "worth the same" as a slower version of the same events. As time becomes something to "save" at home as much as or even more than at work, domestic life becomes quite literally a second shift; a cult of efficiency, once centered in the workplace, is allowed to set up shop and make itself comfortable at home. Efficiency has become both a means to an end—more home time—and a way of life, an end in itself.

A surprising amount of family life has become a matter of efficiently assembling people into prefabricated activity slots. Perhaps the best way to see this is to return to a classic scene in the film *Modern Times*. A team of salesmen is trying to persuade the president of Electro Steel, where Charlie Chaplin works on an assembly line, to install a J. Willicomb Billows Feeding Machine, which, as the mad inventor explains, "automatically feeds your men at work." The sales pitch, an automated recording, continues: "Don't stop for lunch. Be ahead of your competition. The Billows Feeding Machine will eliminate the lunch hour, increase your production, and decrease your overhead." In scientific-looking white lab coats, two sales demonstrators—with the muted smiles and slightly raised eyebrows of French waiters—point to the "automatic soup plate with the compressed air blower" ("no energy is required to cool the soup"); to the "revolving plate with automatic food pusher"; to the "double knee-action corn feeder with its syncro-mesh transition, which enables you to shift from high to low gear by the mere tip of the tongue"; and finally to the "hydro-compressed sterilized mouth wiper," which offers "control against spots on the shirt front."

The hapless Chaplin is chosen to test the machine, and a salesman straps him into it, his arms immobilized. The machine begins to pour soup into his mouth and, of course, finally down his shirt. Chaplin keeps a doubtful eye on the automatic mouth wiper, which periodically spins in to roll over his lips and, if he doesn't stretch up, his nose. Buttered corn on the cob appears, moving automatically back and forth across his mouth. As a deskilled eater, his only job is to bite and chew. However, the corn, like the factory's conveyor belt, soon begins to speed up, moving back and forth so fast that he has no time to chew. The machine breaks. Impassive white-coated salesmen try to fix it, but it only malfunctions again, feeding Chaplin bolts with morsels of sandwich and splashing a cream pie in his face. The mouth wiper leaps out wildly to make a small, clear stripe across his smeared face, and Chaplin drops away from the machine in a faint.

The CEO of Amerco didn't have to introduce a Billows Automatic Feeding Machine. Many of his employees quite voluntarily ate lunch quickly at their desks to save time. This pattern is by no means unique to Amerco. A recent report commissioned by the National Restaurant Association found that these days business lunches are faster and fewer in number. Only 38 percent of adults polled in 1993 said they ate lunch out at least once a week, compared with 60 percent in the mid-1980s. According to Wendy Tanaka, an observer of San Francisco's business district, people take less and less time out for lunch, and many restaurants are being turned into take-out businesses to make ends meet. Customers who do sit down to lunch are more likely to bring work with them. As Tanaka observes, it is no longer unusual for someone to walk in with a laptop computer and have lunch opposite a project not a partner.

Perhaps more significant, though, a feeding-machine atmosphere has entered the home. *Working Mother* magazine, for example, carries ads that invite the working mother to cook "two-minute rice," a "five-minute chicken casserole," a "seven-minute Chinese feast." One ad features a portable phone to show that the working mother can make business calls while baking cookies with her daughter.

Another typical ad promotes cinnamon oatmeal cereal for breakfast by showing a smiling mother ready for the office in her square-shouldered suit, hugging her happy son. A caption reads, "In the morning, we are in such a rush, and my son eats so slowly. But with cinnamon oatmeal cereal, I don't even have to coax him to hurry up!" Here, the modern mothers seems to have absorbed the lessons of Frederick Taylor as she presses for efficiency at home because she is in a hurry to get to work. In a sense, though, Taylor's role has been turned over to her son who, eager for his delicious meal, speeds *himself* up. What induces the son to do this is the sugar in the cereal. For this child, the rewards of efficiency have jumped inside the cereal box and become a lump of sugar.

## A Third Shift: Time Work

As the first shift (at the workplace) takes more time, the second shift (at home) becomes more hurried and rationalized. The longer the workday at the office or plant, the more we feel pressed at home to hurry, to delegate, to delay, to forgo, to segment, to hyperorganize the precious remains of family time. Both their time deficit and what seem like solutions to it (hurrying, segmenting, and organizing) force parents, as shown in earlier chapters, to engage in a third shift—noticing, understanding, and coping with the emotional consequences of the compressed second shift.

Children respond to the domestic work-bred cult of efficiency in their own ways. Many, as they get older, learn to protest it. Parents at Amerco and elsewhere then have to deal with their children, as they act out their feelings about the sheer scarcity of family time. For example, Dennis Long, an engineer at Amerco, told me about what happened with his son from a previous marriage when he faced a project deadline at work. Whenever Dennis got home later than usual, four-year-old Joshua greeted him with a tantrum. As Dennis ruefully explained.

> Josh gets really upset when I'm not home. He's got it in his head that the first and third weeks of every month, he's with me, not with his mom. He hasn't seen me for a while, and I'm supposed to be there. When a project deadline like this one comes up and I come home late, he gets to the end of his rope. He gives me hell. I understand it. He's frustrated. He doesn't know what he can rely on.

This father did his "third shift" by patiently sitting down on the floor to "receive" Josh's tantrum, hearing him out, soothing him, and giving him some time. For a period of six months, Joshua became upset at almost any unexpected delay or rapid shift in the pace at which events were, as he saw it, supposed to happen. Figuring out what such delays or shifts in pace meant to Joshua became another part of Dennis Long's third shift.

Such episodes raise various questions: If Josh's dad keeps putting off their dates to play together, does it mean he doesn't care about Josh? Does Josh translate the language of time the same way his father does? What if time symbolizes quite different things to the two of them? Whose understanding counts the most? Sorting out such emotional tangles is also part of the third shift.

Ironically, many Amerco parents were challenged to do third-shift work by their children's reactions to "quality time." As one mother explained,

> Quality time is seven-thirty to eight-thirty at night, and then it's time for bed. I'm ready at seven-thirty, but Melinda has other ideas. As soon as quality time comes she wants to have her bath or watch TV; *no way*

is she going to play with Mommy. Later, when I'm ready to drop, *then* she's ready for quality time.

A busy doctor married to an Amerco executive offered a similar description of the disruption of her well-laid plan to have "special time" with her children:

> Normally, we pay our neighbor to drop Sam and Grace off at childcare at eight in the morning. Wednesday mornings I give the kids a supposed special treat. I drive them myself and stay and watch them for half an hour. I think of it as a great treat, but usually it's a disaster. Normally, they're pretty happy to be dropped off. But when I do it, they cry. They cling. They get hysterical. And here I am, thinking, "Isn't this great? 'Quality time.'"

In such situations, pressed parents often don't have time to sort through their children's responses. They have no space to wonder what their gift of time means. Or whether a parent's visit to daycare might seem to a child like a painfully prolonged departure. Is a gift of time what a parent wants to give, or what a child wants to receive? Such questions are often left unresolved.

Time-deficit "paybacks" lead to another kind of difficult emotional work. For example, like many salespeople at Amerco, Phyllis Ramey spent about a fifth of her work time traveling. She always kept in touch by phone with her husband and their two children—Ben, three, and Pete, five—and at each sales stop, she bought the boys gifts. Ben enjoyed them but thought little about them; Pete, on the other hand, fixated anxiously on "what mommy's bringing me"— a Tonka truck, a Batman cape, a bubble-making set. As Phyllis put it,

> When I call home and Pete gets on the phone, that's the first thing he'll ask me, "What are you bringing me?" Then he'll tell me what he wants, and he gets disappointed or mad if I don't bring just the right toy. I don't like Pete to care that much about toys. I don't like him to *demand* toys.

Phyllis believed that Pete "really needed more time" with her, and she sensed that she was buying him things out of guilt. Indeed, she talked and joked about guilt-shopping with coworkers. But in Pete's presence she had a hard time separating his anxiety about gifts from his relationship with her.

Amerco parents like Phyllis are not alone, of course. Spending on toys has soared from $6.7 billion in 1980 to $17.5 billion in 1995. According to psychologist Marilyn Bradford, preschoolers looking forward to Christmas ask for an average of 3.4 toys but receive on average 11.6. As employers buy growing amounts of time from employees, parents half-consciously "buy" this time from their children. But children rarely enter into these "trades" voluntarily, and parents are tempted to avoid the "time work" it takes to cope with their children's frustration.

Part of modern parenthood now includes coping with children's resistance to the tight-fitting temporal uniforms required when home becomes work and work becomes home. Like Janey King, some children don't finish their dances, and like Vicky King, some parents try desperately to avoid appeasing their children with special gifts or smooth-talking them with promises about the future.

But even the best of parents in such situations find themselves passing a systemwide speedup along to the most vulnerable workers on the line. It is children like Josh and Pete who signal most clearly the strains in the Taylorized home. Just as a company that is good to its workers need not worry about strikes, so a family without speedups could be less concerned about time-tantrums and might find little need for third-shift work. Of course, some children adapt quietly to the reversal of home and work, as do adults. But many children want more time with their parents than they get, and they protest the pace, the deadlines, the irrationality of "efficient" family life. Parents are then obliged to hear the children's protests, to experience their resentment, resistance, passive acquiescence, to try to assuage their frustrations, to respond to their stubborn demands or whining requests, and in general to control the damage done by a reversal of worlds. This unacknowledged third shift only adds to the feeling that life at home is hard work. Parents are becoming supervisors with stopwatches, monitoring meals and bedtimes and putting real effort into eliminating "wasted" time. If Charlie Chaplin's mechanized dance evoked a speedup in the Taylorized workplace, it is Janey King's interrupted dance that reveals the strains of the Taylorized home.

Children dawdle. Children refuse to leave places when it's time to go, or they insist on leaving places when it's still time to stay. Surely, this is part of the stop and go of childhood itself, but is it also a plea for more control over family time?

---

## Now that you've read

1. What is Hochschild's main argument? What evidence does she offer to support her argument? Do you find that evidence convincing? Why or why not?
2. What are some of the prices we pay to have careers *and* families?
3. What, if anything, should companies do to make it easier on families?

# SEQUENCE 5 ASSIGNMENTS

## Reading 1: Michael C. Murphy and James Archer, Jr., "Stressors on the College Campus: A Comparison of 1985 and 1993"

> Today's world, the U.S. economy, and the problems and experiences that students bring with them are not getting any less complex. Educators have an opportunity to teach students how to manage the many stressors with which they must deal. Educators also have a mandate to confront and change aspects of the campus environment that create stress.

### Prewriting

1. In a few sentences, explain what you understand the quotation above to mean.
2. In the past week, what has made you feel stress most intensely?
3. What are the ways in which you deal with stress?

### Writing assignment

Everyone has to deal with stress, but today's college student has to deal with a *lot* of stress. Write a brief essay in which you discuss the sources of stress for college students and what, if anything, should be done to help students cope with or minimize stress. Does Murphy and Archer's list of the most likely causes of stress make sense to you? What do you make of their claim that women feel more stress than men? On the basis of your experiences and observation, what seem to be the worst stress-causing problems? What are some of the ways you've seen your fellow students deal with stress? Should colleges divert funds from other programs to set up stress-management programs for students? Please draw on your own experience and observation, as well as Murphy and Archer's essay, in responding to this assignment.

## Reading 2: Michael Moffatt, "Coming of Age in a College Dorm"

> At first I mistook Undergraduate Cynical for a privileged form of truth, for what the undergraduates really thought among themselves when all their defenses were down. Eventually I realized that, as a code of spoken discourse, Undergraduate Cynical could be just as mandatory and just as coercive as other forms of discourse.

## *Prewriting*

1. Respond to the above quotation. What do you take the term *Undergraduate Cynical* to mean? Does this seem to be an accurate description of how students at your school express themselves?
2. What were your expectations of dorm life? What were your reactions to some of the things you read in Moffatt's essay?
3. What does dorm life offer a "typical" first-year college student? What are some of the drawbacks?

## *Writing assignment*

Write an essay in which you discuss the importance and relevance (or lack thereof) of dorm life to the undergraduate experience. Consider the Rutgers students' responses to Moffatt's "Martian on Earth" questions, as well as what your own responses would be. Do you see evidence of stress in the interactions among the students Moffatt describes? Also, reflect on the argument between Louis and Carrie. What are the key terms of their disagreement? Do you think gender or class might influence their perspectives? Where do you stand in relation to them?

## Reading 3: Anne Matthews, "The Night Campus"

About 70 percent of students do just fine in higher education; the other 30 percent are a major pain. It is hard to tell, on college applications, who will fall in which category.

## *Prewriting*

1. What do you take the above quotation from Matthews's piece to mean?
2. What stories of violence on campus have you heard?
3. What factors and/or groups of people does Matthews think are responsible for campus violence? List them and state whether you agree with her.

## *Writing assignment*

For this essay, consider the problem of violence on college campuses. To what extent is the problem caused by the 30 percent of students whom Matthews says are a "pain"? To what extent does the "Undergraduate Cynical" style that Moffatt describes or a "party hearty" ethic among students contribute to the problem? To what extent is stress a factor? Of the various factors Matthews discusses, which do you think are the most important? And finally, to what extent is the university responsible for making a campus safe at night? To what extent is it the students' responsibility to protect themselves? Draw on your observations and experience on your own campus to help you make your argument.

## Reading 4: Ellen Rosenberg, "Commuting"

> Very simply, college is not high school. Because you're home, it will only feel like you felt in high school because you're not living away. But every other aspect of commuter life can and will be worlds apart from what high school was . . . if you explore what's available to you and stay on campus long enough after classes to get involved.

### *Prewriting*

1. Respond in a few sentences to the above quotation from Rosenberg's piece.
2. What kinds of organizations and services are available for commuters on your campus?
3. If you are a commuter, how much do you feel a part of your campus community? If you are not a commuter, do you know people who are? Do you think they are missing out on anything by not living on campus?

### *Writing assignment*

College has traditionally been viewed as a period of transition in which students gain increasing independence from their families. Write an essay describing some of the ways in which college might serve that function for commuter students. (Base your comments on your own experience or on your observations or conjectures.) Then speculate on whether college life serves that function better for commuter students or for "traditional" students. If you can, draw on the previous readings in this sequence as well as on "Commuting."

## Readings 5 and 6: Sandy Smith Madsen, "A Welfare Mother in Academy" and "Family Made Graduation More Difficult"

> I have been, and will always think of myself as, a "welfare mother." Two years after my escape from an abusive marriage, I signed up for yet more abuse. I signed up for welfare. And I enrolled in academe. (Madsen)

> I can understand making a fuss when young people graduate because they are at the beginning of their careers, but a degree in "the classics" won't help this woman with the job she's held for 25 years. ("Family")

## Prewriting

1. What are the different ways in which Madsen is defining the word *abuse* in the quotation above?
2. What kind of emotional and financial support of your college ambitions have you received from your friends and loved ones?
3. Why is "Alice" so angry over her middle-aged relative's return to and graduation from college? What is your response?
4. What obstacles is Madsen having to face as she tries to stay in school? What, if anything, should be done to help her and others like her?

## Writing assignment

Write an essay in which you address some of the following questions: What does it take to balance all the demands of family, friends, peers, work, and school? Why is this balance so difficult to maintain? How are the demands different for "traditional" and "nontraditional" students? How are the demands placed on men different from those placed on women, and vice versa? What kinds of obstacles have you faced and what advice can you give others in similar situations? Be sure to offer specific examples and to draw on the readings for this assignment, as well as any of the previous readings that will help you build your argument.

## Reading 7: Arlie Russell Hochschild, "The Third Shift"

> Although work can complement—and, indeed, improve—family life, in recent decades it has largely competed with the family, and won. While the mass media so often point to global competition as the major story of the age, it is easy to miss the fact that corporate America's fiercest struggle has been with its local rival—the family.

## Prewriting

1. Respond briefly to the above quotation. Do you agree with the claim Hochschild makes in this passage? Why or why not?
2. After reading "The Third Shift," what are your goals for balancing your work life and your home life?
3. If you already have a family, is it difficult for your family to balance their schedules and find time to be together? Have you developed any strategies to help you cope with the conflicting demands on your time? If so, describe them.

### *Writing assignment*

Hochschild describes a corporate culture that says its employees can take advantage of "family-friendly" options but then balks when anyone actually tries to do so. She also describes people who find themselves so bewildered or exhausted by their complicated family lives that they actually prefer to spend more hours at work, where their lives are less stressful and they feel more appreciated. What do you make of these findings? Does anything from your own experience support or discredit them? How do you manage to balance your own commitments to work, school, friend, family, loved ones, fun time now? What are your own career goals, and how do you hope to achieve balance as you establish yourself in your career? Be sure to draw on "The Third Shift" and on other readings in this sequence.

## Final Project

Review the essays you've written for this sequence. What do they tell you about college life today, both for you and for your fellow students? Is it different now from how it was in the past? Are you able to strike a satisfactory balance among work, home, and student life? If not, what can you, or your school, do to improve your situation? Have the readings in this sequence taught you anything new about your fellow students? Have they changed your mind about anything? Have they reinforced your views about anything? Mine your essays for a specific issue you'd like to investigate in further detail, and formulate a concise thesis that you can use in a 15- to 20-page research paper. If you can't decide on a topic to investigate further, consider these questions:

What is dorm life like on your campus?

Is your campus safe?

Do students' career plans reflect a desire to balance careers with family or other life goals?

What do students at your school find most stressful about college life? What do they do to relieve their stress?

## Library Research Ideas

Try one or more of the following library research activities, or come up with your own ideas for library research to support your thesis.

1. Search print and electronic indexes of scholarly journals for articles on one of the issues covered in this sequence, and compare what you find to what the author from this sequence wrote. You might even find specific responses to some of the authors in this

sequence. (Arlie Russell Hochschild's work, for example, has received a lot of attention.) Ask your reference librarian for help if you need it.

2. Search the *Reader's Guide to Periodical Literature* for articles on helping welfare recipients get a college education.

3. Find fictional treatments of one of the issues covered in this sequence. Start with your library's online catalog. Also try searching the *MLA International Bibliography* and the *Humanities Index.*

## Field Research Ideas

Try one or more of the following field research ideas, or use your own field research ideas to get data to support your thesis.

1. Interview fellow students about the sources of stress in their lives. Compare responses from different target populations ("traditional" students versus older students with children, for example).

2. Interview college administrators or student services personnel about what your school is doing to ensure students' safety on campus or to help nontraditional students with outside family and work commitments.

3. Find out what sort of "family-friendly" policies your university offers its employees, and survey university workers to see whether they take advantage of these policies.

# College Athletes and Athletics

## Getting Started

This sequence focuses on college athletics. Whether as fans or players, a lot of Americans truly love college-level athletics. But even those who would describe themselves as indifferent are probably aware of some of the stories and myths revolving around college sports. In the readings that follow, Murray Ross in "Football Red and Baseball Green" asks us to consider the larger cultural narratives that sports tell. In "An End to Athletics Dorms," Drake Witham reports on how the special treatment of college athletes has become a hot-button issue on many campuses. Allen Guttmann's "Fair Play for Women?" challenges us to understand that gender differences call for a more complex solution to inequities than Title IX can provide. "Why Men Fear Women's Teams," by Kate Rounds, on the other hand, argues that America's failure to support more professional women's sports reveals profound prejudices in our culture. Leigh Montville playfully suggests adding the position of "Smart Kid" to popular sports in "This Isn't Such a Dumb Idea." And finally, Gary D. Funk's "The Dumb Jock: Fact or Fiction?" seriously addresses whether this stereotype is based on fact or results from longstanding prejudice.

Please reflect on your ideas about the role athletics plays in college life and respond to several of the following questions. I use the Getting Started questions as a preliminary exercise on the first day my class works on a particular sequence. Your teacher may also do this, or he or she may ask that you write out your responses either in a journal or in your notebook. Your teacher may use these questions as a jumping-off place for class discussion as well. No matter how you use these questions in your class, however, you'll still be able to draw on what you write here both in your contributions to class discussion and in your responses to the assignments that follow.

1. When you think of college athletes, what are the first images that come to mind?
2. What benefits do organized sports offer colleges in general? What do they offer yours in particular?
3. Are there any drawbacks to college-level athletics programs? What are they?
4. If you were to make generalizations about college athletes/athletics, what would they be? What would the exceptions to those generalizations be?
5. Where do our images of college athletics and athletes come from?

# READING 1

*Murray Ross*

# Football Red and Baseball Green

Murray Ross's essay, "Football Red and Baseball Green," appeared for the first time in *Chicago Review* in 1971 and was revised in 1993. Ross wants us to understand that sports in our culture are not just important; they're mythical. Sports participation and spectatorship, he argues, make it possible for us to participate in these myths. He's also interested in what sports reveal about our culture. Does his analysis make sense to you?

## Before you read

1. If you're a sports fan, which do you prefer—football or baseball? Why?
2. If you're not a sports fan, which do you dislike more—football or baseball? Why?
3. How do you define the word *myth*? For example, what would a "cultural myth" be?
4. What is the most popular sport on your campus? What do you think makes it most popular?

---

Every Superbowl ever played has rated among the top television draws of its year. By now, after nearly three decades, we know the game has a more than fair chance of being not so hot, some sort of mismatched rout. Even so, everyone—and I mean just about *everyone*—watches. This revelation is just one way of indicating how popular and compelling spectator sports are in this country. Americans, or American men anyway, seem to care about the games they watch as much as the Elizabethans cared about their plays, and I suspect for some of the same reasons. There is, in sport, some of the rudimentary drama found in popular theater: familiar plots, type characters, heroic and comic action spiced with new and unpredictable variations. And common to watching both activities is the sense of participation in a shared tradition and in shared fantasies. If sport exploits these fantasies without significantly transcending them, it seems no less satisfying for all that.

It is my guess that sport spectating involves something more than the vicarious pleasures of identifying with athletic prowess. I suspect that each sport contains a fundamental myth which it elaborates for its fans, and that our pleasure in watching such games derives in part from belonging briefly to the mythical world which the game and its players bring to life. I am especially interested in baseball and football because they are so popular and so uniquely *American;* they began here and unlike basketball they have not been widely exported. Thus whatever can be said, mythically, about these games would seem to apply to our culture.

Baseball's myth may be the easier to identify since we have a greater historical perspective on the game. It was an instant success during the Industrialization, and most probably it was a reaction to the squalor, the faster pace, and the dreariness of the new conditions. Baseball was old-fashioned right from the start; it seems conceived in nostalgia, in the resuscitation of the Jeffersonian dream. It established an artificial rural environment, one removed from the toil of an urban life, which spectators could be admitted to and temporarily breathe in. Baseball is a *pastoral* sport, and I think the game can be best understood as this kind of art. For baseball does what all good pastoral does—it creates an atmosphere in which everything exists in harmony.

Consider, for instance, the spatial organization of the game. A kind of controlled openness is created by having everything fan out from home plate, and the crowd sees the game through an arranged perspective that is rarely violated. Visually this means that the game is always seen as a constant, rather calm whole, and that the players and the playing field are viewed in relationship to each other. Each player has a certain position, a special area to tend, and the game often seems to be as much a dialogue between the fielders and the field as it is a contest between the players themselves: Will that ball get through the hole? Can that outfielder run under that fly? As a moral genre, pastoral asserts the virtue of communion with nature. As a competitive game, baseball asserts that the team which best relates to the playing field (by hitting the ball in the right places) will win.

Having established its landscapes, pastoral art operates to eliminate any reference to that bigger, more disturbing, more real world it has left behind. All games are to some extent insulated from the outside by having their own rules, but baseball has a circular structure as well which furthers its comfortable feeling of self-sufficiency. By this I mean that every motion of extension is also one of return—a ball hit outside is a *home* run, a full circle. Home—familiar, peaceful, secure—it is the beginning and end. You must go out but you must come back; only the completed movement is registered.

Time is a serious threat to any form of pastoral. The genre poses a timeless world of perpetual spring, and it does its best to silence the ticking of clocks which remind us that in time the green world fades into winter. One's sense of time is directly related to what happens in it, and baseball is so structured as to stretch out and ritualize whatever action it contains. Dramatic moments are few, and they are almost always isolated by the routine texture of normal play. It is certainly a game of climax and drama, but it is perhaps more a game of repeated and predictable action: the foul balls, the walks, the pitcher fussing around on the mound, the lazy fly ball to center field. This is, I think, as it should be, for baseball exists as an alternative to a world of too much action, struggle, and change. It is a merciful release from a more grinding and insistent tempo, and its time, as William Carlos Williams suggests, makes a virtue out of idleness simply by providing it:

> The crowd at the ball game
> is moved uniformly
> by a spirit of uselessness
> Which delights them. . .

Within this expanded and idle time the baseball fan is at liberty to become a ceremonial participant and a lover of style. Because the action is normalized, how something is done becomes as important as the action itself. Thus baseball's most delicate and detailed aspects are often, to the spectator, the most interesting. The pitcher's windup, the anticipatory crouch of the infielders, the quick waggle of the bat as it poises for the pitch—these subtle miniature movements are as meaningful as the home runs and the strikeouts. It somehow matters in baseball that all the tiny rituals are observed: The shortstop must kick the dirt and the umpire must brush the plate with his pocket broom. In a sense baseball is largely a continuous series of small gestures, and I think it characteristic that the game's most treasured moment came when Babe Ruth pointed to where he subsequently hit a home run.

Baseball is a game where the little things mean a lot, and this, together with its clean serenity, its open space, and its ritualized action, is enough to place it in a world of yesterday. Baseball evokes for us a past which may never have been ours, but which we believe was, and certainly that is enough. In the Second World War, supposedly, we fought for "Baseball, Mom, and Apple Pie," and considering what baseball means, that phrase is a good one. We fought then for the right to believe in a green world of tranquility and uninterrupted contentment, where the little things would count. But now the possibilities of such a world are more remote, and it seems that while the entertainment of such a dream has an enduring appeal, it is no longer sufficient for our fantasies. I think this may be why baseball is no longer our preeminent national pastime, and why its myth is being replaced by another more appropriate to the new realities (and fantasies) of our time.

Football, especially professional football, is the embodiment of a newer myth, one which in many respects is opposed to baseball's. The fundamental difference is that football is not a pastoral game; it is a heroic one. Football wants to convert men into gods; it suggests that magnificence and glory are as desirable as happiness. Football is designed, therefore, to impress its audience rather differently than baseball.

As a pastoral game, baseball attempts to close the gap between the players and the crowd. It creates the illusion, for instance, that with a lot of hard work, a little luck, and possibly some extra talent, the average spectator might well be playing, not watching. For most of us can do a few of the things the ball players do: catch a pop-up, field a ground ball, and maybe get a hit once in a while. As a heroic game, football is not concerned with a shared community of near-equals. It seeks almost the opposite relationship between its spectators and players, one which stresses the distance between them. We are not invited to identify with Thurman Thomas, Randall Cunningham, or any other of football's megaheroes any more than we are with Zeus. Football's heroes are systematically catapulted into Olympus; they are more than human. Commercial after commercial portrays them as giants of the earth, prodigies to be seen, properly, with awe. Most of us lesser beings could not begin to imagine ourselves playing their game without also imagining our instant humiliation and possible death. The players are that much bigger, that much faster than we are. Watching, we have enough problems figuring out what's going on. In baseball, most of what happens is what meets the eye, but in football each play involves twenty-two men acting simultaneously in combat: It's too much for a single pair of eyes to follow. So we now have two or three television commentators to explain the action as it unfolds, then another three at halftime to evaluate. Coaches have teams of spotters in the stands and hundreds of hours of videos to watch. There is a seemingly infinite proliferation of "meaningful" data; full comprehension remains on the horizon.

If football is distanced from its fans by its intricacy and "superhuman" play, it nonetheless remains a compelling and intense spectacle. Baseball, as I have implied, dissolves time and urgency in a green expanse, thereby creating a luxurious and peaceful sense of leisure. As is appropriate to a heroic enterprise, football reverses this procedure and converts space into time. The game is ideally played in an oval stadium, not in a "park," and the difference is the elimination of perspective. This makes football a perfect television game, because even at first hand it offers a flat, perpetually moving foreground (wherever the ball is). The eye in baseball viewing opens up; in football it zeroes in. There is no democratic vista in football, and spectators are not asked to relax, but to concentrate. You are encouraged to watch the drama, not a medley of ubiquitous gestures, and you are constantly reminded that this event is taking place in time. The third element in baseball is the field; in football this element is the clock. Traditionally heroes do reckon with time, and football players are no exceptions. Time in football is wound up inexorably until it reaches the breaking point in the last minutes of a close game. More often than not it is the clock which emerges as the real enemy, and it is the sense of time running out that regularly produces a pitch of tension uncommon in baseball.

A further reason for football's intensity is that the game is played like a war, with television putting the fans in the war room. The idea is to win by going through, around, or over the opposing team, and the battle lines, quite literally, are drawn on every play. Violence is somewhere at the heart of the game, and the combat quality is reflected in football's army language ("blitz," "trap," "zone," "bomb," "trenches," etc.). Coaches often sound like generals when they discuss their strategy. Woody Hayes, the legendary coach of Ohio State, explained his quarterback option play as if it had been conceived in the Pentagon: "You know," he said, "the most effective kind of warfare is siege. You have to attack on broad fronts. And that's all the option is—attacking on a broad front. You know General Sherman ran an option through the South."

Football like war is an arena for action, and like war football leaves little room for personal style. It seems to be a game which projects "character" more than personality, and for the most part football heroes, publicly, are a rather similar lot. They tend to become personifications rather than individuals, and, with certain exceptions, they are easily read emblematically as embodiments of heroic qualities such as "strength," "confidence," "grace," etc.— clich s really, but forceful enough when represented by the play of a Reggie White, a Troy Aikman, or a Jim Rice. Perhaps this simplification of personality results in part from the heroes' total identification with their mission, to the extent that they become more characterized by what they do than by what they intrinsically "are." At any rate football does not make as many allowances for the idiosyncrasies that baseball actually seems to encourage, and as a result there have been few football characters as eccentric and as recognizably human as, say, the pasta-loving Tommy Lasorda, the surly Jose Canseco, the exuberant Willie Mays.

A further reason for the underdeveloped qualities of football personalities, and one which g ts us to the heart of the game's modernity, is that football is very much a game of modern technology.

Football's action is largely interaction, and the game's complexity requires that its players mold themselves into a perfectly coordinated unit. The smoothness and precision of play execution are insatiable preoccupations, and most coaches believe that the team which makes the fewest mistakes will be the team that wins. Individual identity thus comes to be associated with the team or unit that one plays for to a much greater extent than in baseball. Yogi Berra was not so much a Yankee as a phenomenon unto himself, a man with his own language and a future as a cartoon character. But Mike Ditka, though personally forceful and particular, is mostly a Chicago Bear. Now, relieved of his stewardship, he's a publicly displaced identity, a lost man. The gods of football stand out not only because of their individual acts, but even more because they epitomize the style of the groups they belong to and represent. The archetypal ideal is Camelot, or what Camelot was advertised as: a group of men who function as equal parts of a larger whole, dependent on each other for total meaning.

The humanized machine as hero is something very new in sport, for in baseball anything approaching a machine has always been suspect. The famous Yankee teams of the fifties were almost flawlessly perfect, yet they never were especially popular. Their admirers took pains to romanticize their precision into something more natural than plain mechanics—Joe DiMaggio, for instance, became the "Yankee Clipper." Even so, most people seemed to want the Brooklyn Dodgers (the "bums") to thrash them in the World Series. One of the most memorable triumphs in recent decades— the victory of the Amazin' Mets in 1969—was memorable precisely because it was the triumph of a random collection of inspired rejects over the superbly skilled, fully integrated, and almost homogenized Baltimore Orioles. In baseball, machinery seems tantamount to villainy, whereas in football this smooth perfection is part of the unexpected integration a championship team must attain.

It is not surprising, really, that we should have a game which asserts the heroic function of a mechanized group, since we have become a country where collective identity is a reality. Yet football's collective pattern is only one aspect of the way in which it seems to echo our contemporary environment. The game, like our society, can be thought of as a cluster of people living under great tension in a state of perpetual flux. The potential for sudden disaster or triumph is as great in football as it is in our own age, and although there is something ludicrous in equating interceptions with assassinations and long passes with moonshots, there is also something valid and appealing in the analogies. It seems to me that football does successfully reflect those salient and common conditions which affect us all, and it does so with the end of making us feel better about them and our lot. For one thing, it makes us feel that something can be released and connected in all this chaos; out of the accumulated pile of bodies something can emerge—a runner breaks into the clear or a pass finds its way to a receiver. To the spectator, plays such as these are human and dazzling. They suggest to the audience what it has hoped for (and been told) all along, that technology is still a tool and not a master. Fans get living proof of this every time a long pass is completed; they appreciate that it is the result of careful planning, perfect integration, and an effective "pattern," but they see too that it is human and that what counts as well is man, his desire, his natural skill, and his "grace under pressure." Football metaphysically yokes heroic action and technology by violence to suggest that they are mutually supportive. It's a doubtful proposition, but given how we live, it has its attractions.

Football, like the space program, is a game in the grand manner. Homer would have chronicled it; Beowulf would have played fullback. Baseball's roots are at least as deep; it's a variation of the Satyr play, it's a feast of fools. But today their mythic resonance has been eroded by commercial success. Like so much else in America, their character has been modified by money.

More and more, both baseball and football are being played indoors on rugs in multipurpose spaces. It doesn't make good business sense to play outside where it might rain and snow and do terrible things; it isn't really prudent to play on a natural field that can be destroyed in a single afternoon; and why build a whole stadium or park that's good for only one game? The fans in these stadiums are constantly diverted by huge whiz-bang scoreboards that dominate and describe the action, while the fans at home are constantly being reminded by at least three lively sportscasters of the other games, the other sports, and the other shows that are coming up later on the same stations. Both pro football and pro baseball now play vastly extended seasons, so that the World Series now takes place on chilly October nights and football is well under way before the summer ends. From my point of view all this is regrettable, because these changes tend to remove the games from their intangible but palpable mythic contexts. No longer clearly set in nature, no longer given the chance to breathe and steep in their own special atmosphere, both baseball and football risk becoming demythologized. As fans we seem to participate a little less in mythic ritual these days, while being subjected even more to the statistics, the hype, and the salary disputes that proceed from a jazzed-up, inflated, yet somehow flattened sporting world—a world that looks too much like the one we live in all the time.

Still, there is much to be thankful for, and every season seems to bring its own contribution to mythic lore. Some people will think this nonsense, and I must admit there are good reasons for finding both games simply varieties of decadence.

In its preoccupation with mechanization, and in its open display of violence, football is the more obvious target for social moralists, but I wonder if this is finally more "corrupt" than the seductive picture of sanctuary and tranquility that baseball has so artfully drawn for us. Almost all sport is vulnerable to such criticism because it is not strictly ethical in intent, and for this reason there will always be room for puritans like the Elizabethan John Stubbes, who howled at the "wanton fruits which these cursed pastimes bring forth." As a longtime dedicated fan of almost anything athletic, I confess myself out of sympathy with most of this; which is to say, I guess, that I am vulnerable to those fantasies which these games support, and that I find happiness in the company of people who feel as I do.

A final note. It is interesting that the heroic and pastoral conventions which underlie our most popular sports are almost classically opposed. The contrasts are familiar: city versus country, aspirations versus contentment, activity versus peace, and so on. Judging from the rise of professional football, we seem to be slowly relinquishing that unfettered rural vision of ourselves that baseball so beautifully mirrors, and we have come to cast ourselves in a genre more reflective of a nation confronted by constant and unavoidable challenges. Right now, like the Elizabethans, we seem to share both heroic and pastoral yearnings, and we reach out to both. Perhaps these divided needs account in part for the enormous attention we as a nation now give to spectator sports. For sport provides one place where we can have our football and our baseball too.

---

### Now that you've read

1. Why, in general, do football players get more attention than other athletes? What would Murray Ross say?
2. In what ways do sports have "mythic" qualities, according to Ross?
3. What is the "fundamental myth" that football "elaborates for its fans"?
4. Ross writes, "No longer clearly set in nature, no longer given the chance to breathe and steep in their own special atmosphere, both baseball and football risk becoming demythologized." What do you take him to mean here?

## READING 2

*Drake Witham*

# An End to Athletics Dorms

Drake Witham's article originally appeared in *The Chronicle of Higher Education,* a weekly newspaper that focuses on issues related to higher education. Although his article specifically discusses Division I universities' efforts to integrate athletes into "regular" dormitories, it also points to another issue: the special treatment of athletes involved in the "elite" sports. Here Witham describes changes at a football powerhouse, the University of Florida, discussing both sides of the athletic dorms issue in the context of a larger concern—the special treatment of athletes. As you read, examine the evidence that Witham presents and come to your own decision.

### *Before you read*

1. How important is football on your campus?
2. Are football players treated in special ways, or are they treated pretty much like everyone else?
3. What are some of the arguments for housing athletes together? What are some of the reasons not to?

---

Mo Collins attended the University of Florida because he wanted to play football for a winner and be treated like a winner. Florida's football team is consistently among the best in the country, and the amenities, including Yon Hall, an athletes-only dormitory built right into Ben Hill Griffin Stadium, have always been first-rate as well.

But that changed this year, when Florida boarded up Yon Hall to comply with a National Collegiate Athletic Association rule that will prohibit athletics dormitories at Division I colleges after next July. The rule, which also forbids blocks of rooms made up of more than 49-per-cent athletes, was approved in 1991 as one of several changes aimed at treating athletes more like other students.

Toward that end, Florida moved the athletes into regular dormitories this fall.

Mr. Collins's new campus home has fresh paint and new carpeting. But his room is smaller, and he misses the camaraderie he shared with his teammates in Yon Hall, which provided an anchor to his hectic life as an athlete and a student, he says.

"I could spend a whole day right there, tutoring, eating meals, lifting weights," he says. "We could relate to each other because we had the same hours, the same problems."

## Cohesion or Isolation

Laments like his are common among players and coaches at the 24 Division I colleges that still have athletics dormitories, and at dozens of others that have athletes-only wings or floors. Housing athletes together builds team unity, they say, and makes it easier to arrange study halls and to enforce curfews.

"We think homogeneous living is important to the student-athletes," says Howard Schnellenberger, football coach at the University of Oklahoma. Mr. Schnellenberger, who had athletics dormitories built for his teams at the Universities of Miami and Louisville and inherited one at Oklahoma, says the unity created in the athletics dorms translated into victories on the football field.

While that cohesion has worked well for many coaches and athletes, N.C.A.A. leaders worry that it came at a high cost: isolation for the athletes. When a third of Division I football and basketball players who were required to live together expressed feelings of isolation in a 1987–88 N.C.A.A. survey, the division's members voted overwhelmingly to abolish athletics dormitories.

But if the official aim of the ban was to integrate athletes more fully into campus life, stemming their misbehavior was the N.C.A.A.'s unstated but overriding goal. The college presidents who fought to get rid of the dorms hoped to cut down on the criminal acts and other incidents that have occurred in athletics dormitories, which *Sports Illustrated* called a "cross between *Animal House* and *Animal Farm*" where "anything goes and some students are more equal than others."

As the effective date of the ban approaches, however, it seems unlikely that abolishing athletics dormitories will stop players from misbehaving; reports of incidents involving college athletes continue to appear frequently. But officials at some institutions that already have abandoned athletes-only housing say the change has eased the feelings of isolation felt by many athletes.

"Would I want a child to live in an athletic dorm? No," says Eugene F. Corrigan, the N.C.A.A.'s president and the commissioner of the Atlantic Coast Conference. "The world is bigger than a football team."

That's a tough sell in many places around the South, where football reigns and athletics dormitories got their start. Paul Bryant, the University of Alabama's legendary former football coach, set up a place for his players to live in 1962. "It's the way it's supposed to be," says Jack Rutledge, a former Alabama player who has run the dormitory—known as Bryant Hall—since 1972.

## Increasingly Lavish

In the late 1960s and the '70s, other institutions built athletics dormitories, which as time went on became increasingly lavish, with larger rooms and semi-private baths. The University of Kentucky moved its basketball team into a mansion in 1979.

As was the case with stadiums and weight rooms, the competition to build bigger and better athletics dormitories turned into an "arms race," says Thomas C. Hansen, commissioner of the Pacific-10 Conference. "Once one of these institutions has a palatial dorm, all the other institutions are quickly collecting money to build one."

In an attempt to minimize the recruiting advantage that some colleges gained by building luxurious residence halls, the N.C.A.A. in 1983 adopted a rule that required athletics dormitories to be comparable to other housing on campus. The rule was virtually ignored.

## Incidents of Misbehavior

What could not be ignored were the many incidents of athletes' misbehavior. Within a month in 1989, individual residents of the University of Oklahoma's Bud Wilkinson Hall were arrested in a gang rape, a shooting, and drug trafficking. At the University of Miami in the 1980s, police often were summoned to Foster Hall, which housed only athletes at the time, to break up fights and arrest football players on various charges. Last spring, a football player at the University of Arkansas pleaded guilty to sexual misconduct after being charged with raping a woman at Bud Walton Hall.

"Bad reputation—I think that was the impetus behind this for the presidents," says the N.C.A.A.'s Mr. Corrigan. "They don't like things that cause embarrassment."

"I don't think there ever should have been athletics dorms," says Charles E. Young, chancellor of the University of California at Los Angeles. "I don't think it was good putting together dorms where 100 per cent of the people are strong and vigorous. You don't get the sort of balance."

Forcing athletes to live together also led to isolation, the N.C.A.A.'s 1987–88 study found. While 76 per cent of the athletes who were required to live together liked the arrangement, many of them also said they had frequent or occasional feelings of isolation. Supporters of the ban on athletics dormitories believed that separate living quarters contributed to that feeling. Division I delegates approved the ban overwhelmingly at the N.C.A.A.'s 1991 convention.

## "Difficult to Disguise"

Unlike the largely ignored rule on comparable housing, N.C.A.A. officials and athletics directors agree that the ban on athletics dormitories will be enforced.

"It seems to me that it would be difficult to disguise an athletic dorm," says Charles E. Smrt, an N.C.A.A. director of enforcement. Several athletics directors agree that word would get out if a college continued to maintain such a residence hall.

But 10 months before the prohibition takes effect, dozens of colleges are clinging to some form of athletes-only housing. They plan to comply with the rule by next August, but will do so in different ways.

Some colleges gradually are moving non-athletes into athletics dorms, hoping to conform to the N.C.A.A. rule by having non-athletes make up 51 per cent of their halls' residents by next August. The institutions following this course are trying to keep as many first- and second-year athletes together as possible.

That is the case at Louisiana State University, where Ronnie Haliburton, who played football and lived in an athletics dormitory, is finishing his business degree at the university after a stint in the National Football League.

He is once again living in Broussard Hall, where L.S.U. has begun moving other students in with the athletes. "I really don't like it. I don't think it has the closeness you need," he says. "Football players have different schedules."

Other universities, like Florida, plan to spread athletes all over the campus. "If you're going to integrate, you don't do it at 49 per cent," says James C. Grimm, the university's housing director.

Meeting the N.C.A.A. requirement by introducing non-athlete students into athletics dorms can pose problems. Colleges may have trouble keeping the proportion of non-athletes in the residence hall above 49 per cent, and some may even have a hard time finding students willing to live among dozens of athletes.

"Not too many of our students want to move into the athletics dorm," says Monroe Harrison, housing director at the University of Mississippi. Next year, 49 per cent of the residents in Kinard Hall,which is now an athletics dormitory, are to be athletes.

## A Curfew and Strict Rules

When the University of Arkansas at Fayetteville tried to market its athletics dorm to students two years ago, no one volunteered. "What surprised me most is that it's the only dorm which as a suite arrangement, with two rooms to a bathroom," says Claire Goode, assistant director for residence life. "That's something the students beg us for. Yet they still would not sign up."

Students may have been deterred by last year's sexual assault and several other incidents in Walton Hall, she says. But a curfew and rules that prohibit smoking, drinking, and female visitation may have discouraged them as well, she says.

### Halls for Honors Students

As the ban on athletics dormitories is about to take effect, halls for honors students, foreign students, and students who share academic interests are proliferating. "It's a way to make the campus smaller for the students," says Pat Mielke, housing director at the University of Maryland at College Park.

Mr. Schnellenberger and other opponents of the ban on athletics housing note that trend with some irony. He doesn't understand why athletics dorms are being banned "when universities are going the other way with honors students, engineering students, and people with like interests." Why is segregated housing so distasteful for athletes, he asks, when the "reverse might be true for other students?"

Mr. Hansen, of the Pacific-10, cites a primary difference. Athletes typically have been required to live in athletics dorms, while other specialized residence halls are voluntary. Besides, he says, "Even if we're bucking the trend on campuses, we're going in the right direction" for athletes.

### "A Losing Battle"

Officials at the University of Tulsa agree. When they began integrating non-athletes into the athletics residence hall, neither the athletes nor other students liked it, says Chuck Colby, the student housing director.

But now, "exit interviews show that 95 per cent of the athletes were pleased with the change," says Barry Kinsey, a sociology professor at Tulsa who headed the committee that recommended the change. "A lot of schools are still fighting it, but it's a losing battle. It should be a losing battle. Why would anyone want to separate their athletes?"

Still, Tulsa encountered one major problem in making the transition: "We were playing musical beds trying to find enough seven foot beds for our athletes," says Mr. Colby. The university built a device that extended regular bed frames by 12 inches, but residence halls staff members are still lugging around the seven-foot versions.

After four years, he says, that appears to be about the only glitch in the process.

### *Now that you've read*

1. What are some of the key arguments for and against special housing for athletes, according to Witham?
2. Now that you've read Drake Witham's article, do you think you'd want to live in an athletes' dorm if you were an athlete? Why or why not?
3. Mo Collins, a football player for the University of Florida, is quoted as saying, "I could spend a whole day right there, tutoring, eating meals, lifting weights." What is your response? How is this a good thing? How is it not?

## READING 3

*Allen Guttmann*

# Fair Play for Women?

Allen Guttmann teaches American Studies at Amherst College. In "Fair Play for Women?" he raises complicated questions about the factors involved in placing men and women college athletes on equal ground. His article argues that there are no easy answers for those who seek gender equity in college sports—and that perhaps there are no answers at all. See whether you agree with Guttmann's arguments regarding Title IX and women's increasing participation in college sports.

### Before you read

1. How important are sports on your campus?
2. How important are women's sports on your campus?
3. Have you ever played an organized sport? What kind of support did you get from your school? Did you feel good about that support?
4. What do you predict about the success of professional women's sports as represented, for example, by the Women's National Basketball Association and the U.S. Women's Soccer Association?

It is doubtful that sports participation was an important consideration in the legislative battles that culminated in the passage of Title IX of the Education Act of 1972, but the increases in participation in women's interscholastic and intercollegiate sports have certainly been abetted by legal changes. Title IX made discrimination on the basis of gender illegal in all institutions receiving federal support: "No person . . . shall, on the basis of sex, be excluded from participation in, be denied the benefits of, or be subjected to discrimination under any educational programs or activities receiving federal financial assistance." That the inequalities between men's and women's programs were gross is undeniable. The Syracuse, New York, school board's 1969 budget for extracurricular sports allocated $90,000 to the boys' teams and $200 to the girls'; when money grew tight, the board eliminated the girls' budget. At the University of New Mexico, the 1970–71 budget for men's sports was $527,000 and for women's sports $9,150. In comparison to the University of Washington's budget, New Mexico's was wildly feminist: in Seattle in 1973–74, the men received $2,582,000 and the women $18,000. In response to moral and legal pressure, Washington increased the women's 1974–75 budget to $200,000.

That Title IX has made a difference can also be seen in the before-and-after legal judgments. When Susan Hollander of Hamden, Connecticut, sued her school board for the right to run with the boys' cross-country team because there was no girls' team, John Clark Fitz-Gerald of New Haven Superior Court ruled that

> our younger male population has not become so decadent that boys will experience a thrill defeating girls in running contests. . . . It could well be that many boys would feel compelled to forgo entering track events if they were required to compete with girls. . . . With boys vying with girls . . . the challenge to win and the glory of achievement, at least for many boys, would lose incentive and become nullified. Athletic competition builds character in our boys. We do not need that kind of character in our girls.

In *Gregorio* v. *Board of Education of Asbury Park* (1971), which was also decided before the passage of Title IX, the Superior Court of New Jersey ruled that girls had no right to join the boys' tennis team merely because there was no girls' team. After the new law came into effect, the U.S. Court of Appeals for the 6th District of Michigan ruled, in *Morris* v. *Michigan Board of Education* (1973), that girls had the right to try out for the boys' tennis team even when there was also a girls' team. The drive toward equality was partially blocked, however, when the Supreme Court decided, in *Grove City College* v. *Bell* (1984), that illegal discrimination within a single department was not grounds for action against an entire college or university. If the geologists refuse to hire women, they are liable to lose their own federal grants, but their colleagues in physical education will continue to be funded.

Although Title IX has forced changes, it has not wrought miracles. Walter Byers of the NCAA lobbied hard against Title IX because it spelled "the possible doom of intercollegiate sports." As the bill approached a final vote, the NCAA fought for Senator John Tower's amendment, which would have exempted the "revenue-producing" sports, most of which turn out to be men's sports. The lobbying failed, but most athletic departments are controlled by men and many continue to resist full implementation of the law.

Debates continue on the meaning of equality. The radical view is that parity must be calculated on the basis of the male/female ratio of the entire student body; if 52 percent of the *students* are women, female athletes should receive 52 percent of the funding.

The more moderate view, accepted by the Department of Education, is that the males and females actually participating in sports form the relevant population: if 30 percent of the *athletes* are female, women's sports should receive 30 percent of the money. Having failed to prevent the enactment of Title IX, the NCAA has been less than Draconian in its enforcement efforts. In the spring of 1984, the organization ruled that a school's failure to equalize the number of male and female teams would be punished by a ban on a national competition—for the women's teams. One suspects that some NCAA members are poor losers.

Debates continue about the opportunity for women to play on men's teams. Many male athletes still feel that their masculinity is undermined by women who outperform them. When Jan Merrill, a middle-distance runner, ran against eight men in a two-mile race in 1979, she came in fifth, which so unnerved Fitchburg College coach Jim Sheehan that he cried out, "I'd die before I would ever be beaten by a woman." Of the Auburn University student whom Becky Birchmore defeated while a member of the University of Georgia men's tennis team, Coach Dan Magill lamented, "It ruined him. I really wish I hadn't done it." Ellen Cornish of Frederick, Maryland, had no chance to ruin the lives of the boys from Thomas Johnson High School; she was dragged from the track before she broke the tape.

Even if one feels that male athletes who are defeated by female athletes will have to live with their fates, other questions remain to be answered. Federal law is currently interpreted to mean that girls whose high school have no girls' tennis team have the right to play on the boys' team, but this may not be the best solution. Most of the girls who play on boys' teams are liable to perform at a level below that of their male teammates. Does this cause the girls psychological damage? And what is the equitable solution to the dilemma of boys who want to join the girls' team because their school has no boys' team in their chosen sport? This may seem like a foolish question, but National Public Radio for August 31, 1986, broadcast a report from Annapolis High School, where two boys have requested to be allowed to join the girls' field hockey team.

On average, men are taller and heavier than women, have faster reaction times, more acute vision, better spatial perception, and greater muscular strength. Women, on the other hand, are more flexible than men and surpass men at very long distance running and swimming. With these physiological facts in mind, Jane English has suggested that we "should develop a variety of sports in which a variety of physical types can expect to excel." If the sports in which women outperform men were as salient in the public's imagination as the sports in which men have the physical advantage, then women would more likely be perceived as men's physical equals.

Through their superiority in these "alternative sports" women would have an opportunity to gain in self-respect, which English describes as a "basic benefit" of sports which should be available to all women. Whether such sports can realistically be expected to attain the prestige and popularity of baseball, basketball, football, ice hockey, and other male-dominated sports is, however, questionable.

Some feminists have stressed the cultural factors behind the physical differentials and have concluded that women do not need alternate sports because women have the undeveloped physical potential to equal men's performances in the modern sports now dominated by male athletes. These feminists are correct to assert that socialization, rather than genetic endowment, explains why the average American woman attains her maximum strength at the age of twelve and a half while the strength of the average man continues to increase into his twenties, but it is unlikely that cultural factors can account for *all* the observed gender differences in strength and in sports performance. In official contests (as opposed to recreational situations) a commitment to equality dictates that, as a general rule, men be matched against men and women against women. The ideal legal solution therefore takes into account physical differences when these differences are relevant to athletic performance.

Finally, ethical questions arise for which there are now no satisfactory legal answers. Can those who condemn boxing as brutal and dangerous welcome the entry of women into the ring? Should we rejoice that some women now have the chance to suffer the brain damage that is the boxer's occupational hazard? One might respond that boxing should be made illegal for both sexes, but other questions remain. Is the development of female bodybuilding an indication that women are determined to be strong and independent, as proponents say? Or is it a humiliating sign that they merely wish to imitate men? What is the moralist to make of the use of anabolic steroids by women who seek greater muscle mass than can be obtained by Nautilus workouts alone? Putting the question more generally, *are* there physical and psychological differences between males and females that might allow women to create humane alternatives to some of the distortions and abuses of modern sports?

---

### Now that you've read

1. What do you see as Allen Guttmann's purpose in writing this essay?
2. What is your position in relation to one or two of the issues Guttmann raises?

3. Do you know anyone who has benefitted from Title IX? Anyone who has suffered?

4. Guttmann asks at the end of his essay, "Putting the question more generally, *are* there physical and psychological differences between males and females that might allow women to create humane alternatives to some of the distortions and abuses of modern sports?" What are some of Guttmann's underlying assumptions in asking this question? How do you respond?

# READING 4

*Kate Rounds*

# Why Men Fear Women's Teams

Given the existence of the Women's National Basketball Association and the success of the U.S. Women's Soccer Team, perhaps Kate Rounds's essay "Why Men Fear Women's Teams" is a bit out of date. However, many women athletes would still agree with much of what she says about the status of women's athletics in this country. Rounds is concerned about the scarcity of opportunities for women athletes once they leave the college campus. She has harsh things to say about the roots of discrimination against women athletes on the professional level.

### *Before you read*

1. What are your favorite sports?
2. What are your favorite women's sports?
3. Did you come up with different answers for Questions 1 and 2? If so, why do you think you didn't include any women's sports in your answer to Question 1?
4. What does participation in athletic competition offer men? What does it offer women?
5. Why are women's sports generally less well attended than men's? When there are exceptions (such as gymnastics and ice skating), what are the reasons for those exceptions?

---

Picture this. You're flipping through the channels one night, and you land on a local network, let's say ABC. And there on the screen is a basketball game. The players are sinking three-pointers, slam-dunking, and doing the usual things basketball players do. They're high-fiving each other, patting one another on the butt, and then sauntering to the locker room to talk about long-term contracts.

Now imagine that the players aren't men. They're women, big sweaty ones, wearing uniforms and doing their version of what guys thrive on—bonding. So far, this scene is a fantasy and will remain so until women's professional team sports get corporate sponsors, television exposure, arenas, fan support, and a critical mass of well-trained players.

While not enough fans are willing to watch women play traditional team sports, they love to watch women slugging it out on roller-derby rinks and in mud-wrestling arenas. Currently popular is a bizarre television spectacle called *American Gladiators,* in which women stand on pastel pedestals, wearing Lycra tights and brandishing weapons that look like huge Q-Tips. The attraction obviously has something to do with the "uniforms."

The importance of what women athletes wear can't be underestimated. Beach volleyball, which is played in the sand by bikini-clad women, rates network coverage while traditional court volleyball can't marshal any of the forces that would make a women's pro league succeed.

It took awhile, but women were able to break through sexist barriers in golf and tennis. Part of their success stemmed from the sports themselves—high-end individual sports that were born in the British Isles and flourished in country clubs across the U.S. The women wore skirts, makeup, and jewelry along with their wristbands and warm-up jackets. The corporate sponsors were hackers themselves, and the fan—even men—could identify with these women; a guy thought that if he hit the ball enough times against the barn door, he too could play like Martina. And women's purses were equaling men's. In fact, number-one-ranked Steffi Graf's prize money for 1989 was $1,963,905 and number-one-ranked Stefan Edberg's was $1,661,491.

By contrast, women's professional team sports have failed spectacularly. Since the mid-seventies, every professional league—softball, basketball, and volleyball—has gone belly-up. In 1981, after a four-year struggle, the Women's Basketball League (WBL), backed by sports promoter Billy Byrne, folded. The league was drawing fans in a number of cities, but the sponsors weren't there. TV wasn't there, and nobody seemed to miss the spectacle of a few good women fighting for a basketball.

Or a volleyball, for that matter. Despite the success of bikini volleyball, an organization called MLV (Major League Volleyball) bit the dust in March of 1989 after nearly three years of struggling for sponsorship, fan support, and television exposure. As with pro basketball, there was a man behind women's professional volleyball, real estate investor Robert (Bat) Batinovich. Batinovich admits that, unlike court volleyball, beach volleyball has a lot of "visual T & A mixed into it."

What court volleyball does have, according to former MLV executive director Lindy Vivas, is strong women athletes. Vivas is assistant volleyball coach at San Jose State University. "The United States in general," she says, "has problems dealing with women athletes and strong, aggressive females. The perception is you have to be more aggressive in team sports than in golf and tennis, which aren't contact sports. Women athletes are looked at as masculine and get the stigma of being gay."

One former women's basketball promoter, who insists on remaining anonymous, goes further. "You know what killed women's sports?" he says. "Lesbians. This cost us in women's basketball. But I know there are not as many lesbians now unless I'm really blinded. We discourage it, you know. We put it under wraps."

People in women's sports spend a lot of time dancing around the "L" word, and the word "image" pops up in a way it never does in men's sports. Men can spit tobacco juice, smoke, and even scratch their testicles on national television and get away with it.

Bill Byrne, former WBL promoter, knows there isn't a whole lot women can get away with while they're beating each other out for a basketball. "In the old league," he says, "my partner, Mike Connors, from *Mannix*—his wife said, 'Let's do makeup on these kids.' And I knew that the uniforms could be more attractive. We could tailor them so the women don't look like they're dragging a pair of boxer shorts down the floor."

The response from the athletes to this boy talk is not always outrage. "Girls in women's basketball now are so pretty," says Nancy Lieberman-Cline. "They're image-conscious." The former Old Dominion star, who made headlines as Martina's trainer, played with the men's U.S. Basketball League, the Harlem Globetrotters Tour (where she met husband Tim Cline), and with the Dallas Diamonds of the old WBL. "Everyone used to have short hair," she says. "Winning and playing was everything. I wouldn't think of using a curling iron. Now there are beautiful girls out there playing basketball."

Lieberman-Cline says doesn't mind making the concession. "It's all part of the process," she says. "You can't be defensive about everything."

Bill Byrne is so certain that women's professional basketball can work that he's organized a new league, the Women's Pro Basketball League, Inc. (WPBL), set to open its first season shortly. Byrne talks fast and tough, and thinks things have changed for the better since 1981 when the old league went under. "Exposure is the bottom word," he says. "If you get plenty of TV exposure, you'll create household names, and you'll find arenas. It takes the tube. But I'll get the tube this time because the game of TV has changed. You have cable now. You have to televise home games to show people a product."

There's no doubt that many athletes in the women's sports establishment are leery of fast-talking guys who try to make a buck off women's pro sports, especially when the women themselves don't profit from those ventures. In the old league, finances were so shaky that some players claim they were never paid.

"We weren't getting the gate receipts," says Lieberman-Cline. "They'd expect 2,000, get only 400, and then they'd have to decide to pay the arena or pay the girls, and the girls were the last choice. There was a lot of mismanagement in the WBL, though the intent was good." She also has her doubts about the new league: "There are not enough things in place to make it happen, not enough owners, arenas, TV coverage, or players. It's going to take more than optimism to make it work."

Given the track record of women's professional team sports in this country, it's not surprising that the national pastime is faring no better. When Little League was opened to girls by court order in 1974, one might have thought that professional women's baseball could not be far behind. Baseball is a natural for women. It's not a contact sport, it doesn't require excessive size or strength—even little guys like Phil Rizzuto and Jose Lind can play it—and it's actually an individual sport masquerading as a team sport. Still, in recent years, no one's taken a serious stab at organizing a women's professional league.

In 1984, there was an attempt to field a women's minor-league team. Though the Sun Sox had the support of baseball great Hank Aaron, it was denied admission to the Class A Florida State League. The team was the brainchild of a former Atlanta Braves vice president of marketing, Bob Hope. "A lot of the general managers and owners of big-league clubs were mortified," Hope says, "and some players said they wouldn't compete against women. It was male ego or something."

Or something, says softball hall-of-famer Donna Lopiano. "When girls suffer harassment in Little League, that's not exactly opening up opportunities for women," she says. "Girls don't have the access to coaching and weight training that boys have. Sports is a place where physiological advantages give men power, and they're afraid of losing it. Sports is the last great bastion of male chauvinism. In the last eight years, we've gone backward, not only on gender equity but on civil rights."

Women of color still face barriers that European American women don't, particularly in the areas of coaching and refereeing. But being a woman athlete is sometimes a bond that transcends race. "We're all at a handicap," says Ruth Lawanson, an African American who played volleyball with MLV. "It doesn't matter whether you're an Asian, Mexican, black or white."

Historically, baseball and softball diamonds have not been very hospitable to black men and any women. Despite the fact that even men's softball is not a crowd pleaser, back in 1976, Billie Jean King and golfer Jane Blalock teamed up with ace amateur softball pitcher

Joan Joyce to form the International Women's Professional Softball Association (IWPSA). Five years later, without sponsorship, money, or television, the league was history.

Billie Jean King has her own special attachment to the team concept. As a girl, she wanted to be a baseball player, but her father gave her a tennis racket, knowing that there wasn't much of a future for a girl in baseball. The story is especially touching since Billie Jean's brother, Randy Moffitt, went on to become a pitcher with the San Francisco Giants. But even as a tennis player, Billie Jean clung to the team idea. She was the force behind World Team Tennis, which folded in 1978, and is currently the chief executive officer of TeamTennis, now entering its eleventh season with corporate sponsorship.

On the face of it, TeamTennis is a bizarre notion because it takes what is a bred-in-the-bones individual sport and tries to squeeze it into a team concept. It has the further handicap of not really being necessary when strong women's and men's professional tours are already in place.

In the TeamTennis format, all players play doubles as well as singles. Billie Jean loves doubles, she says, because she enjoys "sharing the victory." What also distinguishes TeamTennis from the women's and men's pro tours is fan interaction. Fans are encouraged to behave as if watching a baseball or basketball game rather than constantly being told to shut up and sit down as they are at pro tour events like the U.S. Open. The sense of team spirit among the players—the fact that they get to root for one another—is also attracting some big names. Both Martina Navratilova and Jimmy Connors have signed on to play TeamTennis during its tiny five-week season, which begins after Wimbledon and ends just before the U.S. Open.

But you have to go back almost 50 years to find a women's professional sports team that was somewhat successful—though the conditions for that success were rather unusual. During World War II, when half the population was otherwise engaged, women were making their mark in the formerly male strongholds of welding, riveting—and baseball. The All-American Girls Professional Baseball League (AAGPBL) fielded such teams as the Lassies, the Belles, and the Chicks on the assumption that it was better to have "girls" playing than to let the national pastime languish. The league lasted a whopping 12 years after its inception in 1943.

The success of this sandlot venture, plagued as it was by the simple-hearted sexism of the forties (the women went to charm school at night), must raise nagging doubts in the mind of the woman team player of the nineties. Can she triumph only in the absence of men?

It may be true that she can triumph only in the absence of competition from the fiercely popular men's pro leagues, which gobble up sponsorship, U.S. network television, and the hearts and minds of male fanatics. The lack of male competition outside the United States may be partly responsible for the success of women's professional team sports in Europe, Japan, South America, and Australasia. Lieberman-Cline acknowledges that Europe provides a more hospitable climate for women's pro basketball. "Over there, they don't have as many options," she says. "We have Broadway plays, movies, you name it. We're over-indulged with options."

Bruce Levy is a 230-pound bespectacled accountant who escaped from the Arthur Andersen accounting firm 11 years ago to market women's basketball. "It's pretty simple," he says. "People overseas are more realistic and enlightened. Women's basketball is not viewed as a weak version of men's. If Americans could appreciate a less powerful, more scientific, team-oriented game, we'd be two-thirds of the way toward having a league succeed."

Levy, who represents many women playing pro basketball abroad, says 120 U.S. women are playing overseas and making up to $70,000 in a seven-month season. They include star players like Teresa Edwards, Katrina McClain, and Lynette Woodward. "A player like Teresa Weatherspoon, everybody recognizes her in Italy," he says. "No one in the U.S. knows her. If there were a pro league over here, I wouldn't be spending all day on the phone speaking bad Italian and making sure the women's beds are long enough. I'd just be negotiating contracts."

Levy claims that U.S. businesswomen aren't supporting women's team sports. "In Europe," he says, "the best-run and most publicized teams are run by women who own small businesses and put their money where their mouth is. "Joy Burns, president of Sportswomen of Colorado, Inc., pleads no contest. "Businesswomen here are too conservative and don't stick their necks out," she says. MLV's Bat Batinovich, who says he's "disappointed" in U.S. businesswomen for not supporting women's team sports, figures an investor in MLV should have been willing to lose $200,000 a year for five years. Would Burns have done it? "If I'm making good financial investments, why should I?"

The prospects for women's professional team sports don't look bright. The reasons for the lack of financial support go beyond simple economics and enter the realm of deep-rooted sexual bias and homophobia. San Jose State's Lindy Vivas says men who feel intimidated by physically strong women have to put the women down. "There's always a guy in the crowd who challenges the women when he wouldn't think of going one-on-one with Magic Johnson or challenging Nolan Ryan to a pitching contest."

Softball's Donna Lopiano calls it little-boy stuff: "Men don't want to have a collegial, even-steven relationship with women. It's like dealing with cavemen."

---

## Now that you've read

1. Do men fear women's teams, according to Rounds?
2. What is Rounds's argument?
3. What evidence does she offer to support her argument?
4. How do you stand in relation to her charge that homophobia is one of the reasons why women's athletics is not as well supported as men's?
5. Do you think she counts women's gymnastics and ice skating in her definition of athletics? Explain your answer.

# READING 5

*Leigh Montville*

# This Isn't Such a Dumb Idea

In this short, humorous piece from *Sports Illustrated,* Leigh Montville satirizes a number of our attitudes about athletes and intellectuals. As so often in satire, the humor teaches us something about ourselves—in this case, our idolization of athletes. What is your initial response to Montville's "idea"?

### Before you read

1. Do athletes receive special treatment on your campus? If so, what forms?
2. Do "smart" students receive special treatment? If so, what forms?
3. Why does our culture tend to look up to athletes so much?
4. What would it take for "smart kids" to receive the same kind of attention lavished on athletes?

---

I've figured out a new rule for all sports. I call it the Smart Kid Rule. I think it will revolutionize college athletics. I think it will return a sense of dignity to the pros that has been disappearing with each Dennis Rodman kick to the groin, with each Robbie Alomar expectoration, with each billion-dollar contract handed to a true knucklehead. I think this rule, done right, can change the fabric of American life.

The Smart Kid Rule.

How does it work?

Every team in every sport has to have a designated Smart Kid. He (or she) is a genius, a scholastic whizbang. He (or she) is a full-fledged member of the team, wearing the entire uniform, the skates in hockey, the pads in football, the battling helmet with the earflap in baseball. There's a special place for him (or her) at the end of the bench. Maybe next to a pile of books and a good reading lamp. The Smart Kid Place.

The Smart Kid doesn't see action often. He (or she) reads, does a little homework, maybe types a thesis. But then, suddenly, if the game ends in a tie: Overtime! Extra innings! That's when the Smart Kid comes into play. Instead of the present system, a shaky way to settle matters because everybody is tired from playing an entire

game, we have a Battle of Smart Kids. Great drama. Great theater.
The best.

How so?

The referee stands in the middle of the court or field or ice or
whatever and announces a topic. The Smart Kid from each team
runs off the bench to answer a question. Or maybe a series of five or
10 questions. The team whose Smart Kid correctly answers the most
questions wins the game. Sometimes we get strung out for a long
time in sudden death as right answer matches right answer. The fans
go crazy at the end. They tear down the goalposts, cut down the
nets, carry the Smart Kid on their shoulders. The Smart Kid is the
hero. Sort of like the Kid Who Kicks the Winning Field Goal.

Can you imagine the change this rule would bring to sports?

Let's see. The game would be close. The camera would focus on
the Smart Kid. The announcers would say, "Look at how calm So-and-
So, the Memphis Smart Kid, is. He just sits there, reading his
Descartes with the game on the line. How does he do it? And there's
So-and-So of Louisville. What's he doing on that personal computer?"

Every college would need Smart Kids, so there would be Smart
Kids recruiting. There would be scholarships. Bob Knight and Jerry
Tarkanian and Tom Osborne and Bobby Bowden would be running
around the country trying to find the smartest Smart Kids. The pros
would need Smart Kids, so there would be bidding wars. There would
be a Smart Kid section at the NFL draft combine. There would be
Smart Kid stats. There would be Smart Kid endorsements. Smart Kids
would become rich, famous, cool. Smart Kids would have agents!

All levels of life would be affected.

You're in high school. Your friend says he's working hard to be a
famous point guard. You say you're working hard to be a famous
Smart Kid.

The captain of the cheerleaders would have to decide between
dating the quarterback or the Smart Kid.

Every night, teenagers would go to bed with posters of Nobel
Prize winners and professors of particle physics on their walls,
right next to the posters of Troy Aikman, Penny Hardaway and Ozzy
Osbourne eating a gerbil.

Smart Kid trading cards! SAT scores and grade point averages
would be listed on the back!

Should the New York Jets take Peyton Manning or Orlando Pace
or a Smart Kid with the first draft pick? Let's face it, you could use a
franchise quarterback or an All-Pro offensive lineman, sure, but you
can't win the close ones without a good Smart Kid.

It's an amazing concept.

Thank you.

How do I think up these things?

I don't know. I'm always wondering whether they should raise the basket, lower the basket or let players play with springs in their sneakers. Or if an obese man would make a good hockey goaltender. Or if the dropkick will ever come back. The Smart Kid Rule just came to me. I thought that maybe it would be good for sports, for our society, if once in a while we showed a Smart Kid on television, made him the same kind of hero that we make our athletes.

How about this? Why don't we have Smart Kids answer questions for points after touchdowns? For free throws? For big situations, bottom of the ninth, bases loaded? Why not have two or three Smart Kids on a team?

Wouldn't work.

Why not?

Too much. The idea of just one Smart Kid on a team is bizarre enough for the American sports mind. Sort of like an obese goaltender.

---

## Now that you've read

1. What is Leigh Montville's "idea"?
2. What makes his idea so silly in our culture? In other words, why do we see this as humor rather than as a genuine suggestion for improving sports?
3. How do you respond to Montville's idea?

## READING 6

*Gary D. Funk*

# The Dumb Jock: Fact or Fiction?

Gary D. Funk's "The Dumb Jock: Fact or Fiction" is a chapter from his book *Major Violation: The Unbalanced Priorities in Athletics and Academics.* He takes the old stereotype of the "dumb jock" as a point of departure for serious research. His findings show how complicated and damaging the stereotype can be, as well as how some athletes have indeed been victimized by college athletics. As you read, consider the evidence he offers, and decide whether you think the stereotype of the dumb jock is "fact or fiction."

### *Before you read*

1. Have you ever heard stories about "dumb jocks"? What were they?
2. Have you ever heard about "smart jocks?" What did you hear?
3. Why do athletes get the reputation of being dumb? What contributes to this reputation?

---

How many Oklahoma University football players does it take to screw in a light bulb?

Only one, but he gets 3 hours of credit for it.

> A well-worn joke in Stillwater,
> home of Oklahoma State University

Current conceptions of intercollegiate athletics and its participants are varied and often negative. Some view big-time athletics with indignation and disgust. These people see athletic departments as an embarrassment, foulers of pristine ivory tower academic environments. Others express outrage or sadness at the present state of affairs. They perceive the Division I monster as corrupt and exploitative, using disadvantaged young people to achieve an end in which the participants reap little and take even less with them after finishing their athletic eligibility. Another, and quite possibly prevailing, public viewpoint is the tacit acceptance of college athletics as a home for good ol' boys, buffoons, and blacks who are incapable of doing anything more than providing entertainment for thousands of screaming fans. This complacent attitude can probably be found on any campus in the country, and it is a major factor in the media harpooning of all aspects of big-time athletics. Historically, though, except in classical culture, the physical and the intellectual have rarely been perceived as related, and one can only imagine (if lampooning history is permissible) the snickers of Roman patricians as gladiators did battle with wild beasts, Christians, and each other.

American intercollegiate athletics and its players have always been shrouded in clouds of doubt and skepticism. In 1869, the very first year that students from Rutgers and Princeton initiated college football competition, the faculties of the two schools canceled a game because they "feared over-emphasis." And, the turn of the century found the president of the United States lamenting the state of college athletics and the *New York Times* comparing football to the "evils" of lynching (there were 23 football deaths in 1905). Although many of the early concerns with college football focused on excessive violence, questions regarding the relationship of academics and athletics manifested themselves throughout subsequent years.

A 1929 study by the Carnegie Foundation for the Advancement of Education urged that "the recruiting from high school . . . the devotion of an undue proportion of time to training, the devices for putting a desirable athlete, but a weak scholar, across the hurdles of examination—these ought to stop." Other critics of the era went further, maintaining that colleges were "inculcating incorrect values by emphasizing athletic excellence over academic excellence; contributing to the moral delinquency of students in gambling, drinking, and 'the other more or less irreparable orgies.'" These attacks inspired the legendary Knute Rockne, innovative Notre Dame coach and staunch defender of football, to argue that more, not less, football was needed and that youngsters should be given "footballs instead of guns."

### Chalk One Up for the Gipper

Unfortunately, even the venerable Rockne was caught in the maelstrom of an intriguing little scandal. It seems that his player George Gipp (of "Win one for the Gipper" fame) was involved in an academic brouhaha that easily could have occurred in the 1990s. Gipp, who lived alone in a South Bend hotel, where he sharpened his skills at cards and pool, was expelled in the spring of 1919 for a variety of academic transgressions. According to Rockne, Gipp was allowed back in school after his performance on an oral examination "amazed" everyone involved. If Rockne's version of the Gipp incident sounds like the hokum passed off on the public by so many of today's coaches, the rest of the story is even more familiar. Father Burns, the

Notre Dame president responsible for Gipp's expulsion, was besieged by outraged local citizens, and it was a petition signed by the most prominent of them (not Gipp's oral wizardry) that finally persuaded the good father to readmit the star halfback. Gipp, meanwhile, used his 6-week hiatus from the university to "hustle pool." Although Rockne and the Gipper would come to be immortalized, concern over the academic-athletic relationship continued to mount. By 1934, 41 different studies had been compiled to show that "non-athletes performed slightly better in schoolwork than did athletes."

For anyone remotely familiar with the history of American intercollegiate athletics, these tidbits are hardly revelations. The entire century has seen arguments over the role of big-time college sports, and many one-time powers (the University of Chicago, the Ivy League schools, and several Catholic colleges) eventually chose to deemphasize athletic competition. Still, the Notre Dames and Michigans remain, and they have been joined by a new breed of cat, the Nevada–Las Vegases and the Alabama-Birminghams. The combination of these athletic powerhouses with an explosion of network and cable television coverage has made college athletics more visible and popular than ever.

Abuses in college sports have always existed, but the recent blitz of media exposure has diminished the public's tolerance for academic wrongdoing. America, at least superficially and politically, has decided to demand excellence and accountability in education. The widely distributed and oft-cited *A Nation at Risk* report (1983) deemed our public education system the equivalent of a foreign invasion and claimed that our illiteracy rate was a threat to national security and technological supremacy. All over the country, state legislatures passed education-oriented bills in a veritable pedagogical frenzy. Exit tests for high school students, standardized teacher eligibility tests, and stiffer entrance requirements for state-supported institutions of higher education became commonplace. Everyone from the president to the local mayor jumped on the educational reform bandwagon, and there were scapegoats aplenty. Naturally, and deservedly, intercollegiate athletics became one of the biggest goats.

Although American society has spent over a hundred years trying to separate the physical from the mental through means as diverse as technology and evangelism, there is a current belief that today's big-time college athlete should be some sort of Astroturf-Renaissance man, spewing forth algorithms as well as play signals. Obviously, such supermen are rare, and the "dumb jock" icon has been a perfect and defenseless target for ridicule and reform. As the sociologist Harry Edwards has stated, "For as long as organized sports participation has been associated with American education, the traditionally somewhat comic, not altogether unappealing 'dumb jock' image of the student athlete has endured."

Is this image based on fact, or is it myth perpetuated by a few sensational and widely publicized scandals? Does "Where there's smoke, there's fire" hold true, or has college athletics become just another scapegoat for an educational system under a barrage of attacks? Only a thorough examination of the facts and available information can shed light on these questions, and, even then, formulating a conclusive opinion may be difficult.

## Academic Achievement of Student-Athletes

A 1990 *NCAA News* headline claimed that "Division I athletes are graduating at higher rate than student body." Is this statement factual, or is it merely propaganda? This is not an easy question to answer. Research data on the relationship between athletic participation and academic achievement on the college level has been sporadic at best, conflicting at worst, and difficult to compare because of methodological, population sample, and reportorial differences. The difficulty in assessing college athletes' academic progress is best illustrated by a 1981 study conducted by the American College Testing Program (ACT) for the NCAA, the governing body for the athletic programs of approximately 800 universities and colleges. The ACT investigation attempted to survey 115 colleges and universities that initially agreed to participate in the study. After repeated efforts by ACT, "sufficient data" was gathered from only 46 of the 115 institutions. Nonetheless, the results of the study received recognition, and the findings were used as justification for the NCAA reforms of the mid- to late 1980s.

While the ACT study was often cited, it was at the same time blistered for "serious methodological problems" resulting from the characteristics of the sample, the quality of the data, and inappropriate data analyses. Another study utilized by the NCAA was conducted by Advanced Technology, Inc. in August 1984. This investigation, the "Study of Freshman Eligibility Standards Technical Report," was also criticized for its sample limitations and lack of appropriate analysis.

The intent here is not to lambaste the efforts of ACT or Advanced Technologies, but to shed light on the difficulties of making a clear-cut determination of the academic status of NCAA student-athletes. Even if all 800 universities and colleges responded to a study or survey, the validity of its results would have to be questioned. The primary problem lies in the reporting bias of the respondents. Athletic directors or other university officials might be inclined to report favorably on the academic progress of their student-athletes. This is not to imply that all or any institutions would blatantly fabricate statistics. However, the mere threat of a reporting bias and the difficulty in verifying data for such a widespread study would ensure that any conclusions would be tentative at best.

Obtaining an accurate overall picture of academic progress by student-athletes would require an independent research team visiting campuses selected by a scientific sampling procedure. Obviously, the cost involved in a study of this magnitude would be a major deterrent. Still, although gaining a consensus on the question may not be feasible, several studies highlighting trends and problem areas are worth reviewing. Although these findings are somewhat limited in their application and degree of generalization, their common denominators invite study.

Two areas of academic progress are constantly under discussion in the media, and they are both areas that can be examined quantitatively. Therefore, classroom performance/grade point average (GPA) and graduation rate can be utilized as barometers to determine if the "dumb jock" is a mere media caricature or if serious academic problems exist in intercollegiate athletics.

### Classroom Performance

Athletes' grade point averages are discussed and scrutinized as if they represented a consistent and reliable measure of academic progress. COSIDA (College Sports Information Directors of America) Academic All-American team selections are based on them, NCAA postgraduate scholarships are granted because of them, and the nationally broadcast praise of a Keith Jackson or a Brent Musburger reflects their loftiness. Unfortunately, the GPA is a limited measure that, at most, signifies a player's progress in a given program at a given institution. Universal comparison of grade point averages is absurd. Is a Vanderbilt University engineering student with a 2.1 GPA a less able student than a University of Nebraska general studies major with a 3.0 average? Probably not, and this very scenario is why the NCAA has been unable (as of 1990) to pass legislation defining satisfactory progress for eligibility by a graduated grade point average scale ranging from a 1.6 minimum requirement after completion of an initial season to a 2.0 minimum after completion of year 3. (The satisfactory progress issue will be discussed in greater detail in chapter 6). Still, grade point averages are a favorite topic of discussion, and the old grads with the inside scoops may giggle at Billy Joe's 1.1 GPA or marvel at the fact that a black kid from Chicago can actually make the dean's list.

How do student-athletes compare with "typical" students in terms of GPA and academic progress? While a multitude of applicable data is not available, several studies present some interesting and relevant findings, both positive and negative.

In one widely recognized study conducted from 1970 to 1980 at Colorado State University, the relationship between sports participation and academic progress was observed. The academic progress of all male and female sports participants was tracked and compared with the achievement of nonathletes. While athletes as a whole entered college only slightly less prepared than nonathletes, their actual college performance differed more substantially. University athletes garnered a lower grade point average (2.56 on a 4.00 scale) than did nonathletes (2.74), and the performance gap widened when the variables of race, sex, and individual sport were considered. It seems that black athletes' GPA achievements were significantly lower than white athletes', and that scholarship athletes were less successful than nonscholarship athletes. Although football players logged the lowest grade point average (2.30), the basketball players' average (2.49) included GPAs of female players during 5 years following the introduction of girls' basketball in the mid-1970s. The inclusion of the female players was reported to have inflated the GPA results for that sport. Another clear-cut conclusion from this study was that athletes in revenue-producing sports (football and men's basketball) were the least successful in terms of academic performance.

The Colorado State study poses an intriguing question: Do all athletes perform less successfully than nonathletes, or are academic deficiencies more likely to be shown by certain athletes in specific sports? Findings from this study seemingly imply that, although the athletes' overall grade point average was lower than that of nonathletes, the former may have been influenced by the less successful academic progress of football and men's basketball players. Also, there is an implication that women athletes tend to perform better than their male counterparts. Are these results isolated, or is this a widespread trend?

A 1981 study apparently substantiates the hypothesis that female athletes perform better than male athletes. In fact, this study "found that female athletes' grade point averages were significantly higher than nonathlete students." (The study also reported that athletes' academic achievement as a whole was *not* significantly lower than that of nonathletes.) These results regarding female athletes' academic achievement were reiterated by a 1986 study, "Athletes and Academic Performance: A Study of Athletes at an NCAA Division I Institution." This extensive investigation categorized student-athletes "by sex, grant-in-aid status, race, and as participating in either a revenue (football and men's basketball) or non-revenue sport." Female athletes, according to the study, achieved significantly higher grade point averages than male athletes participating in both revenue and nonrevenue sports (see Table 1).

**TABLE 1**
**Selected Grade Averages for Sex-Revenue Combinations**

| Athlete category | Total grade point average |
| --- | --- |
| Female athletes | 2.87 |
| Male nonrevenue athletes | 2.47 |
| Male revenue athletes | 2.25 |
| Overall university | 2.57 |

Source [for Tables 1 and 2]: Ann M. Mayo, "Athletes and Academic Performance: A Study of Athletes at an NCAA Division I Institution," *Academic Athletic Journal*, Fall 1986 [27–28, 30].

Like the Colorado State study, this Division I study shows female athletes outperforming all students, and male athletes in the revenue sports of football and basketball lagging behind. These findings were further reiterated by the 1987–88 National Study of Intercollegiate Athletics that found women basketball players earning significantly higher GPAs than men did—an average of 2.640 to 2.440.

A further inspection of the Division I study reveals more illuminating data when athletes' progress is broken down according to grant-in-aid status and race (Table 2).

This table points out two glaring statistical differences. First, full-grant athletes scored significantly lower than partial-grant or no-grant athletes. Second, again in congruence with the findings of the Colorado State study, GPAs of black male revenue sport athletes were significantly lower than those of white male athletes. Obviously, the majority of full grants (full-ride scholarships) usually are awarded in the revenue sports of football and men's basketball, where in the Division I study 41 percent of the participants were black, compared with 5 percent in the nonrevenue sports. Equally disturbing in regard to the minority issue is the academic performance of blacks in basic education requirement classes. While the average black athlete GPA was 1.99, in basic education requirement classes ("core required

**TABLE 2**
**Grade Averages by Grant-in-Aid Status and Race**

| Athlete category | Total grade point average |
| --- | --- |
| Grant-in-aid status | |
| Full grant | 2.44 |
| Partial grant | 2.71 |
| No grant | 2.64 |
| Overall university | 2.54 |
| Race | |
| White male revenue | 2.51 |
| Black male revenue | 1.99 |

classes in the areas of mathematics, humanities, sciences, and social sciences") the average GPA for black male revenue sport athletes plunged to 1.77. This was particularly disturbing to the investigators because a formula using students' high school rank and ACT composite scores had predicted an average GPA of 2.11 for black males participating in revenue sports. The discrepancy between the black males' predicted and actual grade point averages contradicted the findings for female athletes, who overachieved (2.87 total grade point average compared to a predicted 2.75) and for white male revenue sport athletes, who also performed better than anticipated (2.51 total grade point average compared to 2.44 predicted). The achievement gap for black athletes is most distressing because the difference between the basic education requirement GPA (1.77) and the predicted figure (2.11) may be "the best measure of whether a student is attaining his potential." Unfortunately, a 1977-to-1983 study of University of Michigan scholarship football players also found blacks (2.12 grade point average) achieving less than nonblacks (2.44 grade point average). And a 1988, $1.7 million NCAA study conducted by American Institutes for Research (AIR) found that cumulative grade point averages for football and basketball players (2.46) were lower than the average GPAs of players in other collegiate sports (2.61). The NCAA study also reported that black football and basketball players had a cumulative GPA of 2.16 at predominantly white institutions and 2.21 at predominantly black institutions. This compared unfavorably to the 2.48 cumulative GPA for nonblack football and basketball players. Other studies have produced similar findings.

If grade point averages are the sole indicator of academic progress, a problem certainly exists. Athletes in the revenue-producing sports of football and men's basketball apparently perform less successfully academically than female athletes, athletes in nonrevenue sports, and "typical" students making up the overall student body. This unfortunate circumstance is most noteworthy considering the integral, if not primary, roles that black athletes have assumed in Division I football and basketball during the last 2 decades. A glimpse at any NCAA Division I Final Four reveals the prevalence of black players. At the 1990 Final Four, for instance, 37 of the 55 players representing UNLV, Duke, Arkansas, and Georgia Tech were black. Unfortunately, many of these black players may be experiencing the most academic difficulty.

## Graduation Rates

Fortunately, the GPA is not the sole determinant of academic success, and thanks to the Privacy Act, a player—unless he or she is an outstanding scholar—is usually and mercifully spared from having his or her grade point plastered over the print pages or bandied about the airwaves. Although there have been exceptions, graduation rates have usually received the most publicity as a symbol of an athletic program's academic success. Memphis State, for example, had its reputation sullied by published reports that the university graduated only 6 of 58 basketball players between 1977 and 1983. Adding to the embarrassment was the fact that all 6 were white—at a school that has traditionally had many black players. On the opposite end of the spectrum is Duke, a school that, according to reports, graduates 100 percent of its basketball players and is constantly glorified for its academic achievements. However, like grade point averages, graduation rates have some real shortcomings as a measuring stick for a program's academic integrity.

Statistical analysis in itself can be corruptible and misleading; it is erroneous to assume that one school's 25 percent graduation rate for athletes is automatically comparable to another school's 75 percent rate. Here is an example. Assume that School A (25 percent graduation rate) and School B (75 percent) have comparable athletic programs including baseball, basketball, football, and track and field, and that their publicly announced graduation rates reflect the class of 1989, which enrolled in 1985. For the sake of simple mathematics, assume that both schools recruited 100 athletes garnering the academic results shown in Table 3.

School B, obviously, has formulated a creative equation. School A maintains that 100 athletes were recruited and 25 of the recruited athletes graduated, as simple as that. School B, however, has chosen not to include transfers, athletes who quit, and athletes who are staying in school in an attempt to complete degree programs. School B also includes students who quit athletics but remained in school and graduated, whereas even these students are excluded from School A's graduation rate formula. School B's mathematical rationale is that

TABLE 3
**Date for Graduation Rates at Hypothetical Schools**

|  |  | School |
| --- | --- | --- |
| Athlete category | A | B |
| Athletes initially enrolled (1985) | 100 | 100 |
| Athletes who transferred | 10 | 10 |
| Athletes who quit teams and school | 35 | 40 |
| Athletes who quit teams but stayed and graduated in 1989 | 5 | 5 |
| Athletes who used up athletic eligibility and dropped out of school | 5 | 4 |
| Athletes who used up eligibility but are still matriculating | 20 | 34 |
| Athletes who graduated in 1989 | 25 | 7 |

School A claims its graduation rate is 25% (25 / 100 = 25%).
School B claims its graduation rate is 75% (12 / 16 = 75%).

the school had no control over students who transferred or quit, and that athletes continuing their scholarly endeavors should not be included in the calculation until their fate is determined. Admittedly, School B makes a valid, albeit convenient, point.

Neither School A nor School B has contrived a formula that is wrong or unethical. They are, however, both using incorrect graduation rate formulas according to the *NCAA Manual*. Bylaw 5-6-(e)-(4), which requires a Division I institution's chief executive officer to provide annual graduation rate information, states:

> GRADUATION RATES. The report shall include the institution's graduation rate for the entering freshman class that began attendance as full-time, regularly matriculated, degree-seeking students at the institution six years prior to the regular fall term that includes the October 1 deadline established in 30.1, for both recruited student-athletes and students generally. For purposes of this legislation, the "graduation rate" shall be based upon the number of students who entered the member institution with no previous collegiate attendance and graduated from that institution within five academic years of the date of initial enrollment.

> ADJUSTED GRADUATION RATE. The report shall include the institution's adjusted graduation rate for recruited student-athletes in each sport. In calculating the adjusted graduation rate, transfer student-athletes shall be included as a part of the class that had completed degree credit equivalent to the degree credit completed by the transfer student-athletes and accepted by the certifying institution at the time of transfer. A student-athlete who left the institution while in good academic standing and who would have met the satisfactory-progress requirements for athletics eligibility if the student-athlete had returned for the following academic term shall not be included. Student-athletes who did not graduate within the specified five-year period but who continue to be enrolled as full-time students at the same institution and maintain satisfactory progress toward a specific baccalaureate degree also shall not be included.

One can only imagine athletic directors and coaches muddling through that bit of mumbo jumbo, and it is no wonder that graduation rates have a certain air of unreliability about them. Even if Bylaw 5-6-(e)-(4) were followed to the letter, there is nothing to prevent institutions from using an entirely different formula in presenting graduation rates to the media and the public.

Another major problem with comparing institutions' graduation rates is that even if statistical and reporting methods could be standardized, the comparison of these rates might yield little relevant information. As with grade point averages, comparing graduation rates from school to school is like matching apples and oranges. Though a university reporting a 10 percent graduation rate for its athletes should, at the very least, come under scrutiny, an institution flaunting a 100 percent graduation rate might warrant equal suspicion. This is not to say that an immediate investigation of Duke and its reported success should be forthcoming. Duke, Notre Dame, and other prestigious schools have excellent athletic traditions and can maintain high standards and admit quality athletes who are academically capable. However, some situations are peculiarly fishy, and varying degrees of informational latitude may be displayed by individual institutions of higher education. Thus, accurate comparisons of graduation rates may not be feasible or equitable, and comparing institutions with stringent standards to those whose primary requirement is the "feather test" is inherently unjust. (With the feather test, a person who can discernibly blow a feather is admitted; if 4 years later the person can still demonstrate this feat, a diploma is awarded.)

Despite the discrepancies and inequalities, graduation rates remain a prominent topic of discussion. Their perceived utility as a measure of academic integrity is such that two pieces of proposed federal legislation have included graduation rates as a litmus test for an institution's academic propriety.

### Legislating Graduation

In 1985, U.S. Representative James J. Howard (Democrat, New Jersey) proposed a bill (H.R. 2620) that would require colleges and universities to graduate "at least 75% of their scholarship athletes within five years in order for contributions to their athletic departments to qualify as tax deductible." Although Representative Howard's bill failed to become law, as of July 1990 another piece of legislation is awaiting approval from the House of Representatives. Sponsored by two congressional representatives who are former professional basketball players, Tom McMillen (Democrat, Maryland) and Ed Towns (Democrat, New York), the "Student Right-to-Know and Campus Security Act" (H.R. 1454) would require colleges and universities receiving federal funds to "report annually the graduation rates of students with athletic scholarships, and how long it took them compared to all the students." The Senate has already passed a graduation rate disclosure bill, and the two bills must be reconciled before they can be sent to the president's desk. Senator Bill Bradley (Democrat, New Jersey), who sponsored the Senate bill, explained that the motivation for the legislative action was the "single-minded devotion to athletics among our nation's schools and colleges," and he added that this "can lead to exploitation and abuse of our young athletes."

These are lofty words indeed. If graduation rates are to be so scrutinized and effectual in the future, reviewing what knowledge exists about them would be beneficial.

Ascertaining a conclusive national graduation rate for student-athletes is virtually impossible. The hindrances affecting grade point average research and the two previously discussed problems concerning graduation data seriously hamper any efforts to determine credible figures. However, several studies provide a partial glimpse of the graduation rate picture, and individual horror stories and isolated tales of documented neglect abound in today's media and can be located in the libraries' dusty periodical archives (see the accompanying box).

These lamentable happenings should not necessarily be viewed as indictments of the institutions mentioned. In fact, some of these schools should be applauded for admitting what other colleges will not. Although most of these institutions have initiated reform during the past decade, graphic examples of academic neglect continue to be a source of embarrassment for intercollegiate athletics and for institutions that are otherwise highly regarded. Do these examples of poor graduation rates indicate a widespread national problem, or is this yet another case of the dirtiest laundry surfacing in a sensational manner? Answering this question with any degree of certainty is difficult because "few empirical studies exist" that examine the relationship between student-athletes and their academic achievement, particularly in terms of graduation rates. Still, the few existing studies shed some light on the scope of the graduation problems.

### The Party Line

The NCAA contends that its consistent finding has been "that the graduation rate for student-athletes has been higher than that of the student body." To support this contention the NCAA cities its 1989 Division I Academic Reporting Compilation (see Table 4), a comprehensive yet generic overview of student-athlete graduation rates. Graduation rates for 11 men's sports and 10 women's sports (track and cross country considered two sports) are detailed, along with a combined rate for 7 minor men's sports and a combined rate for 4 minor women's sports. In every comparable sport, women did as well as or better than men, and no female sport had a median graduation rate lower than 50 percent. Among males, on the other hand, the report shows 4 different sports' median graduation rates below the 50 percent level, with the revenue-producing sports of football (37.5 percent) and basketball (33.3 percent) settling at rock bottom.

Unfortunately, the NCAA compilation provides no information on the success of minority student-athletes, nor is it possible to compare the student-athlete graduation rates with those of each institution's general study body. Still, reviewing ACT data on national graduation rates does allow for some comparison between the success of student-athletes and their nonathletic peers (see Tables 4 and 5).

Any conclusions from the comparisons of two methodologically different studies should be drawn with caution, however.

## Graduation Rate Horror Stories

- An early 1973 study found that University of Tennessee athletes had more problems than typical students fulfilling graduation requirements because of the amount of time required for sports participation.[a]

- At the University of Texas at Austin, only 39 percent of basketball players *entering* the school between 1975 and 1981 obtained their degrees, whereas 54 percent of the student body as a whole obtained degrees.[b]

- At North Carolina State University, in the classes of 1976, 1977, and 1978, only "two of 80 entering football players graduated. None of the 15 basketball players in those classes earned degrees."[c] According to some reports, the situation in Raleigh improved little during the years Jim Valvano was the head basketball coach.

- More than 200 blacks have played on University of Georgia athletic teams, "but as few as 15 of these athletes may have actually graduated."[d]

- The University of the District of Columbia can only estimate the graduation rate for athletes during the 10 years from 1977 to 1988. James McIver, vice president for the student services, says that between 12 and 16 athletes graduated out of literally hundreds who participated in football, basketball, tennis, and track.[e]

- In 1989 a conference-wide survey of the Big 8 showed that only 9.3 percent of black seniors who played basketball and football during the 1989 season actually graduated.

*Note.* [a]Robert J. Ballantine, "What Research Says: About the Correlation Between Athletic Participation and Academic Achievement." ED233994, 1981, 4. [b]Alvin P. Sanoff and Kathryn Johnson, "College Sports' Real Scandal," *U.S. News and World Report,* 15 September 1986, 62. [c] Jerome Cramer, "Winning or Learning? Athletics and Academics in America," *Phi Delta Kappan,* May 1986, K-3. [d] Ibid., K-2. [e] Susan Oberlander, "New Athletic Director at U. of District of Columbia Will Try to Rescue a Floundering Program," *The Chronicle of Higher Education,* 2 November 1988, A33–A34.

Other studies offer more specific, albeit more isolated, data. The aforementioned Colorado State study found that athletes had a lower graduation rate (34 percent) than did the general CSU student population (44.8 percent). Again, as with grade point averages, football players were the least successful group in the sample, with a graduation rate of 26.8 percent.

**TABLE 4**
**Graduation Rates by Sport**

| | All-male or mixed teams | | | All-female teams | |
| --- | --- | --- | --- | --- | --- |
| Sport | Number of schools in study | Median graduation rate (%)[a] | Sport | Number of schools in study | Median graduation rate (%)[a] |
| Baseball | 238 | 50.0 | Basketball | 263 | 60.0 |
| Basketball | 270 | 33.3 | Field hockey | 71 | 80.0 |
| Football | 194 | 37.5 | Golf | 67 | 66.7 |
| Golf | 179 | 50.0 | Gymnastics | 77 | 66.7 |
| Gymnastics | 37 | 50.0 | Softball | 141 | 66.7 |
| Soccer | 160 | 66.7 | Swimming | 140 | 75.0 |
| Swimming | 145 | 60.0 | Tennis | 190 | 75.0 |
| Tennis | 202 | 66.7 | Track/cross country | 179 | 57.1 |
| Track/cross country | 227 | 47.6 | Volleyball | 202 | 66.7 |
| Wrestling | 108 | 50.0 | All others (4 sports) | | 100.0 |
| All others (7 sports) | | 80.0 | | | |

[a]Graduation rate = $\dfrac{\text{Number of students who graduated by 1988}}{\text{Number of students who entered in 1983}} \times 100$

Source: *The NCAA News*, 13 June 1990, 12.

TABLE 5
**National Graduation Rates by Level of Selectivity**

| Selectivity[a] | Graduation rate (%) | |
|---|---|---|
| | Public university | Private university |
| Highly selective | 61.4 | 82.0 |
| Selective | 54.8 | 66.4 |
| Traditional | 52.4 | 55.6 |
| Liberal | 45.4 | 48.7 |
| Open | 40.7 | 42.5 |

[a]Self-reported

Some research apparently contradicts specific aspects of the Colorado State study findings, however. A study of University of Michigan football players published in 1987 reported that 65.9 percent of the players graduated during a 6-year period under study. While the Michigan figure appears significantly higher than the graduation rate figure for Colorado State athletes, these figures may reflect only the differences between two diverse programs studied at different times. Other studies, however, also seem to negate the Colorado State overall data. Both the ACT and Advanced Technology studies, previously noted as having been criticized for methodological shortcomings, concluded that male athletes graduated at a rate about equal to or higher than that of male nonathletes or students in general.

Although arriving at a conclusion may be presumptuous, it would appear that athletes in general graduate at a rate near or above the 40 to 48 percent national figure. The status of male minority student-athletes is less clear, however, and few definitive studies are available that specifically address minority athletes' graduation figures. While many tangible examples (Georgia, Memphis State, University of the District of Columbia, etc.) seem to point to minority graduation rates as problematic, widespread quantitative data is sparse. Two statistical examples, however, apparently support the consensus portrayed by the media. The Michigan study and its findings on graduation rates mirror the problem experienced by minority student-athletes in the area of grade point averages. Although 65.9 percent of all athletes surveyed in the study graduated, only 52.7 percent of blacks received degrees. The black student-athlete rate pales further when compared to the nonblack graduation rate of 74.4 percent.

Southwest Missouri State University is another example of the discrepancy between the graduation rates of black and white student-athletes. SMSU, a comprehensive regional institution with an enrollment of more than 20,000, has flirted with national success in basketball by appearing in the NCAA Division I postseason tourney for four consecutive seasons. With an overall graduation rate of 46 percent (utilizing the NCAA formula as outlined in Bylaw 5-6-(e)-(4) from the years 1982 to 1990, the basketball program's graduation rate was higher than the national median graduation rate for Division I basketball programs (33 percent) and even bettered the overall SMSU graduation rate of 38 percent. Despite this relevant success, a closer examination of the situation reveals a serious problem. Although the 46 percent team graduation rate may or may not be noteworthy, the glaring difference between the white graduation rate of 93 percent and the black graduation rate of 35 percent *is*. The SMSU figures are supported by the 1989 Big 8 Survey, in which the black graduation figure of 9.3 percent compared unfavorably with the white graduation rate of 48.9 percent. This unfortunate contrast is a national trend. When one considers that 52 percent of Division I basketball players and 36 percent of Division I football players are black, the ramifications are staggering.

## The Bottom Line

Is the "dumb jock" image a myth? Possibly. Does big-time intercollegiate athletics as a whole deserve the criticism it has been forced to endure? Maybe not. Although these questions are answered somewhat cautiously, there is enough evidence to conclude that student-athletes in general are performing satisfactorily in the classroom. In fact, some segments of the student-athlete population outperform their nonathlete counterparts. Many NCAA sports (see Table 4) record outstanding graduation rates, and woman athletes in particular seem to enjoy tremendous success in both the GPA and graduation rate categories. Several theories have been postulated to explain the academic success realized by those young people who are student-athletes in the true sense of the term. Association with achievement-oriented peers, transference of achievement values from sports to the classroom, an increase in self-esteem that creates a higher level of aspiration in other domains, internal and external pressure, and more scholastic and career guidance from significant adults have all been cited as reasons why student-athletes may do as well as or better than typical students. Woman athletes, according to a Texas Tech University researcher, even have a higher degree of moral development. Although moral reasoning abilities do not necessarily correlate with academic performance, women's athletic programs have realized excellent academic success. There is too much quantitative evidence to deny that female student-athletes perform very well in their scholastic endeavors. However, I sincerely doubt that either innate womanhood or superior moral reasoning has anything to do with it. . . .

If the overall student-athlete population performs adequately, and if female student-athletes achieve exceedingly well, then what is causing all the ruckus?

Unfortunately, the public at large just does not care about men's tennis or women's field hockey. Whether it is right or wrong, the majority of the sports associated with outstanding graduation rates simply do not command the attention of the media or the sports-loving public. Certainly each has its own sphere of ardent support, but these nonrevenue sports are just that. Their existence at many Division I institutions is attributed solely to the NCAA requirement that Division I ("major college") institutions "sponsor a minimum of eight varsity intercollegiate sports." Thus, as the remarkable win-loss record of State U's women's volleyball team goes unnoticed, so might the squad's outstanding academic accomplishments. As unreasonable and discriminatory as this may seem, these are, to quote Porter Waggoner, "the cold, hard facts of life."

Football and basketball—men's basketball—are what people care about, and these are the two traditional revenue-producing sports. Some women's programs (i.e., basketball at the University of Tennessee) have become popular, but football and men's basketball are what draw national media attention and generate millions of dollars. These scenarios, however, are predicated on winning, which requires an abundance of extraordinary athletic talent. A large pool of this extraordinary ability can be found in the poor black neighborhoods of inner cities and the equally poor rural regions of the South.

## The Cold, Hard Facts

Bluntly put, academic abuses and problems are most prevalent in the two high-profile revenue-producing sports, and often these problems involve black or minority student-athletes. The problems of educationally disadvantaged black athletes are clear to anyone who has ever seriously studied the high-revenue sports and their relationships to academics. The statistical data does nothing to refute these impressions. The headline cases are troublesome proof of the academic problems surrounding black players. Memphis State University, whose problems have already been detailed, has for years featured a predominantly black basketball team. The University of Georgia fiasco specifically highlighted the academic neglect of black athletes, and there are many other highly publicized educational heresies.

The widespread media attention given to incidents such as these is obviously due in good part to the extreme visibility of the two sports themselves. There is, however, another factor. Though the United States may be one of the planet's more pluralistic nations, there is nonetheless a clear-cut white majority. This white majority is even more evident when the demographics of college graduates and professionals—the financial and working lifeblood of universities and colleges—are considered. Thrust into predominantly white environments are scholastically unprepared blacks from predominantly black communities. It is no wonder that their trials and tribulations are so conspicuous. Freelance writer Jerome Cramer wrote of a conversation with a Washington, DC, sportswriter who stated, "Once the athlete stopped being somebody's tall farm kid from downstate and instead became a strange, big (and increasingly black), dumb kid from the ghetto who no one cared about, then it became clear the athlete really was an outsider." One can only imagine the consequences if George Gipp had been black. And the old rockabilly song may have been most prophetic when it proclaimed in reference to a common crime, "If I'd been a black man, they'd a given me thirty years."

Proclaiming that intercollegiate athletics' academic problems primarily surface in the revenue sports of football and men's basketball and that black student-athletes are often the foci of these problems is not sufficient. This simple statement offers no solutions, and it streamlines an issue laden with complexities and contradictions. Although the student-athlete dilemma may often be "black," many nonblacks are struggling too. More often than not, they may have problems for the same reasons as their black teammates. Unfortunately, grappling with problems steeped in complexity and contradiction is neither easy nor pleasant, and the modern tendency (the NCAA tendency as well) is to plan and implement a short-term and inflexible solution and hope for the best. Quick-fix approaches will not work here, though, and a comprehensive and thorough examination of the student-athletes, the institutions they attend, and the larger society is necessary before any meaningful solutions can be implemented.

---

## Now that you've read

1. What is Gary D. Funk's overall argument in this article?
2. What did you find to be his most convincing example? His least convincing example?
3. Why are the graduation rates so low for athletes?
4. What can schools do to improve this situation? Do they have a moral obligation to do anything, or is it mainly the athlete's responsibility to take care of himself or herself?

# SEQUENCE 6 ASSIGNMENTS

## Reading 1: Murray Ross, "Football Red and Baseball Green"

> There is, in sport, some of the rudimentary drama found in popular theater: familiar plots, type characters, heroic and comic action spiced with new and unpredictable variations. And common to watching both activities is the sense of participation in a shared tradition and in shared fantasies.

### *Prewriting*

1. Respond to the above quotation from Ross's essay. Does his assessment ring true? Can you think of any moments you've witnessed or heard about in sports that seem like "theater"? If so, describe one of them.
2. Look up the word *myth* in the dictionary and then define it in your own words.
3. Why are some athletes and sports given more attention than others? For example, in general, why do football players receive more attention than, say, members of the tennis team or the swim team?

### *Writing assignment*

Murray Ross's essay looks playfully at football and baseball to see what makes them so popular and what their popularity reveals about American culture. He writes, "It is my guess that sport spectating involves more than the vicarious pleasures of identifying with athletic prowess."

For this assignment, use the excerpt from Ross's essay as a jumping-off place to begin your own speculations about the role sports play on the college campus. Pick a college sport you have some knowledge of. What is the "fundamental myth which it elaborates for its fans"? What do you make of this sport's popularity or lack of popularity on your campus? How could this sport be said to belong to a "mythical world"? What elements of drama can be found in the sport, and how does that drama contribute to its "mythic" qualities? How does it compare to other sports on your campus?

## Reading 2: Drake Witham, "An End to Athletics Dorms"

> In an attempt to minimize the recruiting advantage that some colleges gained by building luxurious residence halls, the N.C.A.A. in 1983

adopted a rule that required athletics dormitories to be comparable to other housing on campus. The rule was virtually ignored.

## Prewriting

1. Respond briefly to the above quotation from Witham's article. What do you think of the rule? Why do you think it was ignored?
2. What stories have you heard about special treatment for athletes at your school or elsewhere?
3. What do you make of the high incidence of "misbehavior" (gang rape, shootings, drug trafficking, etc.) committed by those living in athletics dorms? If athletes were integrated into regular housing, do you think such "misbehavior" would happen less often? Why or why not?

## Writing assignment

In his article "An End to Athletics Dorms," Drake Witham writes, "Mo Collins attended the University of Florida because he wanted to play football for a winner and be treated like a winner." What do you take this to mean? In particular, what does it mean for a college athlete to be "treated like a winner"? Is this part of the "mythical" quality of sports that Murray Ross writes about? What do you make of the notion of athletes receiving special treatment? Is this justifiable? If so, when? What about other students, such as honors students?

What are the key arguments being made on both sides of this issue? Where do you stand in relation to those arguments?

## Reading 3: Allen Guttmann, "Fair Play for Women?"

> "No person . . . shall, on the basis of sex, be excluded from participation in, be denied the benefits of, or be subjected to discrimination under any educational programs or activities receiving federal financial assistance." (Title IX of the Education Act of 1972, qtd. in Guttmann)

## Prewriting

1. In your own words, summarize the quotation above.
2. Do you think women should be allowed to play on men's teams? What would be the advantages? What would be the disadvantages?
3. In the last paragraph of Guttmann's essay are a series of provocative questions. Choose the one you find most provocative and write several sentences in response.

## Writing assignment

In this sequence, you've been asked to consider the mythic qualities of college sports and how those qualities may lead to special treatment of the athletes involved. This assignment asks you to continue to think about these issues as they are related to female college athletes.

Guttmann quotes a Connecticut Superior Court ruling: "Athletic competition builds character in our boys. We do not need that kind of character in our girls." What was this judge saying about the differences between male and female athletes? This ruling was written before 1971. Has this kind of attitude disappeared? What are some of the benefits of sports for the female athlete? Are they different from the benefits for male college athletes? How or how not? Is Title IX an example of inappropriate special treatment or does it signify a worthwhile attempt to level the playing field? What is your position in relation to this ongoing debate about support for college women's athletics?

## Reading 4: Kate Rounds, "Why Men Fear Women's Teams"

> "There's always a guy in the crowd who challenges the women when he wouldn't think of going one-on-one with Magic Johnson or challenging Nolan Ryan to a pitching contest."

### Prewriting

1. Respond briefly to the above quotation from Rounds's essay. What do you take this passage to mean?
2. Have you watched any of the WNBA games on television? Why or why not?
3. Do you think the WNBA is here to stay? Why or why not?
4. Why are women's gymnastics and women's iceskating so much more popular than, say, women's fast-pitch softball or women's soccer?
5. How well attended are women's athletics events on your campus?

### Writing assignment

Rounds levels some major charges about why serious women's sports (professional volleyball, for example, rather than beach volleyball) have such a difficult time finding popular support in the United States. What are some of the arguments she makes? What might Guttmann say in response? Where do you stand? What kinds of support should women's athletics receive on your campus? Why? Make your argument using the reading and writing you've done thus far in this sequence.

## Reading 5: Leigh Montville, "This Isn't Such a Dumb Idea"

> I've figured out a new rule for all sports. I call it the Smart Kid Rule. I think it will revolutionize college athletics.

### Prewriting

1. How is being smart valued on your campus?
2. What kinds of prestige are associated with being smart?
3. Why are athletes generally more admired on campus than intellectuals?

### Writing assignments

In "This Isn't Such a Dumb Idea," Leigh Montville uses satire to make several arguments. (To compare this essay with a classic satirical piece of 300 years ago, read Jonathan Swift's "A Modest Proposal.") What is Montville arguing for and against? What makes his arguments satirical? What additional changes to college sports would result from the Smart Kid Rule? Why do we, as a culture, tend to admire athletes more than intellectuals? What might Murray Ross say ("Football Red and Baseball Green")? What might Mo Collins say (look back to "An End to Athletics Dorms")? How do you respond to Montville's arguments and why?

## Reading 6: Gary D. Funk, "The Dumb Jock: Fact or Fiction?"

> For as long as organized sports participation has been associated with American education, the traditionally somewhat comic, not altogether unappealing "dumb jock" image of the student athlete has endured.

### Prewriting

1. Respond briefly to the above quotation from Funk's essay. Do you agree that the "dumb jock" stereotype is "not altogether unappealing"? Why or why not?
2. Have you heard any jokes or anecdotes like the one at the beginning of "The Dumb Jock: Fact or Fiction"? What attitudes do these jokes or anecdotes reveal?
3. What exceptions to the stereotypes can you describe?

### Writing assignment

It has become a clich in our society to describe athletes as all athletic ability and no brains. We need only listen to athletes being interviewed by our local sports reporters to have those stereotypes confirmed. Building on what you've read up to now, consider Gary D. Funk's analysis of the "dumb jock" in "The Dumb Jock: Fact or Fiction?" What factors does Funk believe contribute to the "dumb jock" label? What factors might you add?

Using Funk's essay and your reading and writing so far, discuss the implications of Funk's research and of your own observations and knowledge. Is the "dumb jock" a myth? A vicious stereotype? An accurate label describing a widespread problem? What is the most widespread point of view about this on your campus? What effect does the "dumb jock" label have on college athletes? What suggestions could you make to change either the perception or the reality, as you see it?

## Final Project

Review the essays you've written for this sequence. What is your principal point of view concerning college athletes and athletics? How do you react to the myths and stereotypes discussed in this sequence? Have the readings taught you anything new or changed your mind about anything? Have they reinforced your views about anything? Mine your essays for a specific issue you'd like to investigate in further detail, and formulate a concise thesis that you can use in a 15- to 20-page research paper. If you can't decide on a topic to investigate further consider these questions:

What is the status of "elite" athletes on your campus? Do they enjoy special privileges?

What is the level of support for women athletes and women's athletics on your campus? How would different groups on campus (including women athletes) characterize that support?

What are students' perceptions of college athletes on your campus?

## Library Research Ideas

Try one or more of the following library research activities, or come up with your own ideas for library research to support your thesis.

1. Compare how some Big Ten universities present their athletics programs on their web sites with how they present their academics programs. For example, the University of Michigan, Michigan State University, and Ohio State University all have separate sites devoted entirely to their athletics programs. Check out their "regular" web sites (**http://www.umich.edu, http://www.msu. edu**, and **www.ohio-state.edu**), and compare the layout and design to those of their athletic programs' web sites (**http://www. mgoblue.com, http://www.msuspartans.com**, and **http://www. ohiostatebuckeyes.com**). Note that the athletics programs' sites all have ".com" addresses, indicating commercial sites, rather than the ".edu" addresses used for educational organizations. What does the difference in how these and other schools present

their athletic programs compared to their academic programs say about the value they place on athletics? Can you draw any other inferences from examining these sites?

2. Investigate the history of college athletics at your school, in the United States at large, or in both spheres. What impact have athletics programs had on higher education? What resources do they contribute to universities, and what resources do they absorb? On balance, are athletics programs beneficial to U.S. colleges and universities? Are they beneficial to your school?

3. Do some biographical research on former college athletes who have made a name for themselves in careers outside sports. If you're not aware of any such persons, investigate a number of accomplished individuals whom you admire to see whether they were athletes when they were in college. Look for information on the college careers of former college athletes—and specifically for information on their academic accomplishments. What do these biographies say about the stereotype of the "dumb jock"?

## Field Research Ideas

Try one or more of the following field research ideas, or use your own field research ideas to get data to support your thesis.

1. Survey a random group of students to elicit their opinions and attitudes concerning your school's athletics programs. How do they feel about college athletes? Do they think athletes on campus get special treatment? Would they themselves be college athletes if they had the ability and were given the chance?

2. Survey a random group of professors to get their opinions about the "dumb jock" stereotype. Ask how the athletes in their classes fare academically compared with other students and what they think the university's responsibility is to student athletes' education (particularly athletes in big money-making programs).

3. Interview several student athletes about their experiences in college. Do they like being college athletes? If they're attending your school on an athletic scholarship, are they glad they accepted it, or does it ask too much of them in terms of their time? What are their career goals? If you interview "elite" athletes in money-making programs at large universities, ask whether they feel that what they are getting from the university equals what they are giving to the university.

# Gender and Learning

## Getting Started

The focus of this sequence is how gender does, and how it does not, make a difference in the ways we interact and learn in the classroom and beyond. The title of a recent bestseller claims men and women are so far apart that we're from different planets. The popularity of that book indicates that many people agree there are fundamental differences. Yet, at the same time, we want everyone treated equally. Equality, however, is not so easily defined, as the readings in this sequence demonstrate.

In "Taking Women Students Seriously," Adrienne Rich, writing over 20 years ago, argues that women must be pushed and expected to succeed. Jeffrey Berman's "Hunger Artists" shows how those expectations can have disastrous results. Deborah Tannen argues, in "How Male and Female Students Use Language Differently," that men and women interact differently in different contexts and that teachers must shift those contexts in order to give everyone a chance to excel. Peter Lyman's "The Fraternal Bond as a Joking Relationship" analyzes how even men's and women's senses of humor differ and how those differences can lead to miscommunication.

Sam Keen finds the roots of these differences in men's complicated relationship to the culture of war; he states his case in "The Rite of War and the Warrior Psyche." Finally, in "Grandma's Story," Trinh T. Minh-ha offers us a complex picture of her grandmother's role as storyteller and nontraditional teacher and what that role teaches us about gender.

Please reflect on your ideas about the role that gender plays in your relationships with other students and teachers and in your classes. Then respond to several of the following questions. I use the Getting Started questions as a preliminary exercise on the first day my class works on a particular sequence. Your teacher may also do this, or he or she may ask that you write out your responses either in a journal or in your notebook. Your teacher may use these questions as a jumping-off place for class discussion as well. No matter how you use these questions in your class, however, you'll still be able to draw on what you write here both in your contributions to class discussion and in your responses to the assignments that follow.

1. Are you comfortable participating in class discussions?
2. If you're ever uncomfortable, what makes you feel that way?
3. What kind of discussion do you prefer? Why?
4. Do men and women participate equally in your classes?
5. What suggestions could you offer a teacher who is worried about making sure that everyone gets a chance to talk and no one feels "silenced"?

## READING 1

*Adrienne Rich*

# Taking Women Students Seriously

It was not so long ago that many people, including professors, assumed that women were in college only to find husbands. Over 20 years ago, Adrienne Rich, one of America's foremost poets, gave this talk to teachers of women, arguing that in order for women to achieve, they must be challenged. As you read, think about how much attitudes have (and have not) changed in the past 20 years.

### Before you read

1. Have you ever seen a woman student not taken seriously (or experienced this yourself)? What were the circumstances? How did the woman respond?
2. What do you think about same-sex colleges? Would you want your children to go to a same-sex school? Why or why not?
3. Do you think men and women have different educational needs? If so, describe those different needs.

---

I see my function here today as one of trying to create a context, delineate a background, against which we might talk about women as students and students as women. I would like to speak for a while about this background, and then I hope that we can have, not so much a question period, as a raising of concerns, a sharing of questions for which we as yet may have no answers, an opening of conversations which will go on and on.

When I went to teach at Douglass, a women's college, it was with a particular background which I would like briefly to describe to you. I had graduated from an all-girls' school in the 1940s, where the head and the majority of the faculty were independent, unmarried women. One or two held doctorates, but had been forced by the Depression (and by the fact that they were women) to take secondary school teaching jobs. These women cared a great deal about the life of the mind, and they gave a great deal of time and energy—beyond any limit of teaching hours—to those of us who showed special intellectual interest or ability. We were taken to libraries, art museums, lectures at neighboring colleges, set to work on extra research projects, given extra French or Latin reading. Although we sometimes felt "pushed" by them, we held those women in a kind of respect which even then we dimly perceived was not generally accorded to women in the world at large. They were vital individuals, defined not by their relationships but by their personalities; and although under the pressure of the culture we were all certain we wanted to get married, their lives did not appear empty or dreary to us. In a kind of cognitive dissonance, we knew they were "old maids" and therefore supposed to be bitter and lonely; yet we saw them vigorously involved with life. But despite their existence as alternate models of women, the *content* of the education they gave us in no way prepared us to survive as women in a world organized by and for men.

From that school, I went on to Radcliffe, congratulating myself that now I would have great men as my teachers. From 1947 to 1951, when I graduated, I never saw a single woman on a lecture platform, or in front of a class, except when a woman graduate student gave a paper on a special topic. The "great men" talked of other "great men," of the nature of Man, the history of Mankind, the future of Man; and never again was I to experience, from a teacher, the kind of prodding, the insistence that my best could be even better, that I had known in high school. Women students were simply not taken very seriously. Harvard's message to women was an elite mystification: we were, of course, part of Mankind; we were special, achieving women, or we would not have been there; but of course our real goal was to marry—if possible, a Harvard graduate.

In the late sixties, I began teaching at the City College of New York—a crowded, public, urban, multiracial institution as far removed from Harvard as possible. I went there to teach writing in the SEEK Program, which predated Open Admissions and which was then a kind of model for programs designed to open up higher education to poor, black, and Third World students. Although during the next few years we were to see the original concept of SEEK diluted, then violently attacked and betrayed, it was for a short time an extraordinary and intense teaching and learning environment. The characteristics of this environment were a deep commitment on the part of teachers to the minds of their students; a constant active effort to create or discover the conditions for learning, and to educate ourselves to meet the needs of the new college populations; a philosophical attitude based on open discussion of racism, oppression, and the politics of literature and language; and a belief that learning in the classroom could not be isolated from the student's experience as a member of an urban minority group in white America. Here are some of the kinds of questions we, as teachers of writing, found ourselves asking:

1. What has been the student's experience of education in the inadequate, often abusively racist public school system, which rewards passivity and treats a questioning attitude or independent mind

as a behavior problem? What has been her or his experience in a society that consistently undermines the selfhood of the poor and the nonwhite? How can such a student gain that sense of self which is necessary for active participation in education? What does all this mean for us as teachers?

2. How do we go about teaching a canon of literature which has consistently excluded or depreciated nonwhite experience?

3. How can we connect the process of learning to write well with the student's own reality, and not simply teach her/him how to write acceptable lies in standard English?

When I went to teach at Douglass College in 1976, and in teaching women's writing workshops elsewhere, I came to perceive stunning parallels to the questions I had first encountered in teaching the so-called disadvantaged students at City. But in this instance, and against the specific background of the women's movement, the questions framed themselves like this:

1. What has been the student's experience of education in schools which reward female passivity, indoctrinate girls and boys in stereotypic sex roles, and do not take the female mind seriously? How does a woman gain a sense of her *self* in a system—in this case, patriarchal capitalism—which devalues work done by women, denies the importance and uniqueness of female experience, and is physically violent toward women? What does this mean for a woman teacher?

2. How do we, as women, teach women students a canon of literature which has consistently excluded or depreciated female experience, and which often expresses hostility to women and validates violence against us?

3. How can we teach women to move beyond the desire for male approval and getting "good grades" and seek and write their own truths that the culture has distorted or made taboo? (For women, of course, language itself is exclusive: I want to say more about this further on.)

In teaching women, we have two choices: to lend our weight to the forces that indoctrinate women to passivity, self-depreciation, and a sense of powerlessness, in which case the issue of "taking women students seriously" is a moot one; or to consider what we have to work against, as well as with, in ourselves, in our students, in the content of the curriculum, in the structure of the institution, in the society at large. And this means, first of all, taking ourselves seriously: Recognizing that central responsibility of a woman to herself, without which we remain always the Other, the defined, the object, the victim; believing that there is a unique quality of validation, affirmation, challenge, support, that one woman can offer another. Believing in the value and significance of women's experience, traditions, perceptions. Thinking of ourselves seriously, not as one of the boys, not as neuters, or androgynes, but *as women.*

Suppose we were to ask ourselves, simply: What does a woman need to know? Does she not, as a self-conscious, self-defining human being, need a knowledge of her own history, her much-politicized biology, an awareness of the creative work of women of the past, the skills and crafts and techniques and powers exercised by women in different times and cultures, a knowledge of women's rebellions and organized movements against our oppression and how they have been routed or diminished? Without such knowledge women live and have lived without context, vulnerable to the projections of male fantasy, male prescriptions for us, estranged from our own experience because our education has not reflected or echoed it. I would suggest that not biology, but ignorance of our selves, has been the key to our powerlessness.

But the university curriculum, the high-school curriculum, do not provide this kind of knowledge for women, the knowledge of Womankind whose experience has been so profoundly different from that of Mankind. Only in the precariously budgeted, much-condescended-to area of women's studies is such knowledge available to women students. Only there can they learn about the lives and work of women other than the few select women who are included in the "mainstream" texts, usually misrepresented even when they do appear. Some students, at some institutions, manage to take a majority of courses in women's studies, but the message from on high is that this is self-indulgence, soft-core education: the "real" learning is the study of Mankind.

If there is any misleading concept, it is that of "coeducation": that because women and men are sitting in the same classrooms, hearing the same lectures, reading the same books, performing the same laboratory experiments, they are receiving an equal education. They are not, first because the content of education itself validates men even as it invalidates women. Its very message is that men have been the shapers and thinkers of the world, and that this is only natural. The bias of higher education, including the so-called sciences, is white and male, racist and sexist; and this bias is expressed in both subtle and blatant ways. I have mentioned already the exclusiveness of grammar itself: "The student should test himself on the above questions"; "The poet is representative. He stands among partial men for the complete man." Despite a few half-hearted departures from custom, what the linguist Wendy Martyna has named "He-Man" grammar prevails throughout the culture. The efforts of feminists to reveal the profound ontological implications of sexist grammar are routinely ridiculed by academicians and journalists, including the professedly liberal *Times* columnist, Tom Wicker, and the professed humanist, Jacques Barzun. Sexist grammar burns into the brains of little girls and young women a message that the male is the norm, the standard, the central figure beside which we are the deviants, the marginal, the dependent variables. It lays the foundation for androcentric thinking, and leaves men safe in their solipsistic tunnel vision.

Women and men do not receive an equal education because outside the classroom women are perceived not as sovereign beings but as prey. The growing incidence of rape on and off the campus may or may not be fed by the proliferations of pornographic magazines and X-rated films available to young males in fraternities and student unions; but it is certainly occurring in a context of widespread images of sexual violence against women, on billboards and in so-called high art. More subtle, more daily than rape is the verbal abuse experienced by the woman student on many campuses— Rutgers for example—where, traversing a street lined with fraternity houses, she must run a gauntlet of male commentary and verbal assault. The undermining of self, of a woman's sense of her right to occupy space and walk freely in the world, is deeply relevant to education. The capacity to think independently, to take intellectual risks, to assert ourselves mentally, is inseparable from our physical way of being in the world, our feelings of personal integrity. If it is dangerous for me to walk home late of an evening from the library, *because I am a woman and can be raped,* how self-possessed, how exuberant can I feel as I sit working in that library? how much of my working energy is drained by the subliminal knowledge that, as a woman, I test my physical right to exist each time I go out alone? Of this knowledge, Susan Griffin has written:

> . . . more than rape itself, the fear of rape permeates our lives. And what does one do from day to day, with *this* experience, which says, without words and directly to the heart, *your existence, your experience, may end at any moment.* Your experience may end, and the best defense against this is not to be, to deny being in the body, as a self, to . . . avert your gaze, make yourself, as a presence in the world, less felt.[1]

Finally, rape of the mind. Women students are more and more often now reporting sexual overtures by male professors—one part of our overall growing consciousness of sexual harassment in the workplace. At Yale a legal suit has been brought against the university by a group of women demanding an explicit policy against sexual advances toward female students by male professors. Most young

[1]Quoted from the manuscript of her forthcoming book, *Rape: The Power of Consciousness;* to be published in 1979 by Harper & Row.

women experience a profound mixture of humiliation and intellectual self-doubt over seductive gestures by men who have the power to award grades, open doors to grants and graduate school, or extend special knowledge and training. Even if turned aside, such gestures constitute mental rape, destructive to a woman's ego. They are acts of domination, as despicable as the molestation of the daughter by the father.

But long before entering college the woman student has experienced her alien identity in a world which misnames her, turns her to its own uses, denying her the resources she needs to become self-affirming, self-defined. The nuclear family teaches her that relationships are more important than selfhood or work; that "whether the phone rings for you, and how often," having the right clothes, doing the dishes, take precedence over study or solitude; that too much intelligence or intensity may make her unmarriageable; that marriage and children—service to others—are, finally, the points on which her life will be judged a success or a failure. In high school, the polarization between feminine attractiveness and independent intelligence comes to an absolute. Meanwhile, the culture resounds with messages. During Solar Energy Week in New York I saw young women wearing "ecology" T-shirts with the legend: CLEAN, CHEAP AND AVAILABLE; a reminder of the 1960s antiwar button which read: CHICKS SAY YES TO MEN WHO SAY NO. Department store windows feature female mannequins in chairs, pinned to the wall with legs spread, smiling in positions of torture. Feminists are depicted in the media as "shrill," "strident," "puritanical," or "humorless," and the lesbian choice—the choice of the woman-identified woman—as pathological or sinister. The young woman sitting in the philosophy classroom, the political science lecture, is already gripped by tensions between her nascent sense of self-worth, and the battering force of messages like these.

Look at a classroom: look at the many kinds of women's faces, postures, expressions. Listen to the women's voices. Listen to the silences, the unasked questions, the blanks. Listen to the small, soft voices, often courageously trying to speak up, voices of women taught early that tones of confidence, challenge, anger, or assertiveness, are strident and unfeminine. Listen to the voices of the women and the voices of the men; observe the space men allow themselves, physically and verbally, the male assumption that people will listen, even when the majority of the group is female. Look at the faces of the silent, and of those who speak. Listen to a woman groping for language in which to express what is on her mind, sensing that the terms of academic discourse are not her language, trying to cut down her thought to the dimensions of a discourse not intended for her (*for it is not fitting that a woman speak in public*); or reading her paper aloud at breakneck speed, throwing her words away, deprecating her own work by a reflex prejudgment: *I do not deserve to take up time and space.*

As women teachers, we can either deny the importance of this context in which women students think, write, read, study, project their own futures; or try to work with it. We can either teach passively, accepting these conditions, or actively, helping our students identify and resist them.

One important thing we can do is *discuss* the context. And this need not happen only in a women's studies course; it can happen anywhere. We can refuse to accept passive, obedient learning and insist upon critical thinking. We can become harder on our women students, giving them the kinds of "cultural prodding" that men receive, but on different terms and in a different style. Most young women need to have their intellectual lives, their work, legitimized against the claims of family, relationships, the old message that a woman is always available for service to others. We need to keep our standards very high, not to accept a woman's preconceived sense of her limitations; we need to be hard to please, while supportive of risk-taking, because self-respect often comes only when exacting standards have been met. At a time when adult literacy is generally low, we need to demand more, not less, of women, both for the sake of their futures as thinking beings, and because historically women have always had to be better than men to do half as well. A romantic sloppiness, an inspired lack of rigor, a self-indulgent incoherence are symptoms of female self-depreciation. We should help our women students to look very critically at such symptoms, and to understand where they are rooted.

Nor does this mean we should be training women students to "think like men." Men in general think badly: in disjuncture from their personal lives, claiming objectivity where the most irrational passions seethe, losing, as Virginia Woolf observed, their senses in the pursuit of professionalism. It is not easy to think like a woman in a man's world, in the world of the professions; yet the capacity to do that is a strength which we can try to help our students develop. To think like a woman in a man's world means thinking critically, refusing to accept the givens, making connections between facts and ideas which men have left unconnected. It means remembering that every mind resides in a body; remaining accountable to the female bodies in which we live; constantly retesting given hypotheses against lived experience. It means a constant critique of language, for as Wittgenstein (no feminist) observed, "The limits of my language are the limits of my world." And it means that most difficult thing of all: listening and watching in art and literature, in the social sciences, in all the descriptions we are given of the world, for the silences, the absences, the nameless, the unspoken, the encoded—for there we will find the true knowledge of women. And in breaking those silences, naming our selves, uncovering the hidden, making ourselves present, we begin to define a reality which resonates to *us,* which affirms *our* being, which allows the woman teacher and the woman student alike to take ourselves, and each other, seriously: meaning, to begin taking charge of our lives.

---

### Now that you've read

1. What are some of Rich's main arguments?
2. Is this essay outdated? In what respects, specifically, is it outdated? In what respects, is it still relevant?
3. What advantages might same-sex schools offer? What might be their disadvantages?
4. What do you make of the last paragraph of Rich's essay? Respond briefly to the claims she makes in that paragraph.

# READING 2

*Jeffrey Berman*

# Hunger Artists

In his book *Diaries to an English Professor: Pain and Growth in the Classroom,* Jeffrey Berman categorizes and shares excerpts from diaries his students wrote for him in his classes. This particular chapter focuses on young women who wrote about their eating disorders. These entries from their diaries offer sobering pictures of the struggles many young women go through to overcome a problem that could kill them and to regain control of their lives.

## Before you read

1. What kinds of pressures do young women face? What kinds of pressures do young men face? What similarities and differences are there, and how are they significant?
2. What do you know about eating disorders?
3. Why do you think eating disorders afflict young women more commonly than young men?
4. What makes someone susceptible to developing an eating disorder?

---

> *Just try to explain to anyone the art of fasting! Anyone who has no feeling for it cannot be made to understand it.*
> — FRANZ KAFKA, "A HUNGER ARTIST"

Of all the stories I teach, none is more opaque to male students or more disturbingly transparent to so many female students than Franz Kafka's "Hunger Artist" (1922). Only ten pages long, the tale focuses on a performer who suffers the misfortune of living in an era which no longer values his unusual talent for fasting. Decades earlier, Kafka tells us, life was different. The entire town would turn out to marvel at the emaciated hunger artist sitting in his narrow straw-lined cage, dreaming of shattering his own world record. Rejoicing in the huge crowds gathered around his cage every day, the hunger artist would proudly extend his shriveled arm through the bars of his cage to allow children to feel its skeletal thinness. Despite his death-defying starvation, the hunger artist is never tempted to eat a morsel of food, not even when the permanent watchers at the circus, charged with the task of making sure he does not cheat, turn their backs on him, encouraging him to eat.

Indeed, the spectators do not know how easy it is for the hunger artist to reject food. Perfecting the art of fasting is the only desire in his life. Limited by an impresario's decision that he abstain from food for a maximum of forty days—beyond that period the public apparently loses interest—the hunger artist yearns to fast until the end of his days. "So he live[s] for many years, . . . honored by the world, yet . . . troubled in spirit." When a well-wisher attempts to console him by pointing out that his melancholy is the result of his prolonged fasting, the hunger artist reacts violently, shaking the bars of his cage like a trapped animal. Although the impresario apologizes for these outbursts, attributing them to the irritation caused by fasting, the hunger artist knows that this explanation is a perversion of the truth. "What was a consequence of the premature ending of his fast was here presented as the cause of it!"

To the hunger artist's dismay, the public eventually loses interest in the art of fasting, forsaking him for other performers. Forced to end his partnership with the impresario and hire himself to a large circus, he strives vainly to win a new generation of loyal followers. For a time the old excitement for professional hunger artists returns, and he is exhilarated by the possibility of fasting on and on, with daily placards announcing his record-shattering feat. But soon the fickle crowds tire of the hunger artist's act, his cage is abandoned, and he drops out of sight.

One day an overseer notices the cage and orders attendants to explain why it is standing unused with dirty straw inside it. The attendants poke around in the straw and discover the hunger artist lying in it, close to death. "Are you still fasting?" the overseer asks. "When on earth do you mean to stop?" The dialogue proceeds as follows:

> "Forgive me, everybody," whispered the hunger artist; only the overseer, who had his ear to the bars, understood him. "Of course," said the overseer, and tapped his forehead with a finger to let the attendants know what state the man was in, "we forgive you." "I always wanted you to admire my fasting," said the hunger artist. "We do admire it," said the overseer, affably. "But you shouldn't admire it," said the hunger artist. "Well then we don't admire it," said the overseer, "but why shouldn't we admire it?" "Because I have to fast, I can't help it," said the hunger artist. "What a fellow you are," said the overseer, "and why can't you help it?" "Because," said the hunger artist, lifting his head a little and speaking, with his lips pursed, as if for a kiss, right into the overseer's ear, so that no syllable might be lost, "because I couldn't find the food I liked. If I had found it, believe me, I should have made no fuss and stuffed myself like you or anyone else."

Why does the hunger artist starve himself in order to feel fulfilled? Why does he ask forgiveness for an act that seems both voluntary and involuntary, and for which he wishes to be admired yet not admired? Why does he reach out to others—he almost kisses the overseer—only to spurn communication and connection? In what sense does his artistic performance mask a self-destructive wish? For what does the hunger artist truly hunger? In short, what is the psychology of the man who is, in the impresario's words, a "suffering martyr"—"which indeed he was," Kafka adds cryptically, "although in quite another sense"?

As Kim Chernin has suggested, Kafka's "Hunger Artist" can be read, in part, as a parable on eating disorders, a prophetic warning of our cultural obsession with food and dieting. The hunger artist's anorexic-like behavior will be familiar to anyone who has studied the paradoxical dynamics of this mysterious disease: the need to remain in control while demonstrating out-of-control behavior, the exhibitionistic wish to display one's body while expressing contempt for the corporeal, the effort to preserve the illusion of omnipotence and self-sufficiency while regressing to a state of total infantilism, and the quest for perfectionism while feeling hopelessly imperfect. The hunger artist is a deeply contradictory figure, a self-effacing performer who grandiosely believes he is the greatest faster of all time, a submissive man who reacts violently to those who fail to take him seriously, a loner who becomes irritable and depressed when the multitudes desert his act.

Violence against the body constitutes the essence of the hunger artist's form of expression, violence that reflects narcissistic injury, masochism, and passive aggression. Like his late nineteenth-century American counterpart, Melville's Bartleby the scrivener, the hunger artist "prefers not to." Food becomes the object of his protest, and the decision to stop eating symbolizes nothing less than the repudiation of desire. The cage in which he is imprisoned becomes a metaphor of his diminished body; his self-enclosure stands in sharp contrast to the robust panther which roams the cage after his death. Combining aestheticism and asceticism, the hunger artist finally succeeds in extinguishing his life, thus recalling another tormented Kafka protagonist, Gregor Samsa in *The Metamorphosis* (1912), who, upon hearing his family's lodgers noisily devour their food, sadly thinks" "I'm hungry enough . . . but not for that kind of food. How these lodgers are stuffing themselves, and here am I dying of starvation!"

## The Hunger Artist and Kafka

There are intriguing parallels between the hunger artist's and Kafka's own rejection of food. In the autobiographical "Letter to His Father," written in 1919, Kafka declares that many of the clashes with his father arose over food and drink. Kafka's earliest childhood memory involved a traumatic incident at night in which, whimpering repeatedly for water, he was commanded by his father to remain quiet. When the warning failed to have its desired effect, the father dragged his son out of bed, carried him onto a balcony, and left him there in his nightshirt, outside the shut door. The incident aroused feelings of terror and confusion in the youth; for years afterward he suffered from the tormenting fear that his father, the ultimate authority, would come into his room for no reason and humiliate him again.

In an even more significant passage in "Letter to His Father," Kafka reveals the extent to which his father's attitude toward food had a formative influence on his life:

> Since as a child I was with you chiefly during meals, your teaching was to a large extent the teaching of proper behavior at table. What was brought to the table had to be eaten, the quality of the food was not to be discussed—but you yourself often found the food inedible, called it "this swill," said "that beast" (the cook) had ruined it. Because in accordance with your strong appetite and your particular predilection you ate everything fast, hot, and in big mouthfuls, the child had to hurry; there was a somber silence at table, interrupted by admonitions: "Eat first, talk afterwards," or "faster, faster, faster," or "there you are, you see, I finished ages ago." Bones mustn't be cracked with the teeth, but you could. Vinegar must not be sipped noisily, but you could. The main thing was that the bread should be cut straight. But it didn't matter that you did it with a knife dripping with gravy. Care had to be taken that no scraps fell on the floor. In the end it was under your chair that there were most scraps.

As a result of his father's dictatorial commandments, Kafka came to believe that there were three separate and distinct worlds: a world in which he lived as a slave, forced to obey laws intended only for him; a second world, infinitely remote from the first, where his father lived and governed as a god; and a third world, where everyone else lived happily, free from tyrannical rule. "I was continually in disgrace; either I obeyed your orders, and that was a disgrace, for they applied, after all, only to me; or I was defiant, and that was a disgrace too, for how could I presume to defy you; or I could not obey because I did not, for instance, have your strength, your appetite, your skill, although you expected it of me as a matter of course; this was the greatest disgrace of all."

By rejecting food, Kafka repudiated his father's world of appetite, brute strength, and tyrannical rule. Fasting represented both defiance against his father's domineering control and self-punishment for harboring patricidal feelings. Unable to eat heartily or drink beer with his meals, as his father wished him to do, Kafka, the grandson of a Kosher butcher, became a vegetarian. Nevertheless, conflicts over food continued. "For years he suffered from his stomach," Kafka's friend and future biographer, Max Brod, wrote to Felice Bauer in 1912. Kafka's most recent biographer, Frederick Karl, describes him as "very probably, a secondary anorexic, turning food and the experience of it into a form of warfare, which he could fight and win but at the expense of his well-being.

Kafka's struggle with food appears in his earliest diaries, long before his scarecrow body was ravaged by the tuberculosis that finally consumed his life in 1924 at the age of forty. A fantasy recorded in a 1911 entry reflects the desire for bingeing and purging symptomatic of bulimia:

> This craving that I almost always have, when for once I feel my stomach is healthy, to heap up in me notions of terrible deeds of daring with food. I especially satisfy this craving in front of pork butchers. If I see a sausage that is labeled as an old, hard sausage, I bite into it in my imagination with all my teeth and swallow quickly, regularly and thoughtlessly, like a machine. The despair that this act, even in the imagination, has as its immediate result, increases my haste. I shove the long slabs of rib meat unbitten into my mouth, and then pull them out again from behind, tearing through stomach and intestines. I eat dirty delicatessen stores completely empty. Cram myself with herrings, pickles and all the bad, old, sharp foods. Bonbons are poured into me like hail from their tin boxes. I enjoy in this way not only my healthy condition but also a suffering that is without pain and can pass at once.

A 1913 diary entry records Kafka's fantasy of being nothing more than a slab of meat, ready to be sliced for human consumption. "Always the image of a pork butcher's broad knife that quickly and with mechanical regularity chops into me from the side and cuts off very thin slices which fly off almost like shavings because of the speed of the action. Given his rejection of food, there was a grim irony, as Ernst Pawel observes, in Kafka's final illness, during which he was literally unable to eat. "There is an element of rising savagery in the way in which he progressed from the avoidance of certain foods to what amounted to a self-imposed starvation diet, rendered pathetically ironic by the fact that in the end the very nature of his final illness—tuberculosis of the larynx—made swallowing all but impossible, so that he quite literally starved to death."

And yet despite the parallels between Kafka and the hunger artist, it would be misleading to reduce the author to any of his characters. Whereas Kafka can create, from the depths of his extraordinary imagination, the character of the hunger artist, viewing him as a symbol of a martyred and misunderstood writer, the hunger artist can only starve himself, rejecting life rather than recreating it through art, as his maker did. While the hunger artist undoubtedly reflects his creator's ambivalence toward art, the conviction that writing is both a blessing and a curse, Kafka insisted that art is the antidote to life. "Poetry is disease," he wrote to Gustav Janouch, "yet one does not get well by suppressing the fever. On the contrary! Its heat purifies and illuminates." And whereas the hunger artist falls into oblivion and perishes, unnoticed by the world, Kafka achieved through his art lasting fame, creating imperishable stories that nourish the imagination.

### Eating Disorders as a Cultural Phenomenon

"Fasting would surely come into fashion again at some future date," Kafka prophesies in "A Hunger Artist," a prediction that has come true with a vengeance. The American obsession with dieting has now reached almost epidemic proportions, giving rise to an increased incidence of anorexia and bulimia among college women. Both of these eating disorders are surprising recent cultural developments.

In anorexia, victims starve themselves to the point where, in extreme cases, they take on the appearance of concentration camp survivors. Anorexia reflects a morbid fear of becoming overweight, a fear that persists even when body weight is 15 percent below normal. Psychologists have offered numerous theories to explain the dynamics of anorexia, ranging from the quest for control and perfectionism to the unleashing of violence against the self. Fear of awakening sexuality also plays a key role in a young woman's decision to stop eating. The anorectic frequently stops menstruating and, because of hormonal imbalances triggered by starvation, develops downy hair over her body and takes on a masculine appearance. Although the symptoms of anorexia nervosa were first described more than a century ago—the illness was named by the British physician Sir William Gull in 1874—the disease became well known only in the late 1960s. "One might speak of an epidemic illness, only there is no contagious agent; the spread must be attributed to psychosociological factors," Hilde Bruch remarks in *The Golden Cage* (1978), one of the first books on anorexia. Joan Jacobs Brumberg argues in *Fasting Girls* that anorexia is "clearly a multidetermined disorder that depends on the individual's biologic vulnerability, psychological predisposition, family, and the social climate."

Bulimia is a newer phenomenon. Marlene Boskind-White and William C. White, Jr., two Cornell University psychologists who studied the bingeing and purging eating habits of female college students, coined the word "bulimarexia" in 1975 to describe the psychological dynamics of "perfectionism, obsessive concern with food and body proportions, isolationism, low self-esteem, and a strong commitment to please others, often at the individual's expense." Most researchers now use the term "bulimia nervosa," or simply "bulimia," to describe this disorder.

Anorexia and bulimia have attracted increasing attention in recent years from clinicians, nutritionists, and feminist scholars (the vast majority of people suffering from these disorders are women), but a veil of secrecy persists. Few first-person accounts of anorexia and bulimia exist, and most anorectics and bulimics cannot bring themselves to speak publicly about their illnesses. When they do share their terrible secrets with a relative or friend, they often feel increased shame and isolation.

### Breaking the Silence

One way to break this silence is to encourage students to write diaries about their experiences with eating disorders. "A Hunger Artist" is, of course, a perfect story to read in this context, as is Margaret Atwood's *Edible Woman,* but anorexia and bulimia are so prevalent among college women that they generally submit entries on this subject long before we discuss these texts.

I want to focus in this chapter on five women who were members of the same class; four of them wrote about bulimic behavior, and one wrote about compulsive overeating. None betrayed the skeletal thinness of Kafka's hunger artist, but all discussed the extent to which eating disorders reflected larger conflicts in their lives. They gave me permission to read their diaries to the class, and their writings inspired entries from other students who had never before imagined the "art of fasting."

Diaries on eating disorders illuminate many of the reasons behind self-starvation, and as we shall see, the students offer a variety of explanations involving psychological, cultural, and feminist perspectives. The themes unifying the five women's writings are violence against the female body and the suppression of desire; a profound ambivalence toward food, which is symptomatic of larger issues in students' lives; the need to master inner conflicts and regain self-control; and the search for love, validation, and self-acceptance in a family that is often torn by conflict. Over the years, literally scores of women—but no men—have written diaries about suffering from anorexia and bulimia. Eating disorder diaries are thus female texts. The diaries have been a revelation both to the other students and to me, deepening our understanding of the vexing difficulties of growing up female in the United States.

### BRENDA
*"It All Started Innocently Enough, a Young Girl*
*Being Concerned with Her Looks and Her Weight"*

Brenda, a sophomore, was the first person in the class to write about an eating disorder. Like most of the other women who discussed bulimia, she said that she did not become aware of a problem until long after the onset of its symptoms. She turned in the following diary during the third week of the semester:

> A problem which has been with me for over four years, which I had to enter psychotherapy for, is a disorder which affects many young women in our society. The problem became apparent in my sophomore year of high school, and the symptoms persisted until a little over a year ago. I have bulimia.
>
> In don't know how or why it started, but I can remember as far back as eighth grade being overly concerned with my weight and going so far as to use laxatives to control it. The realization that I had an eating disorder never came until two years later, when my symptoms became impossible to ignore. It all started innocently enough, a young girl being concerned with her looks and her weight. However, some of us possess a predisposition toward letting it go beyond control.
>
> I consider myself a somewhat neurotic or compulsive person to begin with; however, factors like my father's being an alcoholic and leaving me when I was very young surely contributed. As I look back, I see the time when I was in high school as being marked by my father's increasing demands to have me back in his life and to somehow be able to control my life. My problems with him, my stress level, and my bulimia all escalated throughout high school.
>
> Sometime in my sophomore or junior year my mother had me put into counseling, which I hated. I stayed with this ridiculous therapist for six months until I declared myself "all better" so I didn't have to see him anymore. I don't believe I learned anything from that man. Within months, my symptoms were so bad that I missed volleyball practices, taking whole boxes of laxatives and bottles of ipecac on the weekends. My blood pressure dropped to almost too low to donate blood, and I started to become very frightened about what I was doing to myself.
>
> The symptoms of the disease were dictating my whole life: I wouldn't go out with friends on certain occasions because I had planned an evening of bingeing and purging. No one but my mother knew. So finally I had to tell her that I would reenter therapy with another doctor. Everyone thought I was killing myself as I fell in and out of major depressions, my therapist occasionally suggesting antidepressant drugs. But gradually my symptoms became less frightening, and I discontinued therapy when I left for college.
>
> Since I've been here at school, pressures have increased tremendously, my relationship with my father has gotten progressively worse (I refuse to speak with him ever again), I haven't seen a therapist since high school, and yet on my own I've managed to live without symptoms for the past year.
>
> I don't really know how to end this journal. I can't thank anyone for the recovery (which I consider lifelong) but myself: my counselor was all right, my parents think I still make myself sick, and my father never cared. I do know that I have a new sense of confidence, and I feel much better about myself than I have in years. I'm a much more independent person than I ever was and feel much better equipped to handle difficulties in my life.

Brenda apparently has little difficulty writing about her experience with bulimia; she writes factually, without embarrassment, guilt, or shame. She closes the diary on a self-confident note, though not before venting anger toward her father, whom she views, as her next diary demonstrates, as a major source of her problems:

Unfortunately, this week I feel totally uninspired as to what to write about. I attribute that to the fact that I've had so much on my mind lately: I am more than behind in most of my classes, have been having the worst time trying to find a job, am in the negatives as far as my finances go, and have been thinking about how to deal with my father. OK, there's a topic—my relationship with my father. Unfortunately, that subject would require a book to cover, but I'll do my best to condense it.

To give you a little history, my parents got married at an early age. When I was a baby, my father left my family. Whether I did when I was younger or not, I don't hold his leaving us against him now. I feel very aware of that and feel that it has no influence on my feelings for him now, even though he thinks that's one of the reasons I resent him. Anyway, until I was twelve years old, he didn't make much of an effort to see me or my mom or my two brothers.

When he did finally try to become a "part of my life," I had already grown distant from him. He didn't just try to see me more often, but any time our plans didn't work out or I was busy one weekend, he projected his guilty feelings onto me by blaming me for the "horrible" way I was treating him and putting him off. For years I fell for this and actually felt guilty—not just with him, but I now have a chronic guilt complex about everything. Eventually, I caught on to what was happening and told him, with a lot of difficulty and a lot of retaliation on his part.

The poor man is a recovering alcoholic who never should have dropped therapy, because he needs it. To give you an example of his mental condition, I'll quote you a telephone conversation we once had:

ME: I only want a passive relationship with you. I don't know you and don't want you to interfere with my life, but I would like for us to be able to get along.

DAD: All you want is a passive relationship? That's your neurosis, Brenda. All of your relationships are passive!

ME: My neurosis?? How do you know about ANY of my relationships? You don't even know me. So, Dad, why don't you tell me about my neurosis and all of my passive relationships. . . .

DAD: No, you tell me, they're your problems and your relationships.

I don't know how to explain it, but the guy just doesn't have a grip. He keeps meticulous track of every letter I have ever sent him, and his computer remembers every letter he's mailed me. Maybe that's good for him, though, because he distorts the past, and he distorts facts to an unreasonable extent. You just can't argue with him when you're dealing from two different decks. He uses me, he abuses me, he promised to pay for college and then decided a month ago to withdraw his offer. Says he wants to be my father but doesn't know how to give or how to love.

I think the reason he's been on my case so much in the past three years is because my brothers refuse to have anything to do with him. The way it is all ending (I hope) is by my refusal to ever accept another phone call or letter from him.

Brenda's diary recalls those written by Mara, Rachel, and Tracey. . . . We see the same anger toward the father, the same wish to separate her life from his, the same belief that she has nothing in common with him. Brenda's writings suggest that the sins of the fathers have been a major factor in her illness and that her father has exacerbated the situation by labeling her problems a neurosis. For this reason, Brenda can see no hope of reconciliation or compromise with him, no possibility of a useful dialogue. She closes the entry with the vow never to let her father back into her life. She never returned to the subject of her father in any of her later writings.

### MARCY
### "I Felt There Was Power in the Boyish Figure and Weakness in Girlish Curves"

During the same week in which Brenda wrote about her problem with bulimia, Marcy, a senior, turned in the first of four diaries about the difficulty of being a woman in a patriarchal society. She begins by referring to Freud's antifeminist concept of penis envy, insisting that women have been victimized not by anatomy but by culture:

Although I would be the first person to object to Freud's theory of penis envy and the notion that all women have an innate psychological wish to be a man, I must admit that I personally have always felt a certain dissatisfaction with my gender. I am quite certain, however, that this is entirely for social (not psychological) reasons.

I was a tomboy until I was thirteen years old. There are two incidents which I remember very clearly that served to confuse and upset my understanding and acceptance of my gender. The first of these events occurred on a very hot day when I was five years old and playing in a church playground. I was of course playing with the boys because the girls were much too boring (wearing frilly dresses and playing with dolls were not for me—athletics in the dirt were more my style). All the boys decided to take off their shirts because of the heat. So I proceeded to remove my shirt also. Well, you would think that a creature from another planet was standing there from the reaction these boys had. They pointed and laughed, saying, "Tits! Your tits are showing!" Having the limited experience of a five-year-old, I was quite sure that I had no idea what "tits" were. I remember surveying their bodies and then my own and not finding a single difference. I did not understand when they explained to me that since I was a girl, I was not free to cool off on a hot day.

The other incident that stands out in my memory is an argument that ensued between the boys and girls in the second-grade cafeteria. I was sitting at the boys' table as usual when the fight broke out. The boys were calling the girls "corroded," and the girls were telling the boys that they had "cooties." The basic premise was that girls thought they were better, and boys thought they were. There I was, right in the middle of all of this, not knowing which side to take. I knew that I was a girl by definition and that by insulting them I would be insulting myself, and yet I really believed that boys were better. I just sat there silent and confused.

I'm really not sure why I have chosen to discuss these particular things for this diary. I only know that I often still feel that familiar confusion. Why am I valued more if I am physically attractive than intelligent? Why am I expected to be domestic when inside I feel like any other bachelor living alone? The fact is that all women's psyches are messed up by the traditional sex-role stereotypes.

A good example of this is the lack of heroines in the movies. Women sit in movie theaters and identify with the heroes because the director created the movie so that the spectator would identify with the hero. However, at the same time, she knows that she is not like him and cannot be because she is a woman. The majority of the women she sees on the screen (or in the media in general) are portrayed as helpless passive victims who need to be rescued by men. They are also sexually exploited and shown as objects for the satisfaction of male scopophilia or voyeurism. Women then must identify themselves as objects. The internalization of these values can have a significantly destructive impact on the female psyche.

This is a very brief explanation of the psychological confusion I feel just from being a woman. I don't want to be an object or a victim. I want to be a hero, and I've always known I could be, but society keeps trying to tell me that I cannot. That is why I sometimes still wish I were a man. If I were a man, I would not have to face the confusion and the oppression. Sorry Freud, it's not for the penis.

Continuing these meditations in her next diary, Marcy reveals the ways in which women are victimized by a culture that reduces them to a sexual object—a thin object, she adds:

This week I am going to continue what I wrote about last week—that is, the female psyche in a misogynistic society. In particular I want to discuss body perception and eating disorders.

The reason I choose this topic is because it affects nearly every single female I know. (Although I'm not sure about the nationwide statistics, I'm sure this is indicative.) The main problem is the media. It tells us that women should be thin thin thin. Everything is dietetic, and only thin women are shown as models. But the fact is that women have naturally a good deal of fat on their bodies. The result of this dichotomy between media ideal and reality is a society of women obsessed with food and weight.

Perhaps this does not sound so awful. However, in addition to all the deaths caused by bulimia and anorexia every year, even the women who seem "healthy" are victims. All of the women who want that dessert so badly but gather all the willpower in themselves to say no, all the women who have dessert and then feel as guilty as if they had committed a sin, all the women who go to the gym everyday and sweat until they dehydrate—these are the victims as well. Even I am a victim.

I believe that my story is most frightening because if you've ever seen me, you know that I am very skinny. When I was fifteen years old, and I had just developed hips, I wanted to cut them off. This was obviously the product of my still wishing I was a male in a world that favored males. If I had hips and breasts, how was I going to deny my female sexuality?

So I set about to get rid of them. I tried all different methods. I would go a few days with no food and then have some soup or something. Then I found out that all you have to do is vomit afterward and you could eat all you want. So I did this for a while. And don't think I did any of this alone. Two of my close friends, both as thin as I, joined me in my weight loss attempts. An objective observer would probably think that this was a normal stage of development for young women. But obviously, it is not. It is the unhealthy and life-threatening reaction of women to the bogus beauty ideals created by men.

My best friend has a fabulous body. She is thin but not too thin, and she has nice curves. It is the saddest thing to see her grab a handful of her own flesh and look at it with such venomous disgust that you would think it was a cancer or something. You can see nearly every woman do this same thing if you go into the women's locker room in a gym. They get on the scale and pray that more of their bodies will be gone. They literally wish to diminish themselves. They learn to hate their female bodies so much that they will go to any pains to make them disappear. "I don't care if I kill myself doing it. I'm going to burn off those extra pounds." Sound familiar? To me it does.

I have finally learned to love my body because it is the only one I have, and so it is to me beautiful. I think all women need to learn to feel this way about themselves and to ignore the message from the media that says, If you're fat, you're no good. If it took me this long, and I happen to be skinny, how long will it take more voluptuous women? The prospects are bleak.

With each diary, Marcy extends her analysis of a patriarchal society's pernicious influence on the female psyche. In the first entry she explores the dangers of gender stereotyping; in the second she investigates the relationship between body perception and eating disorders; and in the third she responds to a question I had raised in one of my comments: to what extent does a woman's dissatisfaction with her body reflect a fear of sexuality? The question angered Marcy, but she continued to think about it, soon discovering a troubling pattern in her life: an attraction to "male chauvinists." Whereas in the previous entry she identifies the "media" as the major cause of eating disorders, she now writes

about a subject much closer to home—a father's sexist influence
on his daughter:

> In last week's diary you asked whether I was afraid of my female sexual-
> ity. My first response to this was anger. I was defensive. I thought to my-
> self, "I have completely normal and healthy sexual relationships with
> my boyfriends, past and present." But then I realized that my fear is not
> on that level. What I mean is that privately, in the safety of my close
> relationships, I have no problem with my sexuality—in fact, I enjoy it.
> However, in public situations, in front of the whole world, it troubles me
> to be female. I guess this must be because of the many factors about
> misogyny in our society that I discussed in my previous journals, and
> also because my father is a big male chauvinist sexist man. I have re-
> sented his attitude, and only recently did I realize its effect on me.
>
> And yet, when I think about the serious boyfriends I've had in my
> life, all are very different but share one trait—that is, they are male
> chauvinists. Consciously, I find it inconceivable that I would be at-
> tracted to a man who reminds me of my father, and yet here is this evi-
> dence. In fact, my first boyfriend reminds me exactly of my image of my
> father at his age. When I first met him, he was wearing his college foot-
> ball uniform. My father also played football in college, and in most of
> the photographs I have of him he is also wearing a football uniform.
>
> There are other things about my boyfriend that remind me of my
> father as well, but I have never acknowledged the similarities. My rela-
> tionship to my boyfriend was unusual too. He loved me much more than
> I did him; actually, I don't think I ever loved him at all. At times I was even
> sickened by him and his attitudes, and sometimes by his physical being.
> At the same time I liked being with him and being nauseated by him.
> When I think back, this is very self-destructive behavior. I wonder if this
> diary is making sense. Some things are easier to speak of than to write.

After hearing Brenda's and Marcy's diaries read aloud, other
women in the class began writing diaries about eating disorders.
Marcy was surprised by the number of these students, and in her
fourth diary, written in tones ranging from righteous indignation to
caustic sarcasm, she offers additional details of her obsession with
thinness:

> I was never diagnosed as having anorexia or bulimia, but I had, in mild
> form, some of their symptoms. As I mentioned in another diary, when I
> was fifteen years old my body started to change from boyishly skinny to
> round (but still skinny). I became very disconcerted. For reasons that I
> did not understand until later, I felt there was power in the boyish figure
> and weakness in girlish curves. I absolutely despised fat or flab of any
> sort. Fat people repulsed me. To this day I am very turned off by any flab
> on people, and I go out only with thin (some would say skinny) men.
>
> Anyway, I decided to combat my developing body by controlling
> my diet. My most specific memories of dieting and purging were at
> sleep-away camp, where I could get away with not eating because no

one would monitor me (like my mom would at home, who has always been telling me that I am too skinny). Now that I think about this, she gave me an awful lot of attention when the subject of weight and eating came up, and perhaps it was more of this type of attention that I sought when I tried to reduce myself further.

But I think the main reason was a fear of sexuality—a fear of turning into one of those objectified nonhuman things sprawled out all over the pages of dirty magazines and elsewhere. I guess I thought that if I turned into that, others would take over control of my body, and I would no longer have any control. I think that almost all women who starve themselves do so as a form of controlling their own life. It's something that certainly no one else can control, the "rewards" are visible, and sometimes people even comment on them. Sometimes women lose so much weight that they stop menstruating, thus having another visible sign of their own control over their bodies as well as accomplishing the feat of reversing the development of female sexuality.

I remember being really hungry and using willpower not to eat and telling myself to "fight" the temptation to eat. I also remember feeling victorious and powerful after a full day of not eating. When my stomach was so flat that it was concave and my ribs were sticking out, I was strong. I used to drink a lot of diet Pepsi. I always had a can in my hand. I know this one girl who used to buy twenty kinds of diet soda, and that would be all she ate all day. She would pretend that the different flavors were a variety of fruits and foods.

I practiced regurgitating my food every once in a while when I felt that I had eaten an unearthly amount of food, like a whole pint of ice cream. I think I would have done it more, but I really found it to be most unpleasant, so I used the technique only for emergencies. Many times after I ate a big meal I would feel bloated, and I would hate my body and think it was too big. And yet my whole life people, both family and strangers, are constantly telling me how skinny I am. In fact, I often heard men say of me, "She would be attractive if she gained ten pounds," or "Yuk! she's way too skinny." And I am never offended by these remarks.

In a way, they give me a sense of freedom because I think, OK, I'm not fat now and I can even enjoy a few good pig-outs and people will still think I look all right." But I know that I will not be happy with myself if I gained ten pounds, even if the whole world told me how good I looked. I just feel more comfortable in a skinny body. Sometimes I even feel sorry for women with a big chest and a big belly or thighs, but I guess some of them are used to it, and I really believe that they should and could learn to love their own bodies. Maybe not, though, with all the "thin is in" propaganda.

I heard a comedienne do a funny routine. She was talking about how it used to be fashionable for women to be all flabby and fat, like in the classical paintings. She said, "That must have been great. All we women had to do was sit around and eat pastries and get painted. If anyone told us we were gaining a little weight, we could say, "Damn straight, I'm posing for Rubens this afternoon, now pass me a cannoli, you piece of shit!"

I don't use food as a means of control anymore. Now I try to eat healthily without gaining or losing weight. But when I hear the diaries of other women who still have these problems in severe ways, I feel really bad for them. I know that a part of it is due to the media images of ideal women and such. I also know that they must have other problems in their lives to contribute to this disorder.

I wish I could help them, but I don't believe that I can. I think that part of the reason that my condition never got really serious was because my best friend has severe anorexia and was in the hospital for most of our high school years. She almost died from it, and I may have wanted strength or attention, but I did not want to die. She is better now, and I think that therapy helped her a lot. But she still watches her weight and diets. It is sad. That is all I can say. It is very sad.

## LAURIE
### "It Is My Deepest, Darkest, Most Painful Secret"

Unlike Brenda and Marcy, Laurie, a senior, was still caught in the binge-purge cycle. Bulimia was an ongoing problem, creating intense guilt and shame as well as ominous physical symptoms, and she found it painfully difficult to share her secret with anyone. The two diaries she wrote on being bulimic contained an urgency apparent to everyone:

I don't mean to bore you or overemphasize a subject that so many students have chosen to focus their diaries on. In fact, I hesitated to put these thoughts on paper because what I'm about to discuss is something I've kept locked up inside of me for so long; it is something I seem unable to control. None of my friends, housemates, or even my boyfriend knows what I am suffering from and what I'm struggling to overcome every single day. It is my deepest, darkest, most painful secret.

In many ways, hearing that I am not alone with my problem and realizing that others can comprehend what I'm going through gave me the courage to write this journal. If you are still in the dark as to what I am talking about, it is bulimia, more accurately called bulimarexia. It is an extremely destructive and horrible eating disorder that I have been battling for over five years. More than being an embarrassing addiction, bulimarexia is life threatening, and though I am fully aware of this fact, it still is a problem I am incapable of conquering. If people can understand how strong an addiction smoking, biting your nails, or drinking is, then they can understand the seriousness of being bulimarexic.

It starts out as something innocent, a few girlfriends discovering this great weight-loss plan where you can eat as much as you want and never gain weight. What an ideal way to stay thin—thin being the only way for women. Unfortunately for me, this seemingly innocent weight-loss plan progressed into a sick obsession that began to rule my life. Food became an enemy as well as my closest friend; it was something that could make me feel so good and so at ease, yet it was also something that could make me feel ugly, inadequate, and miserable.

I don't know exactly why this problem began. I know it has strong connections with low self-esteem and the desire to be perfect. The media only serve to perpetuate eating disorders, for television, magazines, and billboards brainwash women into believing one needs to have a beautiful face, a beautiful figure, and beautiful hair to be desirable, to be loved, to be accepted. So much emphasis is placed on appearances and thinness in our society. Women are constantly bombarded with messages that they are too fat, too ugly, too wrinkly, too flabby, too greasy: the list is infinite.

I learned early on to internalize and believe these messages sent out in our society. I learned to hate my body, and I learned to take extremely drastic measures to change and improve myself.

I want so badly to overcome this addiction. I desperately want to love and accept myself as I am, with all my flaws and imperfections. To say reaching this point is difficult is a total understatement. Recently, I began group therapy with about nine other girls approximately the same age as I am; we are all suffering from the same eating disorder. We have all admitted that we want to be perfect; we all want so deeply to be that ideal woman whom the media promotes. We all come from similar backgrounds, and all of us have excelled as students. One girl just graduated from Barnard and another from Smith. So, it is quite obvious that bulimarexics are not idiots; most of them are bright, hard-working, ambitious women who simply cannot accept themselves as they are.

I hope that together we can sort through our problems and help each other win this terrible battle. I don't want to die, which is a fear I think about every day. I don't want to go into cardiac arrest or have all my teeth rot and fall out of my mouth. I'm so tired of living with this addiction and hiding it from everyone I am close to. I pray that I can overcome it. I want to be normal; I want to love me as me.

The diary that I handed in two weeks ago, which was read aloud to the class, about "my deepest, darkest, most painful secret," was the first time I have ever discussed my problem with anyone outside of my immediate family, my therapist, and my therapy group. Finally writing about my eating disorder and letting people know about my secret life was a catharsis for me; it felt as if some huge weight was lifted off my shoulders. I honestly cried as I wrote it, realizing just how hard it is coping with bulimia. I cried at how pathetic I am, bingeing and purging day after day, knowing that it can eventually kill me or at least destroy my body.

My therapist had always recommended writing in some sort of journal or diary as a way to help me overcome bulimia. She told me that writing your thoughts down on paper would help you understand yourself more fully and would also help you understand your problem. I never took the time to write, however. I didn't believe keeping a journal would change anything. Writing that diary made me realize how important keeping a journal is; I can "see" myself better, and it just feels good in general to release your pain, fears, and thoughts on paper.

I felt it was important that my diary be read aloud to the class primarily because this problem that affects so many women is frequently misunderstood. I also wanted the other women in the class who may suffer from the same eating disorder to know that they are not alone; I feel for them, I know how deep the pain runs, I know how frightened and helpless they feel. After class a few weeks ago I heard one woman tell another person that she was the one whose diary on bulimia was read aloud. I give her so much credit for having the courage to reveal her identity. I do not feel that I am ready to let people know that I am also bulimic. I'm too scared. I suppose I'm too concerned about what people will think of me.

I wish more people would be aware of this horrible addiction and understand how extremely difficult it is to stop. My brother always says to me, "Why would anyone want to throw up? Puking is disgusting. Why don't you just control yourself?" Believe me, I desperately wish I could control myself. But as I mentioned in that diary, bulimia is an addiction as strong as being addicted to cocaine, cigarettes, or alcohol. It's not something you can just stop without help. I used to think I could stop whenever I wanted. I never thought I needed professional help. Shrinks are for crazy people.

After the problem started getting worse and I found myself completely dominated by bulimia and the whole evil binge-purge cycle, I knew I needed help. I didn't want to acknowledge the fact that I had this sickness, that I was a full-fledged bulimic, so I kept ignoring my parents when they told me to get help. My dad would leave phone numbers of therapists in my bedroom, but I wouldn't call.

Do you know what finally made me give in and call and get help for myself? I went to the dentist, and I had nine cavities. He told me that the enamel on my teeth had been worn off. The same week I had gone to the dentist, one of my teeth shattered from biting into a sandwich. I mean, I never used to get cavities. Like a lead brick it hit me: this was just one sign of how I was destroying my body. I was literally terrified that I was going to lose all of my teeth.

The next day after my dentist appointment, I called the doctor. Something had to be done—enough was enough. I don't want to die! Seeking therapy is an essential part to conquering eating disorders. I do not believe people can cure themselves on their own. I hope all of the women in the class are involved in some sort of therapy now. If not, please go. I know how difficult it is coming to terms with the fact that you have a problem. Just do it. I'm glad I did.

Since I wrote that diary, certain things have changed in my life. In a way, opening up in the diary gave me the courage to open up to my boyfriend. He and I have been dating for over two years. Though we've been together for so long, almost living together for a year, he has never been aware of my problem with bulimia. I kept it a well-hidden secret, and that was no easy task. In fact, he had no idea that I was in therapy twice a week.

I constantly had to lie to him about where I was and what I was doing. The fact that I had to lie to him used to eat away at me; I walked around with a guilty conscience all of the time as well as the fear that one day he would catch me. I wanted to tell him; I wanted to share this ugly part of my life with him, but I could not. I was too ashamed. I didn't want him to think that I was crazy or mentally ill or unstable. I wanted him to think he had the greatest girlfriend, who was "all together" and had her head on straight. I thought if he knew about my problem, he would end things. He would think I was too weak a person to date if I was seeing a therapist.

Last Saturday I was in a miserable mood all day. I had spent two hours talking to my therapy group about bulimia and about hiding it from my friends. I knew I had to tell my boyfriend; I couldn't keep lying to him and deceiving him. It was driving me crazy. Driving to go out to dinner one night this week, I said to him, "There's something I haven't told you that I've wanted to for so long." He grabbed the wheel so tight. He thought I was going to tell him that I cheated on him. When I came out and told him that I had an eating disorder, he seemed relieved; bulimia was easier for him to swallow than infidelity.

When it sank in, he was rather surprised. He wanted to know for how long I had the problem, what I am doing about it, can I stop it, and why didn't I tell him sooner. Well, to make a long story short, it was the best thing I ever did telling him. He was so compassionate and so caring. He said he would help me get through it, that he loves me too much to give up on me now. He even asked me if he could come to therapy with me to learn more about the eating disorder. It feels so good not to have to hide it from him any longer, and to know that he still loves me. I think telling my boyfriend and talking about my eating disorder via these diaries are helping me move closer to conquering the problem. More than anything I want to be normal and eat normally. I want to learn to love and accept myself, no matter what I look like.

Laurie's preoccupation with food shows up in her similes and metaphors. Lying to her boyfriend used to "eat away" at her; when she tells him the truth, while driving to a restaurant for dinner, he feels relieved, since bulimia is easier for him to "swallow" than infidelity. And in disclosing her obsession with self-starvation, Laurie feels "as if some huge weight was lifted off my shoulders."

## JORIE
### "I Am Not As Ashamed of My Bulimia As I Am of the Reasons Behind Being Bulimic"

Jorie, a senior, wrote three diaries about growing up in a troubled family. She saw her problems with bulimia and drug and alcohol addiction as part of a larger pattern of self-destructiveness. She viewed the decision to enter therapy twenty months ago as a turning point in her life:

When we were discussing Kafka's *The Metamorphosis* and "The Judgment," I could relate strongly with both Gregor and Georg and how they felt about their families. The one aspect that I could relate strongly with was Gregor's wish to hurt his family because of the way they had hurt him. I feel, like Gregor, that had my parents maybe showed me love instead of constant abuse, maybe my own actions would not have been so severe.

One of the first acts of defiance that I remember was running away from home. I was thirteen and had been using drugs for about three years. My aunt and uncle lived two hours away from home, and I knew that they understood my situation with my parents and would let me stay with them. I left my home and started to hitchhike to their home. Some woman picked me up and lectured me the whole time that I was in her car about the dangers of a young girl hitchhiking. She dropped me off about a half hour away from my relatives' house. As luck would have it, my uncle was on his way to my parents' house. He picked me up, and I begged him to let me stay in his house. He agreed, knowing what it was like for me in my house. He said I could stay for a week, and he would work on cooling my parents off.

When I returned home, there were no hugs, no asking if I was all right, just glares from my parents. My uncle and aunt left the house quickly because they knew what was going to happen. My aunt later told me that she could feel the hate radiating from me. She said that it frightened her that I could be so angry at such a young age.

I seriously contemplated suicide throughout my pre- and early teens. I felt that there was no way that I could live up to my parents' expectations. I felt, however, that if I could hurt them as much as they had been hurting me, then just maybe they would wake up and realize what they were doing. My actions to hurt them involved a lot of drug use. I could not commit suicide because I could not risk my uncle and aunt's finding me; I was not out to hurt them, just my parents.

Instead, I became a drug addict. Addiction is a slow suicide. I was definitely out to kill myself. I am also bulimic. Although my excuses for bingeing and purging were to stay thin, it was just another way that I could be self-destructive. The whole time I was active in my drug and food addictions, I copped an "I'll show them attitude." I wanted to make my parents sorry for the rotten way they had been treating me.

I could relate to Gregor's metamorphosis. All my life I was reminded what a nothing I was. As a result I became a severe isolator. My favorite thing to do, when I couldn't get high, was to go to my room around 7:30 at night, crawl into bed, and daydream until I fell asleep. This started when I was about ten and ended when I was sixteen. My lack of self-esteem led to my actions of self-destruction. This is definitely apparent in my drug addiction and bulimia. I am also a defeated perfectionist. I will start a project and never finish it, or I will not start a project because I know that I cannot do it perfectly. This is self-destructive because it prevents me from accomplishing anything.

Therapy has done wonders for me as far as my awareness goes. Because my parents' actions were what they were, I have the responsibility to recover from this abuse. I have also come to realize that they are sick people. In a way, I am getting even with them because they will have to live with their miserable little selves while I have the chance to recover. However, like Gregor and Georg, I do love my parents.

Last week when reading Franz Kafka's "Letter to His Father," I felt tears welling up in my eyes. I could really relate to the letter, how Kafka felt toward his father. My father carries many of the same characteristics that Kafka's did.

When Kafka discussed the family dinner table etiquette, I had a rush of memories and feelings. Dinner was always a stressful time in my family. We were not allowed to sing, and God forbid we act the least bit "silly." Though those were the expected norms, hardly ever do I remember a meal in my family that did not end up in a screaming, raging fight. These fights were either between my mother and father, my mother and me, my father and me, or my sister and me.

I could identify with Kafka's father's double standards at the table. While we were expected to act like little adults, my father was allowed to make any racist or misogynistic statement that he felt like making. If my sister criticized Mom's cooking, she received a verbal reprimand, I would receive a verbal and/or physically abusive response, and my dad's criticism was, of course, ignored.

Like Kafka, I never felt capable of living up to my father's set of laws for me. For one thing, I was very feminine. The only thing worse, to my father, was not being a boy. I could understand Kafka's pain regarding the annoyance that he felt he caused his father. I always felt that my father thought I was an annoyance. He was in his late forties when I was born. I was not only unplanned by my parents, I was also another girl.

I have a lot of shame-based issues involving my father. I feel that the only way that I can be at peace with my father is to resolve the shame that is so binding. Like Kafka, I need to hear my father say that I am not guilty. Then, I think, my shame (some of it, anyway) will start working its way out of my feelings. I know I am not guilty, but at the same time I am willing to accept what guilt I actually own.

This week my diary is on eating disorders. I never thought of my eating disorder as a topic of interest; I see it as something I am stuck with and have to deal with on a daily basis. I have always been hung up on my weight. My earliest memory of being self-conscious of my weight is when I was six. I remember the school nurse saying what my weight was, and immediately I felt inadequate, fat. I believe that my eating disorder is a disease, and I will always have it.

I have been abstinent from my symptoms for about fifteen months, but I am still bulimic. I was active in my eating disorder from the time I was ten to the time I was twenty. I am not as ashamed of my bulimia as I am of the reasons behind being bulimic. I don't really remember bulimia being a deep dark secret, but I guess it was because I felt so relieved when I finally admitted it was a problem for me.

Before I was in recovery, I was really embarrassed about my food consumption. I did try to conceal it from my friends. I come from a food-addicted family, so my consumption did not have to be hidden from them. I didn't really have to hide my purging. My purging was a starvation that lasted anywhere from a week to six weeks. I would stop eating. It's scary now, but at the time everyone used to compliment my will-power to stick to my "new diet."

My parents found out about my eating disorder after we had been in family counseling for my drug addiction. Our counselor explained to my parents that it is more common than uncommon for women drug addicts to be bulimic and vice versa. My bulimia isn't as painful as the underlying issues. I have been in therapy for almost two years now. It has not been easy, but it's worth every ounce of pain I have been through. I would highly recommend therapy to anyone.

The origins of my eating disorder are multifold. People will have an eating disorder as a result of being sexually abused; it keeps the bulimic in control of how attractive her body is. People will also be bulimic as a result of the lack of control that they feel regarding their bodies. I was physically and emotionally abused and was never (rarely) allowed to make my own decisions. People will live what they learn.

I come from a dysfunctional family; everyone is addicted either to food or to some other drug. Until I started recovery, I had negative self-esteem. Today it is slowly being rebuilt. My sexuality took a beating. For a long time I was asexual. As my disease progressed, so did my screwed-up sexuality; I also became addicted to sex. The longer I am in recovery, the clearer my sexuality is becoming. My relationship with my parents still has a lot of kinks, but they are being straightened out.

I originally wrote a diary on the subject of addiction, not specifically mentioning bulimia, because they are the same thing. I wrote about it because it is easy to analyze them in a Freudian perspective. I can see a lot of parallels between myself and Kafka's hunger artist. I have a misconception of the word "perfect." I also have a lot of issues with my dad. Psychoanalytically, by starving himself the hunger artist is indicating that he does not like sex. Being the good bulimic that I am, I am addicted to sex. Just like with food, I indulge, then feel guilty.

I don't remember how I felt when I first wrote the diary about my eating disorder. Knowing that other people in the class have the problem doesn't affect me. I am secure in my support system already, so when I hear other people mention that they are also bulimic, I can relate, but it doesn't have the soothing effect of relief. It was easy to write about the eating disorder because of the guaranteed confidentiality. I don't know if I would have been disappointed if you didn't read my diary in class.

I have been as honest as I am capable of being when writing about the experiences. My experience in recovery has been that war stories are just that—war stories. Bragging does not get me better, honesty does. The audience for my diaries has been me. Writing is very therapeutic for me; it helps me get past my shame barrier. I am really glad that there is the confidentiality when reading the diaries. I would feel awkward if people in class knew who I was.

## PAULA
### "I Binged and Binged But Never Quite Made It to the Purge"

Paula, a junior, wrote about the relationship between masochism and the search for love and attention. Her problem with overeating made her almost wish that she was "naturally" anorexic or bulimic. In her early diaries she wrote about her ambivalence toward her

father, whom she resented for divorcing her mother and withdraw-
ing from his family. In the first of three entries included here, Paula
reports how she began to inflict pain upon herself in order to gratify
a self-destructive urge:

> I wonder, is masochism uncommon? Not masochism in the context of
> deriving sexual pleasure from self-inflicted pain, but just plain old pleas-
> ure from experiencing pain one purposefully inflicts on oneself. I am a
> masochist. There is sometimes an ulterior motive for my masochistic
> tendencies—attention. It's strange to admit this, but I have before, and
> probably will again, hurt myself to gain the attention of someone else.
>
> The first time I did it was when I was in high school, and I remem-
> ber being angry at my dad for spending too much time with his wife,
> with whom I did not get along. It wasn't so much the time he spent with
> her, it was the time he didn't spend with me, and the fact that he was in
> some ways becoming very much like her and seemed to want to push
> me away.
>
> While I was at work one afternoon during a weekend I was visiting
> him, I picked up a single-edged razor blade and started slicing up the
> backs of my hands. Nothing worthy of stitches, but I did draw blood.
> My dad did eventually notice at some point during the weekend, and
> I shrugged it off as being bored at work. Funny, I don't remember if I
> achieved the desired effect—more attention from my dad.
>
> I repeated this hand-slashing action a few times during high school
> and my first year of college, primarily as an attention getter from my
> parents. Sophomore year, I remember trying to cut myself with a plas-
> tic knife, which didn't work too well as far as breaking the skin, but it
> was painful, and the pain made me feel better about whatever it was
> that was troubling me.
>
> Another time I cut myself was when I thought my boyfriend was
> becoming attracted again to his old girlfriend, who was in one of his
> classes. Her presence most certainly threatened me, and I needed reas-
> surance that he loved me and not her. One afternoon at work, where I
> have access to single-edged razor blades, I decided that cuts on my
> hands would make me feel better and command attention from my
> boyfriend. This time it worked—not only did the pain make me feel bet-
> ter, but my boyfriend became very concerned and started to show all
> the things he said he felt about me. Why does this kind of pain give me
> pleasure? If it were just the guilt I mean to impose on others, it would
> not be as difficult to understand. At any rate, it would be interesting to
> see what Sigmund Freud would make of this case study.
>
> Like the other women in the class, I obsess over my weight. I was
> always overweight as a child, and as I grew older, my weight always
> bothered me, but never really enough to do much about it. After my
> weight peaked in my freshman year of college, I decided to do some-
> thing drastic—go on a liquid diet. I stuck to it very well and lost fifty-five
> pounds, and I actually felt good about myself; many of my depressing
> moods were gone, and I was much happier.

Going off the diet was scary at first, being a noneater for a period of four months, but eventually I got over my fear of eating (actually, fear of gaining weight, fear of waking up one day just as fat as when I began) and basically lived like a normal person again. Over a course of months I noticed I was gaining a little weight, especially after I began using a prescription medication with a side effect of possible weight gain. I didn't gain all of the weight back, not even half, but I returned to the constant state of depression and unhappiness, and everything around me was falling apart. I tried on my own to lose the extra weight, weight that was not even really noticed by any of my friends, but I had a very difficult time losing it, despite the fact that I was sticking to a low-calorie, low-fat diet.

So I called a nutritionist in the office of the doctor who had supervised my liquid diet and made an appointment to see her, thinking that I would appeal to her to let me return to the diet. All the time I knew that in the long run I was actually avoiding my problem by taking the easy way out, but it was the only thing that I felt I could do to make me mentally stable and not on the verge of being suicidal. The nutritionist agreed with me abut the avoidance thing but saw how emotionally distressed I was and agreed to let me return to the program.

I did very well on it a second time, but one thing strange seemed to be occurring: I kept dreaming that I was eating. It started with my housemate, who told me she had a dream that I was eating ice cream— one of my favorite foods. I laughed and forgot about it, until I had a dream that I had eaten more than just ice cream. I woke up in a cold sweat because I thought I had actually cheated on the diet but then realized that it had just been a dream.

I had another dream that I ate ice cream, and then a third dream that I ate a meal. If I found myself desiring food at a conscious level, I can understand how I might dream about eating it. But on this diet I do not experience hunger or desire for any food—which is one of the reasons why it is so easy for me not to cheat, or even want to cheat. If I longed to eat when I smelled food, or saw food, I could understand why I might dream about it. But I can certainly say that I am lacking any desire for it.

I can go out to dinner with people, look at a menu, and plan out what I would eat if I were eating: it's kind of a joke with my friends, who are used to this. I can sit through a meal and watch people eat without any problems. I don't even desire ice cream, which could very well be my favorite food, and watch my housemate eat it almost nightly. So why am I dreaming about it? I know that dreams are manifestations of unconscious wants, but in this case it doesn't even make sense why I would want food even unconsciously. I must lose weight, and I am in the mind-set for it. Why am I having these dreams?

Sure, I've had an eating disorder—I always ate too much. I binged and binged but never quite made it to the purge. Being a fat person was never fun. I always wished that I was naturally anorexic or bulimic; I used to think, "Boy, how could being too thin be a problem? I would kill to have their problems!" I always envisioned eating disorders as purely physical problems, but after hearing the journals for the past few weeks, I now understand that there are psychological and emotional components to the disorders, and not just physical symptoms.

I must admit that part of me still maintains a desire to have the physical attributes of anorexia or bulimia, but that is largely a reaction to this culture's emphasis on being perfect. I feel guilty for my ignorance of these disorders, which caused my many jokes about them.

Hearing the journals did make me feel uncomfortable, because I have essentially been poking fun at something that should not be taken lightly. I can certainly relate to the feeling of containing a "deep secret" about their disorder, for I did the same thing, except my secret was that I was eating almost whatever I could but pretending that I wasn't. I would deny eating junk food that mysteriously disappeared and would try to carefully rearrange the remaining food so that it looked like it hadn't been touched. I always felt miserable after I binged, but I guess that feeling lifted before I felt the need to get rid of the food I had just eaten.

I have since participated in a rapid weight loss program and have lost a lot of weight, and people who never knew me fat can't even picture me that way, but I still have no problem picturing myself as fat. I am in a constant struggle to keep my weight down, and if I gain weight, I get very depressed. To stay thin I must constantly watch what I eat and make sure that I do not lapse back into my old eating habits—which is sometimes very hard to do. In this way I can certainly understand why an anorectic or bulimic is never satisfied with her appearance, because I suffer from the same complex. I only hope that hearing the journals of others with the same condition has helped them in some way, and that my journal does not sound like I am reducing their problem, or even encouraging it, but serves as another viewpoint of someone who can understand a bit of what they have experienced.

Brenda, Marcy, Laurie, Jorie, and Paula recount different stories in their diaries, yet each would agree that culture plays a powerful role in compelling women to reduce their bodies in order to satisfy patriarchal notions of beauty. Anorexia and bulimia are cultural illnesses, rarely seen in developing countries where food is scarce, and rampant among middle- and upper-class women in developed countries. For all five women, the impulse toward fasting had less to do with the rejection of food than with the craving for another form of nourishment—love, approval, validation. Violence against the body represented their response to the weighty conflicts in their lives.

Although researchers such as Janet Surrey suggest that women with eating disorders have problematic relationships with their mothers, none of the five students revealed this in her diary—perhaps because, by criticizing their mothers, the daughters feared cutting themselves off from a major support system. Instead, four of the five cited a troubled relationship with their father as a serious problem in their lives. The diaries portray the fathers as alcoholic, sexually or physically abusive, controlling or neglectful, and noncommunicative. Like Kafka, who unsuccessfully sought his father's approval— "My writing was all about you," he admitted in "Letter to His Father," "all I did there, after all, was to bemoan what I could not bemoan upon your breast"—the women believed that they could not establish a meaningful dialogue with their fathers.

## Other Diaries on Eating Disorders

The five women were not alone in writing about eating disorders. Three other female students wrote about being anorexic or bulimic in the past, one of them requiring hospitalization for several weeks. Other students said that, although they themselves did not suffer from eating disorders, they knew people who did. One woman, exasperated by what she felt was an abnormal emphasis upon anorexia and bulimia in her classmates' diaries, wrote about how a recent experience confirmed what she was hearing in the classroom:

> Last week as I sat in class and listened to the other diaries being read, I couldn't believe my ears. The very first day of the semester I walked into the classroom and observed my new classmates. Everyone seemed fairly normal. Who knew that I was sitting in the midst of bulimics, drug addicts, sex fiends, and some very disturbed individuals? I don't mean to sound degrading or anything. I understand that many people have different kinds of problems. It's just that I've never known anyone with such serious problems—or at least I never knew about them. My eyes were opened to this fact this weekend.
>
> I learned something that was very disturbing to me. I had gone to a really great party Saturday night where, of course, like countless other college gala events, grain alcohol was served. My best friend at school became violently ill and vomited all over the backyard. I stood with her and tried to comfort her, telling her that getting sick was no big deal and that it happens to people all the time. It was then that she decided to reveal her deep, dark secret to me.
>
> You guessed it. She told me that she used to be bulimic. I was shocked. Even after hearing the countless journals of bulimic girls in class, I was horrified to learn that one of my closest friends felt that she had to hurt herself this way just to have a good body. She also told me that everyone in her family is heavy. She must've been afraid that she, too, would be cursed with love handles and cellulite—so afraid that every night she stuck her finger down her throat as insurance that it wouldn't happen to her. She was very drunk that night, and I don't even know if she remembers that she told me. I've been afraid to bring it up. I guess it's because I really don't know what to say to her.

## The Prevalence of Eating Disorders

The last diary raises three important issues that must be addressed. First, how can a class that seemed "fairly normal" on the first day of the semester contain so many "disturbed" individuals? Was this a representative class? Second, how did Brenda, Marcy, Laurie, Jorie, and Paula evaluate the experience of writing about food conflicts? Finally, how did the other students in the class, particularly the men who had never given much thought to eating disorders, react to these diaries?

To begin with, a majority of the women and *all* of the men were astonished by the number of people who wrote about having eating disorders. Many of the afflicted women were also surprised by this. To determine how many people identified themselves as having an eating disorder, I sent around an anonymous questionnaire at the end of the semester asking male and female students to evaluate their eating patterns. Based on the results of the questionnaire, eight out of the twenty-five women in the class, or 32 percent, believed they had exhibited anorexic or bulimic behavior at one time or another—a figure that is almost double the average percentage of students (17) who write about eating disorders in my other classes. Of the remaining women, six indicated that they knew another person, usually a relative, friend, or roommate, who suffered from an eating disorder. Only one of the ten men in the class wrote about having a problem with food—nighttime overeating.

How do these figures compare with the national statistics on eating disorders? The question is difficult to answer because there have been few good epidemiological studies. The revised edition of the American Psychiatric Association's *Diagnostic and Statistical Manual of Mental Disorders (DSM-111-R)* estimates that anorexia affects from 1 in 800 to as many as 1 in 100 females between the ages of twelve and eighteen; about 4.5 percent of women may be bulimic. These figures may be too low, however, because of narrow diagnostic criteria. *DSM-111-R* defines bulimia as a "minimum average of two binge eating episodes a week for at least three months," but there are many women who could be considered bulimic, even though they binge less frequently than this. Marcy noted, for example, that she resorted to purging only during emergencies. In addition, *DSM-111-R* measures behavior rather than attitude; someone who is technically not bulimic may nevertheless remain obsessed with the bingeing and purging cycle. There is a consensus among researchers that anorexic and bulimic behavior is widespread among college women.

The American obsession with dieting is, of course, well known. Self-report studies suggest that between 50 and 75 percent of American women consider themselves to be overweight and are dieting at various times. A 1982 pilot survey of eating patterns at Wellesley College estimated that 22 percent of the women in the study had a serious eating disorder. Although the questionnaire concluded that most students were close to their ideal weight, there was an "exaggerated level of psychological concern relative to the actual weight loss desired." On the basis of these studies, the 32 percent of the women in my class who identified themselves as having eating disorders would seem to be a fairly accurate reflection of American college students.

## Writing About Fasting

Without exception, Brenda, Marcy, Laurie, Jorie, and Paula concluded in their final diaries that writing was helpful in confronting and working through personal conflicts. Although their diaries reflect different degrees of self-analysis and self-disclosure, all five women were able to look at themselves more objectively and identify conflicts they wished to resolve. They were also gratified that their entries emboldened others to write about similar experiences. Three of the five women expressed reservations about diary writing, however, and their reservations are worth noting.

Brenda, the first person to write about an eating disorder, tried to organize a self-help group in her dormitory for anorexic and bulimic women, but when she received no response, she became discouraged. She was especially annoyed at those people who "suffer, complain, and yet do nothing" about their problems. "It doesn't make a bit of difference to me," she wrote in her final diary, "whether you use my journals in your book. Sorry, but I'm rather indifferent about it. Go ahead."

Brenda may not have realized how difficult it is for most people to write or speak about something as painful as bulimia without the safety of anonymous diaries. Eating disorders are a source of humiliation for many people, and they are not easily convinced to join a self-help group. The ease with which Brenda wrote about bulimia may have prevented her from anticipating how hard it is for others to be self-disclosing. Ironically, as the semester progressed, she asked me not to read her diaries aloud, a pattern that contrasted with the increasing openness of the other students.

Marcy, who wrote four entries on the difficulty of being a woman in a patriarchal society, expressed ambivalence in her final diary over the personal nature of her writings. She viewed the diaries as a "temptation" which she found herself resisting, and she remained suspicious of the opportunity to "purge the self of all the problems that have been building and festering within." She did not want to yield completely to this temptation, she said, because she was a private person. She concluded that while she did disclose a great deal about her life, she held back most of the "good stuff."

Marcy's cautionary note reminds us that, as self-revealing as we may wish to be, we are also self-concealing. We all have a need for privacy, for drawing boundaries between that part of the self which we wish to give to others as a gift and that part which we need to hold back for self-protection. Even Kafka, who was unusually self-revealing, observed that writing means "revealing oneself to excess." If, as the psychoanalyst D. W. Winnicott observes, artists experience both "the urgent need to communicate and the still more urgent need not to be found," then how much greater may this need for self-privacy be among nonartists?

Diary writing allowed Laurie to express her pent-up feelings and take charge of her life. Of all the entries on eating disorders, Laurie's contain the most desperation; bulimia was an ongoing emergency for her, with an uncertain outcome. "I wanted other people to know how frightened I am that I'll never get better, that it might kill me, and how embarrassed and ashamed I am that I have an uncontrollable eating disorder." She singled out as particularly valuable the dialogic nature of classroom diary writing; just as she learned from students who had overcome their eating disorders, so, she hoped, would other students benefit from her knowledge.

Writing encouraged Jorie to explore childhood experiences, helping her to "get in touch with the child within me that I thought had died, or I guess never knew existed." She observed that many of her diaries expressed bitterness toward members of her family. "I know a lot of my diaries were directed at the anger that I feel toward my father, but because I was able to express it and have it validated, I began to start healing from it."

Paula, who wrote about slicing the backs of her hands with a razor blade in order to attract attention from her father, felt that diary writing became tedious during the second half of the semester. She attributed this both to the necessity to type the diaries and to the competition to write compelling diaries that would be read to the class. At first she felt that hearing the diaries was interesting, but after a while it seemed that "everyone was 'competing' to top everyone's problems, as if everyone was going to class to see if *this* week's problems were more intense than last week's."

## Male Responses to Eating Disorder Diaries

Only two of the ten men in the class commented on the eating disorder diaries read in class. One wrote that before hearing the diaries, he had never realized the prevalence of eating disorders or understood why so many women were willing to damage their bodies in order to remain thin:

> I had a huge meal last night, and I tried to envision what it would be like to stick my index finger down my throat. Just the thought made me almost vomit, let alone the act. I see so many attractive women in this class, and I just cannot imagine why they would even think of losing or

rather of torturing off this weight. I've thrown up before from drinking, and that is a nightmare, as anyone in this class can attest to. To do this on a consistent basis is a very frightening thought.

The other man remarked that the diaries sensitized him to the experience of growing up female in a patriarchal culture. "I think that I speak for many of the people in this class when I say that the reading of these diaries has helped to open up our eyes and has given us a chance to learn and experience something that could never happen in a normal classroom setting."

As the semester ended, I asked the students to comment on whether they felt, as a result of hearing so many entries on eating disorders, like the amusement seekers in Kafka's story, who take an early interest in the hunger artist only to turn away in disdain and boredom. Additionally, since we were reading Sylvia Path's poetry, I inquired whether they viewed themselves as part of the "peanut crunching crowd" in the confessional poem "Lady Lazarus," who "shoves in to see/Them unwrap me hand and foot—/The big strip tease." That is, did they feel part of a voyeuristic audience deriving crude entertainment from the artist's anguished cries? A few students acknowledged feeling morbid fascination while listening to the diaries, but most shared the point of view expressed by the following man:

> I really don't think any of us in this class has participated in exploiting the others. There have been times when I have chuckled over a particular phrase in a journal. But I have *never* laughed at any of my classmates' misfortunes. Since I have been lucky to avoid some of their misfortunes, I can only pray that I will never experience what they have experienced. The fact that they have faced their problems and have shared them in class has shown great integrity and courage. I hope that my classmates will never encounter any more tragedies or misfortunes for the rest of their lives. They have had more than enough for one lifetime.

In offering sympathy and understanding, the class thus responded to the female hunger artists differently than the amusement seekers reacted to Kafka's starving character. Insofar as voyeurs lack empathy, the students were not morbid onlookers but caring, attentive listeners. They discovered that Kafka's story, and those of the diarists, have profound psychological, cultural, and feminist implications; and they became more aware of the violent forces directed against the female body and spirit. They grasped the truth of two of Kafka's most starting observations about the power of writing: first, that "a book must be the axe of the frozen sea inside us"; and second, as he wrote to Max Brod, "Writing is only an expedient, as for someone who is writing his will shortly before he hangs himself—an expedient that may well last a whole life." Writing about their own experiences as hunger artists, the students came to understand Kafka—and themselves—a little better.

---

### Now that you've read

1. What did you learn about eating disorders that you didn't already know?
2. Whose story did you find most moving or disturbing? Why?
3. What are some of the factors that contribute to the prevalence of eating disorders in our culture?
4. Who seems most vulnerable?
5. What might we do to try to change people's attitudes about being the "perfect" weight and body shape?

## READING 3

*Deborah Tannen*

# How Male and Female Students Use Language Differently

Deborah Tannen is a professor of linguistics who has made a career of studying how different groups use language. In this essay, she argues that male students generally thrive more in classes that encourage debate and more aggressive interaction, whereas female students tend to thrive in an atmosphere that encourages collaboration. As you read, think about the different classes you're in and the extent to which you and those around you participate. Do you agree with her argument?

### Before you read

1. Do men and women use language differently? How?
2. Have you ever experienced an example of miscommunication that you attributed to gender difference? What happened?
3. What kind of classroom participation do you prefer? Why?
4. Do male and female teachers have different language styles? Explain your answer.

---

When I researched and wrote my latest book, *You Just Don't Understand: Women and Men in Conversation,* the furthest thing from my mind was reevaluating teaching strategies. But that has been one of the direct benefits of having written the book.

The primary focus of my linguistic research always has been the language of everyday conversation. One facet of this is conversational style: how different regional, ethnic, and class backgrounds, as well as age and gender, result in different ways of using language to communicate. *You Just Don't Understand* is about the conversational styles of women and men. As I gained more insight into typically male and female ways of using language, I began to suspect some of the causes of the troubling facts that women who go to single-sex schools do better in later life, and that when young women sit next to young men in classrooms, the males talk more. This is not to say that all men talk in class, nor that no women do. It is simply that a greater percentage of discussion time is taken by men's voices.

The research of sociologist and anthropologists such as Janet Lever, Marjorie Harness Goodwin, and Donna Eder has shown that girls and boys learn to use language differently in their sex-separate peer groups. Typically, a girl has a best friend with whom she sits and talks frequently telling secrets. It's the telling of secrets, the fact and the way that they talk to each other, that makes them best friends. For boys, activities are central: their best friends are the ones they do things with. Boys also tend to play in larger groups that are hierarchical. High-status boys give orders and push low-status boys around. So boys are expected to use language to seize center stage: by exhibiting their skill, displaying their knowledge, and challenging and resisting challenges.

These patterns have stunning implications for classroom inter-action. Most faculty members assume that participating in class discussion is a necessary part of successful performance. Yet speaking in a classroom is more congenial to boys' language experience than to girls', since it entails putting oneself forward in front of a large group of people, many of whom are strangers and at least one of whom is sure to judge speakers' knowledge and intelligence by their verbal display.

Another aspect of many classrooms that makes them more hospitable to most men than to most women is the use of debate-like formats as a learning tool. Our educational system, as Walter Ong argues persuasively in his book *Fighting for Life* (Cornell University Press, 1981), is fundamentally male in that the pursuit of knowledge is believed to be achieved by ritual opposition: public display followed by argument and challenge. Father Ong demonstrates that ritual opposition—what he calls "adversativeness" or "agonism"—is fundamental to the way most males approach almost any activity. (Consider, for example, the little boy who shows he likes a little girl by pulling her braids or shoving her.) But ritual opposition is antithetical to the way most females learn and like to interact. It is not that females don't fight, but that they don't fight for fun. They don't *ritualize* opposition.

Anthropologists working in widely disparate parts of the world have found contrasting verbal rituals for women and men. Women in completely unrelated cultures (for example, Greece and Bali) engage in ritual laments: spontaneously produced rhyming couplets that express their pain, for example, over the loss of loved ones. Men do not take part in laments. They have their own, very different verbal ritual: a contest, a war of words in which they vie with each other to devise clever insults.

When discussing these phenomena with a colleague, I commented that I see these two styles in American conversation: many women bond by talking about troubles, and many men bond by exchanging playful insults and put-downs, and other sorts of verbal sparring. He exclaimed: "I never thought of this, but that's the way I teach: I have students read an article, and then I invite them to tear it apart. After we've torn it to shreds, we talk about how to build a better model."

This contrasts sharply with the way I teach: I open the discussion of readings by asking, "What did you find useful in this? What can we use in our own theory building and our own methods?" I note what I see as weaknesses in the author's approach, but I also point out that the writer's discipline and purposes might be different from ours. Finally, I offer personal anecdotes illustrating the phenomena under discussion and praise students' anecdotes as well as their critical acumen.

These different teaching styles must make our classrooms wildly different places and hospitable to different students. Male students are more likely to be comfortable attacking the readings and might find the inclusion of personal anecdotes irrelevant and "soft." Women are more likely to resist discussion they perceive as hostile, and, indeed, it is women in my classes who are most likely to offer personal anecdotes.

A colleague who read my book commented that he had always taken for granted that the best way to deal with students' comments is to challenge them; this, he felt it was self-evident, sharpens their minds and helps them develop debating skills. But he had noticed that women were relatively silent in his classes, so he decided to try beginning discussion with relatively open-ended questions and letting comments go unchallenged. He found, to his amazement and satisfaction, that more women began to speak up.

Though some of the women in his class clearly liked this better, perhaps some of the men liked it less. One young man in my class wrote in a questionnaire about a history professor who gave students questions to think about and called on people to answer them: "He would then play devil's advocate . . . *i.e.,* he debated us. . . . That class *really* sharpened me intellectually. . . . We as students do need to know how to defend ourselves." This young man valued the experience of being attacked and challenged publicly. Many, if not most, women would shrink from such "challenge," experiencing it as public humiliation.

A professor at Hamilton College told me of a young man who was upset because he felt that his class presentation had been a failure. The professor was puzzled because he had observed that class members had listened attentively and agreed with the student's observations. It turned out that it was this very agreement that the student interpreted as failure: since no one had engaged his ideas by arguing with him, he felt they had found them unworthy of attention.

So one reason men speak in class more than women is that many of them find the "public" classroom setting more conducive to speaking, whereas most women are more comfortable speaking in private to a small group of people they know well. A second reason is that men are more likely to be comfortable with the debate-like form that discussion may take. Yet another reason is the different attitudes toward speaking in class that typify women and men.

Students who speak frequently in class, many of whom are men, assume that it is their job to think of contributions and try to get the floor to express them. But many women monitor their participation not only to get the floor but to avoid getting it. Women students in my class tell me that if they have spoken up once or twice, they hold back for the rest of the class because they don't want to dominate. If they have spoken a lot one week, they will remain silent the next. These different ethics of participation are, of course, unstated, so those who speak freely assume that those who remain silent have nothing to say, and those who are reining themselves assume that the big talkers are selfish and hoggish.

When I looked around my classes, I could see these differing ethics and habits at work. For example, my graduate class in analyzing conversation had twenty students, eleven women and nine men. Of the men, four were foreign students: two Japanese, one Chinese, and one Syrian. With the exception of the three Asian men, all the men spoke in class at least occasionally. The biggest talker in the class was a woman, but there were also five women who never spoke at all, only one of whom was Japanese. I decided to try something different.

I broke the class into small groups to discuss the issues raised in the readings and to analyze their own conversational transcripts. I devised three ways of dividing the students into groups: one by the degree program they were in, one by gender, and one by conversational style, as closely as I could guess it. This meant that when the class was grouped according to conversational style, I put Asian students together, fast talkers together, and quiet students together. The class split into groups six times during the semester, so they met in each grouping twice. I told students to regard the groups as examples of interactional data and to note the different ways they participated in the different groups. Toward the end of the term, I gave them a questionnaire asking about their class and group participation.

I could see plainly from my observation of the groups at work that women who never opened their mouths in class were talking away in the small groups. In fact, the Japanese woman commented that she found it particularly hard to contribute to the all-woman group she was in because "I was overwhelmed by how talkative the female students were in the female-only group." This is particularly revealing because it highlights that the same person who can be "op-pressed" into silence in one context can become the talkative "oppres-sor" in another. No one's conversational style is absolute; everyone's style changes in response to the context and others' styles.

Some of the students (seven) said they preferred the same-gender groups; others preferred the same-style groups. In answer to the question "Would you have liked to speak in class more often than you did?" six of the seven who said yes were women; the one man was Japanese. Most startlingly, this response did not come only from quiet women; it came from women who had indicated that they had spoken in class never, rarely, sometimes, and often. Of the eleven students who said the amount they had spoken was fine, seven were men. Of the four women who checked "fine," two added qualifications indicating it wasn't completely fine: One wrote in "maybe more," and one wrote, "I have an urge to participate but often feel I should have something more interesting/relevant/wonderful/intelligent to say!!"

I counted my experiment a success. Everyone in the class found the small groups interesting, and no one indicated he or she would have preferred that the class not break into groups. Perhaps more instructive, however, was the fact that the experience of breaking into groups, and of talking about participation in class, raised every-one's awareness about classroom participation. After we had talked about it, some of the quietest women in the class made a few volun-tary contributions, though sometimes I had to ensure their partici-pation by interrupting students who were exuberantly speaking out.

Americans are often proud that they discount the significance of cultural differences: "We are all individuals," many people boast. Ignoring such issues as gender and ethnicity becomes a source of pride: "I treat everyone the same." But treating people the same is not equal treatment if they are not the same.

The classroom is a different environment for those who feel comfortable putting themselves forward in a group than it is for those who find the prospect of doing so chastening, or even terrify-ing. When a professor asks, "Are there any questions?" students who can formulate statements the fastest have the greatest opportunity to respond. Those who need significant time to do so have not really been given a chance at all, since by the time they are ready to speak, someone else has the floor.

In a class where some students speak out without raising hands, those who feel they must raise their hands and wait to be recognized do not have equal opportunity to speak. Telling them to feel free to jump in will not make them feel free; one's sense of tim-ing, of one's rights and obligations in a classroom, are automatic, learned over years of interaction. They may be changed over time, with motivation and effort, but they cannot be changed on the spot. And everyone assumes his or her own way is best. When I asked my students how the class could be changed to make it easier for them to speak more, the most talkative woman said she would prefer it if no one had to raise hands, and a foreign student said he wished people would raise their hands and wait to be recognized.

My experience in this class has convinced me that small-group interaction should be part of any class that is not a small seminar. I also am convinced that having the students become observers of their own interaction is a crucial part of their education. Talking about ways of talking in class makes students aware that their ways of talking affect other students, that the motivations they impute to others may not truly reflect others' motives, and that the behaviors they assume to be self-evidently right are not universal norms.

The goal of complete equal opportunity in class may not be attainable, but realizing that one monolithic classroom-participation structure is not equal opportunity is itself a powerful motivation to find more-diverse methods to serve diverse students—and every classroom is diverse.

------

## Now that you've read

1. How is the language use of male students different from that of female students, according to Tannen? Do you agree with her assessment of these differences and their significance? Why or why not?
2. What can teachers do to make sure everyone has an opportunity to be part of the classroom discussion?
3. What, if anything, did you learn about your own participation style as a result of reading this essay?

## READING 4

*Peter Lyman*

# The Fraternal Bond as a Joking Relationship

Peter Lyman is a librarian and professor at the University of California at Berkeley. In "The Fraternal Bond as a Joking Relationship," he analyzes a particular event that occurred in a sorority house on the Berkeley campus of the University of California. Lyman argues that men's friendships operate under very different rules than women's friendships and that these differences caused a profound misunderstanding between the sorority and the fraternity members. Does he seem to you to be on track in his analysis, or has he misinterpreted the evidence?

### *Before you read*

1. What can you tell about the essay from its title?
2. Do men and women have different senses of humor?
3. Where do our senses of humor come from? Why are some things funny to some people and not funny to others?

One evening during dinner, forty-five fraternity men suddenly broke into the dining room of a nearby campus sorority, surrounded the thirty women residents, and forced them to watch while one pledge gave a speech on Freud's theory of penis envy as another demonstrated various techniques of masturbation with a rubber penis. The women sat silently staring downward at their plates listening for about ten minutes, until a woman law student who was the graduate resident in charge of the house walked in, surveyed the scene, and demanded, "Please leave immediately!" As she later described that moment, "There was a mocking roar from the men, 'It's tradition.' I said, 'That's no reason to do something like this, please leave!' And they left. I was surprised. Then the women in the house started to get angry. And the guy who made the penis envy speech came back and said to us, 'That was funny to me. If that's not funny to you I don't know what kind of sense of humor you have, but I'm sorry.'"

That night the women sat around the stairwell of their house discussing the event, some angry and others simply wanting to forget the whole thing. They finally decided to ask the university to require that the men return to discuss the event. When university officials threatened to take action, the men agreed to the meeting. I was asked by both the men and the women involved to attend the discussion as a facilitator, and was given permission to write about the event as long as I concealed their identities.

In the women's view, the joke had not failed because of its subject; they considered sexual jokes to be a normal part of the erotic joking relationship between men and women. They criticized its emotional structure, the mixture of sexuality with aggression and the atmosphere of physical intimidation in the room. Although many of the men individually regretted the damage to their relationship with women friends in the group, they argued that the special group solidarity created by the initiation was a unique form of masculine friendship that justified the inconvenience caused the women.

Fraternal group bonding in everyday life frequently takes the form of *joking relationships,* in which men relate to each other by exchanging insults and jokes in order to create a feeling of solidarity that negotiates the latent tension and aggression they feel toward each other (Radcliffe-Brown, 1959). The humor of joking relationships is generally sexual and aggressive, and frequently consists of sexist or racist jokes. As Freud (1960:99) observed, the jokes men direct *toward* women are generally sexual, tend to be clever (like double entendres), and have a seductive purpose; but the jokes that men tell *about* women in the presence of other men tend to be sexist rather than intimate or erotic, and use hostile and aggressive rather than clever verbal forms. In this case study, joking relationships will be analyzed to uncover the emotional dynamics of fraternal groups and the impact of fraternal bonding upon relationships between men and women.

### The Girls' Story

The women had frequently been the target of fraternity initiation rites in the past, and generally enjoyed this joking relationship with the men, if with a certain ambivalence. "There was the naked Christmas Carol event, they were singing 'We wish you a Merry Christmas,' and 'Bring on the hasty pudding' was the big line they liked to yell out. And they had five or six pledges who had to strip in front of the house and do naked jumping jacks on the lawn, after all the women in the house were lined up on the steps to watch." The women did not think these events were hostile because they had been invited to watch, and the men stood with them watching, suggesting that the pledges, not the women, were the targets of the joke. This defined the joke as sexual, not sexist, and part of the normal erotic joking relation between "guys and girls." Still, these jokes were ritual events, not real social relationships. One woman said, "We were just supposed to watch, and the guys were watching us watch. The men set up the stage and the women are brought along to observe. They were the controlling force, then they jump into the car and take off."

At the meeting with the men, two of the women spoke for the group while eleven others sat silently in the center, surrounded by about thirty men. The first woman began, "Your humor was pretty funny as long as it was sexual, but when it went beyond sexual to sexist, then it became painful. You were saying 'I'm better than you.' When you started using sex as a way of proving your superiority, it hurt me and made me angry."

The second woman said that the fraternity's raid had the tone of a rape. "I admit we knew you were coming over, and we were whispering about it. But it went too far, and I felt afraid to say anything. Why do men always think about women in terms of violating them, in sexual imagery? You have to understand that the combination of a sexual topic with the physical threat of all of you standing around terrified me. I couldn't move. You have to realize that when men combine sexuality and force, it's terrifying to women."

Many of the women began by saying, "I'm not a feminist, but . . . ," to reassure the men that although they felt angry, they hoped to reestablish the many individual friendships that had existed between men and women in the two groups. In part the issue was resolved when the women accepted the men's construction of the event as a joke, although a failed joke, transforming a discussion about sexuality and force into a debate about good and bad jokes.

For an aggressive joke to be funny, and most jokes contain some hostility, the joke teller must send the audience a cue that says "this is meant as a joke." If accepted, the cue invokes special social rules that "frame" the hostile words that are typical of jokes, ensuring they will not be taken seriously. The men had implicitly sent such a cue when they stood *next* to the women during the naked jumping jacks. Verbal aggression mediated by the joke form will generally be without later consequences in the everyday world, and will be judged in terms of the formal intention of jokes, shared play and laughter.

In accepting the construction of the event as "just a joke" the women absolved the men of responsibility for their actions by calling them "little boys." One woman said, "It's not wrong, they're just boys playing a prank. They're little boys, they don't know what they're doing. It was unpleasant, but we shouldn't make a big deal out of it." In appealing to the rules of the joke form (as in saying "That was funny to me, I don't know what kind of sense of humor you have"), the men sacrificed their personal friendships with the women in order to protect the feelings of fraternal solidarity it produced. In calling the men "little boys" the women were bending the rules of friendship, trying to preserve their relationships to the guys by playing a patient and nurturing role.

### The Guys' Story

Aside from occasional roars of laughter, the men interrupted the women only once. When a woman began to say that the men had obviously intended to intimidate them, the men loudly protested that the women couldn't possibly judge their intentions, that they intended the whole event only as a joke, and the intention of a joke is, by definition, just fun.

At this point the two black men in the fraternity intervened to explain the rules of male joking relationships to the women. In a sense, they said, they agreed with the women, being the object of hostile jokes *is* painful. As they described it, the collective talk of the fraternity at meals and group events was entirely hostile joking, including many racist jokes. One said, "I'd had to listen to things in the house that I'd have hit someone for saying if I'd heard them outside." The guys roared with laughter, for the fraternal joking relation consisted almost entirely of aggressive words that were barely contained by the convention that joke tellers are not responsible for what they say.

One woman responded, "Maybe people should be hit for saying those things, maybe that's the right thing to do." But the black speaker was trying to explain the rules of male joke culture to the women, "If you'd just ignored us, it wouldn't have been any fun." To ignore a joke, even though it makes you feel hurt or angry, is to be cool, one of the primary masculine ideals of the group.

Another man tried to explain the failure of the joke in terms of the difference between the degree of "crudeness" appropriate "between guys" and between "guys and girls." He said, "As I was listening to the speech I was both embarrassed and amused. I was standing at the edge of the room, near the door, and when I looked at the guys I was laughing but when I looked at the girls I was embarrassed. I could see both sides at the same time. It was too crude for your sense of propriety. We have a sense of crudeness you don't have. That's a cultural aspect of the difference between girls and guys."

The other men laughed as he mentioned "how crude we are at the house," and one of the black men added, "You wouldn't believe how crude it gets." Many of the men later said that although they individually found the jokes about women vulgar, the jokes were justified because they were necessary for the formation of the fraternal bond. These men thought that the mistake had been to reveal their crudeness to the women; this was "in bad taste."

In part the crudeness was a kind of "signifying" or "dozens," a ritual exchange of intimate insults that creates group solidarity. "If there's one theme that goes on it's the emphasis on being able to take a lot of ridicule, of shit, and not getting upset about it. Most of the interaction we have is verbally abusing each other, making disgusting references to your mother's sexuality, or the women you were seen with, or your sex organ, the size of your sex organ. And you aren't cool unless you can take it without trying to get back." Being cool is an important male value in other settings as well, like sports or work; the joking relationship is a kind of training that, in one guy's words, "teaches you how to keep in control of your emotions."

But the guys themselves would not have described their group as a joking relationship or fraternal bond, they called it friendship. One man said that he had found perhaps a dozen guys in the house who were special friends, "guys I could cry in front of." Another said, "I think the guys are very close, they would do nearly anything for each other, drive each other places, give each other money. I think when they have problems about school, their car, or something like that, they can talk to each other. I'm not sure they can talk to each other about problems with women though." Although the image of crying in front of the other guys was often mentioned as an example of the intimacy of the fraternal bond, no one could actually recall anyone in the group ever crying. In fact crying would be an admission of vulnerability which would violate the ideals of "strength" and "being cool."

The women interpreted the sexist jokes as a sign of vulnerability. "The thing that struck me the most about our meeting together," one said, "was when the men said they were afraid of trusting women, afraid of being seen as jerks." One of the guys added, "I think down deep all the guys would love to have satisfying relationships with women. I think they're scared of failing, of having to break away from the group they've become comfortable with. I think being in a fraternity, having close friendships with men is a replacement for having close relationships with women. It'd be painful for them because they'd probably fail." These men preferred to relate to women as a group at fraternity parties, where they could take women back to their rooms for quick sex without commitments.

Sexist jokes also had a social function, policing the boundaries of the group, making sure that guys didn't form serious relationships with girls and leave the fraternity (cf. Slater, 1963). "One of the guys just acquired a girlfriend a few weeks ago. He's someone I don't think has had a woman to be friends with, maybe ever, at least in a long time. Everybody has been ribbing him intensely the last few weeks. It's good natured in tone. Sitting at dinner they've invented a little song they sing to him. People yell questions about his girlfriend, the size of her vagina, does she have big breasts." Thus, in dealing with women, the group separated intimacy from sex, defining the male bond as intimate but not sexual (homosocial), and relationships with women as sexual but not intimate (heterosexual).

## The Fraternal Bond in Men's Life Cycle

Men often speak of friendship as a group relationship, not a dyadic one, and men's friendships often grow from the experience of shared activities or risk, rather than from self-disclosing talk (cf. Rubin, 1983:130). J. Glenn Gray (1959:89–90) distinguishes the intimate form of friendship from the comradeship that develops from the shared experience of suffering and danger of men at war. In comradeship, he argues, the individual's sense of self is subordinated to a group identity, whereas friendship is based upon a specific feeling for another that heightens a sense of individuality.

In this case, the guys used joking relationships to suspend the ordinary rules and responsibilities of everyday life, placing the intimacy of the fraternal group in competition with heterosexual friendships. One of the men had been inexpressive as he listened to the discussion, but spoke about the fraternity in a voice filled with emotion: "The penis envy speech was a hilarious idea, great college fun. That's what I joined the fraternity for, a good time. College is a stage in my life to do crazy and humorous things. In ten years when I'm in the business world I won't be able to carry on like this [loud laughter from the men]. The initiation was intended to be humorous. We didn't think through how sensitive you women were going to be."

This speech gives the fraternal bond a specific place in the life cycle. The joking relationship is a ritual bond that creates a male group bond in the transition between boyhood and manhood: after the separation from the family where the authority of mothers limits fun, but before becoming subject to the authority of work. One man later commented on the transitional nature of the fraternal bond, "I think a lot of us are really scared of losing total control over our own lives. Having to sacrifice our individuality. I think we're scared of work in the same way we're scared of women." The jokes expressed hostility toward women because an intimate friendship with a woman was associated with "loss of control," namely the risk of responsibility for work and family.

Most, but not all, of the guys in the fraternity were divided between their group identity and a sense of personal identity that was expressed in private friendships with women. Some of the guys, like the one who could "see both sides" as he stood on the edge of the group during the initiation, had reached a point of leaving the fraternity because they couldn't reconcile the tension between his group identity and the sense of self that he felt in his friendships with women.

Ultimately the guys justified the penis envy joke because it created a special kind of male intimacy. But although the fraternal group was able to appropriate the guys' needs for intimacy and commitment it is not clear that it was able to satisfy those needs, because it defined strength as shared risk taking rather than a quality of individual character or personality. In Gray's terms, the guys were constructing comradeship through an erotic of shared activities with an element of risk, shared danger, or rule breaking such as sports, paramilitary games, wild parties, and hostile jokes. In these contexts, strength implied the substitution of a group identity for a personal code that might extend to commitment and care for others (cf. Bly 1982).

In the guys' world, aggression was identified with strength, and defined as loss of control only if it was angry. The fraternal bond was built upon an emotional balance between aggression and anger, for life of the group centered upon the mobilization of aggressive energies in rule-governed activities, especially sports and games. In each arena aggression was defined as strength (toughness) only when it was rule-governed (cool). Getting angry was called "losing control," and the guys thought they were most likely to lose control when they experienced themselves as personally dependent, that is, in relationships with women and at work. The sense of order within fraternal groups is based upon the belief that all members are equally dependent upon the rules, and that no *personal* dependence is created within the group. This is not true of the family or of relations with women, both of which are intimate, and, from the guys' point of view, are "out of control" because they are governed by emotional commitments.

The guys recognized the relationship between their male bond and the work world by claiming that "high officials of the University know about the way we act, and they understand what we are doing." Although this might be taken as evidence that the guys were internalizing their fathers' norms and thus inheriting the rights of patriarchy, the guys described their fathers as slaves to work and women, not as patriarchs. It is striking that the guys would not accept the notion that men have more power than women; to them it is not men who rule, but work and women that govern men.

## References

Bly, Robert. (1982) "What men really want: An interview with Keith Thompson." *New Age* 30–37, 50–51.

Freud, Sigmund. (1960) *Jokes and Their Relation to the Unconscious.* New York: W. W. Norton.

Gray, Glenn J. (1959) *The Warriors: Reflections on Men in Battle*. New York: Harper.
Radcliffe-Brown, Alfred. (1959) *Structure and Function in Primitive Society*. Glencoe: The Free Press.
Rubin, Lillian. (1983) *Intimate Strangers*. New York: Harper & Row.
Slater, Phillip. (1963) "On Social Regression." *The American Sociological Review* 28: 339–364.

---

## Now that you've read

1. What is the point of Lyman's long example of the fraternity joke?
2. What are some of the differences between male and female joking rituals, according to Lyman?
3. What examples can you offer to support or refute Lyman's argument?
4. Lyman writes, "It is striking that the guys would not accept the notion that men have more power than women; to them it is not men who rule, but work and women that govern men." Explain what Lyman is saying here. Do you agree or disagree? Explain your answer.

# READING 5

---

*Sam Keen*

# The Rite of War and the Warrior Psyche

Sam Keen, who holds a degree from Harvard Divinity School, has written extensively about the philosophy of religion. Here he offers a complex exploration of some of the pressures men face from their youngest days. "The Rite of War and the Warrior Psyche" offers a valuable counterpoint to the previous essays; as his essay makes clear, understanding what it means to "be a man" is no less complicated than understanding what it means to "be a woman." Keen locates much of the source of that complication in the "warrior psyche." Think of your own experiences or those of someone close to you as you read "The Rite of War and the Warrior Psyche."

### *Before you read*

1. What does it mean to "be a man"? What does it mean to "take it like a man"? What does it mean to be a "good soldier"?
2. What are some of the pressures placed on young men in terms of standing up for themselves, being able to handle themselves in a fight, standing up to bullies, etc.? How do people generally react when they fail to meet these "standards"?
3. What does *psyche* mean?

---

If men were *Homo sapiens* there would be no war.

I was fourteen when I had my last real fight, with fists and feet and anything handy. I don't remember anymore what it was about, maybe a girl, or a casual insult on the school bus, or maybe it was just because "the enemy" lived across the imaginary line on Bellefonte Street and went to another school. By my reckoning, Charley was a bit of a sissy. Chest caved in, shoulders slumping, he walked with a monkey lope. At any rate, war was declared and we agreed to meet in the vacant lot next to Nancy Ritter's house. At the appointed time, we appeared on the battleground, each accompanied by selected members of our respective tribes. For a while we circled round each other, each waiting for the other to throw the first punch. "You want to start something, you chicken-shit bastard?" "You touch me and I'll bust your ass." We moved closer. Push came to shove, fists flew, and the first one hit me in the nose. "Hell with this," I said. I was better at wrestling than boxing, I strategized. So I ducked, grabbed his legs, and took him to the ground. After much rolling, arm bending, and cursing I ended up on the bottom, unable to move. "Give up," he said. "Or I'll break your arm." He ratcheted my arm up a notch or two and pushed my face into the gravel. "Do you surrender?" "Fuck off." My face hurt, but not as much as my pride. We both knew I was defeated even though I wouldn't surrender, so he released my arm and after a few rounds of mandatory cursing and name-calling we went home.

That night, true to the scenario in the comic books, I vowed I would never again be beaten up by some goddamn sissy. For $3.95 I sent away for a Charles Atlas course and began to transform a ninety-eight-pound weakling into a lean and mean fighting machine. In the secrecy of my room I practiced "dynamic tension," lifted weights, did push-ups and leg lifts. Later I graduated to wrestling. For years, well into my midthirties, I worked out at the YMCA. I perfected my take-downs and pinning combinations and occasionally entered competitions as a light-heavyweight. I was never a champion but I learned to love fighting. And no one rubbed my face in the dirt.

Meanwhile I was studying philosophy and honing the weapons of dialectic, debate, and argumentation. By the time I was a practicing Ph.D. my mind was even more skilled than my body in the art of self-defense. As a professor I engaged in daily combat with colleagues and students. I was good at the academic game, enjoyed it, and played to win. I hardly noticed that, over the years, I had gradually adopted a combative stance toward others—the mind and posture of a warrior. I was much better at fighting than at wondering or loving.

### Agents of Violence

Why has the gender that gave us the Sistine Chapel brought us to the edge of cosmocide? Why have the best and brightest exercised their intelligence, imagination, and energy and managed only to create a world where starvation and warfare are more common than they were in neolithic times? Why has the history of what we dare to call "progress" been marked by an increase in the quantity of human suffering?

Could it be that men are determined to be greedy, aggressive, and brutish? Does some selfish gene, some territorial imperative, drive us blindly into hostile action? Is the story of Cain and Abel etched on our DNA? Does excess testosterone condemn us to violence and early heart attacks?

Because men have historically been the major agents of violence, it is tempting to place the blame on our biology and to conclude that the problem lies in nature's faulty design rather than in our willfulness. But all deterministic explanations ignore the obvious: men are systematically conditioned to endure pain, to kill, and to die in the service of the tribe, nation, or state. The male psyche is, first and foremost, the warrior psyche. Nothing shapes, informs, and molds us so much as society's demand that we become specialists in the use of power and violence, or as we euphemistically say, "defense." Historically, the major difference between men and women is that men have always been expected to be able to resort to violence when necessary. The capacity and willingness for violence has been central to our self-definition. The male psyche has not been built upon the rational "I think; therefore I am" but upon the irrational "I conquer; therefore I am."

In what has come to be the normal state of emergency of modern life, we grant the state the power to interrupt the lives of young men, to draft them into the army, and to initiate them into the ritual of violence. Clich s that pass for wisdom tell us: "The army will make a man out of you," and "Every man must have his war."

Induction into the army or, if you are one of the lucky "few" into the marines, involves the same process of systematic destruction of individuality that accompanied initiation in primitive tribes. The shaved head, the uniform, the abusive drill instructors, the physical and emotional ordeal of boot camp, are meant to destroy the individual's will and teach the dogface that the primary virtue of a man is not to think for himself but to obey his superiors, not to listen to his conscience but to follow orders. Like the rites of all warrior societies it teaches men to value what is tough and to despise what is "feminine" and tenderhearted. Nowhere so clearly as in the military do we learn the primitive maxim that the individual must sacrifice himself to the will of the group as it is represented by the authorities.

In the mythic initiation, the neophyte identifies with the tribal heroes. Their story provides the pattern that will be superimposed on his autobiography. That this mythical-mystical mode of initiation is still in force in our so-called modern mind can be seen in the continual references to the great American hero, John Wayne, in the literature that is now coming out of the Vietnam experience. "The war was billed on the marquee as a John Wayne shoot-'em-up test of manhood . . . I had flashes of images of John Wayne films with me as the hero . . . You see the baddies and the goodies on television and at the movies . . . I wanted to kill the bad guy."[1] Early Christians learned that the authentic life was an "imitation of Christ"; initiates in the mystery cults became the god Dionysius; nice American boys going into battle became John Wayne, the mythic man who had been divinized and made immortal by the media.

For the last four thousand years the baptism by fire has been a great male initiation rite. To win the red badge of courage was the mark of a man. Phillip Caputo reporting on Vietnam states the tradition in classical form: "Before the firefight, those Marines fit both definitions of the word *infantry,* which means either 'a body of soldiers equipped for service on foot,' or 'infants, boys, youths collectively.' The difference was that the second definition could no longer be applied to them. Having received that primary sacrament of war, baptism of fire, their boyhoods were behind them. Neither they nor I thought of it in those terms at the time. We didn't say to ourselves, We've been under fire, we've shed blood, now we're men. We were simply aware, in a way we could not express, that something significant had happened to us."[2]

Although only a minority of men actually serve in the military and fewer still are initiated into the brotherhood of those who have killed, all men are marked by the warfare system and the military virtues. We all wonder: Am I a man? Could I kill? If tested would I prove myself brave? Does it matter whether I have actually killed or risked being killed? Would you think more or less of me if I had undergone the baptism of fire? Would I think more or less of myself? What special mystery surrounds the initiated, the veteran? What certification of manhood matches the Purple Heart or the Congressional Medal of Honor?

Men have all been culturally designed with conquest, killing, or dying in mind. Even sissies. Early in life a boy learns that he must be prepared to fight or be called a sissy, a girl. Many of the creative men I know were sissies. They were too sensitive, perhaps too compassionate to fight. And most of them grew up feeling they were somehow inferior and had flunked the manhood test. I suspect that many writers are still showing the bullies on the block that the pen is mightier than the sword. The test shaped us, whether we passed or flunked.

We are all war-wounded.

### The Warrior Psyche

To understand men and the twisted relations that exist between men and women, we need to look at what happens to a man when his mind, body, and soul are socially informed by the expectation that he must be prepared to suffer, die, and kill to protect those he loves.

These are not the kinds of topics we usually consider when we think about men. Why not? Why do we so seldom wonder if the habit of war has made men what they are rather than vice versa? The warfare system has become such an accepted part of the social and psychological horizon within which we live, that its formative influence on everything we are and do has become largely invisible.

Or to put the matter another way, the warfare system has formed the eyes through which we see war, which means we are encompassed within the myth of war. We assume war is "just the way things are." It is an inevitable outcome of the power dynamics that exist among tribes, groups, nations. And because we rarely examine our basic assumptions about war, generation after generation, we continue to beg the crucial question about the relationship between the warfare system and the male and female psyche.

Lately we have generated a new, and I believe, false hope that women can gain enough power to solve the problems men create. The recent feminist slogan "Peace is Matriotic" reveals in a single phrase the degree to which the warfare system has bewitched us all. It assumes the opposite, that "War is Patriotic," a problem caused by men. But as we will see, the warfare system unfortunately shapes both the male and female psyche equally (although in opposite ways). History offers us the chance to take responsibility and change what we previously considered our fate. What it does not offer is virgin births, pure heroes, guiltless saviors, or morally immaculate groups (the faithful, the bourgeoisie, the moral majority, the sons of God or the daughters of the goddess) whose innocence gives them the leverage to change the course of things in the twinkling of an eye or the length of a sermon.

Our best hope is to see how the war system has been constructed, and then to undertake the hundred-year task of taking it apart piece by piece.

Modern psychology has given us two great intellectual tools that can help us understand the warrior psyche: Freud's idea of "defense mechanisms" and Wilhelm Reich's notion of "character armor."

Freud assumed he was offering an objective, empirical, scientific, and universally valid account of the essential nature of the human psyche. But nowhere was he so much a product of his time as in his assumptions that his own theories were not conditioned by his time and social milieu. Like most nineteenth-century scientists, he assumed he could see reality as if from a god's-eye perspective—the way it really was. But Freud is interesting and useful to us precisely when we see his psychology not as a description of the inevitable structure of the human psyche, but as a psychogram of the way the minds and emotions of men and women have been shaped by the warfare system. His account of the self inadvertently lays bare the logic of the warrior psyche. The psychological landscape he describes, no less than the political landscape Matthew Arnold described in *Dover Beach,* is that of a battlefield where "ignorant armies clash by night."

The psyche, according to Freud, is like a miniaturized nation that is organized to guard against the threats real or imagined, from internal or external sources. It is the scene of a perpetual conflict in which the embattled ego is constantly fending off angelic legions and moralistic forces of the superego and the dark powers of the libidinal underworld. Even in the healthy individual there is a continual conflict between the instinctual drives that propel the organism toward gratification and the defenses and counterforces that oppose the expression and gratification.

The weapons used in this struggle, the defense mechanisms, are well honed but for the most part are used automatically, with little awareness. In fact, defense mechanisms, like the propaganda apparatus of a modern state, function best when they censor awareness of the actual (ambiguous) situation of the self. They foster comforting illusions and keep unpleasant realities out of consciousness.

Consider the obvious parallels between the modus operandi of the warfare state and some of the defense mechanisms Freud considered the armamentum of the ego.[3]

Repression, "the exclusion of a painful idea and its associated feeling from consciousness," is like the repression of our genocide against native Americans and the consequent sense of appropriate guilt.

Isolation, the splitting off of appropriate feelings from ideas, is obvious in our habit of thinking calmly about nuclear destruction.

Reaction formation, "replacing an unacceptable drive with its opposite," is at work in naming the MX missile "the peacekeeper."

Displacement, directing an unacceptable wish away from its original to a less threatening object, e.g., occurs when a man rapes a woman to give vent to the anger he feels toward his mother or toward the authorities who brutalized the "feminine" aspects of himself.

Projection, attributing an unacceptable impulse to somebody else, allows us to claim that the enemy is planning to destroy us.

Denial, remaining unaware of the painful reality, is evident in the pretense that we can use nuclear weapons against an enemy without destroying ourselves.

Rationalization, using reasons to disguise one's unconscious motives, is used when we announce to the world that "We sent arms to the Contras only because we wanted to help them remain free, not because we want to dominate Central America."

Wilhelm Reich added a crucial twist to the notion of defense mechanisms. Not only the mind, but the body is formed by living in the ambiance of threat and violence. When we perceive danger, the body immediately prepares itself for fight or flight, glands and muscles switch to emergency status. Adrenaline courses through our system, the heart rate increases, and we assume a "red alert" stance. In the natural course of things, a threat arises and recedes, the lion approaches and retreats or is killed. But a culture that is at war or constantly preparing for a possible war conspires to create the perception, especially among its male citizens, that the threat from the enemy is always present, and therefore, we can never let down our guard. "Eternal vigilance is the price of liberty." So men, the designated warriors, gradually form "character armor," a pattern of muscular tension and rigidity that freezes them into the posture that is appropriate only for fighting—shoulders back, chest out, stomach pulled in, anal sphincter tight, balls drawn up into the body as far as possible, eyes narrowed, breathing foreshortened and anxious, heart rate accelerated, testosterone in full flow. The warrior's body is perpetually uptight and ready to fight.

Recently, on an ordinary afternoon, I watched an early stage of the education of a warrior in my side yard. Two boys, four and six years old, were swinging on a rope that hung from a tall limb of an old cottonwood tree. For a while they took turns in an orderly way, but then the bigger boy seized power and began to hog the swing. The little boy protested, "It's my turn," and went over and tried to take the rope. "Bug off!" shouted the big boy, and pushed the little boy roughly to the ground. The man-child struggled to his feet, jaw quivering, fighting to hold back his tears, and said defiantly, "That didn't hurt."

Condition a man (or a woman) to value aggression above all other virtues, and you will produce a character type whose most readily expressed emotion will be anger.

Condition a woman (or a man) to value submission above all other attitudes and you will produce a character type whose most readily expressed emotion will be sadness.

Depending on how you look at it, aggression may be man's greatest virtue or his greatest vice. If our destiny is to conquer and control, it is the prime mover. If our destiny is to live in harmony, it is the legacy of an animal past. Or maybe it is only focused energy that may be as easily directed toward making a hospital as making war.

Research has shown it is not simple aggression but aggression mixed with hostility that predisposes Type A personalities to heart attacks. Unfortunately, the majority of men, being novices at introspection, have a hard time separating aggression and anger. Thus, the social forces that encourage a man to be an extrovert, hard-driving and iron-willed, prepare him equally for success and a heart attack. (And why does the heart "attack" a man if not because he has become an enemy to his own heart? And why does it most frequently attack a man at 9 a.m. on Mondays?)[4] Arguably, the fact that men die seven to nine years before women on an average is due to the emotions, behavior, and character-armor that make up the warrior psyche. Statistically, in modern times the traditional female stance of submission has proven to have greater survival value than the traditional male stance of aggression. The meek do inherit the earth for nearly a decade longer than the conquistadors. Men pay dearly for the privilege of dominating. As women enter the arenas where competition and conquest are honored above all other virtues, both their character armor and their disease profiles are likely to begin to resemble men's.

In the psyche no less than in a machine, "form follows function." Thus a man's mind-body-spirit that has been informed by the warfare system will necessarily be shaped by the actuality or anticipation of conflict, competition, and combat. The following are some of the characteristics of the warrior psyche:

- A dramatic, heroic stance. The warrior's world is structured on one of the oldest dramatic principles—the conflict between an antagonist and protagonist, a hero and a villain. It is filled with the stuff of which good stories are made: crucial battles, brave deeds, winning and losing. And violent emotions: hate and love, loyalty and betrayal, courage and cowardice. It is not accidental that we speak of the "theater" of war. The warrior finds the meaning of his life in playing a part in an overarching story of the cosmic struggle between good and evil.

- Willpower, decision and action. The warrior psyche has little time for contemplation, appreciation, and simple enjoyment. It is a mind disciplined to strategic thinking, to the setting of goals and the elaboration of means. It asks "how" rather than "why."

- A sense of adventure, danger, excitement, and heightened awareness that comes from living in the presence of death. Many men who have been to war confess that for all its horror it was the one time in their lives when they felt most alive. The warrior denies death, lives with the illusion of his own invulnerability and his immortality in being a part of the corps, the brotherhood of Valhalla. By remaining in the excitement of the ambiance of violent death he escapes the anxiety (and courage) of having to live creatively with the prospect of normal death.

- The identification of action with force. When politics reaches a point of impotence the warrior's imagination turns immediately to the use of force. Thus the specter of impotence always shadows the warrior. He must constantly prove he is powerful by his willingness to do and endure violence.

- A paranoid worldview. The warrior is marked by a negative identity; his life is oriented against the enemy, the rival, the competition. He moves with others only when he conspires to make them allies in his struggle against a common enemy.

- Black-and-white thinking. The more intense a conflict becomes, the more we oversimplify issues, and screen information to exclude anything that is not relevant to winning the struggle. The warrior's eye and mind narrow to stereotypes that reduce the enemy to an entity that can be defeated or killed without remorse. In the heat of battle life it is: Kill or be killed; You are either for or against us.
- The repression of fear, compassion, and guilt. The warrior psyche automatically manufactures propaganda that allows it to feel morally self-righteous by transferring blame to the enemy.
- Obsession with rank and hierarchy. The military world is organized on the basis of a hierarchy of command and submission, a pecking order in which the private obeys the corporal, the corporal the sergeant, etc. In such a world rank limits responsibility. Because obedience is required there is always a rationale denying one's radical freedom—"I was only following orders, doing my duty."
- The degrading of the feminine. To the degree that a culture is governed by a warfare system, it will reduce women to second-class citizens whose function is essentially to service warriors.

### Cannon Fodder, Gang Rape, and the War System

In the last generation, the women's movement has made us aware of the ways women have been victims of men's violence. Recent estimates[5] are that, in the U.S., three out of four women will be victims of at least one violent crime in their lifetime. Every eighteen seconds a woman is beaten, and the rate of rape is thirteen times higher than in Britain. Short of some theory that attributes violence to the innate sinfulness of men, the only way we can make sense of this propensity to brutalize women is by looking for the factors that cause men to be violent. We must assume, as they say about computers, "Garbage in, garbage out." Violence in, violence out. Men are violent because of the systematic violence done to their bodies and spirits. Being hurt they become hurters. In the overall picture male violence toward women is far less than male violence against other males. For instance, the F.B.I. reports that of the estimated 21,500 murders in the United States in 1989 two-thirds of the victims were males. What we have refused to acknowledge is that these outrages are a structural part of a warfare system that victimizes both men and women.

The advent of total war and nuclear weapons has recently forced women and children to live with the deadweight of the threat of annihilation that men have always felt in times of war or peace. In the old war code, warriors were expendable but women and children were to be protected behind the shield. Granted, the sanctity of innocence was violated as often as it was respected in warfare. The point is: no one even suggested that men's lives have a claim to the sanctity and protection afforded, in theory, to women and children. It is wrong to kill women and children but men are legitimate candidates for systematic slaughter—cannon fodder.

Every man is "the Manchurian candidate," a hypnotized agent of the state waiting to be called into active service by the bugle call of "Duty," "Honor," "Patriotism." While the official stories all rehearse the glory of the crusade, men harbor the secret knowledge from the time we are young that war is more gory than glory. As a boy, I read the names on the Rolls of Honor on the bronze plaques in churches and memorial auditoriums and imagined what it was like for Harvey Jackson 1927–1945, still a boy at eighteen, to die in the mud on a remote island in the Pacific. And we all saw the crippled veterans who had nothing between their bitterness and despair except war stories and wondered if we would still want to live with such perpetual wounds.

The wounds that men endure, and the psychic scar tissue that results from living with the expectation of being a battlefield sacrifice, is every bit as horrible as the suffering women bear from the fear and the reality of rape. Rise a hundred miles above this planet and look at history from an Olympian perspective and you must conclude that when human beings organize their political lives around a war system, men bear as much pain as women. Our bodies are violated, we are regularly slaughtered and mutilated, and if we survive battle we bear the burden of blood-guilt. When we accept the war system, men and women alike tacitly agree to sanction the violation of the flesh—the rape of women by men who have been conditioned to be "warriors," and the gang rape of men by the brutality of war. Until women are willing to weep for and accept equal responsibility for the systematic violence done to the male body and spirit by the war system, it is not likely that men will lose enough of their guilt and regain enough of their sensitivity to weep and accept responsibility for women who are raped and made to suffer the indignity of economic inequality.

If we are to honor as well as be critical of manhood we need to remember that most men went to war, shed blood, and sacrificed their lives with the conviction that it was the only way to defend those whom they loved. For millennia men have been assigned the dirty work of killing and have therefore had their bodies and spirits forged into the shape of a weapon. It is all well and good to point out the folly of war and to lament the use of violence. But short of a utopian world from which greed, scarcity, madness, and ill will have vanished, someone must be prepared to take up arms and do battle with evil. We miss the mark if we do not see that manhood has traditionally required selfless generosity even to the point of sacrifice. "To support his family, the man has to be distant, away hunting or fighting wars; to be tender, he must be tough enough to fend off enemies. To be generous, he must be selfish enough to amass goods, often by defeating other men; to be gentle, he must first be strong, even ruthless in confronting enemies; to love he must be aggressive enough to court, seduce, and 'win' a wife."[6] It was historical necessity and not innate hardness of hearts or taste for cruelty that caused masculinity to evolve into a shell of muscle and will wrapped around a vacuum.

I think what I have said about the warfare system and the warrior psyche is mostly true. But another voice rises up from some primitive depth within myself, the voice of a proud warrior, that I found first in a dream:

I go down into a dark, smoky basement where I am to be initiated into one of the mysteries of manhood. As I enter the room I see that men are sitting around a ring in which two men are fighting. I watch as the fighters batter each other with their fists, but my fascination turns to horror when they pull knives and start slashing at each other. Blood flows. Then one of the fighters stabs and kills the other. I rush from the room in revulsion and moral indignation and report the incident to the police.

I woke from the dream in a sweat, filled with anxiety, unable to go back to sleep. As I began to probe I realized that in the dream I was the "good," moral judgmental observer of the violence and that the fighters were "bad" men. As I lay tossing and turning, it occurred to me to experiment by changing roles in the dream and becoming one of the fighters. After all, it was my dream and all the characters in it were parts of myself. No sooner did I project myself inside the bodies of the fighters than my anxiety vanished and was replaced by a feeling of power and the elation. I was inside the ecstasy of hitting and being hit, lost in the excitement of the battle. I was no longer the moral observer but the warrior lost in the primal battle to survive. And it was not pain I felt but a fierce animal power, raw courage, and the strong knowledge that, if my life was threatened, I would fight with everything in me.

It has been twenty years since my blood-dream, but I remember it vividly because it signaled some kind of change in the depth of my being. It put me in touch with the animal that, if threatened, would defend its life. It told me that although I was moral I was also capable of the primitive amoral violence necessary for survival. After the dream I lost a measure of my fear, paranoia, and feeling of vulnerability, because I knew I would instinctively defend myself if attacked.

This is the dilemma a sensitive man must face: So long as the world is less than perfect the warrior can never wholly retire. It still takes gentleness and fierceness to make a whole man.

*Notes*

1. Mark Baker, *Nam: The Vietnam War in the Words of the Men and Women Who Fought There* (New York: Morrow, 1982), p. 22.
2. Phillip Caputo, *A Rumor of War* (New York: Ballantine, 1978), p. 120.
3. *American Handbook of Psychiatry,* vol. 1 (New York: Basic Books, 1974), p. 750.
4. Larry Dossey, M.D., *Recovering the Soul* (New York: Bantam Books, 1989).
5. *Newsweek* (July 16, 1990); *New York Times* (August 6, 1990).
6. David Gilmore, *Manhood in the Making: Cultural Concepts of Masculinity* (New Haven, Conn.: Yale University Press, 1990), p. 230.

---

## Now that you've read

1. Why does Keen begin with the story of his "lost" fight?
2. What purposes do the personal examples serve throughout the essay?
3. What is Keen's main argument?
4. Where, specifically, do you agree? Where do you question his conclusions?
5. Is it possible to escape "cultural design"? Explain your answer.

# READING 6

## Trinh T. Minh-ha

# Grandma's Story

In this chapter from Trinh T. Minh-ha's book *Woman, Native, Other*, stories serve educational and cultural as well as emotional purposes. Trinh's provocative essay positions us to examine the functions that storytelling serves in a variety of contexts—especially in terms of gender and "truth."

### Before you read

1. Do you or did you ever have a storytelling grandmother? If so, describe some of her stories.
2. Do you think men and women tell stories differently? If so, how?
3. What do you like most about listening to stories or telling them?

---

*See all things howsoever they flourish*
*Return to the root from which they grew*
*This return to the root is called Quietness*
—LAO TZU, *TAO-TE-CHING*, 16 (TR. A. WALEY)

### Truth and fact: story and history

Let me tell you a story. For all I have is a story. Story passed on from generation to generation, named Joy. Told for the joy it gives the storyteller and the listener. Joy inherent in the process of story-telling. Whoever understands it also understands that a story, as distressing as it can be in its joy, never takes anything away from anybody. Its name, remember, is Joy. Its double, Woe Morrow Show.

> Let the one who is diseuse, one who is mother who waits nine days and nine nights be found. Restore memory. Let the one who is diseuse, one who is daughter restore spring with her each appearance from beneath the earth. The ink spills thickest before it runs dry before it stops writing at all. (Theresa Hak Kyung Cha)

Something must be said. Must be said that has not been *and* has been said before. "It will take a long time, but the story must be told. There must not be any lies" (Leslie Marmon Silko). It will take a long time for living cannot be told, not merely told: living is not livable. Understanding, however, is creating, and living, such an immense gift that thousands of people benefit from each past or present life being lived. The story depends upon every one of us to come into being. It needs us all, needs our remembering, understanding, and creating what we have heard together to keep on coming into being. The story of a people. Of us, peoples. Story, history, literature (or religion, philosophy, natural science, ethics)—all in one. They call it the tool of primitive man, the simplest vehicle of truth. When history separated itself from story, it started indulging in accumulation and facts. Or it thought it could. It thought it could build up to History because the Past, unrelated to the Present and the Future, is lying there in its entirety, waiting to be revealed and related. The act of revealing bears in itself a magical (not factual) quality—inherited undoubtedly from "primitive" storytelling—for the Past perceived as such is a well-organized past whose organization is already given. Managing to identify with History, history (with a small letter h) thus manages to oppose the factual to the fictional (turning a blind eye to the "magicality" of its claims); the story-writer—the historian—to the story-teller. As long as the transformation, manipulations, or redistributions inherent in the collecting of events are overlooked, the division continues its course, as sure of its itinerary as it certainly dreams to be. Story-writing becomes history-writing, and history quickly sets itself apart, consigning story to the realm of tale, legend, myth, fiction, literature. Then, since fictional and factual have come to a point where they mutually exclude each other, fiction, not infrequently, means lies, and fact, truth. DID IT REALLY HAPPEN? IS IT A TRUE STORY?

> I don't want to listen to any more of your stories [Maxine Hong Kingston screamed at her champion-story-talker mother]; they have no logic. They scramble me up. You lie with stories. You won't tell me a story and then say, "This is a true story," or "This is just a story." I can't tell the difference. I don't even know what your real names are. I can't tell what's real and what you made up.

Which truth? the question unavoidably arises. The story has been defined as "a free narration, not necessarily factual but truthful in character. . . . [It] gives us human nature in its bold outlines; history, in its individual details." Truth. Not one but two: truth and fact, just like in the old times when queens were born and kings were made in Egypt. (Queens and princesses were then "Royal Mothers" from birth, whereas the king wore the crown of high priest and did not receive the Horus-name until his coronation.) Poetry, Aristotle said, is truer than history. Storytelling as literature (narrative poetry) must then be truer than history. If we rely on history to tell us what happened at a specific time and place, we can rely on the story to tell us not only what might have happened, but also what is happening at an unspecified time and place. No wonder that in old tales story-tellers are very often women, witches, and prophets. The African griot and griotte are well known for being poet, storyteller, historian, musician, and magician—all at once. But why truth at all? Why this battle for truth and on behalf of truth? I do not remember having asked grand mother once whether the story she was telling me was true or not. Neither do I recall her asking me whether the story I was reading her was true or not. We knew we could make each other cry, laugh, or fear, but we never thought of saying to each other, "This is just a story." A story is a story. There was no need for clarification—a need many adults considered "natural" or imperative among children—for there was no such thing as "a blind acceptance of the story as literally true." Perhaps the story has become *just* a story when I have become adept at consuming truth as fact. Imagination is thus equated with falsification, and I am made to believe that if, accordingly, I am not told or do not establish in so many words what is true and what is false, I or the listener may no longer be able to differentiate fancy from fact (sic). Literature and history once were/still are stories: this does not necessarily mean that the space they form is undifferentiated, but that this space can articulate on a different set of principles, one which may be said to stand outside the hierarchical realm of facts. On the one hand, each society has its own politics of truth; on the other hand, being truthful is being in the in-between of all regimes of truth. Outside specific time, outside specialized space: "Truth embraces with it all other abstentions other than itself" (T. Hak Kyung Cha).

### Keepers and transmitters

Truth is when it is itself no longer. Diseuse, Thought-Woman, Spider-Woman, griotte, storytalker, fortune-teller, witch. If you have the patience to listen, she will take delight in relating it to you. An entire history, an entire vision of the world, a lifetime story. Mother always has a mother. And Great Mothers are recalled as the goddesses of all waters, the sources of diseases and of healing, the protectresses of women and of childbearing. To listen carefully is to preserve. But to preserve is to burn, for understanding means creating.

> Let the one who is diseuse, Diseuse de bonne aventure. Let her call forth. Let her break open the spell cast upon time upon time again and again. (T. Hak Kyung Cha)

The world's earliest archives or libraries were the memories of women. Patiently transmitted from mouth to ear, body to body, hand to hand. In the process of storytelling, speaking and listening refer to realities that do not involve just the imagination. The speech is seen, heard, smelled, tasted, and touched. It destroys, brings into life, nurtures. Every woman partakes in the chain of guardianship and of transmission. In Africa it is said that every griotte who dies is a whole library that burns down (a "library in which the archives are not classified but are completely inventoried" [A. Hampate Ba]). Phrases like "I sucked it at my mother's breast" or "I have it from Our Mother" to express what has been passed down by the elders are common in this part of the world. Tell me and let me tell my hearers what I have heard from you who heard it from your mother and your grandmother, so that what is said may be guarded and unfailingly transmitted to the women of tomorrow, who will be our children and the children of our children. These are the opening lines she used to chant before embarking on a story. I owe that to you, her and her, who owe it to her, her and her. I memorize, recognize, and name my source(s), not to validate my voice through the voice of an authority (for we, women, have little authority in the History of Literature, and wise women never draw their powers from authority), but to evoke her and sing. The bond between women and word. Among women themselves. To produce their full effect, words must, indeed, be chanted rhythmically, in cadences, off cadences.

> My great-grandmama told my grandmama the part she lived through that my grandmama didn't live through and my grandmama told my mama what they both lived through and my mama told me what they all lived through and we were supposed to pass it down like that from generation to generation so we'd never forget. Even though they'd burned everything to play like it didn't ever happen. (Gayl Jones)

In this chain and continuum, I am but one link. The story is me, neither me nor mine. It does not really belong to me, and while I feel greatly responsible for it, I also enjoy the irresponsibility of the pleasure obtained through the process of transferring. Pleasure in the copy, pleasure in the reproduction. No repetition can ever be identical, but my story carries with it their stories, their history, and our story repeats itself endlessly despite our persistence in denying it. *I don't believe it. That story could not happen today.* Then someday our children will speak about us here present, about those days when things like that could happen . . . :

> It was like I didn't know how much was me and Mutt and how much was Great Gram and Corregidora—like Mama when she had started talking like Great Gram. But was what Corregidora had done to *her*, to *them*, any worse than what Mutt had done to me, than what we had done to each other, than what Mama had done to Daddy, or what he had done to her in return. . . . (Gayl Jones)

> Upon seeing her you know how it was for her. You know how it might have been. You recline, you lapse, you fall, you see before you what

you have seen before. Repeated, without your even knowing it. It is you
standing there. It is you waiting outside in the summer day. (T. Hak
Kyung Cha)

Every gesture, every word involves our past, present, and future. The
body never stops accumulating, and years and years have gone by
mine without my being able to stop them, stop it. My sympathies and
grudges appear at the same time familiar and unfamiliar to me; I
dwell in them, they dwell in me, and we dwell in each other, more as
guest than as owner. My story, no doubt, is me, but it is also, no
doubt, older than me. Younger than me, older than the humanized.
Unmeasurable, uncontainable, so immense that it exceeds all attempts at humanizing. But humanizing we do, and also overdo, for
the vision of a story that has no end—no end, no middle, no beginning; no start, no stop, no progression; neither backward nor forward, only a stream that flows into another stream, an open sea—
is the vision of a madwoman. "The unleashed tides of muteness," as
Clarice Lispector puts it. We fear heights, we fear the headless, the
bottomless, the boundless. And we are in terror of letting ourselves
be engulfed by the depths of muteness. This is why we keep on doing
violence to words: to tame and cook the wild-raw, to adopt the vertigi-
nously infinite. Truth does not make sense; it exceeds meaning and
exceeds measure. It exceeds all regimes of truth. So, when we insist
on telling over and over again, we insist on repetition in re-creation
(and vice versa). On distributing the story into smaller proportions
that will correspond to the capacity of absorption of our mouths,
the capacity of vision of our eyes, and the capacity of bearing of our
bodies. Each story is at once a fragment and a whole; a whole within
a whole. And the same story has always been changing, for things
which do not shift and grow cannot continue to circulate. Dead.
Dead times, dead words, dead tongues. Not to repeat in oblivion.

> Sediment. Turned stone. Let the one who is diseuse dust breathe away
> the distance of the well. Let the one who is diseuse again sit upon
> the stone nine days and nine nights. thus. Making stand again, Eleusis.
> (T. Hak Kyung Cha)

### Storytelling in the "civilized" context

The simplest vehicle of truth, the story is also said to be "a phase of
communication," "the natural form for revealing life." Its fascination
may be explained by its power both to give a vividly felt insight into
the life of other people and to revive or keep alive the forgotten,
dead-ended, turned-into-stone parts of ourselves. To the wo/man of
the West who spends time recording and arranging the "data" concerning storytelling as well as "the many rules and taboos connected
with it," this tool of primitive wo/man has provided primitive peoples

with opportunities "to train their speech, formulate opinions, and express themselves" (Anna Birgitta Rooth). It gives "a sympathetic understanding of their limitations in knowledge, and an appreciation of our privileges in civilization, due largely to the struggles of the past" (Clark W. Hetherington). It informs of the explanations they invented for "the things [they] did not understand," and represents their religion, "a religion growing out of fear of the unknown" (Katherine Dunlap Cather). In summary, the story is either a mere practice of the art of rhetoric or "a repository of obsolete customs" (A. Skinner). It is mainly valued for its artistic potential and for the "religious beliefs" or "primitive-mind"-revealing superstitions mirrored by its content. (Like the supernatural, is the superstitious another product of the Western mind? For to accept even temporarily Cather's view on primitive religion, one is bound to ask: which [institutionalized] religion does not grow out of fear of the unknown?) Associated with backwardness, ignorance, and illiteracy, storytelling in the more "civilized" context is therefore relegated to the realm of children. "The fact that the story is the product of primitive man," wrote Herman H. Horne, "explains in part why the children hunger so for the story." Wherever there is no written language, wherever the people are too unlettered to read what is written," Cather equally remarked, "they still believe the legends. They love to hear them told and retold. . . . As it is with unlettered peasants today, as it was with tribesmen in primitive times and with the great in medieval castle halls, it still is with the child." Primitive means elementary, therefore infantile. No wonder then that in the West storytelling is treasured above all for its educational force in the kindergarten and primary school. The mission of the storyteller, we thus hear, is to "teach children the tales their *fathers* knew," to mold ideals, and to "illuminate facts." For children to gain "right feelings" and to "think true," the story as a pedagogical tool must inform so as to keep their opinion "abreast of the scientific truth of the time, instead of dragging along in the superstitions of the past." But for the story to be well-told information, it must be related "in as fascinating a form as [in] the old myths and fables." Patch up the content of the new and the form of the old, or impose one on the other. The dis-ease lingers on. With (traditional but non-superstitious?) formulas like "once upon a time" and "long, long ago," the storyteller can be reasonably sure of making "a good beginning." For many people truth has the connotation of uniformity and prescription. Thinking true means thinking in conformity with a certain scientific (read "scientistic") discourse produced by certain institutions. Not only has the "civilized" mind classified many of the realities it *does not understand* in the categories of the untrue and the superstitious, it has also turned the story—as total event of a community, a people—into a *fatherly* lesson for children of a certain age. Indeed, in the "civilized" context, only children are allowed to indulge in the so-called fantastic or the fantastic-true. They are perceived as belonging to a world apart, one which adults (compassionately) control and populate with toys— that is to say, with false human beings (dolls), false animals, false objects (imitative, diminutive versions of the "real"). "Civilized" adults fabricate, structure, and segregate the children's world; they invent toys for the latter to *play* with and stories of a specially adapted, more digestive kind to absorb, yet they insist on molding this world according to the scientifically true—the real, obviously not in its full scale, but in a reduced scale: that which is supposed to be the (God-like-) child's scale. Stories, especially "primitive-why stories" or fairy tales, must be carefully sorted and graded, for children should neither be "deceived" nor "duped" and "there should never be any doubt in [their] mind as to what is make-believe and what is real." In other words, the difference "civilized" adults recognize in the little people's world is a mere matter of scale. The forms of constraint that rule these bigger people's world and allow them to distinguish with certainty the false from the true must, unquestionably, be exactly the same as the ones that regulate the smaller people's world. The apartheid type of difference continues to operate in all spheres of "civilized" life. There does not seem to be any possibility either as to the existence of such things as, for example, two (or more) different realms of make-believe or two (or more) different realms of truth. The "civilized" mind is an indisputably clear-cut mind. If once upon a time people believed in the story and thought it was true, then why should it be false today? If true and false keep on changing with the times, then isn't it true that what is "crooked thinking" today may be "right thinking" tomorrow? What kind of people, we then wonder, walk around asking obstinately: "Is there not danger of making liars of children by feeding them on these [fairy] stories?" What kind of people set out for northern Alaska to study storytelling among the Indians and come round to writing: "What especially impressed me was their eagerness to make me understand. To me this eagerness became a proof of the high value they set on their stories and what they represented"? What kind of people, indeed, other than the very kind for whom the story is *"just* a story"?

## A regenerating force

An oracle and a bringer of joy, the storyteller is the living memory of her time, her people. She composes on life but does not lie, for composing is not imagining, fancying, or inventing. When asked, "What is oral tradition?" an African "traditionalist" (a term African scholars consider more accurate than the French term "griot" or "griotte," which tends to confuse traditionalists with mere public entertainers) would most likely be nonplussed. As A. Hampate Ba remarks, "[s/he] might reply, after a lengthy silence: 'It is total knowledge,' and say no more." She might or might not reply so, for what is called here "total knowledge" is not really nameable. At least it cannot be named (so) without incurring the risk of sliding right back into one of the many slots the "civilized" discourse of knowledge readily provides it with. The question "What is oral tradition?" is a question-answer that needs no answer at all. Let the one who is civilized, the one who invents "oral tradition," let him define it for himself. For "oral" and "written" or "written" versus "oral" are notions that have been as heavily invested as the notions of "true" and "false" have always been. (If writing, as mentioned earlier, does not express language but encompasses it, then where does the written stop? The line distinguishing societies with writing from those without writing seems most ill-defined and leaves much to be desired . . .) Living is neither oral nor written—how can the living and the lived be contained in the merely oral? Furthermore, when she composes on life she not only gives information, entertains, develops, or expands the imagination. Not only educates. Only practices a craft. "Mind breathes mind," a civilized man wrote, "power feels power, and absorbs it, as it were. The telling of stories refreshes the mind as a bath refreshes the body; it gives exercise to the intellect and its powers; it tests the judgment and the feelings." Man's view is always reduced to man's mind. For this is the part of himself he values most. THE MIND. The intellect and its powers. Storytelling allows the "civilized" narrator above all to renew his mind and exercise power through his intellect. Even though the motto reads "Think, act, and feel," his task, he believes, is to ease the passage of the story *from mind to mind.* She, however, who sets out to revive the forgotten, to survive and supersede it ("From stone. Layers. Of stone upon stone between the layers, dormant. No more" [T. Hak Kyung Cha].), she never speaks of and cannot be content with mere matters of the mind—such as mind transmission. The storyteller has long been known as a personage of power. True, she partakes in this living heritage of power. But her powers do more than illuminate or refresh the mind. They extinguish as quickly as they set fire. They wound as easily as they soothe. And not necessarily the mind. Abraham Lincoln, accurately observed that "the sharpness of a refusal, or the edge of a rebuke, may be blunted by an appropriate story, so as to save wounded feeling and yet serve the purpose . . . story-telling as an emollient saves me much friction and distress." Yet this is but one more among the countless functions of storytelling. Humidity, receptivity, fecundity. Again, her speech is seen, heard, smelled, tasted, and touched. Great Mother is the goddess of all waters, the protectress of women and of childbearing, the unweary sentient hearer, the healer and also the bringer of diseases. She who gives always accepts, she who wishes to preserve never fails to refresh. Regenerate.

> She was already in her mid-sixties
> when I discovered that she would listen to me
> to all my questions and speculations.
> I was only seven or eight years old then. (Leslie Marmon Silko)

Salivate, secrete the words. No water, no birth, no death, no life. No speech, no song, no story, no force, no power. The entire being is engaged in the act of speaking-listening-weaving-procreating. If she does not cry she will turn into stone. Utter, weep, wet, let it flow so as to break through (it). Layers of stone amidst layers of stone. Break with her own words. The interrelation of woman, water, and word pervades African cosmogonies. Among the Dogon, for example, the process of regeneration which the eight ancestors of the Dogon people had to undergo was carried out in the waters of the womb of the female Nummo (the Nummo spirits form a male and female Pair whose essence is divine) *while she spoke* to herself and to her own sex, accompanied by the male Nummo's voice. "The spoken Word entered into her and wound itself round her womb in a spiral of eight turns . . . the spiral of the Word gave to the womb its regenerative movement." Of the fertilizing power of words and their transmissions through women, it is further said that:

> the first Word had been pronounced [read "scanned"] in front of the genitalia of a woman. . . . The Word finally came from the ant-hill, that is, from the mouth of the seventh Nummo [the seventh ancestor and master of speech], which is to say from a woman's genitalia.
> The Second Word, contained in the craft of weaving, emerged from a mouth, which was also the primordial sex organ, in which the first childbirths took place.

Thus, as a wise Dogon elder (Ogotemmêli) pointed out, "issuing from a woman's sexual part, the Word enters another sexual part, namely the ear." (The ear is considered to be bisexual, the auricle being male and the auditory aperture, female.) From the ear, it will, continuing the cycle, go to the sexual part where it encircles the womb. African traditions conceive of speech as a gift of God/dess and a force of creation. In Fulfulde, the word for "speech" (*haala*) has the connotation of "giving strength," and by extension of "making material." Speech is the materialization, externalization, and internalization of the vibrations of forces. That is why, A. Hampate Ba noted, "every manifestation of a force in any form whatever is to be regarded as its speech . . . everything in the universe speaks. . . . If speech is strength, that is because it creates a *bond of coming-and-going* which generates *movement and rhythm* and therefore *life and action* [my italics]. This movement to and fro is symbolized by the weaver's feet going up and down . . . (the symbolism of the loom is entirely based on creative speech in action)." Making material: spinning and weaving is a euphonious heritage of wo/mankind handed on from generation to generation of weavers within the clapping of the shuttle and the creaking of the block—which the Dogon call "the creaking of the Word." "The cloth was the Word"; the same term, *soy,* is used among the Dogon to signify both the woven material and the spoken word. Life is a perpetual to and fro, a dis/continuous releasing and absorbing of the self. Let her weave her story within their stories, her life amidst their lives. And while she weaves, let her whip, spur, and set them on fire. Thus making them sing again. Very softly a-new a-gain.

### At once "black" and "white" magic

"The witch is a woman; the wizard is a male imitation" (Robert Briffault). In many parts of the world, magic (and witchcraft) is regarded as essentially a woman's function. It is said that "in primitive thought every woman is credited with the possession of magic powers." Yet she who possesses that power is always the last one to credit it. Old Lao Tzu warned: the wo/man of virtue is not virtuous; the one who never fails in virtue has no virtue at all. Practicing power for the sake of power—an idea implied in the widely assumed image of the witch as exclusively an evil-doer—is an inheritance, I suspect, of the "civilized" mind. She who brings death and disease also brings life and health. The line dividing the good and the evil, magic and witchcraft, does not always seem to be as clear-cut as it should be. In the southern Celebes, for example, "All the deities and spirits from whom sorcerers, whether male or female, derive their power are spoken of as their 'grandmothers.'" Throughout Africa, priestesses are called "Mothers," and the numerous female fetishes served exclusively by women are known as the "Mother fetishes." Among the Butwa, the female hierophants are named "the mothers of the Butwa mysteries." Among the Bir, the women are those who perform the essential ritual of maintaining the sacred fire. In Indonesia, America, northern Asia, and northern Europe, it has been demonstrated that "magical practices and primitive priestly functions formerly belonged to the exclusive sphere of women and that they were taken up [appropriated] by men at a comparatively late epoch." Thus, the adoption of female attire by male shamans and priests is a widespread phenomenon that still prevails in today's religious contexts. Imitating women and wearing women's clothes—priestly robes, skirts, aprons, sottanas, woven loinclothes—are regarded as bestowing greater power: the Mothers' power. Of making material. Of composing on life. Her speech, her storytelling is at once magic, sorcery, and religion. It enchants. It animates, sets into motion, and rouses the forces that lie dormant in things, in beings. It is "bewitching." At once "black" and "white" magic. Which, however, causes sickness and death? which brings joy into life? For white, remember, is the color for mourning in many cultures. The same "medicines," the same dances, the same sorcery are said to be used in both. As occasion arises, the same magic may serve for beneficent *and* maleficent ends. This is why her power is so dreaded; because it can be used for harm; because when it is wielded by one sex, it arouses alarm in the other. The (wizard's) game dates from the times when every practice of this art by women became a threat to men and was automatically presumed to be malignant in intention; when every magic woman must necessarily be a witch—no longer a fairy who works wonders nor a Mother-priestess-prophetess who nurtures, protects, restores, and warns against ill-will. Ill assumption leads to ill action. Men appropriate women's power of "making material" to themselves and, not infrequently, corrupt it out of ignorance. The story becomes *just a* story. It becomes a good or bad lie. And in the more "civilized" contexts where women are replaced and excluded from magico-religious functions, adults who still live on storytelling become bums who spend their time feeding on lies, "them big old lies we tell when we're jus' sittin' around here on the store porch doin' nothin'." When Zora Neale Hurston came back to Eatonville, Florida, to collect old stories, her home folks proudly told her: "Zora, you come to de right place if lies is what you want. Ah'm gointer lie up a nation"; or "Now, you gointer hear lies above suspicion"; or else "We kin tell you some lies most any ole time. We never run outer lies and lovin'." All right, let them call it lie, let us smile and call it lie too if that satisfies them, but "let de lyin' go on!" For we do not *just* lie, we lie and love, we "lie up a nation," and our lies are "above suspicion." How can they be otherwise when they derive their essence from that gift of God: speech? Speech, that active agent in our Mothers' magic; speech, which owes its fertilizing power to . . . who else but the Mother of God?

### The woman warrior: she who breaks open the spell

"Thought-Woman / is sitting in her room / and whatever she thinks about / appears. / She thought of her sisters, / . . . / and together they created the Universe / . . . / Thought-Woman, the spider, / named things and / as she named them / they appeared" (Leslie Marmon Silko). The touch infinitely delicate awakens, restores them to life, letting them surge forth in their own measures and their own rhythms. The touch infinitely attentive of a fairy's wand, a woman's voice, or a woman's hand, which goes to meet things in the dark and pass them on without deafening, without extinguishing in the process. Intense but gentle, it holds words out in the direction of things or lays them down nearby things so as to call them and breathe new life into them. Not to capture, to chain them up, nor to mean. Not to instruct nor to discipline. But to kindle that zeal which hibernates within each one of us. "Speech may create peace, as it may destroy it. It is like fire," wrote A. Hampate Ba, "One ill-advised word may start a war just as one blazing twig may touch off a great conflagration. . . . Tradition, then, confers on . . . the Word not only creative power but a double function of saving and destroying." Her words are like fire. They burn and they destroy. It is, however, only by burning that they lighten. Destroying and saving, therefore, are here one single process. Not two processes posed in opposition or in conflict. They would like to order everything around hierarchical oppositions. They would like to cut her power into endless opposing halves or cut herself from the Mothers' powers—setting her against either her mother, her godmother, her mother-in-law, her grandmother, her daughter, or her granddaughter. One of them has to be wicked so as to break the network of transmission. This is cleverly called jealousy among women, the jealousy of the woman who cannot suffer seeing her daughter or another woman take more pleasure in life than herself. For years and years, centuries and centuries, they have devoted their energies to breaking bonds and spreading discords and confusion. Divide and conquer. Mothers fighting mothers. Here is what an Indian witch has to say on "white skin people / like the belly of a fish / covered with hair":

> . . . . They see no life
> When they look
> they see only objects.
> . . . . They fear
> They fear the world.
> They destroy what they fear.
> They fear themselves.
> . . . . Stolen rivers and mountains
> the stolen land will eat their hearts
> and jerk their mouths from the Mother.
> The people will starve.

These are excerpts of a story passed on by Leslie Marmon Silko. The story is the vision of a witch who, a long time ago, at a contest of witches from all the pueblos, "didn't show off any dark thunder charcoals or red anthill beads" like the other witches, but only asked them to listen: "What I have is a story. . . . . laugh if you want to / but as I tell the story / it will begin to happen." Scanned by the refrain

"set in motion now / set in motion / to work for us" the story thus unfolds, naming as it proceeds the killing, the destruction, the full deed,
the loss of the white man, and with it, the doom of the Indian people.
"It isn't so funny. . . . Take it back. Call that story back," said the audience by the end of the story, but the witch answered: "It's already
turned loose / It's already coming. / It can't be called back." A story
is *not* just a story. Once the forces have been aroused and set into
motion, they can't simply be stopped at someone's request. Once
told, the story is bound to circulate; humanized; it may have a temporary end, but its effects linger on and its end is never truly an end.
Who among us has not, to a certain extent, felt what George Ebers,
for example, felt toward his mother's stories: "When the time of rising came, I climbed joyfully into my mother's warm bed, and never
did I listen to more beautiful fairy tales than at those hours. They
became instinct with life to me and have always remained so. . . . It is
a singular thing that actual events which happened in those early
days have largely vanished from my memory, but the fairy tales I
heard and secretly experienced became firmly impressed on my
mind." The young beautiful fairy and the old ugly witch, remember,
have the same creative power, the same decisive force of speech. As
she names them, they appear . . . The story tells us not only what
might have happened, but also what *is happening* at an unspecified
time and place. Whenever Ebers had the slightest doubt in mind, he
would immediately appeal to his mother, for he thought "she could
never be mistaken and knew that she always told the truth." Lying is
not a mother's attribute. Or else, if lying is what you think she does,
then she will "never run outer lies and lovin'."

> When we Chinese girls listened to the adult talk-story, we learned that
> we failed if we grew up to be but wives or slaves. We could be heroines,
> swordswomen. . . . Night after night my mother would talk-story until
> we fell asleep. I couldn't tell where the stories left off and the dreams
> began, her voice the voice of the heroines in my sleep. . . . At last I saw
> that I too had been in the presence of great power, my mother talking-
> story. . . . She said I would grow up a wife and a slave, but she taught
> me the song of the warrior woman, Fa Mu Lan. I would have to grow up
> a warrior woman. (Maxine Hong Kingston)

She fires her to achievement and she fires her with desire to emulate.
She fires her with desire to emulate the heroines of whom she told
and she fires her with desire to emulate the heroine who tells of the
other heroines, "I too had been in the presence of great power, my
mother talking-story." What is transmitted from generation to generation is not only the stories, but the very power of transmission. The
stories are highly inspiring, and so is she, the untiring storyteller.
She, who suffocates the codes of lie and truth. She, who loves to tell

and retell and loves to hear them told and retold night after night again and again. Hong Kingston grows up a warrior woman and a warrior-woman-storyteller herself. She is the woman warrior who continues to fight in America the fight her mothers fought in China. Even though she is often "mad at the Chinese for lying so much," and blames her mother for lying with stories, she happily *lets the lying go on* by retelling us her mother's "lies" and offering us versions of her stories that can be called lies themselves. Her brother's version of a story, she admits it herself, "may be better than mine because of its bareness, not twisted into designs." Her brother, indeed, is no woman warrior-storyteller. Hong Kingston's apparent confusion of story and reality is, in fact, no confusion at all since it is an unending one; her parents often accuse her of not being able to "tell a joke from real life" and to understand that Chinese "like to say the opposite." Even the events described by her relatives in their letters from China she finds suspect: "I'd like to go to China and see those people and find out what's cheat story and what's not." The confusion she experienced in her girlhood is the confusion we all experience in life, even when we think, as adults, that we have come up with definite criteria for the true and the false. What is true and what is not, and who decides so if we wish not to have this decision made *for* us? When, for example, Hong Kingston yells at her mother: "You can't stop me from talking. You tried to cut off my tongue, but it didn't work," we not only know she is quite capable of telling "fancy" from "facts," we are also carried a step further in this differentiation by her mother's answer: "I cut it to make you talk more, not less, you dummy." (Her mother has already affirmed elsewhere that she cut it so that her daughter would not be "tongue-tied.") The opening story of *The Woman Warrior* is a forbidden story ("No Name woman") that begins with Hong Kingston's mother saying: "You must not tell anyone what I am about to tell you." Twenty years after she heard this story about her father's sister who drowned herself and her baby in the family well, not only has Hong Kingston broken open the spell cast upon her aunt by retelling the story—"I alone devote pages of paper to her"—but she has done it in such a way as to reach thousands and thousands of listeners and readers. Tell it to the world. To preserve is to pass on, not to keep for oneself. A story told is a story bound to circulate. By telling her daughter not to tell it to anyone, the mother knew what she was supposed to say, for "That's what Chinese say. We like to say the opposite." She knew she was in fact the first before her daughter to break open the spell. The family cursed her, she who committed adultery and was such a spite suicide (the aunt); the men (her brothers) tabooed her name and went on living "as if she had never been born"; but the women (Hong Kingston's mother and those who partook in this aunt's death) would have to carry her with(in) them for life and pass her on, even though they condemned her no less. For every woman is the woman of all women, and this one died first and foremost for being a woman. ("Now that you have started to menstruate," the mother warned her daughter, "what happened to her could happen to you. Don't humiliate us.") Hong Kingston has, in her own way, retained many of the principles of her mother's storytelling. If, in composing with "fancy" and "fact," the latter knows when she should say "white is white" and when she should say "white is black" in referring to the same thing, her daughter also knows when to dot her i's and when not to. Her writing, neither fiction nor non-fiction, constantly invites the reader either to drift naturally from the realm of imagination to that of actuality or to live them both without ever being able to draw a clear line between them yet never losing sight of their differentiation. What Hong Kingston does *not* tell us about her mother but allows us to read between the lines and in the gaps of her stories reveals as much about her mother as what she *does* tell us about her. This, I feel, is the most "truthful" aspect of her work, the very power of her storytelling. *The Woman Warrior* ends with a story Hong Kingston's mother told her, not when she was young, she says, "but recently, when I told her I also talk-story." The beginning of the story, which relates how the family in China came to love the theater through the grandmother's passion for it and her generosity, is the making of the mother. The ending of the story, which recalls one of the songs the poetess Ts'ai Yen composed while she was a captive of the barbarians and how it has been passed down to the Chinese, is the making of the daughter— Hong Kingston herself. Two powerful woman storytellers meet at the end of the book, both working at strengthening the ties among women while commemorating and transmitting the powers of our foremothers. At once a grandmother, a poetess, a storyteller, and a woman warrior.

## A cure and a protection from illness

I grew up with storytelling. My earliest memories are of my grandmother telling me stories while she watered the morning-glories in her yard. Her stories were about incidents from long ago, incidents which occurred before she was born but which she told as certainly as if she had been there. The chanting or telling of ancient stories to effect certain cures or protect from illness and harm have always been part of the Pueblo's curing ceremonies. I feel the power that the stories still have to bring us together, especially when there is loss and grief. (Leslie Marmon Silko)

Refresh, regenerate, or purify. Telling stories and watering morning-glories both function to the same effect. For years and years she has been renewing her forces with regularity to keep them intact.

Such ritual ablutions—the telling and retelling—allow her to recall the incidents that occurred before she was born with as much certainty as if she had witnessed them herself. The words passed down from mouth to ear (one sexual part to another sexual part), womb to womb, body to body are the remembered ones. S/He whose belly cannot contain (also read "retain") words, says a Malinke song, will succeed at nothing. The further they move away from the belly, the more liable they are to be corrupted. (Words that come from the MIND and are passed on directly "from mind to mind" are, consequently, highly suspect . . .) In many parts of Africa, the word "belly" refers to the notion of occult power. Among the Basaa of Cameroon, for example, the term *hu,* meaning (a human being's) "stomach," is used to designate "a thing whose origin and nature nobody knows," but which is unanimously attributed to women and their powers. A basaa man said he heard from his fathers that "it was the woman who introduced the *hu*" into human life. In several myths of the Basaa's neighboring peoples, *evu,* the equivalent of the Basaa's *hu,* is said to have requested that it be carried in the woman's belly at the time it first met her and to have entered her body through her sexual part. Thus associated with women, the *hu* or *evu* is considered both maleficent and beneficent. It is at times equated with devil and sorcery, other times with prophecy and anti-sorcery. S/He who is said to "have a *hu*" is both feared and admired. S/He is the one who sees the invisible, moves with ease in the night-world as if in broad daylight, and is endowed with uncommon, exceptional intelligence, penetration, and intuition. Woman and magic. Her power resides in her belly—Our Mother's belly—for her cure is not an isolated act but a total social phenomenon. Sorcery, according to numerous accounts, is hereditary solely within the matrilineal clan; and a man, in countless cases, can only become a sorcerer (a wizard) through the transmission of power by a sorceress (witch). He who understands the full power of woman and/in storytelling also understands that life is not to be found in the mind nor in the heart, but there where she carries it:

> I will tell you something about stories, [he said]
> They aren't just entertainment.
> Don't be fooled.
> They are all we have, you see,
> all we have to fight off
> illness and death.
>
> You don't have anything
> if you don't have the stories. . . .
> He rubbed his belly.
> I keep them here [he said]
> Here, put your hand on it

See, it is moving
There is life here
for the people.

The story as a cure and a protection is at once musical, historical, poetical, ethical, educational, magical, and religious. In many parts of the world, the healers are known as the living memories of the people. Not only do they hold esoteric and technical knowledge, but they are also kept closely informed of the problems of their communities and are entrusted with all family affairs. In other words, they know everyone's story. Concerned with the slightest incident, they remain very alert to their entourage and heedful of their patients' talks. They derive their power from *listening* to the others and *absorbing* daily realities. While they cure, they take into them their patients' possession and obsessions and let the latter's illnesses become theirs. Their actions imply a personal investment of which the healing technics form only a part and are a reflection. "I see the patient's psychic life," many of them say, "nothing is hidden from me." Dis-ease breeds dis-ease; life engenders life. The very close relationship these healers maintain with their patients remains the determining factor of the cure. Curing means re-generating, for understanding is creating. The principle of healing rests on *reconciliation,* hence the necessity for the family and/or the community to cooperate, partake in, and witness the recovery, de-possession, regeneration of the sick. The act of healing is therefore a socio-cultural act, a collective, motherly undertaking. (Here, it is revealing to remember that male healers often claim to be wedded to at least two wives: a terrestrial one *and* a spiritual one. The spiritual wife or the "woman spirit" protects the healer and is the source of his powers. She is the one who "has knowledge" and from whom he seeks advice in all matters. When she becomes too demanding and too possessive, it is said that only one person can send her away: the healer's own mother.) The storyteller, besides being a great mother, a teacher, a poetess, a warrior, a musician, a historian, a fairy, and a witch, is a healer and a protectress. Her chanting or telling of stories, as Marmon Silko notices, has the power of bringing us together, especially when there is sickness, fear, and grief. "'*When they look / they see only objects,*' / They fear / they never stop fearing / but they see not fear the living thing. / They follow not its movements / for they fear not to fear. / *They destroy what they fear. / They fear themselves.*' / They destroy the stories / let these be confused or forgotten / let these be only stories / They would like that . . ."

Stolen rivers and mountains
the stolen land will eat their hearts
and jerk their mouths from the Mother.
The people will starve.

## "Tell it the way they tell it"

It is a commonplace for those who consider the story to be just a story to believe that, in order to appropriate the "traditional" story-tellers' powers and to produce the same effects as theirs, it suffices to "look for the structure of their narratives." *See them as they see each other,* so goes the (anthropological) creed. "Tell it the way *they* tell it instead of imposing *our* structure," they repeat with the best of intentions and a conscience so clear that they pride themselves on it. Disease breeds disease. Those who function best within definite structures and spend their time structuring their own or their peers' existences must obviously "look for" that which, according to their "findings" and analyses, is supposed to be "the structure of their [the storytellers'] narratives." What we "look for" is un/fortunately what we shall find. The anthropologist, as we already know, does not *find* things; s/he *makes* them. And makes them up. The structure is therefore not something given, entirely external to the person who structures, but a projection of that person's way of handling realities, here narratives. It is perhaps difficult for an analytical or ana-lytically trained mind to admit that recording, gathering, sorting, deciphering, analyzing and synthesizing, dissecting and articulat-ing are already "imposing our [/a] structure," a structural activity, a structuring of the mind, a whole mentality. (Can one "look for a structure" without structuring?) But it is particularly difficult for a dualistic or dualistically trained mind to recognize that "looking for the structure of their narratives" already involves the separation of the structure from the narratives, of the structure from that which is structured, of the narrative from the narrated, and so on. It is, once more, as if form and content stand apart; as if the structure can remain fixed, immutable, independent of and unaffected by the changes the narratives undergo; as if a structure can only function as a standard mold within the old determinist schema of cause and product. Listen, for example, to what a man of the West had to say on the form of the story:

> Independent of the content which the story carries, and which may vary from history to nonsense, is the form of the story which is practi-cally the same in all stories. The content is varied and particular, the form is the same and universal. Now there are four main elements in the form of each story, viz. the beginning, the development, the climax, and the end.

Just like the Western drama with its four or five acts. A drama whose naïve claim to universality would not fail to make this man of the West our laughingstock. "A good story," another man of the West as-serted, "must have a beginning that rouses interest, a succession of events that is orderly and complete, a climax that forms the story's point, and an end that leaves the mind at rest." No criteria other than those quoted here show a more thorough investment of the Western mind. *Get them*—children, story-believers—*at the start; make your point* by ordering events to a definite *climax;* then *round out to completion;* descend to a rapid close—not one, for example, that puzzles or keeps them puzzling over the story, but one that *leaves the mind at rest.* In other words, to be "good" a story must be built in conformity with the ready-made idea some people—Western adults—have of reality, that is to say, a set of prefabricated schemata (prefabricated by whom?) they value out of habit, conservatism, and ignorance (of other ways of telling and listening to stores). If these criteria are to be adopted, then countless non-Western stories will fall straight into the category of "bad" stories. Unless one makes it up or invents a reason for its absence, one of these four elements required always seems to be missing. The stories in question either have no development, no climax that forms the story's point, or no end that leaves the mind at rest. (One can say of the majority of these stories that their endings precisely refute such generalization and rationale for they offer no security of this kind. An example among endless others is the moving story of "The Laguna People" passed on by Marmon Silko, which ends with a little girl, her sister, and the people turning into stone while they sat on top of a mesa, after they had escaped the flood in their home village below. Because of the disquieting nature of the resolution here, the storytellers [Marmon Silko and her aunt] then add, as compromise to the fact-oriented mind of today's audience: "The story ends there. / Some of the stories / Aunt Susi told / have this kind of ending. / There are no explanations." There is no point [to be] made either.) "Looking for the structure of *their* narratives" so as to "tell it the way *they* tell it" is an attempt at remedying this ignorance of other ways of telling and listening (and, obviously, at re-validating the nativist discourse). In doing so, however, rare are those who realize that what they come up with is not "structure of *their* narratives" but a reconstruction of the story that, at best, makes a number of its functions appear. Rare are those who acknowledge the unavoidable transfer of values in the "search" and admit that "the attempt will remain largely illusory: we shall never know if the other, into whom we cannot, after all, dis-solve, fashions from the elements of [her/]his social existence a syn-thesis exactly superimposable on that which we have worked out." The attempt will remain illusory as long as the controlled succes-sion of certain mental operations which constitutes the structural activity is not made explicit and dealt with—not just mentioned. Life is not a (Western) drama of four or five acts. Sometimes it just drifts along; it may go on year after year without development, without climax, without definite beginnings or endings. Or it may accumulate climax upon climax, and if one chooses to mark it with beginnings and endings, then everything has a beginning and an ending. There are, in this sense, no good or bad stories. In life, we usually don't know when an event is occurring; we think it is starting when it is already ending; and we don't see its in/significance. The present, which saturates the total field of our environment, is often invisible to us. The structural activity that does not carry on the cleavage between form and content but emphasizes the interrelation of the material and the intelligible is an activity in which structure should remain an unending question: one that speaks him/her as s/he speaks it, brings it to intelligibility.

### "The story must be told. There must not be any lies"

"Looking for the structure of their narratives" is like looking for the pear shape in Erik Satie's musical composition *Trois Pi ces en Forme de Poire* (Three Pieces in a Pear Shape). (The composition was written after Satie met with Claude Debussy, who criticized his music for "lacking of form.") If structure, as a man (R. Barthes) pertinently defines it, is "the residual deposit of duration," then again, rare are those who can handle it by letting it come, instead of hunting for it or hunting it down, filling it with their own marks and markings so as to consign it to the meaningful and lay claim to it. *"They see no life / When they look / they see only objects."* The ready-made idea they have of reality prevents their perceiving the story as a living thing, an organic process, a way of life. What is taken for stories, only stories, are fragments of/in life, fragments that never stop interacting while being complete in themselves. A story in Africa may last three months. The storyteller relates it night after night, continually, or s/he starts it one night and takes it up again from that point three months later. Meanwhile, as the occasion arises, s/he may start on yet another story. Such is life . . . :

> The gussucks [the Whites] did not understand the story; they could not see the way it must be told, year after year as the old man had done, without lapse or silence. . . .
> "It began a long time ago," she intoned steadily . . . she did not pause or hesitate; she went on with the story, and she never stopped. . . .

"Storyteller," from which these lines are excerpted, is another story, another gift of life passed on by Marmon Silko. It presents an example of multiple storytelling in which story and life merge, the story being as complex as life and life being as simple as a story. The story of "Storyteller" is the layered making of four storytellers: Marmon Silko, the woman in the story, her grandmother, and the person referred to as "the old man." Except for Marmon Silko who plays here the role of the coordinator, each of these three story-

tellers has her/his own story to live and live with. Despite the differences in characters or in subject matter, their stories closely
interact and constantly overlap. The woman makes of her story a
continuation of her grandmother's, which was left with no ending—
the grandmother being thereby compelled to bear it (the story) until
her death, her knees and knuckles swollen grotesquely, "swollen
with anger" as she explained it. She bore it, knowing that her granddaughter will have to bear it too: "It will take a long time," she said,
"but the story must be told. There must not be any lies." Sometime
after her death, exactly when does not matter, when the time comes,
the granddaughter picks up the story where her grandmother left it
and carries it to its end accordingly, the way "it must be told." She
carries it to a certain completion by bringing in death where she in-
tends to have it in her story: the white storeman who lied in her
grandma's story and was the author of her parents' death would
have to pay for his lies, but his death would also have to be of his
own making. The listener/reader does not (have to) know whether
the storeman in the granddaughter's story is the same as the one
who, according to the grandmother, "left right after that [after he
lied and killed]" (hence making it apparently impossible for the old
woman to finish her story). A storeman becomes *the* storeman, the
man in the store, the man in the story. (The truthfulness of the story,
as we already know, does not limit itself to the realm of facts.) Which
story? *The* story. What grandma began, granddaughter completes
and passes on to be further completed. As a storyteller, the woman
(the granddaughter) does not directly kill; she decides when and
where that storeman will find death, but she does not carry out a
hand-to-hand fight and her murder of him is no murder in the common, factual sense of the term: all she needs to do is set in motion
the necessary forces and let them act on their own.

> They asked her again, what happened to the man from the Northern
> Commercial Store. "He lied to them. He told them it was safe to drink.
> But I will not lie. . . . I killed him," she said, "but I don't lie."

When she is in jail, the Gussuck attorney advises her to tell the
court the *truth*, which is that it was an accident, that the storeman
ran after her in the cold and fell through the ice. That's all what she
has to say—then "they will let [her] go home. Back to [her] village."

> She shook her head. "I will not change the story, not even to escape
> this place and go home. I intended that he die. The story must be told
> as it is." The attorney exhaled loudly; his eyes looked tired. "Tell her
> that she could not have killed him that way. He was a white man. He ran
> after her without a parka or mittens. She could not have planned that."

When the helpful, conscientious (full-of-the-white-man's-complex-of-
superiority) attorney concludes that he will do "all [he] can for her"

and will explain to the judge that "her mind is confused," she laughs out loud and finally decides to tell him the story anew: *"It began a long time ago . . ."* (my italics). He says she could not have killed that white man because, again, for him the story is just a story. But Thought-Woman, Spider-Woman is a fairy and a witch who protects her people and tells stories to effect cures. As she names Death, Death appears. The spell is cast. Only death gives an ending to the stories in "Storyteller." (The old man's story of the giant bear overlaps with the granddaughter's story and ends the moment the old man—the storyteller—dies.) Marmon Silko as a storyteller never loses sight of the difference between truth and fact. Her naming retains the accuracy and magic of our grand mothers' storytelling without ever confining itself to the realm of factual naming. It is accurate because it is at once extremely flexible and rigid, not because it wishes to stick to certain rules of correctness for reasons of mere conservatism (scholars studying traditional storytelling are often impressed by the storyteller's "necessity of telling the stories correctly," as they put it). It is accurate because it partakes in the setting into motion of forces that lie dormant in us. Because, as African storytellers sing, "the tongue that falsifies the word / taints the blood of [her/]him that lies." Because she who bears it in her belly cannot cut herself off from herself. Off from the bond of coming-and-going. Off from her great mothers.

"May my story be beautiful and unwind like a long thread . . . , she recites as she begins her story. Here she chants the time-honored formula that opens the tales of Kabyle folksingers, but what she chants, in a way, is a variant of what her African griotte-sisters chant every time they set about composing on life: tell me so that I can tell my hearers what I have heard from you who heard it from your mother and your great mother. . . . Each woman, like each people, has her own way of unrolling the ties that bind. Storytelling, the oldest form of building historical consciousness in community, constitutes a rich oral legacy, whose values have regained all importance recently, especially in the context of writings by women of color. She who works at un-learning the dominant language of "civilized" missionaries also has to learn how to un-write and write anew. And she often does so by re-establishing the contact with her foremothers, so that living tradition can never congeal into fixed forms, so that life keeps on nurturing life, so that what is understood as the Past continues to provide the link for the Present and the Future. As our elder Lao Tzu says, "Without allowance for filling, a valley will run dry; / Without allowance for growing, creation will stop functioning." Tradition as on-going commitment, and in women's own terms. The story is beautiful, because or therefore it unwinds like a thread.

A long thread, for there is no end in sight. Or the end she reaches leads actually to another end, another opening, another "residual deposit of duration." Every woman partakes in the chain of guardianship and of transmission—in other words, of creation. Every griotte who dies is a whole library that burns down. Tell it so that they can tell it. So that it may become larger than its measure, always larger than its own in/significance. In this horizontal and vertical vertigo, she carries the story on, motivated at once by the desire to finish it and the necessity to remind herself and others that "it's never finished." A lifetime story. More than a lifetime. One that will be picked up where it is left; when, it does not matter. For the time is already set. "It will take a long time . . . ," the grandmother ends; "it began long ago . . . ," the granddaughter starts. The time is set, she said; not in terms of when exactly but of what: what exactly must be told, and how. "There must not be any lies." Like Maxine Hong Kingston who decided to tell the world the forbidden story of her tabooed aunt, the "No Name Woman," Marmon Silko's granddaughter-storyteller, opens the spell cast upon her people, by re-setting into motion what was temporarily delayed in the story of her grandmother. The burden of the story-truth. She knew that during her own lifetime the moment would come when she would be able to assume her responsibility and resume the grandmother's interrupted story-trajectory. She killed the one who lied to her people, who actively participated in the slow extinction of her race. She killed Him. She killed the white storeman in "her story" which is not "just a story': "I intended that he die. The story must be told as it is." To ask, like the white attorney, whether the story she tells makes any sense, whether it is factually possible, whether it is true or not is to cause confusion by an incorrect question. Difference here is not understood as difference. Her (story) world remains therefore irreducibly foreign to Him. The man can't hear it the way she means it. He sees her as victim, as unfortunate object of hazard. "Her mind is confused," he concludes. She views herself as the teller, the un-making subject, the agent of the storeman's death, the moving force of the story. She didn't know when exactly she would be able to act in concordance with fate (she is also fate), but she planned and waited for the ripe moment to come, so that what appeared as an accident was carefully matured. Her sense of the story overflows the boundaries of patriarchal time and truth. It overflows the notion of story as finished product ("just a story")—one neatly wrapped, that rounds off with a normative finale and "leaves the mind at rest." Marmon Silko's "Storyteller" keeps the reader puzzling over the story as it draws to a close. Again, truth does not make sense. It exceeds measure: the woman storyteller sees her vouching for it as a defiance of a whole system of the white man's lies. She values this task, this responsibility over immediate release (her being freed from imprisonment through the attorney's advice), over immediate enlightenment and gratification (vengeance for the sake of vengeance). Even if the telling condemns her present life, what is more important is to (re-)tell the story as she thinks it should be told; in other words, to maintain the difference that allows (her) truth to live on. The difference. He does not hear or see. He cannot give. Never the given, for there is no end in sight.

> *There are these stories that just have to be told in the same way the wind goes blowing across the mesa*
>
> —Leslie Marmon Silko, "Stories and Their Tellers"

## A BEDTIME STORY

*Once upon a time,*
*an ole Japanese legend*
*goes as told*
*by Papa,*
*an old woman traveled through*
*many small villages*
*seeking refuge*
*for the night.*
*Each door opened*
*a sliver*
*in answer to her knock*
*then closed.*
*Unable to walk*
*any further*
*she wearily climbed a hill*
*found a clearing*
*and there lay down to rest*
*a few moments to catch*
*her breath.*

*The villagetown below*
*lay asleep except*
*for a few starlike lights.*
*Suddenly the clouds opened*
*and a full moon came into view*
*over the town.*

*The old woman sat up*
*turned toward*
*the village town*
*and in supplication*

*called out*
*Thank you people*
*of the village,*
*if it had not been for your*
*kindness*
*in refusing me a bed*
*for the night*
*these humble eyes would never*
*have seen this*
*memorable sight.*

*Papa paused, I waited.*
*In the comfort of our*
*hilltop home in Seattle*
*overlooking the valley,*
*I shouted*
*"That's the END?"*

—Mitsuye Yamada, *Camp Notes*

---

## Now that you've read

1. Trinh claims that both history and storytelling have become gendered in the eyes of "civilized" people. How and why does she think this happened? Do you agree with her?
2. Note that Trinh quotes a number of other woman writers. What effect does incorporating these quotations create in Trinh's own essay?

## SEQUENCE 7 ASSIGNMENTS

### Reading 1: Adrienne Rich, "Taking Women Students Seriously"

> Most young women need to have their intellectual lives, their work, legitimized against the claims of family, relationships, the old message that a woman is always available for service to others. We need to keep our standards very high, not to accept a woman's preconceived sense of her limitations; we need to be hard to please, while supportive of risk-taking, because self-respect often comes only when exacting standards have been met.

#### *Prewriting*

1. What do you take the quotation above to mean, using the context of the essay to help you explain it?
2. What does it mean to have your intellectual life legitimized?
3. After reading this essay, would you opt to change the type of school you attend (coed or same-sex) if you could? Why or why not?

#### *Writing assignment*

Writing in the 1970s, Rich expressed the concern that educators did not have the same expectations of female students as of male students. Write a brief essay in which you address that concern in the context of today's colleges and universities. How much have things changed since Rich began teaching at Douglass College in 1976? Respond specifically to one or two of her questions, using examples from your classes and students you know to back up your responses. Also respond to Rich's list of suggestions for ways in which teachers can "push" women students. Would you make the same argument for teachers to "push" male students? Why or why not?

### Reading 2: Jeffrey Berman, "Hunger Artists"

> The media only serve to perpetuate eating disorders, for television, magazines, and billboards brainwash women into believing one needs to have a beautiful face, a beautiful figure, and beautiful hair to be desirable, to be loved, to be accepted. So much emphasis is placed on appearances and thinness in our society. Women are constantly bombarded with messages that they are too fat, too ugly, too wrinkly, too flabby, too greasy: the list is infinite.

## Prewriting

1. Respond to the above quotation from Berman's book. How much do you think the media are to blame for the prevalence of eating disorders in our culture?
2. How important is weight control to you or to some of your friends? Why does is matter to you, if it does? Why does it not matter to you, if it doesn't?
3. How important are media representations of beauty to you or to your friends? Do you know anyone who strives to be "perfect"?

## Writing assignment

A few years ago, a popular magazine did a survey that included a question that asked women whether they would rather gain 50 pounds or get hit by a truck. Most respondents said they would rather get hit by a truck. What does that indicate about our culture? What did you find surprising about diary entries in this reading assignment? What didn't surprise you? Why are women more likely to have eating disorders than are men? To what extent are the media at fault? What other factors besides the media contribute to this widespread problem? What might Adrienne Rich say? Please draw from Berman's chapter in your response.

## Reading 3: Deborah Tannen, "How Male and Female Students Use Language Differently"

> Talking about ways of talking in class makes students aware that their ways of talking affect other students, that the motivations they impute to others may not truly reflect others' motives, and that the behaviors they assume to be self-evidently right are not universal norms.

## Prewriting

1. Please respond to the above quotation.
2. Are you an enthusiastic participant in classroom discussions? If so, why? If not, why not?
3. Do you notice any patterns in your classes that would support or discredit Tannen's findings?

## Writing assignment

First spend some time working through Tannen's findings and suggestions. What has she observed and how do her observations affect the way she conducts classroom discussion? What might Rich say about Tannen's observations? Next, choose one of your classes in which discussion plays a large part and analyze the participation using Tannen's terms. What patterns do you notice? Who dominates discussion? What forms does that domination take, and how does that student assert himself or herself? How do the other students respond? Now that you've read Tannen's essay, what suggestions could you make that would improve discussion?

## Reading 4: Peter Lyman, "The Fraternal Bond as a Joking Relationship"

> The sense of order within fraternal groups is based upon the belief that all members are equally dependent upon the rules, and that no *personal* dependence is created within the group. This is not true of the family or of relations with women, both of which are intimate, and, from the guys' point of view, are "out of control" because they are governed by emotional commitments.

### Prewriting

1. Respond to the above quotation from Lyman's essay. Does Lyman's claim ring true to you? Why or why not?
2. Have you ever been involved in a joke that one group thought was hilarious and the other group thought was offensive? Describe the situation and the results.
3. Judging on the basis of your own observation, are there differences between men's friendships and women's friendships?

### Writing assignment

Previous readings in this sequence show that men and women can experience communication difficulties. What are some of the differences between male and female joking rituals that Lyman describes in "The Fraternal Bond as Joking Relationship"? How does gender play a role in the problems described in the earlier reading by Tannen? What can Lyman's careful analysis of the dining room event teach us about communication? Cite an example of miscommunication that you've observed since you came to college, and offer your analysis of the difficulties that contributed to it. In what ways is this example different from your observation of classroom participation for your previous writing assignment? In what ways is it similar to that observation?

## Reading 5: Sam Keen, "The Rite of War and the Warrior Psyche"

> To understand men and the twisted relations that exist between men and women, we need to look at what happens to a man when his mind, body, and soul are socially informed by the expectation that he must be prepared to suffer, die, and kill to protect those he loves.

## Prewriting

1. What do you take the above quotation to mean?
2. Why does Keen refer to the relationships between men and women as "twisted"?
3. What are some of the characteristics of the "warrior psyche"?
4. Do you think that the warrior psyche is as ubiquitous as Keen believes it to be?
5. What sense can you make of Keen's dream near the end of his essay? How does it fit into his argument?

## Writing assignment

For the first part of your essay, take some time to work through what Keen means by the "warrior psyche"? What is his argument? How does the warrior psyche affect men's behavior and their relationships with others, according to Keen? Keen compares the "academic game" to combat; what does he mean by this? In the second part of your essay, develop your response to Keen's argument. Where do you agree and where do you disagree? Enlist Rich, Tannen, or Lyman to help you develop your position.

## Reading 6: Trinh T. Minh-ha, "Grandma's Story"

> Tell me and let me tell my hearers what I have heard from you who heard it from your mother and your grandmother, so that what is said may be guarded and unfailingly transmitted to the women of tomorrow, who will be our children and the children of our children.

## Prewriting

1. Please respond to the above quotation from Trinh's essay. What is it that will be "guarded and unfailingly transmitted"?
2. Why must what is heard from one generation to the next be "guarded"?
3. What can you observe about the cultural identity of the storytellers whom Trinh describes? How is this significant to her argument?
4. How would you describe Trinh's tone throughout her essay?
5. How would you describe the structure of her essay?

## Writing assignment

What does Trinh T. Minh-ha mean when she writes, "Truth does not make sense; it exceeds meaning and exceeds measure"? In what ways do her grandmother's stories tell the "truth"? Reflect on Trinh's suggestion that women access a kind of truth through storytelling. How do you respond to her essay and the arguments she makes?

Also consider your own approach to learning and truth. How does gender influence the way you listen to others and express yourself? Are you seeking "truth" at college? If so, where do you think it is to be found? If not, what kind of learning do you hope to do in college? Use this essay as an opportunity to engage in a conversation with Trinh and the other writers in this sequence to consider the role that gender plays in your understanding of truth, knowledge, and learning.

## Final project

Review the essays you've written for this sequence. Have the readings taught you anything new about the effect of gender on identity or about how men and women think, interact, and learn? Have they changed your mind about anything? Have they reinforced your views about anything? Mine your essays for a specific issue related to gender and education that you'd like to investigate in further detail, and formulate a concise thesis that you can use in a research paper. If you can't decide on a topic to investigate further, consider these questions:

How does life on same-sex campuses differ from life on coeducational campuses?

How does gender affect how students treat each other and are treated in the classroom?

How has life as a male (or a female) college student changed from your parents' day to now?

What do male and female students need to know about each other?

What do teachers need to know about their male and female students?

How do the lives of women who are "nontraditional" students differ from those of women who are "traditional" students?

How do the lives of men who are "nontraditional" students differ from those of men who are "traditional" students?

How does culture affect our understanding of gender?

## Library Research Ideas

Try one or more of the following library research activities, or come up with your own ideas for library research to support your thesis.

1. Investigate what has been published about gender and education in the professional education literature. Check journals such as the *Chronicle of Higher Education*, the *American Journal of Education*, the *Harvard Educational Review*, and the *Teachers College*

*Record.* Start with the *Education Index,* or search the ERIC clear-inghouse on the web at **http://ericir.syr.edu.** Much has been pub-lished on this topic; narrow your search to find data relevant to your chosen paper topic.

2. Gather statistics on men's and women's education over the past three decades (such as the number of advanced degrees granted men and the number granted women, the number of women's colleges in the United States, research dollars allocated to women's studies, average age of male and of female college stu-dents, the most common majors among men and among women, and so on) and on gender-related changes in the work force over the same period (the overall number of women and of men in the work force, changes in the numbers of women in specific profes-sions, the number of female CEOs, differences in women's and men's pay scales, and so on). Compare any trends you discover in these two areas to see what they suggest about your chosen paper topic. Look for statistics that you can use to support your thesis, and include them, perhaps in graph or table form, in your paper. If you don't know where to start looking, review Chapter 4 or ask your reference librarian for help.

3. Research cultural stereotypes of men and women. The possibili-ties are virtually limitless, so you will need to focus your search in some way. For example, you could investigate how a certain traditionally male or female icon (for example, "the soldier" for men or "the mother" for women) has been portrayed in litera-ture, films, and the popular press over the past 50 years. Have such portrayals changed recently? Check the *Reader's Guide to Periodical Literature* for articles in the popular press on changing gender roles and images.

4. Look for men's and women's groups on the Internet that might challenge some of the assumptions or points of view expressed in the readings in this sequence. For example, see the list of feminist men's groups at **http://www.feminist.com/pro.htm** and the *Atlantic Monthly* article about conservative women's groups at **http://www.theatlantic.com/trans.atl/issues/96sep/eburkett/ eburektt.htm.**

## Field Research Ideas

Try one or more of the following field research ideas, or use your own field research ideas to get data to support your thesis.

1. Compile a survey to test the widespread assumption that men tend to think alike, women tend to think alike, and men and women tend to think differently. Administer the survey to a large

group of men and women. Ask closed questions designed to elicit respondents' opinions about a wide range of issues (choose issues for which respondents could be expected to express an unambiguous opinion). You might use some of the issues discussed in this sequence. For easy comparison, compile respondents' responses in graph or table form.

2. Survey the men and women in a class or in several classes about patterns of student participation. Ask respondents whether they ever feel reluctant to speak up in class, and ask them to comment on how members of the opposite sex behave in class. Then compare the men's and women's responses.

3. Interview two female professors and two male professors about differences in how their male and female students participate in their classes, about their own teaching styles, and about their attitudes toward students of the opposite sex.

4. Observe and compare how male and female students on campus interact in various contexts (during class discussions, at parties, in lounges, and the like). Observe how male and female professors interact in various contexts, and compare this to how male and female students interact. Observe how male professors interact with female students, and vice versa. Take detailed notes, recording specific examples that you can use in your writing.

# Higher Learning, Cyber-Learning

## Getting Started

As few as ten years ago, personal computers were a luxury that only a small percentage of the population enjoyed. Today colleges like Wake Forest University (a private college) and the University of Florida (a state university) are requiring that all first-year students come to school with their own personal computers. The goal of this sequence is for you to examine critically the impact that computers have had on your education and on your life.

Sherry Turkle's "Hackers: Loving the Machine for Itself" gives us a glimpse of MIT students who develop relationships with their computers that are more satisfying than the relationships they have with most other people. "Computers Help Unite Campuses But Also Drive Some Students Apart," by Trip Gabriel, and "The Computerized Campus," by Theodore Roszak, challenge us to weigh the negatives as well as the positives in the changes computers have brought about in our classes and in our personal lives. Suneel Ratan's "A New Divide Between Haves and Have-Nots?" warns us that the disparity in access to computers and technology among economic classes will have long-term, detrimental consequences. In "Cybercheats: Term-Paper Shopping Online," John N. Hickman warns of some other ominous effects of the availability of technological resources to students. Paul Saffo, in his essay "Quality in an Age of Electronic Incunabula," argues that we are on the verge of truly profound transformations of our society via new technologies. Amy Bruckman's "Finding One's Own Space in Cyberspace" asks us to believe we can find a sense of community in cyberspace much as we do when we choose what groups to join and whom to be with face to face.

Please reflect on your attitudes about the role technology plays in your relationships with other students and teachers and in your classes, and then respond to several of the following questions. I use the Getting Started questions as a preliminary exercise on the first day my class works on a particular sequence. Your teacher may also do this, or he or she may ask that you write out your responses either in a journal or in your notebook. Your teacher may use these questions as a jumping off place for class discussion as well. No matter how you use these questions in your class, you'll still be able to draw on what you write here both in your contributions to discussion and in your responses to the assignments that follow.

1. Would you sign up for a "distance education" course if you had the chance? Under what circumstances would you prefer it?
2. Do you know anyone who "telecommutes"? What are the advantages of working in this manner? What are the disadvantages?
3. What do you like best about using a computer? What do you like least?
4. For what do you most commonly use a computer?

*Sherry Turkle*

# Hackers: Loving the Machine for Itself

Sherry Turkle's "Hackers: Loving the Machine for Itself" allows us to see something of the world of a particular subculture: computer hackers at MIT. This chapter from her book *The Second Self: Computers and the Human Spirit* also gives us a glimpse of what these students find so rewarding about their time with computers—as well as a glimpse of something more disturbing. As you read, think about what it must be like to be so totally immersed in a particular field.

### Before you read

1. What is a hacker? Is the term still widely used? Has its meaning changed since the early 1980s, when Turkle wrote her book?
2. Has the stereotypical image of the computer hacker changed in recent years, with the financial success of Bill Gates and Steve Jobs?
3. How computer-literate are you? Are you satisfied with your level of computer literacy? Why or why not?
4. What do you think about the ethics of hacking, as when hackers break into classified computer files and disrupt the activities of some businesses or universities?

---

Every spring, MIT students hold an unusual contest. It has the form of a beauty pageant, but it is a contest to choose "the Ugliest Man on Campus." For several weeks, the students who think of themselves as most ugly parade around the main corridors of the Institute, wearing placards that announce their candidacy. They flaunt their pimples, their pasty complexions, their knobby knees, their thin, undeveloped bodies. They collect funds to support their campaigns. There is a vote. The proceeds of the campaign collections go to charity.

I spoke with the ex-student, now a professor at another university, who began the contest more than twenty years ago. He is proud of his contribution to MIT culture. "Everyone knows that engineers are ugly. To be at Harvard is to be a gentleman, to be sexy, to be desired. To be at MIT is to be a tool, a nerd, a person without a body. The contest just makes irony of the obvious."

Today's MIT students echo his words. They feel comfortable with a ritual that celebrates a denial of the body, yet at the same time some are upset by the contest. "It hits too close to home. I'm not ugly enough to compete, but I'm not pretty enough to be normal, to have a girlfriend, to know what to do at a party." Some are angry about it, and angry at me for noticing it. "I hate that goddamn contest. It gives the whole place a bad name. It makes me ashamed to be around." Some deny the importance of the whole thing. Others reproach me for being just a "humanist type," oversensitive. Don't I know it's "just a joke"? They point out that good-looking people sometimes compete, "trying to look ugly for a good cause." But most feel that although the contest is a joke it nevertheless expresses a truth. Some might call it the "social construction" of the engineer. These students see it more simply: an engineer is ugly in the eyes of the world, an alien to the sensual.

## The Social Construction of the Engineer

I probably do not have to say the obvious, that many MIT men are involved with and proud of the body and its pleasures. But there is, too, a widespread presence of what has to be described as self-loathing. This is more than the symptom of an individual malady; the illness is social. Our society accepts and defensively asserts the need for a severed connection between science and sensuality, between people who are good at dealing with things and people who are good at dealing with people.

This split in our culture has many social costs, of which the first and most poignant is paid by children, particularly the suffering of many gifted adolescents. MIT students talk about growing up in "all-American" schools. For example, Ron, a junior majoring in astronomy:

> I've always thought of myself as ugly, inept. All of the boys who had friends and were popular were into sports and didn't care about school. Or if they cared about school they were sort of good more or less at everything. But there was I. All alone, fixing used ham-radio equipment. And all of the other kids I knew who were into ham-radio stuff felt just as ugly as I did. We had a club in sixth grade. And we called it "the Gross Club." I'm not kidding. So don't expect me to be surprised to come to MIT and find that all the other loners, doing their math and science and thinking of themselves as losers, make themselves an ugly-man contest.

Ron's sense of himself as ugly is not supported in any way by his physical inheritance, although it is well supported by his grooming and gait. Muscles eventually take their form from the habitual posture of the body and set of the face. Ron's muscles express ambivalence, long felt, toward his body. He sees the power of his mind as a gift that brought him mastery over technology, but for which he has had to pay with shame and misery in the world of people.

The sense of a polarization between science and sensuality is made explicit by Burt, a sophomore majoring in chemical engineering:

> I think of the world as divided between flesh things and machine things. The flesh things have feelings, need you to know how to love them, to take risks, to let yourself go. You never know what to expect of them. And all the things that I was into when I was growing up, well, they were not those kinds of things. Math, you could get it perfect. Chemistry, you could get exactly the right values when you did your experiments. No risks. I guess I like perfection. I stay away from the flesh things. I think this makes me sort of a nonperson. I often don't feel like a flesh thing myself. I hang around machines, but I hate myself a lot of the time. In a way it's like masturbating. You can always satisfy yourself to perfection. With another person, who knows what might happen? You might get rejected. You might do it wrong. Too much risk. You can see why I'm not too pleased with the way my personality turned out.

The chances are that Ron and Burt will make an adaptation. They will emerge one day with diplomas and good job offers to be used as steppingstones to well-paid careers, to a sense of belonging in a social world that contains wives and children and the fabric of a supportive culture. But the transition from pariah to social integration is not easy; getting there is a struggle. Many feel the presence of a choice that can be put off, but that is always there. You are constantly coming to the fork in the road.

One path leads to what many MIT students call the "real world." The other leads to what Ron sees as a continuation of the Gross Club—an even deeper commitment to ways of thinking and living that keep one apart from it. Those who take the second path flaunt their rejection of "normal" society by declaring, "We are the ugly men. You can keep your hypocrisy, your superficial values, your empty sense of achievement. We have something better and purer."

The struggle of the choice is described by Burt, who feels that he and his roommate are choosing opposite branches of the fork:

> For me, MIT isn't the real world. It's sort of a joke around here, to talk of the Institute and to talk of the "real world." But it's not funny. I mean I think of it as a struggle. But my roommate—for him there was no struggle. All there was for him was the ninth floor of Technology Square. I mean where they keep the computers. No struggle at all. Intellectually, I mean when I tried to feel normal about it I always came back to feeling that he had a perfect right to live in any world he wanted to, but when I would see him—and I hardly ever saw him, because he more or less lived there, all nerdy and talking about "foobar, bletch, meta-bletch"—I really hated him. I mean I pitied him. But I can get like that myself. I was like that in high school. I hated him for giving up. I

think that if you become obsessed with computers it makes it easy to give up trying to be a real person.

Burt's anger is not merely a feeling of the moment. It is persistent. He uses his roommate as a foil for his own struggle. It is a struggle to create a bridge between a world of things and a world of people. Like other students who talk about a split between their "people selves" and their "technology selves," Burt is trying to put things together. He wants to believe that intense relationships with technical things need not keep him from productive relationships with the larger culture and caring relationships with other people. In short, Burt wants to be an engineer and live in the real world.

Within every culture, even a culture that wears a collective badge of self-denigration, there is a hierarchy. At MIT, some science is uglier than other science. Some engineering is uglier than other engineering. Some kinds of self-absorption are more unsavory, perhaps even more dangerous than others. And contact with some machines is more contaminating than with others.

### The Image of the Hacker

In the MIT culture it is computer science that occupies the role of the "out group," the ostracized of the ostracized. Computer science becomes a protective screen for the insecurities and self-hate of others in the community. And many of the computer-science students accept this reflection of themselves as archetypical nerds, loners, and losers. On the MIT computer system that is considered to be the most advanced, the most state-of-the-art, the users are referred to as the "lusers." When you "log in" on the system to activate your account, you are given a "luser number" that identifies you to the computer and you are told how many other lusers are working along with you. How many other ugliest men.

Why are the computer-science students seen as the ugliest men or, when they are women, women who are somehow suspect? The self-image of engineering students is already low. Already they fear that quietly, insistently, in a way they do not understand but through paths they dimly suspect, the world of machines has cut them off from people, that they are the "kind of people" who demand perfection and are compelled by the controllable. The formal mechanical and mathematical systems they play with are the externalization of their taste. In the "computer person" they find someone who seems to have taken their taste and carried it to an extreme, someone who has taken their taste, already a source of tension, and transformed it into a perversion.

A fear about oneself is projected onto the perceived excesses of another. Such processes proceed by stereotyping, by mythologizing.

In the case of seeing computation as ugly, as perversion, it is carried by taking a special community within the computer-science world and constructing the image of the "computer person" around it. At MIT, that community is known as "computer hackers." Elsewhere they are known as "computer wizards," "computer wheels," "computer freaks," or "computer addicts." Whatever the label, they are people for whom computers have become more than a job or an object of study, they have become a way of life.

Engineers rationalize, indeed sometimes apologize for, the over-intensity of their relationships with machines by describing them as tools, even as they express their identification by describing themselves as tools as well. The image of the machine as tool is reassuring because it defines a means–ends relationship. With our tools we forge things that can be used by other people. What is different for many hackers is that the means–ends relationship is dropped. The fascination is with the machine itself. Contact with the tool is its own reward. Most hackers are young men for whom at a very early age mastery became highly charged, emotional, colored by a particular desire for perfection, and focused on triumph over things. Their pleasure is in manipulating and mastering their chosen object, in proving themselves with it. It is not hard to understand why these few who "flaunt" the pleasures of the thing-in-itself become the objects for the projection of the nervousness of the many.

We saw the engineering student living with ambivalence, with the sense of being at a fork in the road. One direction leads to engineering being integrated into the everyday flow of relationships with people; the other leads to isolation and ever deeper immersion in the world of machines. Engineering students place great value on those things—books, movies, ideas—that connect their concerns with something larger. *Star Wars* was loved for the way it offered a bridge, even if superficial, between high technology and a romantic humanism. Robert Pirsig's *Zen and the Art of Motorcycle Maintenance* and Robert Florman's *The Existential Pleasures of Engineering* are held in great regard. These works achieved cult status because they describe how intense relationships with technical objects can lead to reflections on the philosophical concerns of the larger culture. They give courage to people like Burt that it is possible to be an engineer and live in the real world as well. By contrast, the hacker crystallizes an image of getting lost in the thing-in-itself.

One of the ways groups mark and protect their boundaries is through the use of language. Engineers develop a language of their own, a jargon. It is a source of pleasure, but also of alienation from nonengineers: "I try not to use it [the jargon] in 'mixed company,' if you know what I mean," says one student. The hacker, however, is lost in the jargon of his machine and its programs. His machine is "intelligent." His machine is "psychological." It offers a language easily applied to people. He uses it in mixed company, and his refusal to talk of other things enrages his engineering colleagues who are struggling to assimilate, to find a language for moving into the real world. This rage helps to set the hacker off as so ugly that the others feel beautiful, at least for the moment, by comparison. The hacker is a threat because he comes to stand for cultural isolation in the enterprise of engineering.

### Passion in Virtuosity

With the computer young people can find channels to a certain kind of virtuosity without passing through the filter of formal education. And a large research environment can benefit from an almost unlimited quantity of this virtuosity. Over the years at MIT there developed what was perceived by both sides as a fair trade. The hackers would supply virtuosity; in return they would be left free to construct their own way of life around one of the most powerful computer systems in the world. To understand what hackers do and how they do it, let us take a case in point: how the MIT hackers built the operating system that controls the computer on which the final draft of this book was typed.

When a company buys a computer, the machine comes with a large collection of programs called the operating system. These are the tools that enable the company's programmers to write special-purpose applications programs with vastly less effort and technical knowledge than would be necessary if they had to work with a bare machine. A simple example of what an operating system does is time-sharing, which allows many users to be served by the same computer in a way that seems to them to be simultaneous. In fact the computer is giving each user a quantum of time so short that he or she does not even notice and become jealous of the attention being paid to the others. This idea is simple, but bringing it about needs so much work that the job of making a time-sharing system of the professional quality of those supplied by a major manufacturer has probably not been carried out as many as a hundred times in the history of computation. The operating system is standard, and may not be optimal from the individual purchaser's point of view, but the purchaser of a computer has little choice but to accept the operating system offered on it. This system would have been constructed by a team of dozens or even hundreds of professionals and would represent the investment of many millions of dollars. To repeat the work and construct an operating system "to one's taste" is unthinkable.

When the Artificial Intelligence Laboratory at MIT obtained its first large computer it did the unthinkable almost without thinking.

There had already grown up a community of gifted and totally dedicated young men, many of whom had dropped out of MIT academic programs in computer science in order to devote themselves more exclusively to computers. They were prepared to be on the job sixteen or eighteen hours a day, seven days a week: they lived and breathed and thought computers. More important for the story of the operating system they developed, they lived and breathed and thought the one computer that the lab had purchased. In record time they built what many considered to be the world's most advanced time-sharing operating system, and one to their taste: ITS. The letters stand for Incompatible Time Sharing, a joking reference to contrast it with the operating system that another, more professionally structured MIT laboratory had recently installed, the Compatible Time Sharing System, CTSS. CTSS was compatible with systems outside MIT to make it easier to run programs written by outsiders. CTSS was practical, but some felt that the system had achieved its practical advantage by compromising its power. ITS was written by people who loved the machine-in-itself. It sacrificed nothing.

ITS was built with little planning and certainly with no formal decisions about the "specs" of the system. It cost a fraction of what it would have cost to make such a system under "industry" conditions. Its development became a model for a mode of production different from the standard, a mode of production built on a passionate involvement with the object being produced. Loyalty was to the project, not to the management; there was no rigid hierarchy, no respect for power other than the power that someone could exert over the computer.

This hacker-style work is not confined to university settings. Industries have learned to profit from intense relationships with computers—some have become quite expert at capitalizing on in-house cultures of passionate virtuosity.

In *The Soul of a New Machine,* Tracy Kidder tells the story of how a new computer, the Eagle, was designed and built by people with uncommon devotion within the Data General Corporation. The book is written as an adventure story, indeed as a "cowboy tale" of a distinctly American variety. There are the "good guys"—the ones who are trying to build the machine. There are the "bad guys"— their rivals working on a competing machine in North Carolina. There is the struggle of the individual to "get back at" the authority of a corporation tempted to take the straight and conservative path when genius and vision offer another.

The word "Soul" in the title of the book is well chosen. It is what the group who created the machine devoted to the task. For the period of production they lived an almost monastic life. Other worldly cares and responsibilities dropped away. A religious leit-motif runs through Kidder's story of their dedicated labors where personal ego and personal reward had no place. What was important was winning. But this is a story in the real world. When the machine goes "out the door" to be marketed, the reality of that dedication is denied.

> The day after the formal announcement, Data General's famous sales force had been introduced to the computer in New York and elsewhere. At the end of the presentation for the sales personnel in New York, the regional sales manager got up and gave his troops a pep talk. "What motivates people?" he asked. He answered his own question, saying, "Ego and the money to buy the things that they and their families want." It was a different game now. Clearly, the machine no longer belonged to its makers.

The Data General hackers created a successful new machine. The MIT hackers associated with ITS also wrote other influential programs and became an integral part of the intellectual life of the MIT Artificial Intelligence Laboratory. In short, hackers play a significant though controversial role in the history of computation. What sets them apart is they work for the joy of the process, not for the product.

### The Hacker Controversies

The roommate who so angered Burt by spending all his time on the ninth floor of Technology Square is following in the footsteps of the senior hackers, most of whom have gone on to other things, some of whom are still around, all of whom are mythologized. As the earlier hackers did in their time, Burt's roommate is finding that the computer allows him rapidly to attain a level of virtuosity that will make him indispensable. And as he moves closer to the center of hacker culture he is moving farther away from academic values, from acceptance of hierarchy, from the "day life" of most of the rest of the world. It is not surprising that he upsets a lot of people.

Indeed, hackers have become objects of criticism and controversy both within and outside the computer community. Their existence challenges assumptions about human motivation ("ego and money") somehow more forcefully because they are technologists than does the existence of priests or poets. People seem ready to accept that artists play with paint or clay, brush or chisel, with a certain disinterest in the final product. However, when an engineer adopts this stance toward his tools, it evokes anxieties about intellectual masturbation. Tools are made to be used, not played with. They should belong to work life, not to intimate life. Public controversies about hackers are fueled by the fact that hackers externalize widespread fears about machines and the dangers of too intimate relationships with them.

Many people first became aware of the existence of hackers in 1976 with the publication of Joseph Weizenbaum's *Computer Power and Human Reason*. The book's description of hollow-eyed young men glued to computer terminals is reminiscent of descriptions of opium addicts and compulsive gamblers:

> Wherever computer centers have become established, that is to say, in countless places in the United States, as well as in virtually all other in- dustrial regions of the world, bright young men of disheveled appear- ance, often with sunken glowing eyes, can be seen sitting at computer consoles, their arms tensed, and waiting to fire, their fingers, already poised to strike at the buttons and keys on which their attention seems to be as riveted as a gambler's on the rolling dice. When not so trans- fixed, they often sit at tables strewn with computer printouts over which they pore like possessed students of a cabalistic text. They work until they nearly drop, twenty, thirty hours at a time. Their food, if they arrange it, is brought to them: coffee, cokes, sandwiches. If possible they sleep on cots near the computer. But only for a few hours—then back to the console or the printouts. Their rumpled clothes, their un- washed and unshaven faces, and their uncombed hair all testify that they are oblivious to their bodies and to the world in which they move. They exist, at least when so engaged, only through and for the com- puters. These are computer bums, compulsive programmers. They are an international phenomenon.

Hackers have been the centerpiece of numerous articles in the popular press expressing grave concern about the dangers of "com- puter addiction." The nature of this concern varies. There are fears that young people will fall victim to a new kind of addiction with druglike effects: withdrawal from society, narrowing of focus and life purpose, inability to function without a fix. Others fear the spread, via the computer, of characteristics of the "hacker mind." And hackers are almost universally represented as having a very undesirable frame of mind: they prefer machines to sex, they don't care about being productive.

Several years ago *Psychology Today* published an interchange called "The Hacker Papers." It was a warning on the part of some, including some hackers, that hacking was dangerous and depleting, and a defense on the part of others that hacking was a creative out- let like any other. The article prompted a flood of electronic mail debating the question. Artificial intelligence scientist Marvin Minsky presented the strongest defense of the hackers. They are no differ- ent from other people seriously devoted to their work, he said. "Like poets and artists they are devoted to developing tools and tech- niques." And as for their alleged ineptness at social relationships, Minsky said that the hackers are superior to the psychologists who trivialize human beings in their rush to stereotype and classify.

In this polemical form the debate is, to say the least, flat and oversimplified. Hackers are caught up with their computers, often to the point where other things in their lives do drop out. But the metaphor of addiction evokes an image of a deadened mind, which does no justice to the hackers' experience of their work as alive and exciting. Minsky is right that hackers are intellectually serious people. But, on the other hand, Minsky contributes to flattening the issue by refusing to allow any difference between hackers, poets, and artists. There are differences between hackers and most poets. Indeed, Minsky might well be betraying the side of himself that is closest to the hacker when he tells us that sees the essence of the work of a poet as developing tools and techniques. This might be true in some cases. But in many, perhaps most, the work of the poet includes exploring the complexities and ambiguities of areas of feeling where, we shall see, the hackers seek simplicities.

Both sides sell the hackers short by saying either that they are just like everyone else or that they are like nobody else except perhaps junkies or poets. A better understanding requires a closer look at hackers as individuals and as part of a culture that expresses and supports the psychological needs they bring to their relationships with computation.

Hackers live a paradox: this is a culture of "lusers" who see themselves as an elite. They are the holders of an esoteric knowledge, defenders of the purity of computation seen not as a means to an end but as an artist's material whose internal aesthetic must be protected. Most paradoxically, they live with a self-image as "lusers" at the same time as they define their relationship with the machine in terms of "winning." They are caught up in an intense need to master—to master perfectly—their medium. In this they are like the virtuoso pianist or the sculptor possessed by his or her materials. Hackers too are "inhabited" by their medium. They give themselves over to it and see it as the most complex, the most plastic, the most elusive and challenging of all. To win over computation is to win. Period.

### Perfect Mastery

The issue of mastery has an important role in the development of each individual. For the developing child, there is a point, usually at the start of the school years, when mastery takes on a privileged, central role. It becomes the key to autonomy, to the growth of confidence in one's ability to move beyond the world of parents to the world of peers. Later, when adolescence begins, with new sexual pressures and new social demands from peers and parents, mastery can provide respite. The safe microworlds the child master has built—the microworlds of sports, chess, cars, literature, or mathematical expertise—can become places of escape. Most children use these havens as platforms from which to test the difficult waters of adolescence. They move out at their own pace. But for some the issues that arise during adolescence are so threatening that the safe place is never abandoned. Sexuality is too threatening to be embraced. Intimacy with other people is unpredictable to the point of being intolerable. As we grow up, we forge our identities by building on the last place in psychological development where we felt safe. As a result, many people come to define themselves in terms of competence, in terms of what they can control.

Pride in one's ability to master a medium is a positive thing. But if the sense of self becomes defined in terms of those things over which one can exert perfect control, the world of safe things becomes severely limited—because those things tend to be things, not people. Mastery can cease to be a growing force in individual development and take on another face. It becomes a way of masking fears about the self and the complexities of the world beyond. People can become trapped.

The computer supports growth and personal development. It also supports entrapment. Computers are not the only thing that can serve this role; people got "stuck" long before computers ever came on the scene. But computers do have some special qualities that make them particularly liable to become traps.

The adolescents who got stuck on ham-radio or fixing cars or playing chess could only with great difficulty take these worlds with them into adult careers. There was room for just so many radio repairmen or auto mechanics or chess masters. Parents, teachers, the educational system didn't support these hobbies—there was pressure to move beyond them, to "grow up." Not so for computer worlds: the gifted high-school programmer can go on to a college major in computer science and on again to lucrative adult work. Other factors in the computer's seduction, and these are the more important ones, have to do with the specificity of the computer as a medium to support the desire, the needs and in extreme cases the obsession for "perfect mastery."

With the computer you can set your own goals. Joe is twenty-three; he dropped out of computer science at Stanford in order to devote himself more fully to computers. The course work was not challenging enough; Joe needed to set his own goals in order to be able to continually surpass them. Now he is part of the support staff for one of MIT's large computer systems. His "official" job is rather undefined. He defines it as continually improving the system by adding features to it (improvements on its editor and mail and message programs) that test the limits of his knowledge. Joe describes himself as "stuck on winning" before he met computers. As a fresh-man at Stanford, he was stuck on the violin.

> I tried to do the same thing with the violin that I am doing now with the computers. But it really couldn't be the same thing. With a musical in-strument, you are continually confronting the physical thing. The violin can only do so much, and your fingers can only do so much. You can work for years and not feel that you are making a real breakthrough. And you are constantly under the pressure of knowing your own limitations. I mean, I knew I was not great. I was obsessed—but I was not great. With programming, whatever you think of—and you are always thinking of something—it can be immediately translated into a challenge. That same night. You can set yourself up to do it in some really esoteric, un-usual way. And you can make a deal with yourself that you won't be sat-isfied, that you won't eat or go out or do anything until you get it right. And then you can just do it. It's like a fix. I couldn't get that kind of fix with the violin. I could be obsessed, but I couldn't get the high.

With the computer as your medium there is no limit to how much you can flirt with losing in your pursuit of winning. There is no limit to the violence of the test.

In *The Right Stuff* Tom Wolfe tells the story of the Air Force test pilots who were chosen to be the first generation of astronauts. As gripping as the story of Project Mercury is what the narrative reveals of the psychology of the test pilot. It is a psychology that de-mands that one constantly test the limits of the physically possible, push "the outer edge of the envelope"; flying aircraft higher than they were designed to be flown, pushing them beyond their maximum in-tended speeds, pulling out of a dive with more acceleration than they were designed to tolerate. Always pushing, playing with the limits until the system failed, the limits of the technology were reached, and only having "the right stuff" could save a man's life. This is the stuff that lets you function as a super-human when you have pushed your-self beyond the edge of the humanly and technically possible. Belief in "the right stuff" allowed a man to feel in control in situations that were set up in advance as situations where control would be lost.

The test pilots didn't put their psychologies away when they left the airfield, when they left their jobs. None of us does. Pushing the "outer edge of the envelope" was translated into rituals of "drinking and driving." They would drink until they were almost out of control and then race cars at speeds almost out of control. And when they survived, they would have further proof that they were the magical few who had the right stuff—which is what they needed to have the courage to go on.

People are not "addicted" to test piloting or race-car driving or computer programming. They are addicted to playing with the issue of control. And playing with it means constantly walking that narrow line between having it and losing it. Computer programming offers this kind of play, and it is a part of the hacker culture. MIT hackers call this "sport death"—pushing mind and body beyond their limits, punishing the body until it can barely support mind and then demanding more of the mind than you believe it could possibly deliver. Anthony, twenty years old, an MIT senior, is a computer hacker who is very aware of the pleasure and the perversion of sport death.

> Computer hacking is kind of masochistic. You see how far you can push your mind and body . . . women tend to be less self-destructive . . . hackers are somewhat self-destructive. They don't take care of their bodies and are in general flunking out. Burnout is common. Women are not so sport death; they are more balanced in their priorities. The essence of sport death is to see how far you can push things, to see how much you can get away with. I generally wait until I have to put in my maximum effort and then just totally burn out.

There are few women hackers. This is a male world. Though hackers would deny theirs is a macho culture, the preoccupation with winning and of subjecting oneself to increasingly violent tests makes their world peculiarly male in spirit, peculiarly unfriendly to women. There is, too, a flight from relationship with people to relationship with the machine—a defensive maneuver more common to men than to women. The computer that is the partner in this relationship offers a particularly seductive refuge to someone who is having trouble dealing with people. It is active, reactive, it talks back. Many hackers first sought out such a refuge during early adolescence, when other people, their feelings, their demands, seemed particularly frightening. They found a refuge in the computer and never moved beyond. Alex is one of these.

Alex spends fifteen hours a day on the computer. "At least fifteen, maybe three for eating, usually a big pancake breakfast with the other guys after a night of hacking. Or sometimes we'll do a dinner in Chinatown at about one in the morning. Six for sleeping. I sleep from about nine in the morning to three, when I go over to the computer center."

> If you look at it from the outside, it looks like I spend most of my time alone. But that is not really true. First of all, there are the other hackers. We eat together a lot, we talk about the system. And then I spend a lot of time, I mean *a lot of time*, on electronic mail. Sometimes I think that electronic mail is more of an addiction for me than the computer is. I talk to people all over the country. When you type mail into the computer you feel you can say anything. A lot of it is just about the system, but sometimes it gets pretty personal. When you type into the machine you can go really fast. The touch is very sensitive. I don't even feel that I am typing. It feels much more like one of those Vulcan mind melds, you know, that Mr. Spock does on *Star Trek*. I am thinking it, and then there it is on the screen. I would say that I have a perfect interface with

592 ■ Sequence 8 Higher Learning, Cyber-Learning

the machine . . . perfect for me. I feel totally telepathic with the computer. And it sort of generalizes so that I feel telepathic with the people I am sending mail to. I am glad I don't have to see them face to face. I wouldn't be as personal about myself. And the telepathy with the computer—well, I certainly don't think of it as a person there, but that doesn't mean that I don't *feel* it as a person there. Particularly since I have personalized my interface with the system to suit myself. So it's like being with another person, but not a strange person. Someone who knows just how I like things done.

The image of computer telepathy comes up often and not just among hackers. It is an important aspect of the holding power of the machine. And it is another reason why people who know computers come to fear them, why, as one architecture student put it, "I swore to myself that this semester I wouldn't touch the machine. It's like making a novena. Promising to give up something for God. But in this case I have promised myself to give it up for myself." He describes himself as "very involved with my work," but "I like to think of my work as 'out there.' And I am 'in here.' The thing with the computer is that you start to lose track of the ins and the outs."

The experience of losing track is captured by Alex's description of the computer as transparent to his thoughts. So much so that he is aware only of a flow of ideas from him to the machine. Programming can be a Zen-like experience. We have seen this quality as the power of the transitional object—the object that is felt as belonging simultaneously to the self and to the outside world. Such objects can evoke an "oceanic feeling" of fusion and oneness. And for Alex, the computer is this kind of object.

Some people don't program straight from their mind. They still have to consciously think about all the intermediate steps between a thought and its expression on a computer in a computer language. I have basically assimilated the process to the point that the computer is like an extension of my mind. Maybe of my body. I see it but I don't consciously think about using it. I think about the design, not implementation. Once I know in my mind exactly what I want to do, I can express it on a computer without much further conscious effort.

I usually don't even hear in my mind the words that I am typing. I think and type ideas expressed in LISP. My hands know which way to go. I think of an idea that I want to express and then I listen to how my hands are saying it. My hands are a really important source of feedback.

Alex's comments evoke the power of the transitional object. His remarks about when he eats and sleeps, about electronic mail, pancakes, and Chinese food touch on something else that makes getting stuck on computers much easier than getting stuck on mathematics or physics, the two things that hackers are most likely to suggest they would have done if they hadn't met the computer. This is the power of belonging to a group, in this case a cohesive and self-protecting computer culture. Most of these young men grew up as loners. Many of them describe a sense, as long as they can remember, of a difference between themselves and other people. Finally, they feel that they belong. Alex is very clear about this: "I always knew I was weird. I mean I didn't know why I was weird, but you could see from how other kids treated me that I must have had a big sign on me saying: 'Weird One—Fold, Bend, Spindle, and Mutilate This One.'"

### Loneliness and Safety

Hackers don't live only with computers; they live in a culture that grows up around computers. The mathematics world that hackers might have joined would have left them alone much of the time. Of course, mathematicians get together, talk about their work, hold departmental colloquia and professional meetings, but the culture of mathematics is a culture of relative isolation. The hacker culture is a culture of loners who are never alone.

It is a culture of people who leave each other a great deal of psychological space. It is a culture of people who have grown up thinking of themselves as different, apart, and who have a commitment to what one hacker described as "an ethic of total toleration for anything that in the real world would be considered strange." Dress, personal appearance, personal hygiene, when you sleep and when you wake, what you eat, where you live, whom you frequent—there are no rules. But there is company.

The people who want to impose rules, the inhabitants of the "real world," are devalued, as is the "straight" computer-science community. They are in a means–end relationship with the computer. They want it to "run" their data, facilitate their experiments. The "straights" control the resources and pay the salaries, but they do not share a true allegiance to the machine. In academic departments, research laboratories, and industries where communities of scientists, engineers, and policy analysts become dependent on complex computer systems and thus on the hackers who maintain them, there is skirmish after skirmish. The hackers are always trying to "improve" the system. This can make the system less reliable as a tool for getting things done, because it is always changing. The hackers also make the system more complex, more "elegant" according to their aesthetic, which often makes it more difficult for other people to use. But the hackers have to keep changing and improving the system. They have built a cult of prowess that defines itself in terms of winning over ever more complex systems.

In most of these settings there is a standoff based on mutual dependency and a measure of mutual distrust. The researchers and administrators can push things only so far, because if the hackers don't get what they want, they will leave. The hacker wants to work on the best systems, but even if he has access to the most state-of-the-art computer he will remain in a work environment only if he feels it is a safe place, that is, an environment where he can work with relative autonomy.

David is a hacker at Stanford. He has moved around a lot looking for safety.

> I only really feel good around the computers at night. It used to be that the night culture got going because that was the time when the turn-around time on the system was the fastest. Now the systems are so powerful that you hardly ever get that feeling of slowdown. If anything, you sometimes get it at night when all the hackers are on. But the night culture remains. Because that is when you are on the machine with your friends, with other people like you. Then it is a secure place where nobody can tell you what to do. And if somebody tries to, you can out-hack them—screw up their programs so that they are kept real busy trying to sort out what hit them. Then they come running to you asking for help and are not exactly in a position to boss you around.
>
> At night there is security. I feel safe from people who think they are smarter than me and from those who want to tell me what to do.

By the standards of the outside world, the hacker culture is tolerant. But it has its own codes and rituals; it provides a framework for living. For Nick, an MIT senior, it is home.

> Hacking is a safe lifestyle, but it's a lifestyle that once you're in it it's hard to get out of it again. Your whole life is amazingly clear. You hack, you talk to other people who hack, etc. There's a society associated with it, there's a culture associated with it, and there's a lifestyle associated with it. It's a whole world. It's always a retreat. There's always things to do, you're never alone.
>
> Deli-Haus, IHOP [a twenty-four-hour-service International House of Pancakes], eating Chinese food at one of the "officially certified" Chinese restaurants—all of these are good, all-American things to do if you're a computer person. The lifestyle grew up from the things hackers did. They stayed up all night, so they always seemed to see the same people, ate at the same open-all-night-type places, they engaged in the same leisure activities, and they grew together, since they always lived together. Newcomers fall into it as if it were natural.

## Being Special

Hackers do fall into the life as though it were natural. Its routines reassure. But it is set up to leave maximum room for people who have defined themselves for a long time, for as long as most of them can remember, as different. Alex makes this point very clear. "Since I was different, different enough so that I wasn't exactly going to fit in with 'the guys,' I guess I decided that I was really going to be different. Really different. I have always wanted to be very special. And when I hack, it is very important to me to have my own territory. I think true hackers all feel this way."

A large computer system is a complicated thing. It leaves plenty of room for territoriality, plenty of room for people who feel that carving out their own terrain and winning at what they are good at might be their only chance of being loved ("I certainly am not going to be loved for being the same as everybody else," Richard says as he points to his hair, a wild Afro that reaches down past his shoulders). And so the hacker culture is held together by mutual tolerance and respect for radical individualism. You can't be a real winner if you are the same as everybody else. Even on the computer system, only difference will make you indispensable. Indispensable means that "they" cannot get rid of you. And indispensable is at least a stand-in for love, as Nick explained:

> I feel a very strong need to be different. I have spent all my life set apart and have been taught that this is the right way to live. My dream, what I want to do, is to be a person that does something, discovers something, creates something, so that people will look at me and say, "Wow, this guy is really something special, let's love this guy." That is all I ever wanted. To be loved by everybody in the whole world.
>
> Hacking . . . it's another world. It was a place where I could make a name for myself because it was stuff I was good at, something I could do, something that makes me different—sets me apart. There are programs on the system right now that can't be fixed without my help, and that makes me happy. I don't know why I need this so bad.

His friend Anthony hacks on the same system, and shares his values. Nick talks about being unique in terms of being loved. For Anthony, being unique is the only way to give life meaning and purpose.

> One thing that bugs me the most whenever I fly home: I look down and see all those houses and all those people who have never done anything that could not have been done by anyone else. That's a terrible thing. I would never want to be like that. It is important not to be common, because if you are your existence is meaningless because it makes no difference if you exist or not. So you must do something out of the ordinary like computer hacking to leave something behind you maybe even more than having kids will.
>
> Computer hackers try to distinguish themselves both from the rest of the world and among themselves. A hacker comes in and he makes sure his personality is different from every other hacker's personality as much as possible even if it means becoming something he's not. Computer hackers have a great fear of drowning in the sea of humanity—all those blank faces. So they set themselves apart.

### *Now that you've read*

1. What is your reaction to the lives these hackers live? Why?
2. How much time do you spend studying in your major field of study? How do you feel about your major?
3. If you could find a field that engaged you this thoroughly, would you consider it good, bad, or a mixture of both? Explain your answer.
4. How do you make sense of the Ugly Man contest? In what ways is it a positive activity? In what ways is it not? How is it related to the rest of the reading?

## READING 2

*Trip Gabriel*

# Computers Help Unite Campuses But Also Drive Some Students Apart

A journalist, Trip Gabriel is himself a frequent user of the Internet and other conveniences that computers make possible. Here he's reporting about the impact computers have had on the campus of Dartmouth College. As you read, consider how similar to or different from Dartmouth your own college campus is, and consider what the significance of those similarities and differences might be.

### Before you read

1. What can you tell about the essay from reading the title? In what ways might computers "help unite campuses"? In what ways might computers "drive some students apart"?
2. How much time do you spend communicating to others via computer? How much time do you spend in face-to-face conversation with others?
3. How common is computer communication on your campus?

---

Hanover, N.H.—Through a plug in his dorm room, Arthur Desrosiers, a Dartmouth College sophomore, pursues all the preoccupations of undergraduate life without leaving his chair: he questions professors, fishes for dates, browses the library catalogue, orders in pizza and engages in 2 A.M. bull sessions on the meaning of it all.

Using the campus E-mail system, known as Blitzmail, he sometimes trades a series of back-and-forth messages with his two roommates—even though they are sitting just a few feet away.

"I guess you could say you're pretty addicted if you're having a long Blitzmail conversation with your roommate, and you happen to be sitting right there in the same room," Mr. Desrosiers said.

Anyone who has not visited a college campus lately might be in for a jolt. Across the country, computer networks are cinching even tighter the already inward-looking communities typical of campuses, transforming the social and academic life of today's students.

Dormitory lounges are being carved up for clusters of computers, student unions are declining as gathering places, and computer-wired dorm rooms are becoming, in some cases, high-tech caves. Some scholars say "plug per pillow" campuses are undermining the ideal of a residential college as a melting pot where people from different social and regional backgrounds meet.

Prof. James Banning, an environmental psychologist at Colorado State University who surveyed some 100 university housing officers last year, remarked: "Universities are saying, 'Oh, my God, they're in their rooms. How can we ever build a sense of community in this building if they don't come out?'"

Dartmouth, one of the most academically competitive colleges in the country, has long had a reputation for encouraging computer use by students. It now has the new distinction of being one of the most E-mail-intensive, delivering about 250,000 electronic messages a day to 5,000 students and 3,000 faculty and staff members, or more than 30 messages apiece.

At public terminals all over the campus (to keep students from having to return to their rooms), 5 to 10 students line up as if at a cash machine, observing rules of Blitzmail etiquette like not reading over the shoulder of the person at the screen. In the Thayer dining hall recently, Stephanie Waddell, a senior studio art major, read a Blitz request from a male friend that began, "Need a date."

James Hunnicutt, a junior English major who was next in line, received five messages from his mother in Charlotte, N.C., asking about his law school plans, a note from a high school girlfriend at a college in Oregon and a message from his roommate vetoing the idea of a party in their room.

Most students say Blitzmail is convenient and indispensable on campuses and gives them an easy way to stay in touch with family and high school friends. But Mark Shahinian, a junior history major, complained that it encouraged one-line electronic bantering while inhibiting meaningful communication.

He compared Blitzmail relationships to the brief encounters typical of those at fraternity parties, which play a big role on the isolated New Hampshire campus. "Blitzmail has a bit of that casualness— knowing a lot of people but not all that well," he said.

Computer technology has come to higher education in many forms, including World Wide Web sites where art professors create digitized galleries, custom software for teaching human anatomy, and "smart" classrooms with a computer for each student to teach engineering or writing. Many college guides now give campuses a "wired rating."

After building momentum for a decade, the wired campus has reached critical mass and will soon be unavoidable, said Kenneth C. Green, the director of the Campus Computing Survey, which collects data annually from 650 colleges and universities.

More than half of all residential campuses in the United States have network connections in dormitory rooms, according to the latest survey, released this year. The number of classes using E-mail to supplement academic discussions and professors' office hours grew to 20 percent in 1995 from 8 percent in 1994. The number that use specialized educational software rose to 18 percent from 12 percent.

Mr. Green, a visiting scholar at the Claremont Graduate School, said that even though there were "a lot of questions about the pedagogical value" of computer technology, academia had largely accepted it, and that there were apparently no efforts to counter any antisocial side effects of systems like Blitzmail.

Paradoxically, it is electronic mail, one of the most mundane and least-examined of computer applications, that is probably having the most profound effect on campuses.

"E-mail is like the god of every college student," said Abigail Butler, who graduated from Vassar College this year with a major in French and political science. "People probably spend easily three hours a day sending and receiving messages. It's the No. 1 way that romances go on at colleges. It's like the dating game on line."

Jeremy Edberg, an undergraduate at the University of California at Berkeley who said he spent 10 hours a day on line, said that almost all his conversations with professors were now by E-mail. Just about the only time he visits them in person, he said, is to try to persuade them to change a grade.

"Students don't meet at rathskellers and hamburger joints and in dorm rooms anymore," said Clifford Stoll, a former researcher at Harvard University and the author of *Silicon Snake Oil: Second Thoughts on the Information Highway* (Doubleday, 1995). "Instead, they poke their heads into computers for hours on end.

"We're turning colleges into a cubicle-directed electronic experience and denying the importance of learning to work closely with other students and professors, and developing social adeptness," Mr. Stoll said.

Professor Banning, the scholar studying dorm life, said that since going to Colorado State in 1978, he had noticed that students were spending more time in their rooms. A once-crowded restaurant across from the residence halls closed three years ago and has not reopened.

"It's kind of odd to think of a restaurant space that's been vacant for three years across from where about 3,000 students live," he said.

But the image of students sitting trancelike in front of computers, cut off from the grit of life, is exaggerated, other experts say. "A certain sector of undergraduates, especially adolescent males," has always focused obsessively on narrow interests, said Steven W. Gilbert, the director of technology projects for the American Association for

Higher Education. "Sometimes it's fixing hot rods. Sometimes it's the Internet. I would bet you wouldn't find any more doing it now than 20 years ago."

To judge by a recent Friday night at Dartmouth, Blitzmail has hardly killed off rathskellers and other gathering places. There were good crowds at Queer Club, a dance presented by the campus gay and lesbian alliance, and off campus at the Dirt Cowboy Cafe, where students sipped carrot juice and cappuccinos.

At the same time, many dorm room windows emitted a bluish glow, the light of a computer screen with a student's head buried in it. A few students said Blitzmail contributed to a feeling of alienation.

Enthusiasts of E-mail praise it as a virtual office system in which students can question professors about courses at any time, and shy students and those for whom English is a second language have a better chance to be heard.

David G. Brown, the provost of Wake Forest University and a professor of economics, said that E-mail had not isolated him from students.

"It's increased the face-to-face communication I've had with my students at least fivefold," he said. "Because we're in communication every day, we feel that we're a group ready to help one another, not only over the network but in person."

This fall, Wake Forest, a private university with 3,700 under-graduates in Winston-Salem, N.C., distributed I.B.M lap-top computers to all its approximately 940 freshmen, paid for with part of a $3,000 tuition increase. It is part of a sweeping Wake Forest plan to use network technology to change the ways students work and communicate.

Professor Brown's freshman economics seminar is already a paperless course that students attend with their lap-top computers, which are all linked together. The professor might ask them to write a one-sentence summary of an economic topic like opportunity cost, what is given up when a choice is made, then electronically forward it to the others.

For homework, he might have students search the Internet for a news article demonstrating opportunity cost, write a short essay about it and then send it to him by E-mail with a picture obtained from the Louvre museum Web site demonstrating opportunity cost. Back in class, essays and pictures spark discussion.

Professor Brown and others who are enthusiastic about wired campuses insist that the cart of technology is being pulled by the horse of learning, rather than the reverse.

But there is concern that the unequal distribution of technology between rich and poor campuses will create a system computer haves and have-nots. Public universities and two-year community colleges are typically less wired because of the high costs. Bringing fiber-optic cable into dormitories and faculty offices for a network can cost millions of dollars. Fitting a classroom with 20 computers and a projection system costs as much as $100,000.

Paradoxically, the highest-tech learning of all—the delivery of lectures over computer screens or cable television, called distance learning—is the subject of the most serious experimentation at cash-strapped public universities. The American Federation of Teachers, in a report this year critical of the sterility of distance learning, noted, "All our experience as educators tells us that teaching and learning in the shared human spaces of a campus are essential to the under-graduate experience."

But the nature of those shared spaces seems to be changing.

At Vassar, students chat electronically between dorm rooms using screen names.

"One woman, an English major, met a physics major who quoted Shakespeare to her, and it was love at first Broadcast," said Ms. Butler, the recent Vassar graduate, who was known on the network as Snow White. "I've also known people who sat at home Friday and Saturday nights, Broadcasting back and forth to people they know only by nicknames, while the rest of the world was going by.

"After a while, it starts to be really unfulfilling," she said. "Every Broadcast conversation with someone new is the same for the first 20 messages, finding out who they are. It's easier to just meet some-one. You learn how much of a difference it makes to see someone in person and actually talk to them."

---

### Now that you've read

1. What are Gabriel's main points?
2. Does it strike you as odd that people living in the same building would communicate with each other on a chatline or via e-mail rather than talking face to face? Explain your answer.
3. If computers both "unite campuses" and "drive students apart," which outweighs the other? Are the benefits worth the draw-backs? Explain your answer.

## READING 3

*Theodore Roszak*

# The Computerized Campus

Theodore Roszak has been an astute observer of American culture since the 1960s. He remains suspicious of the widespread enthusiasm with which computers have been embraced on every campus across the country. His suspicion derives largely from the huge profits that a few giant companies have reaped from this enthusiasm. Read and see if you think he has a point or if he's simply resisting the inevitable.

### Before you read

1. Do you already consider your campus "computerized"? In what ways?
2. Did you grow up with a computer in your household?
3. Do you use a computer regularly for your classes?

---

The computer has entered the world of higher education a great deal more smoothly and decisively than it has made its way into the elementary and secondary schools. Universities, after all, have more internal control over their choices than do bureaucratically congested school systems. This is also the province of learned men and women, scholars and experts who are supposedly prepared to make discriminating judgments that rise above the whims of the marketplace. Yet the campuses have also been targeted for a massive merchandising campaign by the computer makers, and the effort seems to be sweeping all before it.

Many leading universities purchased their first computer in the mid- to late 1960s, one of the IBM hulking giants. It became *the* campus computer, a proud and expensive possession that was frequently displayed as a sign of status. It was usually parked in an air-conditioned computer center and used mainly for administrative data processing. In short order, school records became computer printouts; grades and scheduling were done with punchcards. The better endowed schools, especially those with strong science departments, quickly moved to acquire a few more of these big mainframes for their technicians; these were used as widely as possible on time-sharing arrangements that were often the arena of intense competition and bickering on the part of the faculty.

By the early 1970s, the universities began to set up multiterminal computer labs, where students as well as faculty might be permitted to lay their hands on the technology. Once again, prestigious departments would push to have their own, autonomous labs for their majors as a sign of status. About this time, optional courses in computer programming began to appear, mainly for students in the sciences, engineering, and business. The society was by then becoming highly computerized in all its major sectors; but there were few educators who thought computer literacy, in any interpretation of the term, had an urgent place in higher education. Significantly, things changed in the universities when the market changed. In the 1980s, with the advent of the microcomputer, a readily salable item, the computer industry went after academia with one of the most intense mass marketing efforts in business history. The goal has been nothing less than to place computers in the hands of every teacher and student. With the help of grants, donations, and stupendous discounts ranging up to 80 percent, the companies have succeeded in striking a number of what they hope will be bellwether deals with schools large and small. The campuses have not displayed much sales resistance to these blandishments.

Though there are 3,400 degree-granting institutions in the United States, higher education is one of the richest markets in the information economy. It includes schools like the University of Texas, which owns more computers (18,500 Apple Macintoshes) than any other non-government operation in the world. Through the decade of the 1980s American universities are estimated to have spent some $8 billion dollars on computers. A big school like the three-campus University of Michigan (45,000 students) can budget as much as $50 million a year; but even a small school that sets out to achieve that goal of being fully wired can be a prodigious consumer of computer technology. For example, Carnegie-Mellon University with only 5,500 students has spent as much as $15 million in a single year on the new technology.

Nor is it only the immediate demand they generate that makes the universities so attractive to the data merchants. The schools are the gateway to a student market populated by prospectively high-earning professionals and white collar workers, the ideal computer buyers of the future. When it comes to campaigning for computer literacy, the universities are a far richer prize than the high schools. Even schools as influential as Harvard, Yale, and the University of California at Berkeley have seriously considered imposing such a requirement. Still more welcome than a literacy requirement would be a *property* requirement: namely, that owning a computer should be a condition of admission. This is happening, mainly at engineering schools but also at the three United States service academies. Though the machines may be well-discounted, this is surely a remarkable innovation. Has there ever been another instance of the universities making ownership of a piece of equipment mandatory for the pursuit of learning? One school, Dallas Baptist, which is among those that require every entering student to buy a computer, has gone so far as to reshape its curriculum to emphasize the computer; it insists that at least three assignments per term in each freshman course should require the use of a computer.

The prospect of the fully networked university has made computer makers eager to strike even more advantageous deals with the schools. Companies have resorted to all sorts of inducements, including generous giveaway programs. IBM has been part of $50–$70 million programs at both MIT and Brown. Since the mid-1980s, AT&T, the largest donor, has donated over $285 million in computer labs and equipment to some 60 universities. In addition to offering faculty members discounted or even free computers, some companies have negotiated joint research and development projects that purchase and merchandise courseware developed by professors. The universities are a rich source for instructional innovation and the rewards can be handsome; the most widely marketed educational program, now used in hundreds of schools, is a chemistry course developed at the University of Illinois.

There is no question but that information technology will expand steadily at the universities, most obviously in technical and scientific fields. If only as word processors (the use that predominates among students) the computer has staked out a permanent place in every university department. But even the arts and humanities have a greater stake in the computer. Some of the most ambitious projects for full-text computer access, like the Center for Electronic Texts in the Humanities at Princeton and Rutgers, the E-Text Center at the University of Virginia, or the Center for Scholarly Technology at the University of Southern California, are campus-based. Since the initial euphoria that greeted the computer on campus in the early 1980s, however, some educators have grown cautious about the more extravagant pedagogical claims made for the new technology. In a major national forum in 1989, many teachers cited the troubling issues that arise from unlimited, often unmanageable information access; teaching in a "blizzard of information" raises as many problems as it solves. Some urgently called for a greater emphasis upon the distinction between raw data and knowledge, judgment, and intellectual integration.

Despite these reservations, EDUCOM, the consortium of some 600 universities and 110 corporations that has become the principal lobbying agent on the campuses for new technology, continues to make ambitious predictions about the electronic campus of tomorrow. With each new computer development, EDUCOM spells out a scenario of dazzling possibilities. For example, EDUCOM tells us that when interactive multimedia finally reach the campus in full force, students will be able to find everything they need for a customized, self-paced education in one neat software package. Lecture courses will vanish; modem-to-modem tutorials with the instructor will take the place of class attendance. Instead of being "the sage on the stage," professors will become "the guide at the side" of the magic box.

As if these predictions were not attractive enough, EUIT, EDUCOM's Educational Uses of Information Technology unit, has found a new enticement: cost cutting. Techniques like distance video instruction and interactive programs promise to reach more students with fewer teachers. Computerized instruction may become for the campus what automation has become for the assembly line: the royal road to down-sizing. This is a strong card to play in an era of budgetary restraint; it may even overcome the reservations some might have about the initial cost of the more expensive technology now on the market. The hardware necessary to run "Columbus," IBM's multimedia extravaganza on the life of the great explorer, is priced at $10,000 per system. Costly, but not if one considers how many teaching assistants and lecturers it will cut from the payroll.

Cost cutting is the preferred managerial style of the 1990s. In that respect EDUCOM is in brisk step with the times. But as sophisticated as methods of down-sizing may be, the overall process is a bleak symptom of the nation's economic decline. And quite as much so on the campuses as in manufacturing and the white collar workplace. What EDUCOM's bright prospectus leaves out of account are the ambitions that bring many students to school in the first place. If the computer is used to slash salaries and eliminate teaching positions, what is a college degree going to be worth to those whose goal it is to become educators? There comes a point in the computer enthusiast's image of our cultural destiny that leaves creativity and imagination only one outlet: programming software, designing hardware. The fact that lecturing is an intellectual talent with its own distinct virtues, that the classroom encounter between teacher and student can be a rewarding experience in its own right, even the possibility that there are indispensably valuable things that can be done with the blackboard and the pencil elude the technician's worldview. A great deal that programmers see fit to eliminate in favor of their own narrow skills may be precisely that "human use of human beings" that was supposedly the greatest promise the computer had to offer.

If all works out as the computer makers would have it, there may one day be fully networked campuses where all the students and all the teachers do indeed have micros, and then perhaps they will rarely have to meet at all. They will simply exchange assignments and grades electronically. Networks may even outgrow the campuses that created them—as at the University of Houston, where teachers and students can link up from their own homes. Then, professors can not only grade their students electronically, but network with them at all hours of the day and night, and perhaps watch on line while assignments are processed across the video screen, making helpful suggestions along the way. (Of course, this sort of round-the-clock, unpredictably intrusive fraternization would be possible now by way of telephone. Which is why, in my experience, professors go to great lengths to keep their phone numbers private. I am not certain why the computer terminal, always on and demanding attention, is supposed to make unrestricted teacher-student interaction more enticing.) The ultimate goal of networking on the grandest scale is to become a "wired city" that expands into the surrounding community. Together with Bell Telephone and Warner Communications, which holds the local cable television franchise, Carnegie-Mellon University is planning to do just that in the Pittsburgh area.

One would be hard-pressed to find another time when a single industry was able to intrude its interests so aggressively upon the schools of the nation—and to find such enthusiastic receptivity (or timid surrender) on the part of educators. This is all the more remarkable when one considers that probably no two teachers or computer scientists could come up with the same definition of "computer literacy"—the goal that launched the campaign. As for the general intellectual benefits of that skill, of these there is no evidence to be found beyond the claims of the computer industry's self-promotional literature, filled with vague futuristic allusions to life in the Information Age. Yet if the computer makers succeed in their hard sell, we may soon be graduating students who believe (with their teachers' encouragement) that thinking is indeed a matter of information processing, and therefore without a computer no thinking can be done at all.

"The great university of the future will be that with a great computer system," Richard Cyert, president of Carnegie-Mellon, has announced. A dramatic statement of conviction. Doubtless many educators wish their schools had the resources his university has been able to muster in laying claim to such greatness, even though it remains obscure how quantities of computational power translate into quality of learning. There is no question but that computers have a valuable role to play as computing devices in the technical fields, as electronic record keeping systems, or as word processors. Taken together, this is a sizable contribution for any single invention to make in the daily lives of students and teachers.

But the computer enthusiasts have promised that the new technology will do more than merely replace the slide rule, the typewriter, and the filing cabinet. Its benefits supposedly reach to intellectual values at the highest level, nothing less than the radical transformation of educational methods and goals. The computer, after all, is the bountiful bringer of information, which is widely understood by educators themselves to be the substance of thought. Even Dr. Ernest Boyer, president of the Carnegie Foundation for the Advancement of Teaching, who has raised many keen criticisms on the waste and misuse of computers in the schools, agrees that "in the long run, electronic teachers may provide exchanges of information, ideas, and experiences more effectively (certainly differently) than the traditional classroom or the teacher. The promise of the new technology is to enrich the study of literature, science, mathematics, and the arts through words, pictures, and auditory messages."

How disappointing it is, then, to see so much of this glowing promise come down to mere promotional gimmickry. There is, for example, the image of the fully networked campus which currently stands as the ultimate goal of computerization in the universities. Without leaving their dorms, students will be able to access the library card catalog; they will be able to log on to a student bulletin board to exchange advice, gossip, make dates, find a ride, buy used books. They will be able to submit assignments electronically to their instructors.

Yes, these things and a dozen more *can* be computerized. But why *should* they be? They all get done now by the most obvious and economical means: students walk to the library, the student union, the bookstore, to a nearby coffeehouse or cafe, where they meet other human beings. They talk, they listen, they make arrangements. Outside of disabled students (for whom computers can be a boon), who ever found these ordinary perambulatory activities so burdensome as to be worth the cost of an expensive technology to eliminate them? Indeed, it has always been my thought that an intellectually vital campus is one designed in its architecture, grounds, and general spirit to make such daily human intercourse graceful and attractively frequent—rather than one that spends millions to spare its students the exercise of leaving their dorms.

When enthusiasts come up with artificial uses like these for the computer, they are really doing nothing more than teaching another lesson in technological dependence, a vice already ingrained in our culture. For obvious commercial reasons, they are intruding a machine into places where it was never needed. Similarly, the prospect of having students submit assignments by some form of electronic mail is simply endorsing the sort of pseudo problem (like "static cling" or "wax buildup") that exists only because the hucksters invented it in the first place to sell a product. I have come across computer advertising that seems determined to make me forget that the red pencil—underscoring, circling, working along the margins and between the lines of the page (things no computer can do)—is one of the most practical teaching tools ever invented. Every experienced teacher knows this; but the ads are out to embarrass me into agreeing that, as a full-fledged member of the Information Age, I should be dealing exclusively with floppy disks, light pens, and video screens.

I will admit that, to a degree, one's criteria of educational greatness may invoke matters of personal taste. Some people relish the image of schools where ranks of solitary students in private cubicles sit in motionless attendance upon computer terminals, their repertory of activities scaled down to a fixed stare and the repetitive stroking of a keyboard. I find this picture barely acceptable even where it may be justified episodically for a computer-specific exercise: some drill, computation, or graphics work. The image becomes no more appealing when I am told that working with computers is a marvelous occasion for socializing: the students cluster around the machines, taking their cues from its directives, debating the fine points of this or that response to its queries. As an educational ethos, both these situations strike me as simply another form of technological desiccation in our lives, appearing in the one place we might most want to save from its blight.

My own taste runs to another image: that of teachers and students in one another's face-to-face company, perhaps pondering a book, a work of art, even a crude scrawl on the blackboard. At the very least, that image reminds us of how marvelously simple, even primitive, education is. It is the unmediated encounter of two minds, one needing to learn, the other wanting to teach. The biological spontaneity of that encounter is a given fact of life; ideally, it should be kept close to the flesh and blood, as uncluttered and supple as possible. Too much apparatus, like too much bureaucracy, only inhibits the natural flow. Free human dialogue, wandering wherever the agility of the mind allows, lies at the heart of education. If teachers do not have the time, the incentive, or the wit to provide that, if students are too demoralized, bored, or distracted to muster the attention their teachers need of them, then *that* is the educational problem which has to be solved—and solved from inside the experience of the teachers and the students. Defaulting to the computer is not a solution; it is surrender.

But there are other issues that transcend taste, questions of educational theory, social policy, and professional ethics. It is simply wrong for any priorities about our schools to be set by those with commercial interests at stake. That vice has plagued public schools in the past; it may be more advanced now than ever, as the schools invest in glamorous machines without any clear idea of their use. They are doing so because they have absorbed mindless clich s about "information," its intellectual value and vocational urgency, that are little better than advertising copy. This has led them to overlook the degree to which educational problems are political and philosophical issues that will not yield to a technological fix.

To mention only the most obvious of the issues on which the ethics of the teaching profession require candor:

- Disruptive or alienated students in the schools may reflect an anxiety, even a desperation that stems from their disadvantaged social condition or from the compulsory nature of the school system itself; no matter how equitably the computers are spread through the classrooms, these students are not apt to find the will to learn.

- Students who are being sold on computer literacy as an easy response to their job hunger are simply being deceived; what they are learning in a few computer lab experiences will not make them one iota more employable.

- Teachers who are falling back on flashy software as a convenient classroom entertainment are wasting their students' time and demeaning their own profession.

One senses how distorted the discussion of education has become in the Information Age when educators begin to draw not only upon the products but upon the language and imagery of the industrial marketplace. "Productivity" is the word Dr. Arthur S. Melmed of the Department of Education uses to define "the central problem of education. The key to productivity improvement in every other economic sector has been through technological innovation. Applications of modern information and communications technologies that are properly developed and appropriately used may soon offer education policy makers . . . a unique opportunity for productivity management."

Along the same lines, Richard Cyert of Carnegie-Mellon predicts that his school's computer network "will have the same role in student learning that the development of the assembly line in the 1920s had for the production of automobiles. The assembly line enabled large-scale manufacturing to develop. Likewise, the network personal computer system will enable students to increase significantly the amount of learning they do in the university."

Computers, as the experts continually remind us, are nothing more than their programs make them. But as the sentiments above should make clear, the programs may have a program hidden within them, an agenda of values that counts for more than all the interactive virtues and graphic tricks of the technology. The essence of the machine is its software, but the essence of the software is its philosophy.

## Power and Dependency

Anyone who has watched children almost hypnotically absorbed by the dazzling display of a video game cannot help but recognize the computer's peculiar power to spellbind its users. Fortunately, the most excessive form of this electronic enchantment seems to have lost its hold on the adolescent imagination; the video arcades are fast declining in popularity. But what we have seen there at its extreme is a capacity to fascinate that has been connected with the computer since the earliest stored-program machines arrived in the universities. It reaches back to the first generation of young hackers at a few select computer labs, like that at MIT. Hackers have always been a freakish minority, highly gifted minds for whom the intricacies of the computer can become an obsession, if not an addiction; yet they play a crucial role in the history of the technology. They were the first to give themselves fully to the strange interplay between the human mind and its clever mechanical counterfeit. That interplay deserves the careful attention of educators because it carries within it a hidden curriculum that arrives in the classroom with the computer.

Among the hackers, one of the main attractions of the machine was the enthralling sense of power it gave its user, or rather its master. For one did not simply use a computer, one had to take intellectual control of it. This was a complex machine, an "embodiment of mind," as Warren McCulloch once described it, and it could easily elude effective application. Yet, even when it did so, its misbehavior arose from some rigorously consistent extension of its programming that demanded understanding. It was not like an automobile, which would malfunction simply because a part wore out; its problems were not merely physical. They could only be corrected by tracking the bug through the dense logic of the machine's program. But if the hacker mastered the logic, he could bend the computer to his will. ("His" is historically correct here; notably, nearly all the early hackers, like most hackers since, were male, many of them living in "bachelor mode.") As one computer genius reported to Steven Levy, who has written the best history of the early hackers, there was a day when he came to the "sudden realization" that "the computer wasn't so smart at all. It was just some dumb beast, following orders, doing what you told it to do in exactly the order you determined. You could control it. You could be God."

But the satisfaction of becoming the machine's God, of lowering it to the status of a "dumb beast," is not available to everyone; only to those who can outsmart the smart machine. First it has to be respected as an uncanny sort of mind, one that can perform many mental tricks better than its user. The relationship of the human being to the machine is, thus, an ambivalent one, a complex mixture of sensed inferiority and the need to dominate, of dependence and mastery. "Like Aladdin's lamp, you could get it to do your bidding." That is how Levy describes a certain exhilarating moment of truth in the early hackers' encounter with the computer. But like Aladdin's lamp, the machine holds a genie more powerful than the human being who temporarily commands its obedience.

The word *power* is freely sprinkled through the literature of computers. The computer is a "powerful tool"; it is fueled by "powerful theories" and "powerful ideas." "Computers are not good or bad," Sherry Turkle concludes in her study of the psychology of young computer users. "They are powerful." As we have seen, computer scientists have been willing to exaggerate that power to superhuman, even godlike dimensions. Perhaps it will soon be "an intelligence beyond man's." These heady speculations on the part of respected authorities are not simply whimsical diversions; they are images and aspirations that weave themselves into the folklore of the computer and become embedded in the priorities that guide its development. They are intimately involved in the sense of power that surrounds the machine, even as it is playfully presented to children at the basic level of computer literacy.

This can be a deeply illuminating educational moment for children—if it comes to them in the right way. It is their introduction to the form of power that most distinguishes their species: the power of the mind. At some point, they must learn that the phantom cunning and resourcefulness of the mind provides a greater biological advantage that size and strength, that intelligence counts for more than the brute force of muscles or of engines that replace muscle. In ancient Greece, children learned the value of cunning from the exploits of Odysseus, the man "of many devices." American Indian children learned cleverness from the mythic figure of Coyote the Trickster. All folklore features these masters of guile, who teach that a good trick may outdo the strongest sinews in the risky adventures of life.

In the modern West, the survival power of the mind has come to be concentrated in the "many devices" of our technology, and now most importantly in a smart machine which is the culmination of that technology. Whatever simple, gamelike computer exercises children may learn, they are also learning that the computer possesses what adults regard as the highest kind of power, a power that is similar to what human beings do when they lay plans, store up information, solve problems: something mindlike.

Because of this mindlikeness, the little box with the video screen on top, which doesn't look anything like a person, has come to be surrounded by all sorts of personifications. One "talks" to the computer. It "understands"—or doesn't understand. It "asks" and "answers" questions. It "remembers" things. It says "please" and "thank you." Above all, it "teaches" and "corrects" because it "knows" things and knows them better. If computer literacy takes hold in our schools, students may not be learning these mindlike qualities from another human being, but most often from a machine. Even if they are also learning from a teacher, the teacher will not be a "powerful" device. No one—certainly no computer scientist—has ever described a teacher's mind as "a powerful tool." Why not? Because teachers cannot know as much as the box. The box can hold lots more information. Even if the little computer in the classroom is limited in its capacity, the children know there are other, bigger computers that are running the world they live in. They can be seen in the bank, the store, the doctor's office. And when all the computers are put together, they have a power no teacher can have. They never make mistakes. That is the power which adults respect and would have children aspire to: the power of always being right, quickly and absolutely. But this is a power that can only come through the machine. As one children's book puts it: "Computers never make mistakes. If there is a mistake, it is made by the people who are using the computer or because the computer is broken." The mixture of loose, anthropomorphic metaphors, interactive software, and commercial imagery that accompany the computer into the classroom brings with it a clear, if subliminal, lesson. It is the lesson the computer's inventors and dominant users have ingrained in the technology: a conception of thinking, of order, of intellectual priorities. It goes something like this:

Here is a form of power. It is a power of the mind. It is the greatest power of the mind—the power to process limitless information with absolute correctness. We live in an Information Age that needs that power. Getting a job, being successful, means acquiring that power. The machine has it; you don't. As time goes on, the machine will have more and more of it. It will deserve that power because it fits better with the world than human brains. The only human brains that can be trusted are those that use the machine to help them think.

This lesson can be transmitted in an unthreatening, even inviting way. That is the style of all computer instruction. Start simple. Make it fun. Build confidence. Ideally, the machine should be "user friendly"—a curiously condescending phrase which suggests that the machine is being kind enough to simplify and slow down for less talented users who need to be babied along. Most encouraging of all, the machine will share its power with its users. It can be domesticated and brought into one's home as a mental servant. All one needs to do is adjust to the machine's way of thinking. Becoming computer literate, comments Paul Kalaghan, dean of computer science at Northeastern University, "is a chance to spend your life working with devices smarter than you are, and yet have control over them. It's like carrying a six-gun on the old frontier."

---

## Now that you've read

1. What are some of Roszak's concerns about the computer's effects on the education and on us as individuals?
2. Do you share his concerns? Why or why not?
3. Why have college campuses embraced the computer age so warmly?
4. Are students who don't have their own computers at a disadvantage on your campus? Explain your answer.

## READING 4

*Suneel Ratan*

# A New Divide Between Haves and Have-Nots?

Ratan's article from *Time* helps us see how reduced access to technology in school among those of lower economic status will probably lead to reduced access to technology-related jobs in the future. As you read, think about the effect that access to computers and their related technologies has on your life as a student and beyond.

### Before you read

1. How accessible are computers on your campus for students who don't own their own personal computers?
2. How comfortable are you with computer-related technology?
3. What are some of the advantages of communicating with teachers and other students via e-mail or on video?

---

If there was any lingering doubt that the computer has become ensconced as a member of the American family, it was dispelled at the turn of the year by some startling statistics. For the first time ever, consumers in 1994 bought $8 billion worth of PC's—just a smidgen away from the $8.3 billion they spent on TVs. The sales record in terms of dollars is bound to fall to the computer soon, though the TV's cheaper price guarantees its dominion in numbers for a while yet.

In the nation's poorer areas, however—places like Washington's Anacostia neighborhood, the hollows of Appalachia or Miami's Liberty City—families with IBM Aptivas, NEC CD-ROM drives, modems, Internet connections and all the other paraphernalia so beloved by computer users are few and far between. Therein lies one of the most troubling aspects of the emerging information age. In an era in which success is increasingly identified with the ability to use computers and gain access to cyberspace, will the new technology only widen the gap between rich and poor, educated and uneducated, blacks, whites and Hispanics? As Commerce Secretary Ronald Brown puts it, "How do you create an environment so that once we've built this information infrastructure, you do not create a society of haves and have-nots?"

The stakes are high. Access to the information highway may prove to be less a question of privilege or position than one of the basic ability to function in a democratic society. It may determine how well people are educated, the kind of job they eventually get, how they are retrained if they lose their job, how much access they have to their government and how they will learn about the critical issues affecting them and the country. No less an expert than Mitch Kapor, co-founder of Lotus Development Corp. and now president of the Electronic Frontier Foundation, feels that those who do not have access "will be highly correlated with the general have-nots. Early in the next century the network will become the major conduit through which we conduct our lives. Any disenfranchisement will be very severe."

The fact is that access to the new technology generally breaks down along traditional class lines. Wealthy and upper-middle-class families form the bulk of the 30% of American households that own computers. Similarly, wealthier school districts naturally tend to have equipment that is unavailable to poorer ones, and schools in the more affluent suburbs have twice as many computers per student as their less-well-funded urban counterparts. All this disparity comes to a head in this statistic: a working person who is able to use a computer earns 15% more than someone in a similar job who cannot.

The debate over how to handle the problem pits the freewheeling techno-cowboys of the computer and telecommunications industries against traditional advocates for the poor. The computer and telecommunications industries proclaim a paramount faith in market forces, at least partly because they fear eventual government regulation of access to the infobahn. As they see it, the forces of competition and the marketplace will drive the prices of equipment and online services downward and make both increasingly available to the less affluent.

There is considerable evidence to support that view. The newest computer models sport capabilities far beyond those of their predecessors and are priced lower; presumably, they will continue getting cheaper. Moreover, ever upgrading "heatseekers," who are constantly searching for the latest equipment, are bound to create a vigorous secondhand market. Machines that might otherwise be wasted are instead being sold into the used-computer market, where they can be snapped up by the less advantaged in the same way that poorer people buy used cars instead of new ones.

The problem, as advocates for the poor point out, is that all of today's information roads charge tolls, sometimes hefty ones, that effectively bar even many of those who manage to put together the price of a secondhand computer. The situation is further complicated by the tendency of telecommunications companies to place the new information networks in more affluent communities, by-passing, at least for the moment, poorer rural and inner-city areas. Representative Ed Markey, a Massachusetts Democrat, calls this separating-out process "information apartheid." A coalition of consumer, poverty and religious groups last May petitioned the Federal Communications Commission—which has not yet acted on the matter—to ban what they labeled "electronic redlining," a term derived from the banking practice of refusing loans to people and businesses in areas considered ghettos. "We're talking about something more than plain old TV," says Jeff Chester of the Center for Media Education, a liberal advocacy group. "We're talking about access to the central nervous system of our democracy."

Ensuring that broadband networks are rolled out to inner cities and rural areas at the same time as they are to affluent suburbs would by no means solve all the problems. There is the question of how the undereducated would be able to learn to operate computers—even if they could afford to buy them. M.I.T. Media Laboratory director Nicholas Negroponte argues that the growing pervasiveness of computers in schools and homes, coupled with the increasing ease of computer use, will eventually dispel the techno-illiteracy that haunts the information have-not. Negroponte may be correct, but the transition to widespread computer literacy could easily take 20 or 30 years.

Another part of the debate, now being waged in Washington, is how to expand the 60-year-old concept of universal telephone service to emerging high-speed information services. Part of the problem is that at least 7 million American homes, most of them poor, do not even have the phones that could provide basic access. It is difficult to see people who lack such a necessity of modern American life going out and buying a computer. In January, House Speaker Newt Gingrich raised the idea of giving poor people tax credits to buy laptop computers, but in an era in which middle- and upper-middle-class Americans seem intent on cutting benefits for the poor, meaningful Net-access subsidies seem unlikely.

Yet the information industry is moving so fast that government officials are reluctant to intervene in any way that might slow its dynamism. In a search for creative ways to lessen the technology gap, advocates of wider access are focusing on plans to put computers and Net connections into libraries, post offices and other public places around the country to serve those who do not have home computers.

Many of the early approaches are local and small scale, but they may point the way to the future. New York City's United Community Organization, an umbrella group of neighborhood settlement houses, in February began installing in its project buildings

200 PCs with ISDN (Integrated Services Digital Network) connections to the Internet. Financed by $1.4 million in federal grants and private donations, the machines help the settlement-house staffs coordinate their work and give neighborhood residents the opportunity to cruise the highway, have access to government databases, exchange E-mail and otherwise sample cyberspace's many wonders. The city of Santa Monica, California, has started a public electronic network, installing 15 public-access terminals in places such as banks, community centers and even grocery stores. Anyone who wants to—including the homeless—can get online information about city services, make E-mail connections to city officials and local members of Congress and join discussion groups about contentious local issues like rent control and homelessness.

Mark Cooper, research director of the Consumer Federation of America, argues that there are no panaceas for national concerns about the gap between the information haves and have-nots. Nor, he believes, will eventual computer literacy and Net access do much to end the blight of poverty, illegitimacy, rural isolation and urban decay. "There's always going to be an unequal distribution of income," Cooper says. That's probably true, but at the very least, the new technology should unleash all its considerable energies toward the goal of preventing those problems from getting any worse.

---

## Now that you've read

1. What are Ratan's main concerns in this article? What effects does limited or no access to computers have on "have-nots"?
2. What kinds of things can be done to make computers available to everyone?
3. Do you see this as a concern for the United States in the twenty-first century? Why or why not?

## READING 5

*John N. Hickman*

# Cybercheats: Term-Paper Shopping Online

John N. Hickman's article, which originally appeared in *The New Republic,* probably shocked some readers. Unfortunately, those of us who teach for a living know how easy it is for students to gain access to "services" like this. Hickman makes it clear how prevalent these sources are and shows that even students at the top colleges in the country are plagiarizing with the help of the Internet.

### *Before you read*

1. How comfortable are you doing web searches?
2. Do you know anyone who has ever visited or used an online term-paper source?
3. Why do people cheat? How do you feel about cheating?

---

It's four o'clock in the morning, you're just one page into a 15-page term paper that's due at ten o'clock, and the teaching assistant isn't giving extensions. A few years ago, that would have been it: You would have passed in the paper late, if at all, and dealt with the consequences. But this is 1998, and so, in your most desperate hour, you try a desperate ploy. You log on to the World Wide Web (the university has very generously connected every dorm room to the Internet), enter "term papers" into an online search engine, and find your way to www.a1-termpaper.com. There you scroll down past the big red disclaimer ("All work offered is for research purposes only"), find a paper that fits the assignment, enter your credit card number, and then wait until the file shows up in your college e-mail account. You feel a little ashamed, but, hey, the course was just a distribution requirement, anyway. You put your own name on the title page, print it out, and set the alarm for nine o'clock.

A few years ago, "A1 Termpaper" would have been just another tiny ad in the classifieds of *Rolling Stone* or *National Lampoon*— hardly a temptation for most self-respecting students, and hardly a worry for any serious institution of higher learning. But the Web now features dozens of similar sites—from the "Evil House of Cheat" to "Research Papers Online"—which enable students to purchase ready-made term papers on a wide variety of subjects.

The companies, of course, maintain they are merely providing learning materials for inquisitive students. But there's good reason to think online plagiarism is becoming a real problem on college campuses. The Evil House of Cheat page now boasts over one million hits; A1 Termpaper claims thousands. Although a "hit" is a visit, not a sale, it is hard to imagine that thousands of students—at least 8,000 a week—are visiting these sites, and no one is buying. A spokesman for "The Paper Store" told me that his company's yearly traffic in papers was "well in the thousands." The owner of A1 Termpaper says that he has sold between 1,000 and 2,000 papers in his first year of operation. According to Anthony Krier, a research librarian at Franklin Pierce College in Rindge, New Hampshire, and a widely quoted source on Internet plagiarism (he maintains a database of term-paper websites), the number of term-paper sites has swelled from 28 in the beginning of 1997 to 72 today. "Does the increase in the number of sites translate into an increase in cheating? Certainly," says Krier. "There's no doubt about it. People have got to realize the problem is not going away until they start taking it seriously."

At least one school, Boston University, is. Last year, it became sufficiently worried about online plagiarism that it launched a sting operation, in which a law student posed as an undergraduate in search of a paper on Toni Morrison's *Beloved*. In October, the university—which has been dogging term-paper mills for 25 years—filed suit against eight of the companies it claims to have snagged in the ruse, charging them with mail and wire fraud, racketeering, and breaking a Massachusetts law against term-paper sales.

But B.U. is the exception. Harvard University's Thurston Smith, secretary to the administrative board, is serenely confident that Internet plagiarism is not a problem at Harvard. "I'm sure it's going on somewhere," he says. "I just have to believe Harvard students would have too much respect for the faculty." Just as sanguine are administrators at Bucknell, Dartmouth, and Yale. Terri Barbuto, secretary of the executive committee, Yale's disciplinary body, insists, "It really hasn't been a problem at Yale."

My own sampling of student opinion suggests otherwise. One Yale student, for example, told me that, while researching an essay on Shakespeare, he inadvertently stumbled upon a term-paper site and, after asking around, realized that he wasn't the only student tempted by the ease of Internet plagiarism: "Everyone was finding them and keeping their mouths shut. I mean, at Yale, who would admit to having to buy a paper?" A Princeton freshman admitted to me that he had passed in a pilfered English paper: "Come on," he said, "it's just so easy, and the class was a waste of time, anyway."

Just how easy is it? Punching in "term papers" to an Internet search engine like AltaVista yields more than five million matches.

The vast majority of these sites are, ironically, administrative warnings about online plagiarism, but among the first 100 listings are links to a handful of term-paper sites. If you click on the link to the Evil House of Cheat (www.cheathouse.com), a dark, fiery-fonted homepage will appear on the screen, featuring links to about 40 other term-paper sites. Many of these linked sites are staggering, library-like catalogs of thousands of prewritten papers. At A1 Termpaper's website, which claims to offer "approximately 20,000 prewritten term papers," you could, for example, purchase the 20-page essay, "Hegel's Theory of Religion," for $179, or acquire ten pages on the IMF for a mere $89.50. Or, if that just-right paper isn't already available, The Paper Store will be happy to compose a special one that fits your needs, for about $15 a page.

The proprietors of these services claim that what they do is legal and honorable. "I help people," says Abe Korn, the man behind "The Term Paper, School, and Business Help Line." Korn, who talks a mile a minute in thick Brooklynese and claims to have been a professor at "a very major university," explains that his clients say, "Abe, help me, I don't know how to write a paper. I write them one, as an example, and then they go and pass it in. Is that my fault? No. If I help you in physics and work one problem, and you turn that problem in, am I to blame? No. I'm just a tutor."

Of course, a 1973 Massachusetts law forbids the sale of a term paper by someone knowing or "having reason to know" that it will be submitted as somebody else's work. And Texas passed a similar law last year. But, even if selling term papers is potentially illegal, the law can't do much to shut down sites like "School Sucks"—sites where students generously make their own papers available to others for free. By one count, there are 38 free term-paper sites like School Sucks, a page started in 1996 by a former Florida International University student, Kenny Sahr. By last July, School Sucks, which started with one English paper Sahr borrowed from a friend, had grown into a megasite with 2,000 free term papers and a convenient search engine to locate essays by key words. As of January, according to Sahr, his site registered 1,140,690 hits and advertising revenues of $5,000 a month.

Some of these free papers are, by anyone's standards, awful. One paper on Macbeth begins: "Macbeth is primarily about villains. And the villainy that the play has knows no bounds." Yet other free-paper sites, such as the one designed by Harvard sophomore Dorian Berger, are gems. Dorian's swanky homepage posts about 20 of his generally quite good Harvard papers, free to download.

Even more helpful are pages like "1 Stop Research Paper Shop," which links to 32 scholarly sites, each with free papers posted by altruistically minded academics. Linked to the site: economics papers from the Federal Reserve Bank of Minneapolis, research works from the NASA Laboratories, papers from the Center for Cognitive Science, like "Mechanics of Sentence Processing," and a trove of essays from an assistant professor of economics at the University of Chicago, Casey Mulligan. The homepage of J. Michael Miller, a teacher at Virginia's Episcopal High School, who has a master's degree in history from Georgetown University and a Ph.D. in Russian History from George Washington University, features five of Miller's college papers, ripe for the picking. Miller is only slightly troubled by the prospects of plagiarism. "It's really up to the individual reader," he says, "to do with the information what they will, good or evil. I belong to the school that says teach people to do the right thing and then turn 'em loose."

Concern over Internet plagiarism has led at least a few educators to contemplate high-tech solutions. Two employees of the National Institutes of Health, Dr. Ned Feder and Walter Stewart, have designed a computer program to scan text and recognize word-for-word similarities as short as 32 characters long. Still, the programs have their limits, and, in the end, it's a losing battle. The whole point of the Internet is to share information. To get the benefits of online technology, universities have to cope with the costs. The only real solution to cyberplagiarism, then, is old-fashioned vigilance. Having spent millions of dollars wiring their students to the Internet, universities may have to invest in smaller classes and a better teacher-to-student ratio. A return to some good old analog, face-to-face teaching may be the only way to keep online plagiarism at the fringes, where it belongs.

---

## Now that you've read

1. What do you make of Hickman's discovery that students at prestigious colleges and universities apparently download papers from the Internet and claim them as their own? Did this come as a surprise to you or not? Explain your answer.
2. Who is hurt most by cheating? Is it really "no big deal"?
3. What can teachers do to try to keep their students from resorting to these resources?

# READING 6

*Paul Saffo*

# Quality in an Age of Electronic Incunabula

Paul Saffo is a "futurist" who has written for *PC/Computing* magazine. In "Quality in an Age of Electronic Incunabula," he looks to the future and likes what he sees. He argues that every major technological advance results in a period of adjustment and transition. Soon, he says, things that have us blinking in disbelief now will have become second nature. As you read, consider whether you share his largely optimistic view of the future.

### Before you read

1. What does *incunabula* mean?
2. How much do you read on the computer? For example, do you read e-zines or other longer pieces as a part of your web browsing?
3. Can you imagine reading books on your computer screen? Why or why not?
4. What would be your response if you had to download your college textbooks from the web and read them on your computer screen?

A long-forecast information future is arriving late and in utterly unexpected ways. Paper and its familiars—books, magazines, and newspapers—were supposed to become obsolete, quickly replaced by new forms of electronic media. In fact, the consumption of communications paper in the United States has grown at a rate greater than the growth in gross national product for virtually every year since World War II. Electronics didn't replace paper; it enabled the production of greater volumes of print-based media than ever.

Meanwhile, the diffusion and consumption of new media—the incunabula of our time—have occurred more rapidly yet. From television to Nintendo, wave after wave of electronic novelty has invaded our homes, utterly changing our media habits and desires. Thanks to cable and global news services, consumers today have better access to information on breaking events than President Kennedy enjoyed from the situation room in the White House during the Cuban Missile crisis. The average home today holds more computing power embedded in its appliances than existed in the entire District of Columbia before 1963.

The relationship between burgeoning paper and even more rapid electronic diffusion resembles an expanding sphere, in which volume increases more rapidly than surface area. The information business has become a kind of pi ata: a thin paper crust surrounding an enabling electronic core. Paper has become an artifact of electronic media, but we barely notice because the paper crust conceals the core.

For example, the *Wall Street Journal* is written and edited on computer screens, electronically typeset, and then bounced off satellites to remote printing plants across the country. It assumes its familiar paper form only hours before it appears in our mailboxes. In offices and academic departments, the same pattern explains why we merely create greater volumes of documents than ever; xerographic copiers automate what once was laboriously copied with typewriter and spirit master.

For the moment at least, the social impact of this shift remains hidden beneath the paper skin. For instance, the way we use paper changed fundamentally in the mid-1980s with desktop publishing and new storage technologies. We think of paper as a communications medium, but in fact it had been primarily a storage medium. Consider your favorite book sitting on your bookshelf: how little time it spends in your hands being read, and how much gathering dust. Even a Bible in the hands of the most devout Christian fundamentalist spends more time shut than open.

By 1985, it had become cheaper to store information electronically than on paper, while desktop publishing makes it easier than ever to produce printed copy. The result is that paper is now interface—an increasingly volatile, disposable medium for viewing information on demand. We are solidly on the way to a future where we will reduce information to paper only when we are ready to read it— the phenomenon demonstrated by the *Wall Street Journal*—and then recycle it when done.

Evidence of paper as interface is everywhere. For example, facsimile machines also promote paper as interface. One can subscribe to a growing number of daily customized fax "newspapers" containing only the stories that interest each individual subscriber. The "database publishing" technologies that make these services possible are being used by others to profitably publish everything from customized textbooks to personalized ads in weekly magazines. In four hundred years, our universities have gone from the Stationari of Bologna to the printing press, to the copier, and now the computer to serve up course material.

The forces that made paper as interface possible will have even greater impact in the 1990s. As the communications pi ata continues to expand, holes and thin spots are appearing, making paper more transitory yet. Researchers in theoretical physics and other disciplines have abandoned academic journals for electronic mail to keep up with breaking events in their fields. Meanwhile, financial exchanges have traded electrons for paper as the globe's primary transaction medium. Less than a quarter of our money supply is represented by greenbacks; the rest exists only as phantom memory patterns in huge computer data banks.

The term "electronic book" has suddenly become the hottest buzz-word in the media community, and everyone is getting into the act. One company is selling "expanded books"—computer versions of popular novels like *Jurassic Park*—designed to run on laptop portables. Electronic games-maker Broderbund Software is promoting "living books" on CD-ROM disks, leading with a clever children's title, *Just Grandma and Me*. Another company, Mathcad, is offering interactive technical "electronic handbooks" in partnership with academic publishers.

Software companies aren't the only would-be electronic book publishers. IBM has debuted "illuminated books," interactive educational works developed by Bob Abel. Sony is launching its "BookMan" portable CD-ROM player, and other consumer electronics players are furiously developing electronic book platforms of their own.

All of these products share an emphasis on text as their primary information delivery vehicle. Presumably this is why they have been defined as "books," but the vast penetration of these new media belies their apparent aesthetic inferiority to the best of conventional print. Nothing created on a fax, PC, or laserprinter can match letterpress for sheer sensuous quality. More importantly, the experience offered by electronic media is fundamentally different from anything offered by traditional books.

This latter aspect holds an important clue regarding the prospects for these new media. Our new media will not replace existing media directly; rather, they will penetrate by offering experiences that traditional print does poorly, or cannot do at all. A case in point is hypertext, which is simply a superior electronic alternative to the sort of tasks previously relegated to thesauri and encyclopedias.

The term "electronic book" is misleading, however, because these products are not books at all but something new: the incunabula of our own age. We are living in a moment between two revolutions: one of print, four centuries old and not quite spent, and another of electronics, two decades young and just getting underway. Today's "electronic books" amount to a bridge between these two revolutions, and the term's historic associations can help us through a mind-bending shift in much the same way that "horseless carriage" once eased our grandparents into the age of the automobile.

Of course, just as practical automobiles lay decades beyond the first horseless carriages, it will be some time before our new electronic media even begin to approach the sophistication and subtleties of traditional print. Traditionalists will howl at the vulgarity of it all, much as fans of manuscript writing shuddered at the ugly and unreliable monochrome works that came off the earliest presses.

In fact, events today are unfolding much as they did in the time of the original incunabula, between the 1450s and Aldus's publication of the first modern book in 1501. Recall that the very first books off Gutenberg's press were slavish imitations of what scriveners produced by hand. Just as the inventors of plastic first struggled to make the stuff look like wood and tortoise shell, printing pioneers worked to conceal the novelty of their new books. Mercifully, our new electronic media seem to have passed rapidly through this phase with the first wave of CD-ROM titles.

The current crop of "electronic books" recalls what emerged once the early medieval "print nerds" tired of making simple copies of manuscript works. It takes time to turn raw, untamed information technologies into compelling media that touch user imaginations. It took fifty years in the age of printed incunabula; it is likely to take at least a decade for the first wave of electronic books to be reduced to integral and unremarkable artifacts in our own lives.

This period of diffusion will mask a deeper debate about quality. Are the new electronic books inferior because they remain in their infancy? Or is there something about electronics that is intrinsically inferior to print? Though I welcome today's electronic innovations, I am beginning to suspect that the latter concern has some basis.

It is possible that the very flexibility of our new electronic media constitutes their essential flaw. Several years ago, designer Milton Glaser observed that each new print technology has been infinitely more flexible than its predecessor—and has produced new conventions that were much worse. For Glaser, the essential determinant of aesthetic quality is the "resistance" of a medium; the harder an artist or craftsperson must work, the better the final product is likely to be. Thus, desktop publishing will always tend to produce results inferior to Linotype output, and no matter how hard publishers try, they will never match the quality of letterpress with digital technologies. Moreover, Glaser says, "the computer bears as close a relationship to the production of quality design as the typewriter does to the production of good poetry."

The uneasy traditionalist in me agrees, even as I enter these words into my labor- and aggravation-saving word processor. Of course, "quality" is only one measure of value when it comes to information and society. Cost and availability round out the equation, and virtually every innovation since the printing press has favored both at the expense of quality. The books printed by Aldus in the early 1500s were nothing to look at compared to the work of medieval copyists, but they made information infinitely more accessible and affordable. While a privileged intellectual minority lamented the vulgarity of books in the marketplace, a newly literate population proceeded to change the course of European history.

Today's expanding electronic technologies also serve up an unprecedented explosion in the sheer volume of information assaulting us. A single copy of the Sunday *New York Times* contains more information than a sixteenth-century Venetian merchant was likely to read in a lifetime. Today, more information is stored digitally than on all the shelves of all the libraries in the world.

The resultant "information overload" has fascinated and infuriated us all, but it is something of a red herring; we have been coping with varying degrees of overload for centuries. We will deal with overload in new media in the same way we have always dealt with it—by creating new sense-making tools and social structures tailored to ever richer information environments. Recall that the Di Medicis built their financial empire on a tool for coping with the avalanche of numbers in their brave new world of commerce. Invented by a Benedictine monk, this critical tool was double-entry bookkeeping. Today, the traders of Wall Street are finding increasingly arcane mathematical tools to be essential to survival in what has become an electronic-age "casino of the gods." This ongoing information explosion will have direct effects on our educational structures; continued emphasis on providing students with the intellectual tool kits to cope with information overload is but the most obvious implication.

The *indirect* impacts are far more important. The effect on quality of this explosion in volume is more subtle and worrisome. Quality, by its very nature, tends to be scarce. History suggests that the total amount of quality material in all media has grown slowly over the centuries, but it seems increasingly scarce because the volume of inferior work has grown so much faster. I have little doubt that Gresham's Law applies to media: All things being equal, technological advances will cause the very best to be lost in a burgeoning flow of mediocre works.

Ultimately, quality and quantity in this electronic age converge around changing notions of what constitutes an "original." When a thing is created in a digital environment, every copy made is the equal of the original. In fact, there are no "copies" at all—just multiple originals. This alone guarantees that the information explosion will continue expanding exponentially for the indefinite future. More importantly, though, it may extinguish the very notion of what constitutes an "original" to begin with.

We praise "original" works, and we scorn anything that is "merely derivative." As Picasso once observed, the first man to compare his lover's lips to a rose was quite probably a genius—but everyone to make the comparison thereafter was almost certainly an idiot. The volume of truly original works is actually minuscule; what passes as original is simply a product of our bad memories. Recall that Picasso's "original" work borrowed heavily on themes from African art he observed while a young man. This link, however, is made only by a handful of specialists, while the rest of us consider his work wildly unique.

The search and access power of the digital world will bring our memories back with brutal clarity. Scholars may quickly discover that *nothing* is original and everything is derivative, bordering on plagiarism. Imagine a future electronic book with the ability to link to remote hyperbases and search for sources and content similar to what is being read. The headaches that digital sampling are causing the music industry today are about to be propagated at a much larger scale among scholars. Eventually, we will discover that originality is a myth and that what lifts the great from the merely derivative is not originality at all but passion.

We are entering an age of infinite recall; much more than our information tools are changing. We will become paperless in the same way we once became horseless: Horses are still around, but they are ridden by hobbyists, not commuters. Similarly, new electronic media will creep into our lives, gradually displacing the time we spend with print.

"Electronic books" will mature into new media forms as the age of electronic incunabula comes to a close. Eventually, we will find ourselves in a world that for all intents and purposes will be paperless. We will hardly notice the shift, though, for it will so transform our intellectual lives that comparisons with even the recent past of this century will seem quaint and pointless.

---

### Now that you've read

1. What is Saffo's major argument? Be ready to identify a particular section of the text to support your response.
2. What evidence does he offer to back up his argument?
3. Do you find his arguments convincing or not? Explain your answer.
4. How does the question of "quality" enter the picture, according to Saffo? What determines whether something has "quality" or not?

## READING 7

*Amy Bruckman*

# Finding One's Own Space in Cyberspace

Once you're connected to the Internet and are equipped to send and receive e-mail, you can participate in discussions with people all over the world. Some people are concerned that women are more vulnerable on the net than men are. In "Finding One's Own Space in Cyberspace," Amy Bruckman, however, argues that we all choose the community we're most comfortable in, whether that community is real or virtual.

### Before you read

1. How great a fan of the Internet are you?
2. Do you participate in online discussion groups? Why or why not?
3. Have you ever been "flamed"?
4. At what Internet sites might one's gender make a difference to others? Why? How?

---

The week the last Internet porn scandal broke, my phone didn't stop ringing: "Are women comfortable on the Net?" "Should women use gender neutral names on the Net?" "Are women harassed on the Net?" Reporters called from all over the country with basically the same question. I told them all: your question is ill-formed. "The Net" is not one thing. It's like asking: "Are women comfortable in bars?" That's a silly question. Which woman? Which bar?

The summer I was 18, I was the computer counselor at a summer camp. After the campers were asleep, the counselors were allowed out, and would go bar hopping. First everyone would go to Maria's, an Italian restaurant with red-and-white-checkered table cloths. Maria welcomed everyone from behind the bar, greeting regular customers by name. She always brought us free garlic bread. Next we'd go to the Sandpiper, a disco with good dance music. The Sandpiper seemed excitingly adult—it was a little scary at first, but then I loved it. Next, we went to the Sportsman, a leather motorcycle bar that I found absolutely terrifying. Huge, bearded men bulging out of their leather vests and pants leered at me. I hid in the corner and tried not to make eye contact with anyone, hoping my friends would get tired soon and give me a ride back to camp.

Each of these bars was a community, and some were more comfortable for me than others. The Net is made up of hundreds of thousands of separate communities, each with its own special character. Not only is the Net a diverse place, but "women" are diverse as well—there were leather-clad women who loved the Sportsman, and plenty of women revel in the fiery rhetoric of Usenet's alt.flame. When people complain about being harassed on the Net, they've usually stumbled into the wrong online community. The question is not whether "women" are comfortable on "the Net," but rather, what types of communities are possible? How can we create a range of communities so that everyone—men and women—can find a place that is comfortable for them?

If you're looking for a restaurant or bar, you can often tell without even going in: Is the sign flashing neon or engraved wood? Are there lots of cars parked out front? What sort of cars? (You can see all the Harleys in front of the Sportsman from a block away.) Look in the window: How are people dressed? We are accustomed to diversity in restaurants. People know that not all restaurants will please them, and employ a variety of techniques to choose the right one.

It's a lot harder to find a good virtual community than it is to find a good bar. The visual cues that let you spot the difference between Maria's and the Sportsman from across the street are largely missing. Instead, you have to "lurk"—enter the community and quietly explore for a while, getting the feel of whether it's the kind of place you're looking for. Although published guides exist, they're not always very useful—most contain encyclopedic lists with little commentary or critical evaluation, and by the time they're published they're already out of date. Magazines like *NetGuide* and *Wired* are more current and more selective, and therefore more useful, but their editorial bias may not fit with your personal tastes.

Commonly available network-searching tools are also useful. The World Wide Web is filled with searching programs, indexes and even indexes of indexes ("meta-indexes"). Although browsing with these tools can be a pleasant diversion, it is not very efficient, and searches for particular pieces of information often end in frustration. If you keep an open mind, however, you may come across something good.

### Shaping an Online Society

But what happens if, after exploring and asking around, you still can't find an online environment that suits you? Don't give up: start your own! This doesn't have to be a difficult task. Anyone can create a new newsgroup in Usenet's "alt" hierarchy or open a new chat room on America Online. Users of Unix systems can easily start a mailing list.

If you have a good idea but not enough technical skill or the right type of Net access, there are people around eager to help. The more interesting question is: How do you help a community to become what you hope for? Here, I can offer some hard-won advice.

In my research at the MIT Media Lab (working with Professor Mitchel Resnick), I design virtual communities. In October of 1992, I founded a professional community for media researchers on the Internet called MediaMOO. Over the past three years, as MediaMOO has grown to 1,000 members from 33 countries, I have grappled with many of the issues that face anyone attempting to establish a virtual community. MediaMOO is a "multi-user dungeon" or MUD— a virtual world on the Internet with rooms, objects, and people from all around the world. Messages typed in by a user instantly appear on the screens of all other users who are currently in the same virtual "room." This real-time interaction distinguishes MUDs from Usenet newsgroups, where users can browse through messages created many hours or days before. The MUD's virtual world is built in text descriptions. MOO stands for MUD object-oriented, a kind of MUD software (created by Pavel Curtis of the Xerox Palo Alto Research Center and Stephen White, now at InContext Systems) that allows each user to write programs to define spaces and objects.

The first MUDS, developed in the late 1970s, were multiplayer fantasy games of the dungeons-and-dragons variety. In 1989, a graduate student at Carnegie Mellon University named James Aspnes decided to see what would happen if you took away the monsters and the magic swords but instead let people extend the virtual world. People's main activity went from trying to conquer the virtual world to trying to build it, collaboratively.

Most MUDs are populated by undergraduates who should be doing their homework. I thought it would be interesting instead to bring together a group of people with a shared intellectual interest: the study of media. Ideally, MediaMOO should be like an endless reception for a conference on media studies. But given the origin of MUDs as violent games, giving one an intellectual and professional atmosphere was a tall order. How do you guide the evolution of who uses the space and what they do there?

A founder/designer can't control what the community ultimately becomes—much of that is up to the users—but can help shape it. The personality of the community's founder can have a great influence on what sort of place it becomes. Part of what made Maria's so comfortable for me was Maria herself. She radiated a warmth that made me feel at home.

Similarly, one of the most female-friendly electronic communities I've visited is New York City's ECHO (East Coast Hang Out) bulletin board, run by Stacy Horn. Smart, stylish, and deliberately outrageous,

Horn is role model and patron saint for the ECHO-ites. Her outspoken but sensitive personality infuses the community, and sends a message to women that it's all right to speak up. She added a conference to ECHO called "WIT" (women in telecommunications), which one user describes as "a warm, supportive, women-only, private conference where women's thoughts, experiences, wisdom, joys, and despairs are shared." But Horn also added a conference called "BITCH," which the ECHO-ite calls "WIT in black leather jackets. All-women, riotous and raunchy."

Horn's high-energy, very New York brand of intelligence establishes the kind of place ECHO is and influences how everyone there behaves. When ECHO was first established, Horn and a small group of her close friends were the most active people on the system. "That set the emotional tone, the traditional style of posting, the unwritten rules about what it's OK to say," says Marisa Bowe, an Echo administrator for many years. "Even though Stacy is too busy these days to post very much, the tone established in the early days continues," says Bowe, who is now editor of an online magazine called *Word*.

Beyond the sheer force of a founder's personality, a community establishes a particular character with a variety of choices of how to operate. One example is to set a policy on whether to allow participants to remain anonymous. Initially, I decided that members of MediaMOO should be allowed to choose: they could identify themselves with their real names and e-mail addresses, or remain anonymous. Others questioned whether there was a role for anonymity in a professional community.

As time went on, I realized they were right. People on MediaMOO are supposed to be networking, hoping someone will look up who they really are and where they work. Members who are not willing to share their personal and professional identities are less likely to engage in serious discussion about their work, and consequently about media in general. Furthermore, comments from an anonymous entity are less valuable because they are unsituated—"I believe X" is less meaningful to a listener than "I am a librarian with eight years of experience who lives in a small town in Georgia, and I believe X." In theory, anonymous participants could describe their professional experiences and place their comments in that context; in practice it tends not to happen that way. After six months, I proposed that we change the policy to require that all new members be identified. Despite the protests of a few vocal opponents, most people thought that this was a good idea, and the change was made.

Each community needs to have its own policy on anonymity. There's room for diversity here too: some communities can be all-anonymous, some all-identified, and some can leave that decision up to each individual. An aside: right now on the Net no one is either really anonymous or really identified. It is easy to fake an identity; it is also possible to use either technical or legal tools to peer behind someone else's veil of anonymity. This ambiguous state of affairs is not necessarily unfortunate: it's nice to know that a fake identity that provides a modicum of privacy is easy to construct, but that in extreme cases such people can be tracked down.

### Finding Birds of a Feather

Another important design decision is admissions policy. Most places on the Net have a strong pluralistic flavor, and the idea that some people might be excluded from a community ruffles a lot of feathers. But exclusivity is a fact of life. MIT wouldn't be MIT if everyone who wanted to come was admitted. Imagine if companies had to give jobs to everyone who applied! Virtual communities, social clubs, universities and corporations are all groups of people brought together for a purpose. Achieving that purpose often requires that there be some way to determine who can join the community.

A key decision I made for MediaMOO was to allow entry only to people doing some sort of "media research." I try to be loose on the definition of "media"—writing teachers, computer network administrators, and librarians are all working with forms of media but strict on the definition of "research." At first, this policy made me uncomfortable. I would nervously tell people, "It's mostly a self-selection process. We hardly reject anyone at all!" Over time, I've become more comfortable with this restriction, and have enforced the requirements more stringently. I now believe my initial unease was naive.

Even if an online community decides to admit all comers, it does not have to let all contributors say anything they want. The existence of a moderator to filter postings often makes for more focused and civil discussion. Consider Usenet's two principal newsgroups dealing with feminism—alt.feminism and soc.feminism. In alt.feminism, anyone can post whatever they want. Messages in this group are filled with the angry words of angry people; more insults than ideas are exchanged. (Titles of messages found there on a randomly selected day included "Women & the workplace (it doesn't work)" and "What is a feminazi?".) The topic may nominally be feminism, but the discussion itself is not feminist in nature.

The huge volume of posting (more than 200 per day, on average) shows that many people enjoy writing such tirades. But if I wanted to discuss some aspect of feminism, alt.feminism would be the last place I'd go. Its sister group, soc.feminism, is moderated—volunteers read messages submitted to the group and post only those that pass muster. Moderators adhere to soc.feminism's lengthy charter, which explains the criteria for acceptable postings—forbidding ad hominem attacks, for instance.

Moderation of a newsgroup, like restricting admission to a MUD, grants certain individuals within a community power over others. If only one group could exist, I'd have to choose the uncensored alt.feminism to the moderated soc.feminism. Similarly, if MediaMOO were the only virtual community or MIT the only university, I'd argue that they should be open to all. However, there are thousands of universities and the Net contains hundreds of thousands of virtual communities, with varying criteria for acceptable conduct. That leaves room for diversity: some communities can be moderated, others unmoderated. Some can be open to all, some can restrict admissions.

The way a community is publicized—or not publicized—also influences its character. Selective advertising can help a community achieve a desired ambiance. In starting up MediaMOO, for example, we posted the original announcement to mailing lists for different aspects of media studies—not to the general-purpose groups for discussing MUDs on Usenet. MediaMOO is now rarely if ever deliberately advertised. The group has opted not to be listed in the public, published list of MUDs on the Internet. Members are asked to mention MediaMOO to other groups only if the majority of members of that group would probably be eligible to join MediaMOO.

New members are attracted by word of mouth among media researchers. To bring in an influx of new members, MediaMOO typically "advertises" by organizing an online discussion or symposium on some aspect of media studies. Announcing a discussion group on such topics as the techniques for studying behavior in a virtual community, or strategies for using computers to teach writing, attracts the right sort of people to the community and sets a tone for the kinds of discussion that take place there. That's much more effective than a more general announcement of MediaMOO and its purpose.

In an ideal world, virtual communities would acquire new members entirely by self-selection: people would enter an electronic neighborhood only if it focused on something they cared about. In most cases, this process works well. For example, one Usenet group that I sometimes read—sci.aquaria—attracts people who are really interested in discussing tropical fishkeeping. But self-selection is not always sufficient. For example, the challenge of making MediaMOO's culture different from prevailing MUD culture made self-selection inadequate. Lots of undergraduates with no particular focus to their interests want to join MediaMOO. To preserve MediaMOO's character as a place for serious scholarly discussions, I usually reject these applications. Besides, almost all of the hundreds of other MUDs out there place no restrictions on who can join. MediaMOO is one of the few that is different.

Emotionally and politically charged subject matter, such as feminism, makes it essential for members of a community to have a shared understanding of the community's purpose. People who are interested in freshwater and saltwater tanks can coexist peacefully in parallel conversations on sci.aquaria. However, on alt.feminism, people who want to explore the implications of feminist theory, and those who want to question its basic premises, don't get along quite so well. Self-selection alone is not adequate for bringing together a group to discuss a hot topic. People with radically differing views may wander in innocently, or barge in deliberately—disrupting the conversation through ignorance or malice.

Such gate crashing tends to occur more frequently as the community grows in size. For example, some participants in the Usenet group alt.tasteless decided to post a series of grotesque messages to the thriving group rec.pets.cats, including recipes for how to cook cat. A small, low-profile group may be randomly harassed, but that's less likely to happen.

In the offline world, membership in many social organizations is open only to those who are willing and able to pay the dues. While it may rankle an American pluralistic sensibility, the use of wealth as a social filter has the advantages of simplicity and objectivity: no one's personal judgment plays a role in deciding who is to be admitted. And imposing a small financial hurdle to online participation may do more good than harm. Token fees discourage the random and pointless posting that dilute the value of many newsgroups. One of the first community networks, Community Memory in Berkeley, Calif., found that charging a mere 25 cents to post a message significantly raised the level of discourse, eliminating many trivial or rude messages.

Still, as the fee for participation rises above a token level, this method has obvious moral problems for a society committed to equal opportunity. In instituting any kind of exclusionary policy, the founder of a virtual community should first test the key assumption that alternative, nonexclusionary communities really do exist. If they do not, then less restrictive admissions policies may be warranted.

## Building on Diversity

Anonymity policy, admissions requirements, and advertising strategy all contribute to a virtual community's character. Without such methods of distinguishing one online hangout from another, all would tend to sink to the least common denominator of discourse— the equivalent of every restaurant in town degenerating into a dive. We need better techniques to help members of communities develop shared expectations about the nature of the community, and to communicate those expectations to potential new members. This will make it easier for people to find their own right communities.

Just as the surest way to find a good restaurant is to exchange tips with friends, word of mouth is usually the best way to find out about virtual communities that might suit your tastes and interests. The best published guides for restaurants compile comments and ratings from a large group of patrons, rather than relying on the judgment of any one expert. Approaches like this are being explored on the Net. Yezdi Lashkari, cofounder of Agents Inc., designed a system called "Webhound" that recommends items of interest on the World Wide Web. To use Webhound, you enter into the system a list of web sites you like. It matches you with people of similar interests, and then recommends other sites that they like. Not only do these ratings come from an aggregate of many opinions, but they also are matched to your personal preferences.

Webhound recommends just World Wide Web pages, but the same basic approach could help people find a variety of communities, products, and service that are likely to match their tastes. For example, Webhound grew out of the Helpful Online Music Recommendation Service (HOMR), which recommends musical artists. A subscriber to this service—recently renamed Firefly—first rates a few dozen musical groups on a scale of "the best" to "pass the earplugs"; Firefly searches its database for people who have similar tastes, and uses their list of favorites to recommend other artists that might appeal to you. The same technique could recommend Usenet newsgroups, mailing lists, or other information sources. Tell it that you like to read the Usenet group "rec.arts.startrek.info," and it might recommend "alt.tv.babylon-5"—people who like one tend to like the other. While no such tool yet exists for Usenet, the concept would be straightforward to implement.

Written statements of purpose and codes of conduct can help communities stay focused and appropriate. MediaMOO's stated purpose, for example, helps set its character as an arena for scholarly discussion. But explicit rules and mission statements can go only so far. Elegant restaurants don't put signs on the door saying "no feet on tables" and fast food restaurants don't post signs saying "feet on tables allowed." Subtle cues within the environment indicate how one is expected to behave. Similarly, we should design regions in cyberspace so that people implicitly sense what is expected and what is appropriate. In this respect, designers of virtual communities can learn a great deal from architects.

Vitruvius, a Roman architect from the first century B.C., established the basic principle of architecture as commodity (appropriate function), firmness (structural stability), and delight. These principles translate into the online world, as William Mitchell, dean of

MIT's School of Architecture and Planning, points out in his book *City of Bits: Space, Place, and the Infobahn.*

Architects of the twenty-first century will still shape, arrange and connect spaces (both real and virtual) to satisfy human needs. They will still care about the qualities of visual and ambient environments. They will still seek commodity, firmness, and delight. But commodity will be as much a matter of software functions and interface design as it is of floor plans and construction materials. Firmness will entail not only the physical integrity of structural systems, but also the logical integrity of computer systems. And delight? Delight will have unimagined new dimensions.

Marcos Novak of the University of Texas at Austin is exploring some of those "unimagined dimensions" with his notion of a "liquid architecture" for cyberspace, free from the constraints of physical space and building materials. But work of this kind on the merging of architecture and software design is regrettably rare; if virtual communities are buildings, then right now we are living in the equivalent of thatched huts. If the structure keeps out the rain—that is, if the software works at all—people are happy.

More important than the use of any of these particular techniques, however, is applying an architect's design sensibility to this new medium. Many of the traditional tools and techniques of architects, such as lighting and texture, will translate into the design of virtual environments. Depending on choice of background color and texture, type styles, and special fade-in effects, for instance, a Web page can feel playful or gloomy, futuristic or old-fashioned, serious or fun, grown-up or child-centered. The language of the welcoming screen, too, conveys a sense of the community's purpose and character. An opening screen thick with the jargon of specialists in, say, genetic engineering, might alert dilettantes that the community is for serious biologists.

As the Net expands, its ranks will fill with novices—some of whom, inevitably, will wander into less desirable parts of cyber-town. It is important for such explorers to appreciate the Net's diversity—to realize, for example, that the newsgroup alt.feminism does not constitute the Internet's sole contribution to feminist debate. Alternatives exist.

I'm glad there are places on the Net where I'm not comfortable. The world would be a boring place if it invariably suited any one person's taste. The great promise of the Net is diversity. That's something we need to cultivate and cherish. Unfortunately, there aren't yet enough good alternatives—too much of the Net is like the Sportsman and too little of it is like Maria's. Furthermore, not enough people are aware that communities can have such different characters.

People who accidentally find themselves in the Sportsman, alt.feminism, or alt.flame, and don't find the black leather or fiery insults to their liking, should neither complain about it nor waste their time there—they should search for a more suitable community. If you've stumbled into the wrong town, get back on the bus. But if you've been a long-time resident and find the community changing for the worse—that's different. Don't shy away from taking political action within that community to protect your investment of time: speak up, propose solutions, and build a coalition of others who feel the same way you do.

With the explosion of interest in networking, people are moving from being recipients of information to creators, from passive subscribers to active participants and leaders. Newcomers to the Net who are put off by harassment, pornography, and just plain bad manners should stop whining about the places they find unsuitable and turn their energies in a more constructive direction: help make people aware of the variety of alternatives that exist, and work to build communities that suit their interests and values.

---

## Now that you've read

1. What does someone who is constructing a virtual community have to consider?
2. How is a virtual community similar to a "real" community? How is it different?
3. What are some of the advantages to communicating online rather than face to face? What are some of the disadvantages?
4. Who benefits most from online communities? Why?

# SEQUENCE 8 ASSIGNMENTS

## Reading 1: Sherry Turkle, "Hackers: Loving the Machine for Itself"

> Within every culture, even a culture that wears a collective badge of self-denigration, there is a hierarchy. At MIT, some science is uglier than other science. Some engineering is uglier than other engineering. Some kinds of self-absorption are more unsavory—perhaps even more dangerous—than others. And contact with some machines is more contaminating than with others.

### Prewriting

1. What do you take the quotation above to mean, using the context of the reading to help you explain it?
2. How would you describe your ability with a computer?
3. Do you have any activities or studies that you are this passionately devoted to?
4. How much time do you spend on computers per day?
5. Do you know anyone who is more comfortable with computers than with people?

### Writing assignment

Sherry Turkle wrote her book in 1984. Has computer culture changed significantly on campus since that time? Turkle describes students who identify totally with their major. Do you think this is true in other fields as well? If so, explain your answer. If not, explain why not. Is this still true in computer science? What is your own relationship with computers? What is your response to the "hackers" described in the reading? Use examples from the text.

## Readings 2 and 3: Trip Gabriel, "Computers Help Unite Campuses But Also Drive Some Students Apart," and Theodore Roszak, "The Computerized Campus"

> "We're turning colleges into a cubicle-directed electronic experience and denying the importance of learning to work closely with other students and professors, and developing social adeptness." (Gabriel)

> One would be hard-pressed to find another time when a single industry was able to intrude its interests so aggressively upon the schools of the nation—and to find such enthusiastic receptivity (or timid surrender) on the part of educators. (Roszak)

## Prewriting

1. Respond to the two quotations above. Do you agree that the "intrusion" of computers onto college campuses is a matter to be concerned about? Why or why not?
2. Gabriel quotes an environmental psychologist as follows: "Universities are saying, 'Oh, my God, they're in their rooms. How can we ever build a sense of community in this building if they don't come out?'" Is his concern misplaced? How do you respond?
3. Is anything different in the way you communicate with people online and the way you communicate with them in person? Explain.
4. What are the drawbacks of computer interaction compared with face-to-face interaction?

## Writing assignment

What are Gabriel's and Roszak's concerns about the effects of computers on college campuses? Is it possible that reliance on computers will restrict students' interactions with each other, or will these interactions just take other forms? To support your answer, do a little field research on your campus and observe the effects of e-mail or chat-line participation on some of the students around you (or on you if you frequent cyberspace regularly).

## Reading 4: Suneel Ratan, "A New Divide Between Haves and Have-Nots?"

> The fact is that access to the new technology generally breaks down along traditional class lines.

## Prewriting

1. Respond to the above quotation. Do you agree with Ratan's claim?
2. What do you make of the term *information apartheid*?

## Writing assignment

All students are now being strongly urged to develop their computer skills, and computer literacy is even a graduation requirement for many high schools. Some students are eager to incorporate technology into their learning and even their daily lives, others are resistant, and still others have little opportunity to do either. Many colleges and universities offer courses to help students who have had little exposure to computers become more experienced with technology. What are the advantages of such courses? What are the disadvantages? If you've never taken such a course, try to find someone who has and get that person's feedback to help you provide specific details. In the bigger picture, Ratan is concerned about the distance between technology haves and have-nots. What is your response to his concerns? What are the implications if this gap continues to widen?

## Reading 5: John N. Hickman, "Cybercheats: Term-Paper Shopping Online"

> The only real solution to cyberplagiarism, then, is old-fashioned vigilance. Having spent millions of dollars wiring their students to the Internet, universities may have to invest in smaller classes and a better teacher-to-student ratio. A return to some good old analog, face-to-face teaching may be the only way to keep online plagiarism at the fringes, where it belongs.

### Prewriting

1. Consider and respond to the above quotation. Do you agree that the best way to reduce cybercheating is to lower teacher-to-student ratios and return to face-to-face teaching? Why or why not?
2. Do you know anyone who has ever downloaded a paper from the Internet and turned it in? How would you feel if you learned that someone in one of your classes had cheated in this way? Why?
3. How common do you think cybercheating is?

### Writing assignment

For this assignment, write an essay in which you consider whether or not the boom in educational technology has made cheating easier, more acceptable to students, or both. Before you start writing, find and examine one or more web sites that sell term papers, and report what you find. Are they pitched at specific categories of learners in particular—distance learners, for instance?

In "Cybercheats: Term-Paper Shopping Online," John N. Hickman is surprised to learn that students at Yale and Princeton cheat. Were you also surprised? Do you think differently about why students cheat now that you've read Hickman's article? Drawing on your own experience and observation, as well as on the previous readings, consider what teachers and universities can or should do to try to prevent cybercheating.

## Reading 6: Paul Saffo, "Quality in an Age of Electronic Incunabula"

> Consider your favorite book sitting on your bookshelf: how little time it spends in your hands being read, and how much gathering dust. Even a Bible in the hands of the most devout Christian fundamentalist spends more time shut than open.

## Prewriting

1. Drawing on the context of the essay, explain what you take Saffo's title to mean.
2. Can you think of other electronic devices that we once thought of as luxuries but now see as necessities?
3. How many people do you know who own their own computers? How many had computers five years ago? Has there been a significant increase?
4. Which electronic device would you be least willing to give up? Why?

## Writing assignment

Write an essay in which you respond to Saffo's piece, using as your starting point the question of whether or not computers have changed our intellectual life (including your own). Be sure to address Saffo's definition of quality and to explain why it is an important part of his argument. What is the problem with determining quality in the electronic age? Offer examples from your own experience, and draw on the previous readings in the sequence to back up your arguments.

## Reading 7: Amy Bruckman, "Finding One's Own Space in Cyberspace"

> The question is not whether "women" are comfortable on "the Net," but rather, what types of communities are possible? How can we create a range of communities so that everyone—men and women—can find a place that is comfortable for them?

## Prewriting

1. Respond briefly to the above quote, reflecting upon whether or not you think it would be possible to enable everyone to find a comfortable place in cyberspace.
2. Do you agree with Bruckman that the Web's greatest promise is diversity? Why or why not?

## Writing assignment

According to Bruckman, what goes into developing and choosing a "virtual" community? What was her goal in setting up MediaMOO? She offers advice for negotiating Cyberspace and finding a virtual community in which you are comfortable. If you have participated in online communities, describe your experience, what you liked about it, what you didn't, and what (if anything) made you feel a part of the virtual group. If you haven't participated, get someone to show you how to find and participate in chat lines, and then describe what you experience. Reflect on how your experience did or did not resonate with what Bruckman is saying. Some people, such as Trip Gabriel and Theodore Roszak, feel that belonging to this kind of community prevents us from belonging to other face-to-face communities. Do you agree? Why or why not?

## Final Project

Review the essays you've written for this sequence, and decide where you stand on some of the issues related to technology, education, and society. Is the Internet good for higher education? Is it good for interpersonal communication and development? Have the readings taught you anything new? Have they changed your mind about anything? Have they reinforced your views about anything? Mine your essays for a specific issue related to technology that you'd like to investigate in further detail, and formulate a concise thesis that you can use in a 15- to 20-page research paper. If you can't decide on a topic to investigate further, consider these questions:

How popular is "distance education," or web-based classes, at universities across the country? Is this a trend that will continue to grow?

How prevalent and serious is the problem of students' buying term papers on the web? Is this practice a serious threat to higher education?

Do you know anyone who is "addicted" to the Internet? What forms do those addictions take? What are the causes and effects of Internet addiction?

Do female students interact with computers in the same ways that male students do?

How much of a difference does having a personal computer make to a student's success? Are students who do not have computers at a disadvantage?

Is the goal of wiring every primary and secondary school classroom in the United States for Internet access a worthy one?

## Library Research Ideas

Try one or more of the following library research activities, or come up with your own ideas from library research to support your thesis.

1. Different opinions have been expressed in newspaper editorials and magazine articles concerning the goal of connecting every primary and secondary school classroom to the Internet. Find in

general-interest publications a number of articles that discuss this issue. Also, look in professional journals and in the popular press to find out how many teachers are technologically savvy and trained in how to teach using the Internet.

2. Compare discussions of hacking and of acts by specific hackers in mainstream print newspapers and magazines with discussions of these subjects in online communities and on the web. Is there a big difference in how hackers are treated by these different media? How prevalent is hacker culture on the Internet today? Has it been supplanted by mainstream values? Are hackers admired or reviled by the mainstream press? You might also compare how the print media treated hackers 10 or 15 years ago with how they treat hackers today. Has the meaning of the term *hacker* changed in that time?

3. Compare the print and web versions of a number of newspapers, journals, and magazines. Are the web versions different in any significant ways? Do they reflect a different culture? Or have mainstream print publications appropriated the web's cultural space?

4. See what professional and academic journals that target university professors and administrators (such as the *Chronicle of Higher Education*) have said and are saying about distance learning and educational technology. Do they express great enthusiasm for them? Has their enthusiasm been tempered at all recently?

5. Research the history of electronic publishing and of e-books on the Internet. Are e-books a viable alternative to print books? Are traditional magazines threatened by e-zines? How many people read e-zines? You might also research how people use the Internet and how this has changed over time. Are most uses of the Internet for research or for commercial purposes?

## Field Research Ideas

Try one or more of the following field research ideas, or use your own field research ideas to get data to support your thesis.

1. Survey a group of computer science majors about some of the issues covered in Turkle's piece. You could ask them to define the term *hacker*, or you could provide several different definitions—expressing different views of hackers—and ask them to choose which one they agree with. You could ask for their reaction to the stereotypical image of hackers as being more comfortable with computers than with people. Or you could ask about the ethics of hacking: Is it ever justifiable to hack into a private company's or organization's computer system? You might also want to survey an older target population (such as computer science professors)

and compare their responses to those of undergraduate computer science majors.

2. Subscribe to a relevant mailing list or Usenet newsgroup, and after you've acclimated yourself to the group for a few weeks and become part of it, conduct an online survey on an issue from this sequence. If you explain that you are conducting field research on education technology or on technology and society, you are likely to receive many responses and a lot of input from people who regularly participate in online communities.

3. Survey a group of professors about the problem of term papers purchased on the web. Ask what they are doing to discourage this practice and to catch students who try to pass off as their own work a paper they didn't write.

4. Interview some "distance learning" students about their experiences and their satisfaction with education technology.

5. Survey a random group of students about electronic publishing. Do they read e-zines and e-books? Do they like them? Do they think electronic media will ever supplant traditional print media? You might also survey an older target population and compare the responses of the two groups.

ACKNOWLEDGMENTS

*(continued from page iv)*

Page 115: "The College Mystique" from *The Case Against College*, David McKay Co., 1975, pp. 3–24. Reprinted by permission of the author.

Page 131: Reprinted with the permission of The Free Press, a Division of Simon & Schuster, Inc., from *Lives on the Boundary: The Struggles and Achievements of America's Underprepared* by Mike Rose. Copyright © 1989 by Mike Rose.

Page 148: "Students of Success," *Newsweek*, 1986. Reprinted by permission of the author.

Page 151: "Canto, Locura y Poeisa" from *Women's Review of Books 7*, no. 5, Feb. 1990, pp. 376–385. I wish to thank Ellen Cantarow and Linda Gardiner, editor of *Women's Review of Books*, for having originally published my article in their excellent publication.

Page 170: "College Freshmen More Conservative in Survey." © 1997, The Washington Post. Reprinted with permission.

Page 173: *Generation at the Crossroads: Apathy and Action on the American Campus*, copyright © 1994 by Paul Rogat Loeb. Reprinted by permission of Rutgers University Press.

Page 186: "The Cause of Citizenship" from *Chronicle of Higher Education*, Oct. 6, 1995, B1. Reprinted by permission of the author.

Page 192: From *A Tale of Two Utopias: The Political Journey of the Generation of 1968* by Paul Berman. Copyright © by Paul Berman. Used by permission of W. W. Norton & Company, Inc.

Page 203: Reprinted by permission of the publishers from *The Alchemy of Race and Rights* by Patricia Williams, Cambridge, Mass.: Harvard University Press, Copyright © 1991 by the President and Fellows of Harvard College.

Page 217: "History as Mirror." Reprinted by the permission of Russell & Volkening as agents for the author. Copyright © 1973 by Barbara Tuchman.

Page 239: From *Fear of Falling* by Barbara Ehrenreich. Copyright © 1989 by Barbara Ehrenreich. Reprinted by permission of Pantheon Books, a division of Random House, Inc.

Page 244: "Dirtbags, Burnouts, Metalheads, and Thrashers" from *Teenage Wasteland*, Pantheon, 1991, pp. 145–159. Reprinted by permission of the author.

Page 256: Copyright 1994 from *Teaching to Transgress: Education as the Practice of Freedom* by bell hooks. Reproduced by permission of Taylor & Francis, Inc./Routledge, Inc., http://www.routledge-ny.com.

Page 266: "From Outside, In" originally appeared in *The Georgia Review*, Volume XLI, No. 2 (Summer 1987), © 1987 by The University of Georgia/© 1987 by Barbara Mellix. Reprinted by permission of Barbara Mellix and *The Georgia Review*.

Page 276: "Lost Generation," *The New Republic*, August 2, 1999, pp. 16–18. Reprinted by permission of *The New Republic*, © 1999, The New Republic, Inc.

Page 281: Reprinted with permission from "Sister Outsider" by Audre Lorde, copyright 1984. Published by the Crossing Press, Freedom, CA.

Page 452: Reprinted courtesy of *Sports Illustrated:* "This Isn't Such a Dumb Idea" by Leigh Montville, February 17, 1997. Copyright © 1997, Time Inc., All rights reserved.

Page 455: "The Dumb Jock: Fact or Fiction?" from *Major Violation: The Unbalanced Priorities in Athletics and Academics*, Leisure Press, 1991, 11–29. Reprinted by permission of the author.

Page 481: "Taking Women Students Seriously," from *On Lies, Secrets, and Silence: Selected Prose 1966–1978* by Adrienne Rich. Copyright © 1979 by W. W. Norton & Company, Inc. Used by permission of the author and W. W. Norton & Company, Inc.

Page 489: *Diaries to an English Professor: Pain and Growth in the Classroom* was published by the University of Massachusetts Press in 1994 and is copyrighted © 1994 by the University of Massachusetts Press. Reprinted by permission.

Page 519: "Teachers' Classroom Strategies Should Recognize That Men and Women Use Language Differently" by Deborah Tannen, The Chronicle of Higher Education, June 19, 1991, copyright Deborah Tannen. Reprinted by permission.

Page 525: "The Fraternal Bond as a Joking Relationship" from *Changing Men: New Directions in Research on Men and Masculinity*, ed. by Michael Kemmel, p. 148–163, copyright © 1980 by Sage Publications, Inc. Reprinted by permission of Sage Publications, Inc.

Page 533: From *Fire in the Belly* by Sam Keen, copyright © 1991 by Sam Keen. Used by permission of Bantam Books, a division of Random House, Inc.

Page 545: "Grandma's Story" from *Woman Native Other: Writing Postcoloniality and Feminism*, Indiana University Press, 1989, pp. 119–151. Reprinted by permission of Indiana University Press. Quotes by Leslie Marmon Silko copyright © Leslie Marmon Silko, reprinted with the permission of The Wylie Agency, Inc. Yamada, Mitsuye, *Camp Notes and Other Poems*, copyright © 1992 by Mitsuye Yamada. Reprinted by permission of Rutgers University Press.

Page 579: "Hackers: Loving the Machine for Itself," from *The Second Self: Computers and the Human Spirit*, Simon & Schuster, 1984, pp. 196–216. Reprinted by permission of Brockman, Inc. and the author.

Page 597: "Computers Help Unite Campuses But Also Drive Some Students Apart," *New York Times*, Nov. 11, 1996, p. A12. Copyright © 1996 by the New York Times Co. Reprinted by permission.

Page 602: "The Computerized Campus" from *The Cult of Information: A Neo-Luddite Treatise on High Tech, Artificial Intelligence, and the True Art of Thinking*, University of California Press, 1994. Reprinted by permission of The Regents of the University of California.

Page 614: "A New Divide Between Haves and Have-nots?" from *Time*, Spring 1995. © 1995 Time Inc. Reprinted by permission.

Page 618: "Cybercheats: Term-Paper Shopping Online," *The New Republic*, V. 218, Mar. 23, 1998, pp. 14–15. Reprinted by permission of *The New Republic*, © 1998, The New Republic, Inc.

Page 622: "Quality in an Age of Electronic Incunabula," *Liberal Education*, Winter 1993, pp. 18–23. Reprinted by permission of the author.

Page 628: Republished with permission on *Technology Review* from "Finding One's Own Space in Cyberspace" by Amy Bruckman from *Technology Review 99*, No. 1, January 1996. Permission conveyed through Copyright Clearance Center, Inc.

# Index